INCLUSION

The Wadsworth Special Educator Series

The following Special Education titles are new for 1998/1999 from Wadsworth Publishing Company:

1998

Benner, *Special Education Issues Within the Context of American Society,*
ISBN 0-534-25230-3

Gersten/Jimenez, *Promoting Learning for Culturally and Linguistically Diverse Students,*
ISBN 0-534-34417-6

Rusch/Chadsey, *Beyond High School: Transition from School to Work,*
ISBN 0-534-34432-1

1999

Bigge/Stump/Silberman, *Curriculum, Assessment, and Instruction for Exceptional Learners,*
ISBN 0-534-16770-5

Coutinho/Repp, *Inclusion: The Integration of Students with Disabilities,*
ISBN 0-534-56718-5

Repp/Horner, *Functional Analysis of Problem Behavior: From Effective Assessment to Effective Support,*
ISBN 0-534-34850-5

Inclusion

The Integration of Students with Disabilities

MARTHA J. COUTINHO
East Tennessee State University

ALAN C. REPP, Ph.D.
Northern Illinois University

Wadsworth Publishing Company
I(T)P® An International Thomson Publishing Company

Belmont, CA • Albany, NY • Boston • Cincinnati • Johannesburg • London • Madrid • Melbourne
Mexico City • New York • Pacific Grove, CA • Scottsdale, AZ • Singapore • Tokyo • Toronto

Education Editor: Dianne Lindsay
Editorial Assistant: Valerie Morrison
Marketing Manager: Becky Tollerson
Project Editor: Jennie Redwitz
Print Buyer: Barbara Britton
Permissions Editor: Bob Kauser
Production: Tobi Giannone, Michael Bass & Associates
Copy Editor: Laura Larson
Illustrator: Asterisk Group
Cover Design: Sandy Drooker
Cover Image: Elizabeth Crews
Compositor: Thompson Type
Printer: Malloy Lithographing, Inc.

This book is printed on acid-free recycled paper.

Printed in the United States of America
1 2 3 4 5 6 7 8 9 10

For more information, contact Wadsworth Publishing Company, 10 Davis Drive, Belmont, CA 94002, or electronically at http://www.thomson.com/wadsworth.html

International Thomson Publishing Europe
Berkshire House
168-173 High Holborn
London, WC1V 7AA, United Kingdom

Nelson ITP, Australia
102 Dodds Street
South Melbourne
Victoria 3205 Australia

Nelson Canada
1120 Birchmount Road
Scarborough, Ontario
Canada M1K 5G4

International Thomson Publishing Southern Africa
Building 18, Constantia Square
138 Sixteenth Road, P.O. Box 2459
Halfway House, 1685 South Africa

International Thomson Editores
Seneca, 53
Colonia Polanco
11560 México D.F. México

International Thomson Publishing Asia
60 Albert Street #15-01
Albert Complex
Singapore 189969

International Thomson Publishing Japan
Hirakawa-cho Kyowa Building, 3F
2-2-1 Hirakawa-cho, Chiyoda-ku
Tokyo 102, Japan

Library of Congress Cataloging-in-Publication Data

Inclusion : the integration of students with disabilities / [edited by] Martha J. Coutinho, Alan C. Repp.
p. cm.
Includes bibliographical references and index.
ISBN 0-534-56718-5 (alk. paper)
1. Inclusive education—United States. 2. Handicapped students—Education—United States. 3. Educational change—United States. I. Coutinho, Martha J. II. Repp, Alan C.
LC1201.I537 1999
371.9'046—dc21 98-17646

Dedication

To Bush Hog and Erin

Contents

Acknowledgments

Writing and publishing this text has been a big project, one that has taken considerable time and effort of many, many individuals. Foremost, we would like to thank all of the contributors. Together they have provided professors and teachers with the full breadth of guidance, knowledge, and practical information needed to design and implement responsible and successful inclusive programs at all levels and among students with diverse disabilities. We thank them for making revisions and updates quickly during the editing process.

Our thanks also go to many individuals with Wadsworth Publishing, in particular Valerie Morrison, whose determination to publish this book made everyone's efforts worthwhile. We thank Tobi Giannone of Michael Bass & Associates and Jennie Redwitz of Wadsworth, who worked diligently to keep us on schedule. We are indebted to Laura Larson, our copyeditor, whose professionalism, flexibility, and productivity made it possible to edit such a complex and lengthy manuscript successfully.

Special thanks to Peggy Williams, who has worked from the inception in the preparation of the manuscript. And our thanks to Karen Dayton, who carried out a multitude of tasks under extreme time lines to complete the publication process.

Finally, we would like to thank the following reviewers for their comments and suggestions: Dr. Alice Alexander, Frostburg State University; Dr. Wesley Brown, East Tennessee State University; Dr. Christine Cheney, University of Nevada; Dr. Katherine C. Sacca, Buffalo State College; and Dr. Diane Woodrum, West Virginia University. Their insights and enthusiasm for the text made its publication possible.

Contributors

Mark Alter, Ph.D.
Department of Teaching & Learning
New York University
New York, NY 10003

Lynette K. Chandler, Ph.D.
Department of Educational Psychology, Counseling & Special Education
Northern Illinois University
DeKalb, IL 60115

Martha Coutinho, Ph.D.
Department of Human Development & Learning
East Tennessee State University
Johnson City, TN 37614-0548

Carol M. Dahlquist, M.Ed.
School Association for Special Education in DuPage County (SASED)
Manning School
200 N. Linden
Westmont, IL 60559

Louis Danielson, Ph.D.
Director
Division of Research to Practice
Office of Special Education Programs
Washington, DC 20202

Judith Fein
National Institute on Disability & Rehabilitation Research
Washington, DC 20202

Mary Susan E. Fishbaugh, Ed.D.
Director, Office of Professional Practices
Montana State University–Billings
Billings, MT 59101-0298

Howard Goldstein, Ph.D.
Professor & Chair
Department of Communication Disorders
Florida State University
Tallahassee, FL 32306-1200

Barbara W. Gottlieb, Ed.D.
Lehman College
Department of Specialized Services in Education
Carman Hall, Room B20
Bedford Park Blvd. West
Bronx, NY 10468

Jay Gottlieb, Ph.D.
Department of Teaching & Learning
New York University
New York, NY 10003

Barbara Guy, Ph.D.
Institute on Community Integration
University of Minnesota
430 Wulling Hall
86 Pleasant St. SE
Minneapolis, MN 55455

Sheri L. Hamilton, Ph.D.
c/o Margo A. Mastropieri, Ph.D.
Department of Educational Studies
Liberal Arts & Education Building
Purdue University
West Lafayette, IN 47907-1446

Susan Brody Hasazi, Ed.D.
Department of Education
University of Vermont
448 Waterman Building
Burlington, VT 05405

Jane Hauser
Dissemination Specialist
Division of Research to Practice
Office of Special Education Programs
Washington, DC 20202

Dawn Hunter, Ph.D.
Associate Professor
Chapman University
Orange, CA 92866

David R. Johnson, Ph.D.
Institute on Community Integration
University of Minnesota
102 Pattee Hall
150 Pillsbury St. SE
Minneapolis, MN 55455

Louise Kaczmarek, Ph.D.
Assistant Professor
Department of Instruction & Learning
4F23 Forbes Quad
University of Pittsburgh
Pittsburgh, PA 15260

Susan Wickstrom Kane, Ph.D.
Adjunct Instructor
Department of Communication
University of Pittsburgh at Johnstown
Johnstown, PA 15904

David Malouf, Ph.D.
Educational Research Analyst
Division of Research to Practice
Office of Special Education Programs
Washington, DC 20202

Margo A. Mastropieri, Ph.D.
Department of Educational Studies
Liberal Arts & Education Building
Purdue University
West Lafayette, IN 47907-1446

Margaret J. McLaughlin, Ph.D.
Associate Director
Institute for the Study of Exceptional Children & Youth
University of Maryland
College Park, MD 20742

Susan L. Mortweet, Ph.D.
Post-Doctoral Fellow
Children's Mercy Hospital, Developmental Medicine
2401 Gillham Rd.
Kansas City, MO 64108

Fran O'Reilly, M.Ed.
41 Loomis
Cambridge, MA 02138

Tom Parrish, Ed.D.
Co-Director
Center for Special Education Finance
American Institutes for Research
PO Box 1113
Palo Alto, CA 94302

Alan C. Repp, Ph.D.
Distinguished Research Professor
Department of Educational Psychology, Counseling & Special Education
Northern Illinois University
DeKalb, IL 60115

Ernest Rose, Ph.D.
Dean, College of Education & Human Services
Montana State University–Billings
Billings, MT 59101-0298

Ellen P. Schiller, Ph.D.
Special Assistant
Division of Research to Practice
Office of Special Education Programs
Washington, DC 20202

Patricia F. Schofield, Ph.D.
American Embassy, Bratislava

Thomas E. Scruggs, Ph.D.
Department of Educational Studies
Liberal Arts & Education Building
Purdue University
West Lafayette, IN 47907-1446

Daniel E. Steere, Ph.D.
Assistant Professor
Department of Special Education & Rehabilitation
East Stroudsburg University of Pennsylvania
200 Prospect St.
East Stroudsburg, PA 18301-2999

Cheryl A. Utley, Ph.D.
Assistant Research Professor
Juniper Gardens Children's Project, University of Kansas
650 Minnesota Ave., Second Floor
Kansas City, KS 66101

Toni Van Laarhoven, Ed.D.
Department of Educational Psychology, Counseling & Special Education
Northern Illinois University
DeKalb, IL 60115

Traci Van Laarhoven-Myers, M.A.
Naperville Community Unit School District #203
Naperville, IL 60540

Sandra Hopfengardener Warren, Ph.D.
Faculty Research Associate
Institute for the Study of Exceptional Children & Youth
University of Maryland
College Park, MD 20742

H. Elizabeth Wycoff, M.A., NCSP
School Psychologist
Wheaton Warrenville
Community Unit School District #200
Wheaton, IL 60187

Alisa C. York, M.A., NCSP
School Psychologist
Wheaton Warrenville
Community Unit School District #200
Wheaton, IL 60187

Photo Credits

Page 9	PhotoEdit/Rudi Von Briel
Page 37	Joel Gordon
Page 59	Elizabeth Crews
Page 91	Elizabeth Crews
Page 112	Stock Boston/George Bellerose
Page 135	Jeroboam, Inc./Jane Scherr
Page 152	Stock Boston/Gregg Mancuso
Page 183	PhotoEdit/Amy Etra
Page 206	Jeroboam, Inc./Robert Finken
Page 236	Elizabeth Crews
Page 264	Jeroboam, Inc./Michael Siluk
Page 278	Stock Boston/Bob Daemmrich
Page 312	Joel Gordon
Page 332	PhotoEdit/Paul Conklin
Page 366	PhotoEdit/James Shaffer

Introduction to Integration

MARTHA COUTINHO
ALAN C. REPP

The chapters in this book are arranged in two sections: "Perspectives" and "Integration Efforts." The first section includes chapters on perspectives, trends, and implications (Chapter 1), educational reform (Chapter 2), the challenge of diversity (Chapter 3), the special problems of urban schools (Chapter 4), and the perspective on finance and funding issues (Chapter 5).

The first of these chapters (by Coutinho and Repp) discusses the national context that led to the present form of integration, national trends in placements for students, and implications for research and practice. The authors put into perspective historical movements (for example, the Individuals with Disabilities Education Act [IDEA], mainstreaming, the Regular Education Initiative) toward a continuum of services ranging from the complete segregation of the past to the complete elimination of special education. They also present briefly the perspectives of various organizations on this continuum (such as CCBD, CEC, CED, LDA, NEA, TASH). The placement data show that most students are in either regular education classes (45 percent) or resource rooms (27 percent). There is, however, substantial state-by-state variation (for example, the range for regular class placement is 10 to 84 percent). In addition, percentages vary by disability (for instance, 10 percent for those with mental retardation and 87 percent for those with speech and language impairments), by age (less as students grow older), and over time (some disabilities have increased while others have decreased). The data show that considerable national progress has been made toward implementing the least restrictive principle of IDEA. Nevertheless, the current research base is inconclusive with respect to which approach to inclusion is the most effective.

The second chapter (by McLaughlin, Schofield, and Warren) discusses educational reform and issues it presents for inclusion. The authors argue that if inclusion involves more than moving a student from one locale to another, schools must be restructured. Issues involving testing, changing curricula, education of disadvantaged and culturally diverse students, school finance, school choice, teacher certification, and technology all affect the manner in which inclusion programs would be implemented at the local level. All too often in our experience, we have seen inclusion promoted without careful consideration of these factors and as a result fail for individual students. McLaughlin, Schofield, and Warren show us how complex this program is, and by doing so they present us with a plan that can help make inclusion successful.

The theme of considering inclusion within the context of educational reform is continued in the next chapter (by Utley and Mortweet). The authors discuss the challenge of diversity within reform, noting the special problems of students in economically poor communities. These often include insufficient funding, qualitatively different instruction, and inequitable distribution of instructional materials. Empirical research has shown that as the result of perhaps these and other factors, the amount of time allocated for instruction is less in poverty-level programs, the amount of engaged time is less, materials differ, and teacher behaviors vary. Utley and Mortweet discuss instructional models that can address these problems, concluding their chapter with helpful and specific recommendations for change at the local, state, and federal levels.

The problems of special education students in urban settings are addressed in detail in the next chapter by Gottlieb, Alter, and Gottlieb. The authors, with a long history of research in mainstreaming, report on their database of 91,000 students in New York. The data, which are depressing, indicate that less than 3 percent of the students in self-contained classrooms in the urban schools they studied improved reading test scores from below grade level to grade level. Whereas some argue that such data suggest that special education should be shut down, these authors argue more reasonably that these students *as individuals* cannot develop the academic competencies needed to *succeed* in the mainstream until major changes are made in the curriculum and instructional methods. Their theme, that quality of instruction must be addressed before placement for individuals can be meaningfully discussed, is particularly cogent given the experience of and the amount of data collected over the years by this group.

The final chapter in the "Perspectives" section is on implications that finance and funding issues have on integration. The authors (Danielson, O'Reilly, and Parrish), who have considerable experience with this variable, discuss types of state aid and note that the formulas for providing categorical aid (for special education students) can differ across states, with direct implication for the success of integration efforts. They also discuss the influence of federal funding, and the states' argument that IDEA was overregulated and underfunded. One of the concerns, for example, is that because federal funding under IDEA is based on special education head counts, there is a disincentive for states to provide reform and to reduce the number of identified students. The desire of some states to do so highlights the complexity of funding issues.

The second part of this book, split into two subsections, presents efforts at promoting integration. The first subsection considers general, broad topics and includes discussions on systems change (Chapter 6), assessment and adaptations (Chapter 7), and technology (Chapter 8). The second subsection includes chapters on specific efforts toward integration of students at particular ages. Topics entail the integration of students with mild, moderate, or severe disabilities in the preschool (Chapters 9 and 10), elementary school (Chapters 11 and 12), secondary school (Chapters 13 and 14), and transition to adult life (Chapter 15).

In the first chapter in this section, Hunter argues for a systems change approach, discussing factors promoting and interfering with such change. She advocates a culture of change and suggests eight components for a successful transition to inclusive practices, including developing a vision, valuing professional development, sustaining commitment, providing support, and frequently evaluating progress. Fourteen strategies to promote and effect systems change are then discussed. These can serve as a model or checklist as we try to produce change in classrooms. The chapter concludes with some reflections on change, reflections that support the author's experience with systems change for integration.

The chapter on assessment (Van Laarhoven, Coutinho, Van Laarhoven-Myers, and Repp) goes beyond standardized procedures (for example, WISC) and focuses instead on more functional assessment procedures. These include curriculum-based measurement, functional analysis of problem behavior, curriculum assessment, and assessment of the teacher and concomitant instructional variables. From these results, the authors discuss methods for developing plans for successful integration. Interventions are grouped and presented for students, teachers, environment, and curriculum. The authors take the position that integration will be more successful if the student has more skills, and they suggest teaching students learning strategies, social skills, self-management, and self-advocacy. They also suggest that teacher support will affect the success of integration, and they discuss teacher-planning interventions, training in effective teaching practices, and coteaching arrangements as well as other efforts. Environmental and curricular adaptations are also viewed as critical, and suggestions are provided in each category.

Continuing the theme of adaptations, Schiller, Malouf, Hauser, and Fein discuss the use of technology with students with disabilities. The authors, all with the U.S. Department of Education, bring a wide understanding to this topic and begin with a discussion of the federal legislation that improved the support of technology. They then present cases showing practical examples of its use, followed by an informative discussion of instructional technology to improve academic outcomes. Their major topics are mathematics and reading, and they include sections on incorporating cognitive principles, basic skills, conceptual thinking, and writing. As we all know, assessment is a particularly difficult area in special education, and the authors discuss the relationship of technology to it, including areas like classroom assessment, curriculum-based measurement, and other models of assessment. We are often told that technology is the future of America, and the authors conclude the chapter with a discussion of the future, including topics such as needs, research, and potential.

The next seven chapters form a set on integration at various age and ability levels. The first (by Chandler and Dahlquist) concerns preschool children with mild or moderate disabilities. The authors summarize practices that promote inclusion for preschool-aged children in various programs, including private, community, and federally funded programs. They begin by discussing benefits of inclusion and service delivery options; then, they move to the heart of their chapter with the section on strategies to promote inclusion. They first emphasize ways to arrange environments so that students will share the physical, social, and educational environment within the school. Twenty-three arrangements are provided, all centering around teachers, materials, peer groups, and structure. All suggestions are research based; however, they are presented in a straightforward and practical manner that would allow teachers to develop checklists or lesson plans to help their students. The chapter then moves to behavior management in inclusive programs, and it presents the functional assessment approach that was developed in clinical settings and has only recently been moved to classrooms. Sections on working as a team and on preparing families and children follow. The conclusion discusses evaluating the success of integration, a section that emphasizes the authors' belief that we have a responsibility not just to place students in new environments but also to arrange those environments to promote success.

The second of the pair of chapters on integration in the preschool (by Kane, Goldstein, and Kaczmarek) describes efforts at inclusion of children with severe disabilities. The authors focus on language and social behaviors, as these are crucial to securing and maintaining interactions with other children. Initially, they discuss challenges presented by physical characteristics of both the child and the environment, emphasizing conducting ecological assessments as one way to identify barriers to successful integration. Intervention then follows directly from the assessment data. Next they discuss curricular challenges, including both assessment and intervention challenges. Assessment is divided into two categories, formal and intervention driven. Tests in the former category are criticized, while the ecological assessment approach is preferred because of its emphasis on identifying and changing variables present in the child's environment. Various intervention approaches or areas are discussed, including, for example, functional skill training, mixed modality training, and teaching procedures that promote language acquisition and social interaction. For those unfamiliar with promoting these behaviors, the latter section is a particularly valuable one that defines an array of lesson plans. The authors then discuss challenges to effective integration, focusing again on teaching communication and social skills as well as assessing their effects on peer relationships. They also discuss generalization and maintenance of positive changes in peer relations, and the particular affects and challenges of problem behavior. The chapter concludes with implications for future research.

The next two chapters consider integration in the elementary school. The first (by Mastropieri, Scruggs, and Hamilton) focuses on students with moderate disabilities and reviews evidence on effective instructional and mainstreaming strategies for these students. The purpose is to provide information on validated instructional procedures and on research evidence for inclusion in elementary schools. The section on academic interventions summarizes research on simple concept learning, reading-decoding, word reading, passage reading, and arithmetic. This is followed by a review of social/behavioral interventions and then of life skills intervention. The chapter then moves to a review of mainstreaming studies, again focusing on areas of student learning (including cooperative learning in science and art activities). It ends with a discussion of the research reviewed. Results indicate that (a) the types of interventions reported in the literature are "special education" interventions and are atypical of those that occur in regular education elementary schools; (b) there is very little data on racial, ethnic, or socioeconomic status of the students studied; and (c) that successful integration efforts at this level of schooling are likely to include cooperative group learning, direct instruction, hands-on curriculum, and peer tutoring in more basic skills.

The second chapter on integration of students in elementary school (by Hunter) focuses on children with severe disabilities. The chapter reflects the author's political passions on the topic of integration as well as her practical experience with teaching and coordinating efforts to facilitate integration. Initial sections are on teaching students in general education classrooms (the issue raised as problematic in terms of research in the prior chapter), components of successful schools, collaboration, developing partnerships with families, and assessment. The chapter then moves to curriculum issues, providing specific information on what teachers can do to effect success. The information is very practical and valuable to practicing teachers, administrators, and teacher trainers. Many tables in the chapter present examples of what to do, all arranged around questions such as (a) What can students learn? (b) What do I teach? (c) How do I schedule work? (d) How do I actually teach these students in a general education classroom? (e) What do I do about difficult behavior? and (f) How do I teach students with physical/medical issues? The chapter concludes with discussions of evaluation, grading, resources, and the compelling question, Is inclusive schooling worth the work and the benefits to children?

The third pair of chapters discusses integration of students into the secondary school. The first of these (by York and Wycoff) concerns students with mild or moderate disabilities, and it is divided into two primary sections: general issues and a specific example of evaluation. The former includes (a) assessment of how well separate special education works, (b) how well inclusion/supported mainstreaming works, (c) effects on students, and (d) what is needed for successful inclusion. The second section addresses how we can document and monitor academic progress, and it presents an excellent example of the authors' work on this topic. Data are presented on ten representative students from three districts for which inclusion was mandated by the school board. The data are on reading fluency, which serves as the vehicle to demonstrate several features of the evaluation, including curriculum-based measurement, data analysis, administration and scoring of probes, and research/evaluation design. The authors conclude by discussing where we go from here.

Steere, Rose, and Fishbaugh offer the second of the pair of chapters on secondary schooling, discussing programming for students with severe disabilities.

The authors provide us with a good look at an inclusive high school. They discuss factors affecting success in general but make the factors more specific by relating them to two students in an inclusive high school. They indicate how to organize a secondary-level curriculum, focusing on choosing desirable outcomes and establishing a functional curriculum. They then present factors for success—for example, teaching students to make meaningful choices, providing systematic instruction, experiencing professional development, conducting functional assessments, supporting families, focusing on transition, and providing assistive technology. The authors continue to tie their topics to the two high school students, and they conclude with discussions of the appropriateness of high school for students older than eighteen, follow-up programs for school graduates, and a typical day in high school for these two students.

The last chapter moves beyond formal schooling to a transition from school to adult life. The authors (Guy, Hasazi, and Johnson) initially provide an overview of federal legislation impacting the concept and programming of transition. Then, they discuss necessary and appropriate transition services, focusing on individualized transition planning and activities such as encouraging student participation, selecting strategies, and conducting follow-up study. Components of an inclusive transition are then presented, with a focus on student participation in regular education academics and in vocational education, paid work experiences, and vocational training at employment sites. The chapter concludes with a discussion of community and agency collaboration, a cooperative arrangement that is central to the authors' programs in transition. Topics such as parent and professional partnerships, interagency collaboration, accessing community resources, organizational strategies, and outcome measures are used to demonstrate their approach.

We hope that the reader has been provided with considerable information on both general perspectives and direct efforts toward inclusion of students with disabilities. We sincerely appreciate the efforts of our colleagues who have authored these chapters and who have otherwise contributed to the successful inclusion of students with disabilities.

PART I

Perspectives

1

Enhancing the Meaningful Inclusion of Students with Disabilities

Perspectives, Trends, and Implications for Research and Practice

MARTHA COUTINHO
ALAN C. REPP

Across the country, schools and communities are committing substantial effort and resources to provide for the education and participation of students with disabilities within inclusion environments. Preference for placements within general education is a principal requirement of the Individuals with Disabilities Education Act (IDEA), the federal act that sets forth the requirements to provide a free, appropriate public education to children with disabilities. Thus, researchers, school boards, and teachers focus much of their attention on how best to provide integrated educational programs for students with disabilities that will culminate in acceptable outcomes for all students and that are feasible in schools characterized by financial restraints and restructuring.

Decisions about integration affect a significant number of students, with children with disabilities from birth through age twenty-one comprising about 6.5 percent of the U.S. population (U.S. Department of Education, 1994). For the 1993–1994 school year, for example, the daily educational experience and eventual prospects of approximately 5.17 million children were affected by decisions regarding where and what types of services would be provided.[1]

Today's climate of reform requires that all programs must improve. Wherever services are provided, student achievement and long-term outcomes for all children in America must become better to meet national standards and the challenges of a complex, global economy. Preparedness for adult life, better outcomes, and the implementation of validated, effective instructional approaches are themes that dominate educational discussion and initiatives. Educators are implementing far-reaching general and special education reforms in concert or, frequently, in parallel with one another. Amicably and effectively or not, the services provided through regular and special education converge at the classroom door when seeking to increase the inclusion of children with disabilities within general education environments. This chapter describes the societal commitment, issues, initiatives, national progress, and programmatic implications for meeting this goal.

PRECEDENTS, COMMITMENT, AND ISSUES

The Individuals with Disabilities Education Act is the major legislation for provision of instruction to children with disabilities within integrated educational environments. Among its mandates, IDEA requires educators to implement the "Least Restrictive Environment" (LRE) provision of the act:

1. That to the maximum extent appropriate, children with disabilities, including children in public or private institutions or other care facilities, are educated with children who are not disabled; and

[1] Specifically, in 1993–1994, 5,170,242 children from birth through age twenty-one were served as children with disabilities under IDEA and Chapter 1 of the Elementary and Secondary Act (State-Operated Programs) (U.S. Department of Education, 1994). This figure is a 3.7 percent increase from 1991–1992. Students with specific learning disabilities make up about 52 percent of all children served.

2. that special classes, separate schooling or other removal of children with disabilities from the regular educational environment occurs only when the nature of severity of the handicap is such that education in regular classes with the use of supplementary aids and services cannot be achieved satisfactorily. (34 CFR 300.550)

In addition:

(a) Each public agency shall insure that a continuum of alternative placements is available to meet the needs of handicapped children for special education and related services.

(b) The continuum required under paragraph (a) of this section must:

(1) Include . . . (instruction in regular classes, special classes, special schools, home instruction, and instruction in hospital and institutions)

and (2) make provision for supplementary services (such as resource room or itinerant instruction) to be provided in conjunction with regular class placement. (34 CFR 300.551)

According to Hasazi, Johnston, Liggett, and Schattman (1994), "although the Act and the regulations created a presumption in favor of educating students with disabilities in general education environments, they also acknowledge a need for a range of alternative placement options" (p. 491). To guide decision making, a comment about those regulations offers specific advice to educators: "The overriding rule in this section is that placement decisions must be made on an individual basis" (Office of Federal Register, 1982, p. 822).

Educators and parents have found that IDEA and the implementing regulations did not give enough guidance to know how to provide both a free and appropriate public education (FAPE) and LRE for many children (Turnbull, 1986). Subsequent court decisions were to define FAPE as an education not needing to produce maximum educational benefit but nonetheless leading to meaningful, appreciable, measurable, and adequate gains (*Board of Education of Hendrick Hudson Central School District v. Rowley,* 1982; Osborne, 1996). Many other court decisions have intended to guide how to implement the LRE requirement, have considered how to balance FAPE and LRE, and have weighed the commitment to educate a student alongside his or her nondisabled peers with potentially greater or better services in a segregated setting.

In many early decisions, services in segregated placements were upheld as necessary FAPE (Osborne, 1996). Litigation involving implementation of the LRE requirement has increased, and more recent decisions have favored, although not uniformly, inclusive programming rather than specialized services in segregated classes or schools (*Chris D. v. Montgomery County Board of Education,* 1990; *Greer v. Rome City School District,* 1992; Osborne, 1996). In *Daniel R.R. v. State Board of Education* (1989) a separate class was held as the appropriate placement for a student with mental retardation. However, the court decision also produced a two-part test for determining how to meet the LRE requirement. This test has been used as the basis for a decision in many other court cases and to order inclusive placements. The two-part test includes consideration of such factors as:

> the student's ability to grasp the regular education curriculum, the nature and severity of the disability, the effect the student's presence would have on the functioning of the general education classroom, the student's overall experience in the mainstream, and the amount of exposure the special education student would have to nondisabled students. (Osborne, 1996, p. 108)

The courts' increasing preference for services provided in inclusive settings was illustrated in *Oberti v. Board of Education of the Borough of Clementon School District* (1992, 1993). The *Oberti* decision incorporated the two-part test and reasoning of the *Daniel R.R.* case and tipped the balance in favor of inclusive programs. The *Oberti* decision called for solutions that provide both LRE and FAPE, not one over the other:

> The court in *Oberti* held that IDEA requires school districts to supplement and realign their resources to move beyond the systems, structures, and practices that tend to unnecessarily segregate students with disabilities. The court recognized that including the student in this case in a general education classroom clearly would require a modification of the curriculum, but held that this alone was not a legitimate basis upon which to justify exclusion. Stating that inclusion is a right, not a privilege for a select few, the court placed ultimate responsibility on the school district to show that the student could not be educated in a general education setting with supplementary and services. (Osborne, 1996, p. 112)

An appeals court upheld the district court ruling, adding that association with a nondisabled peer is a right and students with disabilities cannot be excluded from regular classes because they learn in a different manner. In another, similar case, an appeals court rejected a separate class placement even when it represented the better academic setting (*Board of Education, Sacramento City Unified School District v. Holland,* 1992, 1994). The appeals court gave several factors to guide implementation of LRE, including both the educational and nonacademic benefits to a child with disabilities in a regular class, the impact on both other students and the teacher, and costs of providing services.

On the other hand, courts continue to affirm that a continuum of placements be made available and sometimes to order segregated placements (for example, when a student is dangerous or after a significant but failed effort to provide inclusive services). However, the decisions of the appeals courts, particularly in the *Daniel R.R.* and *Oberti* cases, appear to be influencing lower courts to seek implementation of the LRE requirement as one of the primary goals of IDEA.

In addition to extensive litigation, a strident discussion continues among parents, educators, advocates, and other professionals about how to implement LRE. The discussion accompanying efforts of schools has been extensive and sharply discrepant, either promoting inclusion or describing issues and concerns associated with inclusion (Dunn, 1968; Fuchs & Fuchs, 1994a; Hasazi et al., 1994; Stainback, Stainback, East, & Sapon-Savin, 1994).

On the one hand, specialized grouping of some kind characterizes virtually all schools. For example, schools frequently assign groups for classroom instruction, overall class placement, or supplementary instruction, whether conducted within or outside the regular classroom (Jenkins, Jewell, Leicester, O'Connor, Jenkins, & Troutner, 1994). Despite this pattern, criticisms of segregated, compensatory, or "pullout" services of any kind for any student are common and have been based on many arguments. Most notable is the belief that pullout services violate a student's civil rights, arguing that students with disabilities are most appropriately educated alongside their same-age peers and separate education of any kind is inherently unequal (Jenkins et al., 1994). Many recent criticisms have faulted separate programs for children, whether disabled or not, as simply ineffective. Criticisms include the following: (a) services and content are not coordinated, (b) outcomes are not satisfactory, and (c) students learn only basic skills in isolation, missing important, typically more advanced material (Jenkins et al., 1994; Knapp & Shields, 1990).

For well over a decade, initiatives have been developed to enhance and increase the meaningful inclusion of children with disabilities within general education environments. Although similar in their overall purpose, they have varied significantly in their definitions of inclusion, specific goals, approaches, relative alignment with regular education and the reform movement, and target population (for instance, those with mild versus severe disabilities). For example, some initiatives define the full-time inclusion of all children with disabilities in general education classrooms as the ultimate purpose. Others seek to downsize special education but do not contemplate elimination of the continuum of placements. With respect to goals, some efforts have emphasized the academic and social competence of students. Others stress the social acceptance of children with disabilities by nondisabled peers and the social/behavioral competence of students with disabilities. More recent is the goal that the achievement and outcomes of nondisabled students not be affected adversely when services to students with disabilities are provided in general education settings. Some approaches stress far-reaching restructuring and reform of both special *and* regular education and of their joint relationship. On the other hand, some movements have emphasized "making the student ready" through intensive, special education instruction prior to reentry.

Terms and Definitions of Inclusion

Many terms have been used to describe and promote inclusive practices. *Least Restrictive Environment,* known as LRE, has been used since the passage of the federal mandate to describe many general and diverse approaches to fully implement the IDEA. The definition of *full-time regular class* that the U.S. Department of Education provides to states for use when reporting placement settings allows pullout resource room services for up to 20 percent of the school day. Very popular in the 1980s, *mainstreaming* is still used to some extent today. In general, mainstreaming efforts have focused on reintegration of students with disabilities through intensive efforts to ready the student for the demands of mainstream classrooms and to implement interventions prior to referral, thus reducing the number of children referred, identified, and, ultimately, placed in separate environments for services.

The well-known federal call for increased inclusion by former assistant secretary of education Madeleine Will (1986) was represented by the "shared responsibility of the Regular Education Initiative (REI)" to encourage innovative, inclusive models of service delivery. The goals of the REI movement were to restructure the relationships between general and special education, to increase the number of children with disabilities served in regular education classes, and to increase the academic achievement of all children, including those with mild and moderate disabilities (Fuchs & Fuchs, 1994a). Relying primarily on a philosophical preference, advocates of REI noted that positive results had been associated with the integration of students with disabilities (Deno, Maruyama, Espin, & Cohen, 1990; Halvorsen & Sailor, 1990; Madden & Slavin, 1993; Stevens, Madden, Slavin, & Farnish, 1987). Based on their review, Gartner and Lipsky (1987) reported no consistent advantages of placement in full-time special education programs. The tenets, relative success, and tactics of efforts during that time (described now as the REI movement) have been discussed at length (Fuchs & Fuchs, 1994a; Lloyd, Singh, & Repp, 1990; Pugach & Sapon-Shevin, 1987). Particular concerns were that the REI movement remained a *special* rather than regular or joint education initiative and that a decade later, the major goals of the movement had not been achieved.

More recently, the term *inclusion* (inclusive schools, inclusive practices, and so forth) has replaced REI to describe diverse special education reforms that have been forwarded to increase the integration of children with disabilities. For example, after a two-year study of special education focusing on the education reform movement, the National Association of State Boards of Education (NASBE, 1992) recommended "the creation of an inclusive system that strives to produce better outcomes for all students" (p. 4). The inclusive schools movement is defined and interpreted in a variety of ways, making its description and goals difficult to capture. Opinions diverge concerning (a) whether to eliminate the continuum of services and (b) what goals should be emphasized for students.

Inclusive Practices: Varying Approaches

The inclusive schools movement is sometimes associated with the position of Stainback and Stainback (1991), who call for the elimination of special education and its continuum of placements. A similar position in many regards has been presented by the Association of Persons with Severe Handicaps (TASH), which has taken a prominent, active role attempting to influence policy and the public to implement technical assistance and policy initiatives that promote full inclusion. While proposing the end of the special education classes and disability labels, TASH also advocates provision of appropriate supports (for example, specialists and services) that would follow children into the mainstream (Pearpoint & Forest, 1992). A major goal is to improve the social competencies of students with disabilities and promote their acceptance by teachers and nondisabled peers. The inclusive schools movement as forwarded by TASH has been intended to embrace children with all disabilities, although the position departs from that taken by some other professional disability organizations representing students with mild, moderate, and/or sensory disabilities (for example, Learning Disabilities Association, 1993; Commission on the Education of the Deaf, 1988; Council for Children with Behavior Disorders, 1994).

Although described as a part of the inclusive schools movement, many other groups promote somewhat different approaches to enhancing the integration of students with disabilities. The National Education Association (NEA), for example, supports the education of students with disabilities in the least restrictive environment but notes that many requisites (fiscal, personnel, and administrative) are required to implement the mandate. The NEA supports provision of a full array of services and the full continuum of placements (NEA Resolution, 1992). The Council for Exceptional Children (CEC), the largest national professional association of special educators, adopted a position statement describing inclusion as a meaningful goal, but it reiterated the LRE requirement of IDEA that calls for the availability of a full continuum of placements (CEC, 1993). CEC formed a national coalition with 10 other national regular and special education organizations to identify and assist in the implementation of successful instructional practices for students with disabilities. Twelve principles for successful inclusive schools have been described (CEC, 1994), addressing leadership, standards, sense of community, accountability, and changing professional roles, among other themes. They also call for an "array of services" and "flexible learning environments to meet student needs":

> Inclusive schools utilize flexible groupings, authentic and meaningful learning experiences, and developmentally appropriate curricula accessible to all students. Even though full inclusion is a goal, a continuum of educational options is present within inclusive schools to provide choice and to meet the individual needs of each child. Inclusion and cooperation are emphasized within each option, and there is less reliance on pull-out education programs. (p. 14)

This perspective is consistent with efforts to increase the inclusion of children with disabilities through

> decentralization of power and concomitant empowerment of teachers and building-level administrators; a fundamental reorganization of the teaching and learning process through innovations like cooperative learning and thematic teaching; and the redefinition of professional relationships within buildings. (Fuchs and Fuchs, 1994a, p. 299)

A perspective at the federal level has been provided by the assistant secretary of special education and rehabilitative services to guide efforts associated with the inclusive schools movement. Speaking specifically with respect to the integration of children with disabilities in regular classrooms, Judith Heumann (1994) states:

> We need to give a clear message that people with disabilities are capable and should be integrated into the world. We do not advocate a "one size fits all"

approach in making decisions about where disabled students should be educated. Educational placement decision for students with disabilities are made at the local level and must be based on the needs of the individual student. Any other approach is not consistent with the Individuals with Disabilities Education Act (IDEA) and should not be confused with effective educational practices for inclusive classrooms. While there may be some children who would not be appropriately served full time in the regular education classroom, these children represent only a small number of the children with disabilities.

We believe that the regular classroom, with the necessary supports in place, is where most disabled students should be. . . . Both teachers and disabled students may need supports in the classroom to make inclusion work. . . . But the necessary supports depend on individual student and teacher needs.

The United States Department of Education's mission is to ensure equal access to education and to promote educational excellence throughout the nation. Inclusion is consistent with this mission and is an essential component of current school reform initiatives. Consistent with the Individuals with Disabilities Education Act (IDEA), the regular education classroom in the neighborhood school should be the first placement option considered for students with disabilities. . . . The inclusion of students with disabilities in their neighborhood schools must become part of the broader educational reform agenda in this nation. . . . We must share our respective experiences and expertise to design an American education system that promotes equity and excellence for all of the nation's students. (p. 1)

Currently, many other professional organizations, parents, and researchers are describing and advancing specific approaches, also with the purpose of promoting and increasing the meaningful inclusion of children with disabilities within general education environments. For example, the United States, through the U.S. Office of Special Education Programs, has participated in a multinational project sponsored by the Organization for Economic Cooperation and Development (OECD) to study the status of integration for children and youth with disabilities in more than twenty countries. In addition to a comprehensive compilation of the descriptive profile of the integration status of children and youth, the countries are sharing information relative to the historical, legal, and financial basis for special education, relationships between regular and special education, curriculum, teaching training, parental involvement and barriers to integration (Sloan, Denny, & Repp, 1992a). In a second set of reports, countries have prepared a composite case study to illustrate integration practices (Sloan, Alberg, Denny, Hasazi, McLaughlin, & Repp, 1992b). Many researchers and organizations working to increase inclusion have expressed concern that general education does not have the capacity to (a) accommodate student diversity in a manner that provides for successful academic achievement and enhanced social competence (Braaten, Kauffman, Braaten, Polsgrove, & Nelson, 1988; Fuchs & Fuchs, 1994a; Learning Disabilities Association, 1993; Singer, 1988) and (b) provide students with desired socialization experiences (American Council on the Blind et al. (n.d.). Despite philosophical and policy arguments favoring the integration of children with disabilities, some researchers have questioned whether the empirical basis for inclusion is conclusive, particularly for students with mild and moderate disabilities. When reviewed closely, the evidence that more inclusion programs culminate in better academic outcomes for students with mild disablities has been described as neither adequate now nor sufficient at the time the REI movement was launched (Zigmond et al., 1995). In addition to identifying many methodological problems, they note it is not possible to draw firm conclusions because the placements studied varied across studies (for example, some compare self-contained with regular, some omit resource room comparisons, and so forth). In addition, the disability condition of students has varied across studies (students with learning disabilities versus mental retardation, for instance, or those with mild versus severe disabilities).

However, many recent studies reporting on comprehensive efforts to enhance the inclusion of students with disabilities offer reason for considerable optimism (Fuchs & Fuchs, 1994b; Fuchs, Fuchs, & Fernstrom, 1993; Jenkins et al., 1994). For example, Jenkins et al. (1994) report that regular, remedial, and special education students profited from a comprehensive package of interventions. On the other hand, based on additional analyses associated with two of the studies described earlier and an additional study, the substantial and enduring gains implied by "enhanced" integration appear very difficult to attain and maintain (Zigmond et al., 1995). Describing results obtained on a reading achievement measure used in common across the projects, Jenkins et al. found limited gains for students for which comprehensive multiyear planning, implementation, and formative evaluation efforts occurred.

In general, the goals and recommendations of many groups and individuals (a) seek individualized, responsive reintegration and proactive integration efforts for children with disabilities in general education environments; (b) support maintenance of the full continuum of placements; and (c) call for a strong, multifaceted special education system. As described by Fuchs and Fuchs (1994a):

> Now is the time for inventive pragmatists, not extremists on the right or the left. Now is the time for leadership that recognizes the need for change; appreciates the importance of consensus building; looks at general education with a sense of what is possible; respects special education's traditions and values and the law that undergirds them; and seeks to strengthen the mainstream, as well as other educational options that can provide more intensive services, to enhance the learning and lives of all children. (p. 305)

These approaches stress that "a meaningful connection with general education is necessary; that a 'Lone Ranger' strategy for special education is self defeating" (Fuchs & Fuchs, 1994a, p. 295). Too often reforms in special education have run parallel in many states to those in general education, failing to align with large-scale restructuring (McLaughlin & Warren, 1992). Inclusion must be enhanced, not simply increased. The participation of children with disabilities must reflect national commitment to the national education goals and eventual preparedness to assume productive, independent, and satisfying lives in a complex, economically and demographically diverse society.

In conclusion, societal commitment to enhance the inclusion of children with disabilities has been an enduring, although very complex and, in some cases, controversial goal to achieve. Inclusion has been defined in different ways, has emphasized various target populations (such as students with mild versus severe disabilities), and has represented very diverse initiatives and tactics. Though resolved to increase the meaningful inclusion of children with disabilities, educators, parents, researchers, and communities often disagree on many points. Many have discussed the merits of eliminating all pullout services and the actual benefits of returning or maintaining children with disabilities in inclusive environments.

The many inclusion approaches are made up of many strategies to improve or remake the relationship between regular and special education. They reflect differing acknowledgment and accommodation for some of the barriers to enhancing integration, such as the importance of responding to the concerns of parents of children who are not disabled. As described in the next section, recent trends in placement patterns reinforce the opinion that schools, communities, parents, and researchers must work together to provide inclusive services in a responsible, successful manner.

NATIONAL TRENDS IN THE PLACEMENT OF CHILDREN WITH DISABILITIES

What has been national progress in serving children with disabilities within more integrated educational environments? States and locals implement inclusion initiatives, but in which educational environments and with what frequency do children with disabilities receive special education and related services? This section describes national and state trends in placement patterns. It concludes with a discussion of the potential relationship between demographic and fiscal variables and the placement patterns of children with disabilities.

Current National Profile

As required under Part B of IDEA, every year each state reports to the U.S. Office of Special Education Programs the educational environments in which children with disabilities receives services, including data on age and type of disability. As indicated in Table 1.1, for the 1993–1995 school year, about 45 percent of all children with disabilities in the United States received services in the regular class; 27 percent in resource room arrangements; 23 percent in a separate class; and approximately 5 percent in separate facilities (U.S. Department of Education, 1995). Combining categories, we find that over 94 percent of all children with disabilities receive education services at a general education site. However, only 45 percent of all children with a disability are educated in a regular class at least 80 percent of the school day. Figure 1.1 summarizes the federal definitions of educational environments applicable to the tables.

Table 1.1 Percentage of Children with Disabilities Ages Three to Twenty-one Served in Various Educational Environments, 1994–1995 School Year

	Regular Class	Resource Room	Separate Class	Other Separate Facility
United States				
All disabilities combined	45.07	26.96	23.28	4.69
High & Low Range for States				
All disabilities combined	10–84	4–70	5–44	<1–24

SOURCE: *Nineteenth Annual Report to Congress* (U.S. Department of Education, 1997).

Note: "*Other Separate Facilities*" represents percentages for separate schools (public and private), residential facilities (public and private) and homebound/hospital environments combined.

- *Regular class* includes students who receive the majority of their education program in a regular classroom and receive special education and related services outside the regular classroom for less than 21% of the school day. It includes children placed in a regular class and receiving special education within the regular class, as well as children placed in a regular class and receiving special education outside the regular class.
- *Resource room* includes students who receive special education and related services outside the regular classroom for at least 21% but no more than 60% of the school day. This may include students placed in resource rooms with part-time instruction in a regular class.
- *Separate class* includes students who receive special education and related services outside the regular classroom for more than 60% of the school day. Students may be placed in self-contained special classrooms with part-time instruction in regular classes or placed in self-contained classes full-time on a regular school campus.
- *Separate school* includes students who receive special education and related services in separate day schools for students with disabilities for more than 50% of the school day.
- *Residential facility* includes students who receive education in a public or private residential facility, at public expense, for more than 50% of the school day.
- *Homebound/hospital environment* includes students placed in and receiving special education in hospital or homebound programs.

FIGURE 1.1 Definitions of Educational Environments

SOURCE: U.S. Department of Education (1994).

Table 1.1 also summarizes the substantial state-by-state variation in the range of the use of educational placements. Individual states report a range from 10 to 84 percent in the use of regular class placements, 4 to 70 percent for resource room arrangements, 5 to 44 percent for separate classes, and from less than 1 percent up to 24 percent for students served in separate facilities. Services in the regular classroom do not necessarily represent the elimination of all pullout special education services. Using the federal definition, students may still receive special education and related services outside the regular classroom up to one-fifth of the school day.

Table 1.2 presents the percentage of students served in different placement settings in the United States by disability (U.S. Department of Education, 1997). Because of federal reporting requirements, the figures available reflect persons from ages six to twenty-one. As the table indicates, placement varies substantially by specific disability during 1993–1995. Students with a specific learning disability, who comprised 51 percent of all students identified in 1995–1996, were served primarily through regular class and resource room arrangements (81 percent). Students with speech and language impairments, who made up 20 percent of all students served, are the disability group most often served in regular and resource room arrangements: 95 percent. On the other hand, about two-thirds (63 percent) of all students with mental retardation are served through separate classes or separate facilities. Children with mental retardation comprised 11.2 percent of all children served as disabled in the 1995–1996 school year. For students with serious emotional disturbance, who make up the remaining "high-incidence" disability group (8.7 percent in 1995–1996), slightly more than half (54 percent) are served through separate classes or separate facilities.

All other disability conditions represent approximately 7.1 percent of all children served. For each of these, there is also considerable variation in the use of different placements. For example, over three-fourths of all students with multiple disabilities (79 percent) and deaf-blindness (82 percent) are more likely served through separate class and facility arrangements. For the first time, almost 35 percent of students with hearing impairments received services in regular classes, bringing the percentage served in regular and resource rooms to 54 percent. Over four-fifths of children with orthopedic impairments, visual impairments, and other health impairments (91 percent, 83 percent, and 90 percent, respectively) are served in regular or resource room arrangements. Over 80 percent of children with autism are served outside regular classes and resource rooms (U.S. Department of Education, 1997).

Table 1.3 summarizes the percentage of students receiving services in various educational environments for three age groups: six to eleven, twelve to seventeen, and eighteen to twenty-one for the 1994–1995 school year. The use of regular class and resource room arrangements declines from approximately 79 percent for students ages six to eleven, to approximately 69 percent for children ages twelve to seventeen, to 55 percent for students ages eighteen to twenty-one (U.S. Department of Education, 1997). Interpreting similar percentages for the 1990–1991 school year, the U.S. Department of Education (1993) states that as students:

> become older, school personnel may decide that less integrated settings are more appropriate for the delivery of more intensive specialized services. Students age 18–21 may be more likely to be served in less integrated settings because the actual population of these students may represent students with more severe disabilities who have not completed school within the usual time frame. Students with more severe disabilities are typically served in less

Table 1.2 Percentage of Students Ages Six to Twenty-one Served in Different Educational Environments by Disability, 1994–1995 School Year

	EDUCATIONAL ENVIRONMENT					
Disability	**Regular Class**	**Resource Room**	**Separate Class**	**Separate School**	**Residential Facility**	**Homebound/ Hospital**
Specific learning disability	41.1	39.6	18.4	0.6	0.1	0.2
Speech or language impairments	87.4	7.7	4.5	0.3	0.0	0.1
Mental retardation	9.7	27.1	55.9	6.3	0.6	0.5
Serious emotional disturbance	22.1	24.0	35.2	13.6	3.3	1.8
Hearing impairments	35.0	19.4	28.6	6.7	10.2	0.2
Multiple disabilities	9.0	11.8	51.3	21.9	3.5	2.5
Orthopedic impairments	39.0	20.6	31.7	5.6	0.4	2.6
Other health impairments	42.6	28.9	18.6	1.7	0.3	8.0
Visual impairments	45.9	21.1	17.2	4.8	10.4	0.5
Autism	10.7	9.3	55.0	21.6	2.9	0.6
Deaf-blindness	9.4	8.8	36.2	22.9	20.2	2.5
Traumatic brain injury	26.0	24.1	30.4	14.4	2.2	2.9
All disabilities	44.5	28.7	22.5	3.1	0.7	0.6

SOURCE: U.S. Department of Education (1997).

integrated settings. In addition, some 18- through 21-year olds with disabilities may be enrolled in specialized vocational education and transition programs which are likely to be conducted in separate classes and separate schools. (pp. 18–19)

National Trends in Placement Patterns

In recent years, analyses have been conducted to examine relative changes in the use of placement settings over time (Sawyer, McLaughlin, & Winglee, 1992; U.S. Department of Education, 1992, 1993). In general, national placement patterns have changed slowly, in the direction of more children served in less restrictive settings. As Table 1.4 indicates, the number of children served in regular classrooms increased 12 percentage points between the 1989–1990 and 1994–1995 school years. There have been slight decreases in the number served through resource rooms, separate classes, and all other separate facilities combined; −8.5 percent, −1.9 percent, and −2.1 percentage points, respectively.

Table 1.5 summarizes changes in the percentages of children with various disabilities who are served in regular *schools.* Regular school placement represents regular class, resource room, and separate class settings combined. As shown in the table, in the fifteen-year period of 1977–1978 to 1992–1993, for all disabilities combined, regular school placement increased 1.5 percentage points (Sawyer, McLaughlin, & Winglee, 1992; U.S. Department of Education, 1992). The trend for students with orthopedic impairments is the greatest (+17 change in percentage), but for almost all other disabling conditions, there is an increasing trend

Table 1.3 Percentage of Students with Disabilities Ages Six to Eleven, Twelve to Seventeen, and Eighteen to Twenty-one Served in Different Educational Environments, 1994–1995 School Year

	AGE GROUP		
Educational Environment	**6–11**	**12–17**	**18–21**
Regular class	54.4	34.8	28.1
Resource room	24.3	34.1	27.1
Separate class	19.0	25.6	31.0
Other separate facilities	2.4	5.6	13.8

SOURCE: U.S. Department of Education (1997).

Note: *"Other Separate Facilities"* represents combined percentages for separate schools (public and private), residential facilities (public and private), and homebound and hospital environments.

Table 1.4 Percentages of Students Ages Three to Twenty-one Served in Four Educational Environments, 1989–1994 School Years

Environment	**1989–1990**	**1991–1992**	**1992–1993**	**1994–1995**
Regular class	32.5	35.7	39.8	45.1
Resource room	35.5	34.4	31.7	27.0
Separate class	25.2	24.0	23.4	23.3
Other separate facilities	6.8	5.9	5.1	4.7

SOURCES: U.S. Department of Education (1993, 1994, 1995, 1997).

Note: *"Other Separate Facilities"* represents combined percentages for separate schools (public and private), residential facilities (public and private), and homebound and hospital environments.

toward more regular school placement, ranging varies from +22.6 to −3.2 percentage points. An increasing trend was observed for learning disabilities, mental retardation, multiple disabilities, health and orthopedic impairments, hearing impairments, and visual impairments. However, for students with speech or language impairments, serious emotional disturbance and deaf-blindness, negative trends away from regular school placement were noted.

Shifts in *classroom*-level placements between 1985–1986 and 1994–1995 for all disabilities are reported in Table 1.6 (U.S. Department of Education, 1992, 1995, 1997). In this table, data for the classroom environments of regular class and resource room are combined and presented along with that for separate classes. The range in the change in the percentage for regular class/resource room combined is −7.9 percent to +23.9 percent. For all disabilities combined, the change is an increase of +4.2 percent. The shifts were slightly *positive* for all four of the high-incidence disability categories: specific learning disabilities, speech

Table 1.5 Percentage of Children Ages Six to Twenty-one with Various Disabilities Served in Regular Schools Between the 1977 and 1992 School Years

Disability	1977–1978	1981–1982	1985–1986	1989–1990	1992–1993	Percentage Change
All disabilities	93.5	93.9	93.4	94.0	95.1	+1.5
Specific learning disabilities	98.3	98.5	98.6	98.5	98.8	+0.5
Speech or language impairments	99.4	99.3	98.3	98.3	98.5	−0.9
Mental retardation	89.5	88.7	86.1	88.0	90.7	+1.2
Serious emotional disturbance	84.7	82.2	80.2	80.5	81.5	−3.2
Hearing impairments	72.7	76.8	76.3	76.9	77.3	+4.6
Visual impairments	80.9	82.0	81.8	84.1	84.6	+3.7
Deaf-blindness	—	55.7	48.2	55.0	53.4	−2.3
Multiple disabilities	—	70.5	65.0	64.6	71.3	+0.8
Orthopedic impairments	66.6	67.9	79.0	83.6	89.2	+22.6
Other health impairments	77.3	78.8	72.4	77.9	88.0	+10.7

SOURCES: U.S. Department of Education (1992, Appendix I; 1995, Table 1.7).

Note: Data are for students served under IDEA, Part B and Chapter 1 of the Elementary and Secondary Education Act (State-Operated Programs).

and language impairments, mental retardation, and serious emotional disturbance. For the separate class setting, students representing three of the ten disability categories were slightly more likely to be placed in a separate class in 1994–1995 than in 1985–1986. For all disabilities combined, however, there was a decrease of 1.9 percentage points for separate class placements between 1985–1986 and 1994–1995 (U.S. Department of Education, 1992, 1995, 1997).

State Variation in Placement Patterns

Much discussion and controversy accompanied the initial presentation of the substantial variation across states in placement patterns of children with disabilities (Danielson & Bellamy, 1989). The analyses showed each state seeking both to provide an appropriate, individualized program and to implement the Least Restrictive Environment principle. Using a "cumulative placement rate" statistic,[2] Danielson and Bellamy (1989) conducted analyses indicating some states "with the highest [cumulative placement] rates are five to six times more likely to

[2]Cumulative placement rate was defined as the number of students with disabilities within a particular age group who were served in a selected educational placement and all other segregated placements, divided by the state's total population. Dividing by the total state population, rather than the total special education child count, protects a state serving relatively few children with mild disabilities from appearing to serve a large number in more segregated environments (Danielson & Bellamy, 1989). Use of the cumulative placement rate statistic is limited because (a) comparisons between placements is not possible, (b) a cumulative placement means placement in one type of class and all more restrictive placements, and (c) cumulative placement in regular classes and other settings is highly confounded with identification rates (McLaughlin & Owings, 1993). These authors recommend analyses, for example, that represent actual placement rate per the number of students identified as having a specific disability.

Table 1.6 Percentage of Children with Various Disabilities Served in Different Regular School Classroom Environments, 1985–1986 Through 1992–1993 School Years

Classroom Environments	Disability	1985–1986	1989–1990	1992–1993	1994–1995	Percentage Change
Regular class and resource room combined	All disabilities combined	69.0	69.2	71.5	73.2	+4.2
	Specific learning disabilities	77.8	76.8	78.8	80.7	+2.9
	Speech or language impairments	94.7	94.6	92.5	95.1	+0.4
	Mental retardation	28.8	26.5	33.9	36.8	+8.0
	Serious emotional disturbance	44.1	43.5	46.3	46.1	+2.0
	Hearing impairments	43.8	45.3	49.2	54.4	+10.6
	Multiple disabilities	20.6	20.5	26.6	20.8	+0.2
	Visual impairments	62.6	62.8	66.5	67.02	+4.4
	Deaf-blindness	26.0	24.6	21.9	18.1	−7.9
	Orthopedic impairments	48.0	48.6	55.2	60.0	+12.0
	Other health impairments	47.6	53.4	67.4	71.5	+23.9
Separate class	All disabilities combined	24.4	24.8	23.5	22.5	−1.9
	Specific learning disabilities	20.8	21.7	20.1	18.4	−2.4
	Speech or language impairments	3.7	3.8	6.0	4.5	+0.8
	Mental retardation	57.3	61.5	56.8	55.9	−1.4
	Serious emotional disturbance	36.1	37.1	35.2	35.2	−0.9
	Hearing impairments	32.5	31.6	28.1	28.6	−3.9
	Multiple disabilities	44.5	44.1	44.6	51.3	−6.8
	Visual impairments	19.2	21.3	18.0	17.2	−2.0
	Deaf-blindness	22.2	30.4	31.4	36.2	+14.0
	Orthopedic impairments	31.0	35.0	34.1	31.7	+0.7
	Other health impairments	24.8	24.5	20.6	18.5	−6.3

SOURCES: U.S. Department of Education (1992, p. 27; 1995, appendices).

Note: Data are for students six to twenty-one years old, served under IDEA, Part B and Chapter 1 of the Elementary and Secondary Education Act (State-Operated Programs).

have children placed in separate classes or facilities than those with the lowest rates" (p. 452). Several possible explanations for the variability were offered: measurement errors, differences among states in data collection procedures and terminology, and "factors in addition to the characteristics of students" (p. 453). These authors cautioned "placement practices alone should not be interpreted as indicative of the quality of special education in a state" (p. 453). In fact, the U.S. Department of Education (1995) noted that the almost 10 percent increase in regular classroom placements was accounted for largely by improved data collection and reporting in four states: California, Indiana, New York, and Minnesota.

Given limitations associated with the interpretation of the cumulative placement rate statistic (McLaughlin & Owings, 1993), Table 1.7 summarizes actual state-by-state use of various educational environments including those reported for the 1985–1986 (the same year as analyses by Danielson and Bellamy) and 1992–1993 school years (U.S. Department of Education, 1988, 1994).

The most recent profile of states including the District of Columbia and Puerto Rico for the 1992–1993 school year shows that twenty-two states served 50 percent or more of all their children in the regular classroom. The range for regular class placement is 7 to 85 percent. Four states serve more than 50 percent of all their students within resource room arrangements. For resource settings, the range across states is from a low of 3 percent to a high of 69 percent. No state serves more than 43 percent of all children in a separate class. The state with the lowest percentage serves 6 percent through separate classes. The range among states for placement in separate facilities is from less than 1 percent to almost 24 percent. Interpreting the substantial state-by-state variation, the U.S. Department of Education (1992) notes:

> [A]s reported extensively in previous annual reports, placement patterns vary considerably across States. . . . This State variability is likely due to a number of factors including: actual differences in the populations and needs of students, the roles of private schools and separate facilities in the State, different State reporting practices and interpretations of Federal data collection forms, and State special education funding formulas. (p. 24)

Table 1.7 also illustrates changes in placement patterns within states between 1985–1986 and 1992–1993. The national trend reflects an increase in the use of regular class placement over time. Within that time period, twenty-three states increased the use of regular class placement, some dramatically (for example, Alabama, from 0 to 60 percent; Georgia, 1 to 44 percent; Missouri, 2 to 34 percent). Twenty-two states reported a decrease in their relative use of separate classes, and forty-six states reduced the relative percentage served in separate facilities (for instance, Minnesota, from 15 to 7 percent). Table 1.7 illustrates, then, that significant within-state variation over time may be masked by the national percentages.

To better understand individual state efforts to enhance the integration of students with disabilities, additional analyses are needed. These could identify particular state patterns, such as states that serve a relatively high number of students in regular classes but a relatively low number through resource room

Table 1.7 Percentage of Children Ages Three to Twenty-one Served in Different Educational Environments Under IDEA and Chapter 1 of ESEA During the 1985–1986 and 1992–1993 School Years, All Disabilities

LOCATION	REGULAR CLASS		RESOURCE ROOM		SEPARATE CLASSES		ALL OTHER SEPARATE FACILITIES	
	1985–1986	1992–1993	1985–1986	1992–1993	1985–1986	1992–1993	1985–1986	1992–1993
Alabama	0.00	50.99	68.71	22.52	28.45	23.86	2.69	2.60
Alaska	40.89	51.47	37.42	35.34	18.09	12.21	3.60	.97
Arizona	0.27	6.73	72.43	66.04	22.92	22.99	4.39	4.25
Arkansas	25.65	41.22	55.84	39.35	11.61	14.10	6.90	5.34
California	28.92	50.83	38.80	21.34	31.12	24.45	1.16	3.37
Colorado	23.13	24.49	50.98	56.55	19.60	15.44	6.31	3.53
Connecticut	8.39	50.74	49.62	20.23	30.46	22.51	11.53	6.53
Delaware	19.87	35.16	43.11	28.28	19.33	27.06	17.70	9.50
District of Columbia	19.03	11.07	16.82	21.80	39.91	43.20	24.25	23.94
Florida	30.54	43.62	38.26	23.45	23.46	28.27	7.76	4.67
Georgia	1.02	44.08	71.04	29.71	24.84	24.43	3.09	1.77
Hawaii	37.92	38.66	34.96	31.23	24.16	28.96	2.95	1.16
Idaho	37.75	63.40	37.09	22.63	16.96	11.20	8.22	2.77
Illinois	29.52	27.05	32.14	33.37	29.64	31.92	8.69	7.67
Indiana	39.08	60.13	28.57	10.96	26.88	26.04	5.46	2.86
Iowa	25.29	20.11	39.74	60.52	33.33	16.37	1.65	3.02
Kansas	38.20	50.94	33.16	28.61	20.92	15.12	7.72	5.33
Kentucky	27.93	46.95	50.54	38.51	15.08	11.64	6.46	2.89
Louisiana	35.24	34.99	23.27	16.66	30.41	43.62	11.08	4.72
Maine	13.19	49.96	49.57	33.55	17.10	11.28	20.14	5.21
Maryland	39.55	47.33	20.33	18.51	24.65	25.65	15.47	8.51
Massachusetts	8.25	63.88	65.70	14.51	19.28	15.67	6.75	5.94
Michigan	45.27	46.46	21.84	24.85	26.51	23.63	6.39	5.07
Minnesota	12.62	49.46	62.69	31.99	9.83	11.36	14.86	7.19
Mississippi	36.45	33.24	38.13	38.24	22.61	26.76	2.80	1.75
Missouri	2.65	34.49	70.96	39.83	20.52	19.70	5.89	5.97
Montana	59.29	58.93	18.97	29.42	17.71	10.20	4.02	1.45
Nebraska	17.11	61.26	72.54	21.67	7.73	13.54	2.62	3.53

Nevada	27.14	32.15	47.75	43.46	15.80	17.95	9.33	6.44
New Hampshire	61.28	52.48	15.43	22.40	15.91	18.69	7.38	6.43
New Jersey	41.94	32.35	20.48	25.09	28.01	31.93	9.57	10.63
New Mexico	52.84	40.09	27.27	25.53	15.34	32.87	4.54	1.51
New York	9.50	24.40	33.38	25.16	39.62	36.77	17.50	13.67
North Carolina	31.62	57.13	48.94	22.26	13.86	16.78	5.58	3.84
North Dakota	71.85	73.45	8.39	11.84	15.31	11.15	4.45	3.57
Ohio	35.07	35.84	23.41	35.19	27.53	16.84	13.99	12.12
Oklahoma	32.15	49.97	52.17	30.58	12.25	17.17	3.43	2.29
Oregon	59.39	64.56	30.21	22.53	8.19	9.43	2.22	3.49
Pennsylvania	33.90	37.40	28.19	26.52	29.12	30.99	8.78	5.08
Puerto Rico	4.46	12.52	32.89	44.44	27.85	35.60	34.80	7.43
Rhode Island	55.24	51.39	14.77	16.93	24.59	26.35	5.41	5.34
South Carolina	31.30	35.84	44.26	37.11	20.00	24.21	4.45	2.84
South Dakota	6.49	62.74	72.76	22.29	15.11	10.15	5.63	4.84
Tennessee	33.85	50.35	43.20	28.25	17.54	18.24	5.41	3.16
Texas	2.09	25.18	71.93	45.97	18.30	24.70	7.68	4.15
Utah	36.11	41.53	44.20	32.89	13.29	20.66	6.38	4.92
Vermont	50.67	84.74	30.10	2.80	13.17	6.16	6.06	6.31
Virginia	30.83	38.90	36.48	30.00	27.00	27.10	5.69	4.00
Washington	45.42	48.89	24.92	28.85	23.67	20.33	6.00	1.93
West Virginia	46.19	6.75	32.44	69.17	17.86	21.89	3.52	2.19
Wisconsin	39.33	35.71	33.68	37.97	23.19	24.35	3.80	1.98
Wyoming	39.83	50.32	42.08	37.93	13.56	9.07	4.52	2.67
American Samoa	2.40	79.26	63.46	7.65	4.33	2.72	29.81	10.37
Guam	22.31	37.63	20.60	35.76	47.20	24.24	9.88	2.38
Northern Marianas	—	84.06	—	11.01	—	2.03	—	2.90
Palau	—	—	—	—	—	—	—	—
Virgin Islands	—	21.31	—	12.27	—	60.17	—	6.25
Bureau of Indian Affairs	40.57	50.46	46.29	41.00	7.58	6.32	5.55	2.22
U.S. & Insular Areas	26.24	40.53	41.40	29.89	24.49	24.10	7.87	5.48
50 States, D.C., & P. R.	26.23	40.51	41.40	29.88	24.51	24.12	7.87	.90

SOURCES: U.S. Department of Education (1988, 1994).

arrangements (such as Vermont). Also, to avoid misinterpretations based on differential state rates of identification of specific disabilities or identification rate overall, the relationship between rate of identification and placement rates across states should be examined in future analyses.

Analyses are also needed to relate placement rates to those of potentially significant demographic and fiscal variables. McLaughlin and Owings (1993), for example, reexamined state cumulative placement rates for three times: 1976, 1980, and 1983. Seeking to improve state-by-state comparisons, they included state context measures (per-pupil expenditures, per capita personal income, and so forth) and grouped states along these measures for the analyses. Although they noted difficulty interpreting their findings because they used a cumulative placement variable (that is, one comparable to that used by Danielson & Bellamy, 1989), they reported "significant inverse correlations, in the weak to moderate range, between percentage of rural child population and use of special classes and all more restrictive placements" for 1980 and 1983 (p. 254). "Significant positive relationships were also observed in 1980 and 1983 between [personal per capita income] and the cumulative placement rates for special classes and more restrictive environments" (p. 256). The coefficients obtained in the latter analyses were 0.29 and 0.28, respectively.

More recently, Coutinho and Oswald (1996) observed significant relationships between demographic and economic variables and use of different placement settings in children with serious emotional disturbance. Approximately one-half of the variation in states' placement rate in separate facilities was accounted for by three economic variables and the identification rate for children with serious emotional disturbance.

Additional analyses are also needed to interpret trends in state placement patterns over time. For example, Table 1.7 does not account for differences in overall identification rates and/or changes in those rates for the two time periods. Also, additional analyses may well reveal a unique set of complex patterns of placements used by particular states, as educators seek to balance initiatives to provide higher-quality services, respond to fiscal restraints, improve outcomes, and also enhance the integration of students with disabilities.

A study by Dempsey and Fuchs (1993) illustrates the importance of careful examination of individual state placement patterns and trends over time. The results of this study also suggest that shifts in placement patterns may follow, fairly rapidly, a change in the state funding formula for services to students with disabilities. The federal formula for funding special education services is a flat per-child amount. State formulas, however, vary. Some provide additional monies for more expensive, often more restrictive placements. As states responded to numerous fiscal and policy initiatives in the last decade, all but eleven altered their respective funding formula, and many continue to change the mechanisms for funding special education. Many reasons have been offered, including initiatives to promote more integrated placements, efforts to reduce the rate of growth in special education, or a desire to fund special education services at a higher level, or budget restraints (National Association of State Directors of Special Education, 1988). As passed originally in 1975 through PL 94-142, IDEA authorized Congress to spend up to 40 percent by 1982 of the average per-child expendi-

Table 1.8 Funding Available Before and After Changes to a State Funding Formula and Shifts in Use of Various Placement Options

	Placement Option 1: <3 Hrs.	Placement Option 2: 3–20 Hrs.	Placement Option3: 21–27 Hrs.	Placement Option 4: 27+Hrs.
Average level of funding: **"flat"** formula	512	512	512	512
Average level of funding: **"weighted"** formula	333	600	2,693	3,715
Change in use of option after change in funding formula	No change	Decrease	Increase	Decrease

SOURCE: Dempsey and Fuchs (1993).

Note: Hours reflect the time spent in special education per week. Both decreases and the increase, respectively, were statistically significant at $p < .01$.

ture in special education. As of 1992–1993, however, federal spending levels approximated only 8 percent, or a $411 per-child expenditure. "In constant dollars the per pupil allocation is $169, slightly more than the 1978 level of $156" (U.S. Department of Education, 1994, p. 5).

Dempsey and Fuchs (1993) examined the relationship between a change in funding formula and student placement patterns. In this case, the state, Tennessee, switched from a flat rate (the same amount of funds per child regardless of type of disability or amount of service) to a weighted formula. Weights were based on service option to reflect intensity of effort and cost: consultation, partial resource, comprehensive resource, self-contained, and so on. More restrictive options were reimbursed at a higher rate. Table 1.8 summarizes the dollars available per placement option, before and after the change in funding formula.

As Table 1.8 illustrates, Option 3, described as a comprehensive resource room placement, increased significantly. Less restrictive placements decreased or stayed the same. Also during this same time period, 1979–1980 through 1987–1988, special education enrollment decreased by about 10,000 (from approximately 124,000 to 114,000 students). Only ten other states experienced a decline or an annual increase in growth of less than 1 percent during that time period.

In conclusion, national progress in implementing the Least Restrictive Principle of IDEA has been significant: the majority of children with disabilities receive their education within general education environments, and almost three-fourths are served in regular classes or through resource room arrangements. There have been many inclusion initiatives, and placement patterns have been changing slowly. National shifts toward more regular class and regular school placement are being observed. Moreover, for children with specific learning disabilities, visual impairments and mental retardation, hearing impairments, multiple disabilities, orthopedic and other health impairments, the trend toward more inclusive placement is increasing. However, on a national basis, the percentage change is not positive for children with speech or language impairments, serious emotional disturbance, or deaf-blindness. Also, older children are less likely to receive services within regular class and regular school placements. Considerable state-by-state variation in placement patterns also exists. A better understanding of state variation will require investigation of (a) the influence of economic, education, and demographic variables on a state's relative rate of identification of students with disabilities and (b) the role of local procedures and capacity. Rock, Rosenberg, and Carran (1994), for example, provide evidence of the importance of particular experience and training of special educators and of program characteristics (for example, location, public versus private) for the reintegration of children with serious emotional disturbance.

IMPLICATIONS AND DIRECTIONS FOR RESEARCH AND PRACTICE TO ENHANCE INCLUSION

Public opinion and national statistics on the outcomes of children with disabilities point to the urgent need to improve services for children with disabilities (Wagner, 1991; Wagner et al., 1993). For the 1992–1993 school year, only slightly over half of all children with disabilities exiting the educational system received a high school diploma or certificate (U.S. Department of Education, 1994). This percentage is less than for both the previous school year and that reported for the 1985–1986 school year. Analyses of the National Longitudinal Transition Study of Special Education Students (Wagner, 1991) showed that 43 percent of the youth ages fifteen to twenty leaving secondary school over a two-year period simply dropped out. This figure compares with 24 percent of youth in the general population. Concern over poor transitions—namely, the lack of preparedness for adult life and the unsatisfactory outcomes of many youth with disabilities—is, perhaps, the singular other topic that rivals increasing integration for national attention (Wagner, 1991; Wagner et al., 1993).

Despite the many initiatives and evidence of national progress, the current research and knowledge bases appear inconclusive with respect to which particular inclusion approach is most effective, with whom (for example, type of disability) and how (for example, in what relationship with general education). Carefully designed field experiments and more tightly controlled intervention research are needed to learn how best to enhance inclusion. Any discouragement, however, with national progress or the inconclusiveness of the current knowledge base should not allow a return to "same old, same old" strategies. Prospects for children with disabilities when reintegrated within traditionally organized regular education classes remain poor. Evidence also exists that progress is inadequate for students maintained in traditional pullout arrangements (Fuchs et al., 1993). Neither setting, if offering services not specifically validated and effective, is likely to enable educators to address the goals of national education reform for all students.

Based on national progress, societal commitment, and the many inclusion initiatives, two general recommendations can be made to guide both school building initiatives and research to enhance the inclusion of children with disabilities: (a) explicitly define inclusion and the indicators with which to evaluate success and (b) work in partnerships.

First, to assist those seeking to interpret and/or replicate programmatic initiatives to enhance inclusion, those implementing research and system-change initiatives should define terms explicitly and operationally. The particular approach, instructional and curricular strategies, the desired relationships between regular and special educators, and overall goals should be specified. For example, is the goal to eliminate the continuum of placements or to reduce the number of children served through pullout arrangements? Those seeking to adapt and implement particular approaches to enhance integration, to improve practice, or to conduct further research will rely on detailed project descriptions and the findings associated with specific student and system-level indicators.

Differences in the definition of inclusion, the target population, and goals all affect how to implement and evaluate efforts. For example, if the inclusion of children with severe disabilities only is the emphasis, teachers often worry about liability and who will provide the medical assistance some students need. When asked to serve students with mild and moderate disabilities full-time in the regular classroom, teachers frequently ask how they will meet the academic and behavioral needs of students with mild and moderate disabilities, at the same time that they address the needs of all other students. Results of research studies and school-change initiatives are best interpreted against goals, definitions, and approaches that are made explicit.

Child and system-level indicators should be included to evaluate the actual benefits associated with increases in the rate of inclusion. Reliance on important student outcomes is recommended. Outcomes themselves may be defined in terms of short-term objectives or preparedness for adult life roles (such as competitive employment and living independently). Comparative gains made in pullout versus integrated settings should be examined. Outcomes of students with disabilities may also be compared with those attained by students not identified as disabled. Also to investigate are the outcomes of students without disabilities. Is their progress affected when educated in settings alongside nondisabled peers (Sharpe, York, & Knight, 1994)?

Perceived satisfaction by participants with a particular initiative cannot alone be expected to satisfy taxpayer and public demand for improvement and accountability. As described by Green and Shinn (1994):

> [I]t also seems evident that parents must be provided with clear, understandable information about whether and when their children's academic performance is satisfactory. Content analysis of parents' comments suggests strongly that their opinions about their children's achievement are not usually tied to any objective information provided by teachers. In addition, these parents did not have a clear picture of how their children compared to typical peers. In the absence of student outcome data, parents' judgments of their children's progress is impaired and their capacity for oversight is deeply compromised. Parents expressed strong interest in academic performance data that allow comparison to general education peers over time. (p. 279)

Multiple system indicators reflecting resource inputs and necessary training and support, for example, are also needed. Reforms also are implemented to respond to fiscal restraints, not just poor outcomes. Whether an initiative to enhance inclusion succeeds must also be evaluated with respect to the training, technology, and alignment of the fiscal resources needed to produce and maintain significant student gains (Rock et al., 1994). The importance of financial resources and their allocation, for example, when implementing school-based approaches to enhance integration cannot be underestimated. Hasazi et al. (1994) note that in their qualitative policy study of the implementation of the Least Restrictive Principle in several states:

> [F]inance emerged as the cornerstone of influence at all of the sites. It was the "given" or the obvious factor. Time and again interviewees told of the importance of education funding in general, as well as how dependent the educational system had become on the categorical nature of special education for continuous financial support of programs and services. Citing established separate facilities and separate programs as examples, everyone agreed that special education and, in particular LRE, required substantial resources for implementation. Indeed, for those who were moving toward educating increased number of children with disabilities in general education settings, additional resources during the early stages were required beyond what the categorical-funding mechanisms provided. (p. 504)

These authors also observe:

> In the end, however, there were differences in how the high-user sites and the low-user sites chose to view both finance and organization. For the former, finance and organization considerations generally meant literal compliance or close adherence to the strict categorical nature of the systems. If that meant keeping children and youth with disabilities educated in separate programs and facilities to receive necessary financial support, then that is what they did. By contrast, administrators in the low-user sites generally viewed finance and organization not so much as intractable mandates, but as necessary realities that could be "flexed" to push the system to do what they wanted. Compliance meant staying within a more liberal reading of the law so that implementation could be shaped around their own ethical and conceptually defensible view of education. (p. 504)

Regarding the second recommendation offered here, the value of partnerships, investment and collaboration by all sides will be needed to provide better outcomes for students with disabilities served in integrated settings. Partnerships representing general and special educators, administrators, the community, business, higher education, researchers, and parents are needed to identify, implement, and evaluate validated, pragmatic, and innovative instructional strategies and arrangements that meet the needs of all children. When implementing innovations and models, communities and schools embarking on action plans must collectively define services that will represent the student, the system goals, and what will be provided, by whom and where. Results, gains, and obstacles may be expected to differ across schools because of different approaches, goals, and varying levels of resources.

In conclusion, numerous initiatives and the national profile hold much promise and hope for efforts to enhance the inclusion of children with disabilities. To increase the meaningful inclusion of students, we must recall that IDEA defines special education as "specially designed instruction" provided to meet the unique needs of students with disabilities; it is not a "place." As described throughout this text, many instructional, curricular, and programmatic practices can be used to implement inclusion successfully. Numerous strategies employ promising technological innovations, address cultural and demographic diversity, and improve policies and service delivery systems. Using such approaches, educators can provide for the maximum, responsible inclusion of students with disabilities by offering instruction specially designed to meet their unique needs within classroom and community environments.

REFERENCES

American Council on the Blind et al. (n.d.). *Full inclusion of students who are blind and visually impaired: A position statement.* Washington, DC: Author.

Board of Education of Hendrick Hudson Central School District v. Rowley, 458 U.S. 176, 102 S. Ct. 3034, 73. Ed.2d 690, 5 Ed. Law Rep. 34 (1982).

Board of Education, Sacramento City Unified School District v. Holland, 786 F. Supp. 874, 73 Ed. Law Rep. 969 (E.D. Cal. 1992); *affirmed sub nom. Sacramento City Unified School District, Board of Education v. Rachel H.,* 14 F.3d 1398, 89 Ed. Law Rep. 57 (9th Cir. 1994).

Braaten, S., Kauffman, J. M., Braaten, B., Polsgrove, L., & Nelson, C. M. (1988). The Regular Education Initiative: Patent medicine for behavioral disorders. *Exceptional Children, 55,* 21–27.

Chris D. v. Montgomery County Board of Education, 753 F. Supp. 922, 65 Ed. Law Rep. 355 (M.D. Ala. 1990).

Commission on the Education of the Deaf. (1988, February). *Toward equality: Education of the deaf.* Washington, DC: U.S. Government Printing Office. (ERIC Document Reproduction Service No. ED 303 932)

Council of Chief State School Officers. (1992, March). Special education and school restructuring. *Concerns, 35,* 1–7.

Council for Children with Behavior Disorders. (1994). Executive committee approves position statement on inclusion within a continuum of service delivery options. *CCBD Newsletter, 8,* 1.

Council for Exceptional Children. (1993, April). *Statement on inclusive schools and communities.* Reston, VA: Author.

Council for Exceptional Children. (1994). Twelve principles for successful inclusive schools. *CEC Today, 1*(2), 3, 14.

Coutinho, M., & Oswald, D. (1996). Identification and placement of students with serious emotional disturbance. Part II: National and state trends in the implementation of LRE. *Journal of Emotional and Behavioral Disorders, 4,* 40–52.

Daniel R.R. v. State Board of Education, 874 F.2d 1036, 53 Ed. Law Rep. 824 (5th Cir. 1989).

Danielson, L. C., & Bellamy, G. T. (1989). State variation in placement of children with handicaps in segregated environments. *Exceptional Children, 55,* 448–455.

Dempsey, S., & Fuchs, D. (1993). "Flat" versus "weighted" reimbursement formulas: A longitudinal analysis of statewide special education funding practices. *Exceptional Children, 59,* 433–443.

Deno, S., Maruyama, G., Espin, C., & Cohen, C. (1990). Educating students with mild disabilities in general education classrooms: Minnesota alternatives. *Exceptional Children, 57,* 150–161.

Dunn, L. M. (1968). Special education for the mildly retarded—Is much of it justifiable? *Exceptional Children, 35,* 5–22.

Fuchs, D., & Fuchs, L. (1994a). Inclusive schools movement and the radicalization of special education reform. *Exceptional Children, 60,* 294–309.

Fuchs, D., & Fuchs, L. S. (1994b). *A school building model for helping teachers meet the challenge of student diversity: Redesigning education for all children.* Unpublished manuscript, Peabody College of Vanderbilt University, Nashville, TN.

Fuchs, D., Fuchs, L. S., & Fernstrom, P. (1993). A conservative approach to special education reform: Mainstreaming through transenvironmental and curriculum-based measurement. *American Educational Research Journal, 30,* 149–178.

Gartner, A., & Lipsky, D. K. (1987). Beyond special education: Toward a quality system for all students. *Harvard Educational Review, 57,* 367–395.

Green, S. K., & Shinn, M. (1994). Parent attitudes about special education and reintegration. *Exceptional Children, 61,* 269–281.

Greer v. Rome City School District, 967 F. 2d 470, 76 Ed. Law Rep. 26 (11th Cir. 1992): 134.

Halvorsen, A., & Sailor, W. (1990). Integration of students with severe and profound disabilities: A review of the research. In R. Gaylord-Ross (Ed.), *Issues and research in special education.* New York: Teachers College Press.

Hasazi, S. B., Johnston, A. P., Liggett, A. M., & Schattman, R. A. (1994). A qualitative policy study of the least restrictive environment provision of the Individuals with Disabilities Education Act. *Exceptional Children, 60,* 491–507.

Heumann, J. E. (1994, Summer). Heumann speaks out on inclusion. *OSERS News Update.* Washington, DC: U.S. Office of Special Education and Rehabilitative Services.

Individuals with Disabilities Education Act (IDEA), U.S.C., Title 20, §§1400 et seq. Formerly titled the Education for All Handicapped Children Act, originally enacted as PL 94-142 (1975).

Jenkins, J. R., Jewell, M., Leicester, N., O'Connor, R. E., Jenkins, L. M., & Troutner, N. M. (1994). Accommodations for individual differences without classroom ability groups: An experiment in school restructuring. *Exceptional Children, 60,* 344–358.

Knapp, M. S., & Shields, P. M. (1990). Reconceiving academic instruction for children of poverty. *Phi Delta Kappan, 71,* 753–758.

Learning Disabilities Association. (1993, January). *Position paper on full inclusion of all students with learning disabilities in the regular education classroom.* Pittsburgh: Author.

Lloyd, J. W., Singh, N. N., & Repp, A. C. (1990). *The Regular Education Initiative: Alternative perspectives on concepts, issues, and models.* Sycamore, IL: Sycamore.

Madden, N. A., & Slavin, R. E. (1983). Mainstreaming students with mild handicaps: Academic and social outcomes. *Review of Educational Research, 53,* 519–569.

McLaughlin, M. J., & Owings, M. F. (1993). Relationships among states' fiscal and demographic data and the implementation of P.L. 94-142. *Exceptional Children, 59,* 247–261.

McLaughlin, M., & Warren, S. (1992, September). *Issues and options in restructuring schools and special education programs.* College Park: Center for Policy Options in Special Education, University of Maryland. (ERIC Document Reproduction Service No. ED 350 774)

National Association of State Boards of Education. (1992, October). *Winners all: A call for inclusive schools.* Washington, DC: Author.

National Association of State Directors of Special Education. (1989). *State special education finance systems, 1988–89* (Report to the U.S. Department of Education, Contract No. 300-85-0167). Washington, DC: Author.

National Education Association. (1992). *Resolution B-20: Education for all students with disabilities.* Washington, DC: Author.

Oberti v. Board of Education of the Borough of Clementon School District, 789 F. Supp. 1322, 75 Ed. Law Rep. 258 (D.N.J. 1992), 801 F. Supp. 1393 (D.M.J. 1992), aff'd 995 F.2d 1204, 83 Ed. Law Rep. 1009 (3d Cir. 1993).

Office of the Federal Register. (1982). *Code of Federal Regulations Parts 1-399. Chapter III: Office of Special Education and Rehabilitative Services, Department of Education, Part 300.* Washington, DC: U.S. Government Printing Office.

Osborne, A. G. (1996). *Legal issues in special education.* Needham Heights, MA: Allyn & Bacon.

Pearpoint, J., & Forest, M. (1992). Foreword. In S. Stainback & W. Stainback (Eds.), *Curriculum considerations in inclusive classrooms: Facilitating learning for all students.* Baltimore: Brookes.

Pugach, M., & Sapon-Shevin, M. (1987). New agendas for special education policy: What the national reports haven't said. *Exceptional Children, 53,* 295–299.

Rock, E. E., Rosenberg, M. S., & Carran, D. T. (1994). Variables affecting the reintegration rate of students with serious emotional disturbance. *Exceptional Children, 61,* 254–268.

Sawyer, R. J., McLaughlin, M. J., & Winglee, M. (1992). *Is integration of students with disabilities happening? An analysis of national data trends over time.* Rockville, MD: Westat.

Sharpe, M. N., York, J. C., & Knight, J. (1994). Effects of inclusion on the academic performance of classmates without disabilities. *Remedial and Special Education, 15,* 281–287.

Singer, J. D. (1988). Should special education merge with regular education? *Educational Policy, 2,* 409–424.

Sloan, L. J., Denny R. K., & Repp, A. C. (1992a). Integration in the schools: Practices in the United States. In P. Evans & M. McGovern (Eds.), *Active life for disabled youth.* Paris: Organization for Economic Cooperation and Development.

Sloan, L. J., Alberg, J., Denny, R. K., Hasazi, S. B., McLaughlin, M. J., & Repp, A. (1992b). Integration practices in the United States: A composite case study. In P. Evans & M. McGovern (Eds.), *Active life for disabled youth.* Paris: Organization for Economic Cooperation and Development.

Stainback, S., & Stainback, W. (1991). *Curriculum considerations in inclusive classrooms: Facilitating learning for all students.* Baltimore: Brookes.

Stainback, S., Stainback, W., East, K., & Sapon-Savin, M. (1994). Perspective: A commentary on inclusion and the development of a positive self-identity by people with disabilities. *Exceptional Children, 60,* 486–490.

Stevens, R., Madden, N., Slavin, R., & Farnish, A. (1987). Cooperative integrated reading and composition: Two field experiments. *Reading Research Quarterly, 22,* 433–454.

Turnbull, H. R. (1986). *Free appropriate public education: The law and children with disabilities.* Denver: Love.

U.S. Department of Education. (1988). *Tenth annual report to Congress.* Washington, DC: Author.

U.S. Department of Education. (1992). *Fourteenth annual report to Congress.* Washington, DC: Author.

U.S. Department of Education. (1993). *Fifteenth annual report to Congress.* Washington, DC: Author.

U.S. Department of Education. (1994). *Sixteenth annual report to Congress.* Washington, DC: Author.

U.S. Department of Education. (1995). *Seventeenth annual report to Congress.* Washington, DC: Author.

U.S. Department of Education. (1997). *Nineteenth annual report to Congress.* Washington, DC: Author.

Wagner, M. (1991). *Dropouts with disabilities: What do we know? What can we do?* Menlo Park, CA: SRI International.

Wagner, M., Newman, L., D'Amico, R., Jay, E. D., Butler-Nalin, P., Marder, C., & Cox, R. (1991). *Youth with disabilities: How are they doing? The first comprehensive report from the National Longitudinal Transition Study of Special Education Students*. Menlo Park, CA: SRI International.

Will, M. C. (1986). Educating children with learning problems: A shared responsibility. *Exceptional Children, 52,* 411–415.

Zigmond, N., Jenkins, J., Fuchs, L., Deno, S., Fuchs, D., Baker, J. M., Jenkins, L., & Coutinho, M. (1995). Special education in restructured schools: Findings from three multi-year studies. *Phi Delta Kappan, 76,* 531–540.

2

Educational Reform

Issues for the Inclusion of Students with Disabilities

MARGARET J. MCLAUGHLIN
PATRICIA F. SCHOFIELD
SANDRA HOPFENGARDENER WARREN

Inclusion of students with disabilities into the classrooms and routines of regular schools has been at the front of the policy agenda of special education for over a decade. Organizations have issued positions that support or denounce the practice (for example, Arc, 1992; Council for Exceptional Children [CEC], 1993; Learning Disabilities Association of America [LDAA], 1993; National Association of State Boards of Education [NASBE], 1992). Proponents have extolled the benefits of inclusion to students and society (Gartner & Lipsky, 1989; McDonnell & Kiefer-O'Donnell, 1992; McDonnell, McDonnell, Hardman, & McCune, 1991; Sailor, Gee, & Karasoff, 1993; Villa, Thousand, Stainback, & Stainback, 1992), while opponents have debated and dissected the motives as well as the feasibility of the actual practice of inclusion (Fuchs & Fuchs, 1994; Kauffman, 1993).

Despite the depth of discussion and passion associated with the concept of inclusion, only recently has inclusion been addressed within the context of broader education reform of education (Council of Administrators of Special Education [CASE], 1993; McLaughlin, Henderson, & Rhim, in press; McLaughlin & Warren, 1992). Indeed, the inclusion debates often center around placement of children with disabilities and how to fit special education services into an existing classroom or "mapped" onto an existing curriculum. However, inclusion involves more than moving a child from one setting to another and poses major challenges to schools. If students with diverse learning needs are truly to be included in the curriculum and daily fabric of schools, then schools must be restructured. Policies and administrative structures must be reconsidered, and the totality of the general education program—the curriculum standards, assessments, instructional strategies, and professional development—must be made truly inclusive.

This chapter will address those contextual issues. It will begin with an overview of the major themes within the current educational reform movement. Major issues confronting special education programs will also be addressed, and specific policies will be discussed that must be considered if inclusion is to be part of educational reform.

OVERVIEW OF EDUCATIONAL REFORM IN THE UNITED STATES

The momentum for reform in America's schools has been building over almost two decades. The duration of this reform is unprecedented in the history of education in the United States (Fuhrman, 1993; Special Study Panel on Education Indicators, 1991; Toch, 1991). The reform agenda is touching every aspect of education, including changing funding and governance structures, setting content standards, assessing student performance, and enhancing accountability. The sheer number of initiatives makes the current effort more complex than the vast majority of previous "reform" efforts that have focused on isolated curriculum reforms or specific programs or ages. Not only does the current restructuring agenda involve virtually every aspect of education, but, more important, for the first time educators are not in control of their own agenda (Toch, 1991). From the beginning, the current restructuring movement has been part of a larger political agenda involving the nation's governors and business leaders.

Groups such as the National Governor's Association, the Business Roundtable, and the Center for Education and the Economy were responsible for moving education to the forefront of the U.S. attention by linking education to global competitiveness and the creation of a highly skilled workforce for the twenty-first century (Toch, 1991). These influential groups have been joined by a number of scholarly task forces and commissions to improve America's schools.

Major Themes in Educational Reform in the United States

As noted earlier, the current efforts to redefine education are complex. However, certain major themes are evident in the reform agenda.

Improved Student Outcomes A driving force behind the move to change schools is the desire to improve student educational outcomes. The focus on educational outcomes were initially stimulated by a number of national reports (for example, *Reconnecting Youth,* Education Commission of the States, 1985; *A Nation at Risk,* National Commission on Excellence in Education, 1983; *Results in Education: 1991,* National Governors' Association, 1991; and *What Work Requires of Schools,* U.S. Department of Labor, 1991) that viewed flat or declining state and national assessment results as evidence that American education was failing to produce either world-class scholars or competent workers.

There was a call for more than basic literacy as business as well as some professional organizations saw a need for workers who could engage in cooperative problem solving and critical thinking and adapt to changing job demands. Some scholars (Adler, 1982; Goodlad, 1984; Sizer, 1984) argued early on for an overhaul of educational curricula to stress critical thinking, judgment making, and conceptual problem solving.

Goal Setting and Testing During the mid-1980s, the focus of reform narrowed on defining the standards for schools and students and assessing student progress toward those standards. Some of the earliest responses to the need to improve outcomes were state-level mandates such as minimum competency testing for graduation, increased teacher certification requirements, and mandated curriculum or instructional changes that required schools to focus on basic academic skills such as reading and math. Many of these top-down approaches began in the mid-1970s and continued into the next decade. These efforts to legislate learning were largely unsuccessful in improving outcomes (Fullan & Stiegelbauer, 1991). Moreover, they tended to be designed to promote a baseline of minimal literacy skills and did not challenge schools to provide a more authentic education. In fact, testing became the "darling" of policy makers across the country

(Madaus, 1991). The standard-setting process became both a political act involving the nation's governors and the Bush and Clinton administrations as well as a professional endeavor involving almost all of the major content disciplines such as math, English, history, geography, and the arts (McDonnell, McLaughlin, & Morison, 1997). In 1990, the nation's governors and President George Bush met at the Educational Summit in Charlottesville, Virginia, to define a vision for education. This vision was interpreted in terms of six goals that American education was to reach by the year 2000. The goals plus two additional ones have become known as the national education goals.

In 1994, Congress enacted new legislation, Goals 2000: Educate America Act (PL 103-227), designed to define national education goals as well as present a strategy for reaching those goals. This new legislation establishes the eight educational goals in law. Two of these goals directly address improving student achievement: Goal 3 states that by the year 2000, American students will leave grades 4, 8, and 12 having demonstrated competency in challenging subject matter and that all schools will ensure that students be prepared for responsible citizenship, further learning, and productive employment in the modern economy; Goal 4 states that by the year 2000, U.S. students will be first in the world in science and mathematics achievement.

The adoption of Goals 2000 signaled a degree of national consensus surrounding the general concept of standards-based reform. However, participation by states in Goals 2000 is voluntary, and its passage created numerous concerns. As an inducement to states to adopt the national vision of standards-based educational reform, the statute offered modest federal grants to states that agreed to develop education improvement plans adopting both content standards and performance standards. Content standards are defined by the statute as "broad descriptions of the knowledge and skills students should acquire in a particular subject area" (PL 103-227, section 3[4]); performance standards are defined as "concrete examples and explicit definitions of what students have to know and be able to do to demonstrate that such students are proficient in the skills and knowledge framed by the content standards" (PL 103-227, section 3[9]). In accordance with the U.S. emphasis on local control of education, however, the Goals 2000 legislation leaves each state free to set its own content and performance standards and to choose its own means of assessing progress toward its goals. In addition, federal oversight of state compliance with the statute is minimal: the statute has no implementing regulations, and states are no longer even required to submit their plans to the federal Department of Education for review (McDonnell et al., 1997).

Despite its popularity among many state policy makers, Goals 2000 has become controversial at the national level. From its inception, Goals 2000 was intended to embody an ideal of high-quality, equitable schooling based on voluntary standards and to offer states a small amount of funding to help them implement their own approaches to that vision without imposing significant federal mandates on them. Despite having no regulations of the type common to all other federal programs, opponents have portrayed Goals 2000 as a threat to state and local autonomy. In particular, several parts of the original legislation became focal points for dispute.

The original legislation attempted to encourage states to address issues of fiscal equity. Fiscal equity between students in different districts and different states came to be seen as a critical issue to be addressed in educational reform because of both lawsuits challenging the manner in which states distributed educational funding (for example, in 1989, the Kentucky Supreme Court invalidated the entire state system of public education in response to a lawsuit challenging the existing funding system; Schofield, 1996) and public reports such as Kozol's (1992) *Savage Inequalities,* which brought wide public attention to the extreme disparities in funding and resources between the nation's highest- and lowest-spending districts. The need to reduce these disparities has been a recurrent theme in the educational reform movement (McDonnell et al., 1997).

The original Goals 2000 legislation encouraged states to adopt opportunity-to-learn (OTL) standards. These were defined as "the criteria for, and the basis of assessing the sufficiency or quality of the resources, practices, and conditions necessary at each level of the education system (schools, local agencies, and states) to provide all students with an opportunity to learn the material in the voluntary national content standards or state content standards" (PL 103-227, section 3[7]). The OTL standards were intended to assure that disadvantaged students would be provided with the curricular resources to meet the new content and performance standards by which they would be judged. However, because of concerns that the OTL standards could lead to mandated equalization of funding or other intrusions on state and local autonomy, the original OTL standards were specifically stated to be voluntary and nonbinding. Even these watered-down OTL standards were removed, however, when the Goals 2000 legislation was reauthorized in 1996.

Concern for equitable access to a demanding curriculum found expression in two statements in the Goals 2000 legislation. The act stated that "all children can learn and achieve to high standards and must realize their potential if the United States is to prosper" (PL 103-227, section 301[1]) and that "all students are entitled to participate in a broad and challenging curriculum and to have access to resources sufficient to address other education needs" (PL 103-227, section 301[15]). The legislation is also clear that "all students" and "all children" include those with disabilities (section 3[1]).

Other Federal Legislation While direct federal influence is limited under Goals 2000, the Improving America's Schools Act (IASA), the reauthorization of the Elementary and Secondary Education Act (1994), contains major new requirements for obtaining funds under Title I, the largest federal school aid program, which serves poor, underachieving students. The purpose of the new legislation is "to enable schools to provide opportunities for children served to acquire the knowledge and skills contained in challenging state content standards and to meet the challenging state performance standards developed for all children" (PL 103-328, section 1001[d]).

To receive Title I grants, states are now required to submit state plans that provide for challenging content and performance standards, state assessments, yearly reports on meeting standards, and provisions for teacher support and learning aligned with the new curriculum standards and assessments. Assessments and reports must be aligned with the content standards; test at three separate grade levels must be based on "multiple, up-to-date measures that assess higher order thinking skills and understanding"; and "provide individual student interpretive and descriptive reports" as well as aggregated results down to the school level that are broken down by race, gender, English proficiency, migrant status, disability, and economic status (PL 103-328, section 1111).

In addition, for local agencies to receive subgrants, they must have on file with the state education agency a local plan "that is coordinated with other programs under this Act, the Goals 2000: Educate America Act, and other Acts, as appropriate." Among other requirements, the local plans must address how students are assessed in accordance with the state plan and how well they perform relative to state standards.

Because Title I provides well over $7 billion a year in federal funding and includes a detailed set of mandates that local districts must meet as a condition for funding, it is likely that the federal government's influence over the standards and assessments in individual states will be greater through Title I than through Goals 2000. As with Goals 2000, Title I acknowledges students with disabilities and specifies that they are to be included in the teaching and assessment of state content standards. The legislation also indicates that all children are to participate in annual assessments and that reasonable accommodations and adaptations are to be provided students with severe learning needs.

State-Level Activities Besides the federal legislation, standard setting and assessment have been left to individual states. The new content standards are intended to provide direction and vision for significantly upgrading the quality of the content and instruction within all schools in a given state. Beginning even before national educational goals were adopted, several professional subject-matter societies established challenging standards for curriculum content. Perhaps the best known of these efforts are those of the National Council for Teachers of Mathematics (NCTM) and the American Association for the Advancement of Science (AAAS). Standards and curricular frameworks were developed in the disciplines of English, history, geography, mathematics, science, and the arts, most with the support and assistance of the U.S. Department of Education. Yet, many of these have been controversial and criticized as ambiguous or lacking in rigor. Nonetheless, the cumulative effect of many these efforts has been to redefine public school curricula to deemphasize learning of discrete skills and isolated content and instead to demand that students learn more "authentically" using higher-order thinking skills integrating subjectmatter knowledge and content (Blank & Pechman, 1995; McDonnell et al., 1997). State content standards vary significantly in terms of specificity and subject-matter areas.

Equity A driving force behind the creation of standards has been the desire to improve performance of racially and culturally diverse students. During the 1980s, a number of reports, among them *America's Shame, America's Hope: Twelve Million Youth at Risk* (Smith, 1988) and *The Forgotten Half: Non-college Youth in America* (William T. Grant Foundation, 1988), focused attention on the education of disadvantaged and culturally diverse students. In particular, these reports cited the continued tracking of these students into general education classes and the low expectations held for many of these students.

As Toch (1991) notes, the historical approach of public schools has been to educate the middle class and train the lower class, the assumption being that the latter students would fill the jobs on assembly lines and other semiskilled or unskilled positions. However, with the decline in these jobs and the changing composition of American society and schools, a major goal of reform is to ensure equity of access to challenging curriculum. Business leaders in particular cite the need to educate all students and to hold all students to the highest possible standards.

Linked to the issues of equity is the adequacy of school funding. According to Kirst (cited in Kysilko, 1992), state school finance policies began to undergo "rapid-change reconceptualization" in the 1990s. Court cases have been filed in half the states, even in states where courts are rendering second decisions on cases initiated in the 1970s (Kirst cited in Kysilko, 1992).

Numerous proposals have been made to reform school finance, including sales taxes, steeply graduated income taxes, property taxes pooled at the state-level for redistribution, and even voucher systems linked to school choice. An interesting development in school finance cases, evident in court decisions in Kentucky, is that not only must funding be equitably distributed, but student outcomes must also be equalized to ensure that every student receives an "adequate" education.

Restructuring Governance Another theme of the current reform initiatives relates to the notion that schools as organizations need to be fundamentally reconceptualized in order for each student, regardless of social circumstance, to achieve the new level of outcomes. The concept of restructuring represents a shift away from the more top-down model of reform that involves mandated standards for performance and assessments. Restructuring is characterized by changes in policies, organization, and administration as well as in the basic beliefs about schooling held by school staff and the community at large. Frequently, this type of restructuring must begin at the building level.

School restructuring initially was influenced by management theories such as those described in Deming's total quality management (Walton, 1986) and Peters's (1987) *Thriving on Chaos.* The restructuring movement in education has also been influenced by national reports, such as the influential *A Nation Prepared: Teachers for the TwentyFirst Century* (Carnegie Forum on Education and the Economy, 1986) and the "effective schools" literature (see Northwest Regional Educational Laboratory, 1990). The Carnegie report in particular called for changes in the governance of schools in order to create more flexibility at the level of the school building and to empower teachers to make decisions about what and how to teach. These findings have been translated into changes such as the decentralization of authority and decision making from large centralized bureaucracies to local school committees composed of professionals, parents, and community members. Additional changes include developing new collaborative work cultures and fostering new roles for teachers as mentors or coaches (Fullan & Stiegelbauer, 1991; O'Day & Smith, 1993). Other governance changes are evident in state and federal policies that permit waivers or otherwise seek to create greater flexibility in use of targeted resources (McLaughlin & Verstegen, in press). Consolidated funding and flexible use of human and other resources is a keystone of the current governance changes.

School Choice "School choice" initiatives are also included within the arena of school restructuring. Some proponents of school choice see their proposals as efforts to break the monopoly of public education by creating competition among schools for students. Choice programs can take many forms, including open enrollment, the creation of charter and magnet schools within public school systems, and the use of vouchers to access private school education (Ysseldyke, Lange, & Gorney, 1994). School choice in the form of voucher, magnet, and charter schools is also seen as a way to bypass the bureaucracy in creating alternative forms of organization, instruction, and assessment. Proponents claim that choice programs can improve student achievement, reduce dropout rates, and increase teaching authority and autonomy (Lieberman, 1989; Nathan, 1989).

Charter Schools The most prevalent choice option are charter schools, which are independent public schools typically operated by groups of parents or teachers. Advocates claim that independent schools can provide an alternative curriculum and instructional program than that offered at traditional public schools. The charter school movement has gained popular support from both political parties because it increases parental choice, a goal of conservative lawmakers, while theoretically providing equal access for all students without seriously destabilizing currently operating public schools, a goal of liberal lawmakers. As of July 1997, twenty-eight states and the District of Columbia have passed charter school legislation (Schnaiberg, 1997a, 1997b). Approximately 790 charter schools are currently operating across the country (Center for Education Reform, 1997).

Technology A final, significant element of school reform is the increasing use of advanced learning technologies in schools. Researchers are finding that if implemented according to clearly stated instructional goals, technology can be a valuable tool in the hands of good teachers and can effectively support the aims of education reform. Technology can engage students in meaningful learning tasks that foster the complex thinking and communications skills being demanded by the private sector. Proponents claim that students from disadvantaged backgrounds and those with language challenges and special needs stand to gain the most from technology used in these ways.

Technology also holds the promise of increasing student access to high-quality learning experiences regardless of their geographic location—inner cities as well as remote rural areas—through the creative use of broadband telecommunications network (Firestone & Clark, 1991; Office of Technology Assessment, 1989). The Clinton administration explicitly cites educational uses as a rationale for proceeding with the proposed National Information Infrastructure initiative.

The major themes of educational reform are altering every aspect of American education. Traditional organizations and administrative practices are being changed at the same time that new curricula are designed and new demands are made on students and teachers. Further impacting the dramatic changes in schooling is the rapidly changing demographics within the United States. Finally, the attention focused on schools by politicians, business leaders, and the public at large has created the need to make changes quickly and to show results.

REFORM AND SPECIAL EDUCATION: WHERE DOES INCLUSION FIT?

Initially special education had not been specifically acknowledged within the educational restructuring movement (Fuchs & Fuchs, 1994; McLaughlin & Warren, 1992). However, increased attention has recently been paid to the needs of students with disabilities within the various reforms. A National Academy of Science committee has considered the fit between special education policies and practices and reform (McDonnell et al., 1997). Most significant has been some of the recent amendments to the Individuals with Disabilities Act (IDEA) that emphasize accountability for student performance through participation in general education assessments and access to the general education curriculum. In addition, several changes relative to the use of federal special education funds signal the desire to create greater flexibility. When special education is integrated into the fabric of school reform, the most frequent intent has been to create a unified school system (McLaughlin & Warren, 1992).

Efforts to restructure special education programs and services are not driven solely by inclusion. While some authors have drawn parallels between the tenets of inclusion and those of a restructuring school (McDonnell & Kiefer-O'Donnell, 1992; Sailor et al., 1993), other long-standing issues in special education must be negotiated within the current reforms. These are assessment and identification of students who are eligible for special education services, inclusion and the Least Restrictive Environment, and postschool outcomes of special education students.

Assessment and Identification

There are several complex issues related to special education assessment. The first is that assessment for the purpose of determining program eligibility for students with mild to moderate disabilities has been problematic since the passage of IDEA. A number of researchers have documented the inability of assessment tools to differentiate among specific learning disabilities, serious emotional disturbance, and mild mental retardation (Gajar, 1979, 1980; Hallahan & Kauffman, 1977; MacMillan & Hendrick, 1993; Reschly, 1988). The inability to differentially diagnose these students is only part of the problem. Other researchers (Keogh, 1990; Lyon, 1996; Ysseldyke, Algozzine, Regan, & Potter, 1980; Ysseldyke, Algozzine, Shinn, & McGue, 1982) have asserted that many students who have been identified as having a specific learning disability cannot be reliably differentiated from students with learning or behavioral problems. In fact, the differences between the two groups may be only the degree of behavior problems presented to the teacher, teacher intolerance or inability to manage students' problems, parent/family intervention, or parent/family insistence on the identification.

Minority Overrepresentation

Related to the lack of precision in assessment is the troublesome aspect of the overrepresentation of minority males in special education. Whereas some (Reschly, 1988) cite problems with the norms of psychological and educational assessment instruments used for eligibility determination, others (Carpenter, 1992; Fuchs & Fuchs, 1989; Harry, 1992; Ogbu, 1987) strongly suggest that a strong cultural bias exists in the assessment process. This bias represents a mismatch between the language and behaviors of culturally diverse and poor youth and the white, middle-class norms of schools and classrooms. Given the lack of cultural diversity among many teachers in today's schools, the latter researchers suggest that ever greater numbers of culturally and linguistically diverse students are being inappropriately placed into special education. Furthermore, the heavy reliance on IQ assessments as well as educational achievement ensures that many students from low-socioeconomic and other culturally diverse families will continue to be overrepresented in special education programs (Bernard & Clarizio, 1981; Carlson & Stephens, 1986; Harry, 1992).

The costs associated with conducting eligibility assessments also present problems (Chambers & Parrish, 1988; Moore, Strang, Schwartz, & Braddock, 1988). This is particularly difficult given that research relating assessments to Individual Education Plan (IEP) development suggested that rarely does the assessment information result in a functional educational plan (Smith, 1990).

Defining "Least Restrictive Environment"

The issue of what constitutes education in the Least Restrictive Environment (LRE) has been a durable one within special education. The issue of LRE is grounded in statute and regulation as discussed in Chapter 1. The issue also reflects differing beliefs about disability and about the goals of special education. As Fuchs and Fuchs (1994) note, advocates for those individuals with the most significant cognitive and physical disabilities have long pushed for the integration, now inclusion, of those students in regular schools and classrooms. A major impetus for advocating inclusion has been the basic belief that students with the most severe disabilities have a right to be part of the mainstream of society. Inclusion fosters social networks and communication between those who have disabilities and the nondisabled members of the larger society. These networks are considered critical for ensuring that the students with the most significant needs participate in their communities (Sailor et al., 1993).

On the other hand, some students and families and advocates representing other disabilities, such as the deaf, seriously emotionally disturbed, and students with specific learning disabilities, argue that what constitutes LRE is an environment in which students are best served according to their individual needs and that placement should become an issue only after appropriateness of education is determined (Kauffman & Lloyd, 1995). The appropriate educational goals defined for many of the above students include increased academic competence, connection to a specific culture, and emotional well-being or positive social behaviors. Since research (McLaughlin, Warren, & Schofield, 1996) has yet to demonstrate that these important outcomes can always be obtained in the regular classroom, the resulting tension between those who advocate for inclusion and those advocating for maintaining a continuum of placements is strong.

The Postschool Outcomes for Students with Disabilities

There is far less debate about a third major issue in special education. Concerns about what happens to students with disabilities after they leave school have been growing since the mid-1980s, beginning with the publication of a number of follow-up studies that documented the high unemployment and social isolation among former special education students (Edgar, Levine, & Maddox, 1986; Hasazi, Gordon, & Roe, 1985; Mithaug, Horiuchi, & Fanning, 1985). Contributing to the concern was a 1986 Harris poll indicating that unemployment among persons with disabilities was higher and wages lower than for any other group of working-age Americans (Harris & Associates, 1986).

Data from the National Longitudinal Transition Study (NLTS; Wagner, D'Amico, Marder, Newman, & Blackorby, 1992) also pointed to generally high dropout rates and low employment rates for many special education graduates. Many of those students experience continued dependence into adulthood. Although employment and independent living rates improved for some young adults with disabilities after several years out of school, most notably those with more mild disabilities, other young adults with more significant disabilities, or those diagnosed as seriously emotionally disturbed actually did more poorly. Studies such as the NLTS began to focus attention on the outcomes of special education and away from the processes and procedures of providing services. This focus has also shifted to examining how students with disabilities are being included in large national and statewide outcome assessment systems (Westat, 1993).

The effects of this attention have contributed to a beginning awareness of the importance of focusing on the results of special education as measured by student performance in addition to focusing on processes and providing specialized services. There has also been an increased number of activities centered on defining and assessing the valued outcomes for students with disabilities.

OPTIONS FOR THE RESTRUCTURING OF GENERAL AND SPECIAL EDUCATION

The impetus for reform may have emerged separately within the special and general education systems. However, it has created unique opportunities for individual schools and school districts. These opportunities also present significant challenges to leadership in special education. Professionals in special education have acknowledged the power of the general education reform movement to change the way in which special education programs operate. Reform offers an opportunity to move the education of students with disabilities fully into the "mainstream" generation, but this will require leadership with a clear vision for what role special education should play and what it brings to the dialogue.

As noted at the beginning of this chapter, some authors have already identified the parallels between the two movements. Early on the Center for Policy Options in special education at the University of Maryland (McLaughlin & Warren, 1992) investigated school reform efforts in thirty-four local school districts across the country and identified five areas that were critical to school restructuring: (a) the vision and mission, (b) accountability for educational outcomes, (c) governance, (d) curriculum, and (e) professional development.

Within the area of creating a vision and setting the mission for restructuring, McLaughlin and Warren (1992) have identified three options or alternatives. These include creating unified systems, establishing inclusion programs, and maintaining the traditional program structure with a full continuum of services. Table 2.1 provides the assumptions underlying each option. The options are neither mutually exclusive nor philosophically distinct. However, they do reflect how school districts were responding to the restructuring of general and special education.

The unified system option requires the greatest amount of change. This system requires that all aspects of special education, and other special or categorical educational programs, be blended or merged at the administrative and classroom levels. Funding, governance structures, outcome assessments and accountability systems, curriculum and instructional arrangements, and professional certification and development programs must be changed under the unified system option to create fluid services without labels or categorization of students.

The inclusion option is much more child-specific and focuses almost exclusively on the social and educational integration of students with disabilities in general education schools and classrooms. This option does not require the reconceptualization of special education policies or program structures. While certain elements of those structures, such as state-level special education funding formula, may get in the way of moving students from one placement to another, the general categorical structure of special education, including the eligibility requirements, can remain in place. Furthermore, though the unified system option favors the education of students with disabilities within general education classrooms, the goals extend far beyond placement issues.

The traditional program structure option maintains all of the present policy and program structures and emphasizes the need to maintain a separate categorical program along with a full continuum of program placements. Fully including individual students in general education is one of those placements, but this option stresses the individual nature of educational programs and placement decisions. For many advocates of inclusion, maintaining the placement options means providing the opportunity for certain students, specifically those with the more significant disabilities, to be segregated and isolated in special classrooms or schools. Because many advocates of inclusion believe that full inclusion is a right

Table 2.1 Creating a Vision and Setting the Mission for Restructuring: Assumptions Underlying Three Systems

Unified System	Inclusive System	Traditional System with a Continuum of Services
The school system wants to provide equal access to high-quality instruction that results in desired outcomes for all students, regardless of their characteristics or educational needs. Accountability for *all* students is vested in their neighborhood school, and there is one set of outcomes for all students. Decision making and responsibility for students' programs are shared among school and other specialized staff, students, and parents. Generally, all students are educated in their neighborhood schools and fully included in the curricular and extracurricular life of the school, including being educated in age-appropriate regular education classrooms. However, some specialized placements could be made available on a limited-time basis to *any* student who needed intensive services. Most specialized instruction and services are provided without the need to label or otherwise categorize students. A small number of intensive or highly specialized services might be provided on a short-term basis outside the neighborhood school and would be available to any student. Services are provided without labels and use resources from all categorical programs as well as other sources.	All students are educated in their neighborhood school in age-appropriate regular education classrooms and community sites shared by *all* students. Socialization among *all* peers is as important as specific skill attainment. Specialized supports and services are provided within regular education classes and other integrated environments. Special education eligibility requirements and procedures are maintained. Decision making and responsibility for students' programs are shared among school staff, students, and families.	This option requires no policy or program changes except perhaps defining educational outcomes and monitoring those outcomes. Through careful oversight and program monitoring, this option protects students' educational rights. This is considered necessary in the absence of meaningful student outcomes to ensure that students with disabilities receive appropriate services. The option can perpetuate a dual or separate system that conflicts with site-based decision making and school autonomy and works against site-based management and the concept of promoting responsibility and accountability for special education students at the school site. The segregation of students with disabilities occurs as dictated by service needs. However, such segregation can continue into adulthood and allow communities to remain uninformed and uncomfortable with persons with disabilities. This option is meeting increased resistance among some parents, advocates, and professionals. A strong centralized focus of responsibility and advocacy for special education programs is maintained. Some special educators believe some students (e.g., those with behavior disorders) are less accepted by schools and that this option provides the intensive services such students require and shields them from an unaccepting regular classroom. Dual "systems" are maintained that can result in less efficient communication, conflicts across program administrations, and duplication of services and funds. Segregation of students with disabilities from their same-age, "typical" peers can result in a lack of appropriate social relationships.

and not just a wise educational decision, there is no need to maintain other placements. No student should be excluded from his or her neighborhood school. Those advocating a unified system may also take issue with the notion of alternative placements, but they are equally concerned about other issues. They view program efforts to restrict specialized services and resources to specific categories of students as educationally meaningless and fiscally unsound. They also believe that if students with disabilities are to be truly included, then special education programs and services must also be fully included within the organization and structures of general education.

Considerations for Creating a Unified System

The options described earlier provide a conceptual framework for making decisions about a model for change. However, the pathway to decision must begin with a careful consideration of the outcomes of education that are valued by students, their families, and the community at large. Supporting policies concerning funding, outcome-based assessment, curricular frameworks, and professional certification and development also must be considered.

A Student- and Family-Centered Process The process for restructuring special education must begin with the student and his or her family. That is, the conversations about restructuring must begin with defining the goals of education for each student with a disability. Defining an individual student's educational outcomes must be done within the context of broader system standards that have been defined as the critical educational goals. Both special and general educators must confront their beliefs about the purposes of schooling. Parents and advocates for students with disabilities as well as the students themselves must also examine their goals and expectations for special education. Only through such broad stakeholder input can a vision for education be constructed.

For example, if a community endorses the belief that all students, regardless of their characteristics, have a right to the same educational outcomes, then those outcomes as well as the means for assessing progress toward those outcomes must accommodate all students, including those with significant cognitive disabilities. Similarly, if a community believes that students must respect diversity and learn how to communicate and work collaboratively with diverse students, then all students must have regular opportunities to develop those interdependent skills. However, communities that have believed in the primacy of traditional academic outcomes, such as high achievement in math, science, social science, and so forth, will have to address the consequences for those students with disabilities for whom the academic outcomes are not attainable or not relevant.

Decisions about educational outcomes also require examination of what we know about effective education for students with disabilities. Decisions about outcomes will not automatically lead to decisions about how special education programs and services should be structured, but they will determine what is valued in the schools and what knowledge and experiences are offered to students. They should also lead to construction of explicit mission statements and restructuring goals, which in turn will impact policies and school operations.

Supporting Policies Restructuring to implement unified or inclusive schools will require the creation or revision of a number of state and local policies. In addition, fully implementing a unified system will likely require changes in IDEA statute and regulation. The primary change will be to reduce separateness between the program structures supporting students with disabilities and those of general education. Following is a brief overview of major policy areas that will need to be addressed to create a unified system.

Funding Many policy makers and practitioners at the federal, state, and local levels are seeking ways to consolidate educational categorical programs to meet the needs of all children, regardless of the particular funding streams they are eligible to access (McLaughlin & Verstegen, in press). The goal is for full collaboration across categorical programs such as Title 1 and bilingual and migrant education, as well as special education. In other words, the use of resources from special education and the other programs could be used to help any student at risk of school failure.

Because special education is the only federal education entitlement program, blending funds and other resources with other categorical programs is difficult. However, similarities in program structure, student characteristics, and, in some instances, student enrollment, have led to serious interest in collaboration (McLaughlin & Verstegen, in press). Local districts have engaged in a number of efforts to deliver services in a cross-categorical fashion, with some districts combining funds from as many as eight to ten different local, state, and federal categorical sources (McLaughlin & Verstegen, in press; NASBE, 1992).

In addition, some states have begun to change their special education funding formulas to create more flexibility in the system; to sever links among funding, placement, and disability labels; to promote prevention in the service delivery system; and to encourage the notion of special education as a service rather than a place (Parrish, 1997). These changes generally fall into some model of census-based or program-neutral funding (Parrish, 1997). For instance, Oregon, using a program-neutral approach, funds districts from a single source of money called the General School Fund. The formula within the fund takes into account costs for special education by doubling the district payment per pupil identified for special education, up to 11 percent of the average daily membership (Goertz, 1993; NASBE, 1992). Pennsylvania, using a census-based approach, reimburses districts using a two-part formula that provides one flat reimbursement for students identified as mildly impaired, up to 17 percent of the district's average daily membership (including students labeled gifted and talented), and another reimbursement rate for students identified as severely impaired, up to 1 percent of the district's average daily membership (Goertz, 1993; NASBE, 1992). Vermont allocates state special education funds to districts based on a percentage of school population and permits schools to use funds flexibly to serve any student requiring additional learning support.

Outcome-Based Assessment and Accountability In a unified system, there is one set of outcomes that is broad enough to address each learner's needs. There is also an assessment program that enables those outcomes to be monitored for purposes of instructional improvement and program accountability. The assessment program must include multiple methods of assessment as well as adaptations and accommodations that permit each student to be assessed and included in whatever accountability system is in place.

Individual states such as Kentucky, Maine, Maryland, and Vermont, among others, have already made commitments to include students with all disabilities into statewide outcomes and accompanying assessment systems (McLaughlin & Warren, 1992). Some states, such as Kentucky and Vermont, have one set of outcomes although they recognize the need to have alternate assessments for some students with disabilities. Maryland has both a set of differentiated outcomes and assessments for students with significant cognitive disabilities. In all cases, there is explicit recognition that individual and idiosyncratic educational goals and programs cannot exist separate from larger system outcomes or goals. This inclusion of students with disabilities can force accountability for their outcomes onto the general education system and move away from a "your student/my student" mentality (DeStefano, 1993; Jakweth & Frey, 1992).

Moving toward an outcome-oriented system is not without challenges. A report issued by the Center for Policy Options in Special Education (Westat, 1993) identified five key decisions that must be made in the creation of an outcome-based system. These include (a) selecting outcomes that are relevant to all students, (b) establishing performance standards that set appropriately high expectations and that challenge students, (c) accommodating individual disabilities, (d) developing appropriate assessments, and (e) defining who will be held accountable for student progress.

Curricular Frameworks The importance of defining inclusive outcomes is related to the important link between curriculum and outcome assessment. What is measured, gets taught. As Pugach and Warger (1993) point out, the IEP has evolved into the curriculum for many students with disabilities. This approach has often resulted in a fragmented, piecemeal education. Students with disabilities need an opportunity to have a broad and balanced curriculum. At the same time, specific curriculum modifications and adaptations may need to be made to accommodate the learners' needs. The challenge will be to ensure that students with disabilities have access to the content curricula being implemented with the schools while at the same time being provided services that recognize individual differences (McDonnell et al., 1997; Pugach & Warger, 1993). Shriner, Ysseldyke, and Thurlow (1994) discuss several options for considering students with disabilities within the current curriculum reform efforts. These include having one curriculum and set of performance standards and assessments for all students with appropriate accommodations, maintaining differing curricula with different standards and assessments, or having one curricular framework for all students but with differentiated performance expectations. Some combination of all three approaches will likely be required to meet the needs of all students with disabilities.

Professional Certification Standards and Professional Development Another aspect of fragmentation in the special education system is the state-level certification policies that have evolved into very separate and highly specialized delineations of knowledge and competencies. Meanwhile, general education teacher training and certification have, to a great extent, ignored students with disabilities (Field, 1989; Giangreco, Edelman, & Dennis, 1991; Goodlad & Lovitt, 1993).

Everyone involved in the education of students with disabilities agrees that professionals who interact with those students should meet the highest qualification standards of their profession. However, for some of these professionals, those standards are a medical or clinical license and do not include or demand a level of knowledge about education. Many state-level policy makers consider that the IDEA regulatory personnel standards have enforced a medical model on education that has led to overspecialization and a separation from general education curricula and pedagogy (McLaughlin, 1993). This historic emphasis has resulted in a fragmented and often noneducationally relevant set of assessments and "treatments" instead of a comprehensive educational plan that emphasizes access to the general education curriculum. Yet, some argue for maintaining the specialized separate and distinct training programs and certification to promote high quality among special education personnel (Fuchs & Fuchs, 1994; McLaughlin, 1993).

Nevertheless, there is a widespread desire to promote more collaboration between special and general education teachers so that special education practices are infused into the general education environment. A body of literature speaks to the value and importance of collaborative instruction and consultation between general and special educators (Hargreaves & Fullan, 1991; Sugai & Tindal, 1993; Villa et al., 1992). This is seen as the key to promoting the Least Restrictive Environment principle embedded in IDEA, as well as to enhancing instruction within the general education classroom (Hardman, McDonnell, & Welch, 1997).

Calls for increasing flexibility within schools, creating inclusive schools, and other restructuring initiatives have created a tremendous need for professionals who can work collaboratively in schools as problem-solvers, team teachers, and effective consultants (Hardman et al., 1997; Hargreaves & Fullan, 1991; McDonnell et al., 1991; Schumm & Vaughn 1991).

There is general recognition that professionals are the key to any restructuring of special education. In fact, the change literature is explicit about the importance of involving teachers, administrators, and other school staff in the process of defining change as well as providing ongoing professional development to support new practices (Fullan & Stiegelbauer, 1992; Mann, 1978). Policies governing both certification and ongoing professional development need to support these efforts.

SUMMARY

The scope of many of the current reform initiatives—in both general and special education—present a number of challenges and opportunities for special educators. The climate of change existing in many states and local school districts across the country offers the opportunity to reconceptualize special education programs and to create truly inclusive programs. At the same time, change must be responsible and maintain the integrity of special education, which translates to individually designed instruction. Students with disabilities must receive a high-quality education that leads to valued outcomes such as postsecondary education, employment, and full participation in society. Inclusive programs must not sacrifice these values at the expense of philosophy; at the same time, program structures that do not support inclusion must be changed. Restructuring to create inclusive schools can be a positive force for every student, and all stakeholders in education must be involved in defining the reform efforts and ensuring that those reforms respond to the needs of all students.

REFERENCES

Adler, M. J. (1982). *The Paideia proposal: An educational manifesto.* New York: Macmillan.

Arc. (1992). *Position paper on education.* Arlington, TX: Author.

Bernard, R., & Clarizio, H. (1981). Socioeconomic bias in special education placement decision. *Psychology in the Schools, 18,* 178–183.

Blank, R. K., & E. M. Pechman. (1995). *State curriculum frameworks in mathematics and science: How are they changing across the states?* Washington, DC: Council of Chief State School Officers.

Carlson, P., & Stephens, T. (1986). Cultural bias and identification of behaviorally disordered children. *Behavioral Disorders, 11,* 191–198.

Carnegie Forum on Education and the Economy. (1986). *A nation prepared: Teachers for the twenty-first century.* New York: Author.

Carpenter, L. J. (1992). The influence of examiner knowledge based on diagnostic decision making with language minority children. *Journal of Educational Issues of Language Minority Students, 11,* 139–161.

Center for Education Reform. (1997). *The Charter School Workbook: Your road-map to the charter school movement.* Washington, DC: Author.

Chambers, J. G., & Parrish, T. B. (1988). *A survey of expenditures on special education and related services: An analysis of the four oversampled states.* Washington, DC: Decision Resources Corporation.

Council for Exceptional Children. (1993). *Policy on inclusive schools and community settings.* Reston, VA: Author and Council of Administrators of Special Education.

Council of Administrators of Special Education. (1993). *CASE future agenda for special education: Creating a unified education system.* Reston, VA: Author and Council for Exceptional Children.

DeStefano, L. (1993). *The effects of standards and assessment on students in special education.* Minneapolis: National Center on Educational Outcomes, University of Minnesota.

Edgar, E., Levine, P., & Maddox, M. (1986). *Statewide follow-up studies of secondary special education students in transition* (Working Paper of the Networking and Evaluation Team). Seattle: CDMRC, University of Washington.

Education Commission of the States. (1985). *Reconnecting youth.* Denver: Author.

Field, S. (1989). *The special field of special education* (Technical Report 10). Seattle: Center for Educational Renewal, University of Washington.

Firestone, C., & Clark, C. (1991). *Telecommunications as a tool for educational reform: Implementing the NCTM mathematics standards* (report of a conference of the Aspen Institute's Communications and Society program). Washington, DC: Aspen Institute.

Fuchs, D., & Fuchs, L. S. (1989). Exploring effective and efficient pre-referral interventions: A component analysis of behavioral consultation. *School Psychology Review, 18,* 260–283.

Fuchs, D., & Fuchs, L. S. (1994). Inclusive schools movement and the radicalization of special education reform. *Exceptional Children, 60,* 294–309.

Fuhrman, S. H. (1993). The politics of coherence. In S. H. Fuhrman (Ed.), *Designing coherent policy: Improving the system* (pp. 1–34). San Francisco: Jossey-Bass.

Fullan, M., & Stiegelbauer, S. (1991). *The new meaning of educational change.* New York: Teachers College Press.

Gajar, A. (1979). Educable mentally retarded, learning disabled, and emotionally disturbed: Similarities and differences. *Exceptional Children, 45,* 470–472.

Gajar, A. H. (1980). Characteristics across exceptional categories: EMR, LD, and ED. *Journal of Special Education, 14,* 166–173.

Gartner, A., & Lipsky, D. (1989). *The yoke of special education: How to break it.* Rochester, NY: National Center on Education and the Economy.

Giangreco, M. F., Edelman, S., & Dennis, R. (1991). Common professional practices that interfere with the integrated delivery of related services. *Remedial and Special Education, 12*(2), 16–24.

Goertz, M. E. (1993). *School reform and education finance.* Washington, DC: Chesapeake Institute.

Goodlad, J. (1984). *A place called school.* New York: McGraw-Hill.

Goodlad, J. I., & Lovitt, T. C. (Eds.). (1993). *Integrating general and special education.* Upper Saddle River, NJ: Merrill/Prentice Hall.

Hallahan, D. P., & Kauffman, J. M. (1977). Labels, categories and behaviors: ED, LD, and EMR reconsidered. *Journal of Special Education, 11,* 139–149.

Hardman, M., McDonnell, J., & Welch, M. (1997, September). *Special education in an era of school reform: Preparing special education teachers.* Washington, DC: Federal Resource Center for Special Education.

Hargreaves, A., & Fullan, M. (1991). *Teacher development and educational change.* London: Cassell.

Harris, L., & Associates. (1986). *The ICD survey of disabled Americans: Bringing disabled Americans into the mainstream.* New York: Author.

Harry, B. (1992). Restructuring the participation of African-American parents in special education. *Exceptional Children, 59,* 123–131.

Hasazi, S., Gordon, L., & Roe, C. (1985). Factors associated with the employment status of handicapped youth exiting high school from 1979–1983. *Exceptional Children, 51,* 455–469.

Jakweth, P., & Frey, W. (1992, April). *Including students with disabilities in educational evaluation: Implications of unique needs of learners.* Paper presented at the annual meeting of the American Evaluation Association, Seattle, WA.

Kauffman, J. M. (1993). How we might achieve the radical reform of special education. *Exceptional Children, 60,* 6–15.

Kauffman, J. M., & Lloyd, J. W. (1995). A sense of place: The importance of placement issues in contemporary special education. In J. M. Kauffman, J. W. Lloyd, D. P. Hallahan, & T. A. Astuto (Eds.), *Issues in educational placement: Students with emotional and behavioral disorders* (pp. 3–20). Hillsdale, NJ: Erlbaum.

Keogh, B. K. (1990). Narrowing the gap between policy and practice. *Exceptional Children, 57,* 186–190.

Kozol, J. (1992). *Savage inequalities: Children in American schools.* New York: Harper-Perennial.

Kysilko, D. (Ed.). (1992). *State board connection, issues in brief: School finance.* Alexandria, VA: National Association of State Boards of Education.

Learning Disabilities Association of America. (1993). *Position paper on full inclusion.* Pittsburgh, PA: Author.

Lieberman, M. (1989). *Privatization and educational choice.* New York: St. Martin's.

MacMillan, D. L., & Hendrick, I. G. (1993). Evolution and legacies. In J. I. Goodlad & T. C. Lovitt (Eds.), *Integrating general and special education* (pp. 23–48). Upper Saddle River, NJ: Merrill/Prentice Hall.

Lyon, G. R. (1996). Learning disabilities. *The Future of Children: Special Education for Students with Disabilities, 6*(1), 54–76. Los Altos, CA: Center for the Future of Children, David and Lucille Packard Foundation.

Madaus, G. M. (1991). The effects of important tests on students: Implications for a national examination or system of examinations. *Phi Delta Kappa, 73,* 226–231.

Mann, D. (Ed.). (1978). *Making change happen.* New York: Teachers College Press.

McDonnell, J., & Kiefer-O'Donnell, R. (1992). Educational reform and students with severe disabilities. *Journal of Disability Policy Studies, 3*(2), 53–74.

McDonnell, A., McDonnell, J., Hardman, M., & McCune, G. (1991). Educating students with severe disabilities in their neighborhood school: The Utah elementary integration model. *Remedial and Special Education, 12*(6), 34–45.

McDonnell, L. M., McLaughlin, M. J., & Morison, P. (Eds.). (1997). *Educating one and all: Students with disabilities and standards-based reform.* Washington, DC: National Academy Press.

McLaughlin, M. J. (1993). *School reform and students with disabilities: Teachers and educational restructuring.* Washington, DC: Chesapeake Institute.

McLaughlin, M. J., Henderson, K., & Rhim, L. M. (in press). The inclusion of students with disabilities in school reforms and restructuring: An analysis of five local school districts. In S. Vitello & D. Mithaug (Eds.), *Inclusive schooling: National and international perspectives.* Mahwah, NJ: Erlbaum.

McLaughlin, M. J., & Verstegen, D. A. (in press). Increasing regulatory flexibility of special education programs at federal, state, and local levels: Problems and premises strategies. *Exceptional Children.*

McLaughlin, M. J., & Warren, S. H. (1992). *Issues and options in restructuring schools and special education programs.* College Park, MD: Center for Policy Options in Special Institutes for Research, Center for Special Education Finance.

McLaughlin, M. J., Warren, S. H., & Schofield, P. F. (1996). Creating inclusive schools: What does the research say? *Impact, 9*(2), 4–5 (feature issue on Inclusion and School Restructuring).

Mithaug, D., Horiuchi, C., & Fanning, P. (1985). A report on the Colorado statewide follow-up survey of special education students. *Exceptional Children, 51,* 397–404.

Moore, M. T., Strang, E. W., Schwartz, M., & Braddock, M. (1988). *Patterns in special education services delivery and cost* (Contract No. 300-84-0257). Washington, DC: Decision Resources Corporation.

Nathan, J. (1989). *Public schools by choice: Expanding opportunities for parents, students and teachers.* Bloomington, IN: Meyer Share.

National Association of State Boards of Education. (1992, October). *Winners all: A call for inclusive schools* (report of the NASBE study group on special education). Alexandria, VA: Author.

National Commission on Excellence in Education. (1983). *A nation at risk: The imperative for educational reform.* Washington, DC: U.S. Department of Education.

National Governors' Association. (1991). *Results in education: 1991.* Washington, DC: Author.

Northwest Regional Educational Laboratory. (1990). *Effective schooling practices: A research synthesis, 1990 update.* Portland, OR: Author.

Parrish, T. (1997). *Special education in an era of school reform.* Washington, DC: Federal Resource Center for Special Education.

O'Day, J., & Smith, M. S. (1993). Systemic reform and educational opportunity. In S. Fuhrman (Ed.), *Designing coherent education policy: Improving the system* (pp. 250–312). San Francisco: Jossey-Bass.

Office of Technology Assessment. (1989). *Linking for learning: A new course for education.* Washington, DC: Author.

Ogbu, J. (1987). Variability in minority school performance: A problem in search of an explanation. *Anthropology and Education Quarterly, 18,* 312–336.

Peters, T. (1987). *Thriving on chaos.* New York: Harper & Row.

Pugach, M. C., & Warger, C. L. (1993). Curriculum considerations. In J. I. Goodlad & T. C. Lovitt (Eds.), *Integrating general and special education* (pp. 125–148). Upper Saddle River, NJ: Merrill/Prentice Hall.

Reschly, D. J. (1988). Minority MR overrepresentation: Legal issues, research findings, and reform trends. In M. C. Wang, M. C. Reynolds, & H. J. Walberg (Eds.), *Handbook of special education: Research and practice: Vol. 2. Mildly handicapped conditions* (pp. 23–42). New York: Pergamon.

Sailor, W., Gee, K., & Karasoff, P. (1993). Full inclusion and school restructuring. In M. Snell (Ed.), *Instruction of students with severe disabilities* (pp. 1–30). Upper Saddle River, NJ: Merrill/ Prentice Hall.

Schnaiberg, L. (1997a, April 16). EAI seeks to team with developers to build charter school in Arizona. *Education Week,* pp. 1, 27.

Schnaiberg, L. (1997b, July 9). Ohio carries out funding for charter school pilot program. *Education Week,* p. 17.

Schofield, P. (1996). *School-based decision making: Perceived effects on students in special education.* Unpublished doctoral dissertation, University of Maryland, College Park.

Schumm, J. S., & Vaughn, S. (1991). Making adaptations for mainstreamed students: General classroom teachers' perspectives. *Remedial and Special Education, 12*(4), 6–17.

Shriner, J. G., Ysseldyke, J. E., & Thurlow, M. L. (1994). Standards for all American students. *Focus on Exceptional Children, 26*(5), 1–19.

Sizer, T. R. (1984). *Horace's compromise: The dilemma of the American high school.* Boston: Houghton Mifflin.

Smith, R. C. (1988). *America's shame, America's hope: Twelve million youth at risk.* Chapel Hill, NC: MDC. (ERIC Document Reproduction Service No. Ed 301 620)

Smith, S. W. (1990). Individualized education programs (IEPs) in special education: From intent to acquiescence. *Exceptional Children, 57,* 6–14.

Special Study Panel on Education Indicators. (1991). *Education counts: An indicator system to monitor the nation's educational health.* Washington, DC: National Center for Education Statistics.

Sugai, G. M., & Tindal, G. A. (1993). *Effective school consultation: An interactive approach.* Pacific Grove, CA: Brooks/Cole.

Toch, T. (1991). *In the name of excellence.* New York: Oxford University Press.

U.S. Department of Labor. (1991). *What work requires of schools.* Washington, DC: Secretary's Commission on Achieving Necessary Skills.

Villa, R. A., Thousand, J. S, Stainback, W., & Stainback, S. (1992). *Restructuring for caring and effective education: An administrative guide to creating heterogeneous schools.* Baltimore: Brookes.

Wagner, M., D'Amico, R., Marder, C., Newman, L., & Blackorby, J. (1992). *What happens next? Trends in postschool outcomes of youth with disabilities: The second comprehensive report from the national longitudinal transition study.* Menlo Park, CA: SRI International.

Walton, M. (1986). *The Deming management model.* New York: Perigee.

Westat. (1993). *Outcomes-based accountability: Policy issues and options for students with disabilities.* College Park: University of Maryland, Center for Policy Options in Special Education.

William T. Grant Foundation Commission on Work, Family and Citizenship. (1988, January). *The forgotten half: Non-college youth in America.* Washington, DC: Author.

Ysseldyke, J. E., Algozzine, B., Regan, R., & Potter, M. (1980). Technical adequacy of tests used by professionals in simulated decision making. *Psychology in the Schools, 17,* 202–209.

Ysseldyke, J. E., Algozzine, B., Shinn, M., & McGue, A. (1982). Similarities and differences between low achievers and students classified learning disabled. *Journal of Special Education, 16,* 73–85.

Ysseldyke, J. E., Lange, C. M., & Gorney, D. J. (1994). Parents of students with disabilities and open enrollment: Characteristics and reasons for transfer. *Exceptional Children, 60,* 359–342.

3

The Challenge of Diversity

CHERYL A. UTLEY
SUSAN L. MORTWEET

The most prevalent issue in the education reform movement for multicultural/bilingual[1] students with and without disabilities is access to excellence and equality of educational opportunities and experiences (Gay, 1993). Educational inequities exist in the provision and quality of services for poor and multicultural/bilingual students, especially when compared with Caucasian students in more affluent or suburban school districts (Coleman et al., 1966; Kozol, 1991). Neighborhood schools within poor communities emulate constraining factors within the home and school environments that can negatively affect child development and learning. These constraining factors, as manifested in school-based experiences, differ in several important ways: (a) programs in urban school districts, with high concentrations of multicultural/bilingual students, are underfunded (Gottlieb, Alter, & Gottlieb, 1991); (b) students are disproportionately tracked into low-ability or special classes (Oakes, 1985); (c) instructional materials and resources are distributed inequitably to poorer schools, creating inequities in opportunities to learn (Goodlad, 1984); and (d) the content of instruction for multicultural/bilingual students in their school environment is qualitatively different in technical quality, relevance, and appropriateness than the knowledge base of instruction in affluent schools.

Diversity in the composition of our school's population of multicultural/bilingual students presents challenges to regular and special educators, some of which include the following concerns:

1. How can educators view cultural and language differences as strengths and not as handicapping conditions?
2. What are the prereferral services, assessment practices, and teaching strategies that can minimize the inappropriate referral of multicultural/bilingual students into special education?
3. How can teachers develop social skills in multicultural/bilingual students with and without mild disabilities and implement strategies that enhance peer relations among all students?

---

[1]The term *multicultural* refers to students classified according to the Office of Civil Rights (OCR) system. It reads as follows:

> *American Indian or Alaskan Native.* A person having origins in any of the original peoples of North America and who maintains cultural identification through tribal affiliation or community recognition.
>
> *Asian or Pacific Islander.* A person having origins in any of the original people of the Far East, Southeast Asia, the Pacific Islands, or the Indian subcontinent. This area includes, for example, China, India, Japan, Korea, the Philippine Islands, and Samoa.
>
> *Hispanic.* A person of Mexican, Puerto Rican, Cuban, Central or South American, or other Spanish culture or origin—regardless of race.
>
> *Black (not of Hispanic origin).* A person having origins in any of the Black racial groups in Africa.
>
> *White (not of Hispanic origin).* A person having origins in any of the original peoples of Europe, North Africa, or the Middle East. (U.S. Department of Education, 1987, Form ED102, Appendix A)

The term *bilingual,* as defined by Ovando and Collier (1985), refers to an individual who speaks only one language but uses different language varieties, registers, and styles of that language.

4. What polices are needed at the local, state, and federal levels to assist schools in providing equitable programs for multicultural/bilingual students with and without mild disabilities?

The purpose of this chapter is to review the demographic realities of our schools and the characteristics of multicultural/bilingual students in regular and special education. Next, we discuss the use of alternative prereferral services, assessment practices, and strategies to enhance teachers' competencies in teaching academic and social skills to multicultural/bilingual students with and without mild disabilities. Last, we review policies and recommendations at the local, state, and federal levels that will assist administrators and policy makers in making decisions for the future trends in multicultural and special education.

DEMOGRAPHIC REALITIES OF SOCIETY AND SCHOOLS

The United States is becoming an increasingly multiethnic and multilingual society. Estimates suggest that our nation's population will grow to 265 million by the year 2020, with the largest growth among minority groups (Rodriguez, 1990). According to projected data reported by the U.S. Bureau of the Census (cited in Pallas, Natriello, & McDill, 1989), the number of Caucasian students is expected to decline about 13 percent from 1982 to 2020. For Hispanic youngsters, ages zero to seventeen years, trends show that they will have increased from 5.9 million in 1982 to 11.9 million in 2020, an increase of 22 percent.

From 1984 to 2020, estimates are that the number of children in poverty will substantially increase from 14.7 million to 20.1 million. Our educational system will be responsible for teaching approximately 5.4 million more children in poverty in 2020 than in 1984. Additional census data indicated that children living in single-parent homes will have increased from 16.2 million in 1984 to 21.1 million in 2020, an increase of 30 percent. A dramatic rise of 7.6 million children is expected in the number of children residing with mothers with low levels of educational attainment, from 13.6 million to 21.2 million. And finally, the proportion of children from Hispanic backgrounds who speak a primary language other than English is expected to increase from 2.5 percent in 1982 to approximately 7.5 percent by 2020.

Multicultural/Bilingual Students in Special Education

Students are more at risk for special education services when issues of poverty, race, and language are a part of their background (Baca & Almanza, 1991). Cultural, social, and economic factors are strongly linked to the classification of multicultural/bilingual students with disabilities, and the combination of these factors places these children at risk for numerous perinatal, prenatal, and developmental disability problems (Baumeister, Kupstas, Klindworth, & Zanthos, 1991; Edmunds, Martinson, & Goldberg, 1990; Parker, Greer, & Zuckerman, 1988).

According to Tuma (1988), environmental risk factors such as poverty, minority ethnic status, parental psychopathology, physical abuse or other maltreatment, teenage pregnancy, prematurity and low birth weight, parental divorce, and serious childhood illness are associated with higher rates of mental problems in children. In addition, these factors strongly influence "a child's development, parental attitudes toward child-rearing and quality of parent-child interactions, as well as the children's cognition, motivation, personality, and achievement behavior" (p. 189).

Ethnicity and socioeconomic status (SES) variables are intricately linked to the statistical representation of multicultural/bilingual students in special education, with these students disproportionately represented in special education classes (Artiles & Trent, 1994; Artiles & Zamora-Duran, 1997; Chinn & Hughes, 1987; Finn, 1982; Gollnick & Chinn, 1994; Gottlieb et al., 1991; Grossman, 1995; Harry, 1992; MacMillan, 1988; Maheady, Towne, Algozzine, Mercer, & Ysseldyke, 1983) and often underrepresented in classes for the gifted and talented (Gollnick & Chinn, 1990; Sleeter & Grant, 1988). Converging evidence of this phenomenon is provided by the National Longitudinal Transition Study (NLTS) of Special Education Students and student enrollment data collected by the U.S. Department of Education (1992) and U.S. Department of Education's Office for Civil Rights (OCR) (1987) surveys of elementary and secondary schools. Although African-American students constitute 12 percent of the general population, 24 percent of these students are receiving special education services. Similarly, Hispanic children represent 8 percent of the general school population, yet 13 percent of these children are placed in special education. Chinn and Hughes (1987), analyzing OCR data, reported that African-American children continue to be overrepresented in classes for students with educable mental retardation (EMR), students with moderate mental retardation, and students with behavior disorders (BD). Hispanic children, although not statistically overrepresented in classes for students with EMR, are disproportionately represented in classes for students with learning disabilities (LD). Native American children are overrepresented in classes for students with EMR and LD.

Gender and socioeconomic differences also exist in the referral, classification, and placement of multicultural/bilingual students into special classes. According to Gottlieb et al. (1991), boys are referred for special education services twice as often as girls (68 percent versus 32 percent). In a research investigation of 165 public schools in New York State, Gottlieb, Alter, Gottlieb, and Wishner (1994) reported that children in special education are poor, with 90 percent on some form of public assistance. These authors found that approximately 70 percent of children in special education are male and 95 percent of the entire population of 165 schools surveyed in New York State are members from multicultural/bilingual groups. Citing statistics by McLaren and Bryson (1987), Stoneman (1990) provides further evidence for the overrepresentation of males with mild mental retardation, with male-to-female ratios averaging about 1.6:1. In summary, student enrollment in special education classes is heavily weighted with male multicultural/bilingual students.

In analyzing data from the National Institute of Mental Health, Stenho (1982) and Cross, Bazron, Dennis, Issacs, and Benjamin (1989) revealed that cultural traits, behaviors, and beliefs influence differential treatment in the mental health system for African-American, Native American, Hispanic, and Asian-American students when they are compared with the delivery of services for their Caucasian counterparts. For example, African-American students with BD receive mental health services in the juvenile system, whereas Caucasian students with BD receive mental health services in treatment centers. Native American students with BD are removed from their tribal community. Hispanic students with BD are assessed in English or a language that is not their primary language, and Asian-American students with BD do not enter the special education or mental health system.

Cultural Characteristics of Multicultural/Bilingual Students

Children in schools represent differences not only in intellectual and physical capacities but also in cultural and language backgrounds (Anderson & Fenichel, 1989). Culture is a complex phenomenon and extends beyond group membership based on racial, ethnic, and linguistic differences (Park, Pullis, Reilly, & Townsend, 1994). Shade and New (1991) suggest that culture "induces different approaches to how individuals use their minds by providing a set of rules that become preferred methods of acquiring knowledge" (p. 321). The cultural orientation of multicultural/bilingual students to the teaching-learning process is evidenced in their behavioral expectations and social interaction patterns, communication style, and learning style (Shade & New, 1991).

Cultural Factors Affecting Academic Learning Research involving students from various cultural backgrounds indicates that the several psychocultural variables of social organization, sociolinguistics, cognition, and motivation influence the learning processes associated with schooling (Tharp, 1989) (see Table 3.1).

Cultural variables such as those in Table 3.1 are often incompatible with the expectations and routines of schools, leading to educational dissonance between the home and school, with children experiencing educational problems. For multicultural/bilingual students with and without mild disabilities to succeed in school, teachers must develop an understanding of how these cultural and linguistic variables influence the teaching of subject matter, academic skills, and the socialization process (Garcia, 1994). Evidence supporting the position that a deeper understanding of the interactions between a student's home culture and the prevailing school culture is essential for improving the academic achievement of multicultural/bilingual students with and without mild disabilities is provided by Harry (1992) and Boykin (1994) for African-American students; by Weisner, Gallimore, and Jordan (1988) for Hawaiian students; by Garcia (1988) and Moll (1988) for Hispanic students; and by Vogt, Jordan, and Tharp (1987) for American Indian students.

In addition to the characteristics that are associated with a disability, multicultural/bilingual students often exhibit culturally specific behaviors. Multicultural/bilingual students in the process of learning English may also exhibit

Table 3.1 Psychocultural Variables and the Teaching-Learning Process

Social organization refers to the organization of learners and educational experiences during the teaching-learning processes.

Example: Rank-and-file seating and teacher-led, whole-group instruction, followed by individual practice and assessment procedures produce a low level of attention and high levels of attention-seeking among Hawaiian learners.

Sociolinguistics refers to the study of how language varies with social situation and culture (for example, function and differences between home and school language).

Example: African-American learners are sometimes considered below grade level and unresponsive, yet they speak and behave with complexity and competence in home setings.

Cognition refers to the school's expectations that students will follow a certain pattern of cognitive functioning (for example, verbal/analytic thinking rather than visual/wholistic thinking).

Example: Japanese-American and Chinese-American learners apparently have a cognitive function pattern congruent with school expectations.

Motivation refers to the basic reasons and cultural differences that influence what students want to learn or their reasons for participating in learning activities.

Example: Asian-American learners might demonstrate high levels of motivation because of family expectations, while children and adolescents of immigrant families might be motivated to avoid being withdrawn from school and put to work in the fields.

SOURCE: Compiled from Tharp (1989) and McCormick (1990); adapted from *Multicultural Education of Children and Adolescents,* by L. G. Baruth and M. L. Manning, 1992 (p. 297), Needham Heights, MA: Allyn & Bacon. Copyright 1992 by Allyn & Bacon. Adapted with permission.

behaviors similar to those exhibited by students diagnosed as EMR, LD, and BD. As illustrated in Tables 3.2 to 3.5, each ethnic group, once identified as disabled, has specific cultural characteristics and behaviors with profound implications for children and their families.

Cultural Factors Affecting Socialization Although socialization is one of the primary goals of education, research on teaching social skills to multicultural/bilingual children, particularly those with disabilities, is limited (Li, 1992). Peer relationships and peer acceptance have well-documented implications for social adjustment in school and throughout the life span (Asher & Coie, 1990; Cowen, Pederson, Babigian, Izzo & Trost, 1973; Roff, Sells, & Golden, 1972). The importance of positive peer relationships may be an even more pressing concern for multicultural/bilingual students. Huang (1989) interviewed school-age, Southeast Asian refugee children (Vietnamese, Chinese, Cambodian), and found that the majority of them mentioned negative peer interactions (specifically physical altercations) but not academic or language difficulties as their most significant and difficult problem. Unfortunately, just as we have difficulty determining the most influential cause of a multicultural/bilingual student's academic difficulties, our efforts are equally problematic to determine whether such a child's unsuccessful socialization is due to a disability, social skills deficits, or temporary maladjustment to an unfamiliar environment (Li, 1992).

Table 3.2 Characteristics of African-American Students with Mild Disabilities

Condition	Characteristics of Condition	Characteristics of Culture	Possible Implications
Mentally retarded	Limited level of educational achievement	Historically, received little or no schooling	Family may give up on schooling
	Slow thinking	Tolerance for broad range of abilities	May not be perceived as disabled except related to academics
	Poor performance on tests of intelligence and achievement	Poor performance of tests normed on nonblack populations	Misdiagnosis: parental hostility and defensiveness
Learning disabled	Achievement below ability	Ability often misjudged because of test bias	Students with learning disabilities misdiagnosed as mentally retarded
	Faulty perception of sounds, words, and so on	Words not spoken with familiar intonation	Child believed to have auditory perceptual problems when there is a failure to recognize meaning without the cues of dialect
	Hyperactive	Interactive style	Child engaged in interactive process may be viewed as hyperactive
Emotionally disturbed/ behaviorally disordered	Delinquency	Youths may rebel against system when they believe they have little hope for success	Antisocial behavior may be used to achieve status when it cannot be achieved within the system
	Drugs and alcohol	Youths may become drug or alcohol dependent in environment where narcotics are commonly used as an escape	
	Aggressive, acting out, challenging, militant	Desire to assert racial identify	Needs to be directed into positive channels

SOURCE: Based on Nazarro (1981).

Numerous cultural differences exist that affect the social interactions and acceptance of multicultural/bilingual students with disabilities by their peers. Barriers to developing positive peer relations are due to differences in physical appearance, language usage, and cultural practices. Children as young as four years old perceive and react to differences between themselves and others (Diamond, 1993; Sigelman, Miller, & Whitworth, 1986). These reactions toward peers with disabilities are typically negative across all school ages (Gottlieb & Budoff, 1973; Stoneman, 1993) and may be even more discriminatory against multicultural/ bilingual children with disabilities (Brantlinger & Guskin, 1986; Grossman, 1991).

Linguistic differences present another cultural barrier to successful social relationships (Li, 1992). Many cultures do not have extended experiences with the

Table 3.3 Characteristics of Hispanic Students with Mild Disabilities

Condition	Characteristics of Condition	Characteristics of Culture	Possible Implications
Mentally retarded	Limited level of educational achievement	Historically, received little or no schooling	Dropout rate high, even among nonhandicapped
	Slow thinking	Adapts roles and expectations to abilities	Person assured of place in community in spite of limitations
	Poor performance on tests	Most tests are not appropriate, especially timed tests	Frequent misdiagnosis
	Noncompetitive	Noncompetitive	Best to use team approach or cooperative approach learning
Learning disabled	Achievement below ability	Weak skills in both English and Spanish	Problem determining nature of learning problem
	Faulty perception of sounds, words, and so on	Many English words sound alike to Spanish speaker	Problem determining cause of misperceptions
Emotionally disturbed/ behaviorally disordered	Depressed, anxious withdrawn	Youths may turn to drugs or alcohol in situations where family roles have broken down	Requires special extended family and community effort to combat abuse

SOURCE: Based on Nazarro (1981).

communication networks of the majority culture due to social factors such as recent immigration, frequent migration, or living in isolated areas (Heath, 1986). Furthermore, the language and dialectal differences of multicultural/bilingual students in and of itself may be stigmatizing as it is an obvious representation of the broader, minority culture to which they belong. Language learning not only entails acquiring a system of words, sounds, and grammatical rules but also includes understanding language differences within a cultural context so that speech acts and social interactions are meaningful and accepted (Cartledge, 1996). Beyond prejudice elicited by minority language, the lack of verbal communication ability with majority peers is a critical deterrent against effective social interaction and acceptance.

Differences in traditional social practices between minority and majority cultures also contribute to difficulties these children have with social interactions, with both peers and adults. Some dimensions along the continuum of cultural differences that can influence miscommunication and impaired social interactions are manner of coping, emotional expressiveness, individual or group orientation, and egalitarian versus authoritarian social structure (Rotheram-Borus & Tsemberis, 1989). For example, one child's culturally appropriate response to conflict of avoidance may be introversion with minimal eye contact, a response that may be interpreted by an individual unfamiliar with the culture as disrespectful and socially deviant. The majority culture's interpretation of "extreme" emotional behaviors in multicultural/bilingual students with and without mild disabilities

Table 3.4 Characteristics of Asian-American Students with Mild Disabilities

Condition	Characteristics of Condition	Characteristics of Culture	Possible Implications
Mentally retarded	Limited level of educational achievement	Social class and self-esteem determined by level of identity	May have poor self-esteem; family may feel shame
Learning disabled	Achievement below ability	Value placed on high academic achievement, industriousness	Child may try to compensate for disability by working extra hard, memorizing material, and so forth, so as not to bring shame on family
	Faulty perception of sounds, words, and so on	Failure to perceive unfamiliar sounds or to remember words out of context for non-English-speaking children	May lead to confusion in diagnosing problem
	Hyperactive	Self-controlled	Behavior may be a source of shame to parents and self; requires special understanding by educators of traditional cultural expectations
Emotionally disturbed/ behaviorally disoriented	Anxiety, psychosomatic complaints, hysterical blind and deaf reactions; school phobia from not being able to satisfy achievement demands of home and school	Traditionally, child is inhibited, conventional, subservient to authority	Requires special understanding by educators of traditional cultural expectations
	Suicide	Suicide	Japanese culture once reinforced this alternative as a way of ending shameful situation
	Delinquency	Youths refuse to give unquestioning obedience to parental views	Less traditional youths may use crime as a statement of rebellion
	Anxiety, depressive reactions	Youths may become angry at racial barriers, then feel guilty for denying their own ethnicity	Requires special effort to reduce racial barriers so youth will not desire to deny ethnicity
	Aggressive, acting out, challenging, militant	Desire to assert ethnic identity	May be particularly shame producing for more traditional parents

SOURCE: Based on Nazarro (1981).

may represent cultural values or responses to the process of acculturation (Baca & Cervantes, 1989).

Cultural Differences Due to a Disability Children diagnosed as having a disability, by definition, generally bring some maladaptive social functioning to an interaction. For example, children with learning disabilities tend to display negative

Table 3.5 Characteristics of Native American Students with Mild Disabilities

Condition	Characteristics of Condition	Characteristics of Culture	Possible Implications
Mentally retarded	Limited level of educational achievement	Social class and self-esteem determined by level of identity	May have poor self-esteem; family may feel shame
Learning disabled	Achievement below ability	Value placed on high academic achievement, industriousness	Child may try to compensate for disability by working extra hard, memorizing material, and so on, so as not to bring shame on family
	Faulty perception of sounds, words, and so on	Failure to perceive unfamiliar sounds; or remember words out of context for non-English-speaking children	May lead to confusion in diagnosing problem
	Hyperactive	Self-controlled	Behavior may be a source of shame to parents and self
Emotionally disturbed/ behaviorally disordered	Depressed, anxious withdrawn, suicidal	Feelings of unworthiness, due to conflict of values	Common syndrome; may not receive attention
	Delinquency	Inability to succeed may lead to rebellion	Ridicule may be more of an effective deterrent than other punishments
	Alcohol	Alcohol abuse	Requires special extended family and community effort
	Militant	Desire to assert cultural identity	Need to be directed to productive channels

SOURCE: Based on Nazarro (1981).

and rejecting behaviors during social interactions (Bryan, 1978); children with mental retardation may have coordination problems and immature interaction styles (Baca & Cervantes, 1989); and children with autism characteristically exhibit social withdrawal (Sasso, Garrison-Harrell, & Rogers, 1994), all of which may contribute to difficulties in establishing social relationships.

All of these difficulties can create anxiety for multicultural/bilingual students with disabilities, which also may negatively affect social performance and acceptance (Li, 1992). The misperceptions created by cultural and individual differences also influence the typical peer's perceptions of social inadequacy and decisions to avoid or reject multicultural/bilingual students with mild disabilities as friends.

Social and emotional differences are significant factors in a teacher's consideration of potential disabilities in children from diverse cultural backgrounds. Rueda and Forness (1994) point out that an increasing number of immigrant children in the schools must deal with acculturation-related issues that may manifest as behavioral symptoms similar to those featured in depressive disorders. A high degree of stress, guilt, and emotional turmoil can manifest symptoms of childhood depression (Suarez-Orosco, 1989; Trueba, 1987). The lack of cultural knowledge and sensitivity to the culturally specific behaviors of students can lead to the misidentification of these children as LD, EMR, and BD.

THE PREVENTION OF INAPPROPRIATE REFERRALS TO SPECIAL EDUCATION

One significant response to the disproportionate representation of multicultural/bilingual students in special education classes was the formation in 1979 of the Panel on the Selecting and Placement of Students in Programs for the Mentally Retarded with the responsibilities of (a) determining factors that account for the disproportionate representation of minority students and males in special education and (b) identifying placement criteria or practices that do not affect minority students and males disproportionately (Heller, Holtzman, & Messick, 1982). The panel suggested the following six recommendations:

1. Teachers in the regular classroom are responsible for engaging in multiple educational interventions and to note the effects of such interventions on a child experiencing academic failure before referring the child for special education assessment. School boards and administrators are responsible for ensuring that needed alternative instructional resources are available.
2. Assessment specialists are responsible for demonstrating that the measures employed validly assess the functional needs of the individual child for which there are potentially effective interventions.
3. The placement team that labels and places a child in a special program is responsible for demonstrating that any differential label used is related to a distinctive prescription for the educational practices and that these practices are likely to improve outcomes not achievable in the regular classroom.
4. The special education evaluation staff are responsible for systematically demonstrating that high-quality, effective special education is being provided and that the goals of the special education program could not be achieved as effectively within the regular classroom.
5. The special education staff is responsible for demonstrating on at least an annual basis, that a child should remain in the special education class. A child should be retained in the special education class only after a demonstration that he or she cannot meet specified educational objectives and that all efforts have been made to achieve these objectives.

6. Administrators at the district, state, and national levels are responsible for monitoring on a regular basis the pattern of special education placements, the rates of particular groups of children or particular schools and districts, and the types of instructional services offered to affirm that appropriate procedures are being followed or to redress inequities found in the system. (pp. 94–95)

In essence, the panel was recommending a radical change of current educational decision-making practices, where the focus of interventions is on multicultural/bilingual students experiencing academic failure in the regular classroom.

One alternative program to special education intervention is the development of "prereferral intervention teams" or "teacher assistance teams" (TATs), designed to (a) facilitate prereferral screening for special education services so that inappropriate referrals will be reduced; (b) provide immediate peer support for regular classroom teachers working with multicultural/bilingual students experiencing academic problems; (c) assist teachers in the implementation of classroom interventions that are successful with multicultural/bilingual students; and (d) provide continuous staff development for all teachers in the areas of cultural diversity, assessment, instruction, and classroom management (Chalfant & Pysh, 1981; Friend & Cook, 1992; Garcia & Ortiz, 1988).

The prereferral intervention team is essential for multicultural/bilingual students to receive equitable educational services (Gersten & Woodward, 1994). This team is responsible for assessing student language proficiency and dominance, instructional achievement, and cultural influences (Baca & Almanza, 1991). Multicultural/bilingual students with language and cultural differences must be differentiated from the mild categories of disability before referral procedures to special education are implemented. Instructional procedures must be culturally responsive and use strategies that address both cultural and linguistic learning differences and the disability (Hoover & Collier, 1989).

A prereferral model for language minority students has been developed by Garcia and Ortiz (1988) (see Figure 3.1). The prereferral intervention team is composed of school personnel from the regular education system. Special educators and school psychologists may serve as consultants to the team. Responsibilities of the team include conducting follow-up meetings to evaluate interventions, providing recommendations for improving the instructional environment, and making decisions concerning the eligibility of multicultural/bilingual students for special education services. The prereferral model presents questions that address the needs of multicultural/bilingual students at each of the eight steps of the prereferral process.

Step 1: Is the student experiencing academic difficulty? This question assists teachers in determining whether a student's learning problems are due to cultural, linguistic, or socioeconomic variables or due to a disability. Documentation must be provided indicating that student's learning difficulty is because of a limited knowledge of English or lack of opportunities to learn.

Step 2: Are the curricula and instructional materials known to be effective for language-minority students? Efforts should be made to

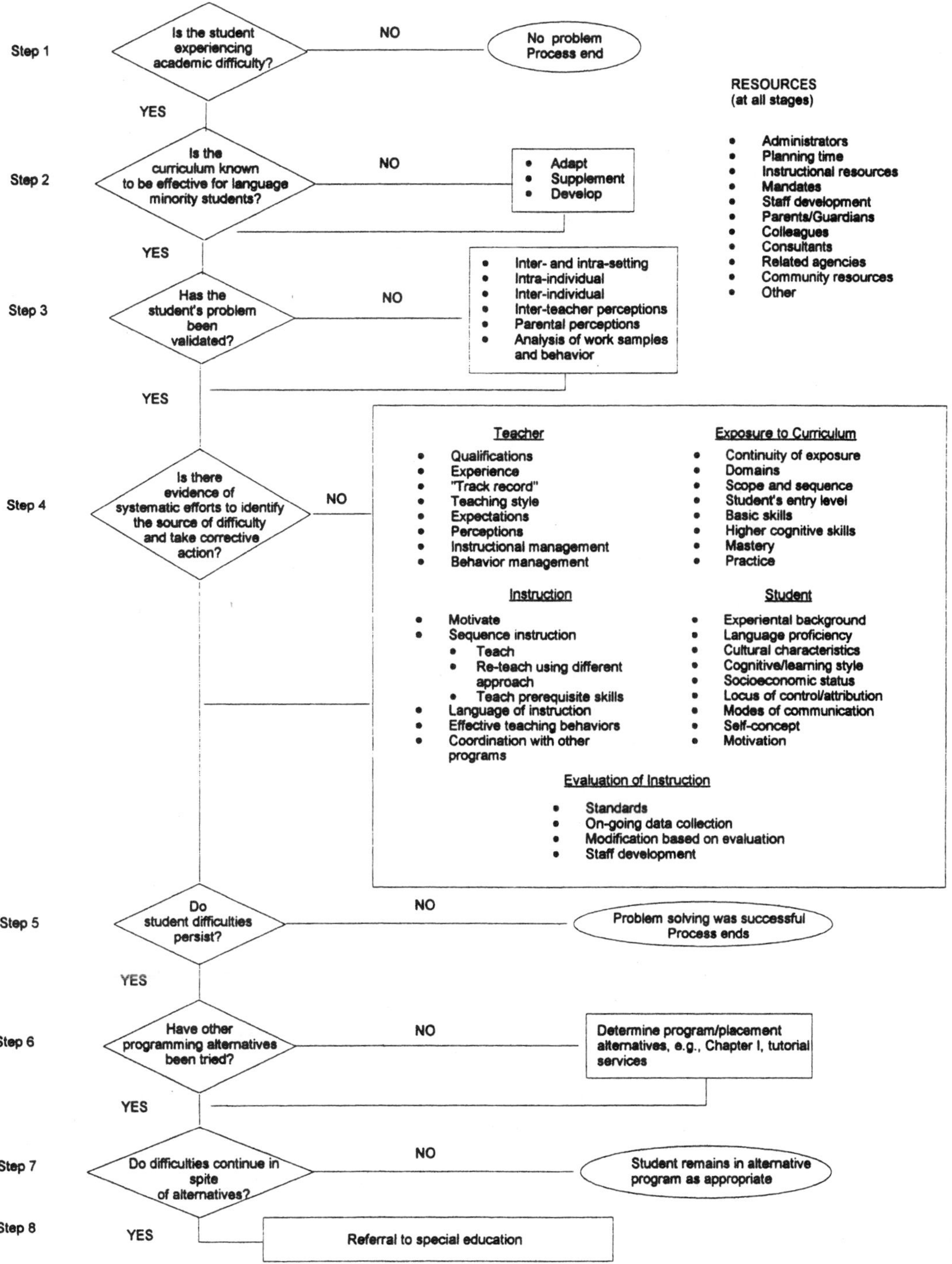

FIGURE 3.1 Preventing Inappropriate Placements of Language Minority Students in Special Education: A Prereferral Process

SOURCE: From *Preventing Inappropriate Referrals of Language Minority Students to Special Education* (p. 3), by S. B. Garcia and A. A. Ortiz, 1988, New Focus Series No. 5. Washington, DC: National Clearinghouse for Bilingual Education.

create more effective instructional programs for these students. The prereferral team should determine whether academic or behavior problems experienced by multicultural/bilingual students are due to (a) the use of ineffective instructional materials and/or (b) poor teaching in general. One such criterion for determining the effectiveness of the instructional curriculum is to see whether the content presents contributions from both minority and majority perspectives. Instructional materials may need to be adapted or modified to meet the cognitive and language skills of multicultural/bilingual students in the regular classroom who are in the process of being referred.

Step 3: Has the problem been validated? This question is designed to have the prereferral team examine several factors and to gather information from multiple sources before deciding that a student's problems are abnormal or deviate from the norm.

Step 4: Is there evidence of systematic efforts to identify the source of difficulty and to take corrective actions? All aspects of the teaching environment must be reviewed, including teacher characteristics, teacher-student expectations, student characteristics, exposure to the curriculum, instructional adaptations, and the evaluation system to determine whether goals and objectives have been met.

Step 5: Do student difficulties persist? Once the sources of the student's difficulties have been determined, we must examine alternative programs offered within the mainstream of the school environment. If the student's problems do not continue to persist, the prereferral process ends.

Step 6: Have other programming alternatives been tried? Other supplemental programs offered within the school district may be a solution to accommodating the needs of multicultural/bilingual students prior to referral. Such alternative programs include compensatory programs, migrant education, Title VII, Chapter 1, tutorial programs, and/or bilingual programs.

Step 7: Do difficulties continue in spite of alternatives? If the prereferral process continues and alternative programs are not successful in solving the student's problems, then a referral to special education is warranted. Diagnostic information must be collected to determine the nature of the disability. In addition, the following information is critical in determining eligibility for special education services: (a) conclusive evidence indicates that the curriculum is appropriate, (b) academic and behavior problems are evident across school and home settings and personnel, (c) problems are documented in the student's native language and in English, (d) the teacher is qualified to teach multicultural/bilingual students, and (e) sound instructional principles are implemented.

Step 8: Should the student be referred for special education services? Once all of the steps of the prereferral process have been completed, there must be ample evidence to suggest that multicultural/bilingual students cannot be adequately taught in the regular classroom. A referral to special education is justified only after these steps have been completed.

In summary, the prereferral model, as described by Garcia and Ortiz (1988), responds to four of the recommendations by the Panel on the Selection and Placement of Students in Programs for the Mentally Retarded (Heller et al., 1982). This model is intended to assist regular education teachers in serving multicultural/bilingual students in the mainstream by providing these students an appropriate education.

CULTURALLY RESPONSIVE ASSESSMENT PROCEDURES

Test Bias Issues

One of the most controversial explanations of the disproportionate representation of multicultural/bilingual students in special education is the allegation of systematic bias, referred to as the inaccuracy of test results that are due to cultural background and the facts of the test rather than actual mental abilities or skills (Reynolds, 1987). Reschly (1982) has argued that "assessment which does not result in effective interventions should be regarded as useless, and biased or unfair as well, if ethnic or racial minorities are differentially exposed to ineffective programs as a result of assessment activities" (p. 215). Critics of the testing movement have suggested that (a) test developers systematically exclude multicultural/bilingual students with and without mild disabilities in the stratification of children in the norming of tests (Haywood, 1977); (b) standardized test norms and indices of reliability and validity are inadequately constructed for use with students with mild disabilities (Fuchs, Fuchs, Benowitz, & Barringer, 1987); (c) standardized intelligence tests do not assess the "functional academic skills" essential for classroom performance (Jones, 1988); (d) testing procedures are biased against low-SES examinees (Fuchs, Fuchs, Daily, & Power, 1986); and (e) test instruments are used for diagnostic purposes and are not prescriptive (Heller et al., 1982).

Components of the psychoeducational process should include information on categories of academically relevant skills, cognitive strategies, and adaptive/motivational skills by using systematic observations of teacher and student behaviors to document problems and the student's progress in regular and special education classrooms (Heller et al., 1982). Collier (1988) and Baca and Cervantes (1989) have suggested that psychoeducational assessment procedures in the prereferral and referral process should include the following relevant information:

1. Prereferral and/or referral data
2. Primary and secondary language data
3. Observational and interview data
4. School records
5. Language proficiency data
6. Educational assessment data

7. Perceptual-motor or psycholinguistic data
8. Adaptive behavior data
9. Medical and/or developmental data
10. Cognitive assessment data

Indicators that signal the presence of specific sociocultural factors that may be contributing to the student's learning and behavior problems should also be considered as valuable information for distinguishing between multicultural/bilingual students with and without mild disabilities. As illustrated in Tables 3.6 and 3.7, several sociocultural factors and samples of behaviors influence the academic and behavior problems of multicultural/bilingual students. A variety of assessment procedures for gathering information that are focused on the "functional" characteristics of multicultural/bilingual students relevant to classroom performance should be used.

EFFECTIVE INSTRUCTIONAL PRINCIPLES

Within the field of special education, process-product research has been conducted to quantify instructional programs in terms of factors such as engagement, academic and transitional activities, and time spent by teachers engaged in academic talk (O'Sullivan, Ysseldyke, Christensen, & Thurlow, 1990). The majority of studies on instructional effectiveness has been acquired through research conducted with low- and middle- to high-SES students. The evaluation of how the behaviors of low-achieving, at-risk, and high-achieving students interact with the instructional environment has revealed that certain classroom factors, as illustrated in Table 3.8, promote lower levels of academic and reinforce negative classroom behavior.

Collectively, the findings of empirical research comparing low-SES versus middle- to high-SES students have shown that the (a) amount of time allocated for academic instruction is correlated with poverty-level programs for at-risk students who spend less time in reading instruction than their middle-class counterparts (Greenwood, Delquadri, Stanley, Sasso, Whorton, & Schulte, 1981); (b) differential gains in students' academic performances were affected by school and classroom processes, with low-SES students significantly less engaged in academic-oriented behaviors than middle-SES students (Greenwood, Delquadri, & Hall, (1989); (c) low-SES children were significantly less engaged in academic behaviors during their daily lessons than were middle-SES, higher-skilled students (Greenwood et al., 1991); and (d) ecological structure of the instructional program serving low-SES students, compared with high-SES students, differed in the materials used, grouping arrangements, and teachers' behaviors (Greenwood et al., 1991).

Research conducted by Arreaga-Mayer, Carta, and Tapia (1994) revealed that bilingual/special education mainstream students spent 67 percent of their instruction time engaged in whole-class instruction formats, 92 percent of their

Table 3.6 Teacher Variables

Experiential Background

1. Does the teacher have the training and experience to work effectively with multicultural populations?
2. What resources has the teacher utilized in attempting to resolve the problem?
   - district resources (instructional supervisors, inservice training, media, and materials)
   - volunteers
   - community resources
   - colleagues
   - external consultants
   - professional associations

Culture

1. Has the teacher gathered cultural information specific to the student and his/her family?
   - native/traditional versus immigrant group
   - parent interviews
   - home visits
2. Does the teacher incorporate aspects of the student's culture into the curriculum?
   - pluralistic goals, perspectives
   - integrating information across subject areas versus isolating units or presenting fragmented bits of information about holidays, festivals, etc.
   - accurate representation of culture and contributions of the group

Language Proficiency

1. Are the teacher's language skills adequate to deliver instruction in the student's native language?
2. If the student is not in bilingual education, what resources have been utilized to provide native language support?
3. Is the teacher adequately trained to provide dual language instruction? English-as-a-second-language intervention?
4. Were the student's linguistic characteristics addressed by the teaching in planning instruction?
   - Comprehensive input is provided
   - Focus of instruction is on meaning rather than error correction
   - There are opportunities for English language acquisition

Teaching Style/Learning Style

1. Is the teacher aware of his/her own preferred teaching style?
2. Is the teacher aware of the student's preferred learning style?
3. Does the teacher use a variety of styles to accommodate various learning styles of students? Is the student's style addressed?

Expectations/Perceptions

1. What are the teacher's perceptions of the student?
2. Are expectations and level of instruction geared to higher levels of thinking?
3. How does the teacher view cultural diversity in the classroom?
4. How do these views influence expectations as well as instructional planning?

SOURCE: From *Preventing Inappropriate Referrals of Language Minority Students to Special Education* (p. 5), by S. B. Garcia and A. A. Ortiz, 1988, New Focus Series No. 5. Washington, DC: National Clearinghouse for Bilingual Education.

Table 3.7 Student Variables

Experiential Background

1. Are there any factors in the student's school history which may be related to the current difficulty?
   - Attendance/mobility
   - Opportunities to learn
   - Program placement(s)
   - Quality of poor instruction
2. Are there any variables related to family history which may have affected school performance?
   - Lifestyle
   - Length of residence in the U.S.
   - Stress (e.g., poverty, lack of emotional support)
3. Are there any variables related to the student's medical history which may have affected school performance?
   - Vision
   - Hearing
   - Illness
   - Nutrition
   - Trauma or injury

Culture

1. How is the student's cultural background different from the culture of the school and larger society?
   - Family (family size and structure, roles, responsibilities, expectations)
   - Aspirations (success, goals)
   - Language and communication (rules for adult, adult-child, child-child communication, language use at home, nonverbal communication)
   - Religion (dietary restrictions, role expectations)
   - Tradition and history (contact with homeland, reason for immigration)
   - Decorum and discipline (standards for acceptable behavior)
2. To what extent are the student's characteristics representative of the larger group?
   - Continuum of culture (traditional, dualistic, atraditional)
   - Degree of acculturation or assimilation
3. Is the student able to function successfully in more than one cultural setting?
4. Is the student's behavior culturally appropriate?

Language Proficiency

1. Which is the student's dominant language? Which is the preferred?
   - Setting (school, playground, home, church, etc.)
   - Topics (academic subjects, day-to-day interactions)
   - Speakers (parents, teachers, siblings, peers, etc.)
   - Aspects of each language (syntax, vocabulary, phonology use)
2. What is the student's level of proficiency in the primary language and in English?
   - Interpersonal communication skills
   - Cognitive/academic literacy-related skills

Table 3.7 Student Variables *(continued)*

Language Proficiency *(continued)*

3. Are the styles of verbal interaction used in the primary language different from those most valued at school, in English?
   - Label questions (e.g., what's this? who?)
   - Meaning questions (adult infers for child, interprets or asks for explanation)
   - Accounts (generated by teller, information new to listener, e.g., show & tell, creative writing)
   - Event casts (running narrative on events as they unfold, or forecast of events in preparation)
   - Stories
4. If so, has the student been exposed to those that are unfamiliar to him?
5. What is the extent and nature of exposure to each language?
   - What language(s) do the parents speak to each other?
   - What language(s) do the parents speak to the chld?
   - What language(s) do the children use with each other?
   - What television programs are seen in each language?
   - Are stories read to the child? In what language(s)?
6. Are student behaviors characteristic of second language acquisition?
7. What types of language intervention has the student received?
   - Bilingual vs. monolingual instruction
   - Language development, enrichment, remediation
   - Additive vs. subtractive bilingualism (transition vs. maintenance)

Learning Style

1. Does the student's learning style require curricular/instructional accommodations?
   - Perceptual style differences (e.g., visual vs. auditory learner)
   - Cognitive style differences (e.g., inductive vs. deductive thinking)
   - Preferred style of participation (e.g., teacher vs. student directed, small vs. large group)
2. If so, were these characteristics accommodated, or were alternative styles taught?

Motivational Influences

1. Is the student's self-concept enhanced by school experiences?
   - School environment communicates respect for culture and language
   - Student experiences academic and social success
2. Is schooling perceived as relevant and necessary for success in the student's family and community?
   - Aspirations
   - Realistic expectations based on community experience
   - Culturally different criteria for success
   - Education perceived by the community as a tool for assimilation

SOURCE: From *Preventing Inappropriate Referrals of Language Minority Students to Special Education* (p. 7), by S. B. Garcia and A. A. Ortiz, 1988, New Focus Series No. 5. Washington, DC: National Clearinghouse for Bilingual Education.

Table 3.8 Alterable Instructional Processes

✓ Low amounts of time devoted to academic instruction
✓ High amounts of time lost to instruction, transitions, and pullout labs
✓ Low academic responding or infrequent opportunities to respond
✓ Infrequent opportunities to learn academic subjects or the exposure to lessons, materials, and independent practice
✓ Instructional materials/media/practices play a role in accelerating or decelerating students' engagement in academic responding and the rate of students' academic growth
✓ Low fidelity of the curriculum
✓ Little use of instructional effectiveness criteria
✓ High use of teacher behaviors that decelerate academic achievement outcomes

SOURCE: Adapted from "The Case for Performance-Based Instructional Models," by C. R. Greenwood, 1996, *School Psychology Quarterly, 11*(4), pp. 283–296.

classroom day not using any language (verbal or written), 8 percent using English, and 1 percent using a non-English language (namely, Spanish). The academic *engagement* time of these students was 44 percent even though they spent most of their day in academic *activities* (math, 20 percent; reading, 18 percent; and language, 16 percent).

The evaluation of instructional practices used during the reading period of African-American and Caucasian students with EMR in self-contained classrooms revealed that both groups of students participated in active academic behaviors 56 percent and 47 percent of the reading period, respectively. African-American students with EMR were engaged in talk academic behaviors. Student responses involved motor and manipulative responses to activities (Utley, Delquadri, Mortweet, Davis, Guess, & Greenwood, 1993). In another study of low-SES and high-SES students with EMR, the results indicated that high-SES students were engaged in more reading (aloud and silently) behaviors, whereas low-SES students with EMR were more engaged in reading readiness behaviors, such as copying words or matching words to pictures (Utley, Delquadri, Mortweet, Thorisdottir, Greenwood, & Dawson, 1993).

Culturally Responsive Instructional Procedures

Another perspective advocated by theorists is that learning is enhanced when it occurs in contexts that are socioculturally and linguistically meaningful (Garcia, 1994; Scribner & Cole, 1981). Recognition of issues (for example, home/native languages) related to the cultural-compatible position is important when designing instruction to address the needs of multicultural/bilingual students. Such practices include the systematic inclusion of students' histories, language, experiences, and values from classroom curricula and activities.

Franklin (1993) has suggested several culturally relevant instructional practices for teaching African-American and other multicultural students with mild disabilities. They are as follows: (a) emphasizing verbal interactions, (b) teaching students to engage in self-talk, (c) facilitating divergent thinking, (d) using small-group and cooperative learning, (d) employing verve in the classroom, (e) focusing on real-world tasks, and (f) promoting teacher-student interactions.

Curricular adaptations will benefit multicultural/bilingual students with mild disabilities, particularly those individuals for whom English is a second language. The Optimal Learning Environment (OLE) curriculum incorporates the following seven principles for teaching language arts effectively (Ruiz, 1989): (a) take into account students' sociocultural backgrounds and their effects on oral language, reading, writing, and second language learning; (b) consider students' possible learning problems and their effects on oral language, reading, writing, and second language learning; (c) follow developmental processes in literacy acquisition; (d) locate curriculum in a meaningful context where the communicative purpose is clear and authentic; (e) connect the curriculum with students' personal experiences; (f) incorporate children's literature in reading, writing, and ESL lessons; and (g) involve parents as active partners in their children's instruction.

The degree of disability will direct modifications of the program's focus, use of specialized knowledge, and use of curriculum materials for multicultural/bilingual students with disabilities (Cloud, 1988; Duran, 1985). Multicultural/bilingual students with moderate-severe disabilities require programs with a developmental focus and the teaching of self-help and communication skills (for example, requesting assistance, giving personal information, daily living skills, and so forth) and in a second language.

CULTURALLY RESPONSIVE TEACHING MODELS

The successful teaching of academic skills and socialization of students begins with educators. Teachers and school personnel provide a model for acceptable attitudes toward others, and the children with whom they have extensive contact will reflect their point of view (Gollnick & Chinn, 1990). Educators have a responsibility to reframe their own biases and low expectations for performance from multicultural/bilingual students with and without mild disabilities (Cummins, 1989) and to begin setting demands and expectations that communicate their belief in the value and promise of these children (Steele, 1992). Simply placing multicultural/bilingual students with Caucasian students in heterogeneous classrooms will not guarantee the development of academic skills and/or positive social interactions (Johnson, Johnson, & Maruyama, 1983). Teachers must be able to create a social structure in the classroom that communicates the notion that all students are responsible for generating an accepting, mutually helpful environment (Reynolds, 1980).

Peer-Mediated Teaching Models

Regular and special education teachers are becoming increasingly concerned about the quality of academic instruction for multicultural/bilingual students with and without mild disabilities (Berliner, 1988). Effective teaching practices have been categorized under the two broad headings of (a) teacher-directed classrooms and (b) peer-mediated lessons. Examples of teacher-directed strategies are the Exemplary Center for Reading Instruction (Reid, 1986) and precision teaching (White, 1986). Teacher-directed procedures are highly structured and consist of a comprehensive system of instructional procedures and curriculum materials.

Peer-mediated approaches, by contrast, are designed to provide direct instruction to target peers. Greenwood et al. (1990) define a peer-mediated approach as one in which peers present prompts or task trials, monitor tutee responses, use error correction procedures, and provide help. This approach is highly structured and based on teacher goals and the classroom curriculum. Aspects of this approach include a continuous program of moderate duration and specific tutor training (that is, encouraging and praising correct responses). Examples of peer-mediated practices are peer tutoring (Delquadri, Greenwood, Whorton, Carta, & Hall, 1986), cooperative learning (Johnson & Johnson, 1986), and social skills training (Strain & Odom, (1986).

Peer Tutoring There is a renewed interest in peer tutoring as a method of individualizing instruction, facilitating effective programming for the entire class, increasing academic responding for all students, and helping multicultural/bilingual students become socially integrated in the regular classroom (Miller, Barbetta, & Herron, 1994; Topping, 1988). Peer tutoring programs, as reviewed in the literature, have been successfully implemented across a variety of student populations (for instance, at-risk; economically disadvantaged; students with EMR, LD, and BD; and multicultural/bilingual students), students in the same grade (same-age students), and older students with younger students (cross-age) (Osguthorpe & Scruggs, 1986). Although several peer tutoring programs have been developed and implemented in regular and special education classrooms, one particular system, ClassWide Peer Tutoring (CWPT), as defined by Carta (1991) and Greenwood, Delquadri, and Carta (1997), has emerged as a systematic instructional procedure using competing teams and a game format. Maheady, Saca, and Harper (1988) describe other components of CWPT as follows: (a) an explicit presentation format, (b) contingent point earning, (c) systematic error correction strategies, and (d) public posting of student performance.

The benefits for multicultural/bilingual students are numerous (Greenwood, Carta, Walker, Arreaga-Mayer, and Dinwiddie, 1988): (a) such tutoring allows teachers to supervise students in a time-efficient manner during instruction, (b) mastery learning occurs because practice and correction procedures are built within the system, (c) subject matter may be taught in primary/secondary languages, (d) second language acquisition is fostered through the context of talking to peers, (e) positive self-esteem and interpersonal attitudes are fostered, and (f) tutoring is a supplemental instructional activity to the classwide instruction.

Cooperative Learning One of the most promising ways of encouraging appropriate interactions among multicultural/bilingual students is to provide tasks that require cooperative effort (Cartledge, 1996; Hudson, 1989; Johnson et al., 1983; Johnson & Johnson, 1986; Kagan, 1992; Reynolds, 1980; Slavin, 1988).

The basic principles fundamental to cooperative learning include simultaneous interaction, positive interdependence, and individual accountability (Kagan, 1992). The most effective interactions within a cooperative context are designed to promote both personal and task-related contact, equal status among participants, opportunities for multicultural/bilingual students to demonstrate skills that are contradictory to stereotypical beliefs, and activities that enhance ethnic relations among students (Johnson et al., 1983; Kagan, 1992). Teachers must structure classroom learning experiences capitalizing on goal interdependence between their heterogeneous groups of children. For certain cultural groups, the use of cooperative structures motivates individuals to work harder because the cultural values within these groups emphasize working for the group and not working individually in a competitive situation. It is also believed that the use of competitive and individualistic structures in the classroom to the exclusion of cooperative learning structures devalues the home culture and the cultural identity of multicultural/bilingual students (Kagan, 1992).

Johnson et al.'s (1983) review revealed that when compared with competitive and individualistic situations, cooperative efforts among children resulted in more positive attitudes, greater interpersonal attraction, more helping behaviors, and more support for using cooperative situations by the children. Children in cooperative learning situations also viewed their class as a more cohesive unit and felt more personally supported, liked, and accepted by their peers, and they had higher expectations for future positive interactions than children experiencing competitive or individualistic learning conditions. Noncooperative instructional arrangements are not conductive to social interaction, and thus allow ethnic prejudice and stereotyping to continue. Successful socialization and the mitigation of such false beliefs, on the other hand, may be possible if "the 'we' feeling developed within cooperative groups . . . outweigh the 'they' perceptions between majority and minority students" (Johnson et al., 1983, p. 34).

Social Skills Training Social skills training focus on the problem of delayed or lack of social skills that are functional and appropriate for successful social interaction with peers. Studies investigating the effectiveness of social skills training for multicultural/bilingual students are limited. Li (1992) reviewed social skills training studies for the general population, students with mild disabilities, and multicultural/bilingual students. She presented an integrated model of social skills training based on her findings that addresses the socialization needs of culturally diverse students with disabilities. According to Li, both the student with the social skills deficit and the entire group must be targeted for change. When selecting their goals for socials skills training, the teacher must consider the existence of ethnic differences both within and between children of different cultures as well as differences in developmental and cognitive abilities. By incorporating these considerations, social skills training will be sensitive to cultural and developmental issues; it will also address both skill and performance deficits.

Finally, as Hartup (1978) so aptly states, "Peer relations are not luxuries in human development; they are necessities" (p. 28). They are necessities not just for Caucasian children but for all children regardless of cultural background or developmental limitations. Regular and special education teachers have a responsibility to provide all children with the necessities to develop to their full, uncompromised potential.

RECOMMENDATIONS

The research described in this chapter addresses some significant questions about how to minimize the placement of multicultural/bilingual students with and without mild disabilities into special education; how to create effective learning and social environments; and how to use effective teaching principles and strategies for enhancing the academic and social skills for these children. Recent education research aimed at restructuring education for these children has generated a set of guidelines for administrators and policy makers at the local, state, and federal levels.

Local Policies

Several recommendations can be addressed at the local level so that multicultural/bilingual students can be provided an equitable and quality education (Federal Resource Center for Special Education, Human Development Institute, 1993). Some of these include, but are not limited to, the following:

1. Initiate school reform polices at the school level that create an inclusionary, positive, and culturally sensitive learning environment for multicultural/bilingual students with and without mild disabilities.
2. Develop and implement alternative assessment and evaluation procedures that consist of valid multilingual, multicultural techniques with the goals of (a) ensuring higher levels of achievement, (b) minimizing the placement of students into special education, (c) increasing opportunities to learn and to have success in integrated classroom settings, and (d) placing students into challenging instructional contexts.
3. Develop polices that require teachers to use instructional-relevant assessments that focus on process and outcome variables.
4. Initiate policies that foster educational experiences and school reform procedures of teaching and service delivery to meet the instructional needs of multicultural/bilingual students with and without mild disabilities.
5. The local education agency will work collaboratively with state agencies to develop in-service programs that require course work and professional training experiences in multicultural education and special education.

State Policies

The National Association of State Boards of Education (1991) has provided several recommendations for infusing multiculturalism in education to meet the needs of multicultural/bilingual students. These recommendations are presented in the document entitled *The American Tapestry: Educating a Nation,* discussing state board leadership, teacher training and staff development, and curriculum and school environment.

1. State boards of education should examine their policies, practices, and procedures to determine their cultural relevancy and appropriateness and develop a process to revise those that do not reflect a multicultural philosophy.
2. State policy makers should assure broad cultural, ethnic, and gender representation on the state board of education, the staffing of the state department of education, and committees and working groups.
3. States should develop more sophisticated systems for gathering and analyzing data showing differential effects on learning. State school data should be compiled according to race, ethnicity, socioeconomic status, and gender to provide continuous information on state diversity and to determine a state's success in educating students from diverse backgrounds.
4. Accreditation of teacher training institutions should be linked to comprehensive inclusion of multiculturalism in teacher education programs, including course work in linguistics, cross-cultural communication, and diverse learning styles. Programs should be evaluated through outcome-based measures to determine the degree to which they meet the board's goals on multicultural infusion.
5. State boards of education must develop and support policies to ensure multiculturalism in staff development and in-service training for teachers, administrators, and other school personnel. They should support ongoing staff development opportunities at the school site and the establishment of state resource centers to ensure continuous systematic exposure to diversity.
6. State boards of education should continue to explore and support opportunities to increase the number of people of color who enter the teaching profession.
7. State boards of education should develop and adopt polices of cultural inclusion that are cross-disciplinary and go beyond the social studies curriculum or any other segment of the curriculum. Multicultural approaches should be infused in reading, language arts, mathematics, science, health, music, and art.
8. State boards of education should develop and support policies that promote integrated multicultural perspectives in the development of textbooks and instructional materials. Adoption criteria should include an assessment of the publishers, the authors, and the editors to ensure accurate and inclusive cultural perspectives.
9. State boards of education should promote and adopt student assessments that are grounded in cultural diversity. Culturally biased assessment should be identified and eliminated. (pp. 10–26)

Federal Policies

Multicultural/bilingual students have been consistently neglected in our schools, and they are more likely to attend schools that are old, overcrowded, and poorly equipped. There is a critical need to have a national education strategy and funding to improve the educational achievements of multicultural/bilingual students with and without mild disabilities in urban and poor communities.

1. Communicate to policy makers at all levels the necessity of providing funds to strengthen the equitable distribution of resources in schools with high concentrations of multicultural/bilingual students with and without mild disabilities.
2. Identify, evaluate, and disseminate nationwide models of culturally competent and exemplary schools that address the needs of multicultural/bilingual students with and without mild disabilities.
3. Establish and support curriculum centers of research, literature, and state-of-the-art materials identifying effective instructional practices for multicultural/bilingual students with and without mild disabilities.
4. Require the inclusion of concepts of multiculturalism and linguistic diversity in projects funded by the U.S. Department of Education.
5. Require federal task forces and advisory panels providing assistance to the U.S. Department of Education to include members from multicultural/bilingual groups in society.

ACKNOWLEDGMENTS

This chapter was supported by grant H029K20029-93 from the Office of Special Education Programs, U.S. Department of Education. The ideas expressed in this chapter are exclusively those of the authors and not the agency.

Reprints of this chapter can be obtained from Dr. Cheryl A. Utley at the Juniper Gardens Children's Project, 1614 Washington Blvd., Kansas City, KS 66102.

REFERENCES

Anderson, P. P., & Fenichel, E. S. (1989). *Serving culturally diverse families of infants and toddlers with disabilities.* Washington, DC: National Center for Clinical Infant Programs.

Arreaga-Mayer, C., Carta, J., & Tapia, Y. (1994). Ecobehavioral assessment of bilingual special education settings: The opportunity to respond. In R. P. Gardner III, D. M. Sainato, J. D. Cooper, T. E. Heron, W. L. Heward, J. Eshleman, & T. A. Groffi (Eds.), *Behavior analysis in education: Focus on measurably superior instruction* (pp. 225–239). Belmont, CA: Brooks/Cole.

Artiles, A. J., & Trent, S. C. (1994). Overrepresentation of minority students in special education: A continuing debate. *Journal of Special Education, 27,* 410–437.

Artiles, A. J., & Zamora-Duran, G. (1997). *Reducing the disproportionate representation of culturally diverse students in special and gifted education.* Reston, VA: Council for Exceptional Children.

Asher, S. R., & Coie, J. D. (1990). *Peer rejection in childhood.* New York: Cambridge University Press.

Baca, L., & Almanza, E. (1991). *Language minority students with disabilities.* Reston, VA: Council for Exceptional Children.

Baca, L. M., & Cervantes, H. T. (1989). *The bilingual special education interface.* Upper Saddle River, NJ: Merrill/ Prentice Hall.

Baruth, L. G., & Manning, M. L. (1992). *Multicultural education of children and adolescents.* Needham Heights, MA: Allyn & Bacon.

Baumeister, A. A., Kupstas, F. D., Klindworth, L. M., & Zanthos, P. W. (1991). *Guide to state planning for the prevention of mental retardation and related disabilities associated with socioeconomic conditions.* Washington, DC: President's Committee on Mental Retardation.

Berliner, D. C. (1988). The half-full glass: A review of research on teaching. In E. L. Meyen, G. A. Vergason, & R. J. Whelan (Eds.), *Effective instructional strategies for exceptional children* (pp. 7–31). Denver: Love.

Boykin, A. (1994). Afrocultural expression and its implications for schooling. In E. R. Hollins, J. E. Kims, & W. C. Hayman (Eds.), *Teaching diverse populations: Formulating a knowledge base* (pp. 243–258). New York: State University of New York Press.

Brantlinger, E. A., & Guskin, S. L. (1986). Ethnocultural and social-psychological effects on learning characteristics of handicapped children. In M. C. Wang, M. C. Reynolds, & H. S. Walberg (Eds.), *Handbook of special education: Research and practice* (Vol. 1, pp. 7–33). New York: Pergamon.

Bryan, T. S. (1978). Social relationships and verbal interactions of learning disabled children. *Journal of Learning Disabilities, 11,* 107–115.

Carta, J. J. (1991). Education of young children in inner-city classrooms. *American Behavioral Scientist, 34,* 440–453.

Cartledge, G. (1996). *Cultural diversity and social skills instruction: Understanding ethnic and gender differences.* Champaign, IL: Research Press.

Chalfant, J. C., & Pysh, M. V. (1981, November). Teacher assistance teams—A model for within-building problem solving. *Counterpoint,* 16–21.

Chinn, P. C., & Hughes, S. (1987). Representation of minority students in special education classes. *Remedial and Special Education, 8*(4), 41–46.

Cloud, N. (1988, December). *ESL in special education.* ERIC Digest. ERIC Clearinghouse on Languages and Linguistics. Washington, DC: Center for Applied Linguistics.

Coleman, J. S., Campbell, E. Q., Hobson, C. J., McPortland, J., Mood, A. M., Weinfeld, F. D., & York, R. L. (1966). *Equality of educational opportunity* (Report of the Office of Education to the Congress and the President). Washington, DC: Government Printing Office.

Collier, C. (1988). *Assessing minority students with learning and behavior problems.* Lindale, TX: Hamilton.

Cowen, E., Pederson, A., Babigian, H., Izzo, L. D., & Trost, M. A. (1973). Long-term follow-up of early detected vulnerable children. *Journal of Consulting and Clinical Psychology, 41,* 438–446.

Cross, T., Bazron, B. J., Dennis, K. W., Issacs, M. R., & Benjamin, M. P. (1989). *Towards a culturally competent system of care: A monograph on effective service for minority children who are seriously emotionally disturbed. Vol. 1.* Washington, DC: Georgetown University Child Development Center.

Cummins, J. (1989). A theoretical framework for bilingual special education. *Exceptional Children, 56,* 111–119.

Delquadri, J. C., Greenwood, C. R., Whorton, D., Carta, J. J., & Hall, R. V. (1986). Classwide peer tutoring. *Exceptional Children, 52,* 535–542.

Diamond, K. E. (1993). Preschool children's concepts of disability in their peers. *Early Education and Development, 4,* 123–129.

Duran, E. (1985). Teaching functional reading in context to severely retarded and severely autistic adolescents of limited English proficiency. *Adolescence, 20,* 433–439.

Edmunds, P., Martinson, S. A., & Goldberg, P. F. (1990). *Demographics and cultural diversity in the 1990's: Implications for services to young children with special needs.* Minneapolis: Pacer Center.

Federal Resource Center for Special Education, Human Development Institute. (1993, May). *Task force report: Cultural and linguistic diversity in education.* Lexington: University of Kentucky Press.

Finn, J. D. (1982). Patterns in special education placement as revealed by OCR surveys. In K. A. Heller, W. H. Holtzman, & S. Messick (Eds.), *Placing children in special education: A strategy for equity* (pp. 322–381). Washington, DC: National Academy Press.

Franklin, M. E. (1993). Culturally sensitive instructional practices for African-American learners with disabilities. *Exceptional Children, 59,* 115–122.

Friend, M., & Cook, L. (1992). *Interactions: Collaboration skills for school professionals.* New York: Longman.

Fuchs, D., Fuchs, L. S., Benowitz, S., & Barringer, K. (1987). Norm-referenced tests: Are they valid for use with handicapped students? *Exceptional Children, 54,* 263–291.

Fuchs, D., Fuchs, L. S., Daily, A. M., & Power, M. H. (1986). The effects of examiners' personal familiarity and professional experience on handicapped children's test performance. *Journal of Educational Research, 78,* 141–146.

Garcia, E. E. (1988). Linguistically and culturally diverse children: Effective instructional practices and related policy issues. In H. C. Waxman, J. Walker de Felix, J. E. Anderson, & H. P. Baptiste (Eds.), *Students at risk in at-risk schools: Improving environments for learning* (pp. 65–86). Newbury Park, CA: Corwin.

Garcia, E. E. (1994). *Understanding and meeting the challenge of student cultural diversity.* Boston: Houghton Mifflin.

Garcia, S. B., & Ortiz, A. A. (1988, June). Preventing inappropriate referrals of language minority students to special education. *New Focus, 5,* 1–12. Washington, DC: National Clearinghouse for Bilingual Education.

Gay, G. (1993). Ethnic minorities and educational equality. In J. A. Banks & C. A. McGee Banks (Eds.), *Multicultural education: Issues and perspectives* (pp. 171–192). Boston: Allyn & Bacon.

Gersten, R., & Woodward, J. (1994). The language-minority student and special education: Issues, trends, and paradoxes. *Exceptional Children, 60,* 310–322.

Gollnick, D., & Chinn, P. (1990). *Multicultural education in a pluralistic society* (3rd ed.). Upper Saddle River, NJ: Merrill/Prentice Hall.

Gollnick, D. M., & Chinn, P. C. (1994). *Multicultural education in a pluralistic society* (4th ed.). New York: Macmillan.

Goodlad, J. I. (1984). *A place called school: Prospects for the future.* New York: McGraw-Hill.

Gottlieb, J., & Budoff, M. (1973). Social acceptability of retarded children in nongraded schools differing in architecture. *American Journal of Mental Deficiency, 78,* 15–19.

Gottlieb, J., Alter, M., & Gottlieb, B. W. (1991). Mainstreaming academically handicapped children in urban schools. In J. W. Lloyd, N. N. Singh, & A. C. Repp (Eds.), *The regular education initiative: Alternative perspectives on concepts, issues, and models* (pp. 95–112). Sycamore, IL: Sycamore.

Gottlieb, J., Alter, M., Gottlieb, B. W., & Wishner, J. (1991). Special education in urban America: It's not justifiable for many. *Journal of Special Education, 27,* 453–465.

Greenwood, C. R. (1996). The case for performance-based instructional models. *School Psychology Quarterly, 11*(4), 283–296.

Greenwood, C. R., Carta, J., & Kamps, D. (1990). Teacher-mediated versus peer-mediated instruction: A review of advantages and disadvantages. In H. C. Foot, M. J. Morgan, & R. H. Shute (Eds.), *Children helping children* (pp. 177–206). New York: Wiley.

Greenwood, C. R., Carta, J., Walker, D., Arreaga-Mayer, C., & Dinwiddie, G. (1988). Peer tutoring: Special education. In T. Husen & T. N. Postlethwaite (Eds.), *The international encyclopedia of education: Research and studies* (Vol. 1, pp. 574–577). Oxford: Pergamon.

Greenwood, C. R., Delquadri, J. C., & Carta, J. J. (1997). *Together we can: ClassWide Peer Tutoring to improve basic academic skills.* Longmont, CO: Sopres West.

Greenwood, C. R., Delquadri, J. C., & Hall, R. V. (1989). Longitudinal effects of classwide peer tutoring. *Journal of Educational Psychology, 81*(3), 371–383.

Greenwood, C. R., Delquadri, J. C., Stanley, S., Sasso, G., Whorton, D., & Schulte, D. (1981, Summer). Allocating opportunity to learn as a basis for academic remediation: A developing model for teaching. *Monograph in Behavioral Disorders,* 22–32.

Grossman, H. (1991). Special education in a diverse society: Improving services for minority and working-class students. *Preventing School Failure, 36*(1), 19–27.

Grossman, H. (1995). *Teaching in a diverse society.* Needham Heights, MA: Allyn & Bacon.

Harry, B. (1992). Restructuring the participation of African-American parents in special education. *Exceptional Children, 59,* 123–131.

Hartup, W. (1978). Peer interaction and the processes of socialization. In M. Guralnick (Eds.), *Early intervention and the integration of handicapped and nonhandicapped children* (pp. 27–51). Baltimore: University Park Press.

Haywood, H. C. (1977). Alternatives to normative assessment. In P. Mittler (Ed.), *Research to practice in mental retardation: Education and training* (Vol. 2, pp. 11–18). Ryde, Australia: International Association for the Scientific Study of Intellectual Disabilities..

Heath, S. B. (1986). Sociocultural contexts of language development. In Bilingual Education Office, California State Department of Education (Ed.), *Beyond language: Social and cultural factors in schooling language minority students* (pp. 143–186). Los Angeles: California State University Evaluation, Dissemination and Assessment Center.

Heller, K. A., Holtzman, W. H., & Messick, S. (1982). *Placing children in special education: A strategy for equity.* Washington, DC: National Academy Press.

Hoover, J. J., & Collier, C. (1989). Methods and materials for bilingual special education. In L. M. Baca & H. T. Cervantes (Eds.), *The bilingual special education interface* (pp. 231–251). Upper Saddle River, NJ: Merrill/Prentice Hall.

Huang, L. N. (1989). Southeast Asian refugee children and adolescents. In J. T. Gibbs & L. N. Huang (Eds.), *Children of color* (pp. 278–321). San Francisco: Jossey-Bass.

Hudson, P. J. (1989). Instructional collaboration: Creating the learning environment. In S. H. Fradd & M. J. Weismantel (Eds.), Meeting the needs of culturally and linguistically different students: A handbook for educators (pp. 106–129). Boston: College-Hill.

Johnson, D. W., & Johnson, R. (1986). Mainstreaming and cooperative learning strategies. *Exceptional Children, 52,* 553–561.

Johnson, D. W., Johnson, R., & Maruyama, G. (1983). Interdependence and interpersonal attraction among heterogeneous and homogeneous individuals: A theoretical formulation and a meta-analysis of the research. *Review of Educational Research, 53,* 5–54.

Jones, R. (1988). *Psychoeducational assessment of minority group children: A casebook.* Berkeley, CA: Cobb & Henry.

Kagan, S. (1992). *Cooperative learning.* San Juan Capistrano, CA: Kagan Cooperative Learning.

Kozol, J. (1991). *Savage inequalities: Children in American schools.* New York: Crown.

Li, A. K. (1992). Peer relations and social skills training: Implications for the multicultural classroom. *Journal of Educational Issues of Language Minority Students, 10,* 67–78.

MacMillan, D. L. (1988). New EMR's. In G. A. Polloway & L. R. Sargeant (Eds.), *Best practices in mental disabilities* (pp. 3–24). Des Moines: Iowa Department of Education.

Maheady, L., Saca, M. K., & Harper, G. F. (1988). The effects of a classwide peer tutoring program on the academic performance of students enrolled in 10th grade social studies. *Exceptional Children, 53,* 52–59.

Maheady, L., Towne, R., Algozzine, B., Mercer, J., & Ysseldyke, J. (1983). Minority over-representation: A case for alternative practices prior to referral. *Learning Disability Quarterly, 6,* 448–457.

McCormick, L. (1990). Cultural diversity and exceptionality. In N. G. Haring & L. McCormick (Eds.), *Exceptional children and youth* (pp. 327–363). Upper Saddle River, NJ: Merrill/Prentice Hall.

McLaren, J., & Bryson, S. E. (1987). Review of recent epidemiological studies of mental retardation: Prevalence, associated disorders, and etiology. *American Journal of Mental Retardation, 92,* 243–254.

Miller, A. D., Barbetta, P. M., & Herron, T. E. (1994). START tutoring: Designing, training, implementing, adapting, and evaluating tutoring programs for school and home settings. In R. P. Gardner III, D. M. Sainato, J. D. Cooper, T. E. Heron, W. L. Heward, J. Eshleman, & T. A. Groffi (Eds.), *Behavior analysis in education: Focus on measurably superior instruction* (pp. 265–282). Belmont, CA: Brooks/Cole.

Moll, L. (1988). Educating Latino students. *Language Arts, 64,* 315–324.

National Association of State Boards of Education. (1991). *The American tapestry: Educating a nation.* Alexandria, VA: Author.

Nazarro, J. N. (1981). Special problems of exceptional minority children. In J. N. Nazzarro (Ed.), *Culturally diverse exceptional children in school.* Washington, DC: National Institute of Education. (ERIC Document Reproduction Services No. 199 993)

Oakes, J. (1985). *Keeping track: How schools structure inequality.* New Haven, CT: Yale University Press.

Osguthorpe, R. T., & Scruggs, T. E. (1986). Special education students as tutors: A review and analysis. *Remedial and Special Education,* 7(4), 15–26.

O'Sullivan, P. J., Ysseldyke, J. E., Christensen, S. L., & Thurlow, M. L. (1990). Mildly handicapped elementary students' opportunity to learn during reading instruction in mainstream and special education settings. *Research Reading Quarterly, 25*(2), 131–146.

Ovando, C. J., & Collier, V. P. (1985). *Bilingual and ESL classrooms: Teaching in multicultural contexts.* New York: McGraw-Hill.

Pallas, A. A., Natriello, G., & McDill, E. L. (1989). The changing nature of the disadvantaged population: Current dimensions and future trends. *Educational Researcher, 18*(5), 16–22.

Park, E. K., Pullis, N., Reilly, T., & Townsend, B. (1994). Cultural biases in the identification of students with behavioral disorders. In R. L. Petersen & S. I. Jordan (Eds.), *Multicultural issues in the education of students with behavioral disorders* (pp. 14–26). Cambridge, MA: Brookline.

Parker, S., Greer, S., & Zuckerman, B. (1988). Double jeopardy: The impact of poverty of early child development. *Pediatric Clinics of North America, 35,* 1–14.

Reid, E. R. (1986). Practicing effective instruction: The Exemplary Center for Reading Instructional Approach [Special Issue]. *Exceptional Children, 52,* 510–519.

Reschly, D. (1982). Assessing mild mental retardation. The influence of adaptive behavior, sociocultural status, and prospects for non-biased assessment. In C. R. Reynolds & T. B. Gutkin (Eds.), *The handbook of school psychology* (pp. 209–242). New York: Wiley.

Reynolds, C. R. (1987). Race bias in testing. In R. J. Corsini (Ed.), *Concise encyclopedia of psychology* (pp. 953–954). New York: Wiley.

Reynolds, M. C. (1980). *A common body of practices for teachers: The challenge of Public Law 94-142 to teacher education.* Minneapolis: University of Minnesota Press.

Rodriguez, F. (1990). Equity in education: Issues and strategies. Dubuque, IA: Kendall/Hunt.

Roff, M., Sells, S. B., & Golden, M. M. (1972). Social adjustment and personality development in children. Minneapolis: University of Minnesota Press.

Rotheram-Borus, M. J., & Tsemberis, S. J. (1989). Social competency training programs in ethnically diverse communities. In L. A. Bond & B. E. Compas (Eds.), *Primary prevention and promotion in the schools* (pp. 297–318). Newbury Park, CA: Sage.

Rueda, R. S., & Forness, S. R. (1994). Childhood depression: Ethnic and cultural issues in special education. In R. L. Peterson & S. I. Jordan (Eds.), *Multicultural issues in the education of students with behavioral disorders* (pp. 40–62). Cambridge, MA: Brookline.

Ruiz, N. N. (1989). An optimal learning environment for Rosemary. *Exceptional Children, 56,* 130–144.

Sasso, G. M., Garrison-Harrell, L., & Rogers, L. M. (1994). Autism and socialization: Conceptual models and procedural variations. *Advances in Learning and Behavioral Disabilities, 8,* 161–175.

Scribner, S., & Cole, M. (1981). Unpackaging literacy. In M. Fart-Whiteman (Ed.), *Variation in writing: Functional and linguistic-cultural differences. Vol. 1: Writing: The nature, development, and teaching of written communications* (pp. 71–88). Hillsdale, NJ: Erlbaum.

Shade, B., & New, C. A. (1991). Cultural influence on learning: Teaching implications. In J. A. Banks & C. McGee Banks (Eds.), *Multicultural education: Issues and perspectives* (pp. 317–329). Boston: Allyn & Bacon.

Sigelman, C. K., Miller, T. E., & Whitworth, L. A. (1986). The early development of stigmatizing reactions to physical differences. *Journal of Applied Developmental Psychology, 7,* 17–32.

Slavin, R. E. (1988). Cooperative learning and student achievement. *Educational Leadership, 46,* 31–33.

Sleeter, C., & Grant, C. A. (1988). *Making choices for multicultural education: Five approaches to race, class, and gender.* Upper Saddle River, NJ: Merrill/Prentice Hall.

Steele, C. M. (1992, April). Race and schooling of black Americans. *Atlantic Monthly,* 68–78.

Stenho, S. M. (1982). Differential treatment of minority children in service systems. *Social Work, 27,* 39–46.

Stoneman, Z. (1990). Conceptual relationships between family research and mental retardation. In N. W. Bray (Ed.), *International review of research in mental retardation* (Vol. 15, pp. 161–202). Orlando, FL: Academic Press.

Stoneman, Z. (1993). Attitudes toward young children with disabilities: Cognition, affect, an behavioral intent. In C. Peck, S. Odom, & D. Bricker (Eds.), *Integrating young children with disabilities in community programs: From research to implementation* (pp. 223–248). Baltimore: Brookes.

Strain, P., & Odom, S. (1986). Peer social imitations: Effective interventions for social skills development of exceptional children [Special Issue]. *Exceptional Children, 52,* 543–552.

Suarez-Orosco, M. M. (1989). *Central American refugees and U.S. high schools.* Stanford, CA: Stanford University Press.

Tharp, R. G. (1989). Psychocultural variables and constants: Effects on teaching and learning in schools. *American Psychologist, 44,* 349–359.

Topping, K. (1988). *The peer tutoring handbook: Promoting cooperative learning.* Cambridge, MA: Brookline.

Trueba, H. T. (1987). *Raising silent voices: Educating the linguistic minorities for the twenty-first century.* New York: Newbury House.

Tuma, J. M. (1988). Mental health services for children: The state of the art. *American Psychologist, 44,* 188–199.

U.S. Department of Education. (1992). *Fourteenth annual report to Congress on the implementation of the Education of the Handicapped Act.* Washington, DC: Government Printing Office.

U.S. Department of Education, Office for Civil Rights. (1987). *1986 elementary and secondary school civil rights survey: National summaries.* Washington, DC: DBS Corporation.

Utley, C. A., Delquadri, J.C., Mortweet, S., Davis, C., Guess, L., & Greenwood, C. R. (1993, June). *Ecobehavorial assessment of minority students with EMR: Validation of academic engaged time.* Poster presented at the annual meeting of the American Association on Mental Retardation, Washington, DC.

Utley, C. A., Delquadri, J. C., Mortweet, S., Thorisdottir, S. A., Greenwood, C. R., & Dawson, H. (1993, May). *The differential effects of socioeconomic status of children with educable mental retardation (EMR) on teacher and student behaviors.* Poster presented at the annual meeting of the Association for Behavior Analysis, Chicago.

Vogt, L. A., Jordan, C., & Tharp, R. G. (1987). Explaining school failure: Producing school success: Two cases. *Anthropology and Education Quarterly, 18,* 276–286.

Weisner, T. S., Gallimore, R., & Jordan, C. (1988). Unpackaging cultural effects on classroom learning: Native Hawaiian peer assistance and child-generated activity. *Anthropology and Education Quarterly, 19,* 327–353.

White, O. R. (1986). Precision teaching—precision learning [Special Issue]. *Exceptional Children, 52,* 522–534.

4

General Education Placement for Special Education Students in Urban Schools

JAY GOTTLIEB
MARK ALTER
BARBARA W. GOTTLIEB

In this chapter we are concerned with the education of academically low-functioning students who are most often classified as learning disabled or emotionally disturbed, and occasionally as language impaired. More specifically, we are concerned with the education these students receive in urban school systems that are plagued by a host of problems, not the least of which is the need to educate a large number of students who are very poor and whose family and community circumstances are often very much disrupted. We address how and where to best educate academically low-functioning students under circumstances that are less than ideal. Our frame of reference focuses on the extent to which such students are likely to receive a better education in general education settings than in special classes. The theme we will develop is that with the current structure of urban education, neither special classes nor general education offers an appropriate instructional environment for substantial numbers of academically low-functioning students. From our perspective, discussions regarding the appropriateness of special classes or general education classes for these students are only meaningful in relation to the quality of instruction that occurs in either setting.

We are taking an unconventional approach to the topic of mainstreaming. It is customary for invited chapters on mainstreaming to focus primarily, if not exclusively, on students labeled as educationally disabled and placed primarily in special classes. In this chapter, however, we are discussing two general issues related to mainstreaming within the larger context of urban education: (a) whether mainstreaming as a placement provides the student with an appropriate education and (b) who is referred to and found eligible for special education.

From the overall perspective of urban education, mainstreaming represents a relatively insignificant consideration. Many more pressing problems confront urban school administrators than whether sufficient numbers of students in special education are mainstreamed. Moreover, when political or court-imposed factors compel urban school administrators to propel mainstreaming to the forefront of the school's agenda, decisions regarding mainstreaming are influenced by a host of factors that often have little to do with students. Among these factors are the general public perception of the quality of the schools; the performance of the general education population; the average class size in the school; the willingness of the classroom teacher to accept a student with disabilities, which is heavily influenced by friendships that exist between general and special education teachers; the willingness of the special education teacher to relinquish a student for part of the school day; and the level of support (or opposition) for mainstreaming offered by the parents of general education classmates. In short, notwithstanding the stridency of the special education debate regarding the need to mainstream or the appropriateness and/or the necessity of placing children with disabilities in inclusive classes, the fact is that in large, urban school districts mainstreaming is of limited political urgency unless the court or the state education department threatens to intervene. In this chapter we treat the topic of mainstreaming as a part of the overall special education system in general, which, in turn, is heavily influenced by the "health" of the general education system.

We begin our discussion by defining some terms employed throughout the chapter. They are common, but at times our usage of them is not. We use the terms *special education* and *special classes* (self-contained) in traditional ways. *Special education* refers to programs and/or services that are available by regulation to students who have been found to be eligible to receive them. *Special classes,* which are part of the continuum of special education, are full-time placement for students who have been classified as having educational disabilities. We use the term *special education services* to refer to education and related services that students can receive without being enrolled in special classes. Resource rooms, consultant teacher services, and related services (for example, speech and counseling) are the special education services to which we most often allude.

We use the term *academically low-functioning students* to denote the population of students who could benefit from special education services and/or from special classes, when these services and classes function effectively with regard to instruction. These students may or may not be disabled according to federal and/or state definitions, but they are not benefiting from the instructional program in the general education class.

The overwhelming majority of students who are found eligible and receive special education in urban settings are not disabled in the sense demanded by federal and state regulation (Gottlieb, Alter, Gottlieb, & Wischner, 1994). They are academically low-functioning students, many of whom also display inappropriate behavior in class, whose educational need has resulted from economic, social and/or cultural disadvantage, and who may experience unstable families, disenfranchised communities, and inadequate schools—a lethal combination of circumstances that renders it difficult for these youngsters to learn and for teachers to teach.

Ironically, the vagaries of urban school systems are such that some general education students who are reared in the same communities and attend the same schools perform as poorly as other students who are identified and placed in special education. For reasons that have as much to do with their teachers as with themselves, these general education students are not referred by their classroom teachers and consequently are never involved in the multidisciplinary assessment process that determines whether they are educationally disabled. The unidentified students remain in general educational classes, usually receive remedial services and/or mental health services from community-based organizations, and remain near the bottom layers of their classes in academic performance.

Finally, we are using the term *mainstreaming* to denote part-time placement in general education classes and *inclusion* to denote full-time placement of identified academically low-functioning special education students in general education classes.

MAINSTREAMING IN THE CONTEXT OF URBAN SCHOOL SYSTEMS

Policies regarding mainstreaming or inclusion are not formulated in a vacuum. They exist and are modified to meet the existing needs of a school system. Sometimes these needs are fiscal and at other times they are forced upon the schools by various political and social forces. Decisions to mainstream or not to mainstream operate in the larger context of the special education and general education structures of the school district. When the special education and general education systems are viewed as separate, yet efficient and effective, pressures are exerted to maintain the status quo. When one or both education systems are viewed as inefficient or ineffective, pressures for change are everywhere: from the state education department, from parents, and from elected officials who fear political retribution from an unhappy constituency.

Whether mainstreaming occurs and how much it occurs are relatively minor considerations in the larger social and political contexts that affect the school system as a whole. The need to maintain control in general education classrooms and the accompanying need to ensure that as many students as possible read at grade level are far more important considerations to urban school administrators than whether an individual student or a small group of students should be mainstreamed. If mainstreaming is seen as interfering with the fulfillment of the larger political goals of the school system, few students will be mainstreamed. Indeed, mainstreaming as a valued goal can only be understood as it relates to and benefits the larger educational missions of the school system, missions that are heavily influenced by a plethora of social and political factors. This state of affairs is just as important today as it was one hundred years ago when difficult social circumstances in the cities were responsible for the establishment of special education in this country. We take a brief digression to illustrate this history and to indicate how decisions that were made one hundred years ago, as well as decisions that were not made, continue to affect the way that we deliver service at the present time.

Special Education in Historical Perspective: The View from the Cities

Although the exact date of the creation of special classes in public schools may be debatable, with a class in Cleveland established in 1893 being the prime candidate for being first (Goodenough, 1949), they were indeed introduced, and prospered, in urban school systems. Their purpose for existing was always subject to a degree of ambiguity. Without doubt, they were introduced, at least in part, for altruistic reasons: to shield academically "backward" students from the unfair competition of more capable classmates. Rhoda Esten (1900), the first director of special classes in Providence, Rhode Island, stated:

> It would be impracticable and unwise to retain the pupils longer in the regular schools, for association with children with whom they are not able to compete will discourage them, and, being unable to comprehend the subjects taught, their already feeble power of attention will be lost, their in-terest destroyed, and the result will be, that they will soon become apathetic, rendering it almost impossible for the special teacher to rouse them to activity. (p. 12)

How best to help the backward students in special classes was never clearly resolved. One approach was that special classes could best serve students by providing special tutoring so that they could eventually return to regular classes. Another view was that the students could be best served by teaching them industrial and vocational training so that they would be able to secure employment when they left school (Goodenough, 1949).

The desire to provide an appropriate education for "backward" students was further complicated by another consideration: relief for classroom teachers from the difficulties of serving backward or disorderly pupils who were sent to special classes. To illustrate, Esten (1900) stated that the development of three auxiliary schools (for backward children) in Providence, Rhode Island, was

> an outgrowth of our schools for special discipline and instruction. Teachers in the regular schools found so much relief when disorderly pupils were transferred to the disciplinary schools, they were not slow to request the removal of backward or mentally deficient children, who were receiving comparatively little benefit in their schools. (pp. 11–12)

The creation and rapid expansion of special classes is further illustrated by Farrell (1908), the inspector of ungraded classes in New York City, the location of the majority of current data we report in this chapter. Referring to conditions that fueled the origins of special classes that are remarkably similar to conditions that currently sustain them, Farrell stated:

> [T]his (special) class . . . was not the result of any theory. It grew out of conditions in a neighborhood which furnished many and serious problems in truancy and discipline. The first class was made up of the odds and ends of a large school. There were over-age children, so-called naughty children and the dull and stupid children. . . . They were the children who could not get along in school. (p. 91)

Between 1899, the beginning of special classes in New York City, and 1903, sixty special classes were opened, educating over a thousand students (Farrell, 1908). The classes were invariably formed in regular school buildings and not in isolated settings to avoid stigmatizing the students.

To the credit of the founders of special classes in urban school districts, they were immediately aware of the need for an accurate assessment system to serve as a basis for assigning students to ungraded classes. They put into place a four-step diagnostic process to determine eligibility for placement in special, ungraded, classes. First, the child suspected of being eligible for ungraded classes was known to the school principal. The principal knew students who needed disciplining, the children who were not promoted with their class, and the children who were truant. Second, students as identified by the principal were required to be examined by a board of health physician to determine whether a physical reason accounted for the academic and behavioral difficulty the child exhibited. Third, during the interval between the identification of the target students and the time that the physicians actually conducted their examinations, the principal required the child's classroom teacher to make detailed observations of the child. The forms used for the observations required teachers to know about the child's economic circumstances, his home, the work he is required to do, his school history, attendance at kindergarten, how many years he has spent in each grade, the regularity of his school attendance, the cause of any irregularity, the quality and character of his mental power, and his nationality and that of the father and mother.

The data collected by the classroom teacher were reviewed by the principal. If the principal decided that the data did not warrant placement in ungraded classes, the child was transferred to another teacher. If the principal believed ungraded class placement was required, the child was referred to the inspector of ungraded classes, who with a medical doctor conducted the diagnostic examination to determine eligibility for placement, which was the fourth and final step in the placement process. The physician looked for anatomical and/or physiological causes of the child's behavior, and the inspector of ungraded classes functioned the way psychologists currently do. That person looked for facts about the child's mental capacity, such as performance under different testing conditions, reactions to new stimuli, as well as his powers of memory, imagination, and attention. Eligible students were sent to ungraded classes, and some who were more severely impaired were rejected from these classes because they were thought to belong in institutions. The elaborate diagnostic process was designed to ensure that ungraded classes accepted only those students who belonged there.

The introduction of intelligence testing in the United States during the first decade of the twentieth century and its application to schools changed the way that schools identified students for special classes. The subjectivity of teachers' estimates of students' performance was replaced by the objectivity that could be obtained from testing students on a uniform set of questions. The new scientific basis for placement of students in special classes did not address the purposes of special classes, however; they were confined mainly to issues related to assessment. The result of the shift of emphasis from pedagogy to assessment had ideological and practical effects. The ideology of placement in ungraded classes was to serve the best interests of the backward child. The practicality of placement was that the classes proliferated to serve the interests of teachers and other, normal, students in class who were being hampered by the presence of slow and disruptive classmates (Fernald, 1903–1904; Goodenough, 1949). It was for an unknown weighting of both reasons, altruism and relief, that special classes in regular school buildings grew exponentially between 1900 and the 1950s.

THE PUSH FOR CHANGE

If *status quo* was the operative descriptor of the educational period until the early 1960s, *change* is the term that best describes the period between the early 1960s and the mid-1970s. The reasons that profound changes were forced on special education are well known and need not be elaborated here. Suffice it to mention that special classes were shown not to be more effective than regular classes in improving the academic achievement of mildly mentally retarded students. This disappointing finding coexisted with the indisputable fact that special classes were overrepresented with minority students at a time when the courts were clamping down on all forms of segregation in the schools. Disenchantment with special classes and the overrepresentation of minority students in those classes were not the sole reasons for the eventual passage of federal legislation (Gottlieb, 1981), but they clearly were important ones.

The enactment of the federal Education of the Handicapped Act in 1975 over the veto of President Gerald Ford, who feared that the necessary funding to support its mandates would not be forthcoming, resulted in several changes at the school level in the decade immediately following. First, special education was transformed from an educational discipline in which the primary concern was for impacting students' academic, social, and vocational performance into one in which the schools' primary concern became focused on complying with federal and state mandates. As examples, far more emphasis was placed on finding students who might be disabled than on ensuring that those who were identified were truly disabled. Also, state auditors and regulators who monitored schools typically investigated whether the teacher had an Individual Education Plan (IEP) in her classroom, not whether the contents of the IEP were appropriate.

The not-so-subtle shift by school districts in emphasizing compliance over educational outcomes was accompanied by a similar shift in the academic community. Research on student outcomes became deemphasized, and literature on philosophical and ideological opinions regarding program effectiveness became ascendant. The push for change was so strong that the academic community was unwilling to seriously entertain the possibility that special classes might benefit from reconceptualization or improvements in pedagogy or in curriculum. Mainstreaming was suddenly the preferred alternative despite an absence of clear empirical support for this belief.

Yet, despite the zeitgeist for mainstreaming, school administrators maintain special classes because they, and classroom teachers, believe that they represent a needed, and an appropriate, placement for substantial numbers of students. This is especially true in urban school districts where, as we indicate later, the quality of general education is often weak and unable to meet the needs of a substantial percentage of the general education population, not to mention the lower end of the general education distribution that is often referred to special education.

The forces that currently sustain special classes in the cities are the same forces that propelled their growth in the first place almost one hundred years ago: poor academic achievement and inappropriate behavior. Chronically poor achievement and inappropriate behavior often coexist with several factors that are prevalent in urban school districts: poverty, crime and unstable families, large numbers of immigrant students who are not fully acculturated into American society, and ethnic (and racial) divisions within the general population. Poor achievement and inappropriate behavior among students are the proximate causes for the creation and maintenance of the vast special education subsystem in urban schools. The host of debilitating societal forces that impact achievement and behavior are the distal causes.

THE STATUS OF GENERAL EDUCATION IN URBAN AREAS

Urban schools differ from their suburban neighbors in many respects, but perhaps none is greater than the general level of poverty that exists and the concentration with which it exists. Poverty contributes to a host of social ills that combine to render many communities and families dysfunctional and not supportive of the school's mission. As a result, there is a pressing need in urban schools for a vast network of social props to provide the support that the family and community would otherwise be expected to offer. Included in this network of social supports are free lunch programs, medical and dental care, social services, big brothers and big sisters, and community volunteers, to name a few.

In recent years, the social structure in the cities has become even more fractured than in prior years, causing additional difficulties for the schools. As one example, the number of immigrant students who are attending school has undergone explosive growth. Between 1990 and 1993 in the New York City public schools, the percentage of elementary school students who are immigrant rose from 8.2 percent to 11.6 percent. The corresponding increase for middle school students was from 11.8 percent to 17.2 percent. An average of 15.2 percent of all students in the urban school system are now classified as limited English proficient, more than double the average of its suburban neighbors. Differences in students' language and culture make it more difficult, and costly, to educate them in ways that will produce grade-level performance, at least in the short run.

Yet, despite the greater need, the available resources to meet the magnitude of need have not been forthcoming. As a bare-bones example, in the 1992–1993 school year, New York City spent $7,495 to educate a child, less than two-thirds of what its suburban neighbors spent (New York State Department of Education, 1994). Educating 36 percent of all students in New York State, the New York City public schools receive only 34 percent of the pool of state aid earmarked for education, despite the substantially higher per capita need (McGivern, 1995).

The lack of support to the entire school system has a very direct bearing on the quality of the classes and their ability to provide an appropriate education for students who are often in dire academic need. Class registers are large. Violence in the schools has increased, and teachers report greater difficulty in controlling their classes. There are too few guidance counselors, and staff development for teachers is severely limited. As the difficulties increase, especially in the poorest sections of the city, teachers leave and are replaced by other teachers who are inexperienced and possess temporary, not permanent, certification. According to the most recent data published by the New York State Department of Education (1994), an average of 67 percent of New York City public school teachers possess permanent certification. By way of comparison, in a contiguous suburban county, the lowest percentage of permanent certification for any of the fifty-six school districts situated in that county is 73 percent. In 70 percent of the school districts in that neighboring county, a minimum of 85 percent of the teachers are permanently certified.

Lack of financial resources to the schools might not be so debilitating if the parents were able to substitute their own resources for those not provided by the schools. This is not possible, however. Residents of the inner-city whose children attend public schools tend to be poor. The relative wealth of citizens in the inner city and those in neighboring suburban communities may be highlighted with the following data produced by the New York State Education Department. Each year, the department calculates a wealth ratio for every school district in the state. The wealth ratio is developed from a weighted combination of property wealth and income. The average for the state as a whole is indexed at 1.0. As of June 1993, the wealth ratio for thirty-two school districts comprising the New York City public school system is 0.98. Nassau County, which borders New York City to the east, contains fifty-six public school districts, only four of which have wealth ratios less than 1.00. Westchester County, which borders New York City to the north, contains fifty school districts, only two of which have wealth ratios less than 1.0.

In the New York City schools, 79 percent of all children in grades K–6 participate in the free or reduced-price lunch program. Thirty percent of five- to seventeen-year-old children are below the poverty level as determined by the 1990 federal census. By contrast, the highest percentage of children in poverty for any of the 106 neighboring school districts in the two contiguous counties is 20, and that percentage exists in only three of the 106 districts.

Poverty is associated with poor academic achievement. In the New York City school system, there is a 0.90 correlation between the percentage of students in 635 elementary schools who participate in the free or reduced-price lunch program and the percentage of children in those schools whose standardized reading test scores fall into the lowest quartile. A -0.94 correlation exists between the percentage of children in the lunch program and the percentage of children whose standardized reading score falls into the fourth quartile.

Direct comparisons on measures of achievement between New York City and its more affluent neighbors can be made from an analysis of reading scores on a third-grade reading test administered annually by the New York State Education Department to students in every school district in the state. In twenty-eight of fifty-six school districts (50 percent) located in Nassau county, 95 percent or more students attained a minimum state reference point score (corresponding to approximately the 25th to 30th percentile); in only eight of the fifty-six school districts (14 percent) did fewer than 90 percent of the students attain this passing score. Only one school district in that suburban county had fewer than 83 percent of its students pass. For the thirty-two school districts comprising the New York City school system, on the other hand, an average of 65 percent attained a passing score. In the highest-scoring community school district in the urban school system, 94 percent of its students passed this state test, the only one of the thirty-two districts that had a 90 percent or higher rate of passing. Half the suburban districts, therefore, performed better than the highest-rated urban school district. The results are similar in Westchester, where in only eight of fifty school districts did fewer than 90 percent pass the state reference point.

The combination of large classes, immigrant students, inexperienced teachers, poverty, and lack of family and community support result in an urban school system where, on average, one-third read at grade level. School policy dictates that students may be referred to special education when they are at least two years below grade level. There is no shortage of qualified candidates.

REFERRALS TO SPECIAL EDUCATION

Teachers are aware which students do not make adequate progress in their classes and require additional supports beyond what is ordinarily available in general education. A lack of resources in general education makes special education the only viable option to provide teachers and students with needed resources: smaller classes, which would allow for more individual attention, and access to guidance counselors and other related service providers. Teachers refer students most often in a sincere attempt to provide those students with much needed services. And many students are referred, indeed.

In 635 elementary schools, educating almost 496,000 students, 4.7 percent of the students are referred for initial evaluations. In 180 middle schools enrolling 184,500 students, 2.1 percent are referred. In 108 high schools enrolling 252,000 students, 0.5 percent are referred. These percentages tally to almost 27,000 referrals annually. Of these, about 90 percent will eventually be found eligible to receive some form of special education service, and about 85 percent will actually receive special education service of some kind. The 5 percent difference between those found eligible and those actually served is the result of parents' unwillingness to allow their children to participate in special education. About one-third of these students will be rereferred and will enter the special education system within two years following the parents' initial refusal.

Resource room placement or self-contained placement are the most common services offered to students who are found eligible for special education. The data we present are confined to students recommended for in-district placement in either resource room or special classes. New York City also educates approximately twenty thousand students in out-of-district public school special classes, referred to as District 75. We have not collected data on students in District 75 or on other, in-district, special education students, although we do know that about 7 percent of all in-district special education recommendations are not for resource room or special class placement but for related services only or other special education programs.

When teachers refer students to special education, they are signaling clearly that they cannot provide them with an appropriate education given the prevailing conditions of their schools and classrooms. They are saying that general education as it currently exists in their schools is not an appropriate placement for the student. Is it reasonable to assume that general education classes in which the teachers do not believe they can provide an appropriate education for low-functioning students are an appropriate placement? We do not think so.

Our doubts regarding the appropriateness of the general education program to educate substantial numbers of children with disabilities are reinforced by other data we have collected from classroom teachers. When we asked 257 classroom teachers who had referred a youngster to special education within the past two months to indicate what resources they would need to retain the youngster in their class, the dominant response was for an additional person, either a related service provider or an aide to assist the student. When we further asked them to indicate what training they themselves would require to be better able to retain the referred youngster, only eighteen provided a specific answer, with the majority of these responses indicating that the teachers felt they needed to be trained in behavior modification. Most teachers had only vague notions of the training they would need to enable them to acquire the skills to provide an effective education for the referred students.

THE MAGNITUDE OF THE SPECIAL EDUCATION SYSTEM IN URBAN SCHOOLS

The combination of academic and behavioral difficulties that are responsible for students entering the special education system also contributes to their remaining in special education. Of the approximately 91,000 elementary, middle, and high school students currently enrolled in special classes in the thirty-two school districts comprising the larger urban school system where we have conducted our research program, 351 were decertified from elementary schools, 432 from middle schools, and 377 from high schools during the 1992–1993 school year. Thus, about 1 percent of students who attended resource rooms or special classes were decertified from the special education registers. There are obviously far fewer decertifications than referrals.

With many new students entering the system and few students leaving, the percentage of students in special education increases as they progress through the grades, until they reach high school. A total of 5 percent of the elementary school population, 8.3 percent of the middle school population, and 6.6 percent of the high school population are enrolled in special classes. When we combine students in special class and students in resource room placements, ignoring students who receive consultant teacher services, related services only, and out-of-district placements, 8.5 percent of all elementary students, 13.7 percent of all middle school students, and 10.5 percent of all high school students receive special education in either resource rooms or special classes. In some districts, about 20 percent of all students in middle school receive resource room or self-contained special education. The drop in the number of high school students who receive special education in either resource rooms or special classes is probably attributable to dropouts, although statistics on dropout rates are hard to document. We do know, however, from a comparison of school registers at the beginning and end of a school year that across all four years of high school, the number of general education students decreases by 11.7 percent between October 31 and June 30. The corresponding decrease for special education students with academic disabilities is 17 percent; for students with behavioral disabilities, the decline is 28.6 percent.

With so many students receiving special education, especially in separate special classes, we may legitimately ask how they fare. This seemingly innocuous question is difficult to answer, however, because no clear-cut criteria are available for what special classes, or mainstreaming options, are expected to accomplish. In the following subsections we elaborate three criteria that we are using to gauge the success of special classes, although we are not certain that the school administration would make similar choices.

The Success of Special Classes

Published studies regarding the ongoing progress of students who are enrolled in special classes has been sparse since the passage of PL 94-142 twenty years ago. Because one purpose of special class education is to improve the academic performance levels of students so that they could return to their general education classes, we may ask how successful we have been in accomplishing this task.

We are employing three criteria to define success. Two of these criteria, number (or percentage) of students decertified and/or mainstreamed, are important because urban school districts are more likely than suburban or rural ones to be under the scrutiny of the courts. The courts and various advocacy groups, most often staffed by attorneys whom the court has empowered to monitor progress, tend to focus on decertifications and mainstreaming as key remedies, with more being better. The third criterion of success, academic progress, is one for which statutes and regulations typically have not held school administrators accountable. We are including it and beginning with it because historically it has played an important role in the debate on special classes and mainstreaming.

Academic Progress The mandates of federal legislation have precluded experimental studies of the effectiveness of different placements; that is, we can no longer randomly assign students to special classes and general education (mainstream) classes. Other methods of data collection are required. Recent data we obtained as part of our research program indicate that as of June 1992, only 52 of 2,234 self-contained students in urban school districts (2.5 percent) improved their standardized reading test scores from below grade level to grade level or above during their final two years in elementary schools. The corresponding figure for middle school students in self-contained classes was 46 of 1,677 (2.7 percent). Other analyses of the same data set indicate that of 4,123 self-contained students whose scores at an initial testing were in the bottom quartile, fewer than 9 percent scored in the second quartile or higher two years later. This figure is aggregated across elementary and middle schools. The data imply, quite convincingly to us, that continued placement of these students in existing special education classes, without introducing major changes in the curriculum and instructional methods, is not likely to provide them with the academic competencies they need to be able to return *successfully* to the mainstream. As special class students progress through the grades without improving their academic competence, the gap between them and their general education age-mates widens, making it increasingly difficult for the special education students to adhere to the academic requirements of the general education class.

We might expect that the continued low performance of students who attend special classes would generate alarm in their teachers, who would then refer them for additional evaluation leading to a change of program or placement. In fact, of 8,193 students who were referred for reevaluation before their triennial evaluation was due, 4,476 (55 percent) were found to be appropriately placed, and no change of services was necessary. Another 35 percent remain in the same special class but are offered a change in the special education services they receive. Only 10 percent of the 8,193 students were moved to a less restrictive environment as a result of the requested reevaluation. Stated somewhat differently, 90 percent of children in self-contained classes remain in self-contained classes, with or without a change in their program, as a result of the reevaluation, and few ever improve their level of academic achievement.

We employed academic progress as one of the indicators of success for special classes, and we portrayed a rather dismal portrait of the level of progress made by students enrolled in these classes. We would be remiss if we did not indicate, however, that the reality of urban schools is that many teachers and administrators do not consider academic progress to be a standard against which to gauge the success of special classes. In impoverished, crime-ridden, inner-city neighborhoods, many children are often referred for special class placement because teachers and administrators believe that students' immediate need is for someone to pay attention to and care for them, treat them with respect and kindness, elevate their self-esteem, teach them appropriate behavior, and provide appropriate standards for what is right and what is wrong. Academic progress as measured by standardized tests of achievement (or by any other measure, for that matter) is viewed as being a far more distal need that can only be successfully addressed after students have learned to feel good about themselves and to be trusting of others. In other words, one reason that achievement scores may be so low is that many special class teachers do not emphasize academic skills.

Mainstreaming A second criterion for the success of special education is the number of special class students who are mainstreamed. Sixteen percent of special class students at the elementary school level are mainstreamed, and 36 percent of middle school students are mainstreamed. These figures represent quantum increases over the 1987–1993 period, when only about 7 percent of students with disabilities were mainstreamed. The fact that more than twice the percentage of middle school students are mainstreamed cannot be explained solely by the 66 percent disparity that exists in the special education populations at the two school levels, however. That is, while 5 percent of all elementary school students are enrolled in special classes, 8.3 percent of all middle school students are in special classes. Compared with elementary school students, many more middle school students are mainstreamed relative to their numbers in the special education population.

We might think that the extent to which students are mainstreamed is a reflection of their academic ability and the likelihood that they will be able to adhere to the academic demands of the general education classroom. However, in analyses of student-level achievement data, we have not detected clear-cut relationships between mainstreaming and academic performance that would explain the substantially higher percentage of mainstreaming that occurs in middle schools. Data we collected during the 1986–1987 school year on a random sample of 9,000 special education students indicated that mainstreamed students had a mean score on tests of reading performance at the 24th percentile, whereas students who were not mainstreamed scored at the 20th percentile, on average. We do not believe that a 4-percentile difference by itself is sufficiently potent or meaningful to explain why some students are mainstreamed and others are not. Departmentalization at the middle schools, coupled with the greater number of options that are available, such as a host of noncore academic subjects like art, music, shop, and so forth, undoubtedly contribute to increases in mainstreaming. More research on this topic is needed.

Decertifications We have previously presented data for decertifications and will not repeat them here. Suffice it to say that the depressed levels of academic achievement among special education students that do not appear to improve over time is undoubtedly responsible, in large, part, for the low decertification rate from special education.

The data we have presented until now do not portray an especially favorable picture of the performance of students enrolled in self-contained classes. In many ways, we have replicated with current data the findings in the literature that revealed a pattern of poor performance by special class students. If anything, our data present a more dismal picture than the literature has typically portrayed. The logical question is, What is the alternative?

The simple answer and the one that springs immediately to mind is to retain students in general education classes. Because school systems are composed of two parallel systems, general and special education, if special education (classes) are viewed as second-rate (Autin & Dentzer, 1993), then at the surface it is easy to suggest that general education is more appropriate.

The problem of providing an appropriate education to academically low-functioning students is considerably more complex, as we shall shortly indicate. We must constantly realize that because special classes are not fulfilling their historic mission in no way addresses the question of whether general education is more appropriate, or at all appropriate, for these students given the difficulties they face.

EDUCATING ACADEMICALLY LOW-FUNCTIONING STUDENTS IN GENERAL EDUCATION CLASSES

One could easily argue that most students who are academically low-functioning could be and should be educated in general education classrooms, as Judith E. Heumann, the assistant secretary for special education and rehabilitation services was recently quoted to say at a recent national conference of the Council for Exceptional Students (Sklaroff, 1994). At one level this is a seemingly innocuous statement with which there is little to disagree. At another level, however, especially as it pertains to inner-city classes, such a view is troublesome. It sheds little light on the question of what we hope to accomplish by educating students who are academically low functioning in general education classrooms. The need to set objective goals and standards for special education students in general education classes is not an idle academic exercise. Without them, we have no way to assess the appropriateness of mainstreamed or inclusive placements. *For students with mild academic disabilities or who are academically low-functioning,* these goals must include a broad array of academic components; social performance is less valued by general education teachers and administrators. In urban schools, the majority of students who are referred for special education, 57 percent in our studies, are viewed by their teachers as either popular or average socially in their general education classes. Teachers view interpersonal competence as a less critical concern; improved academic performance is the central need. Success, therefore, must be defined academically, not interpersonally.

Are we mainstreaming, or including, students with disabilities to promote their academic performance? If so, what standard will we employ to gauge success? Should the students perform somewhere near the average for classes in their own schools, or should they perform near average on a national norm, a more difficult standard? Should they make demonstrable gains in academic performance as determined by portfolio assessments of work products, or should they acquire a level of literacy that might enable them to secure employment when they leave school? If the latter is the standard, recent evidence indicates that educational placement (comprehensive high schools versus segregated special education high schools) did not predict the percentage of time employed, the number of hours employed weekly, or the hourly wage earned of recent academically disabled special education high school graduates in urban schools (Whitehurst, 1994). The only variable that predicted postschool employment was independent work experience obtained by the student during school years—that is, work experience not offered as part of the high school curriculum but obtained at the student's own initiative.

May we decide to promote mainstream and inclusive education as a means of protecting students' civil rights that purportedly are violated when they are placed in self-contained classes? If so, then data on academic or vocational success are irrelevant. Whatever our goals for mainstreaming or inclusive education, we must state them clearly. Without such a clear goals statement, we have no way to determine whether mainstreaming is successful or even appropriate. We do not agree with the view that the retention of all children with disabilities in general education classes is a desirable goal for education. We view this as an appropriate goal for many children with disabilities, but certainly not for all.

THE ISSUE IS INSTRUCTIONAL QUALITY, NOT PLACEMENT

Because we have too often seen general education classes in urban school districts that could not meet the students' needs, we maintain that the location where special education services are delivered is far less important than the quality of the service that is delivered. We believe that sometimes special education can be offered effectively in general education classes and sometimes self-contained placements are likely to be more effective for some students with disabilities. The challenge is to identify correctly both the population and the circumstances that warrant placement in the correct setting.

Once an appropriate placement along the educational continuum has been identified for an individual child who is eligible for special education, the next challenge is to determine a set of instructional conditions and an anticipated level of progress that is to be expected and then determine whether the child is receiving an appropriate education. Continued placement in any environment for an indefinite period is unwarranted unless it can be demonstrated that the child's academic performance or behavior, or language skills, continue to improve. Continued placement in a segregated environment, in the face of performance data indicating a persistent lack of progress is *prima facie* evidence, in our view, that the placement is inappropriate. Yet, this is precisely the state of affairs in most inner-city school districts, as we indicated previously.

The data on academic achievement that we previously presented revealing that only 2.5 percent of students in self-contained classes attain grade-level performance during the final two years of their placement in either elementary or middle school indicate that few students are benefiting academically from self-contained placements. But are there other ways in which students could possibly benefit from self-contained classes?

We have recently found that in a random sample of sixty-two special education youngsters from an impoverished region of an urban school system, students with low IQ scores at the time of admission to special classes posted an average full-scale gain of five IQ points, increasing from an average of 71 to 76 over a period of more than four years between initial and final IQ testing. Students with high Wechsler IQ scores (which in our sample was defined as above 84) who were placed full-time in special classes for an average of forty-four months had a fifteen-point decrease in their full-scale IQ scores, from an average of 96 to an average of 81. The IQ scores of high-IQ students who attended resource room placements held constant over forty-five months, beginning at 94.0 and ending at 93.2. To complete the 2 × 2 matrix of placement and IQ scores, we noted that students with low IQ scores remained at an average score of 74 during the fifty-seven months, on average, that they were enrolled in resource room programs. We are presently attempting to replicate this finding on an additional sample of urban youth.

To the extent that these findings are replicable they may have considerable importance for placement decisions. Clearly, a fifteen-point decrease in full-scale IQ scores for students in special classes whose initial IQ scores average 96 is substantial. The IQ drop, coupled with data that the overwhelming majority of students do not progress academically, suggests that more capable students, those with higher IQ scores, should not be placed in self-contained environments. On the other hand, students with low IQ scores may find self-contained placements a more appropriate environment than general education classes.

FOR WHOM ARE SPECIAL CLASSES APPROPRIATE?

A body of research collectively referred to as the efficacy studies (Kirk, 1964) has frequently been cited as a reason that special classes might not be justifiable and mainstream options would be preferable (see, for example, Dunn, 1968). Not one of the ten efficacy studies conducted between 1932 and 1968 reported superior academic outcomes for educable mentally retarded (EMR) students in special classes. Five studies reported superior academic achievement outcomes for students in general education classes; the remaining five reported no differences. As early as 1964, the findings were subject to many criticisms on methodological grounds when Kirk (1964) published the first comprehensive review of this body of research. One of the criticisms voiced by Kirk and others who followed (for instance, Semmel, Gottlieb, & Robinson, 1979) was that the groups of EMR students in special and regular classes, usually matched on IQ scores, were not comparable for experimental purposes. The argument was advanced that because the general education group was not selected for special class placement, the likelihood was that it was different, more capable, from the group of students that was selected.

Another interpretation to explain the efficacy findings is that the general education group was enrolled in an appropriate educational placement, whereas a portion of the special class group was misplaced and not receiving an appropriate education. The differences in educational outcomes favoring general education may have reflected the inadequacy of the educational program for the higher IQ score group of students who were enrolled in special classes. These more capable students may have been instructed at a level considerably below their abilities. One study attempted to address the issue of an aptitude (ability) × treatment interaction, but it was conducted on a small sample of students who were enrolled in one school building. The study found no significant achievement differences between the special class and mainstreamed group despite the fact that the bulk of the intellectual resources of the investigators were directed at the mainstream group (Budoff & Gottlieb, 1976). Our current findings regarding IQ scores and self-contained placements that were obtained on a random sample renew once again a need to examine the effects of special class placements on specific subgroups of academically low-functioning students.

We recognize the potential for criticism that using IQ as an important, although not the sole, placement criterion was the norm in the past and that abuses in the practice (Berk, Bridges, & Shih, 1980) were responsible for the many assessment safeguards enacted into federal legislation. Those concerns were focused on the disproportionate placement of minority students in special classes. Our study of IQ scores was conducted in one region of an urban school system where 93 percent of the entire student body was composed of minority students. In school districts that are so heavily minority, evidence indicates that the dominant minority group does not get placed disproportionately in special classes, however

(Gottlieb & Alter, 1994). We have also reported elsewhere that high IQ scores serve the purpose of keeping black students out of special education entirely (Kastner & Gottlieb, 1991).

REFORMING URBAN EDUCATION

A combination of circumstances forces us to examine the way that academically low-functioning students, those who most often become part of the special education system, are educated. We have demonstrated that the bulk of special education students, approximately 85 percent of those who are classified as learning disabled, are not disabled in ways that are described in legislation (Gottlieb et al., 1994). The percentage of students who are not educationally disabled is at least as high for students who are classified as emotionally disturbed. We have further presented data in this chapter that demonstrate that few students who are placed in special classes improve their academic test scores in a meaningful way and that few ever leave the special education system. In addition, we have indicated that the situation in general education, bereft of sufficient resources, is not more promising. If we are concerned with improving the academic capability of low-functioning students, what can we do?

Effective change in urban schools of a magnitude likely to impact low-functioning students will only take place, in our estimate, when the schools clearly expand their mission to include custodial, social, and medical services. When students come to school sick, hungry, tired, and scared, the best teachers with ample supports will not make a significant dent in the students' resistive armor.

In inner-city environments, schools cannot be neatly divorced and compartmentalized from society at large. Everyday issues such as whether a youngster will survive another day without being killed or maimed by stray bullets are far more important in the overall scheme of things than whether that youngster spends sixty minutes daily, forty-five minutes daily, or no minutes daily in a general education classroom. The magnitude of social problems in the communities from which many students come make it unlikely that a significant number of students will escape the bottom rungs of the school and society ladder. Some surely will, and if and when they do, we doubt that special education of any kind will have played a major role. In the absence of a well-funded, coordinated attack on the related problems of poverty and crime, we do not expect that education by itself to make major inroads toward a solution.

Given that our major concern is education, what can be done within this domain to help? Several strategies that are important are not new. First, intensive and effective preschool programs, beginning as early as possible, that articulate with the school curriculum must be implemented on a far larger scale than has been done until now. These preschool programs should be under the jurisdiction of the local education agency so as to avoid difficulties over control that invariably arise when different agencies must coordinate their efforts.

Second, a variety of custodial, social, and medical support systems must be brought into the schools so that they might be easily accessed by students who require them. Programs of this kind already exist, but not nearly enough of them are available to meet the need.

Third, the community at large must be involved in efforts to improve the schools. Whether by volunteering as reading aides, classroom management aides, mentors, big brothers and big sisters, or simply neighbors who demonstrate an interest in students, local community members have a critically important role to play.

Fourth, creative attempts to reduce class size must be attempted. Whether classroom aides, nonteaching personnel, high school students who are participating in community service programs as part of their graduation requirements, mental health workers, parents, or siblings, more adult figures must be brought into inner-city classes so that instructional units are effectively reduced.

Fifth, special education should be reserved for students who have demonstrated they are unable to make satisfactory progress when all of these additional resources have been tried and proven ineffective.

Sixth, when students are placed in special education, clear, manageable goals must be established, as well as time lines for achieving the goals. Whichever environment in a particular school system can best deliver the needed services is the appropriate and preferred environment, regardless of whether this is a general education classroom or a special class.

Seventh, if the student fails to progress in special classes within a reasonable amount of time, one year at the maximum, a thorough evaluation of the special education program in that class is needed. This evaluation must include issues related to the adequacy of the placement, the quality of instruction that is offered, the appropriateness of the goals and objectives, the availability of adequate supplemental support for the student and the teacher, and any other considerations that could affect the student's performance.

CONCLUSION

The fervor regarding where to educate students with educational disabilities has been marked by a relative lack of attention to instructional issues. Neither special classes nor general education classes are appropriate when the quality of instruction and educational programming in both locations fails to meet the needs of a substantial percentage of their students. Far too many urban classrooms are in that situation. Until the strident discussions regarding where to educate students are replaced by discussion about how to improve the quality of education, for all low-functioning students, the students will continue to fail regardless of where they are educated. The major question will be whether we want them to fail in general education classes or in special education classes.

Historically, the movement toward mainstreaming and beyond was accelerated by the inability of special classes to demonstrate their worth. When they could not demonstrate that they produced superior outcomes to those offered by general education classes, a variety of other educational arguments were marshaled against special classes, including the alleged stigma that results. Had special classes been demonstrated to be effective in improving academic skills or in improving students' vocational prospects, other arguments would not have gained favor. Other pullout programs exist, such as Reading Recovery, which is designed for a finite period, usually twelve to fourteen weeks, to help first graders in the bottom 20th percentile of their classes. This pullout program has documented evidence of success and is very much in demand in both urban and suburban communities. When a program delivers what the community expects of it, its location becomes unimportant. We believe that it is time to focus on quality instruction, not on the location of instruction.

REFERENCES

Autin, D. M. T. K., & Dentzer, E. (1993). *Segregated and second rate: "Special" education in New York City*. Long Island City: Advocates for Children of New York.

Berk, R. A., Bridges, W. P., & Shih, A. (1981). Does IQ really matter? A study of the use of IQ scores for tracking of the mentally retarded. *American Sociological Review, 46*(1), 58–71.

Budoff, M., & Gottlieb, J. (1976). Special class EMR children mainstreamed: A study of an aptitude (learning potential) × treatment interaction. *American Journal of Mental Deficiency, 81,* 1–11.

Dunn, L. (1968). Special education for the mildly retarded: Is much of it justifiable? *Exceptional Children, 35,* 5–22.

Esten, R. A. (1900). Backward children in the public schools. *Journal of Psycho-asthenics, 5,* 10–15.

Farrell, E. E. (1908). Special classes in the New York City schools. *Journal of Psycho-asthenics, 13,* 91–96.

Fernald, W. E. (1903–1904). Mentally defective children in the public schools. *Journal of Psycho-asthenics, 8*(2–3), 25–34.

Goodenough, F. L. (1949). *Mental testing: Its history, principles, and applications*. New York: Rinehart.

Gottlieb, J. (1981). Mainstreaming: Fulfilling the promise? *American Journal of Mental Deficiency, 86,* 215–226.

Gottlieb, J., & Alter, M. (1994). *Evaluation study of the overrepresentation of children of color referred to special education*. Unpublished final report submitted to New York State Department of Education, Office of Children with Handicapping Conditions.

Gottlieb, J., Alter, M., Gottlieb, B. W., & Wischner, J. (1994). Special education in urban America: It's not justifiable for many. *Journal of Special Education, 27*(4), 453–465.

Kastner, J., & Gottlieb, J. Classification of children in special education: Importance of pre-assessment information and intelligence test scores. *Psychology in the Schools, 28,* 15–23.

Kirk, S. A. (1964). Research in education. In H. A. Stevens & R. Heber (Eds.), *Mental retardation* (pp. 57–99). Chicago: University of Chicago Press.

McGivern, D. O. (1995). *Draft roundtable report to the Regents Subcommittee on Special Education Issues in New York City*. New York: Board of Regents, State University of New York.

New York State Department of Education. (1994). *Report to the governor and the legislature on the educational status of the state's schools: Submitted February 1994*. Albany: State University of New York/State Education Department.

Semmel, M. I., Gottlieb, J., & Robinson, N. (1979). Mainstreaming: Perspectives on educating handicapped children in the public schools. In D. Berliner (Ed.), *Review of research in education. Vol.* 7 (pp. 18–46). Washington, DC: American Educational Research Association.

Sklaroff, S. (1994, April 20). Goals 2000 seen spurring "inclusion" movement. *Education Week,* p. 5.

Whitehurst, K. M. (1994). *The relationships of type of work experience, educational placement, gender, and literacy level to employment outcomes for inner-city youth with mild disabilities.* Unpublished doctoral dissertation, New York University, New York.

5

Finance and Funding Issues and Implications for Integration

LOUIS DANIELSON
FRAN O'REILLY
TOM PARRISH

The importance of finance and funding issues in special education service delivery is probably not self-evident for most people. The fact that funds are allocated from the federal government, state governments, and jurisdictions for special education services is taken for granted today. However, just two decades ago the pattern of financial support was very uneven. As a consequence, services were often unavailable or available only if students attended state-operated facilities.

The amount and nature of special education funding today has been a powerful influence on the way in which services are delivered to students with disabilities. For example, allocation of large amounts of funds to local school districts from federal and state sources has led to the development of community-based programs for students with severe disabilities who were served in institutions twenty years ago. Although changes in the way funds are allocated has promoted positive practices, current funding practices in many states provide fiscal rewards to schools that place students with disabilities in segregated programs that provide little opportunity for interaction with nondisabled children. Finance issues are important for all special educators to understand if we are to continue to develop policies that promote the successful integration of students with disabilities.

Fiscal support for public education is a shared responsibility. In nearly all states, federal, state and local revenues are combined to support the provision of elementary and secondary education programs. Although considerable state-to-state variation is apparent, the share of elementary and secondary education funded by local governments has increased somewhat over the last decade, while federal and state shares have decreased. In the 1982–1983 school year, the percentage contribution of local governments to all elementary and secondary education programs was 45.1 percent, the federal government provided 7.2 percent, and the states furnished 47.7 percent of the funds. By 1992–1993, the local contribution had risen to 46.4 percent, the federal share had fallen to 6.7 percent, and the state share had decreased to 46.8 percent (National Education Association, 1993). The increase in local governments' share of education funding began in 1987–1988, after a period in which the states had provided an increasingly larger proportion of elementary and secondary education funds.

This chapter provides an overview of approaches to special education funding, costs of special education, and current issues. Funding issues that affect efforts to promote integration are also described.

STATE FUNDING APPROACHES

The revenues provided by states for education fall into two major categories: basic support aid and categorical aid. *Basic support* aid, the principal component of a state's education finance system, typically comprises the majority of state education aid provided to local school districts. A primary use of basic support aid is to compensate for differing abilities among local districts to support education. State funds are distributed in inverse proportion to a district's ability to finance education (typically determined based on the district's taxable property base or property valuation.) Thus, less wealthy districts receive more state aid than property-"rich" districts. The resulting combination of state and local revenues enables poor districts to spend at the same rate per pupil as the most wealthy districts in a state.

Basic support aid can also be used to equalize disparities among districts as a result of educational need. Educational need can be determined based on the characteristics of students within a district, or it can reflect varying costs of education programs due to a variety of factors, such as differences in the cost of living throughout the state and adjustments for population sparsity or enrollment growth. A state aid program designed to equalize disparities due to wealth may not necessarily address differences across districts in their educational need.

Categorical aid, a second component of state education finance systems, is designed to address specific educational needs, such as special education, compensatory education, or vocational education. Categorical funds can be provided either in addition to or instead of resources distributed through the basic support program. As with basic support, categorical funds can be distributed in a way that equalizes fiscal capacity as well as educational needs.

Most states distribute special education funds through targeted categorical aid, although special education funds are disbursed in many states through the same formula used to distribute basic support revenues. Categorical funds can be distributed through any number of mechanisms, and each type of aid can have a different distribution formula. For example, special education aid might be distributed as a reimbursement for specific expenditures, while transportation funds could be distributed based on a flat grant in which an additional allocation would be provided for every student needing transportation. The formula used in each state to distribute these resources is virtually unique, having been developed to meet that state's policy goals and priorities.

Approaches to Special Education Funding

All states distribute fiscal resources for the provision of special education services in local education agencies. Of the estimated $19.2 billion expended during 1987–1988 (the latest available data) on services for children with disabilities, state governments provided about 56 percent of the resources, while local governments paid 36 percent and federal sources provided less than 8 percent (U.S. Department of Education, 1992). As shown in Table 5.1, however, these national numbers conceal enormous variability across states. During the 1987–1988 school year, the federal share of special education expenditures was over 10 percent in twenty states (up from sixteen in 1986–1987), whereas in eleven states, localities provided over half the financing for special education services. Still, most states remain as the primary financiers of special education.

The mechanisms that states have developed to distribute resources for special education are complex, often involving complicated interagency structures. The major component of state special education finance systems is the formula used to distribute funds for students with disabilities who are served in local school district programs. Variations on this formula, or separate mechanisms, are often

Table 5.1 Percentage of Federal, State, and Local Funds Expended for Special Education and Related Services, 1987–1988

State	Federal	State	Local
Alabama	11.6	85.4	3.0
Alaska	4.8	70.0	25.2
Arizona	11.4	44.9	43.7
Arkansas	6.3	56.9	26.8
California	6.2	78.6	15.2
Colorado	7.7	40.2	52.1
Connecticut	4.7	38.9	56.4
Delaware	12.9	62.5	24.6
District of Columbia	10.3	89.7	0.0
Florida	5.8	61.9	32.3
Georgia	6.6	75.0	18.4
Hawaii	4.5	95.5	0.0
Idaho	10.2	89.8	0.0
Illinois	7.5	42.1	50.4
Indiana	15.0	52.6	32.6
Iowa	7.6	75.6	16.8
Kansas	6.9	51.2	42.0
Kentucky	11.3	65.3	23.4
Louisiana	6.9	69.8	23.3
Maine	13.9	49.7	36.4
Maryland	7.6	39.3	53.2
Massachusetts	6.9	36.5	56.6
Michigan	7.3	21.9	70.8
Minnesota	3.7	66.8	29.5
Mississippi	13.7	79.9	6.4
Missouri	9.6	90.4	0.0
Montana	10.1	71.5	18.3
Nebraska	11.1	78.9	10.0
Nevada	5.4	55.7	38.9
New Hampshire	5.4	17.4	77.2
New Jersey	10.7	78.5	10.9
New Mexico	8.4	90.6	1.0
New York	3.2	46.9	49.9
North Carolina	13.1	73.7	13.2
North Dakota	7.3	27.6	65.1
Ohio	4.9	56.7	38.5
Oklahoma	9.6	87.7	2.7
Oregon	8.7	17.1	74.2
Pennsylvania	11.0	59.5	29.5
Rhode Island	5.6	94.4	0.0
South Carolina	13.7	55.8	30.5
South Dakota	9.7	34.8	55.5
Tennessee	14.3	63.2	22.5
Texas	11.9	56.1	32.0
Utah	14.2	81.4	4.3
Vermont	9.2	41.3	49.5
Virginia	7.2	17.4	75.5
Washington	6.3	70.2	23.5
West Virginia	12.0	73.7	14.3
Wisconsin	6.1	59.2	34.7
Wyoming	4.5	79.1	16.5
U.S. Total	7.9	56.0	36.1

SOURCE: From *Fourteenth Annual Report to Congress,* by U.S. Department of Education, 1992, Washington, DC: Author.

used to distribute funds for students served in out-of-district placements, such as state-operated facilities or private schools. Some states also have additional funding provisions to address specific situations such as residential care, special education transportation, catastrophic costs, and extended school-year services. The focus of the following discussion is the formula used by states to distribute resources for the provision of special education and related services to school-age students with disabilities who are served by local school district programs.

Over the past twenty years, a number of studies have classified special education funding approaches into various frameworks that group formulas based on their common characteristics (Bernstein, Hartman, Kirst, & Marshall, 1976; Hartman, 1980; Moore, Walker, & Holland, 1982; O'Reilly, 1989; Thomas, 1973). Although some of the details differ, a pattern of six basic formula types has emerged:

1. *Unit* formulas provide a fixed amount of money for each qualified unit of instruction, administration and transportation. Funding is disbursed for the cost of the resources needed to operate the unit, such as salaries for teachers and aides. The amount of funding provided may vary by type of unit. Regulations typically define pupil-teacher ratios or class size and caseload standards, either by disability or by type of program (for instance, resource room). For example, the state may fund one staff unit for each five students with severe disabilities and one staff unit for each forty-five students who are speech impaired.
2. *Personnel* formulas provide funding for all or a portion of the salaries of personnel working with children with disabilities. No other costs are reimbursed. As such, personnel formulas can be viewed as a special case of the unit formula, where funding is provided only for personnel costs. The percentage reimbursement may vary by personnel type. For example, the salaries of certified teachers may be reimbursed at a rate of 70 percent, whereas salaries for aides may be reimbursed at a rate of only 30 percent. Pupil-teacher ratios are typical of this formula type, and minimum state salary schedules are often included also.
3. *Weighted* formulas provide funds for each child with disabilities as a multiple of the general education per-pupil reimbursement. This formula is essentially a per-pupil funding mechanism, with different amounts provided based on a pupil's disability and/or program.
4. *Straight sum* or *flat grant* formulas provide a fixed amount of money for each eligible student with disabilities. The amount may or may not vary by disability of the students served. A cap on the percentage or number of students for whom reimbursement will be provided may be applied to control costs.
5. *Percentage-based* formulas provide to school districts a portion of approved costs of special education programs. The percentage approach can be combined with other formula types, such as personnel, to provide districts with a percentage of special education teacher salaries. Reimbursable costs usually must be in approved categories, and cost ceilings may apply.

6. *Excess cost* formulas are used to reimburse school districts for all or part of the costs of educating children with disabilities that are above the cost of the regular education program.

Recently, Hartman (1992) has suggested a seventh formula type, the *resource-cost model,* which is based on estimating the program requirements for special education and summing the costs to provide the needed resources. No states currently use a resource-cost approach to fund special education programs.

These formula types can be further grouped according to the main factor used for allocating funds: resources, students, or cost (Hartman, 1980). *Resource-based* formulas include unit and personnel mechanisms in which distribution of funds is based on payment for specified resources (such as teachers, aides, and equipment). *Student-based* formulas use the weighted and straight sum formulas and are based on the number and type of children served. *Cost-based* formulas involve the percentage and excess-cost methods, both of which are based on district expenditures for special education programs.

Moore et al. (1982) further classify the types of funding mechanisms according to two dimensions: the main factor on which the allocation is based and the mechanism used to allocate funds, as depicted in Table 5.2. As indicated in the table, these two dimensions can be combined to form nine different types of funding formulas. Only six combinations are feasible: (a) flat grant per student, (b) flat grant per teacher or classroom unit, (c) percentage or excess cost, (d) percentage of teacher/personnel salaries, (e) weighted pupils, and (f) weighted teacher/classroom units.

Special Education Funding in the States

The formulas actually in use by states can be grouped according to any of the traditional classification schemes. Nevertheless, a great deal of overlap occurs among categories, and within any single category formulas vary substantially from state to state. This variation reflects state efforts to be responsive to diverse state and district needs while also meeting state goals. For discussion and comparison purposes, we will classify state funding programs according to a framework. Table 5.3 shows the distribution of state formulas used during the 1992–1993 school year, according to four broad categories: flat grants, pupil weighting, resource-based, and cost-based formulas. Table 5.4 provides a further breakdown of the four categories in an attempt to reflect state special education policies and priorities. That is, for example, states that use a pupil-weighting formula are further classified into three categories according to the type of weight included in the formula: student disability, student program/placement, or a fixed multiplier.

Tables 5.3 and 5.4 indicate that the most common approach to funding special education programs in 1992–1993 was pupil weighting, followed closely by cost-based formulas. Flat grant and resource-based formulas had a similarly small distribution of states. Over the past decade, numerous changes have been made to the formulas used by states to fund special education, with many states moving away from the flat grant approach.

Table 5.2 Types of Special Education Finance Formulas

	FUNDING MECHANISM		
Basic Element	**Flat Grant**	**Percentage**	**Weight**
Students	Flat grant/student	——	Pupil weighting
Resources	Flat grant/classroom or teacher unit	Percentage of personnel salaries	Weighted teacher or classroom units
Costs	——	Percentage cost or excess cost	——

SOURCE: From *Patterns in Special Education Service Delivery and Cost,* by M. T. Moore, E. W. Strang, M. Schwartz, & M. Braddock, 1982, Washington, DC: Decision Resources Corporation.

Although the formulas can be classified according to the broad framework presented here, the basic formula types are inadequate for fully describing differences in philosophy and approach and belie the complexity of the funding systems that exist. Many states incorporate features from multiple funding models. Modifications due to unique state circumstances as well as to political compromises are legion. This has resulted in widely varied use of particular funding prototypes. For example, pupil-weighting formulas are quite diverse across the eighteen states currently using this approach. Alaska includes three weights based on the type of services provided (resource, self-contained, or hospital/homebound). New Jersey's formula, on the other hand, incorporates twenty-six weights based on both student disability and placement.

Theoretically, each of the formula types could be manipulated to result in equal allocations to school districts with similar populations of children with disabilities. As such, the formulas used to allocate special education resources have been described as merely mechanisms for transferring funds from one governmental level to another (Hartman, 1980). But state special education funding programs have the capacity, inadvertently or intentionally, to influence programs at the local level. Funding formulas can affect the number and type of children served, the type of programs and services provided by local school districts, the duration of time students spend in special education programs, the placement of students in various programs, and class size and caseloads. Administrative processes such as record keeping and reporting, as well as program and fiscal planning, can also be impacted by the funding formula.

Funding mechanisms also can be used to support state priorities and initiatives by, for example, earmarking funds for specific activities, establishing service priorities, providing incentives to develop specific types of programs, or instituting disincentives to discourage agencies from serving students in particular placements. The extent to which a formula may impact local district practice must be evaluated by state policy makers. For example, because state aid is distributed in direct relationship to the number of eligible students, flat grants may encourage overidentification of students eligible for special education. Similarly, a pupil-weighting formula may provide an incentive to misclassify students into higher

Table 5.3 Distribution of States Across Special Education Funding Models, 1992–1993

Pupil Weighting (18)	Cost-Based (15)	Flat Grant (9)	Resource-Based (8)
Alaska	Colorado	Alabama	Idaho
Arizona	Connecticut	California	Minnesota
Arkansas	District of Columbia	Delaware	Ohio
Florida	Hawaii	Illinois	Tennessee
Georgia	Louisiana	Kansas	Virginia
Indiana	Maine	Missouri	Washington
Iowa	Maryland	Nevada	West Virginia
Kentucky	Michigan	North Carolina	Wisconsin
Massachusetts	Montana	Pennsylvania	
New Hampshire	Nebraska		
New Jersey	North Dakota		
New Mexico	Rhode Island		
New York	South Dakota		
Oklahoma	Vermont		
Oregon	Wyoming		
South Carolina			
Texas			
Utah			

SOURCE: Center for Special Education Finance Survey data, 1993.

reimbursement categories. With a cost-based formula, if the local share is substantial, an incentive may be provided to identify fewer eligible students in order to minimize program costs.

As Moore et al. (1982) note, the actual model used may be less significant in explaining local district practice than are the other policy decisions made by developing the funding system, such as the level of state spending, equity, or student eligibility for services. Some differences are evident among funding models in their potential to influence local practice, although they are less dramatic than might be expected. Many of the consequences can be mediated by the introduction of additional factors, regulations, and provisions, but this adds to the complexity of the funding system and results in increased administrative and reporting burdens.

Although incentives and disincentives associated with the various funding models have been described in the research literature, very few empirical studies have examined the potential relationships. A longitudinal study by Dempsey and Fuchs (1993) did examine differences in student placement practices at the local level as a function of state reimbursement policy for special education in Tennessee. The researchers concluded that as funding shifted from a flat to a weighted rate, many student placements were shifted toward more financially rewarding options.

Table 5.4 State Special Education Finance Formulas, 1992–1993

	FLAT GRANT		PUPIL WEIGHTING			RESOURCE-BASED		COST		
State	Per Student (2)	Per Class or Teacher Unit (7)	By Disability (6)	By Program or Placement (10)	Single Multiple *r* (2)	Salary Percentage (4)	Classroom Unit (4)	Percentage Reimbursement (9)	Excess Cost (4)	Full State Funding (2)
Alabama		X								
Alaska				X						
Arizona				X						
Arkansas				X						
California		X								
Colorado								X		X
Connecticut								X		X
Delaware		X								
District of Columbia										
Florida			X							
Georgia			X							
Hawaii										
Idaho						X				
Illinois		X								
Indiana			X							
Iowa				X						
Kansas		X								
Kentucky			X							
Louisiana								X		X
Maine								X		X
Maryland									X	
Massachusetts					X					
Michigan									X	
Minnesota						X				
Mississippi*										
Missouri		X								

State									
Montana								X	
Nebraska									X
Nevada		X							
New Hampshire				X					
New Jersey				X					
New Mexico				X					
New York				X					
North Carolina	X								
North Dakota								X	
Ohio							X		
Oklahoma			X						
Oregon					X				
Pennsylvania	X								
Rhode Island									X
South Carolina			X						
South Dakota								X	
Tennessee						X			
Texas				X					
Utah†				X					
Vermont								X	
Virginia							X		
Washington							X		
West Virginia							X		
Wisconsin						X			
Wyoming								X	

*No data are available for Mississippi.

†In Utah, weighted pupil units used in the formula are no longer calculated annually but remain constant, based on the 1989–1990 school year calculation. Adjustments are allowed for growth in average daily membership (ADM).

SOURCE: Center for Special Education Finance Survey data, 1993.

States can introduce regulatory or programmatic provisions to balance the fiscal and programmatic impacts of various funding models. These would include program standards such as student-staff ratios, and fiscal controls such as targeting, or caps or limitations on the number of students eligible for services. The introduction of additional factors into state systems for financing special education adds to their uniqueness and complexity and exacerbates the difficulties for state policy makers faced with evaluating or changing a state's special education finance program. Criteria for assisting policy makers with this task are discussed in the following section.

EVALUATING THE VARIOUS SPECIAL EDUCATION FUNDING MODELS

Given the variety of consequences inherent to each of the funding models, and the competing interests of policy makers and stakeholders likely to be involved in the selection or modification of a state's formula (for example, state legislators and administrators, district administrators, parents and advocates), criteria for evaluating and prioritizing among the various approaches must be established. Over the past fifteen years, a number of researchers have developed criteria for evaluating special education funding formulas (Bernstein, Hartman, Kirst, & Marshall, 1976; Hartman, 1980; Moore et al., 1982). Most recently, Hartman (1992) has synthesized these criteria into a common framework as follows:

1. *Equity* (student and taxpayer). Formulas accommodate varying student needs and concentrations of students with special needs across local districts. Access of students with disabilities to special education and the quality of those programs do not depend on the local district's wealth or location. Variations among districts in their ability to support education are considered. Program or resource equivalence is the goal, not equal spending levels.
2. *Educational programming.* The delivery of appropriate services is encouraged and prioritized. Inappropriate practices are discouraged. Misclassification and the use of categorical labels, as well as overclassification of students with disabilities, is minimized. The principles of least restrictive environment are enforced.
3. *Rationality and simplicity.* The funding formula is easy to understand by all involved parties. The relationships among key policy elements, such as the numbers of children served, personnel required, or actual costs of programs, are straightforward. Implementation procedures are not overly complex.
4. *Comprehensiveness.* All students who are eligible for special education, as well as the resources required to deliver appropriate programs and services, are included in the formula.
5. *Flexibility and responsiveness.* The formula is flexible enough to enable local districts to address local conditions appropriately and efficaciously. Any changes that affect programs and costs can be easily incorporated into the system.

6. *Stability.* The system enables state policy makers to project annual funding requirements accurately. Local districts are assured of predictable revenues to support their programs.
7. *Accountability and cost-effectiveness.* Funding for special education programs at the local level can be tracked using an appropriate cost accounting system. Incentives are included to ensure that local agencies provide programs in a cost-effective manner. The formula includes factors that encourage cost containment.
8. *Efficiency.* Data collection, record keeping, and reporting is minimized at both the state and local levels within the boundaries of appropriate program and fiscal management.
9. *Adequate funding level.* Funding is sufficient for all districts to provide appropriate special education programs to all eligible students with disabilities.

Clearly, a single funding formula cannot accommodate all of these criteria. Support for increased integration, for example, may affect the simplicity or flexibility of a funding formula. State policy makers must prioritize the areas of importance within their state, articulate the goals of the state funding program, and develop appropriate policies that will meet those state goals. Hartman (1992) has suggested four questions to help policy makers with this task:

1. Who is to be served in special education?
2. How are they to be served effectively—what programs and services are to be provided?
3. What are appropriate resources for the programs and services?
4. How are the costs to be shared between local and state agencies?

FEDERAL FISCAL SUPPORT FOR SPECIAL EDUCATION

Currently, the federal government provides aid to states for the education of children and youth with disabilities with funding authorized by Part B of the Individuals with Disabilities Education Act (IDEA), the Preschool Grants Program, and the Part H Early Intervention Program for Infants and Toddlers. In fiscal year 1994, the allocations for states under these three programs were over $2 billion for the Part B program, over $325 million for the Preschool Grants Program, and over $213 million for the Part H program (U.S. Department of Education, 1995a, 1995b). The following discussion will concentrate on the Part B program, which accounts for the vast majority of federal aid for the education of students with disabilities.

Specialized funding for individuals with disabilities dates back to the 1800s (for example, funds were appropriated during the Lincoln presidency to support Gallaudet University to educate students who were deaf). Federal aid to states to share in the costs of educating students with disabilities began with the landmark

Elementary and Secondary Education Act of 1965. Initially, aid was provided for children with disabilities who were served in state-operated or state-supported institutions (PL 89-313). During the early 1970s, Congress demonstrated great concern about the lack of appropriate services for students with disabilities, beginning with the passage in 1975 of the first statute addressed to the education of students with disabilities, the Education of the Handicapped Act. This statute was renamed the Individuals with Disabilities Education Act in 1990. The landmark legislation that was designed to assure that all children with disabilities would be provided a free appropriate public education was enacted in 1975 (PL 94-142), which is largely the same legislation that exists today.

Public Law 94-142 required a great deal of states and local school districts, and it was designed to provide substantial federal assistance to states. The legislation authorized state grants for fiscal year 1978 of up to 5 percent of the national average per pupil expenditure (APPE) for each child with a disability that a state served. The amount authorized was to rise to 10 percent of APPE in 1979, 20 percent in 1980, 30 percent in 1981, and 40 percent in 1982. The fact that the law authorized these amounts was no guarantee that these funds would actually be appropriated by Congress. In fiscal year 1978, the full 5 percent share was allocated to states, which yielded per-child funding of $72 and a total federal appropriation of over $251 million (Parrish & Verstegen, 1994). In fiscal year 1979, the full 10 percent share was appropriated with a per-child allocation of $159 and the federal allocation rising to $566 million. Fiscal year 1979 was the last year for which the federal allocation was at the authorized level. In fiscal year 1980, when the authorized appropriation was 20 percent of APPE, the actual share allocated was 12.5 percent. Since then, the federal share has declined gradually to current levels, which are about 8 percent of APPE. However, the per-child allocation has increased from $72 in 1978 to $420 in 1994. The increase in the per-child allocation has resulted from the increase in the APPE, which rose from $1,430 for the 1978 allocation to $5,108 for the 1994 allocation.

Federal funding under Part B of IDEA has increased every year since 1978. While the federal share of APPE has declined, both the APPE and the number of children with disabilities served have risen substantially during the period. These two factors account for increase in the federal appropriation under this program. To illustrate the impact of growth in the these two factors on the appropriation, between 1993 and 1994 the allocation to states increased by nearly $79 million, yet the federal share declined somewhat. This occurred because the number children served by the states increased by 168,000 students and the APPE increased by $140.

COST OF SPECIAL EDUCATION

While much of this chapter focuses on how we fund special education at the federal and state levels and issues associated with these funding approaches, there is much current interest in the cost of educating students with disabilities. Some critics argue that costs for educating children have risen rapidly over the interval since enactment of PL 94-142 and that these expenditures are reducing funds available to educate nondisabled children. Chaikind, Danielson, and Brauen (1993) reviewed the data that have been amassed to address this issue. Over a period of nearly twenty years across three major national studies of special education expenditures, the costs of serving students with disabilities were found to be remarkably constant (Moore, Strang, Schwartz, & Braddock, 1988; Kakalik, Furry, Thomas, & Carney, 1981; Rossmiller, Hale, & Frohreich, 1970). These studies relied on a cost ratio to express the relative cost of serving a child with a disability. This figure is the ratio of the average per-pupil cost of serving a child with a disability to the per-pupil cost of serving a nondisabled child. In 1968–1969, Rossmiller et al. (1970) found this ratio to be 1.92, which means that the average cost of serving a child with a disability was 1.92 times that of a nondisabled child. Kakalik and his associates found the ratio to be 2.17 in 1977–1978, and Moore and her associates computed a ratio of 2.28 for 1985–1986. For example, the ratio computed by Moore et al. (1988) was based on average per-pupil expenditures for students with disabilities of $6,335 and for the nondisabled of $2,780.

Although the trend has been up somewhat, remarkably, the average cost of serving a disabled child has been nearly twice the cost of serving a nondisabled child for nearly all of the past two decades. This provides evidence that per-pupil special education expenditures have not increased by substantial amounts relative to the increase in per-pupil expenditures for nondisabled students.

CURRENT ISSUES IN FUNDING SPECIAL EDUCATION

A poll of state departments of education (Parrish, 1994) revealed that a major concern is that federal funding under IDEA is not even close to authorized levels. A second important set of issues relates to arguments that current provisions of the IDEA sometimes run counter to state reform efforts designed to enhance the efficiency and effectiveness of special education. Overall, these representatives of the states argued that the IDEA was overregulated and underfunded. Brief descriptions of some of the most important issues regarding the funding of special education follow. The chapter concludes with implications of funding for the integration of students with disabilities.

IDEA Is Not Fully Funded

As discussed more fully earlier in this chapter, the amount of money allocated by the Congress each year to fund IDEA is based on the number of special education students in each state, multiplied by a percentage of the average per-pupil expenditure (APPE) across the nation. For fiscal year 1993, IDEA funding was 8.2 percent of the APPE. At $2.05 billion, this is approximately $7.93 billion below the authorized level of 40 percent of the APPE. Nearly a fivefold increase would be required to fund fully the IDEA at authorized levels.

Census-Based Funding

As the number of special education students continues to grow across the nation, some policy makers have expressed concern about what they argue is a fiscal incentive under the IDEA to continue to identify special education students up to the 12 percent federal funding limit. For example, some states that are involved in funding reform express concern that current federal policies run counter to their efforts. Because the IDEA allocation is based on the number of students identified for special education services (up to 12 percent), states that are serving certain special need students outside of the formal special education system are losing federal funds as their counts of identified special education students drop. One state director argued that

> according to the USDE report, *Patterns in Special Education Service Delivery and Cost,* the cost of the assessment to determine eligibility for special education is $1,206.[1] Assessment is an exercise with little or no instructional benefit, and it is conceivable that states actually lose money by participating in the federal entitlement for special education. . . . At the rate of about $400 per year (per identified student) in federal funds, the costs of the resulting services will be borne by the state for any number of years before any cost-benefit will be realized from the receipt of federal funds. (Tucker, 1993, p. 1)

Since 1992, at least seven states have adopted state special education funding systems that are primarily, or exclusively, based on total district enrollments rather than the number of students assessed and identified as eligible for special education.[2] Primary rationales for this type of system are the removal of fiscal incentives to identify and label students for special education. These incentives are removed because the amount of funds a district receives is based on total district, rather than special education, enrollment. Apart from other types of adjustments that may be contained in the formula, districts with the same overall enrollment will receive the same amount of special education funding regardless of the number of students formally identified for special education services.

Severing the tie between state special education funding and the number of students identified for special education has resulted in a general reduction in the number of students identified for special education services in these reform states. This has been accomplished through such innovations in local practice as allowing special education teachers to work in regular education classrooms with combinations of special and regular education students, allocating resources for prereferral services, and funding the provision of many remedial services outside of special education.

---

[1]The Individuals with Disabilities Education Act requires that students be identified and assessed to be eligible for special education funds. Specific standards for assessment vary from state to state. The $1,206 figure reflects the average assessment cost per pupil in all of the states included in the nationally representative sample used in this U.S. Department of Education study. See Moore et al. (1988).

[2]These states are California, Idaho, Massachusetts, Montana, Pennsylvania, South Dakota, and Vermont.

Generally, these reform states feel that the resultant reduction in the count of special education students is a change for the better (Parrish & Montgomery, 1995). They argue that they are often serving a broader range of students with special learning needs in a less restrictive and more appropriate manner. In short, they believe that some students with special learning needs will be better and more efficiently served outside the formal special education system. Given the trends of escalating special education identification rates and diminishing public resources, reformers argue that this is the type of change in special education policy that the federal government should be encouraging. Rather, because federal funding under IDEA is based on special education head counts, current federal law contains fiscal disincentives for these types of reform.

In arguing that the federal government should also adopt a census approach to special education funding, they say that working outside special education is more cost-effective, overidentification of students is now the major issue, and because all procedural safeguards would remain in place, movement to a census-based funding system would not jeopardize any of the entitlements under current law.

Opponents to census-based funding systems also offer a compelling set of arguments, however. They contend that such systems are not fair to states and districts with higher identification rates and that procedural safeguards cannot be maintained if students are not identified. They also see such a funding system as a retreat from the traditional federal role of fostering and promoting special education services. They say that fiscal accountability would be jeopardized and that current levels of special education funding will be threatened.

Thus, compelling arguments were made for and against changes in federal special education funding policy, including in IDEA as reauthorized in 1997. There are also important potential redistribution effects among the states, although these are being implemented slowly over time. States currently identifying more special education students than average lose under such a system, and states identifying less gain. (For a more in-depth discussion of census-based funding, see Parrish & Verstegen, 1994.

Consideration of the Part B Poverty Adjustment

A major difficulty associated with a census-based funding approach is that it assumes equal special education incidence across states. The current IDEA funding formula, based on the number of identified students, is predicated on the concept that some states serve greater numbers of special education students than others and, therefore, should receive relatively larger allocations of federal special education aid. Although agreement is growing that the number of students identified is as much a matter of choice as of need, as evidenced by the fact that the percentage of students identified for special education services in Massachusetts is more than twice that in Washington, DC, the concept of allowing for varying needs in the funding formula is compelling. However, if funding based on the number of identified special education students is a poor proxy of the true variation in need, and if such a system creates incentives for increased identification, what might be adopted as an independent measure of the need for special education services?

As a result of the reauthorized IDEA, future Part B funding will be adjusted to reflect variations in poverty rates across the states. The rationale is that high concentrations of poverty have been associated with greater numbers of children being identified as eligible for special education and should, therefore, be the basis of targeted resources in an effort to provide more intensive and earlier interventions.

However, one important factor in considering such an adjustment is the exclusionary clause in the learning disabilities definition included in the IDEA, Part B (Section 602a.1.a.15), which states in part:

> The term "children with learning disabilities". . . does not include children who have learning problems which are primarily the result of . . . environmental, cultural, or economic disadvantage.

In addition, although some form of poverty adjustment deserves serious consideration, it brings into further question the most appropriate relationship between special and compensatory education under the federal Title I program. As Title I is designed specifically to allocate supplemental federal funds to poverty areas, a poverty adjustment under the IDEA may further confuse the unique roles of these two federal programs. However, a poverty adjustment under the IDEA may appeal most to those policy makers and scholars who have called for a more coherent education policy that provides an integrated approach across all programs and to those who find preventative services imperative if the growth in special education is to be curtailed. (For a more in-depth discussion of a possible poverty adjustment to IDEA funding, see Parrish & Verstegen, 1994.)

The State Special Education Finance Reform Movement

States are struggling to balance the rights of students with disabilities within a context of limited public resources and a growing demand for social services. As a result, states are actively changing or considering changes in the ways they finance special education programs. In fact, efforts across the states to reform special education finance appear to be at their highest level since the enactment of Education for Handicapped Children Act in 1978 (currently known as IDEA).

The national Center for Special Education Finance (CSEF) conducted a telephone survey in 1995 of all states to learn of any efforts they may be making to reform their special education finance systems. The survey revealed that eighteen states have implemented some type of finance reform since 1990 (seven of these states are again considering reform) and that twenty-nine states were currently considering major changes in fiscal policy. Although nine of these states expected to implement some variation of their existing funding system or have a clear idea for a new one, twenty were as yet undecided about the specifics of the changes they will make.

When states were asked to identify the issues driving reform, they provided more than a dozen answers. However, the consensus was that (a) greater flexibility in the provision of special education services was needed, and (b) disincentives for least restrictive placements had to be eliminated. Reforms are also being driven by fiscal stress as well as more traditional finance goals of accountability, formula simplicity, adequacy of services, and equity.

Rising special education costs and enrollments have become major issues in many states. For example, Pennsylvania faced a $100 million deficit in special education funding before reform. Under the state's prior reimbursement system for special education—which was much more liberal in its funding than the regular education system—some districts had identified up to 36 percent of their students for special education. In Montana, reform was precipitated by a projection made in the mid-1980s of rapid continuing growth in special education enrollments throughout the state.

Resolving tension between special education fiscal and program policy will enhance efforts to increase integration another area of concern. A source for this tension is the groundswell of support for more "inclusionary" educational practices (Parrish, 1994), which have been endorsed by several national organizations and states. For example, the National Association of State Boards of Education (1992) has released a strong policy statement, *Winners All: A Call for Inclusive Schools,* that advocates a shift in education policy to foster the development of well-integrated services for all students. It argues that the linkages among funding, placement, and disability labels, which have traditionally provided the foundation for special education funding, must be broken. Many states are now examining their special education funding systems to see whether they contain any disincentives to integrated classroom placements for students with disabilities.

Finance and funding policies can provide powerful incentives or disincentives to schools as they move to include students with disabilities in regular education settings. One of the most powerful disincentives for including students with severe disabilities in regular education classes is a state funding formula that reimburses schools at a higher rate for the students placed in segregated environments. These formulas are very common because of a historical presumption that more difficult students would be served in restrictive settings and, therefore, that the reimbursement would have to be much higher. If a school district moves these children from segregated placements to inclusive placements, the costs of services might remain high, but the funding formula would not reimburse the district at the same high level. The school district would then lose the funding associated with the segregated placement. Obviously, only a district with a substantial amount of local funding to compensate for these lost funds would change the placement setting for these students. Because of these effects, many parents and professionals are calling for the use of "placement-neutral" funding formulas. One example of a placement-neutral formula is one that reimburses a flat amount for each disabled student served, as the federal formula does. One can see that the funding a school district receives is not impacted if students are served in more inclusive settings.

Another funding issue that is relevant to inclusion of students with disabilities is financial support for training. One current obstacle to inclusion is that regular education teachers and their professional associations feel that regular teachers are unprepared for serving children with disabilities in their classrooms. Teachers' unions may make this issue a collective bargaining issue. Appropriate professional development activities will require funding that may not be readily available at the local level. Unless schools, districts, states, and the federal government are willing to underwrite these costs, the lack of training may prove to be one of the most difficult obstacles.

One interesting funding issue that may serve as an incentive to include more students in regular education classrooms is the perception by some school administrators that it will cost less. At this point, there is no evidence that integration will save money. In fact, if one assumes that training costs will ensue and that services will follow students, the costs could be greater, although savings from transportation expenditures would compensate for some of these expenses.

Although funding policy should be designed to foster the state's programmatic priorities, the reality is often the opposite. Programmatic decisions are often driven by the incentives and disincentives created through the state's funding system. In Vermont, for example, the state director describes several decades in which statewide commissions and workshops had a limited impact on realizing state goals for educating students with disabilities in less restrictive settings. However, after Vermont moved to its new funding system, where dollars were not tied to more restrictive placements, the sentiment supporting restrictive, high-cost placements diminished considerably. In Pennsylvania, once funding was severed from the number of students identified, special education enrollments began to drop.

To address the issues discussed here, states have instituted a variety of fiscal and program reforms. Some states, like California and Oregon, have responded to growing fiscal pressures by capping the growth of special education aid through limits on the number of students eligible for reimbursement (Beales, 1993). In an attempt to remove the fiscal incentive for identifying increasing numbers of special education students, Pennsylvania, Vermont, Massachusetts, and Montana have revised their state finance formulas to decouple funding from the count of special education students. These states now primarily provide special education funds to districts based on some form of a census-based funding system, as described earlier.

Each state will implement reform based on an assessment of local conditions and the goals for program policy it would like the funding system to foster. Although most policy makers believe that funding systems should not encourage overidentification of special education students or more restrictive and costly placements, opinions differ about the types of funding provisions that will most likely realize these policy goals. Whereas some see a need to break the link between funding and placement as a way to discourage restrictive placements, parents and advocacy groups sometimes express concern that it is this very link that ensures fiscal accountability by educators, the receipt of adequate and appropriate services by students with disabilities, and the protection of procedural safeguards.

States attempting to forge new special education finance structures will repeatedly encounter tension among these types of competing policy criteria. A major focus on one criterion may in fact come at the expense of one or more of the others. For example, a formula that is easy to understand and that reduces the local reporting burden may not be the most effective at allocating limited special education resources where they are most needed.

Thus, in attempting to develop an ideal set of special education funding provisions, state policy makers must choose the criteria they wish to foster and recognize that no system, no matter how simple, will be incentive free. Finance and funding issues must be addressed if children with disabilities are to be served appropriately in inclusive settings. We must consider both the costs of services as well as the way in which we reimburse schools for these expenditures. Developing the best fiscal policy for each state will require a full understanding of, and a prioritization among, potentially competing policy goals.

REFERENCES

Beales, J. R. (1993). *Special education: Expenditures and obligations.* Los Angeles, CA: Reason Foundation.

Bernstein, C., Hartman, W., Kirst, M., & Marshall, R. (1976). *Financing educational services for the handicapped: An analysis of current research and practices.* Reston, VA: Council for Exceptional Children.

Chaikind, S., Danielson, L., & Brauen, M. (1993). What do we know about the costs of special education? A selected review. *Journal of Special Education, 26*(4), 344–370.

Dempsey, S., & Fuchs, D. (1993). "Flat" versus "weighted" reimbursement formulas: A longitudinal analysis of statewide special education funding practices. *Exceptional Children, 59*(5), 433–443.

Hartman, W. (1980). Policy effects of special education funding formulas. *Journal of Education Finance, 6*(2), 135–139.

Hartman, W. (1992). State funding models for special education. *Remedial and Special Education, 13*(6), 47–58.

Kakalik, J. S., Furry, W. S., Thomas, M. A., & Carney, M. F. (1981). *The cost of special education* (a Rand Note). Santa Monica, CA: Rand Corporation.

Moore, M. T., Strang, E. W., Schwartz, M., & Braddock, M. (1988). *Patterns in special education service delivery and cost.* Washington, DC: Decision Resources Corporation.

Moore, M. T., Walker, L. J., & Holland, R. P. (1982). *Finetuning special education finance: A guide for state policy makers.* Princeton, NJ: Educational Testing Service, Education Policy Research Institute.

National Association of State Boards of Education. (1992). *Winners all: A call for inclusive schools.* Alexandria, VA: Author.

National Education Association. (1993). *Estimates of school statistics, 1992–93.* Washington, DC: Author.

O'Reilly, F. (1989). *State special education finance systems, 1986–87.* Washington, DC: National Association of State Directors of Special Education.

Parrish, T. B. (1994). *Removing incentives for restrictive placements* (Policy Paper No. 4). Palo Alto, CA: Center for Special Education Finance, American Institutes for Research.

Parrish, T. B., & Montgomery, D. L. (1995). *Politics of special education finance reform in three states* (State Analysis Series No. 1). Palo Alto, CA: Center for Special Education Finance, American Institutes for Research.

Parrish, T. B., & Verstegen, D. A. (1994). *Fiscal provisions of the Individuals with Disabilities Education Act* (Policy Paper No. 3). Palo Alto, CA: Center for Special Education Finance, American Institutes for Research.

Rossmiller, R. A., Hale, J. R., & Frohreich, L. E. (1970). *Educational programs for exceptional children: Resource configuration and costs.* Madison: National Education Finance Project, Department of Educational Administration, University of Wisconsin.

Thomas, M. A. (1973). Finance: Without which there is no special education. *Exceptional Children, 39,* 475–490.

Tucker, J. (1993, March 29). Letter from special education director, Pennsylvania, to the Regional Office of the Inspector General.

U.S. Congress, House of Representatives, Committee on Education and Labor. (1975, June 26). Education for All Handicapped Children Act of 1975, 94th Congress, 1st Session. House Report No. 94-332 (pp. 125–190). In U.S. Senate, Committee on Labor and Public Welfare, Subcommittee on the Handicapped (1976), Education of the Handicapped Act as amended through December 31, 1975 (Report No. 72-611). Washington, DC: Government Printing Office.

U.S. Department of Education. (1992). *Fourteenth annual report to Congress.* Washington, DC: Author.

U.S. Department of Education. (1995a). *Eighteenth annual report to Congress.* Washington, DC: Author.

U.S. Department of Education. (1995b). *Justifications of appropriation estimates to the Congress. Vol. 1.* Washington, DC: Author.

PART II

Integration Efforts

6

Systems Change and the Transition to Inclusive Systems

DAWN HUNTER

More than ever, we are in the process of transition from segregated educational service delivery models to more inclusive models of educating all children, including children with disabilities. This change process is complex, and a glimpse at the national data presented in the *Annual Report to Congress* (U.S. Department of Education, 1995) immediately raises questions concerning educating children with disabilities in the Least Restrictive Environment. For example, the general education class placement for students ages six through twenty-one across all disabilities varies from 1 percent in one state to 87 percent in another. Why might these data vary so greatly? Apparently, in addition to meeting the educational needs of children with disabilities, other factors may be influencing the placement decision-making process in schools, districts, or states. Four such factors include (a) service delivery history, (b) funding formulas, (c) preparedness of the system, and (d) attitudes and perceptions.

The service delivery history of a school, district, and state can greatly impact placement decisions for students with disabilities. Issues include (a) how and when educational services for children with disabilities began; (b) the extent to which schools were constructed specifically for students with disabilities; (c) the extent and influence of court cases and parent and professional advocacy efforts; (d) the availability of fiscal and human resources, including outside support from federal, state, or local grants; and (e) the availability of training activities which brought new instructional technology to the system. For example, if over the last twelve years a school district built three new state-of-the-art self-contained schools for students with disabilities, there may be more reluctance to move to an inclusive schooling model than in a district that never had any self-contained schools. Though the new self-contained schools could be transformed into inclusive general education schools, this effort may require both considerable fiscal resources and time to complete.

Another factor that may affect placement decisions is the formula used to determine special education funding. For example, in states where placement in self-contained schools generates more funds than placement in self-contained classes on general education campuses, there is an incentive to place children with disabilities in self-contained schools. With fiscal resources limited in many districts, this practice may be viewed as either necessary or fiscally prudent. In fact, administrators may view generating this type of additional resources as a way to ensure that children with disabilities will have the services they require. Some states (for example, California) have reviewed their funding formula and determined that changes in reimbursement formulas are necessary to ensure that "placement-neutral" decisions will be made for children with disabilities (that is, decisions in which the services provided do not affect reimbursement).

A third factor impacting placement decisions is the preparedness of the school, district, or state to serve children in general education settings. Because inclusive schooling is relatively new to many, those responsible in the systems may believe they are not adequately prepared to provide educational services to children with disabilities in the general education classroom. For example, teachers, administrators, related service providers, and families may believe personnel are not trained to address the needs of students with disabilities in the general education classrooms. Administrators may find schools do not have adequate support available for students and teachers (for instance, materials, equipment, aides). Administrators may believe that more time is needed to ensure that policies, procedures, strategic plans, and budgets are in place to address the issues that may arise in the transition to a more inclusive schooling model. At times, these may be realistic concerns. At other times, people in the systems may lack confidence in their own ability to provide services. Systems that are committed to a transition to an inclusive schooling model will take steps to become prepared or begin the process on a small scale.

Probably the single most critical factor influencing placement is the attitude of teachers, administrators, parents, professional organizations, school boards, and the community. The influence of this factor simply cannot be overstated. Even with a long tradition of segregated placements, communities that seek more inclusive schooling practices are making it happen.

To educate children with disabilities to the greatest extent possible with typical children, all of these factors as well as others will need to be addressed, and existing structures and behaviors will need to change. This chapter briefly discusses how inclusive schools are implemented through a systems change process, the necessary components for a successful systemic transition to inclusive practice, and strategies for coping with the change process.

INCLUSIVE SCHOOLS DEVELOPED THROUGH THE SYSTEMS CHANGE PROCESS

What Is a System?

As stated previously, systems (for example, a school, a district, a state) are complex creatures. Schalock, Alberto, Fredericks, and Dalke (1993) present four interactive components that conceptualize systems involved in the change process: (a) an underlying philosophical foundation, (b) administrative levels of change (such as national, multiple states; a state, region, local educational agency; neighborhood school, student, or family), (c) the units of analysis and change (that is, whole system, system components, individuals within the system, products of the system), and (d) the targets for change (for instance, mission, vision, policies, laws, culture, services, programs, resources, administration, management, effective practices, personnel, clients, constituents, evaluation, and other agency collaboration).

The Ultimate Goal of a Systems Change Process

Most systems change efforts have at least two goals. One is to accomplish that which is usually stated in a vision, mission, or value statement. The second goal is that the change is a lasting one. These goals are straightforward, but their accomplishment is typically a complex, difficult process.

How Schools, Districts, and States Have Implemented Systems Change

Three approaches to systems change are commonly found in the literature: (a) top-down change, (b) bottom-up change, and (c) shared responsibility for change (Beer, 1980; Greiner, 1967). When reviewing the educational reform and restructuring efforts of those who are making a transition to inclusive schooling models, we find that all three of these strategies are being used (Karasoff, Alwell, & Halvorsen, 1992; Regional Resource and Federal Centers Program, 1993). Sailor (1991) suggests that change efforts should proceed from both top-down and bottom-up directions. Parents seeking inclusive schooling arrangements also have used a variety of change strategies to secure inclusive placements for their children with disabilities (Ryndak, Downing, Jacqueline, & Morrison, 1995).

Unfortunately, sufficient data are not available about the effectiveness of the various change approaches. Moreover, because the change process requires that goals and strategies be "custom tailored" to individual systems, determining what aspects of the change process may be generalized to other systems change efforts is difficult.

What Produces Change, and Why Is Change Often Not Enduring?

System components are interactive, and changes in one part of the system frequently affect other components. As a consequence, the interdependence of system components must be taken into account to foster lasting change. Too often, an approach is directed toward change in only one or a few of a system's components. For example, a state developing and disseminating a policy encouraging inclusive schooling may have little impact on actual practices unless additional components of the system also change (for example, the attitudes of local administrators or teachers, parental support of the policy, provision of professional development activities, availability of adequate resources and planning time, and provision of transportation arrangements). Changing state policy facilitates change, but actions in isolation of other change efforts will not be effective. For example, the inclusive schooling initiative is linked closely to larger restructuring efforts in the school, district, or state.

Must all components of the system be identified, and must an exact plan for change be developed? Fullan (1993b) argues that even if we could construct a detailed analysis, it still would not constitute reality because of the changes among system components and the impact of changes on all system components. For example, a change within one part of the system may be inconsistent or incompatible with goals or procedures in another part of the system (Fullan & Miles, 1992). Consequently, the exact outcomes of change efforts often are unpredictable and cannot be planned. Systems do not remain stable for very long, a phenomenon referred to as "dynamic complexity" (Kilmann, 1989; Senge, 1990). The best plans may result in little lasting change unless they are accompanied by provision for ongoing planning and evolution. The third year of a change process, for example, is often critical. Tye (1987) indicates that in her experience

> most change efforts begin to falter in about the third year of implementation. A change that cannot survive the "Year-3 Crisis" is apt to have been a change that was undertaken without sufficient attention to all the systemic pressures and consequences involved. (p. 283)

Systems change efforts produce only temporary rather than enduring change for several reasons. For example, systems have failed to change because of (a) a lack of administrative support (McDonnell & Hardman, 1989); (b) organizations either overmanaging or underleading, which is typically found in bureaucratic structures (Kotter, 1990); (c) insufficient time allowed to see the change (Elmore & McLaughlin, 1988); and (d) players reverting to old ways of doing things when they implement changes that initially may feel awkward and forced (Kilmann, 1989).

The factors perhaps most likely to make enduring systems change difficult are the deep structure and culture of systems. Tye (1987) states, "The elements of schooling that I have called deep structure are rooted in the values and assumptions of our society, they are part of the conventional wisdom about schooling, and they have come to be accepted without question" (p. 283). Consequently, challenging the deep structure of schooling is very difficult. In many respects, the inclusive schooling change effort has been based on civil rights or value-based ideologies. Not all professionals and parents share the belief that children with disabilities should be educated with their peers without disabilities in general education classrooms. They cannot imagine how inclusive schooling could work. In this way, the inclusive schooling movement has challenged the deep structure of the educational system. All of these reasons, though not exhaustive, are intended to illustrate common problems that prevent real and lasting change.

Kotter (1990) states that leadership produces change and that constructive change is achieved through three processes:

> 1. *Establishing direction*—developing a vision of the future, often the distant future, along with strategies for producing changes needed to achieve that vision.
> 2. *Aligning people*—communicating the direction to those whose cooperation may be needed in order to create coalitions that understand the vision and that are committed to its achievement.
> 3. *Motivating and inspiring*—keeping people moving in the right direction despite major political, bureaucratic, and resource barriers to change by appealing to very basic, but often untapped, human needs, values, and emotions. (p. 5)

Kotter (1990) also notes that motivation and inspiration are created by

> (a) articulating again and again a vision in a way that stresses the key values of the people being communicated to; (b) involving those people in deciding

how to achieve that vision or some portion of the vision; (c) supporting their efforts with coaching, feedback, role modeling, and a lot of enthusiasm; and (d) sincerely recognizing them in public and rewarding their successes. (p. 73)

EIGHT COMPONENTS FOR A SUCCESSFUL TRANSITION TO INCLUSIVE PRACTICE

Schools, districts, and states that are successfully moving from separate models of schooling to more inclusive models must address many factors. These include policies, attitudes, practices, and school structure, each of which must be understood in an unique way, depending on the school, district, or state implementing the systems change effort. Eight key components for successful inclusive school practices are presented next.

Establishing Vision and Commitment

Schools, districts, or states initiating a transition to inclusive schooling must articulate a vision that defines what is to be achieved through the change process. Although there is some discrepancy in the literature regarding when a vision statement should be established, it must be developed (Fullan, 1993b; Karasoff, Alwell, & Halvorsen, 1992; Schalock et al., 1993). According to Kotter (1990), "Typically a vision is specific enough to provide real guidance to people, yet vague enough to encourage initiative and to remain relevant under a variety of conditions" (p. 36). Vision statements provide the values and beliefs that serve as the foundation for making decisions and implementing changes. Vision statements for inclusive schooling models typically include statements affirming a sense of community, full membership for all students, and respect and valuing of diversity and individual differences.

The vision must align with other ongoing, significant reform or restructuring efforts. A vision that ignores or conflicts with the larger reform or restructuring efforts may compete for resources and attention and will produce little enduring change. The term *inclusive schooling* should be defined clearly and be widely disseminated to avoid misunderstanding among those who will participate in the change process. Linking the vision to other systemwide reform initiatives and clarifying the definition of inclusive schooling promotes communication and understanding of the process among all concerned.

In addition to stating a vision, leaders have a responsibility to fulfill the vision. Specifically, there must be congruence between the actions of key players and the message they communicate (Kotter, 1990). The vision statement must be supported by the entire school community (for example, teachers, administrators, secretaries, custodians, bus drivers, families, students). Therefore, when inconsistencies with the vision (such as "handicapisms," teasing, inappropriate jokes) arise, they are dealt with swiftly and in an educational manner.

Valuing and Providing Professional Development

The transition to an inclusive model will require many people to develop new skills. Therefore, another critical component for successful inclusive schooling is that "cutting-edge" professional development is valued and provided. Onetime, isolated in-service sessions will not prepare staff for new roles and responsibilities needed. Consequently, ongoing and sustained training will be needed. Selection of the specific professional development activities should be guided by the vision statement and definition.

Individual teachers and administrators demonstrate different strengths and weaknesses. Therefore, when professional development is planned, we should ask what skills and support they feel they need to be successful. "Inclusive schooling" initiatives, per se, may be familiar to participants. However, only by individualized needs' assessments can the support and skills be provided to implement changes in a particular community. Many times, predicting what someone will need to feel supported is impossible. Asking teachers and administrators what they need sends the message that all are valued and respected.

The roles and expectations of teachers, support staff, related service providers, and administrators also must be outlined clearly. Actual roles and expectations can be developed in many ways (for example, through collaborative teams, work groups, task forces, or administrative recommendations). Key players who are part of the process will feel more comfortable and more ownership in their new roles. Once expectations and needs are understood, the professional development activities that are needed become apparent and attractive to everyone involved.

As part of the professional development process, schools, districts, or states often seek consultants and mentors who demonstrate the expertise that is needed. Consultants and mentors should have expertise in the change process, knowledge and experience working in inclusive settings, and excellent interpersonal skills. In addition to professional development, consultants also can perform other critical roles that will assist in the change process. For example, a competent consultant who is respected and supported by policy makers can (a) be objective and assist in reorienting perceptions, if necessary, (b) bring new ideas and possible solutions, (c) challenge the behaviors of managers, if necessary, and (d) influence other decision makers (Beer, 1980).

Mentoring strategies have been used very successfully as a means of providing ongoing professional development on a one-to-one basis in the classroom or at the administrative level. Mentoring strategies can be implemented in a variety of ways. For instance, two teachers in the same school can become a mentoring pair, sharing skills with one another; one teacher can serve as a head teacher, assisting a teacher with less experience; a collaborative team can serve the mentoring function with a teacher or administrator; or a general and special educator can co-teach inclusive classes to learn respective approaches. Keys to successful mentoring relationships are easy and consistent access to the mentor and creation of a nonthreatening learning environment for all participants. Arrangements such as these can be very beneficial to teachers and administrators and experienced as an enjoyable and supportive way to learn new skills.

Professional development and support for change are also needed within many institutions of higher education. For example, many college and university faculty have not been trained to implement inclusive practices through a systems change process. Schools and districts seek teachers and administrators, prepared through teacher and leadership preparation programs, who can implement inclusive educational practices successfully. As increasing numbers of new employees come prepared, schools and districts increasingly can focus professional development activities on second-generation issues, including how to make services more efficient and how to improve student outcomes.

Making a Sustained Commitment to Planning

Because inclusive schooling efforts require systemic planning, a commitment must be made to the planning process over time at several levels. The type of planning, at various stages should be influenced by several factors, including (a) the scope of the vision; (b) how far the system has progressed in the change process; (c) the resources available for planning; (d) the skills, styles, and experience of leaders in the system; and (e) the history of the system when seeking to make changes that alter the system's deep structure and culture. Planning that supports major changes requires a great deal of skill. Probably the most difficult skills are (a) offering support that assures that the vision and direction of the systems change effort are maintained, (b) implementing evaluative strategies that permit midcourse corrections, and (c) providing the capacity to revise plans to achieve goals as system components are affected during the change process.

Plans never unfold exactly as they are designed; there are always surprises (Kilmann, 1989). Kilmann (1989) notes that "human nature and human systems do not lend themselves to an entirely predictable path" (p. 42). This is especially true in the case of inclusive schooling efforts because of the multidimensional and interdependent nature of this type of systemic change. Kilmann describes five aspects that must be considered for planned change: (a) culture, (b) management skills, (c) team building, (d) strategy structure, and (e) reward system. He cautions that the process must be implemented in an integrated and flexible manner and that there are no "quick fixes." Only sustained commitment to planning will facilitate lasting change.

Support for planning is also a central issue at the school building and classroom levels. Administrators must ensure a commitment to allocate time for planning at these levels. The amount of time needed for planning will vary greatly. As inclusive schooling becomes more familiar to everyone involved, the amount of time necessary for planning tends to decrease slightly. However, there will always be a need for teachers, aides, related service providers, families, collaborative teams, and administrators to engage in a variety of planning activities (for example, determining and making curriculum or environmental adaptations, solving problem situations before they become crises, communicating progress and concerns). Time for planning should be set aside during normal school hours and sustained throughout the school year. Fragmented planning time should be avoided whenever possible. This is often not easy to do and will require administrative support to ensure that adequate time and resources are provided for planning.

Implementing Collaborative Practices Among School Staff, Service Providers, and Families

Collaborative relationships and interactions will need to occur at all levels—classroom, school building, district, and state—to promote the structural, political, and attitudinal changes for systems making the transition to more inclusive schooling models. Idol, Paolucci-Whitcomb, and Nevin (1986) state that collaboration is an interactive process that enables people with diverse expertise to generate creative solutions to mutually defined problems. Collaboration appears to be most effective when there is a shared agenda among the participants (Graden & Bauer, 1992; Thousand & Villa, 1992), the right players are at the table (Morsink, Thomas, & Correa, 1995), roles of the players are clearly defined (Morsink et al., 1995), and a serious commitment is made to the collaborative process (Graden & Bauer, 1992). These issues are addressed further by Morsink, Thomas, and Correa (1995); Pugach and Johnson (1995); and Sugai and Tindal (1993).

Most believe that collaboration is a skill readily demonstrated. However, true collaboration skills often must be taught and not be assumed to come naturally. Until recently, many educator preparation programs did not teach critical collaboration skills, including (a) how to collaborate effectively, (b) how to work as a team, (c) how to solve problems creatively and effectively, (d) how to work effectively with families from diverse backgrounds, and (e) how to negotiate and resolve conflicts. These are some of the foundational skills that are necessary to ensure a collaborative process. Fox and Williams's (1991) Team Member Checklist (see Table 6.1) can be a useful tool to evaluate one's own participation in a collaborative team meeting.

Collaboration among school staff, related service providers, and families is another critical component of the process. Families must be valued team members and included in the decision making process. Family values, priorities, and time constraints need to be respected, and practices and policies should be "family friendly." Hilton and Henderson (1993) found that teachers with more pre-service training regarding family involvement were more likely to involve parents once they were actually teaching. In addition, professionals need to be careful not to promote actively the expectation of "superfamilies" (Mlawer, 1993).

To support families and school staff adequately, we need to develop collaborative relationships with a variety of community service providers (such as mental health services, rehabilitation services, public health nursing services, community-based physical or occupational therapists). For instance, if a child demonstrates significant behavioral problems in a general education classroom, we may need to collaborate not only with the school psychologist, teachers, administrators, and family members but also with community mental health services. As another example, for a family to be able to raise its child at home and for the child to participate fully in the activities of the neighborhood school, the family may need access to periodic respite care, and the teacher may need two sessions a month with the child's mental health worker to communicate progress and address problems as they arise.

Table 6.1 Team Member Checklist

1. I contributed my ideas.
2. I encouraged others to contribute their ideas.
3. I listened to and expressed support and acceptance of others' ideas.
4. I expressed my feelings.
5. I offered my personal and professional resources to support the team.
6. I asked for clarification and help when needed.
7. I helped the group keep working.
8. I maintained a sense of humor.
9. I recorded group and individual tasks.
10. I enjoyed myself.

SOURCE: From *Best Practice Guidelines for Meeting the Needs of Students in Local Schools,* T. Fox & W. Williams, 1991, Burlington: University of Vermont, Center for Developmental Disabilities.

Embracing Differentiated, Flexible Instructional Approaches

One of the fears of inclusive schooling is that the quality of instruction will diminish for other students. Teachers and administrators have to ensure that meaningful, dynamic, quality, and flexible instruction is being provided to all students served through inclusive schools. Teachers must be proficient in a variety of teaching strategies that support successful inclusive practices, and administrators must support them in their implementation of these strategies. These instructional strategies include, for example, cooperative learning, experiential learning, theme-based projects, incidental teaching, computer-assisted instruction, various peer-assisted and peer-mediated strategies, and co-teaching.

Providing Adequate and Responsible Support

Another component that is consistently identified with successful inclusive schooling efforts is the planning and presence of adequate and responsible supports. Commitment to responsible support necessitates an active process of determining and offering the supports both students and teachers need to be successful. Support includes "people" supports such as classroom teaching assistants, consultants, mentor teachers, and peer tutors. "Natural supports" (that is, those people who would typically be in the given environment) are used whenever possible. Support also includes providing appropriate curriculum, material, equipment, environmental modifications, or enhancements when they are necessary. Friendships and social networks are important elements of the educational process. Therefore, the school program should also provide supports that foster the development of friendships and social networks between students with disabilities and their peers. Support is best defined by the people who request it; therefore, we need to ask students, families, and staff to define the supports they need to be successful and not assume we know what they will need. (For additional information about what constitutes support, see York, Giangreco, Vandercook, & Macdonald, 1992.)

Because fiscal resources frequently and increasingly are limited in American schools, those implementing a systems change effort must be creative in identifying the available supports (for example, people, resources, materials, space) and opportunities to generate additional resources. Those implementing systems change efforts in schools, districts, and states must look carefully at the way resources are currently being used and whether alternative allocations could speed up or enhance change. New collaborative relationships with the community at large must be considered. For example, if additional resources are needed to support students in developing computer skills in the general education classroom, systems could develop a partnership with a community business that is interested in establishing a school volunteer program.

Evaluating Progress and Outcomes Frequently and Systematically

A central question when evaluating the progress and outcomes of the systems change effort is "How will we know when we get there?" An answer will require a review of system status and progress on a recurring and candid basis. From the onset, those involved in the change process should document (a) specifically what is to be accomplished by the end of the change process; (b) indicators of change, including those that examine effects for all students; (c) the types of information needed to measure the indicators; and (d) the methods the system will use to identify any unintended outcomes of the change effort. The evaluation strategy will vary depending on the vision of the system and the types of outcomes the system is interested in measuring, but both formative and summative elements are needed. Examples of questions to be addressed in an evaluation include these:

1. Are goals in the student's Individual Education Plan (IEP) achieved at the desired rate and level?
2. Are students benefiting from inclusive schooling as measured by achievement levels in core subject areas?
3. What feedback is offered by parents, students, and teachers regarding support for inclusive practices?
4. What is the rate of turnover among teachers?
5. Has the student absenteeism rate changed?
6. Have incidents of handicapism, sexism, and racism in the system decreased or increased?

Other areas that may be important to address are (a) whether the rate of change is occurring at a desirable pace, (b) "things we would do differently next time," and (c) whether the evaluation strategy evolved with the transition to an inclusive system. Best practices remain best practices briefly, only until better practices are developed. The outcomes and indicators established initially may not be the most relevant as time passes. Therefore, evaluators and those implementing the changes must incorporate ongoing innovations into the systems change plan and evaluation strategy. This may be difficult for those who initiate the change process. Mechanisms can be put in place to support continuing change and evolution that is consistent with the vision. Advisory committees; mentor schools, districts, or sites; consultants; and feedback sessions can provide ongoing input and can support changes as a system moves to a more inclusive model.

Because of the interdependence of system components, the measurement of outcomes of the change process is a difficult task. As described, the change process is complex, and there is almost always an interactive effect among components. When one critical element is changed, there likely will be significant consequences for the change process. Examples of critical elements include changes in state certification requirements or policies, cuts in resources, turnover in key personnel, and the unanticipated provision of funds for statewide personnel development. Evaluation strategies should incorporate methodologies to determine (a) whether changes and outcomes were the result of the strategies implemented, (b) whether initial changes continue over time, and (c) in what way other systemwide initiatives (for example, school reform or accountability efforts) have influenced and, conversely, been affected by the change effort.

Systems change can be fostered in many ways. When we evaluate and examine change efforts, attempts to generalize procedures to attain comparable outcomes must proceed with caution. What works in one system may not work in another. In addition, we must be willing to acknowledge that mistakes or inefficient practices occurred. There are many gray areas, and given the differences within and across schools, districts, or state cultures, the path of change may be uncharted at various points. Successful systems change efforts are represented by open decision making and self-appraisal, particularly when unanticipated events and obstacles occur. Participants acknowledge setbacks and develop alternatives to move ahead. Systems that embrace effective communication channels support systems and build collaborative relationships not only survive setbacks but also foster problem-solving strategies that may lead to better outcomes. The systems change efforts should support objective and ongoing examination of efforts and obstacles such that teachers and administrators feel supported and share information to solve problems rather than ignore or cover up issues to avoid censure.

Recognizing Change as a Process

Because significant and lasting improvements and changes are difficult to implement today, multidimensional and dynamic approaches are needed. Recognition that change is an ongoing process and not a onetime event helps those involved address the inevitable ebb and flow of progress and the many day-to-day issues that occur. Resources are available to support participants through the change process (Fullan, 1992, 1993a, 1993b; Fullan & Miles, 1992; Fullan & Stiegelbauer, 1991), and this type of information should be shared with all involved with the transition. Fullan (1993b), for example, identifies eight lessons about educational change:

1. You cannot mandate what matters.
2. Change is a journey, not a blueprint.
3. Problems are friends.
4. Vision and strategic planning come later.
5. Individualism and collectivism must have equal power.
6. Neither centralization nor decentralization works.
7. Connection with the wider environment is critical for success.
8. Every person is a change agent. (pp. 125–130)

Information about the change process, as experienced in the change to inclusive school systems, should be incorporated into the ongoing professional development activities provided to teachers, related-service providers, administrators, support staff, families, and faculty at institutions of higher education.

STRATEGIES FOR COPING WITH THE CHANGE PROCESS

Any change is a difficult process for most of us. We feel most comfortable with experiences that are familiar. Consequently, implementing a new model of educating students can produce a great deal of anxiety and fear as well as excitement. Those participating in a systemic change to a more inclusive school system often experience these feelings. As a result, coping with change can be very challenging for everyone involved. Listed here are fourteen strategies or guidelines that can be used by teachers, support staff, administrators, and families to cope better with the change process.

1. *Keep the vision of inclusive schooling ever present.* There will be days when you will wonder whether the stress of change is worth all of the aggravation. Posting your vision will give you some energy as well as keep you centered. Therefore, you may wish to post the vision (or key words of the vision) on your desk, inside your calendar, in the school foyer, in your car, and so forth.
2. *Seek support.* You are not alone, although at times you will seriously doubt this statement. Support may come from surprising places. You may want to maintain a list of allies at various levels (building, district, state, national). Read the list whenever you are feeling overwhelmed. Make some calls to reach out to others who may also be feeling unsupported in their efforts. Do not forget that families of children with disabilities are also needing support and can provide support to you as well.
3. *Be informed.* Read, read, and read some more. Keep abreast of the literature (for instance, current research, effective teaching strategies, examples of where model programs are located). Professional and family organizations can serve as both support and a source of knowledge (for example, conferences, journals, meetings) and experience for you.

4. *Take care of yourself.* You need to be healthy (physically, mentally, spiritually) during the change process. You must be willing and able to say no at times. This will be difficult to do, but you simply cannot be involved in everything that is happening. Choose your activities wisely.
5. *Understand that supporting an inclusive schooling agenda may not help you win any popularity contests.* Being or looking like a martyr is not the answer, either. Martyrdom may bring you some comfort for a while, but it is not an effective or healthy strategy. When discouraged, review suggestions 1 and 2 yet another time.
6. *Be a role model for the kind of teacher or administrator with whom we all would want to work.* When change is occurring, fears can run high. When fears run high, so can tempers. During these stressful times, ask yourself, "Am I being the kind of professional others would want to work with on a daily basis?" If the answer is yes, wonderful. If the answer is no, take a serious look at how you might act differently. Change often comes through personal relationships and modeling behavior. If you are not collaborative and approachable, you may miss the opportunity to support the beginnings of change.
7. *Remember, students are the top priority.* Many temptations will arise to pull you away from the responsibilities of teaching. Consistently model good teaching practices. Do not let your teaching suffer because you are involved and too busy with the change process. If you allow yourself to be distracted and unfocused, it will without a doubt come back to haunt you. For example, the rate of student progress will be affected adversely, and others who look to you as a role model will observe a discrepancy between the goals of inclusive schooling and implementation practices.
8. *When in doubt, always take the high road.* So much is at stake, there is no room for unethical shortcuts. Your integrity is the foundation for credibility. You may be confronted with activities with which you feel professionally uncomfortable; do not be dragged into situations that will result in all participants looking bad. If you are tempted to make an unflattering comment about a colleague who does not share your values about inclusive schooling, think twice. Make your dialogue and behavior evidence of your commitment to respect for all individuals.
9. *Listen, listen, listen.* Often the concerns colleagues or parents are voicing are serious concerns. Effective listening and dialogue support individuals through the change process and increase opportunities for identifying solutions to problems.
10. *Remain flexible.* Most situations are not black and white—gray areas are ever present. Situations can be addressed in numerous ways, and sometimes we simply do not have all the answers. Encourage suggestions from others, and remain open to these suggestions. Be a collaborative team player.
11. *Become fluent in problem-solving and conflict resolution strategies.* Numerous effective problem-solving and conflict resolution strategies are found in the literature or are commercially available. Become knowledgeable about these

strategies and use them. At times, asking a facilitator to mediate the process may be useful. Maintain a list of readily available facilitators who are skilled in these processes.

12. *Maintain a sense of humor.* When was the last time you really laughed? Yes, this is serious business, but we cannot take ourselves too seriously. We must keep a sense about our humor and when to use it. However, during the change process we often forget the importance of humor and laughter. Laughter often eases tension and is restorative. It can also be a bridging experience. Seek opportunities to share laugher.
13. *Be patient and learn to live with chaos.* Change is not easy and it takes time. Look for opportunities to make small inroads and celebrate these successes. Remember, the situation you are experiencing will eventually pass. However, with the unpredictable and complex nature of change, a new situation will no doubt arise. By accepting that chaos is often a critical and necessary part of the change process, you can accommodate chaos more readily.
14. *Keep the faith.* Hundreds of examples of schools have successfully made the transition to inclusive schooling. The process has not been easy. However, the expressed benefits to the children, teachers, and families of these schools indicate that the results are worth the effort.

SOME CONCLUDING THOUGHTS

In the Beginning

In reflecting on the history of inclusive schooling, I find that in many cases school systems have been reluctant to change; thus, persons interested in changing the system have had to push to initiate the beginning of the transition process. These efforts were critical at the beginning of the change effort. Without beginning somewhere, we simply could not change things. Parents felt they could not wait for the promised changes to come. Educators who were seeing the benefits of inclusive schooling could not stand by and wait until the systems were ready to change. Administrators could not wait until they had all of the answers and until the teachers and the community were totally prepared for all of the challenges they were sure to encounter as they suggested a new way of educating all children. Consequently, families and professionals took the risk of beginning the effort.

Although the concept of inclusive schooling was not necessarily a totally new concept and some educators and families were stating it is the right thing to do for many years, until recently there was not a critical mass of people who shared this vision, had the energy to tackle the effort, and felt able "to rock the boat." Often, the effort was met with great resistance. Educators or families who disagreed with the concept of inclusive schooling were the "enemy." Strategies were developed and implemented to "conquer the enemy." Some of these strategies resulted in more children with disabilities educated in general education classes with the supports both the children and the teachers required to be successful. In other situations, battle lines were drawn, and professionals and families representing both sides of the issue immersed themselves in the trenches, securing and strengthening their positions on the battlefield. Kilmann (1990) states, "Strong-willed individuals with competing visions can create war-like atmospheres which squander resources, accomplish little, and exhaust everyone" (p. 89). Some of the battles were won by supporters of inclusive schooling; others were won by supporters of the status quo. Whatever the outcome, battles were typically won at great expense to everyone involved.

The Present and Hope for the Future

With working examples of inclusive schooling in every state and a growing literature and research base, now is the time to seek the implementation of inclusive schools through a planned, systems change process. The search for a vision that reflects common ground for all is a critical step. Also important is the implementation of strategies that address concerns and obstacles and provide a collaborative environment in which support for change is provided. Moving forward will be accompanied by honest dialogue, flexibility, continuing evolution of goals and strategies, highly ethical and professional standards in our interactions, discovered ways to help people develop new skills, and recognition that the transition to an inclusive system occurs within a larger system in which ongoing change and adequate progress must occur.

Is this all possible? Absolutely. Will it take time? Absolutely. The future prospects for all children and the design and delivery of educational services are up to all of us. Any change effort begins with people willing to take a leadership role. I challenge each of you to examine your values and beliefs and become actively involved in the process of change to ensure that the future of our nation's children is bright and one in which all children feel a sense of belonging and purpose.

REFERENCES

Beer, M. (1980). *Organization change and development: A systems view.* Glenview, IL: Scott, Foresman.

Elmore, R. F., & McLaughlin, M. W. (1988). *Steady work: Policy, practice and the reform of American education.* Santa Monica, CA: Rand.

Fox, T., & Williams, W. (1991). *Best practice guidelines for meeting the needs of students in local schools.* Burlington: University of Vermont, Center for Developmental Disabilities.

Fullan, M. G. (1992). *Successful school improvement: The implementation perspective and beyond.* Philadelphia: Open University Press.

Fullan, M. G. (1993a). *Change forces: Probing the depth of educational reform.* New York: Falmer.

Fullan, M. G. (1993b). Innovation, reform, and restructuring strategies. In G. Cawelti (Ed.), *Challenges and achievements of American education* (pp. 116–133). Alexandria, VA: Association for Supervision and Curriculum Development.

Fullan, M. G., & Miles, M. B. (1992). Getting reform right: What works and what doesn't. *Phi Delta Kappan, 73*(10), 744–752.

Fullan, M. G., & Stiegelbauer, S. (1991). *The new meaning of educational change.* New York: Teachers College Press.

Graden, J. L., & Bauer, A. M. (1992). Using a collaborative approach to support students and teachers in inclusive classrooms. In S. Stainback & W. Stainback (Eds.), *Curriculum considerations in inclusive classrooms: Facilitating learning for all students* (pp. 85–100). Baltimore: Brookes.

Greiner, L. E. (1967, May–June). Patterns of organizational change. *Harvard Business Review,* pp. 119–128.

Hilton, A., & Henderson, C. J. (1993). Parent involvement: A best practice or forgotten practice? *Education and Training in Mental Retardation, 28,* 199–211.

Idol, L., Paolucci-Whitcomb, A., & Nevin, A. (1986). *Collaborative Consultation.* Austin, TX: PRO-ED.

Karasoff, P., Alwell, M., & Halvorsen, A. (1992). *Systems change: A review of effective practices.* San Francisco: California Research Institute.

Kilmann, R. H. (1989). *Managing beyond the quick fix: A completely integrated program for creating and maintaining organizational success.* San Francisco: Jossey-Bass.

Kotter, J. P. (1990). *A force for change: How leadership differs from management.* New York: Free Press.

McDonnell, A., & Hardman, M. (1989). The desegregation of America's special schools: Strategies for change. *Journal of the Association for Persons with Severe Disabilities, 15,* 68–74.

Mlawer, M. (1993). Who should fight? Parents and advocacy expectation. *Journal of Disability Policy Studies, 4,* 105–116.

Morsink, C., Thomas, C., & Correa, V. (1995). *Interactive teaming: Consultation and collaboration in special program.* New York: Macmillan.

Pugach, M. C., & Johnson, L. J. (1995). *Collaborative practitioners, collaborative schools.* Denver: Love.

Regional Resource and Federal Centers Program. (1993). *Education reforms and special education: The era of change for the future.* Plantation: South Atlantic Regional Resource Center, Florida Atlantic University.

Ryndak, D. L., Downing, J. E., Jacqueline, L. R., & Morrison, A. P. (1995). Parents' perceptions after inclusion of their children with moderate or severe disabilities. *Journal of the Association for Persons with Severe Handicaps, 20,* 147–157.

Sailor, W. (1991). Special education in the restructured school. *Remedial and Special Education, 12,* 8–22.

Schalock, M., Alberto, P., Fredericks, B., & Dalke, B. (1993). The house that TRACES built: A conceptual model of delivery systems and implications for change. *Journal of Special Education, 28,* 203–230.

Senge, P. (1990). *The fifth discipline.* New York: Doubleday.

Sugai, G. M., & Tindal, G. A. (1993). *Effective school consultation: An interactive approach.* Pacific Grove, CA: Brooks/Cole.

Thousand, J., & Villa, R. (1992). Collaborative teams: A powerful tool in school restructuring. In R. Villa, J. Thousand, W. Stainback, & S. Stainback (Eds.), *Restructuring for caring and effective education* (pp. 73–108). Baltimore: Brookes.

Tye, B. B. (1987, December). The deep structure of schooling. *Phi Delta Kappan, 69,* 281–284.

U.S. Department of Education. (1995). *Annual report to Congress.* Washington, DC: Author.

York, J., Giangreco, M. F., Vandercook, T., & Macdonald, C. (1992). Integrating support personnel in the inclusive classroom. In S. Stainback & W Stainback (Eds.), *Curriculum considerations in inclusive classrooms: Facilitating learning for all students* (pp. 101–116). Baltimore: Brookes.

7

Assessment and Adaptation of the Student, Instructional Setting, and Curriculum to Support Successful Integration

TONI VAN LAARHOVEN
MARTHA COUTINHO
TRACI VAN LAARHOVEN-MYERS
ALAN C. REPP

The Individuals with Disabilities Education Act (IDEA) provides that "specially designed instruction" be implemented to meet the unique needs of students with disabilities. Additionally, it requires that students with disabilities are educated to the maximum extent possible with students without disabilities. Known as the Least Restrictive Environment (LRE) requirement, these procedures ask that students with disabilities be given supplementary services and aides in order to succeed in general education environments. Planning and providing appropriate adaptations to promote efforts to maintain students with disabilities within integrated environments and to reintegrate students previously served through separate arrangements are necessary. Selecting the appropriate adaptations requires assessment of the student, the instructional setting, and the curriculum.

The goal of this chapter is to provide a framework for determining how to meet the needs of students with mild, moderate, or severe disabilities in the LRE. Specifically, we propose a framework for planning and implementing instruction within integrated environments that culminates in a match between the individualized needs of students with disabilities and the educational services provided. The approach is represented by (a) ongoing assessment of the student, educator, setting, and the curriculum and, based on the assessments, (b) the selection of interventions and adaptations that meet requirements for successful integration.

A FRAMEWORK FOR ASSESSING AND ADAPTING VARIABLES RELATED TO THE STUDENT, TEACHER/SETTING, AND CURRICULUM

Designing instruction that leads to successful adult outcomes underlies the provision of a quality education for students with disabilities. Providing meaningful instruction within the context of integrated educational arrangements is a priority for all students with disabilities. As provided for in IDEA, teams composed of educators, related service providers, and parents are responsible for planning an Individual Education Plan (IEP) that supports services provided in integrated environments. Identifying meaningful educational opportunities requires (a) coordinated assessment of the student, teacher/setting, and curriculum; (b) identification of the existing match among the student, the instructional setting, and curriculum; (c) selection of interventions and adaptations consistent with the student's skill or knowledge, teacher/setting, and curriculum needed to support successful integration and outcomes; and (d) implementation of the interventions and/or adaptations. Figure 7.1 summarizes the approach.

As part of the assessment process, the team assesses the opportunity for integration in the educational setting (for example, school, community) to identify factors that will enhance or prevent successful integration of students. Throughout, the focus is "student driven"—that is, guided and evaluated with respect to

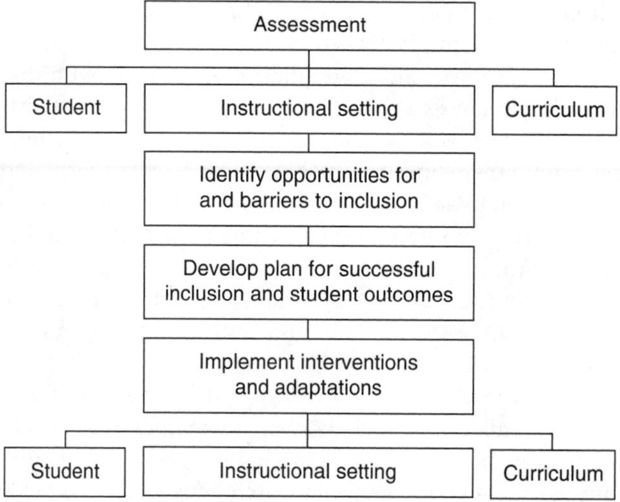

FIGURE 7.1 A Framework for Assessing and Adapting Variables Related to the Student, Teacher/Setting, and Curriculum

the individual goals and the specific accommodations needed to prepare students with mild or severe disabilities for adult life.

Assessment of the Student

Assessment determines current levels of functioning with respect to the skills, behaviors, and knowledge relevant for success from preschool through the school years and into adult life. Typically, these competencies are reflected in the goals established in the IEP or the Individual Transition Plan (ITP) for each student. Assessment of the student should be closely related to the current curricula, instructional techniques, and settings in which instruction is expected to occur. Goals typically represent one or more of the following domains (with examples in parentheses): (a) academic/functional academics (skills in reading, mathematics, science, money handling, time management, language arts, and so forth), (b) adaptive behavior (social skills and adaptive behaviors necessary for learning and succeeding in classroom, home, or community settings), (c) vocational skills (work habits, finding jobs, specific job skills), (d) domestic or daily living skills (self-care, meal planning, budgeting), (e) community skills (shopping, banking, recreation/leisure options), (f) recreation/leisure (extracurricular activities, clubs, hobbies), and (g) embedded skills (knowledge and use of learning strategies, communication skills, motor skills). These domains encompass most aspects of life and are intended to guide instruction that will prepare students to succeed in life after school (Brolin, 1992; Brown, Branston-McLean, Baumgart, Vincent, Falvey, & Schroeder, 1979; Ford, Schnorr, Meyer, Davern, Black, & Dempsey, 1989).

Several different assessment approaches may be implemented to determine priority educational goals for students with disabilities. Assessment strategies should provide for the collection of both norm-referenced and criterion-referenced information. Norm-referenced assessments often are represented by an individual intelligence test, standardized achievement test, or domain-specific achievement or process battery (*Key Math-R,* see Connolly, 1988; *Wechsler Intelligence Scale for Children,* Wechsler, 1974; *Woodcock Reading Mastery Test—Revised,* Woodcock, 1987; *Woodcock-Johnson Psychoeducational Battery—Revised,* Woodcock & Johnson, 1989). Norm-referenced measures indicate the relative skill levels of students as compared with those of same-age students or other relevant norm groups. This information helps identify a student's overall strengths and weaknesses, and it guides more detailed assessments needed to develop instructional plans for integrated educational environments. The additional assessments typically are criterion referenced (that is, information indicates the student's level of performance with respect to an earlier point in time), a standard (for example, a National Education Goal), or a particular domain (such as math computation).

To support instructional planning for placement within integrated environments, criterion-referenced assessment strategies should emphasize both formal (for example, *Brigance Diagnostic Inventories,* Brigance, 1980) and informal criterion-referenced assessments (for instance, teacher-developed informal measures or performance assessments). Curriculum-based assessment (CBA) is a criterion-referenced approach that may be implemented in a formal or informal manner. Curriculum-based measurement, a form of CBA, incorporates a formal methodology that determines how well a student is performing within a given curricular area (Deno, 1985). The objectives of the curriculum are used to assess and evaluate student progress through brief repeated testing and/or observations. By using CBA approaches, educators can determine the current functioning levels of students in relation to the curriculum being used. Particularly when supported through computer-based applications, CBA provides specific information related to instructional placement, diagnosis of specific student strengths and weaknesses, and ongoing assessment of student progress in academic areas such as reading, mathematics, and spelling (Fuchs & Allinder, 1993; Fuchs, Fuchs, & Hamlett, 1993). This type of assessment procedure is extremely useful in integrated environments because it allows direct measurement of student progress within the current curriculum (Fuchs, Deno, & Mirkin, 1984; Fuchs & Fuchs, 1986a). For example, if students are experiencing difficulty with curricular content, the educator can provide additional instruction or individualized adaptations that will ensure success.

Curriculum-based assessment can be used for any curriculum area. For instance, Brolin (1992) developed CBA instruments that measure life skills of students in special education. These assessment batteries coincide with the *Life Centered Career Education Program* (LCCE). The LCCE is a curriculum that emphasizes the competencies associated with daily living, personal-social, and occupational skills. Information from the assessment generates outcome goals and instructional objectives for individual students and suggests relevant areas of instruction. Because students with disabilities do not make satisfactory progress in many unadapted regular education curricula, teams must select relevant educational goals and identify adaptations that can be embedded within a regular education setting. Overall, the curriculum should represent one that leads to self-sufficiency and preparedness in adult life.

The Syracuse Community-Referenced Curriculum Guide (Ford et al., 1989) is an excellent resource for students with moderate to severe disabilities. This guide offers a functional curriculum that can be incorporated into the curriculum of a regular school. It provides scope and sequence charts for academic, daily living, vocational, community, recreation/leisure, and embedded skills. These charts are valuable in assisting educators in identifying relevant educational goals that match the needs of the student in integrated environments. Through ongoing assessment, educators can monitor student progress and plan instruction accordingly.

Increasingly, assessment strategies may also include performance and authentic assessments. Performance assessments are those that require students to construct a response, allow teachers opportunities to observe the thinking and learning process of students, and represent tasks reflecting real-world requirements (Office of Technology Assessment, 1992). Performance assessments may be particularly relevant when seeking to enhance the integration of students with disabilities because of the emphasis on what students can "do," not just know, and reliance on tasks that are needed to function successfully in real-world environments. There are many questions about performance and authentic assessments (for example, regarding the technical characteristics, design of scoring rubrics, and types of assessment decisions that are possible). However, the limitations of traditional assessments, particularly paper-and-pencil tasks, and the goals of education reform in both regular and special education have led to increasing experimentation and use of performance assessments by both special and regular educators at the classroom and system (statewide) level. Resources are becoming increasingly available to assist educators seeking to design performance assessments (Council for Exceptional Children, 1994; Hart, 1994).

Success in integrated school, community, and, ultimately, adult environments depends on the demonstration of adaptive behavior as well as academic and occupational skills. Assessment of the student, therefore, also examines behaviors that may be needed or interfere with services provided in integrated settings. Students who engage in problem behavior pose a challenge for both regular and special educators. To be successfully integrated, students must adapt to the behavioral expectations of the setting. In a classroom, for example, typically students are expected to sit quietly in their seats and comply with teacher requests. Some students may have skill deficits in the area of social competence (Epstein & Cullinan, 1987). Assessment procedures should be conducted to identify specific social skills that may require remediation.

Several different measures can be used to assess social functioning, including adaptive behavior scales, rating scales, checklists, or interviews that are completed by parents, teachers, or the student (Korinek & Polloway, 1993). Direct observations of students in naturalistic settings, including job or work experience environments, should be conducted to verify the results of more formal testing and to identify specific skill deficits in relevant environments. In some instances, students may be asked to respond to specific social situations that are presented in a simulated format (Korinek & Polloway, 1993). This procedure may assess how students might respond in environments that are not directly observable to the evaluator. Once specific skills are identified, instruction can be planned. Providing social skills instruction will enhance the likelihood of successful integration of students within educational as well as vocational environments.

Functional assessment is another very useful technique that yields possible reasons for problem behavior and guides educators toward an intervention based on the cause (Repp, Felce, & Barton, 1988). Functional analysis procedures assist in the identification of variables within the environment that may occasion or maintain problem behavior (for example, easy versus difficult tasks, attention/no attention, escape from tasks, active versus passive tasks) (Cooper, Wacker, Thursby, Plagmann, Harding, & Derby, 1992; Dunlap, Kern-Dunlap, Clarke, & Robbins, 1991; Kern & Dunlap, in press; Lalli, Browder, Mace, & Brown, 1993; Mace, Lalli, & Lalli, 1991; Repp & Karsh, 1994). Once these variables are identified, interventions aimed at controlling these variables can be initiated.

A helpful tool that can be used to assess student behavior in educational settings is the *Functional Assessment and Program Development for Problem Behavior: A Practical Handbook* (O'Neill, Horner, Albin, Sprague, Storey, & Newton, 1997). This guide contains an interview form that can be completed by members of a transdisciplinary team, a student-directed interview form, a data sheet for conducting direct observations of the student, instructions for conducting environmental manipulations, and other forms for summarizing data and planning interventions. The interview form helps identify possible reasons for problem behavior. It also assists team members in identifying possible environmental variables that may be maintaining problem behavior. For example, some students may have difficulty when the schedule changes or their routine is upset. This information is extremely valuable for staff members to know so that interventions can be planned based on these findings. For instance, staff could provide structured routines for the student and could inform the student when there will be changes in the schedule to reduce the occurrence of maladaptive behavior. This information could also assist educators in identifying instructional environments that would enhance or hinder integration. An unstructured educational environment may not be the best match for this particular student, particularly if activities are very different from day to day.

Assessment of Educator and Setting

A number of variables affect the probability with which students with disabilities will maintain adequate rates of progress within integrated settings. Assessment procedures also should be conducted on environmental factors present in the instructional setting to achieve a match between the educational needs of the student and the integrated environment in which services are provided. Munk and Repp (1994), for example, have identified several instructional variables that can be modified to control or reduce problem behavior in integrated instructional settings. Some of these include student choice of task, variation in task, pacing of instruction, interspersal of high probability of success tasks, and reducing the difficulty of the task. Specific variables are manipulated in a hypothesis-testing format to determine their influence on problem behavior during instruction.

Educators can plan lessons with this information to reduce the likelihood of maladaptive behavior. Assessing both student responding within different curricular areas and across different instructional contexts can provide valuable information for enhancing the integration of students in regular education settings.

Assessment of educators and integrated environments also can be done using ecological inventories. Ecological inventories or environmental analyses are assessments of environments where students are currently receiving instruction or where they will receive instruction in the future (Brown, Branson, et al., 1979). The results provide educators with a list of activities and specific skills that are required to function successfully within a given environment (Sailor & Guess, 1983). Ecological inventories are typically completed by educators who observe nondisabled persons performing all of the skills within the targeted environment or through a survey that is completed by persons knowledgeable of the expectations required in the environment (Wilcox & Bellamy, 1982). These inventories can be completed in any environment where the student will be expected to perform targeted skills (for example, community, home, and school settings).

Fuchs, Fuchs, and Fernstrom (1993) used ecological inventories to conduct environmental assessments of mainstreamed math classes. In their approach, ecological inventories were used within the context of transenvironmental programming (Anderson-Inman, 1981, 1986), a conservative procedure for reintegrating students into general education settings. The ecological inventories were composed of classroom observations and teacher interviews. For the classroom observations, three setting dimensions were assessed: physical environment (for example, number of students, noise level, small-group areas), teacher behavior (such as frequency and quality of praise, instructional pacing, monitoring of student work, tolerance for student movement), and rules and procedures (for instance, rules used in the classroom and how they were communicated). During the interviews, teachers were asked to describe their overall behavioral expectations and expectations for academic work (for example, cooperative peer interaction, use of "appropriate language"). They also described their grouping patterns (large, small, individual), preferred pedagogic style (lecture versus interactive), and their use of various instructional strategies (for example, seat work, peer tutoring, self-instruction). Additional information gathered included the type of guidance given to students (oral direction, written or posted information), amount of chalkboard use, the nature of assignments and homework given, and the names of the text and supplemental materials used. This information was used in conjunction with curriculum-based measurement of student progress to formulate plans for the reintegration of students with disabilities.

The information gathered from ecological inventories can be used to determine the match between current students' skills and the skills expected or necessary in the integrated environment. The process also identifies possible barriers for successful integration. Once barriers or problem areas are identified, they can be addressed through direct interventions with the student and, if necessary, the use of additional supports, adaptations, or modifications in the environment. However, another important variable to consider when planning for integration is the curriculum that is being used in the integrated environment.

Assessment of the Curriculum

Curriculum plays a major role in determining how successful students with disabilities will be in general education classrooms. In the past, students with disabilities have been removed from general education classes because of their inability to progress at a satisfactory rate through a standard educational curriculum. For this reason, assessment should be conducted for the curriculum areas that a student will be expected to master. In some cases, a student will be expected to master all of the content. Another student may be expected to master only some of the goals specified in the scope and sequence of the curriculum. As before, curriculum-based assessment techniques can assist educators in determining what skills and knowledge have been mastered, whether prerequisite skills must be taught in order to achieve satisfactorily, and relative rates of progress.

Areas for which the relevance and suitability of the curriculum should be assessed include (a) the curriculum goals (are the curriculum goals compatible with the student's individualized goals; does the student have the skills required to complete the objectives within the curriculum?), (b) the reading level of the text and supplementary materials (is the student reading at the grade level presented in the text, and can the student understand the vocabulary used?), (c) the presentation of material (are skills and knowledge taught through rule-based or discovery methods; are the provisions made for practice completed through in-class activities, discussion, and homework; is student competency addressed through traditional grading methods or through performance assessments?), and (d) the relevance of curriculum in meeting transition goals (will the curricular content assist the student's transition from preschool to first grade; is the eleventh grade "general track" curriculum relevant to the student's functioning in adult life?).

Several of the questions posed throughout the curriculum assessment process are answered in a straightforward manner. For instance, identifying the curriculum goals, determining the reading level of the materials, and identifying the way in which materials are presented, can be accomplished with relative ease. Determining the relevance of the curriculum in meeting transition goals and providing integrated opportunities for learning to occur, however, require much more assessment and thoughtful planning, particularly at the secondary level. Throughout the assessment and planning process, teams must reconcile the relevance of the curricular goals in a particular environment (for example, a tenth-grade mainstream world cultures class); the particular transition and outcome goals established for a student with a mild, moderate, or severe disability; and the desire to provide educational services in integrated school and community environments.

Assessment of the curriculum should support the many transitions that occur throughout the school careers of students with disabilities. Often, transition means something different to students, parents, teachers, counselors, administrators, and the general public. The term *transition,* as used within the field of special education, refers to the movement from one educational environment to another (Polloway & Patton, 1993a). The transitions that are made in special education can be conceptualized as being either vertical (movement throughout educational environments across the life span) or horizontal (movement between the special education–regular education settings) (Polloway, Patton, Smith, & Roderique, 1991). Important vertical transitions for students with special needs might include preschool transition, middle school transition, high school transition, and transition from school to community.

When determining the relevance of curricular areas to a student's life, one must realize that each student is in school on a time-limited basis. The real test of what has been taught is how useful it is once students leave the program (Polloway & Patton, 1993a). Educators must consider future outcomes and be sensitive to the subsequent environments in which students will need to adapt and function.

During the preschool years, much of the curricular emphasis focuses on experiential activities. Language arts, social skills, self-care, creative arts, fine-/gross-motor skills, and academic areas are often presented in a "hands-on" fashion. Students with disabilities are generally able to participate successfully in this learning environment. However, educators must consider the type of instruction that will occur in the next learning environment. During the first grade, for instance, instruction begins to shift more toward basic academic skills, and the behavioral expectations become more stringent (for example, students are expected to spend more time in their seats).

Few question that an academic focus is integral in the education of students with mild to moderate disabilities during the elementary school years. As students reach middle and high school, however, teams must carefully evaluate the continuation of only that focus for some students. Academic instruction for individuals not bound for postsecondary educational settings should shift to include a school-to-work orientation and more functional, practical, and applied instruction (Polloway & Patton, 1993b).

Schloss and Sedlak (1986) describe curriculums as being either developmental (sequenced by students' chronological age or developmental level) or functional (crucial skills or behaviors required for independent, normalized, adult living). The authors suggest that a developmental curriculum should be used if the student (a) acquires new skills fairly efficiently, (b) keeps pace or is only slightly behind the level of his or her peers, (c) spends a substantial part of the school day engaged in instruction, and (d) will receive several years of instruction before graduation. They also recommend that a functional curriculum should be used if the student (a) has significant difficulty learning new tasks, (b) has not kept pace with his or her peers in the total number of skills acquired, (c) is engaged in instructional activities for a very small portion of the day, and (d) is approaching graduation.

As students move from preschool through environments, the course content of the curriculum tends to shift from basic, concrete skills to more involved, abstract skills. This shift from easier to more difficult content can create a larger gap between student capabilities and the curriculum requirements. For instance, students are no longer learning to read; rather, they are reading to learn. The relevance of the curriculum in meeting the needs of the students prior to their exit from high school settings must be evaluated carefully. High school graduation requirements and other factors determining course selection must relate to future plans for postsecondary education, vocational training, integrated employment (including supported employment), continuing education, adult services, independent living, or community participation (IDEA, Amendments, 1990, Section 602[A], 20 U.S.C. 1401[A]). The settings that provide the best opportunities for integration and that allow IEP and ITP objectives to be addressed may be expected to extend beyond traditional classroom to vocational, job site, and community environments.

The transition from school to community has received the most attention from professionals in the field. The initial focus on transition was largely a response to the alarming data on the high dropout rates of students and the high rates of unemployment and underemployment of adults with disabilities (Will, 1984). The primary vehicle that specifically documents transitional planning is the ITP. With the passage of IDEA, transition planning must be part of a student's IEP. More specifically, IEPs must include

> a statement of the needed transition services beginning no later than age 16 and annually thereafter (and when determined appropriate for the individual, beginning at age 14 or younger), including when appropriate, a statement of the interagency responsibilities or linkages (or both) before the student leaves the school setting. (IDEA Amendments, 1990, Section 602[A], 20 U.S.C. 1401[A])

To assist promoting "linkages" between the high school environment and post–high school environments, the needs identified for the students should include the name of the person, organization, or agency responsible for supplying services after high school as well as the extent of the services provided. If no annual needs are identified or written, an explanation of why they are not addressed must be included on the IEP.

Because of the increasing focus on transition, teams must conduct assessments to determine the relevance and adaptability of curriculum, particularly at the secondary level. The assessment guides the selection of curricular content that accommodates the skill level of the student and is relevant given the subsequent environments in which the student will eventually live and work. In summary, systematic, coordinated assessment of the student, the instructional setting, and the curriculum provides for the development of educational plans based on relevant student goals, current performance in various instructional settings, relevant curricula, and strategies to accommodate opportunities for and barriers to integrated instruction.

DEVELOPING A PLAN FOR SUCCESSFUL INTEGRATION AND STUDENT OUTCOMES

Once assessment information has been collected and analyzed, special and regular educators, the student, parents, and other members of the IEP team determine the match between the current level of functioning of the student and his or her readiness to succeed in the relevant, integrated educational environments.

The information from the assessment procedures guides the determination of the most relevant settings in which instruction is to take place. Figure 7.2 summarizes the specific steps in the development of a plan to support successful integration and student outcomes.

To begin, the team identifies goals for the student. Goals should be prioritized according to student assessment information and should reflect the curricula the student needs to succeed in adult life environments. The team then identifies integrated environments in which goals may be addressed. Environments are also identified for goals that do not appear to be achievable in integrated settings.

When identifying relevant educational environments, the team must consider the following points: (a) students with disabilities should be educated with their same-age peers and should be engaged in age-appropriate activities (Brown, Branston, Hamre-Nietupski, Pumpian, Certo, & Gruenwald, 1979), (b) students with disabilities should be integrated in natural proportions (that is, the same proportion that occurs within the population at large) (Brown et al., 1989), and (c) students with disabilities should be integrated in educational environments that will match or accommodate their individualized needs (based on findings from the assessments, including ecological inventories).

Students should be integrated with their same-age peers so that they will share similar experiences and may develop friendships that will continue throughout their school years and beyond. Selecting age-appropriate environments should be based on the students' chronological age rather than developmental level. For example, some adolescents with moderate or severe disabilities may be functioning at a developmental level similar to that of much younger students. Integrating these students with younger ones does not provide them with age-appropriate social models and will not assist them in making friends. Additionally, students with disabilities should engage in activities that are chronologically age-appropriate. For example, if students are reading below grade level, efforts should be made to locate reading materials that cover similar topics for their age range and have been written at lower reading levels. This will increase the students' interest in the content while reducing the stigma of doing "baby work." Sharing similar experiences and learning similar information will help students acquire common knowledge that fosters socialization with peers.

When identifying integrated environments for students with disabilities, one should follow the principle of natural proportions (Stainback, Stainback, & Jackson, 1992). Students with moderate or severe disabilities make up only a small portion of the population. When integrating these students, educators should try to follow natural proportions so that an overabundance of students with disabilities is not in one class. The same principle holds for integration in community settings. Community training and/or vocational training should be conducted with small groups in a variety of settings.

Assessment-based IEP and ITP goals may be used to identify specific academic, vocational, independent living, behavioral or other interventions. As described in Figure 7.2, team members identify who will provide the services (instruction in solving math problems, speech therapy, and so forth). The team

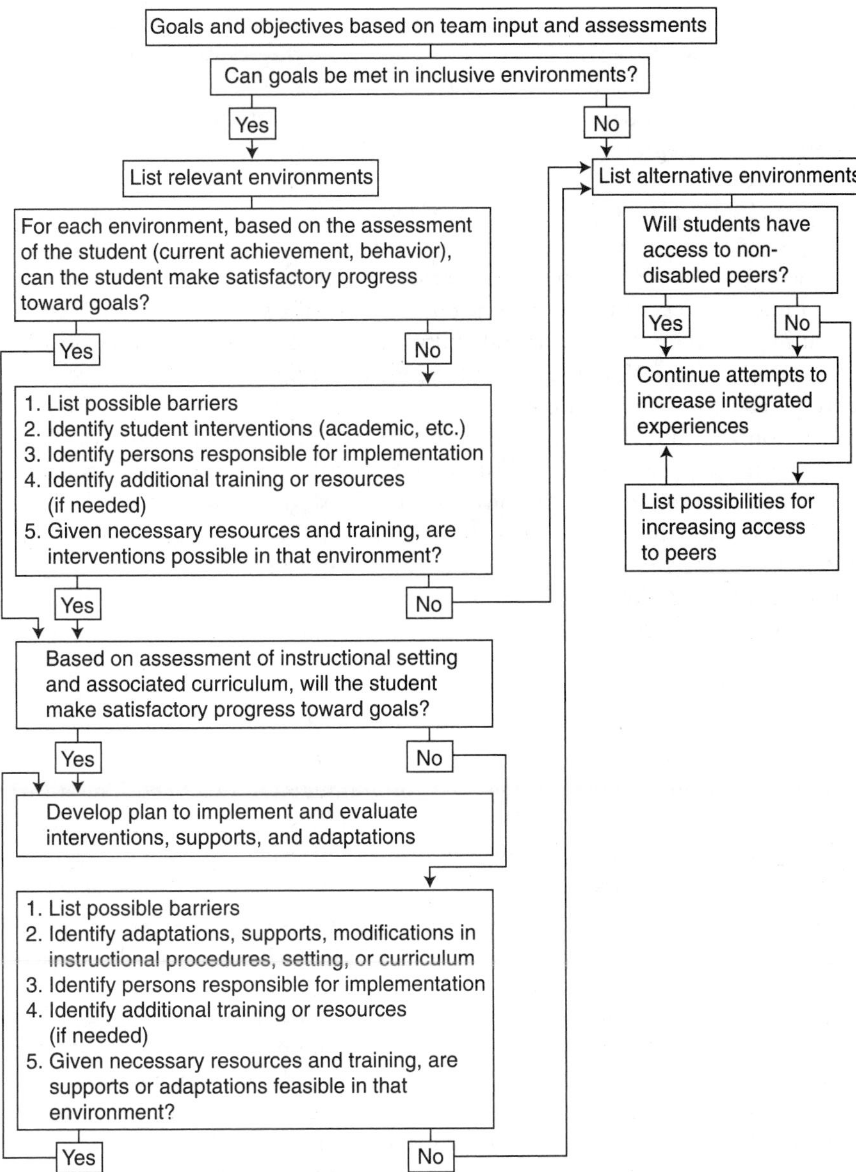

FIGURE 7.2 Steps in the Development of a Plan to Support Successful Integration and Student Outcomes

must also determine where services will be provided. Based on the assessment of the instructional settings, it must evaluate the feasibility of providing these interventions in integrated environments and identify training and additional resources that are needed (for example, an instructional aide). For each goal and relevant environment, the team should consider specific student variables that may enhance or interfere with integration (for example, current level of functioning, behavioral competence) with respect to the results of the assessment of the teacher and setting variables. Fuchs et al. (1993), for instance, have identified several teacher and setting variables that influence the success students with disabilities experience in integrated settings (for example, class size, teacher behavior, behavioral expectations, expectations for academic work, grouping patterns, instructional strategies, type of guidance given, pedagogical style, instructional strategies, nature of homework and assignments). When we compare student skill level with the setting variables, we may be able to identify discrepancies that would impede successful integration. For example, if a student with an attention deficit hyperactivity disorder has difficulty attending to lengthy lectures or problems remaining seated, the team could predict that this student may have problems in classroom environments that use lecture as the primary mode of instruction and in classrooms that require extended periods of seatwork. With this information, team members can identify possible adaptations that could increase successful integration. For instance, (a) the student could be taught a self-monitoring procedure to increase attending skills (Maag, Reid, & DiGangi, 1993), (b) the teacher could increase the amount of active responding during instruction (Munk & Repp, 1994), (c) the teacher could use response cards to increase student participation (Gardner, Heward, & Grossi, 1994), or (d) a support person could assist the general educator in implementing behavior management programs.

Other teacher variables that should be evaluated include (a) the flexibility of the teachers in modifying instruction to support student differences and (b) the philosophical beliefs of the teachers regarding integrated practices. These variables are important because students with disabilities will succeed more readily with teachers who can accommodate individual differences and value integration procedures. Students may have difficulty in classroom settings if the teacher demands that all students master concepts in a similar manner or expects students to perform all the skills required of students without disabilities. In addition, teachers who do not agree with or value integrated practices may not alter the educational environment or may not accept students in their classes. Attempting to place students in these types of environments would be fruitless unless attempts were made to change attitudes and, if necessary, provide training and supports.

Once relevant educational environments based on a match between student's skills and the teacher/setting are selected, team members look at the curricula to determine whether they are relevant and presented so that the student will be able to make satisfactory progress. If they are not able to master curricular content independently, adaptations or supports that assist students in acquiring skills and knowledge will need to be identified. For example, a student with disabilities may have difficulty acquiring concepts in a traditional manner. These students may need to be provided with instruction on learning strategies or may work on individualized objectives within the curriculum. The most crucial component of determining the match between the student and curriculum is that it must be relevant in meeting the individualized goals of the student.

In summary, guided by the student's particular goals and needs, the team should identify specific adaptations applicable to the student, the instructional setting, and the curriculum. Implementation requirements should be determined, and the persons responsible for providing or securing supports should be identified. These may include training, financial resources, transportation, or modifications in the classroom or community facility. A time line for implementation of the plan should then be developed. The plan may represent a gradual increase in opportunities for more integrated educational opportunities as both the student and environment are prepared, or it may reflect a plan to design an entire system that immediately provides for full integration of the student. As indicated in Figure 7.2, team members also search for and identify strategies to increase access to students not identified as disabled.

IMPLEMENTING INTERVENTIONS AND PROVIDING ADAPTATIONS

Successive chapters of this text provide detailed suggestions for interventions and adaptations that may be undertaken to support students with mild, moderate, or severe disabilities at the preschool, elementary, and secondary levels within integrated environments. The following section describes the kinds of adaptations that may be provided to support successful integration and/or reintegration with nondisabled peers in natural educational and community settings. Specifically, the following section will include (a) interventions to support the student, (b) adaptations to enhance the capacity of integrated settings to support student diversity, and (c) adaptations of the curriculum.

Adaptations to Support the Student

When integrating students with mild, moderate, or severe disabilities, we may need some adaptations to teach students the skills they will need to be successful. Some areas for which adaptations and interventions may be developed include (a) instruction in learning strategies, (b) instruction in social skills, (c) procedures for self-monitoring and self-management, and (d) self-advocacy and self-determination. These adaptations to support students directly enhance their capacity to learn effectively within integrated educational environments.

Learning Strategies Instruction A number of strategy approaches are available to assist the student with mild disabilities in acquiring content and succeeding within integrated educational environments (Deshler & Schumaker, 1988; Mercer, 1994). The most important goal of strategies instruction is that the student gain the target content, skill, or information through strategic thinking. A comprehensive approach to strategy instruction is the Strategies Intervention Model (SIM) (Deshler & Lenz, 1989; Lenz, Clark, Deshler, Schumaker, &

Rademacher, 1990). Developed as a secondary intervention model, the programming components of the SIM are the Strategic Curriculum Component, the Strategic Instructional Component, and Strategic Environment Component. Within the Strategic Curriculum Component, for example, are strategies representing "what" will be taught. "Learning Strategies" comprise a group of these and include, for instance, the "Word Identification Strategy," "Paraphrasing Strategy," and "Multipass Strategy." The Strategic Instruction Component designates "how" strategies may be taught and includes a number of procedures that may be implemented by educators within integrated environments to improve the delivery of content for students with mild disabilities. An example of these are the "Content Enhancement Procedures" represented by routines and other procedures teachers may use to convey subject matter in a way that is understood and retained by students (Lenz, Bulgren, & Hudson, 1990).

Many strategy-specific approaches are also available. For example, semantic webs (Anders & Bos, 1984) and semantic feature analysis (Bos & Anders, 1987) represent teaching routines that incorporate a visual organizer to help students with mild disabilities learn important concepts and connect what they already know with what they are learning. Several mnemonic devices, implemented as instructional devices may be used to assist the student with mild disabilities to acquire and remember content (Mastropieri, Scruggs, McLoone, & Levin, 1985). Depending on the specific strategy or overall approach selected (for example, strategy-specific or a comprehensive model addressing curriculum, instructional procedures, and so forth), instruction may be provided within integrated or pull-out environments with application of the skill demonstrated through mastery of current content area knowledge and skills. Advantages of strategies instruction is that it addresses the need of students with mild disabilities to accommodate the demands of regular classroom environments, and, in many cases, procedures may be implemented by regular educators in integrated environments to support students at risk of educational failure (Schumaker & Deshler; 1988).

Social Skills Instruction Persons with disabilities often have more social and behavioral difficulties than most persons in the general population (Patton & Polloway, 1990). Some professionals have argued that providing social skills training is critical to facilitate successful integration in educational settings and to improve outcomes for students with disabilities (Polloway & Smith, 1988). Typically, training is concerned with the development of interpersonal skills that will be appropriate in different environments. Because students with disabilities often have more difficulty acquiring social skills, efforts should be made to provide direct instruction of these skills through effective instructional procedures (Korinek & Polloway, 1993).

Targeted skills for instruction would include those that the student would need to be successful across a wide range of environments. Therefore, efforts should be made to promote generalization and maintenance of these skills through systematic instruction. Bauwens, Hourcade, and Friend (1989) suggest that generalization of social skills could be enhanced through collaboration between general and special educators. Social skills could be taught within general education environments so that learned skills will transfer to integrated environments. Other techniques for teaching social skills include social skills groups (Kamps et al., 1992), peer-mediated interventions (Goldstein, Kaczmarek, Pennington, & Shafer, 1992; Haring & Breen, 1992; Odom, Chandler, Ostrosky, McConnell, & Reaney, 1992; Odom & Strain, 1986), self-management and self-evaluation techniques (Kern-Dunlap, Dunlap, Clarke, Childs, White, & Stewart, 1992; Kern-Koegel, Koegel, Hurley, & Frea, 1992), and video-assisted instruction (Kern-Dunlap et al., 1992; Morgan & Salzberg, 1992). Teaching students how to socialize in an adaptive manner will increase the likelihood that they will succeed and be accepted within integrated educational environments.

Self-Monitoring and Self-Management Procedures Self-monitoring or self-management techniques have been used to increase the independence of students with disabilities in integrated settings. Self-monitoring has been used to enhance on-task responding when students monitor either attention or academic responding (DiGangi, Maag, & Rutherford, 1991). This type of procedure is appealing because it can heighten student independence in a simple and practical way (Lentz, 1988). As a result, this type of student adaptation can be implemented more easily within integrated environments to improve, for example, the attending or academic skills of students with disabilities. For example, Maag et al. (1993) studied the effects of self-monitoring on on-task behavior, academic productivity, and academic accuracy with six students with learning disabilities who were receiving math instruction in general education settings. All of the interventions resulted in improvements in on-task responding; however, self-monitoring academic productivity and accuracy resulted in superior performances.

Self-management procedures are also helpful in increasing independent performances of students with disabilities. These techniques can be used to assist students with performing daily living skills throughout the day. For example, Pierce and Schreibman (1994) effectively taught daily living skills to three students with autism through the use of pictorial self-management procedures. Skills included getting dressed, setting the table, making lunch, doing laundry, making a drink, and making a bed. All students learned to perform these skills in the absence of a treatment provider. In addition, these skills generalized across settings and across tasks. Cuvo, Davis, O'Reilly, Mooney, and Crowley (1992) used written task analyses to serve as textual prompts for students with mild disabilities who were performing functional tasks.

Providing students with written or pictorial representations of sequenced activities can reduce the amount of dependence on staff while increasing independence of the student. For example, self-management procedures could be used to teach students to dress independently in locker rooms, assist students in following their daily schedule, or help students in performing job-related skills. This type of adaptation has practical implications for increasing independent functioning within integrated environments.

Self-Advocacy and Self-Determination Another way to increase the independence of students with disabilities is to promote self-advocacy and self-determination. As defined by Wehmeyer (1992), self-determination is represented by attitudes and abilities that allow students to make choices about their quality of life while not being overly influenced by others. Self-advocacy can provide students with the opportunity to make decisions about what they want to do with their lives while in school and once they graduate. In addition, students can be given an opportunity to communicate their preferences when determining course selection and when making other decisions. By learning self-advocacy skills, students with disabilities may have more control over planning their own future. The LCCE curriculum described earlier (Brolin, 1992), for example, includes a self-determination curriculum package.

Adaptations to Support Educators: Enhancing the Capacity of Integrated Settings to Support Student Diversity

Teaching always has been a complex and demanding career. Current school reform and budget initiatives call on teachers to support an increasingly diverse population of students within the classroom. As a result, educators are searching for effective, feasible alternatives to the practice of pulling students out of the general education classrooms for additional assistance. To support the shift in providing quality education to all students, more and more special education teachers are coming into the general education classrooms to create dynamic, high-energy classrooms that promote increased learning (Friend & Cook, 1992).

Based on the plan developed to support the successful inclusion of the student, several teacher and setting variables may be identified for which adaptations may be needed to accommodate the increasing diversity of students. The following subsections describe examples of strategies and adaptations to support the teacher, including (a) teacher-planning interventions, (b) effective teaching practices, (c) co-teaching, (d) collaboration/consultation, (e) in-class support by other service providers, (f) peer tutoring and cooperative learning, and (g) ongoing professional development. Examples of strategies and adaptations to accommodate the environment will also be included—namely, (a) physical changes, (b) class and group size, (c) paraprofessionals and volunteers, and (d) community-based instruction.

Teacher-Planning Interventions The Unit Planning Pyramid and Lesson Planning Pyramid represent teacher-planning interventions that may be used to help educators focus on what content will be learned by all students, what content will be learned by some students, and how to give all students an opportunity to learn (Schumm, Vaughn & Leavell, 1994; Joint Committee on Teacher Planning for Students with Disabilities, 1995). Teachers use a graphic device (the Planning Pyramid), self-questioning techniques, and a Unit Planning Form. The latter organizes target concepts, instructional strategies, and adaptations; identifies materials and resources; and records evaluation procedures. A Lesson Planning Form is also used to help teachers focus on what will be taught within each lesson of the unit. Teachers consider how the classroom is organized for instruction (for example, class size) and factors at the school level that affect the classroom environment (for example, schedules, holidays).

Another teacher planning intervention that directly supports the successful integration of students with disabilities is the Course Planning Routine (Lenz et al., 1993). Teachers engage in a series of steps to create a course that accommodates a wide range of student academic diversity. The stages of the Course Planning Routine include selecting critical content outcomes (referenced to ten questions all students will be able to answer at the end of the unit), creating course content maps, making decisions to ensure all students are involved as a community of learners, tracking the progress of high-, average- and low-achieving students, and planning and reflecting on instruction throughout the year. Accompanying the Course Planning Routine are the Unit Planning Routine and the Lesson Planning Routine to align decision making at the unit and lesson plan level, respectively. These interventions help teachers dedicate time before instruction occurs to identify the content, strategies, classroom variables, and evaluation procedures that support successful outcomes for students with disabilities within integrated environments.

Effective Teaching Practices Teacher-directed group instruction has received much attention in published literature over the past fifteen years. This type of instruction refers to activities led primarily by the teacher and aimed at meeting a small number of instructional objectives (Hendrickson & Frank, 1993). Support for the effectiveness of these teaching practices with students with disabilities is growing (Sindelar, Espin, Smith, & Harriman, 1990). Research indicates that teacher-directed instruction will assist students with disabilities in experiencing much more educational success (Hendrickson & Frank, 1993; Joyce & Weil, 1986; Montague & Bos, 1986; Paine, Carnine, White, & Walters, 1982; Palinscar & Brown, 1987). Such instruction includes (a) concise lessons with specific objectives and procedures to be followed, (b) modeling through visual demonstration and verbalization, (c) guided practice with semi-independent and independent work under close teacher supervision, and (d) questions and teacher feedback. A brief description of these variables is provided in the next section.

Effective teachers design lessons that are engaging to all students. The specific needs of each student are considered. Effective teachers focus on the objective(s) for each student and the skills necessary for students to succeed. For example, planning may include preparation of task-analyzed or scripted formats developed prior to instruction and used to assist teachers in presenting information clearly and at an appropriate pace (Montague & Bos, 1986; Paine et al., 1982; Schunk & Cox, 1986). Through careful planning, only the relevant features of the task are identified and presented during instruction. Sorting out relevant features of instruction will help students with disabilities focus on the critical features of the task and will reduce confusion.

Modeling through demonstration and "thinking out loud" has been used as an effective instructional technique. Following direct instruction of steps involved in a learning process, teachers model each step within the problem while thinking out loud (that is, verbalizing each step) (Schunk & Cox, 1986). Another form of modeling, called the Demonstration Plus Permanent Model (Blankenship & Baumgartner, 1982; Rivera & Smith, 1987), involves providing a step-by-step verbalization of the task and a permanent visual model. Both forms of modeling have been found to improve student performance. Implementing these types of procedures will provide students with clear examples of how a task is performed and will assist them in learning the task.

Guided practice is an instructional technique used to allow students to practice a new skill with teacher guidance. It differs from modeling in that students actually work through tasks while the teacher guides them through each step. This approach allows students to "learn by doing" and assists students with disabilities in acquiring new skills. In addition, teachers are given the opportunity to observe how students perform the skill, which can help them determine whether additional instruction is necessary. Students receive feedback while they perform the task and chances to practice the skill without practicing errors. Once students are proficient, guidance is faded systematically. The students eventually practice the behavior without assistance while receiving feedback from the teacher when necessary.

The importance of providing students feedback and increasing academically engaged time has received much attention in current literature. Maintaining a brisk teaching pace (Silbert, Carnine, & Stein, 1990), using questions effectively (Rosenshine, 1983), minimizing student errors (Neef, Iwata, & Page, 1980; Wolery, Bailey, & Sugai, 1988), maximizing choral responding (Heward, Courson, & Narayan, 1989), and monitoring student progress on a continuous basis (Fuchs & Fuchs, 1986a) are all effective teaching practices that highlight the use of feedback and promote engagement of all students during small-group instruction and independent practice (Hendrickson & Frank, 1993; Karsh & Repp, 1992; Repp & Karsh, 1992). These variables have been effective with students with and without disabilities. Incorporating feedback and many opportunities to respond will increase the likelihood that students with disabilities will acquire skills successfully.

Co-teaching A teaching team can be defined as an organizational and instructional arrangement of two or more members of the school and community who divide planning, instructional, and evaluation responsibilities for the same group of students on a regular basis for an extended period of time (Thousand & Villa, 1990). Friend and Cook (1992) highlight several ways in which co-teaching takes place: (a) one teacher leads instruction for the group while the other circulates around the room, paying particular attention to the needs of the students with disabilities; (b) the teachers divide the class in half and teach the same information to smaller groups; (c) one of the teachers provides remediation for students who need it, while the other offers enrichment for the rest of the class; or (d) both teachers teach the group simultaneously (one models a skill while the other describes it, both role-play for the students, or both share a presentation).

Co-teaching provides students with an educational environment that lends itself to an increased potential for individualized instruction to meet the needs of all students. With multiple instructors, there is increased grouping and scheduling flexibility (Olsen, 1968), greater opportunities to take advantage of specialized knowledge and instructional approaches of the team members (Bauwens et al., 1989), and a higher teacher-student ratio that allows for more immediate attention to student needs and more active student participation (Thousand & Villa, 1990).

Collaboration/Consultation Professional peer collaboration/consultation is an additional strategy used to meet the needs of a diverse student population. Peer collaboration is a teacher support system that builds on natural relationships many teachers have already established in their schools. Additionally, peer collaboration facilitates the development of alternative educational practices to assist students who are experiencing difficulty (Pugach & Johnson, 1990).

Consultation has been defined in a variety of ways. Harris (1990) thinks of it as a process that enables individuals with differing areas of expertise to work together to plan and conduct educational programs for diverse students who are learning together in integrated environments. To be proficient in the art of collaboration/consultation, one must possess basic skills such as technical expertise, effective communication, and the ability to coordinate instructional services to ensure quality education for all students (Goldstein & Sorcher, 1974; Harris, 1990).

No single educator has all the skills necessary to meet the needs of all students. The people who consult with one another share their expertise with the student and any other individual providing services to that student. This team develops and implements educational programs together (Harris, 1990). They must be willing to listen and learn from one another and to work in a coordinated fashion to provide well-integrated educational services to the student. When done correctly, collaboration/consultation can be a dynamic and worthwhile process that provides more than any one teacher can offer.

In-Class Support by Other Service Providers Increasingly, special educators are beginning to assume the role of support facilitators as they work as co-teachers and collaborators/consultants in general education classrooms. Support facilitators are often responsible for (a) building a sense of ownership among school personnel and community members; (b) seeking extra support (for example, additional teaching assistants, volunteers, state or federal grants); (c) establishing peer support committees within general education classrooms; (d) organizing teacher and student assistance teams; (e) serving as a co-teacher; (f) analyzing and adapting curriculum as needed; (g) locating specialists, materials, and equipment; (h) arranging for sharing of information between the home and the school; and (i) fostering professional peer collaboration (Stainback & Stainback, 1990a). This list of responsibilities is not intended to be all-inclusive or to peg the support facilitator as the sole provider of support to educators and students in integrated environments. There are specialists or consultants in speech, hearing, vision, physical therapy, reading, technology, and behavior management. The students themselves, teachers, job coaches, teaching assistants, volunteers, parents, and other school personnel also offer a wide range of expertise. The job of the support facilitator is to assist in organizing and coordinating these resources into a comprehensive support network for students and teachers in integrated settings (Stainback & Stainback, 1990b).

Peer Tutoring and Cooperative Learning Peer tutoring and cooperative learning strategies fit well with the current movement to individualize instruction and to support and meet the needs of all students. Evidence of the instructional, social, and cost-effective benefits of peer tutoring is mounting. The practice of tutoring allows for increased academically engaged time and for more repetition and practice on individualized academic tasks (Jenkins & Jenkins, 1981). This strategy supports research that stresses the need for repeated practice on individualized tasks (Rosenshine & Stevens, 1986) and the importance of increased opportunities to respond (Hall, Delquadri, Greenwood, & Thurston, 1982).

There are several designs of tutoring programs. Each can be adapted in terms of student age, subject matter, school organization, and teacher preference (Gartner & Lipsky, 1990). Two examples of peer tutoring include classwide student tutoring teams (Delquadri, Greenwood, Whorton, Carta, & Hall, 1986; Slavin, Karweit, & Madden, 1989) and cross-age tutoring programs (Jenkins & Jenkins, 1981).

In cooperative learning environments, positive student interdependence is encouraged. Goals are structured so that students learn to be concerned about how well all members of the group have learned the skills or concepts (Hendrickson & Frank, 1990). Each member of the group is accountable for helping bring success to the entire group. One way to ensure that all students of the group are cooperating is to assign various roles within the group (for example, leader, checker, praiser) (Sapon-Shevin, 1990). Each of these roles would be taught and rotated among all group members. Cooperative learning arrangements can be adapted to support all students in settings that include small-group instructional activities and cooperative instructional or recreational game activities (Sapon-Shevin, 1990). These instructional procedures are arranged to ensure that students will acquire skills that match their level of functioning.

Ongoing Professional Development An additional strategy for supporting school personnel, family members, students, and community members is to provide educators with strategies, information, and exposure to specific practice that underlie successful integration practices (Thousand & Villa, 1990). Through participatory and hands-on workshops, guest speakers, and observation of practices in place at other schools, teachers can come together to express concerns and to learn about best practices on a number of current topics. Potential topics might include crisis intervention, classroom management, direct instruction, strategies instruction, collaborative teaching, transition, and community-based instruction.

Strategies and Adaptations to Accommodate the Environment

Physical Changes The classroom environment is a critical determinant of successful teaching and learning. Although the physical environment is separate from the teacher-student relationship, it is an extension of the teaching-learning paradigm (Polloway & Patton, 1993b). An effective teaching environment facilitates student learning by (a) being aesthetically pleasant; (b) having adequate and appropriate equipment; (c) entailing areas for conducting a variety of instructional and social activities and reinforcement; (d) including instructional adjuncts such as bulletin boards, study carrels, and interest centers; (e) providing optional seating and work surfaces; (f) being barrier-free; and (g) being organized yet flexible (Polloway & Patton, 1993c). Arranging classroom environments in this way will assist in accommodating the learning styles of all students.

Class and Group Size As described earlier in this chapter, the relative success of integration practices is influenced by the provision of effective instruction procedures in the classroom setting. Research highlights the importance of creating an engaging environment that provides each student with several opportunities to respond during instructional activities. A valuable first step in conducting teacher-directed lessons may be to form small groups of students (Carnine, Silbert, & Kameenui, 1990). To support and provide quality small-group instruction, teachers may wish to incorporate others in the classroom environment.

Paraprofessionals and Volunteers The paraprofessional's position (in facilitating integrative practices) is one of support and assistance in a variety of settings (for example, inclusive environments, job sites, community environments) and a number of roles (such as supervising small groups, tutoring individuals). As we now focus on supporting all students within educational and community environments, the need for all significant persons to work together as a team is evident. Additional support persons might include family members, all school personnel, peers, volunteers, student employers, community members, and local businesspeople.

Community-Based Instruction Parents and professional educators have become increasingly aware of the importance of supporting individuals with disabilities in integrated environments. They have also recognized the need to teach functional skills that relate to living in the "real world." For many students, the goal of becoming active participants and contributing members of society may require instruction that cannot be provided in the traditional classroom environment. Alternate environments may need to be selected to accommodate the needs of individual students. Community-based instruction offers students an opportunity to receive direct instruction in a variety of community environments (banks, grocery stores, job sites, and so forth). Students are provided with practical instruction that will assist them in accessing and making their way around their own community once they leave the educational environment (Ford et al., 1989). As students approach graduation, community work experiences and job placements represent important transition goals.

Adaptations of the Curriculum

Some students with disabilities will be able to perform most of the skills required within traditional curriculum areas, whereas others may need the curriculum to be adapted to meet their specific needs. Depending on the skill level of the student and the particular goals, we may need to adapt a curriculum slightly or significantly. The following section has been adapted from Davern and Ford (1989, pp. 252–253).

Adapting the Content Some students may be able to master most of the content within the regular education curriculum. Their goals may be similar to their nondisabled peers. For these students, modifications may need to be made on a lesson-by-lesson basis. For instance, if a lesson requires a lot of reading and the student has difficulty with reading, a tape could be made so that the student could get the information in a different format while still covering the same content. Other students may be required to master only some of the curricular content. For these students, more adaptations or modifications will be required. In this instance, educators need to determine what constitutes the most critical components of the curriculum so that students can master the concepts that are important. Once identified, students could be given guided notes to assist them in focusing on the relevant information. In addition, students could be given homework or practice activities that focus on the content that they are expected to master. This level of adaptation requires more systematic planning to ensure that essential skills are identified and taught effectively.

Some students may not be able to master the skills or content from a particular curriculum area. These students may be able to participate in educational activities that are drawn from the curriculum, but they may be working on embedded skills (motor, social, communication). For instance, a student with severe disabilities may be integrated into music, band, or chorus. Although the student may not have the skills to read music or play an instrument, he or she may be able to participate by working on individualized objectives. For example, if the student has goals involving improving motor, social, and communication skills, he or she may be able to work on these goals by walking with peers to class, activating a pressure switch to tape-record songs for the group, assisting with turning pages, and socializing with students in the class. In this scenario, the student would participate during the class but would be working on specific individualized goals.

Sometimes students will have goals that are more functional in nature. These goals will have relevance to the student's daily functioning both in and out of school. In this case, the goals and objectives would not be drawn from the regular curriculum, as typically offered. Instead, students would work from a curriculum that is more functional in nature. For example, if a student is working on budgeting money, he or she may need to practice budgeting and related skills in applied contexts to make instruction more meaningful. This student may be engaged in a series of activities that revolve around the goal of budgeting. For example, the student could be taught banking skills in community environments. The students may be working on depositing and withdrawing money earned from a cooperative job. They could work on budgeting their money by planning for necessary expenses (for example, lunch money, gas money) and recreational or desired expenses (money to go to the movies, say, or purchasing a new CD or budgeting for a vacation). Problem-solving activities would need to be designed to assist students in determining the best way to budget their money. Math skills would also be taught within this context. Students might be required to balance a checkbook or determine how much interest they will earn in a savings program. All of these skills would assist students in learning skills that they would need to function effectively as adults. These skills are important for all students. At various points, activities would include students with and without disabilities. Nondisabled students would probably need less intensive instruction and could learn these skills on a short-term rotating basis.

Other functional skills may be included within naturally occurring times of the school day (Stainback, Stainback, & Moravec, 1992). For example, students could be taught (a) food preparation and eating skills during lunch, snack, or home economics classes; (b) dressing skills during physical education class; and (c) purchasing skills during lunch and at the school store. In some instances, however, students may require more intensive instruction on these skills than are offered within the routine of a typical school day. Opportunities to practice functional skills would need to be scheduled into the daily routine. For example, a student may have a goal to work on vocational skills. To accommodate the student, a teacher could schedule time for students to engage in classroom jobs while allowing the student with disabilities to have the most opportunities (Ford, Davern, & Schnorr, 1992). Curricular content needs to be presented in a flexible manner to accommodate the needs of all students.

Changing Student Response Requirements to Demonstrate Mastery of Material Some students may have difficulty expressing what they know in response modes that are typically used in school settings (for example, written essays, multiple-choice tests). The response requirements may be problematic and may interfere with student achievement. Changing or modifying response requirements may enhance the student's ability to access or demonstrate knowledge or curricular content. There are several different options for modifying response requirements. For example, some students may have difficulty with written work. In this case, the student may perform better using a word processor that has a spell-check and grammar program or presenting information orally. Other students may have difficulty with paper-and-pencil tests. If the student has difficulty reading or writing answers on the test, it could be presented orally and the student could respond orally or with short answers.

For some students, the only accommodation required may be additional time to complete assignments and tests. If the time required to complete tasks becomes extremely burdensome to the student, educators might consider modifying the requirements by reducing the amount of work within assignments and tests or the number of required assignments. Students who are expected to master only some of the concepts within the curriculum may be given different assignments that are suited to their learning style or preference (for example, making oral presentations, drawing a picture to demonstrate comprehension). The students' skills would be evaluated with different criteria than other class members. Using alternative forms of assessment will also enhance successful integration of students with disabilities. As described earlier, performance and authentic assessments can provide information about what a student can do, not just "knows," with respect to a real-world task.

Using alternative methods of assessment for particular students may require adjustment of the grading system. Typically, students are graded based on normative methods, curved grades, or universal methods (Ford et al., 1992). This type of grading system may adversely affect a student's chances of being successful. Students may need to be evaluated based on their individualized goals. However, grading students based on individualized objectives may yield misleading information when comparing grades across students. For example, some students may master all of the skills required in the curriculum, earning an A. Another student may have had the curriculum adapted significantly and receive the same grade. Although the students received the same letter grade, they did not perform at the same level of proficiency. This issue becomes increasingly problematic when students' grade point averages are used to obtain scholarships or to gain entrance into college. Therefore, school systems should develop a grading policy that is recognized as fair and also facilitates communication between and readiness for postsecondary education opportunities.

CONCLUSION

This chapter has described a framework for meeting the needs of students with mild, moderate, or severe disabilities within inclusive educational environments. We have considered a system for determining the match among student characteristics and needs, instructional setting, and curriculum variables, discussing examples of possible adaptations to enhance integrated experiences. The rationale of this framework is to propose a systemic approach for meeting the individual goals of students with disabilities within the Least Restrictive Environment. The assessment, decision-making, and intervention components are intended to ensure that students with disabilities receive relevant educational experiences that meet their needs and prepare them for life beyond school.

REFERENCES

Anders, P. L., & Bos, C. S. (1984). In the beginning: Vocabulary instruction in content classrooms. *Topics in learning and learning disabilities, 3,* 53–65.

Anderson-Inman, L. (1981). Transenvironmental programming: Promoting success in the regular class by maximizing the effect of resource room assistance. *Journal of Special Education Technology, 4,* 3–12.

Anderson-Inman, L. (1986). Bridging the gap: Student-centered strategies for promoting the transfer of learning. *Exceptional Children, 4,* 562–572.

Baumgart, D., Brown, L., Pumpian, I., Nisbet, J., Ford, A., Sweet, M., Messina, R., & Schroeder, J. (1982). Principle of partial participation and individualized adaptations in educational programs for severely handicapped students. *Journal of the Association for the Severely Handicapped,* 7, 17–27.

Bauwens, J., Hourcade, J. J., & Friend, M. (1989). Cooperative teaching: A model for general and special education integration. *Remedial and Special Education, 2,* 17–22.

Blankenship, C., & Baumgartner, M. (1982). Programming generalization of computational skills. *Learning Disability Quarterly, 5,* 152–162.

Bos, C. S., & Anders, P. L. (1987). Semantic feature analysis: An interactive teaching strategy for facilitating learning from text. *Learning Disability Focus, 3,* 55–59.

Brigance, A. H. (1980). *Brigance diagnostic comprehensive inventory of basic skills.* North Billerica, MA: Curriculum Associates.

Brolin, D. (1992). *Life Centered Career Education: Competency assessment batteries.* Reston, VA: Council for Exceptional Children.

Brown, L., Branston, M. B., Hamre-Nietupski, S., Pumpian, I., Certo, N., & Gruenwald, L. (1979). A strategy for developing chronological age appropriate and functional curricular content for severely handicapped adolescents and young adults. *Journal of Special Education, 13,* 81–90.

Brown, L., Branston-McLean, M. B., Baumgart, D., Vincent, L., Falvey, M., & Schroeder, J. (1979). Using the characteristics of current and subsequent least restrictive environments as factors in the development of curricular content for severely handicapped students. *AAESPH Review, 4,* 407–424.

Brown, L., Long, E., Udvari-Solner, A., Davis, L., VanDeventer, P., Ahlgren, C., Johnson, F., Grenewald, L., & Jorgenson, J. (1989). The home school. *Journal of the Association for Persons with Severe Handicaps, 14,* 1–7.

Carnine, D., Silbert, J., & Kameenui, E. (1990). *Direct instruction reading* (2nd ed.). Upper Saddle River, NJ: Merrill/Prentice Hall.

Connolly, A. J. (1988). *KeyMath—revised: A diagnostic inventory of essential mathematics.* Circle Pines, MN: American Guidance Service.

Cooper, L. J., Wacker, D. P., Thursby, D., Plagmann, L. A., Harding, J., & Derby, K. M. (1992). Analysis of the role of task preferences, task demands, and adult attention on child behavior in outpatient and classroom settings. *Journal of Applied Behavior Analysis, 25,* 823–840.

Council for Exceptional Children. (1994). *CEC mini-library: Performance assessment.* Reston, VA: ERIC/OSEP Special Project, ERIC Clearinghouse on Disabilities and Gifted Education.

Cuvo, A. J., Davis, P. K., O'Reilly, M. F., Mooney, B. M., & Crowley, R. (1992). Prompting stimulus control with textual prompts and performance feedback for persons with mild disabilities. *Journal of Applied Behavior Analysis, 25,* 477–489.

Davern, L., & Ford, A. (1989). Scheduling. In A. Ford, R. Schnorr, L. Meyer, L. Davern, J. Black, & P. Dempsey (Eds.), *The Syracuse community-referenced curriculum guide for students with moderate and severe disabilities* (pp. 247–255). Baltimore: Brookes.

Delquadri, J., Greenwood, C., Whorton, D., Carta, J., & Hall, R. (1986). Classwide peer tutoring. *Exceptional Children, 52,* 535–542.

Deno, S. L. (1985). Curriculum-based assessment: An emerging alternative. *Exceptional Children, 52,* 219–232.

Deshler, D. D., & Lenz, B. K. (1989). The strategies instructional approach. *International Journal of Learning Disability, Development, and Intervention, 36,* 203–224.

Deshler, D. D., & Schumaker, J. B. (1988). An instructional model for teaching students how to learn. In J. L. Graden, J. E. Zins, & M. J. Curtis (Eds.), *Alternative educational delivery systems: Enhancing instructional options for all students* (pp. 391–411). Washington DC: National Association of School Psychologists.

DiGangi, S. A., Maag, J. W., & Rutherford, R. B., Jr. (1991). Self-graphing of on-task behavior: Enhancing the reactive effects of self-monitoring on on-task behavior and academic performance. *Learning Disability Quarterly, 14,* 221–230

Dunlap, G., Kern-Dunlap, L., Clarke, S., & Robbins, F. R. (1991). Functional assessment, curricular revision, and severe behavior problems. *Journal of Applied Behavior Analysis, 24,* 387–397.

Epstein, M. H., & Cullinan, D. (1987). Effective social skills curricula for behaviorally disordered students. *Pointer, 31,* 21–24.

Ford, A., Davern, L., & Schnorr, R. (1992). Inclusive education: "Making sense" of the curriculum. In S. Stainback & W. Stainback (Eds.), *Curriculum considerations in inclusive classrooms: Facilitating learning for all students* (pp. 37–61). Baltimore: Brookes.

Ford, A., Schnorr, R., Meyer, L., Davern, L., Black, J., & Dempsey, P. (1989). *The Syracuse community-referenced curriculum guide for students with moderate and severe disabilities.* Baltimore: Brookes.

Friend, M., & Cook, L. (1992, March). The new mainstreaming. *Instructor,* pp. 30–37.

Fuchs, D., Fuchs, L. S., & Fernstrom, P. (1993). A conservative approach to special education reform: Mainstreaming through transenvironmental programming and curriculum-based measurement. *American Educational Research Journal, 30,* 149–177.

Fuchs, L. S., & Allinder, R. M. (1993). Computer applications in the schools for students with mild disabilities: Computer-assisted instruction and computer-managed instruction. In R. A. Gable & S. F. Warren (Eds.), *Strategies for teaching students with mild to severe mental retardation* (pp. 49–70). Baltimore: Brookes.

Fuchs, L., Deno, S., & Mirkin, P. (1984). The effects of frequent curriculum-based measurement and evaluation on pedagogy, student achievement and student awareness of learning. *American Educational Research Journal, 21,* 449–460.

Fuchs, L. S., Fuchs, D., & Hamlett, C. L. (1993). Technological advances linking the assessment of students' academic proficiency to instructional planning. *Journal of Special Education Technology, 12,* 49–62.

Fuchs, L. S., & Fuchs, D. (1986a). Curriculum-based assessment of progress toward long- and short-term goals. *Journal of Special Education, 20,* 69–82.

Fuchs, L. S., & Fuchs, D. (1986b). Effects of systematic formative evaluation: A meta-analysis. *Exceptional Children, 53,* 199–208.

Gardner, R., III, Heward, W. L., & Grossi, T. A. (1994). Effects of response cards on student participation and academic achievement: A systematic replication with inner-city students during whole-class science instruction. *Journal of Applied Behavior Analysis, 27,* 63–72.

Gartner, A., & Lipsky, D. K. (1990). Students as instructional agents. In W. Stainback & S. Stainback (Eds.), *Support networks for inclusive schooling: Interdependent integrated education* (pp. 81–93). Baltimore: Brookes.

Goldstein, A. P., & Sorcher, M. (1974). *Changing supervisor behavior.* Elmsford, NY: Pergamon.

Goldstein, H., Kaczmarek, L., Pennington, R., & Shafer, K. (1992). Peer-mediated intervention: Attending to, commenting on, and acknowledging the behavior of preschoolers with autism. *Journal of Applied Behavior Analysis, 25,* 289–305.

Hall, R. V., Delquadri, J., Greenwood, C. R., & Thurston, L. (1982). The importance of opportunity to respond in children's academic success. In E. Edgar, N. Haring, J. Jenkins, & C. Pious (Eds.), *Mentally handicapped children: Education and training.* Baltimore: University Park Press.

Haring, T. G., & Breen, C. G. (1992). A peer-mediated social network intervention to enhance the social integration of persons with moderate and severe disabilities. *Journal of Applied Behavior Analysis, 25,* 319–333.

Harris, K. C. (1990). Meeting diverse needs through collaborative consultation. In W. Stainback & S. Stainback (Eds.), *Support networks for inclusive schooling: Interdependent integrated education* (pp. 139–150). Baltimore: Brookes.

Hart, D. (1994). *Authentic assessment: Handbook for educators.* New York: Addison-Wesley.

Hendrickson, J. M., & Frank, A. R. (1993). Engagement and performance feedback: Enhancing the classroom achievement of students with mild mental disabilities. In R. A. Gale & S. F. Warren (Eds.), *Strategies for teaching students with mild to severe mental retardation* (pp. 11–47). Baltimore: Brookes.

Heward, W., Courson, F., & Narayan, J. (1989). Using choral responding to increase active student response. *Teaching Exceptional Children, 21,* 72–75.

Individuals with Disabilities Education Act of 1990, PL 101-476 (1990 Education for the Handicapped Act Amendments, October 30, 1990), 20 U.S.C. 55, 1400–1485.

Jenkins, J. R., & Jenkins, L. M. (1981). *Cross age and peer tutoring: Help for children with learning problems.* Reston, VA: Council for Exceptional Children.

Joint Committee on Teacher Planning for Students with Disabilities. (1995). *Planning for academic diversity in America's classrooms: Windows on reality, research, change, and practice.* Lawrence: University of Kansas Center for Research on Learning.

Joyce, B., & Weil, M. (1986). *Models of teaching* (3rd ed.). Upper Saddle River, NJ: Prentice Hall.

Kamps, D. M., Leonard, B. R., Vernon, S., Dugan, E. P., Delquadri, J. C., Gershon, B., Wade, L., & Folk, L. (1992). Teaching social skills to students with autism to increase peer interaction in an integrated first-grade classroom. *Journal of Applied Behavior Analysis, 25,* 281–288.

Karsh, K. G., & Repp, A. C. (1992). The Task Demonstration Model: A concurrent model for teaching groups of persons with severe disabilities. *Exceptional Children, 59,* 54–67.

Kern, L., & Dunlap, G. (in press). Assessment-based interventions for children with emotional and behavior disorders. In A. C. Repp & R. H. Horner (Eds.), *Functional analysis of problem behavior: From effective assessment to effective support.* Pacific Grove, CA: Brooks/Cole.

Kern-Dunlap, L., Dunlap, G., Clarke, S., Childs, K. E, White, R. L., & Stewart, M. P. (1992). Effects of a videotape feedback package on the peer interactions of children with serious behavioral and emotional challenges. *Journal of Applied Behavior Analysis, 25,* 355–364.

Kern-Koegel, L., Koegel, R. L., Hurley, C., & Frea, W. D. (1992). Improving social skills and disruptive behavior in children with autism through self-management. *Journal of Applied Behavior Analysis, 25,* 341–354.

Korinek, L., & Polloway, E. A. (1993). Social skills: Review and implications for instruction for students with mild mental retardation. In R. A. Gables & S. F. Warren (Eds.), *Strategies for teaching students with mild to severe mental retardation* (pp. 71–97). Baltimore: Brookes.

Lalli, J. S., Browder, D. M., Mace, F. C., & Brown, D. K. (1993). Teacher use of descriptive analysis data to implement interventions to decrease students' problem behaviors. *Journal of Applied Behavior Analysis, 26,* 227–238.

Lentz, F. E. (1988). On-task behavior, academic performance, and classroom disruptions: Untangling the target selection problem in classroom interventions. *School Psychology Review, 17,* 243–257.

Lenz, B. K., Bulgren, J., & Hudson, P. (1990). Content enhancements: A model for promoting the acquisition of content by individuals with learning disabilities. In T. Scruggs & B. Wong (Eds.), *Intervention research in learning disabilities* (pp. 122–165). New York: Springer.

Lenz, B. K., Clark, F. L., Deshler, D. D., Schumaker, J. B., & Rademacher, J. (Eds.). (1990). *SIM training library: The strategies instructional approach.* Lawrence: University of Kansas Institute for Research in Learning Disabilities.

Lenz, B. K., Deshler, D., Schumaker, J., Bulgren, J., Kissam, B., Vance, M., Roth, J., & McKnight, M. (1993). *The Course Planning Routine: A guide for inclusive course planning* (Research Report). Lawrence: University of Kansas Center for Research on Learning.

Maag, J. W., Reid, R., & DiGangi, S. A. (1993). Differential effects of self-monitoring: attention, accuracy, and productivity. *Journal of Applied Behavior Analysis, 26,* 329–344.

Mace, F. C., Lalli, J. S., & Lalli, E. P. (1991). Functional analysis and treatment of aberrant behavior. *Research in Developmental Disabilities, 12,* 155–180.

Mastropieri, M. A., Scruggs, T. E, McLoone, B., & Levin, J. R. (1985). Facilitating learning disabled students' acquisition of science classifications. *Learning Disabilities Quarterly, 8,* 299–309.

Mercer, C. D. (1992). *Students with learning disabilities.* Upper Saddle River, NJ: Merrill/Prentice Hall.

Montague, M. & Bos, C. S. (1986). The effect of cognitive strategy training on verbal math problem solving performance of learning disabled adolescents. *Journal of Learning Disabilities, 19,* 26–33.

Morgan, R. L., & Salzberg, C. L. (1992). Effects of video-assisted training on employment-related social skills of adults with severe mental retardation. *Journal of Applied Behavior Analysis, 25*(2), 365–383.

Munk, D. D., & Repp, A. C. (1994). The relationship between instructional variables and problem behavior: A review. *Exceptional Children, 60,* 390–401.

Neef, N., Iwata, B., & Page, T. (1980). The effects of interspersal training versus high-density reinforcement on spelling acquisition and retention. *Journal of Applied Behavior Analysis, 13,* 153–158.

Odom, S. L., Chandler, L. K., Ostrosky, M., McConnell, S. R., & Reaney, S. (1992). Fading teacher prompts from peer-initiation interventions for young children with disabilities. *Journal of Applied Behavior Analysis, 25,* 307–318.

Odom, S. L., & Strain, P. S. (1986). A comparison of peer-initiation and teacher-antecedent interventions for promoting reciprocal social interaction of autistic preschoolers. *Journal of Applied Behavior Analysis, 19,* 59–71.

Office of Technology Assessment. (1992). *Testing in the American schools: Asking the right questions* (OTA-SET-519). Washington, DC: U.S. Government Printing Office. (ED 340 770)

Olsen, C. O. (1968). Team teaching in the elementary school. *Education, 88,* 345–349.

O'Neill, R. E., Horner, R. H., Albin, R. W., Sprague, J. R., Storey, K. S., & Newton, J. S. (1997). Functional assessment and program development for problem behavior: A practical handbook (2nd ed.). Pacific Grove, CA: Brooks/Cole.

Paine, S. C., Carnine, D. W., White, A. T., & Walter, G. (1982). Effects of fading teacher presentation structure (covertization) on acquisition and maintenance or arithmetic problem-solving skills. *Education and Treatment of Children, 5,* 93–107.

Palinscar, A. S., & Brown, D. A. (1987). Enhancing instructional time through attention to metacognition. *Journal of Learning Disabilities, 20,* 66–75.

Patton, J. R., & Polloway, E. A. (1990). Mild mental retardation. In N. G. Haring & L. McCormick (Eds.), *Exceptional children and youth* (5th ed., pp. 195–237). Upper Saddle River, NJ: Merrill/Prentice Hall.

Pierce, K. L., & Schreibman, L. (1994). Teaching daily living skills to children with autism in unsupervised settings through pictorial self-management. *Journal of Applied Behavior Analysis, 27,* 471–481.

Polloway, E. A. & Patton, J. R. (1993a). Career development, life skills preparation, and transition planning. In E. A. Polloway & J. R. Patton (Eds.), *Strategies for teaching learners with special needs* (pp. 459–483). New York: Macmillan.

Polloway, E. A., & Patton, J. R. (1993b). Curriculum development and program design. In E. A. Polloway & J. R. Patton (Eds.), *Strategies for teaching learners with special needs* (pp. 165–182). New York: Macmillan.

Polloway, E. A., & Patton, J. R. (1993c). Strategies for classroom management: Organizational strategies. In E. A. Polloway & J. R. Patton (Eds.), *Strategies for teaching learners with special needs* (pp. 55–91). New York: Macmillan.

Polloway, E. A., Patton, J. R., Smith, J. D., & Roderique, T. W. (1991). Issues in program design for elementary students with mild retardation: Emphasis on curriculum development. *Education and Training in Mental Retardation, 26,* 142–150.

Polloway, E. A., & Smith, J. D. (1988). Current status of the mild mental retardation construct: Identification, placement, and programs. In M. C. Wang, M. C. Reynolds, & H. J. Walberg (Eds.), *The handbook of special education: Research and practice* (Vol. 2, pp. 1–22). Oxford: Pergamon.

Pugach, M. C., & Johnson, L. J. (1990). Meeting diverse needs through professional peer collaboration. In W. Stainback & S. Stainback (Eds.), *Support networks for inclusive schooling: Interdependent integrated education* (pp. 123–137). Baltimore: Brookes.

Repp, A. C., Felce, D., & Barton, L. E. (1988). Basing the treatment of stereotypic and self-injurious behaviors on hypotheses of their causes. *Journal of Applied Behavior Analysis, 21,* 281–289.

Repp, A. C., & Karsh, K. G. (1992). An analysis of a group teaching procedure for persons with developmental disabilities. *Journal of Applied Behavior Analysis, 25,* 701–712.

Repp, A. C., & Karsh, K. G. (1994). Hypothesis-based interventions for tantrum behavior of persons with developmental disabilities in school settings. *Journal of Applied Behavior Analysis, 27,* 21–31.

Rivera, D. M., & Smith, D. D. (1987). Influence of modeling on acquisition and generalization of computational skills: A summary of research findings from three sites. *Learning Disability Quarterly, 10,* 69–80.

Rosenshine, B. (1983). Teaching functions in instructional programs. *Elementary School Journal, 83,* 335–352.

Rosenshine, B., & Stevens, R. (1986). Teaching functions. In M. C. Wittock (Ed.), *Handbook on research on teaching* (pp. 376–391). New York: Macmillan.

Sailor, W., & Guess, D. (1983). *Severely handicapped students: An instructional design.* Boston: Houghton Mifflin.

Sapon-Shevin, M. (1990). Student support through cooperative learning. In W. Stainback & S. Stainback (Eds.), *Support networks for inclusive schooling: Interdependent education* (pp. 65–79). Baltimore: Brookes.

Schloss, P. J., & Sedlak, R. A. (1986). *Instructional methods for students with learning and behavior problems.* Boston: Allyn & Bacon.

Schumaker, J. B., & Deshler, D. D. (1988). Implementing the regular education initiative in secondary schools: A different ball game. *Journal of Learning Disabilities, 21,* 36–42.

Schumm, J. S., Vaughn, S., & Leavell, A. (1994). Planning Pyramid: A framework for planning for diverse student needs during content area instruction. *Reading Teacher, 47,* 608–615.

Schunk, D. H., & Cox, P. D. (1986). Strategy training and attributional feedback with learning disabled students. *Journal of Educational Psychology, 78,* 201–209.

Silbert, J., Carnine, D., & Stein, M. (1990). *Direct instruction mathematics* (2nd ed.). Upper Saddle River, NJ: Merrill/ Prentice Hall.

Sindelar, Q., Espin, C., Smith, M., & Harriman, N. (1990). A comparison of more and less effective special education teachers in elementary-level programs. *Teacher Education and Special Education, 13,* 9–16.

Slavin, R., Karweit, N., & Madden, N. (1989). *Effective programs for students at risk.* Boston: Allyn & Bacon.

Stainback, W., & Stainback, S. (1990a). The support facilitator at work. In W. Stainback & S. Stainback (Eds.), *Support networks for inclusive schooling: Interdependent integrated education* (pp. 37–48). Baltimore: Brookes.

Stainback, S., & Stainback, W. (1990b). Support networking for inclusive schooling. In W. Stainback & S. Stainback (Eds.), *Support networks for inclusive schooling: Interdependent integrated education.* Baltimore: Brookes.

Stainback, S., Stainback, W., & Jackson, H. J. (1992). Toward inclusive classrooms. In S. Stainback & W. Stainback (Eds.), *Curriculum considerations in inclusive classrooms: Facilitating learning for all students* (pp. 3–17). Baltimore: Brookes.

Stainback, W., Stainback, S., & Moravec, J. (1992). Using curriculum to build inclusive classrooms. In S. Stainback & W. Stainback (Eds.), *Curriculum considerations in inclusive classrooms: Facilitating learning for all students* (pp. 65–84). Baltimore: Brookes.

Thousand, J. S., & Villa, R. A. (1990). Sharing expertise and responsibilities through teaching teams. In W. Stainback & S. Stainback (Eds.), *Support networks for inclusive schooling* (pp. 151–166). Baltimore: Brookes.

Wechsler, D. (1974). *Manual for the Wechsler Intelligence Scale for Children—Revised.* San Antonio, TX: Psychological Corporation.

Wehmeyer, M. L. (1992). Self-determination and the education of students with mental retardation. *Education and Training in Mental Retardation, 27,* 303–314.

Wilcox, B., & Bellamy, G. T. (1982). *Design of high school programs for severely handicapped students.* Baltimore: Brookes.

Will, M. C. (1984). *OSERS programming for the transition of youth with disabilities: Bridges from school to working life.* Washington, DC: U.S. Department of Education, Office of Special Education and Rehabilitation Services.

Wolery, M., Bailey, D., & Sugai, G. (1988). *Effective teaching: Principles and procedures of applied behavior analysis with exceptional students.* Boston: Allyn & Bacon.

Woodcock, R. W. (1987). *Woodcock Reading Mastery Tests—Revised.* Circle Pines, MN: American Guidance Service.

Woodcock, R. W., & Johnson, M. B. (1989). *Woodcock-Johnson Psycho-Educational Battery—revised: Tests of cognitive ability.* Allen, TX: DLM Teaching Resources.

8

Technology and Children with Disabilities

ELLEN P. SCHILLER
DAVID MALOUF
JANE HAUSER
JUDITH FEIN

As an integral part of special education, technology has enhanced the lives of many individuals with disabilities. Simply put, technology has been used quite successfully to provide greater access to the world. One need only see a child with cerebral palsy using a sonic head point and a computer to communicate with families and friends to appreciate the power that technology provides children with disabilities.

Technology, however, is not a panacea. Assistive technologies for children with disabilities can mean increased independence and easy access to others, and instructional technology enhances good teaching and helps teachers facilitate learning. But technology alone cannot improve outcomes for children with disabilities. The challenge is to find the right mix, for technology embedded in well-designed educational approaches can mean the difference between being left behind and moving forward. Clark (1983) said it most clearly: "instructional technologies are mere vehicles that deliver instruction but do not influence student achievement any more than the truck that delivers our groceries causes changes in our nutrition" (p. 445).

Teachers can draw on a wide variety of technologies to establish the kinds of learning environments that promote (a) problem solving and critical thinking, (b) skill and concept development, and (c) social and emotional well-being. When carefully chosen, technology can assist in attaining explicit instructional goals, especially when the selected technology incorporates procedures known from research to have a high probability of meeting the instructional needs of students with disabilities.

If instructional technology is to have optimal impact, then, it must be used by teachers in a systematic manner as part of a well-planned instructional program. In short, instructional technology will be effective only when teachers link it to curricular needs of students with disabilities (Okolo, 1990a). Not an end in itself, technology must be considered in relation to the needs, practices, and principles of effective instruction.

In this chapter, we will highlight the opportunities for using technology for teaching academic content and for gaining access to independence and learning. We also will offer some cautions and discuss the limitations of technology. We will draw upon existing empirical research to determine the best practices in technology use and recommend how technology may be used.

ASSISTIVE TECHNOLOGY AND INDEPENDENCE

More and more classrooms have increasing numbers of students with disabilities who use assistive technology. This increase is due to advances in technology and to the passage of federal legislation that gives schools greater responsibility for providing devices to students in special education settings.

The terms *assistive technology device* and *assistive technology service* were defined by Congress in the Technology-Related Assistance for Individuals with Disabilities Act of 1988 (PL 100-407) and later included in the Individuals with Disabilities Education Act (PL 101-476):

> ***Terms***
>
> The term "assistive technology device" means any item, piece of equipment, or product system, whether acquired commercially off the shelf, modified, or customized, that is used to increase, maintain, or improve functional capabilities of individuals with disabilities. (20 U.S.C. Chapter 33, Section 1401 [25])
>
> The term "assistive technology service" means any service that directly assists an individual with a disability in the selection, acquisition, or use of an assistive technology device. Such term includes:
>
> (A) the evaluation of the needs of an individual with a disability, including a functional evaluation of the individual in the individual's customary environment;
>
> (B) purchasing, leasing, or otherwise providing for the acquisition of assistive technology devices by individuals with disabilities;
>
> (C) selecting, designing, fitting, customizing, adapting, applying, maintaining, repairing, or replacing of assistive technology devices;
>
> (D) coordinating and using other therapies, interventions, or services with assistive technology devices, such as those associated with existing education and rehabilitation plans and programs;
>
> (E) training or technical assistance for an individual with disabilities, or, where appropriate, the family of an individual with disabilities; and
>
> (F) training or technical assistance for professionals (including individuals providing education and rehabilitation services), employers, or other individuals who provide services to, employ, or are otherwise substantially involved in the major life functions of individuals with disabilities. (20 U.S.C. Chapter 33, Section 1401[26])

Assistive technology devices can help students who have physical, cognitive, or emotional disabilities; and devices are often used as alternative ways of performing actions, tasks, and activities to produce outcomes of independence, inclusion, productivity, and an improved quality of life. Table 8.1 summarizes and provides examples of ten areas in which assistive technologies are being used in classrooms (Blackstone, 1990).

Assistive devices run the gamut from adapted spoons and switch-adapted, battery-operated toys for young students to complex devices such as computerized systems that are operated through particular software programs. Technology is often characterized as low-, medium-, or high-tech (Thorkildsen, 1994). Low-tech devices are simple, nonelectric, relatively inexpensive devices such as the white cane used by blind students. Medium-tech devices are aids that might use electricity but are not computer driven, such as an electric wheelchair that allows students with a disability to attend school and participate in a regular education classroom. High-tech devices require computerized systems that are operated

Table 8.1 Applications and Examples of Assistive Technology

Application	Intended Outcomes	Equipment Examples
Positioning	Increased function and participation through stable and comfortable positioning	Adapted seating; standing tables; cushions and wedges to maintain posture
Access	Enhancement of speed, accuracy, endurance, independence	Switches; head pointers; electronic communication devices; text enlargement
Environmental control	Manipulation and control of environment to allow access and independence	Battery-operated items; remote control units; power door openers
Augmentative and alternative communication	Independent means of speech or written communication	Nonelectric communication boards or books; laptop computers with special software and hardware
Assistive listening	Appropriate signal-to-noise ratio	Hearing aids; personal FM units
Visual aids	Enhancement or interpretation of visual information	Braille note-taking systems; recording devices; large-screen monitors
Mobility	Independent movement, exploration, social interaction, and learning	Electric or conventional wheelchairs; crutches; canes; orthotics
Physical education, recreation, leisure, play	Access to materials/activities allowing peer interaction, hobby development	Outdoor adaptations; computer games; board game adaptations; painting with a head wand
Self-care	Independent self-care activities	Modified eating utensils; page turners; adapted personal hygiene aids

SOURCE: Adapted from Blackstone (1990).

through a particular software program. The microcomputer, one of the most popular high-tech devices, has the primary advantage that most schools already have access to them. So versatile is this device that it can be used by students with speech impairments to synthesize a voice, students with learning disabilities to receive individualized instruction, or students with mobility impairments to use as a network to access places that might not be otherwise reachable. In terms of schooling, however, any technology must be examined in terms of the student and the teacher.

Assistive Technology and the Student

The impact of available technology is important to consider for the simple and often-stated reason that the goal of assistive technology is to increase the student's ability to interact independently with his or her physical and social environment. In some cases, assistive devices achieve this goal very effectively and seem to open up new worlds for the student. In other cases, these devices fall short of their potential. Todis and Walker (1993) report on the assistive technology experiences of Rose and Sara (two real students, although not their real names). Those cases are summarized here to provide practical examples of technology applications.

Rose

Rose is an eleven-year-old fifth-grade student with cerebral palsy. She is unable to walk unassisted but can move around by crawling or by using handrails or a walker. Much of the time, she gets around in a motorized wheelchair with electronic, programmable controls and a joystick. Rose uses a variety of other assistive devices, including adapted pencils, eating utensils, and scissors, that allow her to function nearly independently in school and at home.

Last year Rose's mother obtained funding to buy Rose a computer. This portable computer is mounted on Rose's wheelchair. It has a word processor with word prediction capabilities, so Rose can type the first letters of a word then choose the desired word from a list. This is important because Rose uses only one finger on her right hand to type and tires quickly. The computer also has voice output that allows Rose to produce messages in spoken form.

Rose is independent and social and plans to attend college and have a career. She talks with friends on the phone, which is preprogrammed with their numbers. She likes horseback riding, swimming, summer camp, and slumber parties.

Sara

Sara is a fifteen-year-old student in a rural middle school. She has cerebral palsy and is unable to support her weight or grasp objects. She communicates primarily through eye gaze or by moving her right or left hand to indicate yes or no. She has used a motorized wheelchair for four years, but she has grown to the point that the chair no longer "fits." Reaching the joystick has become more difficult, requiring her to twist her body in a way that aggravates her scoliosis and is intensely uncomfortable. Problems with the wheelchair culminated in Sara running into a door frame and breaking her leg. Sara's parents cannot afford to replace the wheelchair, so makeshift solutions have been applied, such as making a strap from pantyhose to hold Sara's arm in place.

Sara communicates through both high- and low-tech devices. She uses a plastic board that allows her to communicate by looking at items. She also uses an electronic communication device with voice output, and she does academic work on a classroom computer. Sara cannot use a keyboard, so the communication device and the computer use "scanning" (that is, words, letters, or phrases are illuminated in sequence), and she makes a selection by pressing a headswitch. Even though Sara is a good scanner, she only produces about five letters per minute. The school staff feels that Sara has more to say than her current technology allows. The electronic communication device seems to be too slow and limited, and the messages sometimes make no sense to the staff. Her writing is hard to interpret, perhaps in part because she had no means for developing expressive communication in her early years.

To a school staff faced with meeting Sara's educational and personal care needs, Sara's technology seems to represent simply an additional responsibility. They complain about the technology and often forget to use it.

All of Sara's technology, except for a standard wheelchair, stay at school. The family says there is no room for it in their house, and they understand her nonverbal communications well enough. Their minivan is not equipped with a lift, and Sara has grown too tall to fit in it when she is in her power chair. Besides, there is no place to drive a power chair in their rural area. The family sees Sara as bright and sweet and do not seem to see increased independence as an important goal for her. They plan to have her with them indefinitely. Sara seems to enjoy new experiences and independence but shies away from increased responsibilities. It is hard to know her view of her future.

What do these two cases tell us about the use of assistive technology? Perhaps the clearest implication is that no single factor determines the success of an assistive device. To begin with, each device has a variety of characteristics that increase or decrease its effectiveness. Some of the most important characteristics, taken from Thorkildsen's (1994) review of research and clinical studies, are (a) operability, (b) dependability, (c) affordability, (d) durability, (e) flexibility, (f) ease of maintenance, (g) portability, (h) compatibility, (i) learnability, (j) personal acceptability, (k) physical comfort, and (l) supplier repairability. However, a variety of other factors interact to enhance or diminish the benefits of assistive devices. Some of those extremely important factors are:

- the attitudes of parents, students, and teachers;
- the nature of school and community environments; and
- the availability of funds and services.

Assistive Technology and the Teacher

As the number of students who use technology increases, teachers need even more to (a) acquire information about technology devices, (b) assume skills in technology services provision, and (c) be cognizant of the many individuals who can serve as important sources of knowledge. As we learned from reading about Sara, technology can represent an additional responsibility and burden to school staff. This responsibility can be minimized by having teams of professionals and family members working together to determine the most effective device a student should be using and how the student can use it most efficiently.

Individuals who can serve on such teams include regular and special education teachers, counselors, occupational, physical, and speech and language pathologists, administrators, health care workers, and parents. As each technology device has a variety of characteristics that increases or decreases its effectiveness, each person has his or her own unique expertise to contribute to the provision of technology that children can easily operate.

The extent of the teacher's involvement in the selection of a device for a student can vary considerably. Ideally, though, the teacher should be a key member of the team that determines the potential for assistive technology, since the teacher is responsible for setting and meeting the student's instructional goals (Todis & Walker, 1993). The team approach works most effectively when teachers, other professionals, parents, and the student are cooperatively involved in the decision-making process.

There may be times when a teacher's first knowledge of and contact with a child is seeing the student in the classroom using an assistive device. In such instances, the teacher cannot assume (a) that the student has been evaluated adequately, (b) that the best device has been selected, (c) that appropriate training has been provided, or (d) that ongoing support is available to student and staff (Todis & Walker, 1993). If the teacher has not been trained in selecting and using technology equipment in the classroom, she or he should seek the advice of other individuals who are familiar with that process. For example, a speech and language pathologist can suggest ways to maximize a student's speech, language, and communication during various activities, such as use of a communication device during circle time and a miniboard at home during bath time. The physical therapist, after evaluating the student's posture and mobility, can recommend various techniques, devices, and strategies that will appropriately position the student to facilitate comfort, proper development, safety, and increased mobility (Flexer, 1992). In addition, and equally important, a person with a disability who has experience with the technology can be used as an invaluable source of information regarding the effective use of some technology.

Following the student's assessment and placement in the classroom, the teacher should work with the specialist who conducts training in the use of the device to avoid the problem of classroom activity focusing on the technology itself, rather than on the goal the technology was acquired to achieve. The teacher should be aware of the fact that the goal is not just to teach the student to use the device but to show the student how to use the device to complete specified tasks and work toward educational goals.

The teacher also should be involved with encouraging family participation in the use of technology at home and in the community. As we previously indicated, the student should not be taught to use a device unless it will facilitate his or her acquisition of a particular goal. Conversely, a piece of equipment should not be used if it disrupts or impedes the completion of a task.

Teachers particularly need to consider the emotional reactions of families of children with disabilities and be sensitive to their ability to solve their own problems. Teachers also must be aware of the possible negative effects that using a device can have on a student (for example, it takes time to learn to use it, it can cause feelings of self-consciousness, it may be a challenge to learn to use it skillfully, it can be frustrating, and it can be dangerous). In short, technology alone is of little use. Having said that, we will now consider the uses of technology as a tool in teaching math, reading, and writing and how teachers can use technology to assess academic performance of children with learning problems.

INSTRUCTIONAL TECHNOLOGY TO IMPROVE ACADEMIC OUTCOMES

For technology to have an impact on academic outcomes for children with learning problems, teachers must use principles of effective instruction designed to accommodate the individual learning characteristics of children with disabilities. Children with learning problems use inefficient strategies for remembering information and inefficient strategies for acquiring and using content knowledge (Baker, Kameenui, & Simmons, 1993; Wong, 1986). To accommodate these learning characteristics,[1] teachers can design effective instruction, both a technology-based delivery system and a teacher-delivered system, to ensure students will derive optimum benefits to learn basic skills, problem solve, and reason.

Students with learning problems need explicit instruction, whether delivered by the teacher or computer. This instruction must incorporate (a) sequenced, appropriately paced, and a full range of examples; (b) opportunities for frequent responding; (c) graphics and animation or pictures that contribute to rather than distract from learning; (d) frequent and informative feedback, enabling students to locate and correct errors; (e) an adequate number of practice opportunities; and (f) appropriately distributed review opportunities during the instruction (Okolo, Bahr, & Rieth, 1993). They also need strategy instruction—often called cognitive and metacognitive strategies. Strategy instruction is the opportunity to give students the opportunity to learn what experts know.

In a computer-supported environment, teachers must select well-designed software that includes menus, prompts, maps, activities, and searching options that help students use strategies to learn. Students will learn more when computer-based instruction activities are preceded or accompanied by teacher-directed instruction (Okolo et al., 1993).

The following recommendations for teaching math, reading, and writing promote the use of efficient learning strategies and delivery of effective instruction for students with learning problems.

Instructional Technology and Teaching Mathematics

National assessments of mathematics performance show that American students do poorly on mathematical problem solving. In fact, American elementary and secondary students are behind other industrialized nations. It seems that one reason for this lackluster performance is that whereas American education is good at teaching students mathematical skills, it falls short in helping youngsters understand the concepts that underlie those skills. Too much time is spent on drill and practice. Not enough time is devoted to mathematical conceptual understanding, problem solving, and reasoning. Without this conceptual knowledge to apply

[1]"Learning characteristics" are to be distinguished from "learning styles." Although *learning styles* is a popular term, no research base supports the identification of learning styles and for matching instructional approaches to learning styles. (See Arter & Jenkins, 1978, for a complete discussion.)

what they know to solving problems, it is unlikely that young people can make appropriate use of the skills they do have (Scheid, 1990).

Concerned not only with the test results but also with the demands of living and working in an information age, the National Council of Teachers of Mathematics (1989) published a comprehensive set of guidelines and standards for curriculum, instruction, and assessment. Those guidelines take into consideration the changing nature of mathematics knowledge in society. The standards encourage problem solving as the focus of mathematics curriculum and stress that math principles and concepts as well as processes should be taught.

The guidelines do not take explicitly into account the needs of children with disabilities. However, as Scheid (1990) points out, "[T]he fostering of independent problem solving skills that enable youngsters to apply math procedures in functional, vocational, and career settings has been a long-standing goal in special education" (p. 2). Meaningful math learning requires the acquisition of conceptual as well as procedural knowledge, and students' independent problem-solving capabilities need to be nurtured.

Although basic skills are not enough, basic skills training must be a part of the curriculum of students with disabilities. Until those skills become automatic, students cannot tackle those skills requiring higher-order thinking (Okolo et al., 1993). In this regard, technology can be a helpful tool. The computer, equipped with a well-designed computer-assisted instruction (CAI) program, can help a student practice computation. In fact, the ability to deliver large amounts of effective practice is one of the most established strengths of CAI. As Okolo (1992) notes, technology can automate certain skills, and CAI as a tool can be highly interactive and infinitely patient. It can present information in a variety of ways and can adjust to respond to learner needs.

Beyond the basics, if it is used well and grounded in a sound program of instruction, technology can support higher-order thinking by engaging students in authentic, complex tasks within collaborative learning contexts (Means et al., 1993). Successful problem solvers consciously or unconsciously use self-instruction, self-questioning, and self-monitoring to gain access to strategic knowledge, guide execution of strategies, and regulate use of strategies and problem-solving performance. Research has demonstrated that these cognitive and metacognitive strategies can be taught (Montague, 1992).

One of the challenges facing contemporary education is how to provide students with realistic situations in which to practice solving problems. In traditional math, problems have one correct answer. Life problems, on the other hand, are complex and require multiple tasks. In approaching problem solving, the goal of cognitive research has been to break out of the word problem mode and focus on the situation. "Our primary goal is to create shared learning environments that permit teachers and students to explore together the kinds of general problem situations they encounter outside of school" (Bottge & Hasselbring, 1993, p. 38). One such activity occurs in a series of videos that make up *The Adventures of Jasper Woodbury,* developed by the Cognition and Technology Group at Vanderbilt University (1991). "Rescue on Boone Mountain," for example, requires students to figure out how to rescue a wounded eagle. An ultralight plane that can carry only a limited amount of weight is to be the rescue vehicle. The students need to determine such things as how much spare gas can be carried in a plane already filled with both the cage for the eagle and the weight of the pilot. The class must plot the best route to the site and the amount of time it has to successfully complete the rescue. Problem solving for this activity involves teams working out time, rate, and distance factors as well as using statistics, geometry, and geography. Integrated media such as audio, videodisc, videotape, maps, and still photos are used.

Teachers need to know about cognitive processes to ensure students with disabilities acquire and use math (Means et al., 1993). How can a teacher use cognitive-based methods for teaching math? Scheid (1994) suggests seven ways to incorporate cognitive principles into math instruction:

1. Plan the lesson by identifying underlying concepts and relationships that students need to understand, and explicitly teach them—do not assume anything is readily apparent to the students;
2. When introducing new concepts, draw connections between what students already know and understand and what they are about to learn—present math in the context of situations that are familiar to students;
3. Actively involve students by presenting instruction from a perspective of the problem to be solved—a problem that could have more than one answer;
4. Teach children strategies to help them solve problems—a picture showing the problem, a diagram to chart progress—and the reasons for using certain strategies;
5. Ask "how" and "why" questions and listen to determine whether the students really understand;
6. Use learning groups—it helps students communicate with and rely on one another to solve problems being addressed; and
7. Be aware of the role of attitudes and beliefs in the learning process. Students in need of special education may not have much confidence in themselves after years of failure. They need to know it is smart to ask questions when they do not know an answer and that math knowledge from everyday experiences is relevant to understanding what is taught about math in school. (pp. 6–7)

This guidance can benefit most learners, not just those with disabilities. Teaming these strategies with technology can be a powerful combination. Papert (1980) believes that computers can be designed so that learning to communicate with them could be a natural process. He also believes that learning to communicate with the computer may change the way other learning takes place. He does not see CAI as the computer being used to "program the child"; rather, the child programs the computer, and in doing so, gains contact with rich and conceptually deep ideas from science, mathematics, and intellectual model building.

What we now know about using technology with children with learning problems tends to bear Piaget out.

Instructional Technology and Teaching Reading

Difficulties in learning to read are major reasons for referrals to special education (Wong, 1986). The National Longitudinal Transition Study of Special Education reports that students who leave school without having acquired functional literacy skills have only a 50 percent chance of becoming employed (Wagner, Blackorby, Cameto, Hebbeler, & Newman, 1993). Difficulties in acquiring cognitive and metacognitive skills for reading to learn are characteristic of students who have learning problems (Peters & Levin, 1986; Wong, 1986).

Successful readers read quickly and effortlessly. They recognize whole words at a glance, gleaning appropriate meaning at once (Adams, 1990). How do they do this? What are the instructional implications for unsuccessful readers, particularly for students with disabilities for whom the reading curriculum is judged appropriate? What, too, are the implications for using technology to teach reading to students with disabilities?

In addressing these questions, we know that skillful readers can accomplish the following:

1. Recognize familiar words as a whole while visually processing every letter of those words
2. Recall all the meanings of a word in context before selecting the most appropriate meaning from the alternatives (contextual guidance does not preselect the meaning of words)
3. Translate spellings to sounds as they read (the ability to read long words depends on the ability to break words into syllables) (Adams, 1990; Baker, Kameenui, Simmons, & Stahl, 1994)

To teach reading to students with learning problems effectively, we need to balance the role of technology with the role of teacher. Although the technology may be seductive, the characteristics of the learner need to be considered first when selecting instructional tools. Multimedia, for example, is a very exciting technology currently being developed to deliver and facilitate instruction. Texts, such as textbooks, can be transferred to a multimedia environment. In one such environment, called macrostructures, learners can ask for help with unknown words via a speech synthesizer for reading the unknown word or via video segments to help with definitions of unknown words. Students with disabilities, however, often do not ask for help. They will finish tasks before many of the other students in the class because they do not stop and ask themselves questions, such as "Do I understand what I am reading? What is the meaning of this new word?" Asking and answering these kinds of questions are cognitive strategies in which good readers engage and excel. Thus, achievement gains suffer when students are given small amounts of control or are permitted to make choices about contextual rather than essential features of reading instruction (Okolo et al., 1993).

Technology can enhance learning outcomes for two types of reading: (a) practicing basic skills and (b) promoting conceptual thinking (Hasselbring, Russell, & Woodward, 1987).

Practicing Basic Skills Basic skill instruction lends itself to implementation of drill-and-practice activities that have characterized much of educational computing. Essentially, effective computer-based interventions have been developed to promote automaticity[2] in decoding (Hassebring, Goin, & Bransford, 1988) and word recognition (Roth & Beck, 1986). Researchers have explored ways in which technology can enhance vocabulary knowledge (McKeown & Beck, 1988).

When teachers used a computer program called Hint and Hunt I (Beck & Roth, 1984) with mildly disabled learners for fifteen minutes a day for ten weeks, reading increased by 27 percent (Jones, Torgesen, & Sexton, 1987). More impressively, students with mild disabilities showed an accompanying 20 percent increase (to almost 100 percent) in accuracy on a list of generalized words that were never practiced during the training. Thus, students demonstrated improvements in decoding skills, not just simply improvements in reading a limited set of practice words.

When Hint and Hunt I was used with Hint and Hunt II and Construct-a-Word (Beck & Roth, 1984a; 1984b), the authors found that the decoding skill of poor readers was increased by 25 percent, resulting in a 17 percent increase in sentence reading speed (Akolo, 1990b). The contrast group showed a negligible increase—only a 3 percent rise in sentence reading speed. From these studies, specific instruction provided by the computer appears to be effective in increasing the fluency of essential phonological decoding skills in learners with mild disabilities.

Promoting Conceptual Thinking Although more limited in its scope, there is an emerging body of research on using multimedia environments for delivering instruction in higher-order skills such as reading comprehension and reasoning. New technologies such as hypermedia and videodiscs may offer potential avenues for supporting a broader variety of reading instruction. Already, videodiscs have been used to create "macrocontexts"—contexts sufficiently broad and rich to facilitate instruction in a variety of skills and content areas. Video macrocontexts can supply the background knowledge that students with disabilities often need to construct meaning from text successfully (Cognition and Technology Group at Vanderbilt University, 1994).

Multimedia environments that organize and support learning through teaching (MOST environments) are designed to support differences among learners in acquiring conceptual skills. This growing technology allows teachers to present more integrated, complex information, particularly if the information is dependent on visual images and motion. For example, the MOST environment can be composed of the following elements:

---

[2]The principle of automaticity is that basic skills (such as math facts) should be practiced until they require little conscious effort and can thus be incorporated into more complex tasks.

1. The Peabody Literacy Program, which facilitates comprehension and fluency instruction. The original version of the program mediates instruction in word recognition and decoding as well as students' comprehension of text passages that are centered on contemporary topics and presented via videodisc. An animated tutor guides the learner and gives feedback, and a voice recognition system allows learners to interact with the tutor. Both fluency instruction and comprehension are emphasized.
2. The Multimedia Producer, which is a Macintosh-based program that allows students to create their own multimedia productions
3. The Two-Way Videoconferencing System, which also is a Macintosh-based system that brings together teachers and students with content area specialists, designers, and other schools (Cognition and Technology Group of Vanderbilt University, 1994)

Kelly and O'Kelly (1993) posit that most children learn to read and write early in life. Children hear stories and connect events in the stories to events in their own life. In the MOST project, children are given an opportunity to explore all aspects of writing and take control of their environment by collaborating with each other and in some cases tutoring their younger peers. Using the MOST environment, preschoolers began by collaborating in multimedia environments and taking turns being the teacher. Helping each other, they use multimedia's tools to script and videotape their own stories. As a teacher noted, the children are using technology as a tool that has meaning to them. They tell stories, print them out, videotape them, and take them home. This is a task where the kids producing stories feel in control and in charge, and they are unflagging. "MOST environments . . . engage students in authentic tasks that place students in a position to create interesting and important multimedia products that teach their peers, parents, and others about important life topics" (Cognition and Technology Group of Vanderbilt University, 1994, p. 23).

Instructional Technology and Writing

Writing is a complex process involving motor, cognitive, and social skills, and many students with disabilities reasonably find the process of writing to be a daunting experience. Children and youth with language-related disabilities may have difficulty organizing their thoughts or may need practice and specific instruction to improve their skills. Students with physical impairments may have difficulty with small motor movements. Those with sensory impairments may be unable to see or to hear information relevant to what they need to learn.

Technology has the potential to mitigate some of the difficulties of certain disabilities and to support some of the instructional activities related to writing. For example, word processing seems to have burgeoned in the past ten years. This could attest to a growing sense within schools of the importance of writing, not only as an avenue for expression but as an indicator of a child's progress in other subjects. In addition, some of the newer technologies have capabilities such as keyboard adaptations for specific physical impairments or voice recognition or speech-to-text conversion to aid children and youth who present a variety of physical or sensory impairments.

However, a decade of research in writing has shown that technology alone, and word processing in particular, does not improve the overall quality of student writing. In fact, focus has shifted from merely expecting the computer to solve problems to examining the interaction of the computer with other instructional factors (Morocco, Dalton, & Tivnan, 1992).

Many factors, after all, are involved in the process of writing, and they are often difficult to isolate. For example, how do teachers' attitudes and experience about how writing should be taught affect their thinking about writing in general? What type of writing is actually being done in the classroom? How much time is spent on writing, and in what setting is writing accomplished? What impact does a child's disability have on the process of writing itself?

As in any instructional activity, looking at writing in a broad context is useful, as the act of writing is more than simply putting thoughts on paper. Writing, as it becomes an intrinsic part of a child's educational repertoire, fosters the process of communication.

More specifically, accepted research regards writing as a set of processes involving planning, composing or drafting, and revising or editing. Furthermore, accomplished writers move back and forth among these phases. Morocco, Dalton, and Tivnan expressed this idea as early as 1989. They stated the goal of a writing process is for students to develop their own skills to plan, generate, and express ideas and revise and edit their writing that is meaningful to them. The writing processes are completed on automatic writing tasks and as students help one another write, edit, and revise.

The teacher's role in this process is as complex as the writing process itself (Kelly & O'Kelly, 1993). Not only do teachers help students master the skills and strategies necessary to becoming effective writers, but they also provide specific direction in planning, writing, and revision (Zorfass, Corley, & Remz, 1994). The teacher's role has become even a more important part of the mix, with the advent of technology adding a new dimension to instructional responsibilities (Means et al., 1993; Okolo et al., 1993). Some of the instructional features teachers will want to use are as follows (Stein, Dixon, & Isaacson, 1994):

- *Provides explicit strategies* for all phases of the writing process: planning, text structures, and revising
- *Supports* students to succeed, eventually leading to independence and self-regulation. These supports should include feedback to learners and guidance as they apply new knowledge.
- *Provides a review* that is adequate, distributed over time, and cumulative

Finally, teachers need to allocate time to writing. Teachers can provide an atmosphere conducive to writing instruction by serving as an audience for the student's work, arranging the classroom to encourage and support writing, and recognizing writing as an important activity (Scheid, 1991). As discussed earlier, such environments seem to be evolving as part of the MOST environments for teaching children with learning problems reading and writing.

Ultimately, the teacher must evaluate the curriculum content and the student's progress to choose the most effective instructional approach. Examining various technology-based assessment approaches will help the teacher make decisions.

TECHNOLOGY FOR ASSESSING CLASSROOM PERFORMANCE

In special education, assessment has a number of different functions, including (a) determining eligibility for placement, (b) guiding instructional planning, and (c) tracking student progress. In recent years, technology has found its way into virtually all these functions. In some cases, technology simply facilitates processes that can be accomplished without technology. For example, school psychologists sometimes use a computer program to score a test or prepare an assessment report. In other cases, technology enhances assessment in ways that cannot be duplicated without the technology. Computer-tailored tests that instantly adapt themselves on the basis of the student's responses, or interactive video-based systems that test student responses to realistically portrayed situations, or artificial intelligence systems that analyze student assessment results and make complex decisions about student classifications and educational interventions are all good examples of "pure" technology at work.

Classroom Assessment

Perhaps of greatest relevance to classroom teachers are the roles technology can play in the assessments performed in everyday classroom instruction. Most of today's instructional software programs, although they differ in how they collect and use this information, record data on student performance. Some programs gather information continuously by recording each response the student makes; others administer and record periodic tests. In reporting the results, some programs break the information down into simple forms, such as percentage accuracy, whereas others provide complex analyses of subskills and types of errors. Some programs automatically adjust instruction on the basis of student performance.

The assessment components of these commercial software products tend to be based on fairly simple assessment principles: they test how accurately (and sometimes how quickly) the student can respond to items taken directly from instruction. Actually, despite their computerization, most of these assessment components can be classified as "informal classroom assessments,"[3] similar to weekly spelling tests, chapter quizzes, teacher-developed tests, and so on. Informal classroom assessments (in computer or noncomputer forms) have been a mainstay of classroom instruction for many years, but they are easily misapplied in subjective and unsystematic ways.

---

[3]The word *informal* is not intended to imply poor quality. Instead, it means that formal techniques of test development, such as standardization, technical analysis, and validation, have not been applied.

Over the years, special education researchers have developed and studied several systematic approaches for linking classroom assessment and instructional decisions. These approaches, which include precision teaching and curriculum-based measurement, involve the frequent collection of data on student performance and the analysis of the data (usually by means of graphs) as a basis for making instructional decisions.

These approaches were developed prior to the introduction of classroom microcomputers. However, as computers became available, the advantages of computerizing these assessment approaches were recognized, and software versions began to appear. One of the earliest such revisions was AIMSTAR, a computerized tool for precision teaching (Hasselbring & Hamlett, 1983).

Curriculum-Based Measurement and Computers

A good example of long-term research and development on computerized classroom assessment can be found in the work on computer applications in curriculum-based measurement conducted at Vanderbilt University (Fuchs, Fuchs, & Hamlett, 1993). Curriculum-based measurement (CBM) is a method for testing students on an ongoing basis and using the results to guide instructional decisions. For example, each week a student may take a timed test on a set of math problems sampled from the year's curriculum, and the number of correct answers per minute may be displayed on a graph. If satisfactory learning is occurring, the graph will trend upward. If the student is experiencing difficulties, the graph may be flat or even trend downward. This indicates that the teacher should alter instruction for that student.

Curriculum-based measurement can be very labor intensive for the teacher. Tests must be prepared, administered, and scored on a regular basis, and student performance must be graphed and analyzed. Thus, in the mid-1980s, a series of projects began to study the use of computers to automate CBM. Computer systems were developed to administer the tests, store the responses, and prepare various types of reports for the teacher, including graphs and subskill analyses. Eventually, "expert systems"[4] were added to analyze the data and to make instructional recommendations. These projects have consistently found that computerized CBM leads to improvements in certain aspects of teaching and, most important, in student achievement.

Other Models of Assessment

Approaches like precision teaching and curriculum-based measurement are primarily intended to answer such questions as "How well does the student know the material?" "Is learning progressing satisfactorily?" "With which information or skills is the student having difficulty?" Because they are not standardized on large samples of students, these approaches do not answer such questions as "Is

---

[4]Expert systems are a type of artificial intelligence that can store expert knowledge in the form of rules and apply this knowledge to individual cases.

the student on grade level?" or "How does the student compare with other students of the same age?" Also, because they do not draw very extensively on cognitive or instructional theories, such approaches are not intended to provide much insight into underlying factors or processes of learning.

Approaches like precision teaching and curriculum-based measurement are deliberately focused on observable features of instruction and behavior. They reflect a general reluctance to make inferences about processes or factors that cannot be observed. In this way they differ from a number of other approaches that try to look beyond observable behavior to discern general patterns or underlying factors and processes that may have implications for instruction. In these approaches, inferences are made on the basis of theories of assessment, learning, and cognition. Because they tend to involve complex analyses of student responses, these assessment approaches often depend on the use of technology.

For example, the assessment component of the DLM Math Fluency Program (Hasselbring & Goin, 1989) uses patterns of accuracy and response speed to make inferences based on cognitive theories of automaticity and stages of learning. The student first practices math facts in a computer activity that encourages accuracy, not speed. This is called the *acquisition stage.* When the student reaches a criterion of accuracy on a math fact, instruction for that fact shifts to a computerized game that encourages both accuracy and speed. This is called the *fluency stage,* and it continues until automaticity can be inferred from sufficient speed. At this point, the math fact is considered to be learned to a useful level, and the student begins working on a new math fact.

Malouf and Taymans (1988) tested a similar approach in two studies on computerized instruction and assessment in teaching functional abbreviations and vocabulary. Drawing upon cognitive theories of automaticity, stages of learning, semantics, and memory, the authors studied various methods for using student accuracy and response speed to determine when items had been learned well enough to be retained and applied to more complex tasks. Findings suggested that predictive validity[5] was increased when assessments were based on more complete models of underlying learning processes. For instance, the findings suggested that response speed had value as an indicator of learning only after accuracy had been achieved and that assessment was more accurate when it took this factor into account. Findings further suggested that assessment was more accurate when response speed was divided into components representing the cognitive and physical responses involved in the learning task.

Other assessment approaches have applied much more complex models, often using artificial intelligence or expert system software to represent systems involving numerous elements and processes. Examples can be found in the TORUS program for mathematics assessment, which uses expert system technology to analyze student errors and to discern patterns of conceptual misunderstanding (Woodward, Freeman, & Howard, 1992), and DynaMath, a computerized system

[5]The term *predictive validity* refers to the ability of a test to predict performance in other important activities. It is one of several types of "validity" used to judge tests.

for assessing student learning in mathematics (Gerber, Semmel, & Semmel, 1994), which incorporates computerized models of the teacher, student, and instructional domain to analyze errors and identify an optimal range of instruction for the student.

What Does This Mean for the Teacher?

Will sophisticated approaches such as TORUS or DynaMath ever find their way into the classroom? Maybe, but only if some challenges can be overcome. The capacity of technology to accommodate complex assessment models strains the capacity of educational research to develop and validate them. Thus, such systems can be difficult and time-consuming to produce, and the ultimate results can be disappointing. Commercial software companies may see no benefit in investing money in such systems, unless teachers demand them. Teachers, it has been noted, often make little use of the assessments currently available in commercial software (MacArthur & Malouf, 1991), despite the fact that technology serves simply to expand the already existing variety of available strategies for conducting classroom assessments.

Ultimately, the teacher must select approaches to classroom assessment and decide what role technology will play. Used in combination with other assessment strategies and in a manner consistent with the curriculum and the teacher's instructional approaches, technology can be a powerful aid in assessing and understanding student learning.

TECHNOLOGY AND THE FUTURE

Considering the promise of technology for children and youth with disabilities is exciting. Imagine children with mild disabilities using integrated multimedia technology *routinely* to call up historic images from other times and cultures, write collaborative short stories with friends, and take an active involvement in their own education.

Imagine persons with physical disabilities using such assistive technologies as computer peripherals, robotics, and virtual reality to gain access to and control over environments and experiences once closed to them. Imagine telecommunications satellites being used to provide networked instruction to persons with disabilities who are homebound or live in remote geographic areas.

Of course, a serious examination of current research studies and economic indicators can bring such thoughts rapidly down to Earth, as examination calls into question the manner in which we currently educate children with disabilities and the extent to which we are preparing them for the changes occurring in society and the work environment of the future.

Recent studies generally agree about the kinds of skills the future workforce will need as there continues to be a shift from a manufacturing to a service economy and from an industrial to an information-based society. Elements comprising the foundation of success in the workplace are basic skills, higher-order thinking skills, and interpersonal skills, which means that future workers will (a) need to apply fundamental mathematics concepts to their work, (b) write brief communication, and (c) be able to work effectively as part of a team (U.S. Department of Labor, 1991). Beyond basic skills, those who succeed will have to possess broader intellectual abilities in (a) abstraction, (b) system thinking, (c) experimentation, and (d) collaboration (Reich, 1991).

Responding in advance to future demands, the U.S. Department of Labor (1991) report summarizes five key areas in which all high school students should be competent. Future workers should be able to demonstrate an ability to (a) manage resources, (b) communicate with others, (c) manage information, (d) understand systems, and (e) use technology appropriately, which itself implies that without effective preparation, special education students will likely join what Johnston and Packer (1987) describe as the "growing underclass" of workers who will fill low-paying service sector jobs.

In time, such an underclass could be subject to increasingly pronounced patterns of unemployment. This is borne out by the findings of the National Longitudinal Transition Study of Special Education Students (Wagner et al., 1993), which illustrated a sizeable gap between the unemployment rates of out-of-school youth with disabilities and youth in general; and those workers with disabilities who *are* employed were more likely to hold low-status jobs with less hope for advancement than young workers in general.

The challenge for the future is for educators not only to make some fundamental changes in how they think about instruction but also to make changes in planning how to deliver more diverse special education and related services. The use of technology, embedded in a sound instructional program, has the potential to bridge what Johnston and Packer (1987) call "the gap" between the low education skills of new workers and the advancing skill requirements of the work world.

One example of technology's potential is an ongoing effort by Technical Educational Research Centers (TERC). For the past ten years, TERC has been using computer networks and telecommunications in a variety of projects to move learning beyond the boundaries of the classroom. In one instance, a project linked groups of classrooms to one another and to professional scientists who helped students explore pressing global problems. The students conducted experiments and shared their findings with other students. This gave students an opportunity to use more analytical thinking as well as to "experience" the excitement of science (Means et al., 1993).

As exciting as the use of technology can be in educating children with disabilities, there are not enough computers in schools today to infuse technology-based learning into the curriculum. In truth, most schools do not have the upgraded systems necessary to make technology an integral part of the instructional program. Typically, in most schools one computer is available for every thirty students, which approximates little more than one hour a week of available time per student (Hasselbring, 1991). This situation will need to change, as getting appropriate technology into the hands of educators and giving them training and support in its use is critical to the future of students with disabilities.

This is not to say that schools are totally bereft of technology. Although computer use is not widespread in all schools, almost every school district has video and audio equipment; and most classrooms have access to a VCR. More than half of the states, particularly those with a rural or geographically widespread population, have begun to explore the use of telecommunications technology in distance learning.

Some school districts have developed programs to meet specific needs of students with particular disabilities. Other districts use technology as part of an overall instructional program, networking with other students and other classrooms. Still other schools rely on technology in the training and support of teachers and encourage the use of technology in general (Hauser, 1994).

Today computers and other devices are being used in schools as tools in the learning process rather than as instructional delivery devices. Multimedia environments can mirror the technology to be used at home or in future workplaces; and word processors, spell checkers, and on-screen calculators can also serve students as they learn (Means et al., 1993).

Used effectively, computer technology has the potential to enhance students' work and perform routine, basic skills tasks, freeing students to learn to operate at higher cognitive levels within the context of overall instruction. Some projects approach this by providing information and technology tools for student inquiry. The Education Development Center, for example, is field-testing MAKE IT HAPPEN!, a program that guides the development of inquiry-based thematic units, integrating a variety of technology applications.

A suburban New York site developed a unit on the human body, with teachers and students using simulations, a CD-ROM magazine index, videos, and word processing. A rural community in New Hampshire focused on the history of the town, developing a unit that relied on such technological support as a teacher-made video, a database, and word processing (Means et al., 1993).

Such applications of diverse technologies now need to occur on more than just a random basis. On the one hand, as we have seen, major advances in rehabilitation and multimedia technologies have clear benefits for children and youth with disabilities. At the same time, the new technologies will demand that a large number of students with disabilities and their teachers become proficient in computers and other high technology instructional systems.

The questions, for the present, remain as follows:

1. How can technology influence or change learning?
2. What do we know now about how students learn and how technology can strengthen that process?
3. As technologies advance in fields beyond education, how can we adapt what they know to the teaching of children with disabilities?
4. How can we get powerful tools directly into the hands of our teachers and give them the training and support they need?

However long addressing these questions may take, if students with disabilities are to be meaningful participants in the society of the future, we must most particularly examine and question "business as usual," so that fundamental change can occur.

REFERENCES

Adams, M. (1990). *Beginning to read: Thinking and learning about print.* Cambridge, MA: MIT Press.

Arter, J., & Jenkins, J. (1979). Differential diagnosis and prescriptive teaching: A critical review. *Review of Educational Research, 49*(4) 517–555.

Baker, S., Kameenui, E. D., & Simmons, D. (1994). *Characteristics of student with diverse learning and curricular needs* (Technical Report). Eugene: University of Oregon, National Center to Improve the Tools of Educators.

Baker, S., Kameenui, E. D., Simmons, D., & Stahl (1994). Beginning reading: Educational tools for diverse learners. *School Psychology Review, 23,* 372–391.

Beck, I., & Roth, S. (1984a). *Research and instructional issues related to the enhancement of children's decoding skills through a microcomputer program.* Paper presented at the annual meeting of the American Education Research Association, New Orleans.

Beck, I., & Roth, S. (1984b). *Hint and hunt I and II* (computer program). Allen, TX: DLM.

Blackstone, S. (1990, November). Assistive technology in the classroom: Issues and guidelines. *Augmentative Communication News, 3*(6), 1–4.

Bottge, B. A., & Hasselbring, T. S. (1993). Taking word problems off the page. *Educational Leadership, 50,* pp. 36–38.

Clark, C. (1983). Reconsidering research on learning from media. *Review of Educational Research, 53,* 445–460.

Cognition and Technology Group at Vanderbilt University. (1994). Multimedia environments for developing literacy in at-risk students. In B. Means (Ed.), *Technology and education reform: The reality behind the promise.* San Francisco: Jossey-Bass.

Education of the Handicapped Act Amendments of 1990, PL 101-476, Section 602,104 Stat. 1105 (1990).

Flexer, C. (1992). *Listening and hearing.* Rockville: MD: American Speech-Language Hearing Association.

Fuchs, L. S., Fuchs, D., & Hamlett, C. L. (1993). Technology advances linking assessment of students' academic proficiency to instructional planning. *Journal of Special Education Technology, 12,* 49–62.

Gerber, M. M., Semmel, D. S., & Semmel, M. I. (1994). Computer-based dynamic assessment of multidigit multiplication. *Exceptional Children, 61,* 114–125.

Hasselbring, T. S. (1991). Improving education through technology: Barriers and recommendations. *Preventing School Failure, 35,* 33–37.

Hasselbring, T. S., & Goin, L. I. (1989). *DLM Math Fluency Program* [computer program]. Allen, TX: DLM Learning Resources.

Hasselbring, T. S., Goin, L. I., & Bransford, J. D. (1988). Developing math automaticity in learning handicapped children: The role of computerized drill and practice. *Focus on Exceptional Children, 20,* 1–7.

Hasselbring, T. S., & Hamlett, C. (1983). AIMSTAR: A data management and decision-making system [computer program]. Portland, OR: ASIEP Education Company.

Hasselbring, T., Russell, S. J., & Woodward, J. (1987). *Academy for effective computer use.* Reston, VA: Council for Exceptional Children.

Hauser, J. (1994, February). Rollerskating on the information superhighway: Access and equity for children with disabilities. *Education SatLink* [magazine and program guide]. Columbia: Missouri School Board Association.

Johnston, W., & Packer, A. (1987). *Workforce 2000.* Indianapolis: Hudson Institute.

Jones, K., Torgesen, J. K., & Sexton, M. (1987). Using computer guided practice to increase decoding fluency in learning disabled children: A study using the Hint and Hunt I program. *Journal of Learning Disabilities, 20,* 122–128.

Kelly, A. E., & O'Kelly, J. B. (1993). Emergent literacy: Implications for the design of computer writing applications for children. *Journal of Computing in Childhood Education, 4,* 3–14.

MacArthur, C. A., & Malouf, D. B. (1991). Teachers' beliefs, plans, and decisions about computer-based instruction. *Journal of Special Education, 25,* 44–72.

Malouf, D. B., & Taymans, J. M. (1988). *The validity of response latency as a measure of learning during computer-assisted instruction.* Paper presented at CEC/TAM International Conference on Technology and Special Education, Reno, NV.

McKeown, M., & Beck, I. (1988). Learning vocabulary: Different ways for different goals. *Remedial and Special Education, 9,* 42–52.

Means, B., Blando, J., Olson, K., Middleton, T., Morocco, C. C., Remz, A. R., & Zorfass, J. (1993). *Using technology to support education reform.* Washington, DC: Government Printing Office.

Montague, M. (1992). The effects of cognitive and metacognitive strategy instruction on the mathematical problem solving of middle school students with learning disabilities. *Journal of Learning Disabilities, 25,* 230–248.

Morocco, C. C., Dalton, B., & Tivnan, T. (1989). *The impact of computer-supported writing instruction on the writing quality of learning-disabled students: Final report* (Grant Number G008630149). Washington, DC: U.S. Department of Education.

Morocco, C. C., Dalton, B., & Tivnan, T. (1992). The impact of computer-supported writing instruction on fourth-grade students with and without learning disabilities. *Reading and Writing Quarterly: Overcoming Learning Difficulties, 8,* 87–113.

National Council of Teachers of Mathematics. (1989). *Curriculum and evaluation standards for school mathematics, assessment standards for school mathematics, professional standards for teaching mathematics.* Reston, VA: Author.

Okolo, C. M. (1990a). *Classroom uses of instructional technology: Recommendations for future research and related activities.* Washington, DC: COSMOS.

Okolo, C. M. (1990b). Effects of an introductory computer course on special educators' attitudes and evaluations of instructional software. *Journal of Special Education Technology, 10*(4), 233–240.

Okolo, C. M. (1992). Reflections on the effect of computer-assisted instruction format and initial attitude on the arithmetic facts, proficiency, and continuing motivation of student with learning disabilities. *Exceptionality, 3,* 255–258.

Okolo, C. M., Bahr, C. M., & Rieth, H. J. (1993). A retrospective view of computer-based instruction. *Journal of Special Education Technology, 12,* 1–27.

Papert, S., (1980). *MINDSTORMS: Children, computers, and powerful ideas.* New York: Basic Books.

Peters, E. E., & Levin, J. L. (1986). Effects of a mnemonic imagery strategy on good and poor readers' recall of prose. *Reading Research Quarterly, 21,* 179–192.

Reich, R. (1991). *The wealth of nations.* New York: Knopf.

Scheid, K. (1990). *Cognitive-based methods for teaching mathematics to students with learning problems.* Unpublished manuscript, Information Center for Special Education Media and Materials, Linc Resources, Columbus, Ohio.

Scheid, K. (1991). *Effective writing instruction for student with learning problems.* Unpublished manuscript, Information Center for Special Education Media and Materials, Linc Resources, Columbus, Ohio.

Scheid, K. (1994). Cognitive-based methods for teaching mathematics: Matching classroom resources to instructional methods. *Teaching Exceptional Children, 26*(3), 6–10.

Stein, M., Dixon, R., & Isaacson, S. (1994). Effective writing instruction. *School Psychology Review, 23,* 392–405.

Technology Related Assistance for Individuals with Disabilities Act of 1988, PL 100-407.

Thorkildsen, R. (1994). *Quality and availability of assistive devices* (Technical Report No. 7). Eugene: University of Oregon, National Center to Improve the Tools of Educators.

Todis, B., & Walker, H. (1993). User perspectives on assistive technology in educational settings. *Focus on Exceptional Children, 26*(3), 1–16.

U.S. Department of Labor. (1991). *What work requires of schools. A SCANS report for America 2000.* Washington, DC: Author.

Wagner, M., Blackorby, J., Cameto, R., Hebbeler, K., & Newman, L. (1993, December). *A summary of findings from the national longitudinal transition study of special education students.* Menlo Park, CA: SRI International.

Wong, B. (1986). Metacognition and learning disabilities. In D. L. Forrest-Pressley, G. E. MacKinnon, & T. G. Waller (Eds.), *Metacognition, cognition and human performance* (pp. 137–180). San Diego, CA: Academic Press.

Woodward, J., Freeman, S., & Howard, L. (1992). *TORUS: Computer-based analysis of subtraction* [computer program]. Eugene, OR: Eugene Research Institute.

Zorfass, J., Corley, P., & Remz, A. (1994). Helping students with disabilities become writers. *Educational Leadership, 51*(7), 62–66.

9

Integration in the Preschool for Children with Mild or Moderate Disabilities

LYNETTE K. CHANDLER
CAROL M. DAHLQUIST

The inclusion of young children with special needs in settings with typical children is supported by social, educational, and legislative imperatives. Inclusion has been advocated as a value-driven and empirically based recommended practice for over twenty years by early childhood special educators and organizations for young children and individuals with disabilities such as the Division for Early Childhood and the National Association for the Education of Young Children (1993), and the Council for Exceptional Children (1993). Federal commitment to the inclusion of young children with special needs was underscored with the passage of PL 99-457 in 1986 (Education for All Handicapped Act Amendments, PL 99-457) and reinforced by the Individuals with Disabilities Education Act in 1990 (PL 101-476) and PL 102-119 in 1991 (Individuals with Disabilities Education Act Amendments). These laws specify that children with disabilities from three to five years of age should receive a free and appropriate education in the Least Restrictive Environment (LRE). Although the laws do not identify inclusive or integrated settings as LRE, their intent is that the location of services and method of providing services should support maximum participation in the mainstream, based on the principle of normalization (Salisbury & Smith, 1993).

Inclusion is one of many terms that refer to placing children with special needs in settings with typically developing peers. Other terms such as *mainstreaming, integration,* and *reverse mainstreaming* also have been used to describe this practice. Early childhood special educators have recently criticized these alternative terms for highlighting the differences between children rather than focusing on similarities and rights of all children to education in the Least Restrictive Environment. For example, Odom and McEvoy (1988) describe mainstreaming as the placement of children with disabilities in educational settings for and with normally developing children. They define integration as the process of actively mixing the two groups of children. Salisbury (1991) suggests that the definitions of these terms imply that young children with disabilities are being placed into the mainstream, into programs that were developed *for* other children (that is, "typical" children). These definitions further imply that if placing children with disabilities in regular education or community day care programs does not work, these children can be pulled out and placed in segregated special education programs. Salisbury maintains that the definition and underlying philosophy of inclusion is different. Inclusion implies that young children with disabilities are placed in classes that they would attend if they did not have a disability. Children with special needs are included as part of the class (as are all children) rather than being integrated or mainstreamed into a class for typically developing children.

The philosophy of inclusion is based on attitudes and values that celebrate diversity (Council for Exceptional Children, 1993). Within this philosophy the assumption is that all classes and settings consist of children with varying levels of ability and diverse needs. These diverse needs should be accommodated and programs adapted to meet the needs of all children rather than the majority of children. Alternative placements for children with special needs should be explored *only* after adaptations and supports in the inclusive program have been implemented and shown not to be sufficient to meet the child's needs.

The number of preschool-aged children enrolled in inclusive settings and the number and type of programs that include typical children and children with disabilities are increasing. Although an accurate estimate of the number of young children attending inclusive programs in the United States is not available, Lamorey and Bricker (1993) indicate that in Oregon approximately 30 percent of preschool-aged children with developmental disabilities attended programs with typical peers. Wolery and Fleming (1993) report that 75 percent of the nine hundred preschools they surveyed across the country indicated they had included at least one child with disabilities between 1989 and 1990.

The commitment to inclusion presents many challenges to teachers, parents, and administrators as they strive to develop models of inclusion that (a) meet the needs of all children in a program, (b) are feasible to employ within early childhood settings, and (c) are supported by staff, parents, school personnel, and the community. There is no one accepted or recommended model for developing and delivering inclusive services for preschool-aged children. For example, some programs have engaged in extensive preparation and teacher education prior to adopting inclusion. Other programs have enrolled children with special needs and then developed methods to foster inclusion based on the characteristics and needs of those children, families, and program staff. Variability in methods and models to promote inclusion is to be expected and, in fact, desired. No single method or model of inclusion can be effective across all children, families, and programs (Spodek & Saracho, 1994). Rather, inclusion practices, just like other aspects of early childhood special education, must be individualized to meet the diverse needs of children, programs, and families. This does not mean however, that educators are without direction in designing inclusion programs. Fortunately, several methods and strategies to promote inclusion and models of inclusion programs have been provided through demonstration and research projects and through topical issues of early childhood and special education journals and books (for example, Division for Early Childhood, 1993; Fewell & Neisworth, 1990; Mori & Garwood, 1981; Odom, 1989; Peck, Odom, & Bricker, 1993). These models and strategies provide a variety of practices that educators may consider as they design inclusion programs for their communities.

The purpose of this chapter is to summarize practices that promote inclusion in programs that serve preschool-aged children, with and without disabilities. The term *inclusion* will be used to indicate the practice of enrolling children with special needs in programs that they would attend if they did not have a disability. This may include community or family day care programs, community preschool programs, private preschool programs, and federally or state-funded at-risk programs such as Head Start and prekindergarten programs. This chapter will present the rationale for and benefits of inclusion for young children, program options for inclusion, strategies and recommended practices to promote and evaluate the success of inclusion, and behavior management practices in inclusive settings. In this chapter the term *teacher* will be used to indicate all adults in the classroom setting and will refer to teaching assistants, inclusion facilitators, principals, therapists, volunteers, parents, and teachers.

BENEFITS OF AND RATIONALE FOR INCLUSION

In 1978, Guralnick edited one of the first books concerning integration for young children. This seminal book identified several potential and expected benefits to inclusion. Positive outcomes were described for (a) children with special needs, (b) typical children, (c) family members, (d) teachers and other educators, and (e) the society or the immediate community.

Children with special needs who attended integrated programs were expected to gain skills in social, behavioral, and educational or developmental domains. The efficiency of learning and the quality and quantity of skills attained were expected to be greater in inclusive settings than in segregated settings. Inclusive settings were expected to provide opportunities for more stimulating, responsive, and normalizing experiences than would segregated settings that enrolled children with similar or limited repertoires. An assumption was that inclusion would provide children with special needs the opportunity to observe, imitate, and interact with typical, and often more advanced, peers who would model communication, play, and social skills, as well as other adaptive behaviors (Bricker, 1978; Guralnick, 1990; Peterson, 1987).

Typically developing children, their parents, and educators were expected to benefit from inclusion as they adopted attitudes that respected differences and disabilities (Vincent, Brown, & Getz-Sheftel, 1981). These positive attitudes and accepting behaviors also were expected to impact the local community and society at large. In addition, inclusion advocates anticipated that no detrimental effects would ensue for typical children from participation in inclusive programs; that is, typically developing children were expected to show gains in development that would be expected from participation in early childhood programs that did not include children with special needs.

Several of the expectations and benefits articulated by inclusion advocates have indeed been realized. Many studies have documented that typically developing children do not show detrimental effects from participation in inclusive programs and in fact make gains that are on par with or that exceed gains that would be expected from maturation alone (Odom & McEvoy, 1990). In addition, typically developing children, parents, and teachers do generally exhibit positive attitudes concerning children with disabilities (Bailey & McWilliam, 1990).

Many studies also have documented social, behavioral, and educational or developmental benefits for children with special needs who participate in inclusive settings. Inclusion programs often produce greater gains in social, cognitive, play, and communication skills than do segregated programs (Guralnick, 1990; Salisbury & Smith, 1993). However, other investigators have reported equivalent development between segregated and inclusive settings (Bailey & McWilliam, 1990; Jenkins, Speltz, & Odom, 1985; Odom & McEvoy, 1988), and a small number of studies have documented detrimental effects from inclusion. In one such study, Cole, Mills, Daley, and Jenkins (1991) report that although children with mild disabilities performed better in integrated classroom settings, children with moderate disabilities made more developmental gains in segregated settings than they did in reverse mainstream settings. Outcomes in social and behavior skills and parent perceptions were not assessed, however, in this study.

Lamorey and Bricker (1993) reviewed sixteen studies, conducted between 1988 and 1992, concerning the effects of inclusion on children and their parents. They examined outcomes in the areas of social interaction, general developmental or educational skills, and parent attitudes and perceptions. They report two consistent findings in the area of social interaction: (a) planned and structured interventions in inclusive setting did successfully increase peer interaction and social skills, and (b) teacher behavior strongly influenced the level of and opportunities for peer interaction. In terms of developmental or educational outcomes, Lamorey and Bricker note that although the group of studies indicated significant improvements in social competence and play skills, no consistent significant effects in preacademic, motor, cognitive play, or language domains were noted. In this collection of studies, children did as well in inclusion settings as they did in segregated settings. Lamorey and Bricker do state, however, that the broad outcome measures obtained from the norm-referenced assessments used in these studies may obscure some benefits, and they recommend that future research examine more specific and less global outcomes. Finally, Lamorey and Bricker report that parent attitudes regarding inclusion generally were positive; however, parents of children with special needs and parents of typical children seldom interacted with one another.

Lamorey and Bricker's (1993) review points to several important factors that influence the success of inclusion. These factors must be considered if we are to realize the benefits of inclusion identified by Guralnick and his colleagues in 1978 and more recently by Peck, Odom, and Bricker (1993). Placing children with special needs in inclusive preschool programs is the beginning of an opportunity, but an opportunity that must be supported with planning and proactive interventions (Johnson & Johnson, 1980). Merely placing children with special needs in inclusive settings is not sufficient to promote the gains in development that are expected from inclusion. Inclusion requires active planning and interventions that focus on specific skills (for instance, incidental teaching to promote communication skills, environmental arrangements to provide opportunities for social interaction). For example, increased social and play skills, interaction with typical peers, and communication skills are often cited as benefits of inclusion, but these benefits usually are only found in those programs that actively promote such skills (Odom & McEvoy, 1988, 1990). Many now assume that the specific curriculum and instructional strategies employed and the quality of instruction have a more powerful influence on outcomes in inclusive programs than the mere process of placing children in the same setting. When placement in natural settings and active interventions are combined, maximum effects are found for inclusive versus segregated programs (Jenkins, Odom, & Speltz, 1989; Odom & McEvoy, 1990; Strain & Odom, 1986).

Based on our current knowledge regarding the benefits of inclusion, the challenge to educators and families is to design programs that maximize the effectiveness of inclusion (Guralnick, 1990). This effort will require resources, personnel, and the development of a variety of service delivery options and intervention strategies that blend into existing programs.

SERVICE DELIVERY OPTIONS

Public schools are required by federal law to provide special education and related services to preschool-aged children with developmental disabilities or delays in the least restrictive environment, which for many children is an inclusion program. Unfortunately, most public schools do not provide programs for typically developing preschoolers. As a result, public schools must "be creative in their efforts to provide young children with integrated or normalized education opportunities" (Rose & Smith, 1994, p. 1). Until recently, the majority of inclusion programs were associated with universities and funded as model demonstration programs. As the practice of inclusion expands, there is a great need for additional programs within the community to serve as inclusion sites. Increasing numbers of children are being served in community-based neighborhood programs such as family day care homes, church-based day care programs, and private and public preschool programs. Options for community-based programs may include Head Start programs, at-risk or prekindergarten programs, private day care and preschool programs, family day care homes, and preschool special education programs that are located in public school buildings.

Within these programs are many options for service delivery and intervention. Options for inclusion may include (a) enrollment with no special education or support services, (b) enrollment with minimal special education and support services such as adaptive equipment and adapted curriculum activities and materials, (c) enrollment with special education and support services provided by consulting personnel (namely, an inclusion facilitator), (d) enrollment in a program that is co-taught by an early childhood educator and early childhood special educator, (e) dual enrollment in an early childhood program and a special education preschool program, and (f) primary enrollment in a special education preschool program with opportunities to interact with typical peers during some activities. Educators and families should consider the intent of the least restrictive environment mandate when selecting service delivery options and program placement. The LRE mandate implies that education in inclusive programs is preferable to segregated education and should be used unless there are compelling reasons for alternative placement. It further implies that all children with special needs, regardless of the severity of disability or delay, should spend some portion of the day in settings with typical peers. The law's intent is to view special education as a service that may be provided in a variety of placements. Parents and staff are encouraged to identify the type and frequency of special education and related services that are required and then to identify how these can be obtained in the placement(s) that parents prefer.

Theoretically, any early childhood program can be an appropriate setting for inclusion. However, the amount of effort involved in planning and implementing an inclusion program will vary as a result of factors that are present when a program is selected. Several factors will facilitate the process of inclusion. If these factors are not in place when a program is selected, time and effort will need to be devoted to developing these factors. The absence of these factors, however, should not preclude a program from including children with and without special needs.

Many educators consider teacher attitudes and abilities the most important factors contributing to successful inclusion (Cook, Tessier, & Armbruster, 1987; Safford, 1989; Thompson, 1994). Educators and parents may look for programs that employ staff who are willing to work with children of varying abilities, who have a developmental facilitation verses custodial approach to care, and who have a generally positive attitude concerning disability and inclusion (Bruder, 1993). As Thompson (1994) indicates, procedures are more easily changed than are philosophies or values. Staff should be willing to individualize and adapt interventions and to collaborate in planning and implementing the inclusion program.

Educators and parents might consider prior experience and training of staff with respect to regular early childhood and early childhood special education programs. They also might consider the hours of service and days of the week when services are provided; the cost to parents (if applicable); the options for family involvement; the type of approach staff employ when interacting with families (for example, a family-centered approach) (Bruder, 1993; Thompson, 1994); and the accessibility of environmental features such as space, materials, peers, and adults (Bailey & McWilliam, 1990). The ratio of children with special needs to typically developing children also may be considered. Current recommended practices concerning such a ratio follow the concept of natural proportions in which the number of children with special needs per program reflects the natural proportions of disability in the population. For example, the Circle of Inclusion preschool programs developed by Thompson and her colleagues (1994) generally have eighteen to twenty-two typically developing children and one to two children with special needs.

STRATEGIES TO PROMOTE INCLUSION

Successful inclusion involves the participation of all children in all aspects of the classroom routines and activities. Children with and without disabilities should share the physical environment, as well as the social and instructional or educational environment.

Sharing the Physical Environment

Sharing the physical environment is the first step to successful inclusion. When children share the physical environment, they spend the majority of the day in the same areas and engage in the same activities as their peers. Inclusion is not realized when children with disabilities are placed in one segregated area of the room, while typically developing children work and play in other areas. In an inclusive program, all children work and play in proximity to one another for a majority of the daily activities and routines. For example, all children should sit together during snack and circle activities, play at the same tables or theme areas (that is, centers), and participate in outdoor and out of class activities. This might require teachers to (a) help a child who is nonambulatory move to various areas as activities change (such as from the block area to the story area), (b) position or support a child who typically is in a care chair on the floor during circle time or in the pool during a swimming activity, or (c) give a child intravenous feedings during snack time near or at the snack table.

When typical children and children with special needs share the physical environment, they have opportunities to interact and play with one another and to observe and learn from one another. However, as mentioned earlier, sharing the physical environment is only a preliminary step to promoting inclusion for many children. Physical proximity must be paired with additional proactive strategies that help children share the social and educational environments as well.

Sharing the Social Environment

Positive social interactions, independent and group play skills, and friendships with peers are some of the most important benefits that may result from inclusion. Social competence with peers has been related to general developmental progress, cognitive development, communicative competence, and academic or educational success (Guralnick, 1986; Hendrickson, Strain, Tremblay, & Shores, 1982; Strain & Odom, 1986). Teachers have identified positive interaction with peers and appropriate play skills as important behaviors for success within early childhood and early childhood special education programs (Murphy & Vincent, 1989; Odom, McConnell, & Chandler, 1994).

During the preschool years most children develop friendships, establish appropriate styles of interaction, and engage in positive group play. Other children, however, especially children with moderate and severe disabilities, do not develop appropriate peer interactions without specific experiences that provide opportunities to interact with and receive feedback from socially competent peers. In fact, as mentioned earlier, the social benefits that accrue in inclusive settings have primarily occurred only when social interaction was actively promoted by teachers. For children to share the social environment, teachers must plan for and arrange daily interactions between children.

Within inclusion programs for preschool-aged children, strategies to promote social interaction can be divided into three categories: environmental arrangements, adaptations of regularly scheduled activities and routines, and direct and indirect teaching strategies.

Arranging the Environment The environment has a strong influence on social behavior and can either facilitate or inhibit the frequency and type of peer interaction. Within preschool settings, investigators have identified four variables that

Table 9.1 Factors to Consider When Arranging the Physical Environment

Categories	Factors	Environmental Arrangements That May Promote Peer Interaction*
Adults	Presence versus absence	Teach absence
	Type of behavior adults promote	Teacher presence; low rate of teacher-child interaction
	Rate of adult-child interaction	Teacher presence; prompt peer interaction
		Reinforcement provided following an activity
Materials	Number and variety	Somewhat limited number and variety
	Distribution among children	Part of materials given to each child
	Type of material	Materials that promote social play (e.g., sociodramatic activities, water play, games, motor activities, blocks)
		Familiar materials
		Materials that generally match developmental level of children
		Materials that can be used in multiple ways by children of varying play levels
Peer groups	Size	Small group size: 2–4 children
	Composition	Children with social delays paired with children with appropriate social skills
		Children with special needs paired with children with more advanced skills
		Heterogeneous or integrated group
		Peers of same chronological age
Structure	High versus low structure	Teacher describes activity theme and goals
		Teacher determines group composition
		Teacher assigns roles
		Teacher distributes limited materials
		Teacher prompts peer interaction or leaves the area
		Teacher designates small play area approximately 10' × 10'
		Teacher designates seating arrangements
	Goal of activity	Cooperative goal for the activity

*This category provides examples of how some of the factors may be arranged to promote peer interaction. It does not offer examples to match each factor that may be considered.

SOURCES: These factors were derived from the following sources: Chandler et al. (1992); Guralnick and Groom (1988); McEvoy, Nordquist, Twardosz, Heckaman, Wehby, and Denny (1993); Odom (1988); Odom et al. (1993); Odom and Strain (1984); Quilitch and Risley (1973); and Strain and Odom (1986).

influence behavior: adults, materials, peer groups, and activity structure. These variables can be arranged to set the occasion for or to actively promote social interaction. Table 9.1 presents factors within these four categories that teachers may consider when arranging the classroom along with examples of environmental arrangements that have been shown to promote peer social interaction.

Thoughtful organization of the preschool environment should be a first step, a building block to helping children share the social environment (Chandler, Fowler, & Lubeck, 1992; Odom et al., 1993). In arranging the classroom environment to promote peer interaction, teachers should (a) consider the abilities and needs of children in the program, (b) examine the classroom environment to determine whether it provides opportunities for all children to interact, (c) observe the extent of positive peer interactions, (d) identify existing environmental arrangements that should be maintained, and (e) introduce new arrangements where needed to promote social interaction for their children. In addition to examining general classroom features, Chandler et al. (1992) recommend that teachers develop one activity center that is specifically designed to promote peer interaction.

Adapting Regularly Scheduled Activities and Routines A second strategy focuses on arranging or modifying daily activities and routines and modifying teacher behavior during them. Within this framework, teachers consider the various activities and routines that occur throughout the day and decide which of these might promote social interaction. Teachers then adapt activities and routines so that they include a social component. Daily activities and routines might include free play, circle time, transitions, snack, story time, large- or small-group activities, table activities, and cleanup.

Perhaps the best-known example of adapting classroom activities to promote social skills is friendship activities, identified in previous literature as affection training (McEvoy, Spicuzza, Davis, Cooper, & Neimeyer, 1993). Friendship activities involve adapting traditional preschool games, songs, and other group activities to include a friendship component. For example, when playing the game Simon Says, the teacher might include, "Simon says, pat your friend on the back" or "Simon says, look at your neighbor." Or when singing "If You're Happy and You Know It," the teacher may add, "If you're happy and you know it, smile and say hi to your friend" or "shake hands with the friend next to you" (see McEvoy et al., 1988, and Twardosz, Nordquist, Simon, & Botkin, 1983, for additional information on affection or friendship activities).

Other examples of adapting daily activities and routines to promote peer interaction and friendship include these:

1. Pair children as buddies during routine activities or activity transitions. For example, buddies can sit next to each other, share a cleanup duty or school job, line up together before recess, or take turns on the computer in a joint game.
2. During circle activities, such as talking about the weather, show and tell, or story time, have children face and talk to the other children instead of the teacher. Have children direct their questions to other children and encourage responses from peers.
3. At the end of an activity, have children go to the next activity in pairs or small groups based on a common characteristic such as the color of shirt or socks they are wearing.
4. Add a friendship component to the end of an activity such as cleanup by having children give each other a high five for working together.
5. During a large-group music activity, ask children to hold hands and dance in a circle or with a partner.
6. Adapt board game cards to include a friendship component (Foxx, McMorrow, & Schloss, 1983). For example, if children are playing Candyland, the card they pick might have a friendship task for them to complete before they

move their game piece. Friendship tasks may be to "Shake hands with the friend next to you," "Tell us the name of the friend sitting next to you," or "Give a friend a warm fuzzy."

Direct and Indirect Teaching Strategies Adapting daily activities and routines and arranging the classroom environment to promote social skills often work best with children whose peer interaction skills are not exhibited frequently enough or are of poor quality. For many children, however, more intensive strategies are needed to teach skills that will allow them to share the social environment with their peers. Several direct and indirect teaching strategies have been used in inclusive programs to promote peer interaction.

A set of indirect strategies that may be used to teach, as well as to promote, the use of social skills can be described under the category of incidental teaching. Incidental teaching originally was developed to promote communication and was defined as "interaction between an adult and a single child, which arises naturally in an instructional situation such as free play and which is used by the adult to transmit information or give the child practice in developing a skill" (Hart & Risley, 1975, p. 11). Several other strategies such as milieu, mand-model, and activity-based interventions expand the focus of the incidental teaching model to include a variety of developmental domains and specific skills such as peer interaction. These indirect teaching strategies allow teachers to take advantage of natural opportunities for promoting a skill or to arrange the environment to provide opportunities to promote desired skills such as social interaction.

To implement this procedure, the teacher would (a) notice what interests the child, (b) decide whether this presents an opportunity to teach social interaction, (c) establish joint attention between the child of interest and another child, (d) prompt social interaction, and (e) reinforce social behavior with praise and natural consequences. For example, if during snack Gerald tells the teacher, "I know what we're having for snack," the teacher might decide that this presents an opportunity to promote social interaction. She might prompt Gerald to tell the whole class and then prompt the class to listen. She then can praise Gerald for talking to the class and bring out the snack that he described (natural consequence). Or, if Jalica is showing Sal her picture and he is ignoring her, the teacher might tell Sal to look because Jalica is showing him something, and then prompt Jalica to show him the picture again. She can then praise Sal for listening to Jalica and for looking at her picture and praise Jalica for showing her picture to Sal. The natural consequence for the children is the peer interaction itself.

Ostrosky and Kaiser (1991) have identified seven strategies teachers might use to arrange situations that would provide an opportunity to use incidental teaching: (a) use interesting materials, (b) place some materials out of reach, (c) provide inadequate portions, (d) present choices, (e) create situations in which the child needs assistance, (f) sabotage or alter the activity, and (g) set up silly situations. For example, a teacher might place some materials out of reach and then prompt a child to ask a peer for help in retrieving them. Or, the teacher might introduce a game that one child cannot do alone. The teacher can prompt the child to find a friend to play, prompt and praise peer interaction, and then allow the natural consequence of completing the game or activity to provide reinforcement.

A second indirect teaching strategy that teachers have used to promote peer interaction is correspondence training, also known as say/do training. Correspondence training helps children identify the behavior that they will do prior to engaging in an activity. For example, a child may indicate that he or she will share toys with Natalie during free play. At the end of the activity, the child reports or discusses with the teacher whether he had engaged in the behavior that had been identified. The child receives reinforcement if there is a match between the verbal and nonverbal behavior (that is, say/do). The goal of correspondence training is to help children achieve correspondence between saying and doing. For instance, Guevremont, Osnes, and Stokes (1986) used correspondence training to increase peer-directed talk for a preschool child who seldom interacted with peers. The child was prompted to describe the behavior that she would emit during a play session (for example, "I'm going to talk to Jerome today"). The child then discussed her behavior with the teacher and received reinforcement if she had talked to Jerome during the activity.

Direct teaching strategies typically involve the teacher in a mediator or coaching role as children are taught specific social skills to use with peers. Direct teaching strategies include sociodramatic script training, teacher-mediated interventions, and peer-mediated and comprehensive interventions. These strategies often require more teacher time, adaptations of daily routines and activities, and interactions with children than do indirect teaching strategies. The primary purpose of the more direct teaching activities is to teach children with social delays social skills and behaviors that would allow them to interact and share the social environment with peers. One or a combination of the following strategies may be used in direct teaching: instructions, discussion, modeling, role-play, prompting, feedback, and reinforcement. As with all previous strategies, direct teaching strategies may be implemented by teachers, teaching assistants, parents, and other adults in a classroom or home setting.

Goldstein and his colleagues have developed sociodramatic scripts that teachers may use to help children participate in a variety of sociodramatic activities such as McDonald's Hamburger Shop, Pet Shop, Doctor, and Magic Show (Goldstein & Cisar, 1992; Goldstein, Wickstrom, Hoyson, Jamieson, & Odom, 1988). Through sociodramatic script training, children role-play one or more parts of prepared scripts for sociodramatic activities (for instance, salesperson or customer, doctor or parent). During training, the teacher assigns children to roles, provides an overview of each role and the general behaviors that are required to complete the role, and then prompts children to demonstrate the behaviors specified for each role. The behavior identified should vary across children based on each child's abilities. For example, one child may point to french fries to place an order, another may say, "French fries," and yet another may say, "I want some french fries, please." The teacher provides frequent prompting at the beginning of training and fades the level of prompts as children independently engage in pretend play. Variation in the behaviors associated with each role also is encouraged.

For example, a child who learned to say "french fries" when placing an order would be reinforced for expanding the role and ordering "french fries and a Coke" or "a large order of fries." Sociodramatic script training facilitates peer interaction in familiar routines and helps children learn to take turns, follow the activity theme, and engage in similar and predictable exchanges.

Teachers may add a direct teaching component to regularly scheduled group activities such as circle time or snack. For instance, during morning circle time when the children and teacher review what will happen during the day, a direct teaching activity that focuses on how to play with your friend might be introduced. This teacher-mediated activity begins with the teacher talking about playing together or being friends and reviewing classroom rules for appropriate social behaviors (for example, say please, ask for a toy, share with friends). The teacher then asks the children questions about the discussion and encourages them to respond either in unison or individually. The teacher might then role-play different situations with each child (such as asking for a toy) and then ask children to role-play with each other.

To provide more in-depth training, the teacher might teach specific skills for children to use in social situations. In doing so, the teacher would create a task analysis of the steps involved in each skill (for example, entering a play group, sharing toys, asking for help), discuss and model each step, and then ask children to role-play the skill. As children role-play, the teacher would provide prompts and feedback. For example, to make an initiation to a friend, children may learn to "say your friend's name or tap your friend on the shoulder, wait for your friend to look at you, and ask your friend to play." To respond to a friend, children may learn "when your friend says your name or taps you on the shoulder, look at your friend and answer your friend." At the end of this activity teachers can model, prompt, and reinforce children's use of the social behaviors throughout the day.

In peer-mediated strategies, children, rather than teachers, promote and consequate social behaviors. Teachers train peers to use specific behaviors and intervention strategies with children who exhibit delays in social skills. For example, peer mediators may prompt social behavior, model appropriate behavior, or use incidental training techniques (McGee, Almeida, Sulzar-Azaroff, & Feldman, 1992; Odom, Chandler, Ostrosky, McConnell, & Reaney, 1992). Peer mediation training typically involves (a) teacher-child discussions concerning the skills peers are to use, (b) the teacher's modeling of correct and incorrect examples of the skills with child feedback and correction, and (c) child role-play with feedback and praise provided by the teacher and other peers. Peer mediators then are asked to use the skills with their peers in a structured play activity. During the structured play activity, peer mediators may receive prompts, feedback, and reinforcement from the teachers. As peer mediators become proficient at using the skills, teacher prompts, feedback, and reinforcement are reduced.

A recent variation on peer-mediated strategies were identified by Odom et al. (1993) as a comprehensive intervention. This variation includes *all* children with and without social delays in the training and provides *all* children with prompts and/or reinforcement for interacting during structured play activities. This reduces the potential stigmatization and segregation of children with disabilities who do not participate in the training sessions in peer mediation training. It also may promote more normalized interactions between children. Haring (1992) cautions that children who have been taught to view their role as helper may interact differently with children with special needs if they see their role as playmate. The comprehensive intervention places all children at an equal status; all children are peer mediators. Odom and his colleagues (1993) provide detailed descriptions on how to select and train peer mediators and how to implement peer mediation and comprehensive intervention strategies.

In summary, using a variety of techniques to help children share the social environment is important. Both verbal and nonverbal social behaviors should be available to include children with language delays in social activities. Although participation by children should be voluntary, teachers should encourage and reinforce participation. Friendship activities and other adapted activities and routines should be conducted for ten to fifteen minutes daily and then faded as children begin to interact independently. Teachers also should evaluate social activities to identify those that children (and teachers) prefer and those that are most successful at helping children share the social environment (McEvoy et al., 1988).

Sharing the Educational or Instructional Environment

Sainato and Lyon (1989) have indicated that although the why of integration was clear, the how was not so evident. This point is especially true when considering the educational or instructional aspects of inclusion. Yet, children need to share the educational environment as well as the physical and social environment if the benefits expected from inclusion are to be realized. When young children share the educational environment, they have opportunities to learn from one another during child-centered and teacher-directed group activities and to participate in normal classroom activities and routines.

In inclusive programs, the curriculum and materials used by teachers and teaching assistants and expectations for children should reflect the range of abilities and needs of all children in the classroom. The goal of inclusion is for all children to participate in classroom routines and activities and to be educated in the same manner as much as possible using similar or adapted materials and individualized methods of instruction. Individualization may occur across a number of factors including type and frequency of cues and prompts, pace of instruction, task goals, anticipated behavior, type and frequency of teacher attention and assistance, and adaptations to curricular materials.

Many of the strategies that may be used to promote physical and social inclusion also will be useful in helping children share the educational environment. These strategies include placing children near each other during educational activities, arranging the educational environment, adapting existing educational activities and materials, using indirect and direct teaching strategies, and using peers as mediators during educational activities. Additional strategies are described in the following paragraphs.

Use the Same or Similar Classroom Materials and Activities for All Children Thompson and her colleagues (Thompson, 1994) identified several strategies that may be used to help children share the educational environment. One of these is to use existing classroom materials and activities to meet individual needs. When teachers use special or different materials or different activities for one child, they set that child apart from typical activities and routines and peers. In a more normalizing and cost-effective strategy, the teacher would identify how typical classroom activities and materials could be used to teach skills to each child. This may require adapting materials, providing assistance to children, and identifying the variety of skills that may be promoted during an activity or with educational materials. For example, puzzles can be used to promote grasp and release skills in the fine-motor domain; identification of shapes, colors, and pictures, and matching in the cognitive domain; following directions and conversation in the communication domain; and taking turns and sharing in the social skills domain. An art activity might be used across children to (a) build fine-motor strength in holding a crayon correctly, (b) promote independence and making choices as children determine what colors they will use and what picture they will make, (c) enhance speech and language skills by providing an opportunity for child-child or adult-child conversation about the picture, (d) promote social skills as children ask for and share crayons or color a group picture, and (e) practice identifying and naming colors and objects on the picture.

When teachers adapt materials and activities, they should consider the type of adaptation needed to help children participate. For some children, participation may be enhanced through cognitive adaptations such as simplifying the task or reducing the number of steps required. For others, physical adaptations to match individual characteristics will be most beneficial (for instance, stabilize materials, enlarge visual materials, add texture or color to materials, add an auditory component to materials, or provide physical assistance).

Use Facilitative and Natural Positioning Techniques A second strategy suggested by Thompson and her colleagues (Thompson, 1994) is to use facilitative and natural positioning techniques. Good posture and positioning fosters participation in activities by promoting normalized muscle tone, respiration, stability, and balance. These provide the child with opportunities to make eye contact, and to reach for, touch, and hold materials. For children with physical disabilities, support should be as natural as possible and provide positions that are as similar to those of other children as possible. For instance, a child with physical disabilities should be seated at the same level as other children. Support and physical prompting should be offered from behind the child so that the child faces the other children and has a clear view of the activity.

Cooperative Group Strategies During educational activities, children are more likely to interact and share the educational environment if interdependent group goals are used and each child has something to contribute to the activity. For example, if the group goal is to design a Mr. Potato Head, complete a puzzle, or build a tower, then each child would have pieces to contribute to the final product.

The buddy system is another strategy that may be used during educational activities and transitions such as going to the restroom, preparing for snack, or cleaning up. The buddy system involves pairing a child with a typically developing peer who may provide assistance, model appropriate behavior, or serve as a peer mediator. Assistance may be physical (such as helping a child open a bottle of glue), verbal (providing visual, gestural, or vocal cues or prompts following an instruction), and/or visual (following child's focus). When children are paired as buddies, teachers should identify a joint, cooperative goal and assign roles for achieving the goal. Buddy systems also decrease child dependence upon the teacher, and enhance peer interaction skills that contribute to peer relationships and friendship such as taking turns, providing assistance, and working cooperatively (Tremblay, Strain, Hendrickson, & Shores, 1981).

Partial Participation The principle of partial participation implies that all children should and can participate at some level in all classroom activities and routines. No child should be excluded because of a disability or special need. In applying the principle of partial participation, the teacher identifies children who cannot independently participate throughout an activity and then develops strategies to foster reduced or adapted levels of participation.

One way to identify children for partial participation is to analyze a task or skill and then identify steps the child can do independently. For example, a task analysis for putting different shaped pieces in a container might include these steps: (a) take cubes out of container, (b) pick up one cube, (c) place it over the correct hole, and (d) release the cube. A task analysis also identifies prerequisite and corequisite skills that are needed. For example, to independently complete the task described earlier, a child would need to be able to grasp and release small objects and to identify either visually or through touch the hole in the container in which the cubes are to be placed.

If a child cannot complete a task independently, the teacher can develop strategies for partial participation. The teacher might provide peer or teacher assistance, adapt materials, or accept a variety of response forms. For instance, if the child is not able to grasp and release objects, participation with other children might involve pouring the cubes out of the container. Alternatively, the child may receive physical assistance from the teacher or a peer to release the block or participate by shaking her head yes and no to indicate where to place the cubes.

Individualized Participation Within Groups Teachers may use individualized participation to promote inclusion during educational or preacademic activities. Individualized participation involves identifying individual goals and methods of working toward those goals during group activities. For example, many programs have a daily circle activity in which children discuss today's weather or yesterday's field trip. Within this activity, teachers might individualize the form of response each child uses to answer questions, the type of questions each child answers, and the frequency of answering questions. For instance, in reply to a question about whether it is sunny or rainy outside, one child may point to pictures of the sun or rain, one may shake his or her head yes or no, another may answer, "Rainy," another may answer, "It is rainy outside," and yet another may use sign language to answer the question. Or, the teacher may ask one child whether it is rainy or sunny outside and then ask another to tell what the weather is like today. Within individualized participation, expectations are based on each child's goals and capabilities rather than on a set curriculum that expects the same goals and responses for all students. Teachers also can individualize participation by using multisensory materials, activities, and teaching strategies that address different learning styles and a variety of physical and sensory abilities.

Activity and Play-Based Strategies The structure and teaching practices of many early childhood programs are based on the belief that typically developing young children learn skills in the context of self-initiated play and during daily activities and routines. The goal of many early childhood programs is to provide a developmentally appropriate environment that promotes development as children manipulate and interact with toys, materials, adults, and peers (Bredekamp, 1987). The role of the teacher is to support self-initiated, active learning by the child (Bailey & Wolery, 1992). This activity- and play-based approach to learning is increasingly being used in both early intervention and segregated preschool special education programs as well as in community-based preschool programs (Bredekamp, 1993; McLean & Odom, 1993).

Several procedures may be included within the concept of activity- and play-based strategies. These include naturalistic and milieu teaching; incidental teaching; activity-based intervention; transition-based teaching; teacher-supported play; and child-initiated, child-centered, or child-directed play. Although there are differences among all of these procedures, they all embed teaching strategies and opportunities for learning within the context of play and other daily activities and routines. With each of these strategies, the teacher arranges the environment to include toys, materials, activities, and routines that are appropriate to the child's age and interests. The teacher then uses the activity or toy as a vehicle to promote skill acquisition or to promote fluency and generalization. For example, the teacher might place a variety of interesting materials such as sponges, finger paints, markers, glue and string, stickers, and stencils in the art area. When a child expresses an interest in making a picture, the teacher can use the art activity as a vehicle to provide experience in making choices. To do this, the teacher might allow the child to choose a set of materials. When the child is finished with those materials, the teacher would ask him or her to choose additional materials. Alternatively, children's interest in an art activity might be used to promote social skills by developing a group art project.

In activity- and play-based strategies, the teacher may (a) ask questions or request information related to the activity, (b) provide information about or describe the child's behavior, (c) prompt behavior, (d) imitate the child's behavior, (e) model or prompt expansions of the child's behavior, and (f) reinforce appropriate skills. For instance, if a teacher saw children pretending to be firefighters during free play, she could join the activity and within the context of the play activity discuss yesterday's field trip to the fire station. During this play activity, the teacher might (a) ask for information ("What did we do at the fire station yesterday?"), (b) provide information, ("We saw a big dog at the fire station, and Joni got to wear a fire hat"), (c) prompt behavior ("What sound did the fire truck make? Why do they use a siren?"), (d) imitate the siren sounds made by the children and repeat the answers they provide concerning the siren ("It's loud"), (e) model expansions of child behavior ("Yes, it was loud; the siren tells people the fire truck is coming"), and (f) reinforce behavior ("I'm glad you remembered our trip to the fire station").

Several resources can assist teachers in designing and implementing activity- and play-based teaching strategies. Among these are Bailey and Wolery (1992); Bricker and Cripe (1992); Bredekamp (1987); Cripe, Slenz, and Bricker (1993); Johnson-Martin, Attermeier, and Hacker (1990); Linder (1993); and Ostrosky and Kaiser (1991).

Activity- and play-based strategies are particularly suited to inclusion programs because they can be used to address multiple goals for one child or for a group of children within a single activity, promoting skills across a variety of developmental domains (Bricker & Cripe, 1992). Children share the educational environment because learning is embedded in activities in which all children participate. For example, a block activity can be used to promote grasp and release skills (fine-motor), color identification (cognitive), adult-child or child-child conversation (communication), and turn-taking skills (social). These skills also could be promoted in other daily activities such as art and puzzle activities or snack and cleanup routines.

Several additional benefits make activity- and play-based teaching useful in inclusion programs. Regular education teachers may be more likely to implement Individual Education Plan (IEP) or Individualized Family Service Plan (IFSP) goals when they do not require major adjustments in existing teaching styles and routines (Peck, Killen, & Baumgart, 1989). Activity and play-based strategies also may foster family involvement in the child's educational program. These strategies can be easily used by family members to promote skills during normal family activities including preparing dinner, watching television, reading books, playing together, and dressing. For example, parents can provide language models by naming the parts of clothing while dressing. Or, parents may ask children to identify concepts while reading books or watching television. A final benefit may be the generalization and maintenance of previously learned behavior. Skills that are learned during play and during daily routines and activities are learned in the context of naturally occurring antecedents and consequences, and are practiced across a variety of settings, activities, individuals, and materials (Haring, 1992).

Although there are many advantages to using activity and play-based interventions, a cautionary statement is warranted. Even though many children learn skills through play activities, acquisition cannot be left to chance, even when the environment is developmentally appropriate. As McLean and Odom (1993) point out, developmentally appropriate practice and play-based interventions should be the foundation of classroom teaching for all children. However, they may not be sufficient for all children with special needs. Some children may require additional opportunities to practice skills, may need to be guided to play in centers that address specific needs or IEP goals, may need to experience a wider variety of generalization situations, and may require teacher-mediated instruction in addition to child-centered play activities (Cook et al., 1987).

Behavior Management in Inclusive Programs

Many children with special needs and children at risk for disability evidence challenging behavior at both a higher incidence and a higher prevalence than do typically developing children (Breiner & Forehand, 1982; Walker, 1993). Challenging behaviors may require inordinate amounts of teacher time and effort, decrease the amount of time available for promoting functional behavior skills, reduce children's positive interactions, and result in exclusion from activities or referral for more restrictive placement (Hains, Fowler, & Chandler, 1988; Repp & Karsh, 1990).

Few teachers and families have adequate training and experience in treating challenging behavior in early childhood programs (Watkins & Durant, 1992). This lack of training often leads to the misconception that challenging behaviors are related to or caused by the child's disability. This misconception may result in failure to address challenging behaviors or in the application of ineffective behavior management strategies. Both of these practices allow challenging behaviors to become further ingrained in the child's repertoire, thus increasing the risk of lifelong behavior problems and exclusion from inclusive settings.

Functional assessment is a proactive positive approach that focuses on the environmental conditions that directly promote both appropriate and challenging behaviors (Repp & Karsh, 1990). Environmental conditions may include variables that are present prior to the occurrence of behavior and that set the occasion for behavior to occur (identified as setting events and antecedent events) and consequences that follow the occurrence of behavior. Setting events and antecedent events include the type of activity, task difficulty, activity instructions, frequent errors, the time of day, location of the activity, and lack of peer or adult attention. Consequences include variables such as termination of a task, access to a preferred item, the introduction or removal of adult or peer attention, and removal from the setting (for example, time-out).

Information about setting events, antecedent events, and consequences enables teachers and families to identify the function of behavior from the child's perspective. For example, functional assessment would determine whether running out of the classroom functions to produce attention, terminate or prevent participation, or increase activity level for the child. In other words, functional assessment helps teachers and families determine what the child obtains by engaging in the behavior.

Within the functional assessment model intervention is designed to address the hypothesized function of behavior. Functional assessment interventions are designed to (a) modify the environment so that variables that are associated with the problem behavior are removed or changed and/or (b) replace the challenging behavior with a more appropriate behavior that achieves the same function. For example, the program team observes that Rhonda consistently throws toys when she is not receiving teacher attention (antecedent) and that this behavior usually results in immediate attention from the teacher (consequence). They hypothesize that the function of throwing toys is to obtain attention. An intervention for this hypothesis would be to provide frequent attention when Rhonda engages in appropriate toy play and to withhold attention when she throws toys. In another example, the team identifies mouthing toys as a problem behavior for Peter. Using functional assessment, they find that Peter does not mouth all toys, only those that he does not know how to use. They hypothesize that the function of mouthing toys is to increase stimulation. The intervention for this hypothesis would be to teach Peter how to play with new or unfamiliar toys.

This approach to behavior management is congruent with the philosophy of inclusion in that it provides individualized programming across children and modifies the environment in order to promote appropriate behavior. Several resources can assist the program team in learning about and in conducting functional assessment (see, for example, Arndorfer & Miltenberger, 1993; Carr, Robinson, & Palumbo, 1990; Foster-Johnson & Dunlap, 1993; Repp & Karsh, 1990).

Working as a Team

Inclusion represents a new partnership among early childhood and early childhood special education philosophies, teaching practices, and program staff (Guralnick, 1990). This partnership has resulted in new and unfamiliar roles for both early childhood and early childhood special educators. In an inclusive program, early childhood educators may find that they are expected to work with children with special needs and their families and to collaborate with early childhood special educators and therapists. Early childhood special educators may find that they no longer have a self-contained classroom; instead, they are expected to provide services through indirect service delivery models such as consultation, technical assistance, and staff development programs. Other areas of concern that program staff have identified are related to (a) time and effort to plan for and implement inclusion strategies, (b) new and changing roles and responsibilities, (c) training and expertise of staff, (d) philosophical differences, (e) lines of authority, (f) individualized education plans, (g) legal requirements, and (h) family involvement (Thompson, 1994).

The success of inclusion is largely dependent on the development of a collaborative partnership that promotes communication between early childhood and early childhood special education and related services staff. Strain (1990) points out that successful inclusion requires identification of the roles of all individuals and the resources that are available to assist in fulfilling those roles. In an inclusion program, the special educator should work with the early childhood staff to blend goals for children with special needs into classroom activities and routines. To do this, they will need to be familiar with the physical aspects of the classroom, curriculum, and materials and teaching philosophy and practices used by regular education staff. They must be willing to share their expertise, collaborate with team members, and allow the early childhood educator to serve as the primary teacher for all children (unless both educators served as co-teachers). They also must be able to adapt curricula, teaching procedures, and materials to promote the development of children with special needs and to address IEP goals within the early childhood classroom (Stayton & Bredekamp, 1994).

The role of the early childhood staff will be to serve as the primary teacher for all children enrolled in the program, regardless of developmental status. Therefore, they must be willing to work with children with special needs and their families, adapt the classroom environment and teaching practices to accommodate children with special needs, share expertise regarding early childhood teaching practices, and ask for and receive suggestions and recommendations from the special educator and the families of children with special needs (National Association for the Education of Young Children, 1994).

The role of administrators will be to develop interagency agreements that describe (a) a shared philosophy regarding inclusion, (b) the roles that staff members will assume, (c) a plan for transition into and from inclusion programs, (d) the way financial costs are to be met, (e) a system for family involvement, and (f) a plan for evaluating the effectiveness of inclusion. Lack of administrative support can be a significant factor that decreases the success of inclusion (McEvoy, Peterson, & McConnell, 1991). Administrators must support staff in their roles as members of the inclusion team, and provide staff training in inclusion, disabilities, team building, working with families, and other areas of interest identified by team members.

Transdisciplinary Teams The transdisciplinary model of teaming has been proposed for inclusion programs at the preschool level (Bruder, 1993; Templeman, Fredericks, & Udell, 1989). Within this model, staff members share the same vision and philosophy regarding inclusion and working with children. Team members collaborate in developing goals and strategies and in adapting the classroom to accommodate the diversity of children enrolled in the program (Peck et al., 1989). In a transdisciplinary model, staff are committed to (a) sharing resources, (b) teaching each other, (c) learning from each other, and (d) working together. To fulfill this commitment, staff engage in role release and acceptance by sharing information about their specific area of expertise and by crossing professional boundaries in working with children (Salisbury & Smith, 1993). For example, the physical therapist may share information about positioning children with physical disabilities and then train other staff members to use positioning techniques. In the transdisciplinary model, the child with special needs is not viewed as the sole responsibility of the special educator; all staff are willing and able to work with both typical children and children with special needs (Odom & McEvoy, 1990). The benefits of a transdisciplinary model include the following:

1. The team develops a picture of the whole child versus compartmentalizing the child by developmental domain or the child's development.
2. Strategies are synthesized across disciplines and individuals who work with the child.
3. There is increased consistency across team members in working with the child and family.
4. The knowledge base, problem-solving potential, and expertise of team members increase through role release and collaborative activities.

5. The team members are able to discuss concerns that may arise regarding inclusion and specific children.

Although the transdisciplinary model offers many benefits, establishing a good working team involves considerable planning and effort. The effectiveness of the transdisciplinary model will depend on the commitment of team members to inclusion and teamwork, time constraints, and administrative support.

Family Participation on the Team Parents and other family members are important members of the transdisciplinary team. They can provide information about their child, identify materials and activities within the classroom that their child will enjoy, and offer suggestions for adapting the classroom to accommodate their child. Participating as a team member also can be beneficial for families. It can reduce some of the stress and uncertainty that may be associated with inclusion and help families and team members address concerns that parents may have. Parents often are concerned about teacher expertise and willingness to work with a child with special needs, the acceptance of their child by other children in the program, and whether the teachers will have time to address their child's individual and special needs. Concerns such as these may be addressed through participation in IEP meetings, visiting the program, and talking with other team members.

Preparing Families and Children for Inclusion

One of the decisions the team will make is whether to prepare classroom peers and their families for inclusion. Some programs and families routinely provide preenrollment activities for classroom peers and/or their families. Preenrollment activities range from simple activities such as informing children and families that a new child with special needs will be entering the program, to more extensive activities such as discussions concerning disabilities. Preenrollment activities might be used if the program staff and the child's family feel that some of the typical peers will need help adjusting to any physical or behavioral differences of a child with special needs (Hanline, 1993). Prior training activities might help children who share an inclusion classroom acquire positive attitudes regarding disabilities and be comfortable interacting with peers who have special needs.

Other programs and families do not actively prepare peers and their families for inclusion, feeling that preenrollment activities emphasize differences between the child with special needs and other children in the program (Thompson, 1994). Instead, these parents and professionals answer questions and discuss issues when they are raised by families or children in the context of daily routines.

Few studies have examined the benefits or drawbacks of preparing preschool-aged children for inclusion (Odom & McEvoy, 1990). Investigators who have conducted preenrollment activities have documented both positive and negative outcomes (for example, Raab, Nordquist, Cunningham, & Bliem, 1986; Vandell, Anderson, Ehrhardt, & Wilson, 1982). As a result, a consensus on which practice is most beneficial does not exist. Families and programs should consider whether they want to address the issue of child preparation and then identify methods either to prepare children or to respond to questions and concerns that children may raise. Parents and professionals might consider the age of children in the program and characteristics of the child with special needs in deciding if they wish to use child and family preparation activities.

Preenrollment Activities for Children There are many activities that parents and programs might consider if they decide to use activities to prepare children for inclusion:

1. Parents might visit the preschool program and talk to the other children about their child and then respond to questions from the children. The parents may also show pictures or videotapes of their child during this activity.
2. Teachers can read and discuss stories or watch and discuss television programs that include children with special needs (such as *Sesame Street*).
3. Simulation activities can be used to help children understand specific disabilities. For example, children might wear gloves on their hands while completing a fine-motor activity, wear a blindfold while walking around the classroom, wear earplugs while listening to a story, or experience using a wheelchair.
4. Puppets such as the Friends on the Block can be used to illustrate and prompt discussion regarding special needs.
5. Parents and/or program staff might develop a book about the child and his or her special need (Klein & Sheehan, 1987). The book can be used to introduce the child and his or her special needs to peers. If the child uses equipment such as braces or a wheelchair, examples of these can be made available for children to explore and discuss with an adult.

Talking with Children About Special Needs Preschool-aged children often are aware of and curious about disabilities in other children. They may have questions about the cause of a disability or why a child cannot perform a skill, uses adaptive equipment, and behaves in different ways. When parents and professionals discuss special needs with children and families, whether it is part of preenrollment activities or in response to questions, they should (a) show that they are comfortable talking about the child's special needs, (b) provide honest and accurate information appropriate to the child's developmental level, (c) convey respect for the child, (d) focus on the child's strengths and abilities as well as special needs, (e) describe the child's unique communication and coping strategies if applicable, (f) highlight the similarities between all children and acknowledge the worth of all children, and (g) when possible redirect questions that are directed to an adult to the child with special needs, even if the adult helps the child respond to the question (Stoneman, 1993; Thompson, 1994).

Adult attitudes and behavior are important determiners of acceptance and peer relationships (Hanline, 1993). Teachers and parents can foster positive attitudes by developing cooperative group activities and by modeling positive interaction with children who have disabilities. In doing so, teachers must be careful not to model or promote a sense of feeling sorry for the child or a sense that typical children are to be commended because they are playing with the child with disabilities. Teacher behavior should send the message that "I like to play with this child" and that playing with this child is as normal as playing with any child in the class (Kugelmass, 1989).

Strategies to Prepare Parents for Inclusion Some of the concerns or questions often expressed by parents are (a) "Will there be a reduction in the amount of teacher attention to their child?" (b) "Will there be negative outcomes for their child such as modeling inappropriate behaviors?" (c) "Are there adequate resources for all children?" and (d) "What is the ratio of children with disabilities to typical children and to adults in the classroom?" (Peck, Carlson, & Helmstetter, 1992; Stoneman, 1993; Thompson, 1994). To address concerns such as these, programs and families have provided published material about inclusion, developed articles for parent newsletters that present the program's philosophy and plans for inclusion, and created newsletters that introduce and welcome the family and the child with disabilities to the program. Another strategy invites the family and/or program staff to attend a parent meeting and talk about inclusion, the child, and the family. Parent preparation activities should describe the vision for inclusion, discuss expected benefits of inclusion, address concerns and questions that parents may have, promote parent-parent interaction, and foster positive attitudes that reflect all children and families are equal and welcome members of the program.

EVALUATING THE SUCCESS OF INCLUSION

Evaluation is an important component of any inclusion program. It will identify for the transdisciplinary team those components of inclusion that should be maintained and those that should be revised. Evaluation should address child adjustment and the progress of children with special needs and of typically developing children, family perceptions and satisfaction, and the needs and satisfaction of program staff.

In many programs, child evaluation is accomplished through standardized, norm-referenced assessments. Unfortunately, these assessments may not identify small increments of change or change in the quality of behavior. They also may either fail to assess or assess inadequately many of the outcomes that are expected from participation in an inclusion program (for instance, imitation of advanced peer's behavior, development of positive attitudes regarding disability). Therefore, additional methods other than standardized measures are needed to evaluate inclusion adequately. For example, play- or curriculum-based assessments can be used in conjunction with or in place of norm-referenced assessments. Programs also should evaluate progress on a child's specific goals (such as IEP goals) and document qualitative and small changes in behavior (Bruder, 1993). For example, judgment-based assessments can be used to document engagement, social interaction with peers, fluency of skills, and generalization of skills across activities, individuals, and settings (Wolery & Fleming, 1993).

In developing an evaluation protocol, we should remember that teachers do not have unlimited resources and time to conduct evaluation. Care should be taken to develop methods that are feasible within the classroom setting and that teachers are likely to use (Odom et al., 1994). Wolery and Fleming (1993) recommend that teachers collect one- to three-minute probe data on child behavior twice a month. The role of all adults in the classroom also may be considered when designing a protocol and collecting evaluation data. For example, the inclusion facilitator or classroom assistant might collect data while the teacher conducts an activity in which IEP goals are addressed.

Evaluation of parents and program staff should assess their perceptions of and satisfaction with the inclusion program. Questionnaires, checklists, or Likert scale evaluations often are used in parent and staff evaluation. Other forms of evaluation might include focus groups, interviews, analysis of team meetings and outcomes, documentation of skill acquisition, and analysis of periodic needs assessments.

CONCLUSION

The Division for Early Childhood and National Association for Young Children (1993) have endorsed inclusion as the recommended service delivery option for young children with special needs. This endorsement is based on the conviction that young children with special needs are more similar to than different from their typically developing peers and that all young children benefit from sharing the learning environment. As Salisbury and Smith (1993) point out, "the reality of today's society is that any child, on a given day, may be a child with special needs" (p. 2). Individuals who work in inclusive programs for young children should be prepared to address the diverse abilities and needs of all children in their programs. In addition, early childhood programs will need to develop models of inclusion that reflect the concerns, resources, and priorities of families, program staff, and members of the community. This goal can only be accomplished through collaborative efforts that include families, early childhood educators, early childhood special educators, administrators, related service personnel, and related community agency personnel.

REFERENCES

Arndorfer, R. E., & Miltenberger, R. G. (1993). Functional assessment and treatment of challenging behavior: A review with implications for early childhood. *Topics in Early Childhood Special Education, 13*(1), 82–105.

Bailey, D. B, & McWilliam, R. A. (1990). Normalizing early intervention. *Topics in Early Childhood Special Education, 10*(2), 33–47.

Bailey, D. B., & Wolery, M. (1992). *Teaching infants and preschoolers with disabilities* (2nd ed.). Upper Saddle River, NJ: Merrill/Prentice Hall.

Bredekamp, S. (1987). *Developmentally appropriate practice in early childhood programs serving children from birth through age 8*. Washington, DC: National Association for the Education of Young Children.

Bredekamp, S. (1993). The relationship between early childhood education and early childhood special education: Healthy marriage or family feud? *Topics in Early Childhood Special Education, 13*(3), 258–273.

Breiner, J., & Forehand, R. (1982). Mother-child interactions: A comparison of a clinic-referred developmentally delayed group and two nondelayed groups. *Analysis and Intervention in Developmental Disabilities, 3,* 35–57.

Bricker, D. D. (1978). A rationale for the integration of handicapped and nonhandicapped preschool children. In M. J. Guralnick (Ed.), *Early intervention and the integration of handicapped and nonhandicapped children* (pp. 3–26). Baltimore: University Park Press.

Bricker, D., & Cripe, J. (1992). *An activity-based approach to early intervention*. Baltimore: Brookes.

Bruder, M. B. (1993). The provision of early intervention and early childhood special education within community early childhood programs: Characteristics of effective service delivery. *Topics in Early Childhood Special Education, 13*(1), 19–37.

Carr, E. G., Robinson, S., & Palumbo, L. W. (1990). The wrong issue: Aversive vs. nonaversive treatment. The right issue: Functional vs. nonfunctional treatment. In A. C. Repp & N. N. Singh (Eds.), *Perspectives on the use of nonaversive and aversive interventions for persons with developmental disabilities* (pp. 361–380). Sycamore, IL: Sycamore.

Chandler, L. K., Fowler, S. A., & Lubeck, R. C. (1992). An analysis of the effects of multiple setting events on the social behavior of preschool children with special needs. *Journal of Applied Behavior Analysis, 25,* 249–264.

Cole, K. N., Mills, P. E., Daley, P. S., & Jenkins, J. R. (1991). Effects of preschool integration for children with disabilities. *Exceptional Children, 58,* 36–45.

Cook, R. E., Tessier, A., & Armbruster, V. B. (1987). *Adapting early childhood curricula for children with special needs*. Upper Saddle River, NJ: Merrill/Prentice Hall.

Council for Exceptional Children. (1993). *CEC policy on inclusive schools and community settings*. Reston, VA: Author.

Cripe, J., Slenz, K., & Bricker, D. (1993). *AEPS curriculum for birth to three years. Vol. 2*. Baltimore: Brookes.

Division for Early Childhood. (1993). *DEC recommended practices: Indicators of quality in programs for infants and young children with special needs and their families*. Reston, VA: Council for Exceptional Children.

Division for Early Childhood, & the National Association for the Education of Young Children. (1993). *Position on inclusion*. Reston, VA: Council for Exceptional Children.

Education for All Handicapped Act Amendments of 1986, PL 99-457 (1986, October 8), Title 20, U.S.C. 1400 et seq: *U.S. Statutes at Large, 100,* 1145–1177.

Fewell, R. R., & Neisworth, J. T. (Eds.). (1990). Mainstreaming revisited. *Topics in Early Childhood Special Education, 10*(2).

Foster-Johnson, L., & Dunlap, G. (1993). Using functional assessment to develop effective individualized intervention for challenging behaviors. *Teaching Exceptional Children, 25*(3), 44–50.

Foxx, R. M., McMorrow, M. J., & Schloss, C. N. (1983). Stacking the deck: Teaching social skills to retarded adults with a modified table game. *Journal of Applied Behavior Analysis, 16,* 157–170.

Goldstein, H., & Cisar, C. L. (1992). Promoting interaction during sociodramatic play: Teaching scripts to typical preschoolers and classmates with developmental disabilities. *Journal of Applied Behavior Analysis, 25,* 265–280.

Goldstein, H., Wickstrom, S., Hoyson, M., Jamieson, B., & Odom, S. (1988). Effects of sociodramatic script training on social and communicative interaction. *Education and Treatment of Children, 11,* 97–117.

Guevremont, D. C., Osnes, P. G., & Stokes, T. F. (1986). Programming maintenance after correspondence training interventions with children. *Journal of Applied Behavior Analysis, 19,* 215–219.

Guralnick, M. J. (Ed.). (1978). *Early intervention and the integration of handicapped and nonhandicapped children.* Baltimore: University Park Press.

Guralnick, M. J. (1986). The peer relations of young handicapped and nonhandicapped children. In P. S. Strain, M. J. Guralnick, & H. M. Walker (Eds.), *Children's social behavior: Development, assessment, and modification* (pp. 93–140). Orlando, FL: Academic Press.

Guralnick, M. J. (1990). Major accomplishments and future directions in early childhood mainstreaming. *Topics in Early Childhood Special Education, 10*(2), 1–17.

Guralnick, M. J., & Groom, J. M. (1988). Peer interactions in mainstreamed and specialized classrooms: A comparative analysis. *Exceptional Children, 54,* 415–426.

Hains, A. H., Fowler, S. A., & Chandler, L. K. (1988). Planning school transitions: Family and professional collaboration. *Journal of the Division for Early Childhood, 12,* 108–115.

Hanline, M. F. (1993). Facilitating integrated preschool service delivery transitions for children, families, and professionals. In C. A. Peck, S. L. Odom, & D. D. Bricker (Eds.), *Integrating young children with disabilities into community programs: Ecological perspectives on research and implementation* (pp. 133–146). Baltimore: Brookes.

Haring, N. (1992). The context of social competence: Relations, relationships, and generalization. In S. Odom, S. McConnell, & M. McEvoy (Eds.), *Social competence of young children with disabilities: Issues and strategies for intervention* (pp. 277–306). Baltimore: Brookes.

Hart, B., & Risley, T. R. (1975). Incidental teaching of language in the preschool. *Journal of Applied Behavior Analysis, 8,* 411–421.

Hendrickson, J. M., Strain, P. S., Tremblay, A., & Shores, R. E. (1982). Interactions of behaviorally handicapped children. *Behavior Modification, 6,* 323–353.

Individuals with Disabilities Education Act of 1990, PL 101-476 (The 1990 Education for the Handicapped Act Amendments, October 30, 1990), 20 U.S.C. 55, 1400–1485.

Individuals with Disabilities Education Act Amendments of 1991, PL 102-119 (October 7, 1991), Title 20, U.S.C. 1400 et seq: *U.S. Statutes at Large, 105,* 587–608.

Jenkins, J. R., Odom, S. L., & Speltz, M. L. (1989). Effects of social interaction of preschool children with handicaps. *Exceptional Children, 55,* 420–428.

Jenkins, J. R., Speltz, M. L., & Odom, S. L. (1985). Integrating normal and handicapped preschoolers: Effects on child development and social interaction. *Exceptional Children, 52,* 7–18.

Johnson, D. W., & Johnson, R. T. (1980). Integrating handicapped students into the mainstream. *Exceptional Children,* 47, 90–99.

Johnson-Martin, N. M., Attermeier, S. M., & Hacker, B. (1990). *The Carolina curriculum for preschoolers with special needs.* Baltimore: Brookes.

Klein, N., & Sheehan, R. (1987). Staff development: A key issue in meeting the needs of young handicapped children in day care settings. *Topics in Early Childhood Special Education,* 7(1) 13–27.

Kugelmass, J. W. (1989). The "shared classroom": A case study of interactions between early childhood and special education staff and children. *Journal of Early Intervention, 13,* 36–44.

Lamorey, S., & Bricker, D. D. (1993). Integrated programs: Effects on young children and their parents. In C. A. Peck, S. L. Odom, & D. D. Bricker (Eds.), *Integrating young children with disabilities into community programs: Ecological perspectives on research and implementation* (pp. 249–270). Baltimore: Brookes.

Linder, T. W. (1993). *Transdisciplinary play-based intervention: Guidelines for developing a meaningful curriculum for young children.* Baltimore: Brookes.

McEvoy, M. A., Nordquist, V. M., Twardosz, S., Heckaman, K. A., Wehby, J., & Denny, R. K. (1988). Promoting autistic children's peer interaction in an integrated early childhood setting using affection activities. *Journal of Applied Behavior Analysis, 21,* 193–200.

McEvoy, M. A., Peterson, C., & McConnell, S. (1991). Early education: Which path to inclusion? *IMPACT: Institute on Community Integration, 4*(2), 1, 15.

McEvoy, M. A., Spicuzza, R., Davis, C., Cooper, C., & Neimeyer, J. (1993, December). Increasing social skills of young children: Old methods and new user friendly alternatives. Symposium presented at the Division for Early Childhood Conference, San Diego.

McGee, G. G., Almeida, C., Sulzar-Azaroff, B., & Feldman, R. (1992). Promoting reciprocal interactions via peer incidental teaching. *Journal of Applied Behavior Analysis, 25,* 117–126.

McLean, M. E., & Odom, S. L. (1993). Practices for young children with and without disabilities: A comparison of DEC and NAEYC identified practices. *Topics in Early Childhood Special Education, 10*(2), 274–292.

Mori, A. A., & Garwood, S. G. (1981). Mainstreaming: A challenge for the 1980s. *Topics in Early Childhood Special Education, 1*(1).

Murphy, M., & Vincent, L. J. (1989). Identification of critical skills for success in day care. *Journal of Early Intervention, 13,* 221–229.

National Association for the Education of Young Children. (1994). *NAEYC guidelines for preparation of early childhood professionals.* Washington, DC: Author.

Odom, S. L. (1989). Topical issue on mainstreaming. *Journal of Early Intervention, 13.*

Odom, S. L., Bender, M., Stein, M., Doran, L., Houden, P., McInnes, M., Gilbert, M., DeKlyen, M., Speltz, M., & Jenkins, J. (1988). *The integrated preschool curriculum: Procedures for socially integrating handicapped and nonhandicapped children.* Seattle: University of Washington Press.

Odom, S. L., Chandler, L. K., Ostrosky, M., McConnell, S., & Reaney, S. (1992). Fading teacher prompts from peer-initiation interventions for young children with disabilities. *Journal of Applied Behavior Analysis, 25,* 307–318.

Odom, S. L., McConnell, S., & Chandler, L. K. (1994). Acceptability and feasibility of classroom-based social interaction interventions for young children with disabilities. *Exceptional Children, 60,* 226–236.

Odom, S. L., McConnell, S., Ostrosky, M., Peterson, C., Skellenger, A., Spicuzza, R., Chandler, L., McEvoy, M., & Favazza, P. (1993). *Play time/social time: Organizing your classroom to build interaction skills.* Tucson, AZ: Communication Skill Builders.

Odom, S. L., & McEvoy, M. A. (1988). Integration of young children with handicaps and normally developing children. In S. L. Odom & M. B. Karnes (Eds.), *Early intervention for infants and children with handicaps: An empirical base* (pp. 241–267). Baltimore: Brookes.

Odom, S. L., & McEvoy, M. A. (1990). Mainstreaming at the preschool level: Potential barriers and tasks for the field. *Topics in Early Childhood Special Education, 10*(2), 48–61.

Odom S. L., & Strain, P. (1984). Classroom-based social skills instruction for severely handicapped preschool children. *Topics in Early Childhood Special Education, 4*(3), 97–116.

Ostrosky, M. M., & Kaiser, A. P. (1991). Preschool classroom environments that promote communication. *Teaching Exceptional Children, 23*(4), 6–11.

Peck, C. A., Carlson, P., & Helmstetter, E. (1992). Parent and teacher perceptions of outcomes for typically developing children enrolled in integrated early childhood programs: A statewide survey. *Journal of Early Intervention, 16,* 53–63.

Peck, C. A., Killen, C. C., & Baumgart, D. (1989). Increasing implementation of special education instruction in mainstream programs: Direct and generalized effects on nondirective consultation. *Journal of Applied Behavior Analysis, 22,* 197–210.

Peck, C. A., Odom, S. L., & Bricker, D. D. (Eds.). (1993). *Integrating young children with disabilities into community programs: Ecological perspectives on research and implementation.* Baltimore: Brookes.

Peterson, N. L. (1987). *Early intervention for handicapped and at-risk children: An introduction to early childhood special education.* Denver: Love.

Quilitch, H. R., & Risley, T. R. (1973). The effects of play materials on social play. *Journal of Applied Behavior Analysis, 6,* 573–578.

Raab, M. M., Nordquist, V. M., Cunningham, J. L., & Bliem, C. D. (1986). Promoting peer regard of an autistic child in a mainstreamed preschool using pre-enrollment activities. *Child Study Journal, 16,* 265–284.

Repp, A. C., & Karsh, K. G. (1990). A taxonomic approach to the nonaversive treatment of maladaptive behavior of persons with developmental disabilities. In A. C. Repp & N. N. Singh (Eds.), *Perspectives on the use of nonaversive and aversive interventions for persons with developmental disabilities* (pp. 331–348). Sycamore, IL: Sycamore.

Rose, D. F., & Smith, B. J (1994). *Providing public education services to young children with disabilities in community-based programs: Who's responsible for what?* Pittsburgh, PA: Research Institute on Preschool Mainstreaming.

Safford, P. L. (1989). *Integrated teaching in early childhood: Starting in the mainstream.* White Plains, NY: Longman.

Sainato, D. M., & Lyon, S. R. (1989). Promoting successful mainstreaming transitions for handicapped preschool children. *Journal of Early Intervention, 13,* 305–314.

Salisbury, C. L. (1991). Mainstreaming during the early childhood years. *Exceptional Children, 58,* 146–155.

Salisbury, C. L., & Smith, B. J. (1993). *Effective practices for preparing young children with disabilities for school* (ERIC Digest E519, Clearinghouse on Handicapped and Gifted Children). Reston, VA: Council for Exceptional Children.

Spodek, B., & Saracho, O. N. (1994). *Dealing with individual differences in the early childhood classroom.* White Plains, NY: Longman.

Stayton, V., & Bredekamp, S. (1994, October). DEC forum: Collaborative activities between NAEYC, ATE, and DEC in developing personnel standards. Symposium presentation at the International Early Childhood Conference on Children with Special Needs, St. Louis, MO.

Stoneman, Z. (1993). The effects of attitude on preschool integration. In C. A. Peck, S. L. Odom, & D. D. Bricker (Eds.), *Integrating young children with disabilities into community programs: Ecological perspectives on research and implementation* (pp. 223–248). Baltimore: Brookes.

Strain, P. S. (1990). LRE for preschool children with handicaps: What we know, what we should be doing. *Journal of Early Intervention, 14,* 291–296.

Strain, P. S., & Odom, S. L. (1986). Peer social initiations: Effective intervention for social skills development. *Exceptional Children, 52,* 543–551.

Templeman, T. P., Fredericks, H. D., & Udell, T. (1989). Integration of children with moderate and severe handicaps into a day care center. *Journal of Early Intervention, 13,* 315–328.

Thompson, B. (1994). A circle of inclusion. Preconference workshop presented at the annual Illinois Early Childhood Conference, Peoria.

Tremblay, A., Strain, P. S., Hendrickson, J. M., & Shores, R. E. (1981). Social interactions of normally developing preschool children: Using normative data for subject selection and target behavior selection. *Behavior Modification, 5,* 237–253.

Twardosz, S. L., Nordquist, V. M., Simon, R., & Botkin, D. (1983). The effect of group affection activities on the interaction of socially isolated children. *Analysis and Intervention in Developmental Disabilities, 3,* 311–338.

Vandell, D. L., Anderson, L. D., Ehrhardt, G., & Wilson, K. S. (1982). Integrating hearing and deaf preschoolers: An attempt to enhance hearing children's interactions with deaf peers. *Child Development, 53,* 1354–1363.

Vincent, L., Brown, L., & Getz-Sheftel, M. (1981). Integrating handicapped and typical children during the preschool years: The definition of best educational practice. *Topics in Early Childhood Special Education, 1*(1), 17–24.

Walker, G. R. (1993). Noncompliant behavior of people with mental retardation. *Research in Developmental Disabilities, 14,* 87–105.

Watkins, F. P., & Durant, L. (1992). *Complete early childhood behavior management guide.* New York: Center for Applied Research in Education.

Wolery, M., & Fleming, L. A. (1993). Implementing individualized curricula in integrated settings. In C. A. Peck, S. L. Odom, & D. D. Bricker (Eds.), *Integrating young children with disabilities into community programs: Ecological perspectives on research and implementation* (pp. 109–132). Baltimore: Brookes.

10

Integration in the Preschool Classroom for Children with Severe Disabilities

SUSAN WICKSTROM KANE
HOWARD GOLDSTEIN
LOUISE KACZMAREK

Children with severe disabilities are those who because of the intensity of their physical, mental, or emotional problems need educational, social, psychological, and medical services beyond those that are traditionally offered by regular and special education programs, in order to maximize participation in society and self-fulfillment. Such children may have severe language or perceptual-cognitive deprivation and evidence a number of abnormal behaviors including failure to respond to even the most pronounced stimuli, self-mutilation, manifestations of durable and intense temper tantrums, and the absence of even the most rudimentary forms of verbal control. They may also have extremely fragile physiological conditions (U.S. Office of Education, 1975, Section 121.2).

Severe disability in preschool children can be defined formally or informally. Although formal definitions of severe disability such as the one given here are helpful, an informal definition may prove more enlightening for our purposes. Children with severe disabilities are often thought of as those children who present the greatest challenge to the practice of inclusive education. The challenges that arise are likely to concern teachers, the child's parents, other students, and their parents. For example, teachers may feel unprepared for a child's unique needs, a child's parents may question the quantity and/or quality of appropriate instruction in the inclusive classroom, and classmates' parents may fear a loss of instructional time. These are reasonable concerns if we assume that the preschool site chosen for inclusion will operate in a fairly traditional manner. A call for effective inclusion of any child is a call for systems change. In the case of children with severe disabilities, the change may be significant.

The argument for normalization via classroom and community inclusion has been made quite eloquently by others (Brown, Long, Udvari-Solner, & Davis, 1989; Guralnick, 1990). Brown, Long, Udvari-Solner, and Schwarz (1989) describe the historical evolution of service delivery models for students with severe disabilities, culminating with the current issue: Should these children be based in regular or special education classrooms in their home school? We are proposing an alternative answer to this question: that all children, including those with severe disabilities, deserve an "irregular" classroom, a classroom where the needs of each individual child are met in creative and effective ways. Preschools may be particularly well suited to such irregularity. Because variation in the entry skills, aptitudes, and learning styles of preschoolers is expected, some degree of flexibility is already built into many programs. Thus, the necessary systems change can build on existing mechanisms for handling diversity.

Often, those least prepared will carry the responsibility for implementing a systems change. This is certainly true of inclusive education efforts. The traditional training and experience of professionals in special education, early childhood education, communication disorders, physical and occupational therapy, psychology, and other fields may run counter to the demands of creating learning environments for all children. Even family members and other caregivers may be expected to take on new roles, like case manager or educational consultant, that they may not be prepared to enact.

Indicators of best practice for early intervention are blurring distinctions across disciplinary boundaries. New emphases are being placed on family issues, transdisciplinary service delivery, collaborative consultation, and individualized activity-based curricula (for example, Catlett, 1993). Changes in professional training programs will help the next generation of service providers, but most current practitioners are learning through a combination of in-service training and experience. Furthermore, although efforts continue to expand, full inclusion of preschoolers with severe disabilities is not common.

To focus our exploration of the issues surrounding inclusion of preschoolers with severe disabilities, we will primarily be taking the perspective of a speech-language pathologist. We believe, however, that this discussion is applicable to other service providers, because many parallels and shared experiences are involved. The traditional modes of service delivery for speech-language pathologists share many features with special education and other therapies (for instance, physical, occupational, vision, hearing). The special needs of the children served by these professionals have traditionally translated into special (domain-specific) assessments, special intervention providers (teachers and therapists working separately), special (separate) environments for each service, and special curricula (different goals and approaches for each service).

One of the most compelling arguments for desegregating services concerns the development of social and communicative skills (Goldstein & Kaczmarek, 1992; Guralnick, 1990; Odom & McEvoy, 1990). Certainly there are potential benefits of integration in other domains, but the interactive nature of communication and social behavior makes acquiring truly functional skills nearly impossible without exposure to the opportunities inherent in an integrated setting. Speech-language pathologists have great opportunities to help the children they serve through effective inclusion, but the challenges faced also may be great.

Three levels of integration must be considered if children are to be included fully in preschool settings (Noonan & Hemphill, 1988). Children must be integrated physically into the program, with attention to both the physical characteristics of the environment and the physical challenges and needs of the child. Children must be integrated into the curricular aspects of the program, including assessment, instructional planning and implementation, and evaluation of outcomes. Finally, children must be affectively integrated into the program, with opportunities to be a valued and integral part of the group. We will consider physical integration first, then curricular integration, and finally affective integration of children with severe disabilities. We will review the literature with emphasis on communication intervention and discuss factors that challenge and support normalized service delivery at each of the levels.

CHALLENGES TO PHYSICAL INTEGRATION

A number of barriers faced in integration involve the physical environment and/or the child's physical characteristics and needs. Some preschool settings are inaccessible or dangerous for children with various disabilities. Even if the primary site (for instance, a classroom) is accessible, all the activity-related areas such as bathrooms, playgrounds, and vans for trips may not be. Because a great deal of functional communication and socialization takes place in areas other than the classroom, these areas must be accessible and safe for all children. Toys and play equipment must be carefully considered, not only in terms of the instructional or interactional value but also for safety, particularly when children are likely to bite, throw, or ingest nonedibles.

Sensory and motor impairments must also be taken into account when designing and/or adapting the preschool environment (Utley, 1986). Such factors as lighting, noise level and sound reverberation, arrangement of seating and tables, and placement of activity centers take on additional significance when children with disabilities are in the classroom. Many of these adaptations, such as improved listening environments, can be beneficial to all children, not just those who have identified disabilities (Berg, 1987; Finitzo, 1988).

The use of adaptive and prosthetic devices such as glasses, hearing aids, and communication boards by preschoolers with severe disabilities is another area of concern. Staff and family members may need specialized training and support to assure that these devices are properly maintained and used (English, 1991; Individuals with Disabilities Education Act, 1977, Section 121).

One of the newer and potentially most helpful tools for physical integration of children with disabilities is ecological assessments. As described in the literature (Barnett, Macmann, & Carey, 1992; Carta, Atwater, Schwartz, & Miller, 1990; Carta, Sainato, & Greenwood, 1988; Cipani, 1991; Neisworth & Bagnato, 1988), these involve examining and recording features of current and future environments and activities. The assessment of individuals within their natural settings as well as assessment of the setting itself are included in the process.

An ecological assessment can be conducted in the potential setting prior to placement to determine what areas or activities present potential dangers or challenges. One possible strategy would be to conduct an ecobehavioral assessment of a typically developing child in the setting, then an assessment of the target child. A thoughtful analysis of these results should provide information regarding changes to be made in the physical setting and lead to goals for intervention with the child, as will be discussed later. The input of various team members is vital in such an assessment, as each member brings his or her own insights and concerns to the process. The speech-language pathologist, for instance, may be looking specifically for room arrangements and materials that support interaction between children and for activities or toys that encourage communication at different levels.

A number of rating scales are available for assessing preschool environments. Perhaps the best known of these is the *Early Childhood Environment Rating Scale* (ECERS) (Harms & Clifford, 1980). Originally designed for use in settings for typical children, it has been applied successfully in programs that serve children with disabilities, although not necessarily those with severe disabilities. The scale is used to assess furnishings and displays, language-reasoning experiences, fine- and gross-motor activities, creative activities, social development, personal care routines, and adult needs. Incorporating special needs into the assessment procedure seems quite reasonable. For example, how are the furnishings and displays appropriate for a child with visual impairment?

Balancing adaptations in the environment that are necessary for safety and access against curricular and affective concerns may be challenging at times. Bailey, Clifford, and Harms (1982) compared the richness of typical preschool programs and those for children with disabilities, and they found that the typical programs were rated higher on each of twelve dimensions. Although this finding can and should be used to support mainstreaming by using the argument of enrichment and normalization for students with disabilities, it also raises some concerns. To some extent, the limited range of available toys, activities, and other stimuli may have been influenced by child characteristics. For example, noise and flashing lights may provoke seizure activity, too many distractions may inhibit attention, and toys with small or hazardous elements (for example, staplers, sequins, sand in a table) may be eaten or thrown. The challenge in effective physical integration is to determine arrangement and selection of toys and activities that will benefit all children. Creative solutions will be required in many cases and may be provided by a number of interventionists, including the speech-language pathologist. The speech-language pathologist may suggest that certain toys be out of reach yet visible, for instance. This allows for control of these materials while simultaneously encouraging communication.

A broad review of research regarding environmental arrangement can be found in a special issue of *Education and Treatment of Children* (McEvoy, 1990). More specialized reviews examine the effects of setting variables on preschool behavior problems and social-communicative interaction (McEvoy, Fox, & Rosenberg, 1991; Sainato & Carta, 1992). Most of the studies on environmental arrangement have been conducted in nonintegrated settings and tend to look at general effects of setting variables across groups of children without disabilities. In Sainato and Carta's (1992) review, for example, only one of the spatial density studies and one of those that explored use of toys and materials included subjects with disabilities. Furthermore, the inclusion of children with disabilities in studies does not assure that the findings apply to all children. Cars, gross-motor equipment, and sociodramatic play materials may promote peer interaction in general (see McEvoy et al., 1991) but not the participation of children with certain severe disabilities. Typical sociodramatic play materials and schemes may not incorporate roles easily taken by children with limited cognitive, linguistic, or motor skills.

Although many of the current findings may be useful or may suggest adaptations, more research is needed to explore the relationships between environmental (setting) variables and the behavior of children with various types and severity of disabilities in inclusive classrooms. The broad use of frequent ecological assessments and specific data collection in the classroom can also provide guidance in selecting and adapting toys and activities.

CURRICULAR CHALLENGES

Speech-language pathologists and related service providers traditionally have had little direct impact on general curriculum development. Assessment by related service providers has been domain specific (such as communication), geared to identifying eligible children and determining deficit skills that lead to individual treatment goals. Once a treatment program is begun, the classroom teacher may be asked to modify activities and routines to encourage behaviors or to probe for generalization of learned behaviors. More recently, primary and related service providers have sought input from each other regarding program development, but the line between "my" and "your" program often remains.

Early childhood programs today reflect a variety of influences and may fall anywhere on a continuum, from highly structured programs that emphasize academic skills to those that are more experiential and child directed with emphasis on social-emotional skill development (Bricker & Cripe, 1992). Although the latter is generally considered more amenable to inclusion, children who are "dumped" into programs at either end of this continuum might be expected to have different but equally serious problems. The goals and approaches used in an academically oriented program will likely be far removed from the abilities and needs of a preschooler with severe disabilities. On the other hand, a child who is placed in an experientially oriented program may not be able to access and/or profit from the available learning opportunities. Among these children will be those who display challenging behaviors that are likely to lead to removal from integrated settings. More passive and/or "acceptable" children may stay in the classroom but receive a less than optimal educational experience.

Much current debate centers around the theoretical and practical relationship between early childhood education (ECE) and early childhood special education/ early intervention (ECSE/EI) (see, for instance, Wolery, 1993). The recent publication of guidelines for recommended practices by both the National Association for the Education of Young Children (NAEYC) and the Division for Early Childhood (DEC), Council for Exceptional Children, has spurred discussion of the many similarities as well as the differences between ECE and ECSE/EI. We lend support to the position of others (Carta, Atwater, Schwartz, & McConnell, 1993; McLean & Odom, 1993) that the Developmentally Appropriate Practices (DAP) recommended by the NAEYC provide a solid context but may not be sufficient for meeting the needs of children with disabilities in the preschool classroom.

Some degree of specialized services will be needed to assure that these children adapt to new classrooms and that teachers and peers adapt their behavior as well as classroom structures to these children. Such adaptations may require service providers to take on new roles. Because a number of agencies and individuals may be involved, team members must collaborate. A number of models for team building and supports for the process are becoming available. Transdisciplinary consultation (Pennington, Kaczmarek, & Goldstein, 1993; Rainforth, York, & Macdonald, 1992) is a particularly appealing model for use in inclusive preschool settings. This approach allows classroom team members with different areas of expertise to assist each other in "developing and refining skills that facilitate child behaviors identified by the team" (Pennington et al., 1993, Module 1-3).

For individual team members, effective inclusion of preschoolers with severe disabilities will require flexibility and individualization at all levels of service delivery, including assessment, intervention, and evaluation. Changes may be needed in many current practices to meet new demands.

Assessment

Guidelines for recommended practice in assessment support processes and instruments that meet standards of treatment utility, social validity, and comprehensiveness (Neisworth, 1993). *Treatment utility* refers to the usefulness of assessment strategies for making eligibility and programming decisions. *Social validity* refers to the power of the assessment to tap those behaviors that others in the child's environment view as important or useful. *Comprehensiveness* involves collecting data in many ways, so that an overall picture of functioning is obtained, not one dictated by the parameters of one particular instrument.

The question of eligibility for communication intervention is unlikely to be an issue for children with severe disabilities, because nearly all these children will have deficits in communication skills. A possible exception may occur when exclusionary practices like cognitive referencing are employed. Cognitive referencing has been suggested by some as a means of determining eligibility or setting priorities for provision of speech-language services. Using the cognitive referencing model, the children who are in greater need of services are those whose cognitive skills are more highly developed than their linguistic skills.

Speculation that children with larger gaps between their cognitive levels and their communication levels would profit more from intervention than children with smaller gaps has not been borne out in the research literature (Notari, Cole, & Mills, 1992). Two corollary assumptions of the model—that cognition sets the upper bound for language development and that certain cognitive skills are prerequisites for learning language—are also questionable (Notari & Cole, 1993). For instance, Romski and Sevcik (1992) found that children who are essentially presymbolic and have not attained the level of cognitive skill thought to be necessary for language development can learn to use alternative and augmentative communication (AAC) systems.

Although cognitive skills support linguistic development, they are not always prerequisites. An interactive relationship between the two areas is more plausible. Practically speaking, working on causal reasoning by prompting/shaping the sign "more" to continue a desired activity would be just as logical (and probably more immediately functional) than prompting banging a hammer to make a ball drop into a box. Perhaps training in certain communicative behaviors can spur development of other, more strictly "cognitive" skills. Further study of AAC, prelinguistic, and early linguistic learning of young children might help elucidate the relationship between cognitive and linguistic development and the emergence of symbolic skills.

Preschoolers with severe disabilities will include children for whom the function of communication is at least as important as the form. Many of them will be preverbal. They may have related difficulties (for example, in initiating interactions) or relative strengths in social and/or symbolic abilities. Incorporating caregivers into the process of assessment is important for all young children, but it is vital for children with severe disabilities whose interaction may be idiosyncratic or elicited differentially by familiar people. In light of these probable assessment needs, examining some of the more frequently used assessment instruments is disturbing.

Wetherby and Prizant (1992) critiqued ten commonly used assessment instruments for young children. These instruments were identified through a survey of graduate school programs in communication disorders as being most frequently taught and used in their training programs. Although several of the instruments included limited assessment of communicative functions and social-affective signaling, none addressed these areas in depth. Only one of the instruments, the *Birth to Three Checklist of Learning and Language Behavior* (Bangs, 1986), analyzed preverbal communication in any depth. The *Birth to Three Checklist* was also the only one to profile social, communicative, and symbolic abilities. Spontaneous child-initiated language was used for assessment in just two of the ten instruments (only one in depth). Fewer than half used both caregiver informants and direct child assessment to collect information, and none involved caregivers as active participants to a great extent (two did so in a limited way). Interestingly, the second most frequently taught and used assessment instrument in the Wetherby and Prizant survey, the *Preschool Language Scale* (Zimmerman, Steiner, & Evatt, 1969), did not address any of these characteristics.

Few formalized instruments used by speech-language pathologists currently meet the assessment needs of young children with severe disabilities, although the *Communication and Symbolic Behavior Scale* (Wetherby & Prizant, 1990), which has recently been standardized, holds much promise.

Models of assessment guided by intervention design, rather than the search for developmental delays, are generally better suited to the needs of children with severe disabilities. The key tasks in intervention-driven (our term) assessment are to define problem situations, determine goals and strategies for changing behavior, evaluate environmental supports, and explore the possible roles of caregivers, family members, and peers as service providers (Barnett et al., 1992). Some of the techniques used for intervention-driven assessment are observational measures (Miller, 1981; Neisworth & Bagnato, 1988), criterion-referenced or curriculum-based measures (Bricker & Cripe, 1992; Neisworth & Bagnato, 1988), ecologically based assessments (Campbell, 1988; Wilcox, 1988), and dynamic assessment (Olswang, Bain, & Johnson, 1992). Although observational measures and criterion-referenced measures are familiar to most service providers, adaptation to the assessment needs of children with severe disabilities in inclusive settings may present new challenges.

Observational measures include behavior sampling, such as communication ("language") sampling, and observational coding. Computer packages are available to assist in the analysis of communication samples (for instance, SALT1 by Miller & Chapman, 1986), but context effects and interpretation of results continue to be problematic. Systematic observation and coding (Neisworth & Bagnato, 1988) can provide information about naturally occurring communicative interactions between the target child and significant others, including teachers and typical peers. Although most coding protocols were initially developed for use in research studies, they may be adapted for use by practitioners. Observational assessment of children in inclusive settings can include measurement of specific communicative acts (for example, nonverbal/verbal, initiations/responses, requests/comments) for both target children and communication partners.

Criterion-referenced and curriculum-based assessments look at skill development within logical sequences or continua of behavior. In curriculum-based assessment, the logical sequences are part of a curriculum. An exhaustive review of criterion-referenced assessments is not attempted here, but two that might well be used for preschoolers with severe disabilities include the *Assessment, Evaluation and Programming System for Infants and Young Children* (AEPS) (Bricker, 1992) and *Transdisciplinary Play-Based Assessment* (TPBA) (Linder, 1993a, 1993b).

Ecologically based measures focus on the child's participation in naturally occurring activities, with particular attention to the interaction between personal variables and environmental variables. Environmental variables include physical features, such as room layout and availability of materials; social features, such as peer or teacher responsiveness; and learning variables, such as setting events, cues, and contingencies. Information for ecological assessments can be collected primarily through observation, as in ecological inventories, or by report of significant adults, as in ecobehavioral interviews. Descriptions and examples of ecological inventories can be found in the literature (Campbell, 1988; Goldstein, Kaczmarek, & Hepting, 1996; Rainforth et al., 1992), but they tend to be informal measures. One instrument developed for older children that might be adapted for preschool use is the *Assessment of Student Participation in General Education Classes* (Macdonald & York, 1992). The primary use of ecobehavioral interviews has been to develop hypotheses about the factors controlling challenging behaviors that are then tested experimentally (Arndorfer & Miltenberger, 1993; O'Neill, Horner, Albin, Storey, & Sprague, 1990; Reichle & Wacker, 1993). An ecological approach seems to be a valuable framework for assessing children's behavior generally and the behavior of children in inclusive settings specifically.

Decisions about a child's readiness to learn new behaviors can be based on both assessment of current status and perceived impact of instruction on behavior change. One way to test more directly the impact of instruction on a child's performance is through dynamic assessment. Dynamic assessment basically uses a systematic "test-teach-test" approach to make inferences about the child's learning potential, identify factors that influence performance, and develop some facilitative strategies for learning. Dynamic assessments may help bridge the gap between assessment and intervention, as suggested by Olswang et al. (1992), but we need to know more about their use and interpretation. For instance, little is known about the relationship between assessment outcomes and subsequent success in learning.

Intervention-driven assessment promises to contribute to the efficient development of goals and approaches that are functional, developmentally appropriate, and socially valid. The assessment process can be further enhanced by team involvement in the early stages of assessment and the logical sequencing of assessment efforts to gain increasingly specific information.

Team members can collaborate from the start of the process, working together to develop an overall plan for assessment (Goldstein, 1993). Because of the focus on natural sequences of behavior and the functions served by these behaviors, initial assessments are less likely to be domain specific and more likely to be administered jointly by team members, thus requiring some knowledge and skills in cooperative assessment. Some possible formats for conducting team assessments include arena assessment (Foley, 1990; Wolery & Dyk, 1984) and transdisciplinary play-based assessment (Linder, 1993a). After problems are identified and a broad framework for intervention is established, more in-depth assessment of certain areas may be indicated. Once a general communication problem in the class is identified, such as the need to establish or refine request behavior, the speech-language pathologist may need to assess current abilities further to determine the most appropriate form(s) to teach and the best methods of instruction. The function of requesting, for example, may be accomplished using various forms, such as prelinguistic vocal or nonvocal behavior, signs or speech, or using an adaptive communicative device. The speech-language pathologist can then use commercially available tests that are strong in particular areas or design individualized "test" items or probes to obtain the desired information (Goldstein, 1993).

Intervention

The communication behaviors and specific intervention needs of preschoolers with severe disabilities are likely to be diverse. For example, a child with autism who has limited functional speech may be able to imitate words and phrases. Another child may not speak at all but may interact readily with staff and peers using gestures and vocalization with obvious intent. A third child may communicate wants and needs only in a rudimentary way, such as crying, facial expressions, and preintentional vocalizations. In any case, the direct service providers will need input on the systems and techniques that both adults and peers can use to facilitate communicative interaction.

Relatively few data-based reports of intervention with preschoolers with severe disabilities in regular classrooms have appeared in the literature. Furthermore, most literature has focused on mainstreaming and integration, which emphasize fitting a child with disabilities into the norm rather than creating environments for all children, as is the emphasis with inclusion. To make recommendations for practice, we must extrapolate from studies of older or younger children with disabilities, mainstreamed preschoolers with mild-moderate disabilities, and children in segregated settings. However, in the absence of data to support the differential effectiveness of most intervention techniques with this specific population of children, these recommendations for practice should be considered tentative.

Communication skills interventions for preschoolers with severe disabilities will be enhanced by the following: (a) training functional skills, (b) incorporating natural cues and contingencies, (c) using a variety of effective teaching techniques, (d) distinguishing form and function of behavior, (e) training in mixed modalities, (f) utilizing classroom supports, and (g) accessing professional/technical resources.

Functional Skill Training Functional interventions focus on behaviors that are directly related to the child's ability to operate successfully in a particular environment. For example, requesting juice may be more important to the child in a preschool classroom than naming objects on presentation. Although some activities are inherently more functional than others (for example, those that relate to basic human needs), the determination of functional behaviors will vary for each child depending on current abilities and the demands of the child's everyday environment.

Naturalistic Approaches Intervention is naturalistic to the extent that elements of the child's typical environment are incorporated as cues and contingencies for target behaviors. An intervention that uses visual presentation of juice at snack time to stimulate the request behavior "juice" and consequently rewards the request with a drink is more naturalistic than one that uses pictures as stimuli and rewards production with praise or tokens.

Intervention that takes place within the ongoing activities in a child's classroom is more likely to produce generalized behavior change than intervention delivered in a separate room with cues and contingencies not typically or frequently encountered in the classroom. Although there is support for the general effectiveness of naturalistic classroom-based teaching strategies (Kaiser, Yoder, & Keetz, 1992; Warren & Kaiser, 1986), studies that compare the effectiveness of individual and classroom-based treatment have produced mixed results. When we examine the studies that include young children with cognitive impairments, however, the evidence more clearly supports the relative effectiveness of classroom-based treatment (Wilcox, Khouri, & Caswell, 1990) and treatment that follows the child's lead (Yoder, Kaiser, & Alpert, 1991).

There may be times when a more traditional pull-out approach is warranted with a particular child, but we believe that an integrated approach should be the "default" mode (Goldstein et al., in press). Pull-out intervention would be temporary in this conception, and the goal would be to prepare the child and/or the environment for continued integrated services. We would also note that many of the advantages claimed for pull-out intervention can be achieved in the classroom as well. For example, separate areas of the classroom can be designated where children go for activities that require concentration or quiet. Massed-trial training can be incorporated naturally into certain activities, such as greeting other children or requesting snack items. One-to-one teaching also can occur in the context of group instruction, as when interventionists circulate among children engaged in a particular activity, encouraging certain behaviors or experiences. These strategies can be a part of the curriculum for all children, thus creating normalized and effective services for the children with disabilities.

Much of the impetus for naturalistic intervention came from those interested in teaching language skills (Hart & Risley, 1980; Warren & Kaiser, 1988). The concept of milieu language teaching, and related naturalistic approaches, calls for embedding communication training in the child's regular ongoing activities: the treatment is conducted within the milieu.

The regular ongoing activities of preschoolers tend to cross developmental and academic domains. The transition to closing circle, for example, is accomplished through successful integration of communication skills (such as following directions, imitating a cleanup song, asking for or offering assistance), motor skills (such as moving between carpet and circle area, grasping and carrying carpet, maneuvering from stand to sit), cognitive skills (such as finding a color carpet, knowing locations of items), and social skills (such as waiting a turn for carpet, finding a buddy to sit near). Once the activities that will be part of children's classroom experience are identified, intervention can be individualized to fit the requirements of individual children.

Although naturalistic approaches share many features, they differ somewhat in specific teaching techniques used. One distinction between milieu teaching and other approaches (for example, MacDonald, 1985; Weiss, 1981; Wilcox, 1992) is the use of explicit prompts for target behavior. Some see this as unnatural, thus likely to interfere with natural discourse development (MacDonald, 1985). Others view prompting as an important feature of intervention for children who do not interact with enough frequency to create many naturalistic teaching opportunities (Yoder & Warren, 1993). Most likely, the effectiveness of prompting depends on characteristics of the child, the type of interaction, and the nature of the prompt. Further research is needed to elucidate these relationships.

Although most of the studies involving milieu teaching procedures focus on development of speech (Kaiser et al., 1992), milieu teaching has also been used to facilitate sign acquisition (Oliver & Halle, 1982) and the use of speech output communication devices (Romski & Sevcik, 1992). Prelinguistic milieu teaching has been suggested in the literature (Yoder & Warren, 1993) and been used with young children with mental retardation (Warren, Yoder, Gazdag, Kim, & Jones, 1993). Yoder and Warren (1993) suggest that a milieu approach, with its use of explicit prompts for target behaviors, may be most effective for children who are prelinguistic but already demonstrating communicative intent. They suggest that other approaches, such as the responsive interaction approach proposed by Wilcox (1992), might be better suited to the needs of preintentional communicators. In the responsive interaction approach, care providers are instructed in providing consistent and contingent responses to the child's early communicative behavior.

A number of curricular approaches have been specifically designed to incorporate functional and naturalistic teaching strategies, including Activity Based Intervention (Bricker & Cripe, 1992) and Individualized Curriculum Sequencing (Guess & Helmstetter, 1986). These approaches have intuitive appeal for use in inclusive preschool settings, because they work within the ongoing activities and interactions that typically occur in preschools. It is more likely that a teacher or aide will be able to prompt requesting during snack than it is that the teacher will be able to conduct an individual lesson with massed trial training of signs or words. Although consumer satisfaction data are seldom collected and reported in the literature, there are anecdotal reports of teacher enthusiasm for more naturalistic approaches (Guess & Helmstetter, 1986).

Teaching Techniques Evaluating the relative effectiveness of specific teaching techniques is difficult, if not impossible. Individual techniques are rarely used in isolation but nearly always employed as a package. Some of the techniques that have been found to be effective in communication intervention with preschoolers are described here (adapted from Kaczmarek, Hepting, & Dzubak 1992).

Environmental arrangement creates opportunities for children to communicate. For example, toys can be put out of reach but clearly in view. Activities may be designed to require some communication, as when one child holds the flashlight and others must tell the child when to turn it on and off. Interventionists may deliver inadequate portions or amounts of materials or create needs for assistance or protesting, perhaps by hiding jackets or sitting in a child's boat and taking up all the space. Sabotage and violations of routine expectations also can be used to spur communication. For example, the children may be asked to fill cups that have holes in the bottoms, or the children's names may be said incorrectly in a greeting song. Although these tactics can be useful, care must be taken against overuse to the point where the child cannot count on anything.

Prompted imitation is a prompt that requires a child to imitate production of verbalizations, signs or gestures, or selections on an augmentative device. It helps children improve imitation skills, add more forms (for example, words) to their communicative repertoire, combine existing forms into more complex productions, and associate these forms with specific events.

Manding is a question or an imperative that obligates children to communicate in a particular way. The child may be asked to request or provide objects, actions, or information. This technique teaches children to respond appropriately to verbal or signed cues with a particular (category of) behavior.

Time delay is a period of silence marked by expectant attention during the presentation of a salient object or occurrence of an event that provides children with an opportunity to use their communication skills (for instance, to request). This teaches the child to initiate independently, as the time delay is lengthened and nonverbal cues are faded out.

Interrupting chained behavior involves removing an item needed to complete a multiple-step activity, thus allowing the child to initiate a request within the context of the activity.

Modeling is the demonstration of target behaviors, in this case unaccompanied by requests for production. This technique teaches children the appropriate initiation of various forms of communication behaviors through observational learning.

Sustained attention is a period of silence with expectant and/or joint attention providing the child with opportunities to comment. This technique teaches children that their communication partner is "listening."

Expansion, recast, and repetition can all follow a child's utterance. Repetition is verbatim imitation of the child's production. Expansion involves elaboration of the child's production into a more complex form. A recast is a grammatically correct version of the child's ungrammatical utterance. These techniques teach the child that their repertoire of forms can be understood or expanded and modified.

Listener preparatory training prepares children to go beyond dependent and/or respondent communication toward more spontaneous initiation of communication. Kaczmarek (1990) proposes a matrix model for training language that includes behaviors like selecting an appropriate listener, establishing proximity, and obtaining attention before delivering messages.

Distinguishing Between Form and Function of Behavior Communication intervention research and practice reflect a growing awareness of the difference between pragmatic form and social function in communication (Reichle, Halle, & Johnston, 1993). This distinction is particularly relevant in working with young children with severe disabilities who will likely need intervention for both of these areas and will benefit from a careful analysis of form and function. Several classification systems have been devised for describing communicative functions (see Reichle et al., 1993, for a comparison of taxonomies), but the terminology and descriptions of early functions are fairly consistent. Gaylord-Ross, Stremel-Campbell, and Storey (1986) observed and classified the social functions of emerging language/communication behaviors for subjects of various ages. They found that the earliest emerging functions for all ages were protesting/rejecting, requesting an object/action, and requesting continuation. In addition, the preschool children frequently used greeting and offering functions.

Opportunities to express these early-emerging functions occur repeatedly throughout the day in a preschool setting. Presenting all children with chances to protest or request objects, actions, or continuations is normalizing and can be fun for all. Teachers and peers can provide numerous models for receptive and expressive language development. All children can take turns communicating "up," for instance, to make a large parachute go up in the air. An alternate vocal or gestural behavior can be used by nonverbal children, or appropriate verbal behavior can be used by more sophisticated children to initiate the action. General developmental information and the particular abilities of the child are considered in selecting forms that are slightly more complex or more effective socially than those currently employed by the child.

Mixed Modality Training Speech-language pathologists who help preschoolers with severe disabilities develop functional communication skills will require knowledge about preverbal, early verbal, nonverbal, and augmented communication modes. Although a relative wealth of literature addresses the selection of the optimal communication mode for learners, we would agree with Reichle and Keogh (1986) that this may really be a pseudo-issue. Simultaneous training in multiple modalities appears preferable. Use of several communication modes may increase listener participation and improve message understanding. Furthermore, the objection of learner confusion is not supported in the literature (Reichle & Keogh, 1986).

Emphasis on deciding the "best" communication mode can, in practice, preclude the ongoing assessment of what works for a particular child in a particular situation. Some benefits of communication books with iconic symbols over use of manual signs have been noted in community settings. Rotholz, Berkowitz, and Burberry (1989), for instance, found that teenage students with severe disabilities experienced greater success in ordering food at McDonald's using communication books than sign language. A nonverbal preschooler might learn quickly to use a communication book or object display to indicate a preference for certain activity centers, whereas the signs for the various activities might be difficult to train and not easily interpreted by communication partners. This same child may use a natural gesture or vocalization to communicate quickly and effectively in situations where use of a communication book or display system is cumbersome, as when the child is using playground equipment.

Utilizing Classroom Supports To maximize the effects of intervention, we should tap into the human resources that already exist in the classroom (teachers and peers) and explore the recruitment of additional resources, such as parents, aides, or volunteers. Because these additional adults function basically as assistant teachers, we will focus our discussion on peer- and teacher-mediated intervention techniques.

A teacher can do many things to facilitate general communication interaction in the classroom and to elicit specific behaviors from children during ongoing activities (Campbell, Stremel-Campbell, & Rogers-Warren, 1985). The teacher can set the stage for communication, use specific elicitation techniques, and prompt and provide reinforcement for target behaviors in much the same manner as a speech-language pathologist. For instance, teachers at a residential treatment facility were taught to use time delay within their classroom routine with positive effects on the spontaneity of students' speech (Schwartz, Anderson, & Halle, 1989). The question regarding teacher implementation of communication intervention strategies is not whether they can implement these strategies but rather whether they will choose to implement them over a period of time. Teachers will need adequate training and support to continue such interventions. Strategies that are adopted for regular use will be those that are incorporated comfortably into the teacher's role and/or are highly successful in eliciting target behaviors.

Although teachers seem always to be asked to do *more* in this model of communication intervention, they may at times be asked to do *less,* or to substitute one type of interaction for another. For instance, several investigators have found that the presence of the teacher had a negative impact on peer interaction (reported in Chandler, Fowler, & Lubeck, 1992). The primary problem may be the nature of the teacher's participation: directing play may decrease peer interaction by increasing reliance on the teacher, whereas providing structure and directing children to interact with each other may have a positive impact. Studies of script training for sociodramatic play (Goldstein & Cisar, 1992; Goldstein, Wickstrom, Hoyson, Jamieson, & Odom, 1988) demonstrate that children's interaction can be facilitated by establishing roles and behavioral repertoires before sociodramatic play activities, then prompting and reinforcing continued interaction. The behaviors that were modeled for target children in the Goldstein and Cisar study (1992) included nonverbal, minimal verbal, and elaborated response forms. This typology provides a framework for the kind of adaptations necessary to implement script training with children who have severe disabilities.

Teachers also can encourage interaction by interpreting the idiosyncratic communication efforts of children with severe disabilities and can encourage the peers to interpret and respond to these efforts (Goldstein & Gallagher, 1992). The responsive interaction strategies that have been suggested primarily for parental use (for instance, Wilcox, 1992) might well be employed by teachers (and perhaps peers) in the classroom. Further exploration of the issues surrounding teacher-mediated communication intervention is warranted.

Peers are a valuable resource for intervention efforts not only because of their ready availability in the classroom but also because of the strong social motivations that exist among children. In peer-mediated interventions, peers are taught to supply instructional supports and encouragements for target children. Although most of the peer-mediated intervention literature focuses generally on social skills (McConnell, McEvoy, & Odom, 1992), more specific efforts have been made to target communicative interaction. Goldstein and Wickstrom (1986) taught peers to use a set of strategies to encourage the communicative interaction of preschoolers with autism and related disorders. These strategies were further refined in a subsequent study by Goldstein and Ferrell (1987) and included (a) establishing eye contact, (b) initiating joint play, (c) using descriptive talking, and (d) responding to the utterance of the target child. Peers in both studies succeeded in eliciting more communicative interaction from target children. Goldstein, Kaczmarek, Pennington, and Shafer (1992) found that a less directive set of procedures (for example, attending to, commenting on, and acknowledging the behavior of preschoolers with autism) also was effective in increasing social-communicative interaction.

Venn, Wolery, Fleming, DeCesare, Morris, and Cuffs (1993) taught preschool peers to use a mand-model procedure during snack to elicit requests from children with disabilities. They found that the peers were able to implement the procedure correctly after training. The preschoolers with disabilities responded to the mand models of their peers, and two of three subjects increased their spontaneous requesting. One interesting finding was the initial increase in inappropriate behavior by the target children when the mand-model procedure was introduced followed by a decrease over time. The authors attributed the increase to the new demands for communication and the decrease in replacement of inappropriate behavior with a more efficient functional equivalent (requesting).

Peer-mediated interventions for communication skills are promising, but our knowledge base for designing and implementing effective strategies is limited at present. Many potential applications of peer-mediated intervention have yet to be explored. For example, can preschool peers be trained to facilitate augmentative and alternative communication (AAC) use in a manner similar to the adult interaction partners trained by Light, Dattilo, English, Gutierrez, and Hartz (1992)? The lack of published curricular materials for facilitating peer-mediated interventions is another problem for speech-language pathologists collaborating with classroom teachers.

Accessing Professional and Technical Resources The population of preschool children with severe disabilities is quite heterogeneous with regard to the specific cognitive, sensory, and motor impairments they have and possible medical conditions that might affect their program planning. Unless a speech-language pathologist is working in a highly specialized setting, such as those run by university research programs, they are unlikely to be expert in their knowledge of all the disabling conditions that may be encountered. Many speech-language pathologists working in rural areas are by necessity generalists. To be certain, some skills particular to the generalist come of broad experience with many very different people and problems. One of the skills required of generalists is the awareness of problems that require specialized knowledge and/or skills—in other words, knowing when to make referrals or recruit assistance. At the other end of this process, resources must be readily available to interventionists and support rather than undermine service delivery efforts.

One way to gain technical knowledge is to study the available literature and/or participate in continuing education programs. These general educational efforts take on added importance when rapid change is occurring in an area of practice. This is the case with early intervention in general and is especially true with inclusion of young children with severe disabilities. We have tried throughout this review to present some of the interventions that have been used or might be adapted for use with this population of children in inclusive settings. As mentioned before, however, much of the information is extrapolated from research with different populations. The literature on preschoolers in inclusive settings that is disability specific is generally scant, with the possible exception of autism. In reviews of social interaction and communication issues specific to children with hearing impairments (Antia & Kreimeyer, 1992) and visual impairments (Skellenger, Hill, & Hill, 1992), for example, only one study of intervention with mainstreamed preschoolers is reported.

Another way to obtain help for particular problems or students is by accessing various technical assistance programs. Technical assistance programs are available for specific areas of concern, such as the assistive technology programs sponsored by individual states, but the specific structure of these programs and ease of access to them depend largely on one's geographical situation.

Technical assistance that comes to the site and/or uses local resources will probably be more successful than externally generated programming recommendations. Janney and Meyer (1990) describe a consultation model for problem behavior that uses locally available resources and expertise and specific intervention efforts to support integrated placement for individual students. They report success with the model in general, and 75 percent of placements were maintained at follow-up.

EVALUATION AND INSTRUCTIONAL DECISION MAKING

One advantage in conducting adult-directed, massed trial training over more naturalistic, distributed trial training is the relative simplicity of evaluation procedures. By recording the procedures used, trials presented, and percentage correct responses in each session, the interventionist can keep track of treatment fidelity and progress or lack of progress for target behaviors. The meaning of this "progress" is debatable, as the maintenance and generalization of the behaviors will need to be evaluated, but initial data collection is simpler.

The effective implementation of naturalistic approaches will require creative solutions to the problems of ongoing data collection and their use in decision making. Both the Activity Based Intervention and Individualized Curriculum Sequencing models provide guidance for collecting and analyzing data. Bricker and Cripe (1992) recommend the use of a formalized probe system for collecting observational data on child progress, with flexible administration in terms of time and personnel factors. Other methods of evaluation include rating scales, anecdotal records, and permanent products/portfolios. Once data are collected, the next problem is how to use the data to make programming decisions. Conducting a meta-analysis of applied behavior analysis studies, Haring, Liberty, and White (1980) found greater improvement in student performance when instructional decisions were based on data evaluation rules than when based on teacher judgment. Evidence indicates that among well-trained, experienced teachers of children with disabilities, data collection and review is fairly common, but systematic use of the data to modify programs is not (Farlow & Snell, 1989).

Because naturalistic teaching strategies rely heavily on the occurrence of teaching episodes, data should be collected periodically on the opportunities provided for use of target behaviors. The data can be used to modify the program for particular students but can also be generally useful in designing environments and activities that support communicative skill development.

CHALLENGES TO AFFECTIVE INTEGRATION

Researchers have found that typically developing young children will interact with peers who have disabilities and that both groups of children can benefit from this interaction (Strain, 1990). On the other hand, typically developing children will generally select peers without disabilities as playmates over children with disabilities (Odom, McConnell, & McEvoy, 1992). Playmate preference is not always based on severity of disability or even the child's level of social competence, but it may be predicted by variables such as physical attractiveness, toy play skills, the extent of disruptive behavior, and athletic prowess (Strain, 1985). The expectation is unrealistic that children with multiple deficiencies in these regards will establish and maintain friendships without an intervention that targets children with and without disabilities.

Other limitations on the affective integration of children with severe disabilities are imposed by the attitudes and behaviors of significant adults. Many common practices, such as traditional pull-out therapy, can be stigmatizing for children if they are treated as remedial procedures used only for children who have problems.

Affective integration must be supported by early, effective, and sensitive service delivery systems. Although preschoolers may already be positively or negatively predisposed toward certain physical and behavioral characteristics, they are still fairly adaptable. Practices that stigmatize and detract from a child's social status within the preschool setting can be replaced by neutral practices or, better yet, by those that improve social status. The child with disabilities can, whenever possible, be made a key player in activities. For instance, peers can assemble themselves as "mountains" and produce echoes when the target child vocalizes, or the target child may be the DJ who activates a tape recorder to start and stop dancing. The child also may be given interaction supports (for example, communication boards, toys) that are particularly attractive to peers and thus act as a kind of prosthesis for social interaction.

With the blending of traditional domain boundaries, new roles are available for speech-language pathologists in areas that contribute to affective integration. Two areas in which speech-language pathologists may have important roles are promoting social skill development and managing challenging behavior.

Communication overlaps with many areas of development, but it is integrally tied to social skill development. Indeed, many behaviors are hard to classify as one versus the other. For example, is saying "Excuse me" a communication or social skill? Is smiling or waving? A child can have highly developed verbal skills and poor social skills or can be socially competent with poor language skills, but these exceptions prove the rule. As is apparent from the review of peer-mediated intervention, researchers who are interested in social skills and those who are interested in communication skills share many goals and approaches.

Social survival skills seem to be more important than academic skills in determining success in mainstreamed classrooms (see Chandler, 1992). Although preschool programs that nurture the development of social skills are quite common, formal social skills training is a relatively new focus for preschool curricula. However, a significant body of research documents the effectiveness of environmental arrangement, teacher-directed procedures, and peer-mediated procedures for increasing rate and quality of peer interactions (McEvoy, Odom, & McConnell, 1992; Peterson & McConnell, 1993). Curricular packages are available for social skills training.

Analysis of interactions of preschoolers with profound disabilities and typical classmates is sparse. One exception is a descriptive study conducted by Hanline (1993) that explored spontaneous peer interactions in a full-inclusion preschool. In designing the program for these children, Hanline augmented with loosely structured interventions an existing preschool curriculum that already stressed social interaction: children were placed/positioned to encourage interaction; appropriate interaction behavior was modeled by interventionists, then prompted and reinforced for peers; the idiosyncratic behaviors of children with disabilities were interpreted for peers; and questions about the children with disabilities were answered.

Differences were found in the behavior of the three profoundly disabled children and three typically developing peers. The quantity and effectiveness of initiations was quite a bit higher, and the total number of interactions was greater for the typical peers; but the children with disabilities had frequent opportunities to interact, and the length of time for each interaction was comparable. The children without disabilities were more persistent in their initiations to children with disabilities, seeming to derive satisfaction in successfully eliciting a response. Differences were also noted among the children with disabilities. One interesting difference was the relatively low rate of interaction observed for a child with visual impairment.

Generalization and maintenance of changes in peer interaction continue to be a problem. Some solutions to these difficulties may be offered by training procedures that can be easily implemented within the typical structure of the classroom and/or rely on less intrusive teacher prompting and reinforcement. These procedures include affection training (McEvoy et al., 1992; McEvoy, Twardosz, & Bishop, 1990), correspondence training (McEvoy et al., 1992; Osnes, Guevremont, & Stokes, 1986), and the sociodramatic script training discussed earlier. In affection training, typical preschool group activities (for instance, songs, games) are modified to incorporate prompts for interaction, typically some kind of affectionate response. These procedures are apparently most effective in encouraging increased interaction among children who already know how to interact (McEvoy et al., 1992). Some modifications of affection training procedures may be needed for children who are learning to interact or who are averse to certain kinds of interaction (such as touch). Correspondence training uses a "say/do" procedure to encourage peers to interact with children who have disabilities and subsequently rewards them for appropriate behaviors (Osnes et al., 1986). Such training can be worked into the planning and wrap-up discussions in many preschool programs.

The management of challenging behavior is another area of potential involvement for speech-language pathologists. Behaviors that are problems in the classroom may serve various functions for the child. The identification of antecedents and consequences of particular problem behaviors through functional analysis provides interventionists with some insight into the function of the behavior for a particular child (Arndorfer & Miltenberger, 1993; O'Neill et al., 1990; Reichle & Wacker, 1993). Some of the most likely functions are self-regulation, play, and social-communicative functions (Meyer & Evans, 1986). Examples of behaviors with social-communicative functions include head banging to escape/terminate interaction, biting to gain attention, and screaming to indicate toy ownership. When the function is social-communicative in nature, Meyer and Evans (1986) suggest that curricular goals for related communication behaviors are overdue.

Carr and Durand (1985; Durand & Carr, 1991) have conducted several investigations of functional communication training for the remediation of challenging behaviors. Their work is based on the notion of functional equivalence, which allows for "equivalent" categories of behavior in terms of the consequences that are elicited. The behavior selected for training should fulfill the same function as the problem behavior, but more appropriately and, hopefully, more efficiently.

A more appropriate communication form can be selected based on the child's abilities and the likelihood that others will interpret it accurately and provide the desired consequences. If the child already has words or signs in his or her repertoire, these may be prompted at the appropriate times. For example, "No more" or "All done" could be used to terminate interaction, "Mine" could be used to keep a toy, or new forms of communication could be taught. Unfortunately, in some situations a more appropriate form is not as efficient as the challenging behavior. Preschool peers may be more likely to give in to screams or head banging than to respond to a child's more conventional communication attempts. To maximize success, we should work with others in the child's environment to be sure that they are responding to the child's new efforts.

Most of the communicative behaviors selected to replace challenging behaviors have been linguistic forms. The potential usefulness of functional communication training for children at the prelinguistic level is suggested by Carr and Kemp (1989), who successfully trained pointing as a functional replacement for the "leading" behavior of preschoolers with autism. Given evidence that the presymbolic communication of young children with disabilities is interpreted inconsistently by their partners (Wilcox et al., 1990), supporting consistent responses to the target behavior is even more important. Functional equivalence training for communicative behaviors is a promising technique for the treatment of challenging behavior. Further investigations could address the relative "power" of various communicative forms, the effectiveness of the technique for prelinguistic children, the types of support needed for classroom communication partners, and the social validity of such interventions.

IMPLICATIONS AND AVENUES FOR FUTURE RESEARCH

Inclusion efforts are just beginning for preschoolers with severe disabilities. Many of our recommended practices have been extrapolated from research with older children, preschoolers with mild and moderate disabilities, and preschoolers with severe disabilities in segregated settings. To provide quality services for these children in inclusive programs, specialists from many disciplines will be asking similar questions with a slightly different focus. Researchers from many disciplines need to look at the usefulness of specific assessment and intervention strategies and techniques within preschool classrooms.

Careful research on new techniques combined with systematic replication of current applied clinical research will allow us to evaluate better the general usefulness of particular strategies for preschoolers with severe disabilities in inclusive settings. Subpopulations (for example, preschoolers who are blind or who use AAC) should also be studied with reference to the effectiveness of particular strategies. A number of specific research questions for researchers interested in the communication skills of preschoolers with severe disabilities have been suggested throughout this review. Major areas for exploration include (a) the influence of environmental or setting variables on the communication behavior of these children; (b) the ability of traditional and nontraditional measures to provide complete and useful information regarding communicative functioning and evaluation of progress; (c) the adaptations necessary to apply assessments and intervention procedures designed for other populations to this population; (d) the effects of communication interventions on other areas of functioning, such as cognitive or social-emotional functioning, and vice versa; and (e) the long-term effects of inclusive education on the communication and affective development of children with and without disabilities.

The quality of the research process may well depend on the success of efforts to bridge the clinician-researcher gap. The problems created by dichotomizing the pursuits of clinicians and researchers have been discussed in the literature. Recommendations for closing this gap include training speech-language pathologists to be "clinical scientists" and providing structural supports for cooperative interaction between researchers and clinicians (Fey, 1990; Ringel, 1972). Cooperative interaction will certainly be needed in research on inclusion. Only a combination of the experience and insights of the clinician with the theoretical base and scientific rigor of the researcher will produce the kind of high-quality, clinically applicable findings needed to advance practice.

CONCLUSION

Although this review has concentrated on the issues and challenges facing speech-language pathologists, we believe that other service providers face similar challenges. The role of the specialist is evolving in many ways. Children with severe disabilities, by definition, will require a great deal of support to function optimally in their environment. Unless adequately trained and readily available support staff work collaboratively with the primary service provider(s), efforts to include preschoolers with severe disabilities may be doomed to failure. On the other hand, when support services are incorporated into the classroom creatively, the result can be improved opportunities for all children. Our vision is similar to that of Hobbes (1975), who describes a classroom in which

> the mainstream is actually many streams, sometimes as many streams as there are individual children, sometimes several streams as groups are formed for special purpose, sometimes one stream only as concerns of all converge. We see no advantage in dumping exceptional children into an undifferentiated mainstream; but we see great advantages to all children, exceptional children included, in an educational program modulated to the needs of individual children, singly, in small groups, or all together. Such a flexible arrangement may well result in functional separations of exceptional children from time to time, but the governing principle would apply to all children: school programs should be responsive to the learning requirements of individual children, and groupings should serve this end. (p. 197)

The challenge for inclusive education is to strike a balance between accepting individual differences and encouraging all children to achieve their "personal best."

REFERENCES

Antia, S. D., & Kreimeyer, K. H. (1992). Social competence intervention for young children with hearing impairments. In S. Odom, S. McConnell, & M. McEvoy (Eds.), *Social competence of young children with disabilities: Issues and strategies for intervention* (pp. 135–164). Baltimore: Brookes.

Arndorfer, R. E. & Miltenberger, R. G. (1993). Functional assessment and treatment of challenging behavior: A review with implications for early childhood. *Topics in Early Childhood Special Education, 13*(1), 82–105.

Bailey, D. B., Clifford, R. M., & Harms, T. (1982). Comparison of preschool environments for handicapped and nonhandicapped preschoolers. *Topics in Early Childhood Special Education, 2,* 9–20.

Bangs, T. (1986). *Birth to three checklist of learning and language behavior.* Allen, TX: DLM Teaching Resources.

Barnett, D. W., Macmann, G. M., & Carey, K. T. (1992). Early intervention and the assessment of developmental skills: Challenges and directions. *Topics in Early Childhood Special Education, 12*(1), 21–43.

Berg, F. (1987). *Facilitating classroom listening: A handbook for teachers of normal and hard of hearing students.* Austin, TX: PRO-ED.

Bricker, D. (Ed.). (1992). *Assessment, evaluation, and programming system (AEPS) for infants and young children: Vol. 1. AEPS measurement for birth to three years.* Baltimore: Brookes.

Bricker, D., & Cripe, J. (1992). *An activity-based approach to early intervention.* Baltimore: Brookes

Brown, L., Long, E., Udvari-Solner, A. & Davis, L. (1989). The home school: Why students with severe intellectual disabilities must attend the schools of their brothers, sisters, friends, and neighbors. *Journal of the Association for Persons with Severe Handicaps, 14,* 1–7.

Brown, L., Long, E., Udvari-Solner, A., & Schwarz, P. (1989). Should students with severe intellectual disabilities be based in regular or special education classrooms in home schools? *Journal of the Association for Persons with Severe Handicaps, 14,* 8–12.

Campbell, C. R., Stremel-Campbell, K., & Rogers-Warren, A. (1985). Programming teacher support for functional language. In S. Warren & A. Rogers-Warren (Eds.), *Teaching functional language* (pp. 309–339). Austin, TX: PRO-ED.

Campbell, P. H. (1988, October). *Child-environmental assessment through a process of ecological inventories.* Tallmadge, OH: Family Child Learning Center.

Carr, E. G., & Durand, V. M. (1985). Reducing behavior problems through functional communication training. *Journal of Applied Behavior Analysis, 18,* 111–126.

Carr, E. G., & Kemp, D. C. (1989). Functional equivalence of autistic leading and communicative pointing: Analysis and treatment. *Journal of Autism and Developmental Disorders, 19,* 561–578.

Carta, J. J., Atwater, J. B., Schwartz, I. S., & McConnell, S. R. (1993). Developmentally Appropriate Practices and early childhood special education: A reaction to Johnson and McChesney-Johnson. *Topics in Early Childhood Special Education, 13,* 243–254.

Carta, J. J., Atwater, J. B., Schwartz, I. S., & Miller, P. A. (1990). Application of ecobehavioral analysis to the study of transitions across early educational settings. *Education and Treatment of Children, 13,* 298–315.

Carta, J. J., Sainato, D. M., & Greenwood, C. R. (1988). Advances in the ecological assessment of classroom instruction for young children with handicaps. In S. L. Odom & M. B. Karnes (Eds.), *Early intervention for infants and children with handicaps* (pp. 217–239). Baltimore: Brookes.

Catlett, C. (Ed.). (1993). *A compendium of early intervention training activities.* Rockville, MD: American Speech-Language-Hearing Association.

Chandler, L. K. (1992). Promoting children's social/survival skills as a strategy for transition to mainstreamed kindergarten programs. In S. Odom, S. McConnell, & M. McEvoy (Eds.), *Social competence of young children with disabilities: Issues and strategies for intervention* (pp. 245–276). Baltimore: Brookes.

Chandler, L. K., Fowler, S. A., & Lubeck, R. C. (1992). An analysis of the effects of multiple setting events on the social behavior of preschool children with special needs. *Journal of Applied Behavior Analysis, 25,* 249–263.

Cipani, E. (1991). Functional language assessment. In E. Cipani (Ed.), *A guide to developing language competence in preschool children with severe and moderate handicaps* (pp. 22–42). Springfield, IL: Thomas.

Durand, V. M., & Carr, E. G. (1991). Functional communication training to reduce challenging behavior: Maintenance and application in new settings. *Journal of Applied Behavior Analysis, 24,* 251–264.

English, K. (1991). Best practices in educational audiology. *Language, Speech, and Hearing Services in the Schools, 22,* 283–286.

Farlow, L. J., & Snell, M. E. (1989). Teacher use of performance data to make instructional decisions: Practices in programs with moderate to profound disabilities. *Journal of the Association for Persons with Severe Handicaps, 14,* 13–22.

Fey, M. E. (1990). Understanding and narrowing the gap between treatment research and clinical practice with language-impaired children. *ASHA Reports, 20,* 31–40.

Finitzo, T. (1988). Classroom acoustics. In R. Roeser & M. Downs (Eds.), *Auditory disorders in school children* (2nd ed., pp. 221–233). New York: Thieme Medical Publishers.

Foley, G. (1990). Portrait of the arena evaluation: Assessment in the transdisciplinary approach. In E. Gobbs & D. Teti (Eds.), *Interdisciplinary assessment of infants: A guide for early intervention professionals* (pp. 271–286). Baltimore: Brookes.

Gaylord-Ross, R., Stremel-Campbell, K., & Storey, K. (1986). Social skills training in natural contexts. In R. Horner, L. Meyer, & H. Fredericks (Eds.), *Education of learners with severe handicaps: Exemplary service strategies* (pp. 161–187). Baltimore: Brookes.

Goldstein, H. (1993). Interventions to promote communication skills. In S. Odom & M. McLean (Eds.), *DEC recommended practices: Indicators of quality in programs for infants and young children with special needs and their families* (pp. 69–76). Reston, VA: Council for Exceptional Children.

Goldstein, H., & Cisar, C. L. (1992). Promoting interaction during sociodramatic play: Teaching scripts to typical preschoolers and classmates with disabilities. *Journal of Applied Behavior Analysis, 25,* 265–280.

Goldstein, H., & Ferrell, D. R. (1987). Augmenting communicative interaction between handicapped and nonhandicapped preschoolers. *Journal of Speech and Hearing Disorders, 19,* 200–211.

Goldstein, H., & Gallagher, T. M. (1992) Strategies for promoting the social-communicative competence of young children with specific language impairment. In S. L. Odom, S. R. McConnell, & M. A. McEvoy (Eds.), *Social competence of young children with disabilities: Issues and strategies for intervention* (pp. 189–213). Baltimore: Brookes.

Goldstein, H., & Kaczmarek (1992). Promoting communicative interaction among children in integrated intervention settings. In S. F. Warren & J. Reichle (Eds.), *Causes and effects in communication and language intervention* (pp. 81–111). Baltimore: Brookes.

Goldstein, H., Kaczmarek, L., & Hepting, N. (1996). Recommended practices for interventions to promote communication skills. In S. Odom & M. McLean (Eds.), *Recommended practices in early intervention.* Austin, TX: PRO-ED.

Goldstein, H., Kaczmarek, L., Pennington, R., & Shafer, K. (1992). Peer-mediated interventions: Attending to, commenting on, and acknowledging the behavior of preschoolers with autism. *Journal of Applied Behavior Analysis, 25,* 289–305.

Goldstein, H., & Wickstrom, S. (1986). Peer intervention effects on communicative interaction among handicapped and nonhandicapped preschoolers. *Journal of Applied Behavior Analysis, 19,* 209–214.

Goldstein, H., Wickstrom, S., Hoyson, M., Jamieson, B., & Odom, S. L. (1988). Effects of sociodramatic play training on social and communicative interaction. *Education and Treatment of Children, 11,* 97–117.

Guess, D., & Helmstetter, E. (1986). Skill cluster instruction and the individualized curriculum sequencing model. In R. Horner, L. Meyer, & H. Fredericks (Eds.), *Education of learners with severe handicaps: Exemplary service strategies* (pp. 189–248). Baltimore: Brookes.

Guralnick, M. J. (1990). Major accomplishments and future directions in early childhood mainstreaming. *Topics in Early Childhood Special Education, 10,* 1–17.

Hanline, M. F. (1993) Inclusion of preschoolers with profound disabilities: An analysis of children's interactions. *Journal of the Association for Persons with Severe Handicaps, 18,* 28–35.

Haring, N. G., Liberty, K. A., & White, O. R. (1980). Rules for data-based strategy decision in instructional programs. In W. Sailor, B. Wilcox, & L. Brown (Eds.), *Methods of instruction for severely handicapped children* (pp. 159–192). Baltimore: Brookes.

Harms, T., & Clifford, R. M. (1980). *Early childhood environment rating scale.* New York: Teachers College Press.

Hart, B. M., & Risley, T. R. (1980). In vivo language intervention: Unanticipated general effects. *Journal of Applied Behavior Analysis, 7,* 243–256.

Hobbes, N. A. (1975). *The futures of children: Categories, labels, and their consequences.* San Francisco: Jossey-Bass.

Individuals with Disabilities Education Act, Public Law 94-142, Section 121a, 303 (*Federal Register,* 1977).

Janney, R. E., & Meyer, L. H. (1990). A consultation model to support integrated educational services for students with severe disabilities and challenging behaviors. *Journal of the Association for Persons with Severe Handicaps, 15,* 186–199.

Kaczmarek, L. A. (1990). Teaching spontaneous language to individuals with severe handicaps: A matrix model. *Journal of the Association for Persons with Severe Handicaps, 13,* 160–169.

Kaczmarek, L., Hepting, N. H., & Dzubak, M. (1992, December). *Teaching children with severe disabilities to communicate spontaneously.* Paper presented at the meeting of the Division for Early Childhood, Washington, DC.

Kaiser, A. P., Yoder, P. J., & Keetz, A. (1992). Evaluating milieu teaching. In S. F. Warren & J. Reichle (Eds.), *Causes and effects in communication and language intervention* (pp. 9–47). Baltimore: Brookes.

Light, J., Dattilo, J., English, J., Gutierrez, L., & Hartz, J. (1992). Instructing facilitators to support the communication of people who use augmentative communication systems. *Journal of Speech and Hearing Research, 35,* 865–875.

Linder, T. (1993a). *Transdisciplinary play-based assessment: A functional approach to working with young children* (rev. ed.). Baltimore: Brookes.

Linder, T. (1993b). *Transdisciplinary play-based intervention: Guidelines for developing a meaningful curriculum for young children.* Baltimore: Brookes.

Macdonald, C., & York, J. (1992). An assessment of student participation in general education classes. In B. Rainforth, J. York, & C. Macdonald (Eds.), *Collaborative teams for students with severe disabilities* (pp. 256–257). Baltimore: Brookes.

MacDonald, J. D. (1985). Language through conversation. In S. Warren & A. Rogers-Warren (Eds.), *Teaching functional language* (pp. 89–122). Baltimore: University Park Press.

McConnell, S. R., McEvoy, M. A., & Odom, S. L. (1992). Implementation of social competence interventions in early childhood special education classes: Current practices and future directions. In S. Odom, S. McConnell, & M. McEvoy (Eds.), *Social competence of young children with disabilities: Issues and strategies for intervention* (pp. 277–306). Baltimore: Brookes.

McEvoy, M. A. (Ed.). (1990). Special issue: Organizing caregiving environments for young children with handicaps. *Education and Treatment of Children, 13* (4).

McEvoy, M. A., Fox, J. J., & Rosenberg, M. S. (1991). Organizing preschool environments: Suggestions for enhancing the development/learning of preschool children with handicaps. *Topics in Early Childhood Special Education, 11*(2), 18–28.

McEvoy, M. A., Odom, S. L., & McConnell, S. R. (1992). Peer social competence intervention for young children with disabilities. In S. L. Odom, S. R. McConnell, & M. A. McEvoy (Eds.), *Social competence of young children with disabilities: Issues and strategies for intervention* (pp. 113–134). Baltimore: Brookes.

McEvoy, M. A., Twardosz, S., & Bishop, N. (1990). Affection activities: Procedures for encouraging young children with handicaps to interact with their peers. *Education and Treatment of Children, 13,* 159–167.

McLean, M. E., & Odom, S. L. (1993). Practices for young children with and without disabilities: A comparison of DEC and NAEYC identified practices. *Topics in Early Childhood Special Education, 13,* 274–292.

Meyer, L. H., & Evans, I. M. (1986). Modification of excess behavior: An adaptive and functional approach for educational and community contexts. In R. Horner, L. Meyer, & H. Fredericks (Eds.), *Education of learners with severe handicaps: Exemplary service strategies* (pp. 315–350). Baltimore: Brookes.

Miller, J. (1981). *Assessing language production in children: Experimental procedures.* Austin, TX: PRO-ED.

Miller, J., & Chapman, R. (1986). *Systematic analysis of language transcripts (SALT1)* [computer software]. Madison: University of Wisconsin Press.

Neisworth, J. T. (1993). *DEC recommended practices: Indicators of quality in programs for young children and their families.* Reston, VA: Division for Early Childhood, Council for Exceptional Children (Task Force on Recommended Practices).

Neisworth, J. T., & Bagnato, S. J. (1988). Assessment in early childhood education: A typology of dependent measures. In S. Odom & M. Karnes (Eds.), *Early intervention for infants and children with handicaps* (pp. 23–49). Baltimore: Brookes.

Noonan, M. J., & Hemphill, N. J. (1988). Comprehensive curricula for integrating severely disabled and nondisabled students. In E. Meyen, G. Vergason, & R. Whelan (Eds.), *Effective instructional strategies for exceptional children* (pp. 157–172). Denver, CO: Love.

Notari, A., & Cole, K. (1993). Language intervention: Research Implications for service delivery. In C. A. Peck, S. L. Odom, & Bricker, D. D. (Eds.), *Integrating young children with disabilities into community programs: Ecological perspectives on research and implementation* (pp. 17–37). Baltimore: Brookes.

Notari, A. R., Cole, K. N., & Mills, P. E. (1992). Cognitive referencing: The (non)relationship between theory and practice. *Topics in Early Childhood Special Education, 11*(4), 22–38.

Odom, S. L., McConnell, S. R., & McEvoy, M. A. (1992). Peer-related social competence and its significance for young children with disabilities. In S. Odom, S. McConnell, & M. McEvoy (Eds.), *Social competence of young children with disabilities: Issues and strategies for intervention* (pp. 3–35). Baltimore: Brookes.

Odom, S. L., & McEvoy, M. A. (1990). Mainstreaming at the preschool level: Potential barriers and tasks for the field. *Topics in Early Childhood Special Education, 10*(2), 48–61.

Oliver, C. B., & Halle, J. W. (1982). Language training in the everyday environment: Teaching functional sign use to a retarded child. *Journal of the Association for the Severely Handicapped, 8,* 50–62.

Olswang, L. B., Bain, B. A., & Johnson, G. A. (1992). Using dynamic assessment with children with language disorders. In S. F. Warren & J. Reichle (Eds.), *Causes and effects in communication and language intervention* (pp. 187–215). Baltimore: Brookes.

O'Neill, R., Horner, R., Albin, R., Storey, K., & Sprague, J. (1990). *Functional analysis of problem behavior: A practical assessment guide.* Sycamore, IL: Sycamore.

Osnes, P. G., Guevrement, D. C., & Stokes, T. F. (1986). If I say I'll talk more, then I will: Correspondence training to increase peer-directed talk by socially withdrawn children. *Behavior Modification, 10,* 287–299.

Pennington, R., Kaczmarek, L., & Goldstein, H. (Eds.). (1993). *Transdisciplinary consultation: A staff development model.* Pittsburgh, PA: University of Pittsburgh, Transdisciplinary Consultation Project.

Peterson, C. A., & McConnell, S. R. (1993). Factors affecting the impact of social interaction skills interventions in early childhood special education. *Topics in Early Childhood Special Education, 13*(1), 38–56.

Rainforth, B., York, J., & Macdonald, C. (1992). *Collaborative teams for students with severe disabilities.* Baltimore: Brookes.

Reichle, J., Halle, J., & Johnston, S. (1993). Developing an initial communicative repertoire: Applications and issues for persons with severe disabilities. In A. P. Kaiser & D. B. Gray (Eds.), *Enhancing children's communication: Research foundations for intervention* (pp. 105–136). Baltimore: Brookes.

Reichle, J., & Keogh, W. J. (1986). Communication instruction for learners with severe handicaps: Some unresolved issues. In R. Horner, L. Meyer, & H. Fredericks (Eds.), *Education of learners with severe handicaps: Exemplary service strategies* (pp. 189–219). Baltimore: Brookes.

Reichle, J., & Wacker, D. (1993). *Communicative alternatives to challenging behavior: Integrating functional assessment and intervention strategies.* Baltimore: Brookes.

Ringel, R. L. (1972). The clinician and the researcher: An artificial dichotomy. *ASHA,* pp. 351–353.

Romski, M. A., & Sevcik, R. A. (1992). Developing augmented language in children with severe mental retardation. In S. F. Warren & J. Reichle (Eds.), *Causes and effects in communication and language intervention* (pp. 113–130). Baltimore: Brookes.

Rotholz, D. A., Berkowitz, S. F., & Burberry, J. (1989). Functionality of two modes of communication in the community by students with developmental disabilities: A comparison of signing and communication books. *Journal of the Association for Persons with Severe Handicaps, 14,* 227–233.

Sainato, D. M., & Carta, J. J. (1992). Classroom influences on the development of social competence in young children with disabilities. In S. L. Odom, S. R. McConnell, & M. A. McEvoy (Eds.), *Social competence of young children with disabilities: Issues and strategies for intervention* (pp. 93–109). Baltimore: Brookes.

Schwartz, I. S., Anderson, S. R., & Halle, J. W. (1989). Training teachers to use naturalistic time delay: Effects on teacher behavior and on the language use of students. *Journal of the Association for Persons with Severe Handicaps, 14,* 48–57.

Skellenger, A. C., Hill, M., & Hill, E. (1992). The social functioning of children with visual impairments. In S. Odom, S. McConnell, & M. McEvoy (Eds.), *Social competence of young children with disabilities: Issues and strategies for intervention* (pp. 165–188). Baltimore: Brookes.

Strain, P. S. (1985). Social and nonsocial determinants of handicapped preschool children's social competence. *Topics in Early Childhood Special Education, 4*(4), 47–59.

Strain, P. S. (1990). LRE for preschool children with handicaps: What we know, what we should be doing. *Journal of Early Intervention, 14,* 291–296.

U.S. Office of Education. (1975). *Estimated number of handicapped children in the United States, 1974–1975.* Washington, DC: Office of Special Education Programs.

Utley, B. L. (1986). Characteristics and special needs of severely handicapped preschoolers. In L. Bickman & D. L. Weatherford (Eds.), *Evaluating early intervention programs for severely handicapped children and their families* (pp. 21–49). Austin, TX: PRO-ED.

Venn, M. L., Wolery, M., Fleming, L., DeCesare, L. D., Morris, A., & Cuffs, M. S. (1993). Effects of teaching peers to use the mand-model procedure during snack activities. *American Journal of Speech-Language Pathology, 2,* 38–46.

Warren, S. F., & Kaiser, A. P. (1986). Incidental language teaching: A critical review. *Journal of Speech and Hearing Disorders, 51,* 291–299.

Warren, S. F., & Kaiser, A. P. (1988). Research in early language intervention. In S. Odom & M. Karnes (Eds.), *Early intervention for infants and children with handicaps: An empirical base* (pp. 89–108). Baltimore: Brookes.

Warren, S. F., Yoder, P. J., Gazdag, G. E., Kim, K., & Jones, H. A. (1993). Facilitating prelinguistic communication skills in young children with developmental delay. *Journal of Speech and Hearing Research, 36,* 83–97.

Weiss, R. S. (1981). INREAL Intervention for language handicapped and bilingual children. *Journal of the Division for Early Childhood, 4,* 40–51.

Wetherby, A., & Prizant, B. (1990). *Communication and symbolic behavior scales—Research edition.* Chicago: Riverside.

Wetherby, A. M., & Prizant, B. M. (1992). Profiling young children's communicative competence. In S. Warren & J. Reichle (Eds.), *Causes and effects in communication and language intervention* (pp. 217–253). Baltimore: Brookes.

Wilcox, M. J. (1988). Designing an ecologically-based communication assessment. *Clinical Connection, 3*(1), 1–4.

Wilcox, M. J. (1992). Enhancing initial communication skills in young children with developmental disabilities through partner programming. *Seminars in Speech and Language, 13*(3), 194–212.

Wilcox, M. J., Khouri, T. A., & Caswell, S. (1990). Partner sensitivity to communication behaviors of young children with developmental disabilities. *Journal of Speech and Hearing Disorders, 55,* 679–693.

Wolery, M. (Ed.). (1993). Relationship between general and special early childhood education. *Topics in Early Childhood Special Education, 13*(3).

Wolery, M., & Dyk, L. (1984). Arena assessment: Description and preliminary social validity data. *Journal of the Association for the Severely Handicapped, 3,* 231–235.

Yoder, P. J., Kaiser, A. P., & Alpert, C. L. (1991). An exploratory study of the interactions between language teaching methods and child characteristics. *Journal of Speech and Hearing Research, 34,* 155–167.

Yoder, P. J., & Warren, S. F. (1993). Can developmentally delayed children's language development be enhanced through prelinguistic intervention? In A. P. Kaiser & D. B. Gray (Eds.), *Enhancing children's communication: Research foundations for intervention* (pp. 35–61). Baltimore: Brookes.

Zimmerman, I., Steiner, V., & Evatt, R. (1969). *Preschool language scale.* Upper Saddle River, NJ: Merrill/Prentice Hall.

11

Integration in the Elementary School for Students with Moderate Disabilities

MARGO A. MASTROPIERI
THOMAS E. SCRUGGS
SHERI L. HAMILTON

This chapter reviews available research evidence on effective instructional and mainstreaming/inclusion strategies for students with moderate disabilities. A variety of effective interventions has been documented through research; however, effective mainstreaming strategies for this population have far less research evidence. Students with moderate disabilities have been integrated with nondisabled students in regular education settings, and, generally, positive interactions between the groups have increased. However, less evidence is available on the ability of regular classroom settings to address the unique curriculum needs of students with moderate disabilities. Schools considering mainstreaming/inclusive programming for students with moderate disabilities should carefully attend to the instructional and curriculum needs of such students, and monitor setting effectiveness in meeting these needs.

Persons with moderate mental retardation have been characterized by the American Association on Mental Retardation (AAMR; formerly the American Association on Mental Deficiency) as those who display significant deficits in adaptive behavior and who function intellectually within the 35–40 to 50–55 range of psychometric intelligence (Grossman, 1983). In 1992, the AAMR moved away from the previous system of classification based solely on IQ score and adaptive behavior measures and toward a model intended to reflect the level of support needed to maximize their potential levels of competent functioning. According to this new classification scheme, persons previously characterized as having moderate mental retardation would correspond most closely to what the AAMR termed "limited." This term means that the level of support needed is consistent over time, time limited but not intermittent, and requires fewer resources than more intense levels of support (AAMR Ad Hoc Committee on Terminology and Classification, 1992). It is not yet known whether this new classification will replace the older version in actual practice (Hallahan & Kauffman, 1994).

Individuals with moderate disabilities comprise between 6 and 10 percent of all persons with mental retardation (Patton, Payne, & Beirne-Smith, 1986). In overall performance, persons with moderate disabilities perform slightly below those with mild retardation, and they may require instructional strategies that are somewhat different from those used with students with mild disabilities (see, for example, Scruggs & Mastropieri, 1993). Educational programs concentrate on communication, functional, vocational, and daily living skills (Salend, 1994). Many individuals with moderate disabilities learn functional academic skills, can be employed, and live independently in the community (Espin & Deno, 1988).

In 1991, a panel of persons representing university special education programs, advocacy organizations, and school personnel reached consensus on the following characteristics of students with moderate mental disabilities:

> Children with moderate mental disabilities exhibit a wide range of academic achievements. To varying degrees, they learn to tell time, count money, and use a calculator. By adulthood, some individuals can count or match to sample while others have an understanding of basic addition, subtraction, and occasionally multiplication. Typically, these students read at first- or second-grade levels with limited comprehension. They do, however, develop functional reading skills such as reading signs, simple forms, and menus. Within

> this group, considerable variability in written communication exists. . . . Since acquisition, transfer, and generalization of skills and knowledge are difficult for individuals with moderate cognitive impairments, instruction is provided in domestic, vocational, and leisure skills. (Copel, 1991, p. 1)

Although the population of students with moderate disabilities comprises up to 10 percent of the total population of individuals with mental retardation and has been described as exhibiting characteristics that distinguish such students from those with mild or severe mental retardation, evidence indicates that the characterization of "moderate" disabilities is disappearing from the literature. For example, in the second edition of a popular introductory text on mental retardation, Patton et al. (1986) devote a brief section (pp. 80–81) to the definition and characteristics of moderate mental retardation. In the fourth edition of the same text, however (Beirne-Smith, Patton, & Ittenbach, 1994), a definition and characteristics of this subpopulation are not discussed separately; instead, they are included within separate chapters on mild mental retardation (Chapter 6) or on severe and profound mental retardation (Chapter 7). Further, a recent research volume (Gable & Warren, 1993) is divided into two parts: one dealing with mild disabilities and another focusing on severe disabilities. In a chapter in another recent text (Wolery & Haring, 1994), moderate disabilities is included but discussed alongside severe and profound disabilities. Given these recent publishing developments and the new AAMR definitional guidelines, students identified as having moderate disabilities may receive even less attention in the future (J. Patton, personal communication, April 13, 1994). Nevertheless, there appear to be a number of common characteristics of these learners that warrant our attention.

To what extent can students with moderate disabilities be integrated into the regular elementary school classroom environment, and to what extent can contemporary regular elementary classrooms meet the needs of students with moderate disabilities? To address these questions, we undertook a thorough literature review of intervention research with students of elementary age with moderate disabilities. We gathered information on the instructional procedures validated by research, as well as the existing research evidence on inclusion of students with moderate disabilities in elementary school settings. With such information at hand, we would be able to provide specific recommendations on the type and nature of effective mainstreaming/inclusion activities for students with moderate disabilities.

In the remainder of this chapter, we will describe the results of our literature search and the studies we identified. Finally, we will provide some overall recommendations for further research and practice for accommodating students with moderate disabilities in elementary school settings.

LITERATURE SEARCH PROCEDURE

We conducted a search of sources listed in the ERIC database from 1985 to present. Articles were included if they provided original research on samples of individuals with an IQ range of 30 to 55 or if the samples were defined as having moderate, mild/moderate, or moderate/severe mental retardation. Articles also were delimited by inclusion of students from elementary school ages (or early adolescence) or elementary settings. An ERIC search was also conducted on the following special education topics: attitudes, assessment, interventions, and mainstreaming/inclusion. Documents located through this procedure were searched for samples of students with moderate mental retardation. In addition, the following journals, from 1985 to present, were hand-searched for intervention studies that included students with moderate mental retardation: *Education and Treatment of Mental Retardation, American Journal of Mental Retardation, Mental Retardation, Journal of the Association for the Severely Handicapped, Exceptional Children, Journal of Special Education, Remedial and Special Education,* and *Exceptionality.* Finally, we conducted an ancestry search on reference lists of all identified articles for additional sources. We also consulted earlier reviews (for instance, Ault, Wolery, Doyle, & Gast, 1989) for concordance with our own conclusions.

Each identified article was searched for the following variables: purpose of the study; sample description, including number of subjects, sex, age/grade, IQ/developmental functioning measures, race/ethnicity, socioeconomic status (SES), and school/community location; type of research (intervention, assessment, and so forth); independent variables; dependent variables; and results of the study. When available, these variables were recorded.

RESULTS

Initially ERIC identified 238 references to the descriptor "moderate mental retardation." However, using the search criteria described previously, we found that only seventeen of these articles met all criteria for inclusion. Fifteen investigations described the results of academic or social interventions provided by teachers or researchers with students with moderate disabilities in special education settings. These investigations are indirectly relevant to the issue of mainstreaming/inclusion because they provide evidence about optimal intervention strategies as well as curriculum needs of students with moderate disabilities. Two articles described the results of interventions that involved the interaction of students with moderate disabilities and nondisabled students, and they are directly relevant to the issue of mainstreaming. All reports are discussed separately in the following sections.

Academic Interventions

Simple Concept Learning Tateyama-Sniezek (1989) compared single or multiple (four) examples in training acquisition and generalization of the concept of color names to five boys and three girls with moderate retardation (age range, six to ten years; IQ range, 25 to 50). Greater generalization occurred when multiple examples of each color were used during training.

Reading-Decoding Hoogeveen and his colleagues have conducted a number of investigations that have attempted to improve the reading decoding performance of students with moderate disabilities. Hoogeveen, Smeets, and Lancioni

(1989) describe a model of mnemonic elaboration for teaching letter sounds to three boys and a girl with mild and moderate mental retardation. Students were from eight to thirteen years old and had IQ scores ranging from 47 to 68. The materials included letters that had been pictorially enhanced to resemble objects where the first letter was the same as the target letter (see also Ehri, Deffner, & Wilce, 1984). For instance, the letter *v* was drawn to resemble a bird (the word for *bird* in Dutch, where this study was conducted, begins with a "v" sound). Over time, the pictorial elaboration was faded until only the original letter remained. A sequence of two-letter to two-syllable words was taught, but students made differential progress through the program. All students learned to read by this method, and transfer to similar but untrained words was very high, presumably because of the phonic approach employed. However, comprehension of transfer passages was more limited.

Hoogeveen, Birkhoff, Smeets, Lancioni, and Boelens (1989) describe a program for training phonemic segmentation in moderately retarded children. Participants included nine boys and seven girls six to nineteen years old, with IQ scores between 35 and 72. Neither direct phoneme instruction nor picture cues appeared to facilitate isolation of the final phoneme in consonant-vowel-consonant (CVC) words. In a second experiment, use of longer pauses, later faded, between initial CV and final C phonemes resulted in higher levels of recall and generalization, for both meaningful and nonmeaningful CVC words. These findings were supported by the results of an investigation by Hoogeveen, Kouwenhoven, and Smeets (1989), who report that training without pictorial prompts resulted in better blending of trained and untrained CVC items than pictorial prompts and direct teaching of eleven boys and eleven girls who ranged in age from seven to sixteen years and had IQ scores from 40 to 67.

Word Reading Four reports addressed strategies for facilitating word reading. Singh and Solman (1990) trained five-letter nouns to four boys and four girls, seven to nine years of age, with Down's syndrome and diagnosed as having moderate mental retardation. All students made the most errors when pictures were presented alone, followed by presentation of the picture with written label. Students made fewest errors when words were initially presented without pictures. Generalization of learned skills was not addressed. Gast, Ault, Wolery, Doyle, and Belanger (1988) compared the constant time delay procedure and the procedure of least prompts in teaching food words to four female students eight and ten years old with IQ scores of 44 to 51. The constant time delay procedure involved a delay of four seconds between presentation of the written and verbal stimulus ("What word?") and provision of the model. The least prompts procedure provided a sequence of prompts, including verbal descriptions and pictorial prompts, before providing a model response. The constant time delay necessitated fewer sessions and minutes of instructional time and resulted in fewer errors. Learned responses generalized across settings and persons, and two of the eight students, who apparently had some word segmentation knowledge, responded correctly to untrained words.

Wolery, Ault, Doyle, Gast, and Griffen (1992) compared the use of choral and individual responding in teaching community-sign words to two boys and two girls (age range, ten to thirteen years) with moderate mental retardation (IQ range, 33 to 48), in three experiments in which opportunities to respond and stimulus exposures varied across conditions. Individual responding was more effective when opportunities to respond were equated, but choral responding was superior when exposures per stimulus were equated. Generalized responding was not addressed.

Barudin and Hourcade (1990) compared three methods of teaching simple nouns to nineteen boys and thirteen girls with moderate and severe mental retardation (IQ range, 27 to 54; age range, nine to twenty years). Sight word, picture fading, and tactile-kinesthetic presentations were all found to be superior to a noninstructional control condition but did not differ among themselves in effectiveness. Transfer effects were evaluated but were found to be very limited.

Passage Reading Singh (1989) describes the behaviors of four female teachers as they monitored the passage reading of eighteen students with moderate disabilities (twelve to seventeen years old) who read at about the first-grade level. Teachers most frequently corrected errors by providing the correct pronunciation, although a variety of other corrective prompts were employed. Teachers used positive comments about ten times as frequently as negative comments.

Arithmetic Baroody (1987) investigated whether a sample of twenty-four individuals with moderate disabilities and six with mild disabilities (age range, six to twenty years; IQ range, 31 to 66) would spontaneously invent more efficient calculational procedures and abstract basic arithmetic relationships. More experimental ($N = 15$) subjects, who received computational training, than control subjects did invent computational short cuts, including counting fingers, and principles, such as commutativity, and facts with zero and one.

Social/Behavioral Interventions

Watson, Bain, and Houghton (1992) taught five girls and two boys (six to eight years old) to refuse the advance of a stranger making an inappropriate request, to leave the scene of the interaction, and to report the interaction to a safe adult. Training was conducted over fifteen 25-minute lessons. After training, six of the seven students displayed improvement in self-protective skills, which generalized across time, individuals, and situations.

Horner, Sprague, O'Brien, and Heathfield (1990) analyzed the aggressive behavior of a fourteen-year-old boy with moderate mental retardation, concluding that task difficulty was functionally related to aggression. Teaching the student to press a single key signifying "Help, please" on an electronic communication device was associated with substantial decreases in aggression, while training the high-effort response of typing out "help please" was not associated with decreased aggression. A coincident increase in a pointing response suggested that some generalization had occurred.

Wilson, Rusch, and Lee (1992) increased the level of correspondence between verbal and nonverbal behavior in an exercise room with correspondence training. Four thirteen-year-old boys (IQ range, 41 to 49) were given verbal praise or tangible reinforcement when their exercise behavior matched their stated intentions prior to exercise. Levels of correspondence increased, but generalization was not addressed.

Kim, Lombardino, Rothman, and Vinson (1989) used prompting and modeling to promote symbolic ("pretend") play in a sample of two boys and two girls (total sample age range, five to ten years; mental age range, two to three years), characterized as functioning in the "trainable" mentally retarded range. Compared with four control students, experimental students exhibited a marked positive increase in symbolic play after training.

Life Skills Interventions

Sisson, Kilwein, and Van Hasselt (1988) used verbal prompts and faded physical prompts to teach self-dressing skills to two boys with moderate disabilities, five and nine years old, with visual impairments. After approximately twenty and ninety sessions, respectively, students successfully exhibited self-dressing skills. These skills were observed to maintain over eighteen to thirty-six weeks and to generalize to other garments.

Mainstreaming/Inclusion Studies

Surprisingly, we located only two studies that impacted directly on mainstreaming/inclusion students with moderate disabilities in regular elementary school settings. One additional investigation of cross-age student tutoring also appeared relevant and is included in this section. Each report is described separately in the section that follows.

Cooperative Learning in Science Putnam, Rynders, Johnson, and Johnson (1989) used cooperative learning as a strategy to include students with mild to moderate mental retardation in regular class science lessons. Noting that "most studies on mainstreaming and cooperative learning have involved students with mild handicapping conditions" (p. 551), Putnam et al. selected three boys and thirteen girls with IQ scores ranging from less than 35 to 72 (including five with Down's syndrome and two characterized as autistic) for their investigation. These students were drawn from three self-contained "trainable mentally handicapped" classrooms in an elementary school and ranged in age from nine to fourteen years.

Cooperative groups were formed that included three students each. Each group included two nondisabled students taken from two regular education fifth-grade classrooms and one student with disabilities. For half of the groups, students were instructed in collaborative skills. These skills included sharing materials and ideas, encouraging everyone to participate, saying at least one nice thing to everyone in the group, and checking to see whether everyone understands and agrees with answers. Instruction in collaborative skills was not provided to students in the other eight groups. All groups participated in ten hands-on science lessons involving the study of buoyancy, provided over a period of three weeks. Each lesson consisted of about thirty-five minutes of group activity followed by about ten minutes of free play. During the lessons, observations of student interactions were made and coded. At the end of the lessons, the frequency of various interactions was compared across groups. When all students' interactions were analyzed, no differences were found between conditions. However, when interactions of nondisabled students toward students with disabilities were analyzed, statistically significant differences between conditions were found on three variables: orienting toward the student, cooperative participation, and neutral vocalizations to student. All differences favored the groups that had been instructed in collaborative skills. The authors also found that teachers made more direct interventions, either verbally or by manipulating materials, with the groups that had been instructed in collaborative skills.

Results of the investigation by Putnam et al. (1989) suggest that students trained in collaborative skills may interact more in cooperative group situations than students who have not received such training. However, several questions for further research can be generated from the results of this investigation. First, the overall frequencies of interactions between students with disabilities and their nondisabled peers appears rather low, even among students trained in collaborative skills (averaging less than one occurrence in five 10-second observation periods). Establishing standards for desirable levels of interaction, and monitoring progress toward realizing these standards, would be a helpful accomplishment for future cooperative learning researchers.

Second, Putnam et al. (1989) placed disappointingly little emphasis on academic outcomes, stating paradoxically that "academic achievement was not a focus of this study, but is an important consideration in mainstreaming efforts" (p. 555). The authors state that nondisabled students in the two treatment conditions did not statistically differ on unit posttest scores. However, since all groups included students with disabilities, we cannot determine whether the inclusion of such a student in each group affected academic outcomes of the nondisabled students, either positively or negatively. Further, the lack of pre- and posttest data precluded the analysis of what gains nondisabled students realized from the beginning to the end of the lesson. Finally, the lack of any academic outcome data on the students with disabilities precluded any analysis of possible differences in learning outcomes as a function of training in collaborative skills or of whether anything at all was learned about buoyancy by students with disabilities. Although "partial participation . . . was encouraged" (p. 556), such as pouring water or recording from dictated spelling, the academic or behavioral gains realized from such participation is unknown from the stated results of the study. Enhanced interaction with nondisabled students is a desirable outcome; thus, the consequences of such interaction in both social and academic domains would be important to know.

Finally, we were again disappointed that no information was provided on the amount of interaction observed during unstructured free play activities that immediately followed each science activity. These free play intervals appear to have been an ideal time for observing the transfer of social interactions from structured to unstructured activities of students, trained and untrained in collaborative skills. The lack of observational data provides no evidence regarding whether the collaborative skills training was sufficient in promoting generalization of interactions to free play settings.

Inclusion in Art Activities Schleien, Ray, Soderman-Olson, and McMahon (1987) describe an effort to integrate students with moderate to severe cognitive deficits into a community museum program. Nine second-grade students with moderate to severe mental disabilities were included in this investigation (age range, seven to ten years), along with twenty-seven students from two regular second-grade classes. Ages ranged from seven to ten years, with a mean age of 7.7. Training was provided to all regular education students and teachers and museum staff in awareness of persons with cognitive deficits, attitudes toward individuals with disabilities, and methods for fostering appropriate social interaction. All students met together once a month for six months, studying architectural design. Gallery experiences allowed students to learn about design elements through hands-on interaction with holograms, light columns, wall panels, and so forth. In the studio phase of each visit, students met in groups of three nondisabled students and one student with disabilities to create individual and group works of art. For the final art project, a "Fantasy City" was constructed. At the end of the project, results showed the number of interactions between students with and without disabilities had increased. Although the frequency of interactions received by students with disabilities was clearly seen to increase over time, the trend of the frequency of interactions initiated by students with disabilities was less clear, although the highest number of initiations by students with disabilities occurred during the last visit.

These results are in concordance with the research synthesis of Mastropieri and Scruggs (1985–1986), who concluded that preschool students with disabilities were less likely to initiate interactions with nondisabled peers before they were explicitly trained and reinforced to do so. Nevertheless, the results of Schleien et al. support those of Putnam et al. in that social interactions initiated by nondisabled students increased over time in the context of group activities. Again, academic gains, on either students with moderate disabilities or nondisabled students, were not evaluated.

DISCUSSION

The results of this review provide implications for the integration of students with moderate disabilities in the elementary school, evidence of the effectiveness of some initial mainstreaming/inclusion efforts, and implications for further research on the regular classroom integration of students with moderate disabilities. Each will be discussed separately.

The results of recent research on intervention strategies supports previous characterizations of students with moderate disabilities as individuals who can benefit from basic academic, social, and life skills instruction. Students with moderate disabilities were successfully trained in color recognition, sight word reading, decoding skills, arithmetic computation, appropriate social responding to a variety of situations, and self-dressing skills. However, in all cases, interventions were (a) delivered on the individual or small-group level, (b) intensive and highly structured, and (c) implemented over relatively extensive time periods. These characteristics are commonly associated with interventions found in the special education literature (for example, Mastropieri & Scruggs, 1994). Consistent with previous research on students with disabilities, generalization outcomes were realized only as a result of explicit generalization training; when generalization effects were not targeted and programmed, they typically were not obtained (Scruggs & Mastropieri, 1994a). Results of these investigations, overall, are in strong agreement with the results of previous reviews of the literature, such as those of Ault et al. (1989), who report on the effectiveness of such instructional strategies as error correction, stimulus shaping, prompting, and time delay.

Unfortunately, the interventions described in these studies do not bear a close resemblance to methods and materials typically observed in elementary grade, regular class settings. Many of the behaviors trained (for instance, color recognition, symbolic play, self-dressing) have been mastered by most nondisabled students before they enter first grade. Some negative behaviors exhibited by at least some students in these reports, such as "hitting, kicking, and pulling the hair of the teacher, tipping over tables and chairs" (Horner et al., 1990, p. 92), are not commonly observed with typical students in regular class settings. Even the academic skills trained in reading and arithmetic are typically learned at a much younger age, and at a much faster pace, than the training described in the present set of investigations. Finally, the training procedures and teacher behaviors described in these studies, characterized by low student-teacher ratios, intensive instruction, frequent verbal and tangible reinforcement, do not appear to be typical of contemporary regular education classroom methods. For example, the methods for teaching reading described in these studies bear little resemblance to the "whole language" methods of reading and language arts instruction that have become popular in regular classrooms (see, for example, Routman, 1991).

How, then, can learning take place for students with moderate disabilities in regular elementary class settings? Clearly, instruction will have to be very different from contemporary models of elementary class instruction, or students will need to be taught in new (and presently nonvalidated) ways. If this second option strains credibility, it does seem possible that regular elementary classes can be to some degree reconstructed. For example, Burts (1990) reports on the successful implementation of a program in which nondisabled high school students tutored high school students with moderate disabilities in basic skills. Students learned basic skills, and interactions between students with and without disabilities increased over time. Although this program took place in special class settings, it is conceivable that such a program could also take place within a regular classroom. However, whether elementary-aged students can function effectively as long-term tutors for students with moderate disabilities awaits research validation.

Kozleski and Jackson (1993) describe the full-time inclusion of a student with severe disabilities in regular fourth- and fifth-grade classes. This investigation is relevant to the inclusion of student with moderate disabilities in regular elementary classrooms because the student clearly had different learning and curriculum needs than did the nondisabled students in those classrooms. Nevertheless, the authors provide evidence that the student increased in social interactions over time with the nondisabled students and that the student improved over time in sociometric ratings by nondisabled students. However, claims that progress had been made on specific learning needs of the target student were insufficiently documented, leaving unanswered the question of whether the regular classroom was really the optimal setting for learning such skills as communication, mobility, and life skills (see also Salisbury, Palombaro, & Hollowood, 1993, for a qualitative description of an inclusive setting for students with severe disabilities).

Other more inclusive options include placing special education teachers and support staff into the regular classroom to deliver instruction that students with moderate disabilities are less likely to receive in those settings. This "pull-in" approach would be similar to that used in some settings with students with learning disabilities, which is presently receiving much current research attention. However, whether this arrangement is optimal for students with learning disabilities is at present far from certain (Zigmond et al., 1995). Further research will certainly be necessary to validate such approaches with students with moderate disabilities.

Nevertheless, when students with moderate disabilities have been integrated with nondisabled students, the results have been promising. The two studies identified in the present review that evaluated the effects of including students with moderate disabilities in regular class activities reported that social interactions increased over time among students of different ability levels. Unfortunately, academic outcomes were not reported in either investigation, so evaluating the learning consequences, on both students with and without disabilities, in those contexts is difficult. Interestingly, in both investigations, students were involved in small-group, hands-on activities, in science and art/architecture. Such activities have been recently recommended as providing positive opportunities for including students with disabilities in regular classes (see, for instance, Mastropieri & Scruggs, 1993).

We were disappointed to find that very little data were provided on the racial/ethnic or SES of the subjects studied in these investigations. Such information could potentially have led to additional insights on how the characteristics of moderate disabilities interact with the characteristics of race/ethnicity or SES. For example, schools of different SES may be differentially receptive to mainstreaming/inclusion efforts. Additionally, student race/ethnicity may interact in some way with inclusion efforts. Further research could be helpful in addressing these issues.

The results of the present review, then, suggest that restructured regular elementary classrooms, which incorporate hands-on curriculum, cooperative group learning, direct instruction, and peer tutoring in more basic skills, may hold the greatest promise for accommodating the learning needs of students with moderate disabilities. These conclusions are in essential agreement with the findings of a three-year qualitative investigation of science classrooms that had successfully included students with a variety of special needs (Mastropieri, Scruggs, & Bohs, 1994; Scruggs & Mastropieri, 1994b). All successful classrooms had the following elements in common: administrative support, appropriate curriculum, accepting environment, effective teaching, peer assistance, and disability-specific instructional modifications. Further research can provide important information on the extent to which implementation of these variables can facilitate the inclusion of students with moderate disabilities in regular classes.

REFERENCES

Ault, M. J., Wolery, M., Doyle, P. M., & Gast, D. L. (1989). Review of comparative studies in the instruction of students with moderate and severe handicaps. *Exceptional Children, 55,* 346–356.

AAMR Ad Hoc Committee on Terminology and Classification. (1992). *Mental retardation: Definition, classification, and systems of support* (9th ed.). Washington, DC: American Association on Mental Retardation.

Baroody, A. J. (April, 1987). *Addition learning by mentally handicapped children.* Paper presented at the biennial meeting of the Society for Research in Child Development, Baltimore. (ERIC Document Reproduction No. ED 288 282)

Barudin, S. I., & Hourcade, J. J. (1990). Relative effectiveness of three methods of reading instruction in developing specific recall and transfer skills in learners with moderate and severe mental retardation. *Education and Training in Mental Retardation, 25,* 286–291.

Beirne-Smith, M., Patton, J. R., & Ittenbach, R. (1994). *Mental retardation* (4th ed.). Upper Saddle River, NJ: Merrill/ Prentice Hall.

Burts, M. E. (1990). *A staff development program to implement a student tutorial program for the trainable mentally handicapped.* Fort Lauderdale, FL: Practicum Report, Nova University, Center for the Advancement of Education. (ERIC Document Reproduction Service No. ED 329 091)

Copel, H. (1991). *Students with moderate cognitive abilities: Tech use guide: Using computer technology.* Reston, VA: Council for Exceptional Children, Center for Special Education Technology. (ERIC Document Reproduction Service No. ED 339 159)

Ehri, L., Deffner, N. D., & Wilce, L. S. (1984). Pictorial mnemonics for phonics. *Journal of Educational Psychology, 76,* 880–893.

Espin, C. A., & Deno, S. L.(1988). Characteristics of individuals with mental retardation. In P. J. Schloss, C. A. Hughes, & M. A. Smith (Eds.), *Mental retardation: Community transition* (pp. 35–55). Boston: College Hill.

Gable, R. A., & Warren, S. F. (Eds.). (1993). *Advances in mental retardation and developmental disabilities.* Baltimore: Brookes.

Gast, D. L., Ault, J. J., Wolery, M., & Doyle, P. M., & Belanger, S. (1988). Comparison of constant time delay and the system of least prompts in teaching sight word reading to students with moderate retardation. *Education and Training in Mental Retardation, 23,* 117–128.

Grossman, H. J. (1983). *Classification in mental retardation.* Washington, DC: American Association on Mental Deficiency.

Hallahan, D. P., & Kauffman, J. M. (1994). *Exceptional children: Introduction to special education* (6th ed.). Boston: Allyn & Bacon.

Hoogeveen, F. R., Birkhoff, A. E., Smeets, P. M., Lancioni, G. E., & Boelens, H. H. (1989). Establishing phonemic segmentation in moderately retarded children. *Remedial and Special Education, 10*(3), 47–53.

Hoogeveen, F. R., Kouwenhoven, J. A., & Smeets, P. M. (1989). Establishing sound blending in moderately mentally retarded children: Implications of verbal instruction and pictorial prompting. *Research in Developmental Disabilities, 10,* 333–348.

Hoogeveen, F. R., Smeets, P. M., & Lancioni, G. E. (1989). Teaching moderately mentally retarded children basic reading skills. *Research in Developmental Disabilities, 10,* 1–18.

Horner, R. H., Sprague, J. R., O'Brien, M., & Heathfield, L. T. (1990). The role of response efficiency in the reduction of problem behaviors through functional equivalence training: A case study. *Journal of the Association for the Severely Handicapped, 15,* 91–97.

Kim, Y. T., Lombardino, L. J., Rothman, H., & Vinson, B. (1989). Effects of symbolic play intervention with children who have mental retardation. *Mental Retardation, 27,* 159–165.

Kozleski, E. B., & Jackson, L. (1993). Taylor's story: Full inclusion in her neighborhood elementary school. *Exceptionality, 4,* 153–176.

Mastropieri, M. A., & Scruggs, T. E. (1985–1986). Early intervention for socially withdrawn children. *Journal of Special Education, 19,* 429–441.

Mastropieri, M. A., & Scruggs, T. E. (1993). *A practical guide for teaching science to students with special needs in inclusive settings.* Austin, TX: PRO-ED.

Mastropieri, M. A., & Scruggs, T. E. (1994). *Effective instruction for special education* (2nd ed.). Austin, TX: PRO-ED.

Mastropieri, M. A., Scruggs, T. E., & Bohs, K. (1994). Mainstreaming an emotionally handicapped student in science: A qualitative investigation. In T. E. Scruggs & M. A. Mastropieri (Eds.), *Advances in learning and behavioral disabilities* (Vol. 8, pp. 131–146). Greenwich, CT: JAI.

Patton, J. R., Payne, J. S., & Beirne-Smith, M. (1986). *Mental retardation* (2nd ed.). Upper Saddle River, NJ: Merrill/Prentice Hall.

Putnam, J. P., Rynders, J. E., Johnson, R. T., & Johnson, D. W. (1989). Collaborative skill instruction for promoting positive interactions between mentally handicapped and nonhandicapped children. *Exceptional Children, 55,* 550–557.

Routman, R. (1991). *Invitations.* Portsmouth, NH: Heinemann.

Salend, S. (1994). *Effective mainstreaming: Creating inclusive classrooms* (2nd ed.). New York: Macmillan.

Salisbury, C. L., Palombaro, M. M., & Hollowood, T. M. (1993). On the nature and change of an inclusive elementary school. *Journal of the Association for Persons with Severe Handicaps, 18,* 75–84.

Schleien, S. J., Ray, M. T., Soderman-Olson, M. L., & McMahon, K. T. (1987). Integrating children with moderate to severe cognitive deficits into a community museum program. *Education and Training in Mental Retardation, 22,* 112–120.

Scruggs, T. E., & Mastropieri, M. A. (1993). Teaching students with mild mental retardation. In R. A. Gable & S. F. Warren (Eds.), *Advances in mental retardation and developmental disabilities* (Vol. 5, pp. 117–125). Baltimore: Brookes.

Scruggs, T. E., & Mastropieri, M. A. (1994a). The effectiveness of generalization training: A quantitative synthesis of single subject research. In T. E. Scruggs & M. A. Mastropieri (Eds.), *Advances in learning and behavioral disabilities* (Vol. 8, pp. 259–280). Greenwich, CT: JAI.

Scruggs, T.E., & Mastropieri, M.A. (1994b). Successful mainstreaming in elementary science classes: A qualitative investigation of three reputational cases. *American Educational Research Journal, 31,* 785–811.

Singh, J. (1989). Teacher behavior during oral reading by moderately mentally retarded children. *Journal of Reading, 32,* 298–304.

Singh, N. N., & Solman, R. T. (1990). A stimulus control analysis of the picture-word problem in children who are mentally retarded: The blocking effect. *Journal of Applied Behavior Analysis, 23,* 525–532.

Sisson, L. A., Kilwein, M. L., & Van Hasselt, V. B. (1988). A graduated guidance procedure for teaching self-dressing skills to multihandicapped children. *Research in Developmental Disabilities, 9,* 419–432.

Tateyama-Sniezek, K. M. (1989). The effects of stimulus variation of the generalization performance of students with moderate retardation. *Education and Training in Mental Retardation, 24,* 89–94.

Watson, M., Bain, A., & Houghton, S. (1992). A preliminary study in teaching self-protective skills to children with moderate and severe mental retardation. *Journal of Special Education, 26,* 181–194.

Wilson, P. G., Rusch, F. R., & Lee, S. (1992). Strategies to increase exercise-report correspondence by boys with moderate mental retardation: Collateral changes in intention-exercise correspondence. *Journal of Applied Behavior Analysis, 25,* 681–690.

Wolery, M., Ault, M. J., Doyle, P. M., Gast, D. L., & Griffen, A. K. (1992). Choral and individual responding during small group instruction: Identification of interactional effects. *Education and Treatment of Children, 15,* 289–309.

Wolery, M., & Haring, T. G. (1994). Moderate, severe, and profound disabilities. In N. G. Haring, L. McCormick, & T. G. Haring (Eds.), *Exceptional children and youth* (6th ed., pp. 258–299). Upper Saddle River, NJ: Merrill/Prentice Hall.

Zigmond, N., Jenkins, J., Fuchs, L., Deno, S., Fuchs, D., Baker, J. N., Jenkins, L., & Coutinho, M. (1995). Special education in restructured schools: Findings from three multi-year studies. *Phi Delta Kappan, 76,* 531–540.

12

Integration in the Elementary School for Students with Severe Disabilities

DAWN HUNTER

> Not long ago, we thought children with severe disabilities could not learn and, therefore, did not need to attend school. However, some educators and families did not accept this idea and began trying to teach these children—and the children learned.
>
> Not long ago, we thought children with severe disabilities needed to learn in separate schools "with their own kind." However, some educators and families did not accept this idea and began trying to teach these children in self-contained classes within the regular school—and the children learned.
>
> Not long ago, we thought children with severe disabilities needed to learn in self-contained classes within the regular school. However, some educators and families did not accept this idea and began trying to teach these children in selected general education classes (e.g., art, physical education, music)—and the children learned.
>
> Not long ago, we thought children with severe disabilities could learn only in selected general education classes. However, some educators and families did not accept this idea and began trying to teach these children in the general education classroom with necessary supports—and the children learned. (Hunter, 1994, p. 1)

Elementary classrooms have changed a great deal over the past ten years. We have seen major changes in the demographics and home environments of the children attending public schools. For example, public schools are seeing an increase in the numbers of students who (a) are living in poverty, (b) have families experiencing unemployment, (c) are homeless, (d) are from single-parent families or living with relatives other than their natural parents, (e) come from homes in which English is not the main language, and (f) are living within undesirable situations in their homes and communities (such as drug and alcohol abuse, violence, physical abuse).

In addition, many of the federal and state programs (for example, special education, bilingual, migrant, disadvantaged) in schools that have operated rather autonomously in the past are becoming blurred because many students do not "fit" into any one program but rather may have multiple needs for educational support. Consequently, teachers are attempting to educate students who, as a group, are far more heterogeneous than we have seen in the past. All of this is occurring at a time when school districts are experiencing tremendous hardships because of shrinking federal, state, and local fiscal resources. Therefore, there has never been a time more critical for educators, families, and communities to work closely together to meet the educational needs of their children.

In addressing the diverse needs of the students they are serving, elementary schools are making numerous structural, personnel, and instructional changes. For example, some schools have created democratic structures and processes where curriculum is created to give students democratic experiences (Beane & Apple, 1995). Others have created humanistic schools, child-centered schools, or outcome-based educational schools. These changes in structure have necessitated a change in the way the schools deploy teachers, instructional aides, and related service personnel (for instance, team teaching or co-teaching, inclusion facilitators). In addition, many elementary schools are using new or renewed instructional strategies such as multilevel instruction, cooperative learning, experienced-based learning, theme-based instruction, and computer-assisted instruction to enhance the learning process.

To create positive and productive learning environments, Epanchin, Townsend, and Stoddard (1994) proposed that "teachers and other school personnel need to be:

1. *Excellent instructional leaders,* capable of stimulating students' thought and motivating students to become actively involved in the learning enterprise;
2. *Competent, caring, and ethical decision makers* who are affectively connected to their students and willing to act in order to create safe and affirming learning environments;
3. *Appreciative of multiple perspectives,* understanding that multiple realities may exist within a school. Judging that one perspective is right and others wrong or inappropriate can antagonize, alienate, and limit understanding, while learning about the affirming differences can enrich and strengthen the school climate;
4. *Sensitive to ethnic, gender, and religious differences,* realizing that heritage impacts people in profound ways that include language, attitudes, values, and expectations self and others;
5. *At ease with their own sense of self-efficacy and personal power* so that they can deal with the multitude of personal challenges to their beliefs and knowledge;
6. *Focused on their goals* so that they can react to immediate, short-term problems as well as think about and plan for long-term solutions;
7. *Reflecting on their practice,* constantly evaluating and thinking about their teaching so that they can learn from and grow in their profession; and
8. *Capable of a systems view of school,* acknowledging that school and classrooms are complex systems, intricately connected to other systems, particularly the families of children in school. When family and school work together, solutions that benefit the child are possible; when family and school are in conflict, the child usually suffers." (pp. 6–7)

Therefore, to address the needs of a diverse student body, educators, administrators, and other school workers may need to develop new skills and attitudes to meet the needs of all students in our elementary schools.

TEACHING STUDENTS WITH SEVERE DISABILITIES IN THE GENERAL EDUCATION CLASSROOM

We are amazed when we realize that many children with severe disabilities did not even attend public schools until the passage of the Education of All Handicapped Children's Act (EHA) in 1975. Our ability to educate children with severe disabilities successfully has come a long way in a relatively short time. Advances in pedagogy, instructional and assistive technology, and early intervention can account for much of this advancement. However, just as important is the change in attitudes and expectations demonstrated toward people with severe disabilities. This change has been due largely to teachers, administrators, families, and communities witnessing, through their own experiences, the numerous benefits of educating students with severe disabilities alongside their peers without disabilities in general education classrooms. Often the impetus for these programs has come from the families of these children (for instance, *Ronker v. Walters, Oberti v. Clementon Board of Education, Daniel R.R. v. State Board of Education, Holland v. Sacramento*) and from collaboration with professionals and parent/professional organizations (for example, The Association for Persons with Severe Handicaps [TASH]).

In the past, children with severe disabilities were often labeled and sent away from the general education environment where they remained until they could demonstrate the skills they needed to reenter the general education setting. Frequently, this practice ignored and violated both the least restrictive environment and individualized education program requirements of EHA and its subsequent amendments (that is, the Individuals with Disabilities Education Act [IDEA]). This practice served to reinforce the readiness, deficit, and medical models, which were often detrimental to the education of children with severe disabilities. However, more recently we have seen a paradigm shift in the way in which we approach educating children with severe disabilities. That is, there has been substantial movement away from a readiness model (which by definition encourages segregation) to an inclusive schooling model, where diversity is valued. There is a recognition that diverse learning styles, abilities, cultural, ethnic, and linguistic backgrounds bring a richness to the learning environment for all students. This type of experience can only facilitate building the skills all students will need to live in our diverse world. As Margaret Mead (1935) so articulately stated, "If we are to achieve a richer culture . . . , we must weave one in which each diverse human gift will find a fitting place" (p. 322).

The words *inclusion* or *inclusive schooling* mean many different things to different people. *Inclusion* is used in this chapter to refer to children with disabilities going to the same schools as their brothers and sisters and other children in the neighborhood and receiving their education full-time in the general education class with the supports necessary for success within the classroom. All students, including those with disabilities, are a valued part of the school community and contribute unique talents and perspectives to the school. In addition, all students are ensured equal opportunities to access activities, materials, equipment, and classrooms throughout the entire school building. Inclusive schools employ a coordinated service delivery model in which teachers, parents, and related service personnel work collaboratively to determine student needs and provide appropriate interventions in naturally occurring contexts (Catlett, Hunter, & Brady, 1998). At the heart of inclusion are two beliefs: (a) all children with disabilities can learn when given the necessary supports, and (b) all children have a right to learn alongside their peers without disabilities.

Currently, many schools, districts, and states are transitioning toward developing inclusive schooling models of educating children. Consequently, several teachers may have many questions about "who these students are." As discussed in other chapters in this book, children who have been labeled as having a severe disability are a very heterogeneous population. Many of the children may have cognitive, physical, or sensory disabilities or multiple disabilities (for example, deaf-blindness, cerebral palsy and mental retardation). In addition, some of the children demonstrate challenging behaviors, and a small number of these children have complex medical conditions. Consequently, students with severe disabilities may have difficulty in the areas of expressive and receptive language, ambulation, and daily living.

Because educating children with severe disabilities in the general education classroom is a relatively recent paradigm shift, we do not have all of the answers yet. However, emerging best practices have been identified (Fox & Williams, 1991; Meyer, Eichinger, & Downing, 1994). In addition, an abundance of materials is available to educators and families interested in pursuing inclusive schooling for children with severe disabilities (Vandercook, Walz, Doyle, York, & Wolff, 1995).

KEY COMPONENTS OF SUCCESSFUL INCLUSIVE SCHOOLS

Inclusive schooling can look very different from community to community. Although there is no one inclusive school model, most successful inclusive schools do share certain characteristics. Several of these key components for successful inclusive education are identified here:[1]

1. A *clear vision* has been developed at the school, which supports a sense of community in which there is full membership for all students and in which individual differences and diversity are valued and respected. This vision is supported by all school staff, families, and students. When inconsistencies with the vision arise, they are dealt with swiftly and in an educational manner.
2. *Collaboration between school staff and families* is evident. Families are valued team members and are included in the decision-making process. In addition, family values, priorities, and time commitments are respected. Schools make every

[1]These components are described in detail in Chapter 6.

attempt at being "family friendly." School staff have been trained in the art of collaboration, teamwork, creative problem solving, and conflict resolution.

3. There is a *commitment to planning,* and this commitment is sustained throughout the school year. Fragmented planning is avoided, and time is set aside during normal school hours for planning.
4. *Adequate and responsible supports* are in place (for example, human supports such as classroom teaching assistants, consultants, and peer tutors, with "natural supports" being used whenever possible; appropriate modifications of curriculum, environment, materials are made as needed; necessary equipment is provided). An active process is used to determine the supports both students and staff need to be successful, and these supports are provided. In addition, there is a recognition that friendships and social networks are important elements of the educational process. Therefore, the school program also offers support that will foster the development of both friendships and social networks between students with disabilities and their peers without disabilities.
5. *Meaningful, flexible, and dynamic instruction* is occurring in the school. Teachers have been well trained in preservice programs, and there is administrative support for proactive staff development in the school. Consequently, staff are proficient in using a variety of strategies that have proved effective in inclusive schools, and all students are learning.
6. A commitment is made to taking a careful and *objective look at all aspects of the school program regularly* to ensure that adequate progress is being made. This includes a commitment to keep abreast of "best and emerging practice." Consequently, the program remains open to change.
7. There is an *understanding* of the change process and that change is truly a dynamic process.

THE PROCESS OF COLLABORATION

Effective collaboration is a key element for successful inclusive schooling. Many resources have been developed to assist educators and parents in understanding the collaboration process and developing collaborative teams (Graden & Bauer, 1992; Morsink, Thomas, & Correa, 1991; Pugach & Johnson, 1990, 1995; Stainback & Stainback, 1992; Sugai & Tindal, 1993; Thousand & Villa, 1992). Graden and Bauer (1992) state that collaboration has two distinct goals: (a) to address concerns related to student performance and (b) to prevent future problems for the student or others. Therefore, the collaborative process involves people who are interested in the education of all students and who share a common goal for those students. Typically, this process includes general education teachers, instructional aides, special educators, related service personnel, administrators, and families. However, other personnel such as computer support personnel, librarians, school counselors, custodians, support staff, and cafeteria workers also play a key role in facilitating the learning process for each child.

The collaborative process includes both formal (such as collaborative teams, teacher assistance teams, problem solving teams) and informal (such as good communication between teachers and custodians) structures. To meet the goals of collaboration, teams may need to fulfill many roles. Johnson, Pugach, and Hammitte (1988) describe four roles that form the framework to schoolwide collaboration: (a) the supportive role, (b) the facilitative role, (c) the informative role, and (d) the prescriptive role.

Because collaborative teams will be called on to play a variety of roles, both teams and individual team members need to be skillful and flexible. In addition, the collaborative process must facilitate team skills that are supportive rather than judgmental. While many of us assume we are skillful collaborators, we often are not. Collaboration is truly an art and a skill we have to learn (Morsink et al., 1991). In addition, building teams that truly are collaborative takes time; collaborative teams do not "just happen." Most of the time, a great deal of work takes place before members gel as a team.

Fox and Williams (1991) have developed the following "team member checklist" describing valuable behaviors team members should feel they exhibited in the course of collaboration:

1. I contributed my ideas.
2. I encouraged others to contribute their ideas.
3. I listened to and expressed support and acceptance of others' ideas.
4. I expressed my feelings.
5. I offered my personal and professional resources to support the team.
6. I asked for clarification and help when needed.
7. I helped the group keep working.
8. I maintained a sense of humor.
9. I recorded group and individual tasks.
10. I enjoyed myself. (p. 77)

Initially, teams will need time to identify and agree on the kinds of tasks they will address and to clarify the roles (individual and shared) they will perform. A basic tenet of collaboration is that the leadership and responsibility for implementing solutions are shared across team members equitably (Thousand & Villa, 1992). If this type of balance does not occur, the collaborative process will be in serious jeopardy, resentments may build, and teams may actually see ineffective hierarchical forms of leadership begin to evolve. These effects will defy the very concept of collaboration. Consequently, teams must pay close attention to this basic tenet.

As mentioned earlier, collaborative teams may play a variety of roles in the inclusive schooling process. Effective problem-solving skills are central to all the identified roles. Numerous examples of problem-solving processes and strategies appear in the literature (Osborne, 1963; Parnes, 1981, 1985, 1988; Pugach & Johnson, 1990; Sugai & Tindal, 1993; Turnbull, Turnbull, Shank, & Leal, 1995; Zins, Curtis, Graden, & Ponti, 1988). Some of these strategies lend themselves better to certain situations (for instance, solving problems with the children, identifying and solving administrative challenges, thoughtfully delineating activities that will require substantial follow-through, brainstorming creative solutions to future issues), whereas others are more generic problem-solving strategies. In addition, problem-solving activities can be classroom specific or schoolwide (Pugach & Johnson, 1995) and therefore, may require different problem-solving processes. Consequently, team members must become skillful problem solvers and familiar with a variety of problem-solving processes to have a broader base from which to make decisions.

DEVELOPING FAMILY-PROFESSIONAL PARTNERSHIPS

Learning can be greatly facilitated when families and school personnel work closely together toward a common goal of ensuring that all children in a school reach their greatest educational and social potential. For an effective partnership to occur, the relationship must have parity. An effective partnership between schools and families requires demonstrated mutual respect, honest and open communication, and a foundation built on trust that both parties are committed to making decisions based on what is best for the student.

The attitudes of both families and professionals play an enormous role in whether partnerships are formed. Professionals must refrain from making judgments about families who are not interested in forming partnerships. Identifying these families as "unmotivated," "uncooperative," "resistant," "uncaring," or "bad" families is neither helpful nor accurate.

Families either do not want to be involved or simply cannot be involved in school meetings, activities, and functions for several reasons. For example, families may feel intimidated in schools or may feel as though they are unwanted guests. Family members who had troublesome school experiences when they were growing up may find being involved in their own child's educational program difficult. In addition, many families simply do not have the time or resources (for instance, incompatible work schedules, economic constraints, lack of transportation or babysitting) to develop partnerships. Families may have little energy remaining for school involvement when they are encountering numerous competing family responsibilities. Cultural constraints may prevent more active involvement of families, and in some families meeting even basic educational responsibilities may be difficult because of the limited schooling of the family, language barriers, and the family's literacy skills.

Interestingly, a recent study found parents would be willing to be more involved in the schools if (a) they had more knowledge about how the system works (51 percent), (b) they had more time (49 percent), (c) they felt professionals respected their observations and point of view (33 percent), (d) they had child care available for their children at home (24 percent), (e) professionals used language that was easy to understand (22 percent), (f) attempting to change something was less frustrating (22 percent), and (g) professionals listened to the needs of the family better (14 percent) (Sontag & Schacht, 1994).

Another factor that educators often overlook is that discussions concerning family involvement often focus on what families lack and consequently what *they* need to do at home to improve the learning situation for the child with disabilities. This need can be extremely frustrating for families who may already be struggling. Furthermore, professionals frequently miss the opportunity to begin a dialogue by not asking how *they* can support the family. Professionals often assume they know what a family needs when, more often than not, they do not. Ensuring that supports and services emerge around needs identified by family members demonstrate a commitment to the partnership by professionals. Children with severe disabilities will have a better quality of life, both at school and at home, if they are living in healthy families that feel supported and nurtured.

Consequently, schools must create opportunities for families and professionals to define collaboratively what the desired partnership will look like. This visioning and joint goal setting will set the stage for the partnership. However, goals that are outlined must be realistic and take into account the time and energy parameters of both families and professionals to avoid producing yet another overload situation for either party. Both parties should discuss any expectations they have about the frequency or type of interactions that may occur and acknowledge the need for flexibility as new situations arise.

ASSESSMENT OF ACADEMIC, SOCIAL, AND BEHAVIORAL SKILLS

If there is an assumption that a student with a severe disability will be educated in the general education classroom with same-aged peers, one looks at the assessment process quite differently right from the start. Energy is not spent on making sure the child is "ready" to participate but rather on ensuring that the child *will* participate as a valued and respected member of the classroom and school. Consequently, both assessment and instruction focuses on building on the student's strengths and skills.

How do we assess the academic, social, and behavioral skills of children with severe disabilities in the general education classroom? Because students with severe disabilities often have numerous instructional needs, deciding where to begin the assessment process can be very difficult. One way to start is by asking, What should our students' lives be like once they leave school? This question facilitates looking at the "bigger picture." Once we know what skills with which a student should leave high school, we can begin to work backward to determine what needs to be taught at the elementary school. For example, if ultimately we want all children to experience a high quality of life, in which they are valued and fully participating members of their communities (for example, enjoying their leisure time, participating in community events, using community services, experiencing friendships, working, being part of a strong family unit), we must begin to address the academic, communication, mobility, social, and behavioral needs of students with severe disabilities during the elementary school years.

Although a myriad of psychometric educational, social, and behavioral assessments have been developed for children with severe disabilities, the types of information measured by these instruments are often not useful to teachers. In fact, in many cases, achieving either accurate or meaningful results from these assessments is difficult. Additionally, many times the way in which the results are presented provides teachers and families with little guidance on how to use the assessment information. That is, how does the assessment information actually impact teaching and learning?

Consequently, a variety of nontraditional assessment strategies are more frequently being used in schools that have moved to inclusive models. These methods include (a) portfolio assessments; (b) curriculum-based assessments; (c) direct observation across settings; (d) family inventories and interviews; (e) ecological assessments of school, home, and community environments; (f) inclusive-schooling checklists; and (g) discrepancy analyses of the school environment. These types of assessment strategies are also effective in determining the communication, mobility, social, and behavioral goals for the student. For example, by using an ecological inventory approach, we can assess the students' communication, social, and behavioral skills during naturally occurring social times such as before school, in cooperative group and large-group activities, at lunch, during recess, at assemblies, while on field trips, during after-school activities, and while waiting to leave school for the day. Although many of these strategies have been in use for some time and are described in the literature, many individuals may be unfamiliar with the strategies and, consequently, somewhat reluctant to use them.

CURRICULUM ISSUES (ACADEMIC, SOCIAL, BEHAVIORAL)

Four questions frequently asked by general education teachers in elementary schools who have not previously worked with students with severe disabilities are as follows: (a) What can students with severe disabilities learn in the general education classroom? (b) What do I teach students with severe disabilities in my general education classroom? (c) When does everything get taught? (d) How do I actually teach students with severe disabilities in the general education classroom? Each of these questions is addressed in the subsequent sections.

What Can Students with Severe Disabilities Learn in the General Education Classroom?

The general education classroom provides numerous learning opportunities for all students. The Institute on Disability at the University of New Hampshire (1990) has identified seven types of learning opportunities available to students in the general education classroom, including (a) friendships; (b) academic skills; (c) learning to interact in small-group tasks; (d) organizational and process skills (for example, initiating, preparing materials, socializing, communicating, and terminating actions); (e) special interests (for instance, the development of lifelong leisure and vocational interests); (f) communication, movement, and social skills; and (g) functional life skills.

What Do I Teach Students with Severe Disabilities in My General Education Classroom?

After the assessment process is completed, the student's Individualized Education Plan (IEP) is developed. This document will be the blueprint for what will be taught in the classroom. Excellent resources provide suggestions both for developing useful and effective IEPs and for ensuring that the IEP process is individualized, user friendly, and productive (Giangreco, Cloninger, & Salce-Iverson, 1993; Giangreco, Dennis, Edelman, & Cloninger, 1994). (Those general education teachers unfamiliar with the mandated requirements of the IEP process can obtain many resources from local and state education agencies, the U.S. Department of Education, state parent training organizations, professional organizations, and through national resources such as the NICHCY Clearinghouse.)

Because students with severe disabilities are a very heterogeneous group, individual educational goals will vary considerably. Figure 12.1 provides a sampling of the types of educational goals that may be developed for some third grade students with severe disabilities. Though limited, this sample demonstrates how such goals could be addressed in the daily activities of a typical classroom. Depending on the needs and characteristics of the student (that is, whether the student walks or uses a wheelchair; talks or is just beginning to use an alternative communication system; is gregarious or is socially withdrawn; is experiencing behavioral difficulties; is independent in self-care skills or requires a great deal of assistance) and the preferences and needs of the family, these types of goals may or may not be appropriate.

When Does Everything Get Taught— That Is, How Does the Scheduling Work?

Once the goals and objectives have been determined, the task then becomes incorporating these goals and objectives into the daily routine of the general education classroom. Generally there are numerous opportunities to teach specific goals and objectives in the daily routines of any general education classroom schedule. Although students need adequate opportunities to learn the skills articulated in their IEPs, not every IEP objective must be included in every activity. However, without careful planning, opportunities to work on specific goals may be overlooked. A variety of tools (namely, matrices and checklists) have been developed to facilitate incorporating student goals into daily activities of the general education classroom (Giangreco et al., 1993; Neary, 1992).

Scheduling Elementary schools are undergoing a great deal of change, and identifying characteristics of a typical elementary school has never been more difficult because of the diversity in philosophies, governance, structure, resources,

FIGURE 12.1 Possible Goals That Third Grade Students with Severe Disabilities May Have in Their IEPs

Academic Skills

- Identify printed name.
- Print name.
- Copy printed words.
- Trace printed words.
- Sequence three events in story.
- Identify the main characters in a story.
- Listen to a short story and identify the main characters in the story and the sequence of critical events.
- Demonstrate comprehension to a story by answering five questions about the story.
- Expand vocabulary by at least five new words each week.
- Increase reading vocabulary.
- Point to key words as they are read in a story.
- Dictate a story about an assigned topic.
- Create a story with at least two characters.
- Write a short story.
- Select pictures of objects when requested.
- Identify numbers 1 through 10.
- Develop one-to-one correspondence skills.
- Use a calculator to perform single- and double-addition tasks.
- Tell time to the hour and the half hour.
- Identify the days of the week.
- Identify primary and secondary colors.
- Relay information about one current event daily.
- Identify what is happening next in the school schedule.
- Develop a new interest in some aspect of science.
- Increase basic knowledge of science (e.g., human body, rain forest, animals, heat, light, rocks, environments, energy, plants, whales).
- Develop a new interest in some aspect of social studies.
- Increase knowledge of social studies (e.g., responsibility, cultures, geography, democracy, voting, heroes, living peacefully with others, concept of fairness).

Self-Care (could be performed either independently or with assistance)

- Button and zipper clothing.
- Comb hair.
- Wash face and hands.
- Eat complete lunch within thirty minutes.
- Prepare snack.
- Deposit trash in basket after lunch.
- Go through lunch line taking all appropriate items needed to eat lunch (tray, lunch, silverware, napkin, milk).
- Empty colostomy bag.
- Wash hands.

Self-Determination

- Make choices.
- Indicate preferences in social activities.

(continued)

FIGURE 12.1 *(continued)*

Self-Determination *(continued)*

- Provide assistance to others in some way.
- Problem solve everyday situations that arise.
- Control the environment using adaptive switches (e.g., activating VCR, tape recorder, CD player, lights, battery-operated toys).

Mobility

- Get from room to room with minimal assistance.
- Carry lunch tray to table without dropping tray.
- Play safely on two outdoor pieces of equipment (jungle gym, swings, merry-go-round).
- Maintain current physical condition (i.e., do not develop any new contractures).
- Walk twenty feet using walker.
- Hold lightweight objects in hands for at least ten seconds without dropping objects.

Social skills

- Develop friendships that extend beyond the school day.
- Develop turn-taking skills.
- Play computer games with peers.
- Interact appropriately in small groups.
- Say "please" and "thank you" (either verbally or with communication system).
- Participate in art class without disturbing classmates.
- Initiate in some way (verbally, communication board, eye glance) at least one interaction every class period.
- Learn the names of classmates.
- Participate in after-school events with classmates.

Recreation Skills

- Develop one new leisure activity that can be done independently (e.g., painting, coloring, cutting and pasting, putting stickers in a book, listening to music using headphones, playing a musical instrument).
- Develop one new leisure activity that can be done with a small group (e.g., play computer game, card game, table or board game, outdoor game).
- Learn the words and melodies to three new songs.
- Sing songs with others (starting and stopping the song when others do).

Communication Skills

- Indicate yes or no to questions.
- Expand functional use of alternative communication system (pictures, sign language).
- Increase the number of spoken words.
- Use compound sentences.
- Indicate wants or needs through gestures or sign language.

and curriculum. Clearly, some models mentioned earlier in the chapter will embrace and facilitate inclusive schooling more than other models (schools subscribing to the "back to the basics" philosophy in which children sit in rows with the teacher presenting the curriculum through lectures and seatwork will have more difficulty meeting the educational needs of students with severe disabilities than schools in which students work in small groups or experience participatory learning opportunities with their peers). In addition, we cannot describe a typical student with severe disabilities, given the individual characteristics of this heterogeneous population of students. Thus, to present an example of a school schedule for a particular grade that generalizes across elementary schools and students with severe disabilities is virtually impossible. An example is provided to help the reader picture how the goals of a student with severe disabilities could be incorporated into the daily routine. Figure 12.2 briefly describes the daily activities and the various ways in which a student's goals could be incorporated into classroom activities. Please note that I assume that modifications or adaptations are made to the typical general education activities only when the student cannot participate in the activities in the same way peers without disabilities can. The literature contains other examples of IEP goals and corresponding schedules for individual students with severe disabilities that may also be helpful to the reader (Ford, Davern, & Schnorr, 1992; Neary, 1992).

How Can Related Services Be Delivered in an Inclusive School?

Another concern often voiced is how related services (for example, physical therapy, occupational therapy, speech therapy) can be provided in inclusive elementary schools. Many schools (not only inclusive schools) have shifted from using isolated therapy models to integrated therapy models. In integrated therapy models, related service personnel work collaboratively with teachers to incorporate therapeutic activities into the student's schedule. This process allows the student to practice the skill in the natural setting rather than in isolation. If a student requires intensive direct therapy, these sessions can occur before or after school or at some time during the day when the class members are engaged in individual work. With therapy scheduled in this manner, the student will not be missing key opportunities for learning with peers and will not have unnecessary attention drawn by being removed from the group.

How Do I Actually Teach Students with Severe Disabilities in the General Education Classroom?

Without a doubt, educating children in the general education classroom can be a challenging experience for educators. As discussed in other chapters, we already know a great deal about teaching children with severe disabilities. An extensive pedagogy has been developed over the past twenty-five years. Initially, strategies were developed for teaching students primarily in self-contained classrooms or in the community, and clearly many of these strategies can be used in the general education classroom. Consequently, one of the roles of special educators in inclusive schools is to teach general educators how to incorporate these teaching strategies into their repertoire of skills. Interestingly, many of these strategies may be useful to all students in the general education classroom, as well as to students with severe disabilities. In addition, many strategies frequently used in general

FIGURE 12.2 Example of How Various Goals and Activities Could Be Incorporated into the Daily Schedule of a Third Grade General Education Classroom

Time	Classroom Activity	Possible Activities
9:10–9:20	Arrive at school; put things in lockers; take attendance; sharpen pencils; get ready and organized for the day.	Peers assist student in getting to class and putting things in locker. Peers assist student in delivering attendance and lunch count to the office. Student may be able to assist others in sharpening their pencils by using an electric pencil sharpener.
9:20–9:40	Teacher writes a topic on the overhead; students write a story about the topic in their journals; teacher calls on students to share their story—students can either read or pass.	Student could dictate a story and have someone else write it down. Student could have a variety of pictures available and create a story from the pictures. Student could practice writing key words related to the topic in a journal (the teacher could write the words to copy in the student's journal as a model). Students could either share work with the class (e.g., show the work done, tell a story related to the topic verbally or with the use of an alternative communication system).
9:40–10:05	Students get out math log books or go to math computer stations, complete assigned math activities (individual or small group depending on the day and activity).	Peers assist student in getting out math log or find computer station. If the class was working individually, the student would work individually too on math-related goals. Student could participate in the small group in numerous ways depending on the student's goals, including counting materials while distributing them, checking the group's work using a calculator (or pointing to numbers on the calculator when called out), holding flash cards for the group, or calling on group members, activating a tape recorder that contains story problems the group is to solve.
10:05–10:15	Draw picture to accompany the story students had written earlier in the morning; share pictures and put into their journal porfolio.	Have peer reread the topic that was on the overhead, and student could select relevant pictures from a pile of pictures and paste pictures on paper after finishing his or her "picture." If the student was learning colors, peers could request that the student hand them specific colors or crayons. If portfolios had photographs of peers on them, the student could locate the portfolio for the peer. If the student was working on writing his or her name, it could also be done at this time.
11:05–11:30	Students break into pairs and take turns reading the story out loud that the teacher began; when finished they complete some type of worksheet together (e.g., story mapping).	Key words or pictures could be placed in front of student, and student could point to the words or pictures as peer reads the story. Peer could read story, stopping periodically to ask the student to "tell" the story up to that point. If necessary, student could work on reading goals individually with teacher, aide, or at a computer. Worksheet could be adapted using pictures to accommodate student who is a nonreader.

Time	Classroom Activity	Possible Activities
11:30–12:00	Small-group activities (cooperative groups, problem solving, games, worksheet) that focus on the vocabulary that was generated from the story the teacher read.	Student could take a variety of roles in cooperative groups (e.g., encourager, timekeeper using a timer, collector, distributor of materials, word holder, monitor) and in game activities. Student could find pictures for the group that could enhance peers learning the vocabulary words. Student could practice identifying the words in match-to-sample games or worksheets with peers.
12:00–12:25	Students use the bathroom and eat lunch.	May need adult assistance with using the bathroom—opportunity to work on personal care skills. Eat with peers; may need assistance with going through lunch line (the student may require special food), eating lunch, and cleaning up after lunch.
12:25–1:00	Recess outdoors unless it is raining (in that case, students have recess in the gym).	Play games with peers (peers could problem-solve how they could adapt games to include the student). "Chat" with peers using alternative communication system.
1:00–1:10	Cool off from recess (unstructured time in the classroom—students can do whatever they wish during this time).	Could work on individual academic or social goals either with or without peers (e.g., play a table game, read a story with someone, extra time to practice alternative communication, rest inside if necessary).
1:10–1:30	Read magazine articles on current events and complete activities to prepare for Friday's "news notes" test (this activity is performed individually at student's desk).	Peer could read or summarize articles to the student. Student could use a headphone to listen to a summary of the current events. A nonreading student could review materials via pictures and describe the pictures. Student could watch a video clip of current events. Student could use a computer to addess student bulletin board on current events.
1:30–2:20	Either science or social studies depending on the day of the week, usually the teacher presents the material in a large-group activity (slides, video, story, discussion, demonstration); then students break into small groups for a cooperative activity (experiential learning) on picture board that the songs were about).	During large-group activity: **Slides or video:** Assist teacher by loading or activating VCR or slide projector, turning off lights using switches if necessary. **Story:** Follow along in a book that displays the lesson in pictures. **Discussion:** Answer questions verbally or using pictures or alternative communication systems. Selects peers for ther turn to participate in discussion, by either pointing or using a class picture board. **Demonstration:** Peers assist student in holding materials. Student assists teacher by handing teacher materials when requested. Student is asked to identify particular objects as they are used in the demonstration.

(continued)

FIGURE 12.2 *(continued)*

Time	Classroom Activity	Possible Activities
1:30–2:20 *(continued)*		During large-group activity *(continued)*: **Experiential learning:** In science activities, student is involved in activity by measuring and mixing materials, holding materials, distributing materials. In social studies, student is involved in activity by wearing designated costumes with peers (which will also give the student the opportunity to practice buttoning and zippering skills, hair combing skills if hair gets messed up), having a role in drama activities.
2:20–3:00	Either gym, music, or computer lab, depending on the day of the week	Peers could assist the student in participating. If necessary, the student could work on individual goals with the teacher or aide that had not been incorporated into the schedule during this time. **Gym:** Rules could be modified to allow greater participation if necessary. If student needs hands-on physical therapy, it can be done at this time. **Music:** If student used an alternative form of communication, it could be reinforced during music class (using sign language in addition to signing, pointing to pictures on picture board that the songs were about). Materials could be adapted if necessary to allow for greater participation (e.g., put Velcro on a drumstick and student's hand, use switch to activate CD player). Student could assist in distributing materials and putting them away. **Computer:** Individual work on computer using either existing programs or programs that have been tailored specifically for the student, with assistance if necessary (e.g., making choices, preparing schedule for next day, engaging in number or time activities, reading activities, accessing programs on topics of particular interest to the student or that support other goals.).
3:00–3:10	Write in "responsibility book" (books students write homework assignments in—parents sign these each night).	Student could paste pictures of homework assignments in the book (or paste in the book activities they had completed that day or something that happened that day). Peer could assist student in writing or drawing pictures of assignments, activities completed that day, or something that happened that day. Student could identify from a list of assignments read by a peer which ones he or she needs to complete that night. Teacher or aide could review with student the activities they completed that day and write a note home to families (which would also help foster communication between school and families).

FIGURE 12.2 *(continued)*

Time	Classroom Activity	Possible Activities
3:10–325	Teacher plays music, and students clean up the room and their desks (tasks are assigned weekly to cooperative groups).	Student assists in selecting the music that will be played. Student is responsible for putting the tape in the tape recorder (if necessary, could activate tape using an adaptive switch). Student assists in classroom cleanup tasks, with peer assistance if necessary (e.g., washing off overhead transparencies with a sponge, dumping shavings from pencil sharpener into trash can, watering plants that are brought to student).
3:25	Leave school.	Peers could assist student in getting to bus or by walking home with the stuent.
After school	After-school activities are sponsored by either the community or community education extension services.	Students participate in activities with their peers such as community organizations and clubs (e.g., Girl Scouts, Boy Scouts), classes (e.g., computer, microwave cooking, drama, art), or recreational activities (e.g., swimming). Peers could provide support for the students in these activities. Activities could be modified (e.g., rules changed to be more inclusive, materials adapted, or expectations changed) to meet the interests and needs of the students.

education classrooms (for instance, cooperative learning, multilevel instruction) have been shown to be effective in teaching students with severe disabilities. Simply stated, good teaching is good teaching.

The collaborative team may need to address several issues to ensure that the learning experience will be beneficial to all students in the general education classroom and that the necessary support will be provided to the student, the classroom teacher, and the student's peers. Tashie et al. (1993) have outlined a very useful strategy for evaluating the types of support that may be necessary. In this model, a collaborative team determines (a) the amount and type of adult support (for example, teachers, aides, related service personnel, volunteers) and peer support (for instance, peer tutors, cross tutors, instructional strategies such as cooperative learning); (b) the extent to which the curriculum may need to be modified (that is, the addition, adaptation, or substitution of materials); and (c) the extent to which expectations (academic, social, physical, and so forth) may need to be modified (namely, modifying the demonstration of learning, the quantity of work, or the priority of goals). A few additional comments on each of these issues are briefly discussed next.

Student and Teacher Support All teachers bring their own set of skills, strengths, and styles to the classroom. In some situations teachers will feel confident; in others they may not. Determining the level and type of teacher and student support can be quite complex. Administrators, families, and others can help by recognizing that teachers may (a) have the skills they need but lack confidence, (b) have the skills but be afraid they will not measure up to the expectations of others, (c) lack the skills but be willing to learn, (d) have the skills, but have negative attitudes that prevent them from becoming fully involved, (e) not have the skills and have no desire to learn new skills, (f) be experiencing fears that are preventing them from being fully involved (for example, being afraid of potential lawsuits), or (g) lack the skills but be embarrassed to ask for assistance. Understanding these types of situations will greatly influence how the issue of support should be approached and delivered. York, Giangreco, Vandercook, and Macdonald (1992) state that support can be classified into four different types: resource, moral, technical, and evaluative. Because of the heterogeneity of student and teacher needs and skills, support may look very different across students and teachers. Teachers often feel unsupported with the "support" they receive. Frequently, teachers are not asked about the kind or amount of support they need: instead, support decisions are made at an administrative level.

Support can also be contagious; that is, both students and teachers can quickly become dependent on support when it may be unnecessary. One example is the use of classroom instructional aides. Frequently, teachers, families, and administrators feel that a classroom aide should be placed in the general education classroom full-time to work with the student with severe disabilities. Such a placement can be both a costly and instructionally unsound decision. Although students may require the support of an instructional aide (especially at the beginning of the school year or when a child first begins attending the general education classroom), rarely is an instructional aide needed full-time in the general education classroom (given reasonable class sizes). In addition, though an instructional aide can provide a student assistance, the aide's presence can serve as a barrier to natural interactions between the student and peers. Consequently, decisions about support must be determined on an individual basis and reevaluated frequently.

Curriculum Modifications, Adaptations, and Enhancements Numerous resources are now available that provide excellent practical suggestions for supplementing the curriculum with additional materials, adapting existing materials, or substituting materials (Ebling, Deschenes, & Sprague, 1994; Kronberg & Filbin,1993; McCoy, 1995; Neary, Halversen, Kronberg, & Kelly, 1992; Salend, 1994; Stainback & Stainback, 1992; Wood, 1992). Although some of these resources do not focus specifically on students with severe disabilities, we can easily generalize many strategies to students with severe disabilities in the general education classroom. Margolis and McGettigan (1988) found that if adaptations are to be successful, teachers must be given the opportunity to (a) build on what they know, (b) be central participants in decision making, (c) own the adaptations that are selected, (d) have support, (e) receive ample feedback and reinforcement, (f) become familiar with types of adaptations, (g) be invited to adapt strategies to increase compatibility with their customary approach to teaching, and (h) gain positive recognition for their efforts.

In addition to curriculum modifications, at times we must make environmental modifications that allow students with severe disabilities full access to the classroom. For example, the actual layout of the classroom may be a factor that the teacher will need to consider. Because some students with severe disabilities will use wheelchairs for mobility, the classroom will need to be arranged to allow the student easy access to all parts of the classroom. Some students with severe disabilities may also need to use a variety of equipment (such as adapted chairs, bolsters to ensure the student is positioned well for instruction, and communication devices) that will require additional space in the classroom. In addition, some students may require additional environmental accommodations for either health or safety reasons (for example, sitting out of a heavy traffic flow pattern if a student is using a ventilator, providing air conditioning if a student has serious allergies). Any specialized equipment must be integrated into the classroom in a manner that does not cause unnecessary attention or detract from classroom learning (Knight & Wadsworth, 1993).

Other changes in the environment may also be necessary for instructional reasons. Some students may be distractible, focusing on what else is happening in the immediate environment rather than on instruction. Other students may be sensitive to sound. In these situations, we might make sure the student's desk and cooperative group learning activities are not located close to the door if the hallway tends to be busy or noisy. At other times, we might structure the environment to enhance the likelihood that opportunities for learning will occur (for instance, some games facilitate more social interactions than others).

Environmental modifications will most often be child specific, and frequently there is no way to predict what modifications, if any, will need to be made. Therefore, educators must be alert to the academic and social behaviors of the children and not overlook the possibility that simple classroom modifications may greatly impact the learning environment. Often, these modifications are easy to make and will produce immediate results.

Whether modifying, adapting, or enhancing the curriculum or the environment, teachers should ensure that instruction is age appropriate and of the highest quality and that students are grouped appropriately (Tashie et al., 1993).

Expectations and Attitudes In addition to modifying expectations about how students with severe disabilities will demonstrate learning (for instance, through sequencing pictures rather than writing or verbalizing, using a computer instead of handwriting), how much work is to be expected (for example, one-third of the math story problems instead of all of them, three spelling words instead of ten), or the priority of goals (such as concentrating on reading more than on science), the teacher may also look at the attitudes and expectations that students, teachers, and other school staff have about students with severe disabilities. As we all know, expectations can become self-fulfilling prophecies. Consequently, we should set high, yet reasonable, expectations for all students.

If elementary school students are interacting with students with severe disabilities for the first time, they may feel somewhat uncomfortable or fearful. Therefore, we may need to teach students how to interact appropriately with students with severe disabilities. For example, to facilitate effective communication between students with severe disabilities and their peers, we may demonstrate to elementary school children how to use alternative communication boards.

At times, students may act inappropriately toward students with severe disabilities by teasing, calling them names, or intentionally excluding students from activities. In addition, Evans, Salisbury, Palombaro, and Goldberg (1994) state:

> It seems inevitable that when students with severe disabilities are educated in regular academic settings, the instructional demands placed on them are going to differ somewhat from those of their peers without disabilities. If typical children are not skilled in judging the fairness of such situations, they may develop resentments toward the less able peers, or be less effective as their advocates or both. (p. 326)

Therefore, these authors suggest that we need to "examine the issue of equity and justice in light of classroom social relations" (p. 326). If these types of situations occur, they should be addressed immediately in an educational and nonthreatening manner.

A variety of strategies for addressing these issues are found in the literature. For example, numerous materials are available that promote a sense of community, class cohesiveness, an understanding of differences, and mutual respect and caring among students (Charney, 1991; Salend, 1994). In addition, a variety of attitude change strategies (for instance, simulation of disabilities, shared experiences, guest speakers, class discussions) can be used with elementary school students. However, teachers should use attitude change strategies cautiously, and only after becoming fully informed about the pros and cons that each type of strategy can have on students. Salend (1994) summarizes a variety of attitude change strategies and issues that should be considered when using these strategies in the classroom.

Teaching Children with Difficult Behaviors in the General Education Classroom

Though the majority of children with severe disabilities will not exhibit behaviors that will be extremely challenging in the general education classroom, a few students will. We should also note that students who do not have this label may also present behavioral challenges to an elementary classroom teacher. Consequently, the general education teacher needs to be prepared to handle behavioral situations in the classroom. In inclusive schools (as in all schools), we want to ensure that the strategies we use will maintain the dignity of children, enhance learning opportunities (social and instructional), support a sense of community in the classroom, provide a safe environment for all children, and model the types of behaviors we wish to see in children.

If our goal is to create a sense of community where all students are valued, respected and supported, we will need to use strategies that (a) attempt to prevent behavioral situations from developing in the first place, (b) avoid criticizing children (as well as others in the environment), and (c) avoid reacting in a manner that creates negative interactions between a child and others. Reacting is a natural phenomenon. Consequently, in situations that catch us off guard we generally rely on strategies with which we are familiar. Therefore, we should reflect on how we typically react in situations and examine whether we might want to develop a broader array of effective strategies for dealing with these situations.

Often we are too close to the situation to see clearly how our own behavior may be influencing a child's behavior. Therefore, working with others in problem-solving difficult behaviors is often very helpful. In addition, we should seek the support and advice of others in handling any situation where a child's behavior is threatening the safety of another child, him- or herself, staff, or family members.

Children may be exhibiting less than desirable behaviors in the classroom for a multitude of reasons. Though at times the reasons for this type of behavior may appear obvious, often they are not. To develop a clear picture of what is actually occurring, we may need to look first at (a) our own behavior (and that of others in the environment), (b) the culture and climate (for instance, philosophy of school and classroom, degree of collaboration, rules), (c) the teaching and learning environment in the classroom (such as flexibility in adapting to a variety of learning styles, availability of materials and support), (d) the physical characteristics of the classroom (for example, space, size, appearance of classroom), and (e) the structure of the classroom and school and the way we move throughout the school day (that is, time schedules, traffic patterns, school routines). Only after understanding the context of the behavior are we in a good position to begin to solve problems.

A series of questions that may assist educators in gaining contextual clarity is provided in Figure 12.3. Behavioral, environmental, structural and collaborative interventions or strategies are embedded in the questions.

Teaching Children with Physical/Medical Issues in the General Education Classroom

Because of better nutritional, physical, and medical care, more children with severe disabilities are living than in the past. Some of these children may require medical technology to assist them in breathing and maintaining bodily functions. Controversy continues about the extent of nursing services that should be provided in public schools, but an increasing number of children who are dependent on medical technology are being educated in public schools (Haynie, Porter, & Palfrey, 1989). Therefore, elementary teachers and students may be interacting for the first time with children with severe disabilities who are also dependent on medical technology. Some of the medical technology may include ventilators or oxygen masks to assist in breathing, gastrostomy tubes (G-tube) or nasogastric tubes (NG-tube) to assist in feeding, central venous catheters (CVC) (a long-term intravenous line), clean intermittent catheterization (CIC) to assist in bladder elimination, and colostomies to assist in bowel elimination. In addition, some students may require nasal or mouth suctioning to facilitate breathing.

Although in most cases the classroom teacher will not be responsible for implementing all the necessary medical procedures, at the very least the teacher

FIGURE 12.3 What Is the Child's Behavior All About?

Any time we want to change a child's behavior, we should stop, give serious thought to the situation, and ask ourselves a series of questions. Some questions may include the following:

1. **As a teacher I need to ask myself the following questions:**
   a. Why am I wanting to change the behavior? Can the behavior be tolerated?
   b. Whose problem is it (e.g., is it really the child's, mine, an adminstrative problem, a personality conflict)?
   c. What role is my behavior playing in the situation (e.g., am I ignoring the child, am I unintentionally putting the child down, am I paying too much attention to the child, does the behavior remind me of an experience I am dealing with at home with one of my own children)?
   d. Is there a communicative intent in the child's behavior (e.g., angry but cannot come out and say it, bored, frustrated, unhappy, nervous, scared)? If so, what is the child trying to tell me? What can I do to help the child express the concern in a more positive way?
   e. Are there cultural factors (e.g., shyness in front of a group, needing to appear macho to preserve a family image) or other life experiences that may be influencing the learner's behavior (e.g., divorce, death in family, violence, drugs)?
   f. Have I established a quality teacher-learner relationship that will serve as a good foundation for trust, support, and change?
   g. Have I structured activities that will promote positive student-student relationships that will serve as a good foundation for trust, support, and change?
   h. Have I looked for simple solutions (environment and structure) before moving to more complex solutions?
   i. Do I want to be teaching? Am I under stress—is it affecting my performance?
2. **As a teacher I need to ask myself the following questions dealing with motivation or instructional issues:**
   a. Do I know the skills the child has? Is the work I am assigning at an appropriate level to allow the child to remain motivated? Have I allowed enough time for the activity?
   b. Am I relating the instruction to the child's background and experience? Am I presenting the material in a way that makes sense to the child? Am I making learning fun? Is there a balance in class activities (e.g., challenging/comfortable, alone/group, alive/quiet)?
   c. Is the quality of the student-teacher relationship good? If not, what can be done to improve the relationship? (If there is a good relationshp, the child will often be more motivated to do the work.)
   d. Is the quality of the student-student relationships good? Does the child have at least one or two friends in class? If not, what activities can be implemented to improve student-student relationships in class?
   e. Is the child interested in or committed to changing his or her behavior? If not, what can be done to interest the child? In what is the child interested? Toward what will the learner work?
3. **What changes can I make in the environment that may positively influence the child's behavior?**
   a. Does the child have adequate "space" (e.g., for belongings)?
   b. Is the environment comfortable (e.g., noise level, temperature, lighting) and safe?
   c. Are the children grouped in a manner that is conducive for learning (e.g., are activity groups too large or too small for the child, and is the composition of group right for the child)?

SOURCE: Questions have been adapted from Espanchin et al. (1994).

FIGURE 12.3 *(continued)*

d. What is the attitude of the teacher? Do people smile? Is there a sense of humor in the environment? Is learning fun in the classroom?

e. Is the environment one in which you would want to be for an extended period of time? If not, what could be done to change it?

f. Does the child have a "voice" in the classroom? Is having a "voice" encouraged and respected?

g. What is the pace of the instruction? Is the child able to keep up? Is the child bored?

h. Are there exciting things happening in the class? Is there a good mix of project-based activities, individual work, group work, and so on?

i. Does the child have an opportunity to make choices? Is the child required to make too many choices?

j. Are there adequate and interesting materials for the child?

k. How do I interact with the child? What is the nature of the interactions (e.g., warm, supportive, caring)?

l. Do other children interact with the child? If so, how? What is the nature of the interactions (e.g., supportive, caring, fun)?

m. What will be the fallout (both positive and negative) of either addressing or not addressing the issue? To the child? To the rest of the class? To the school? To me, the teacher? To the family? (Am I prepared to handle the consequences of intervening? Things may get worse before they get better.)

4. What changes can I make in the structure of the school day that may positively influence the behavior?

a. Is the structure of the school day affecting the behavior?

b. Are there unnecessary rules in the environment in which the behavior is occurring? If so, can these be eliminated or modified?

c. Could changes in routines or schedules positively affect the behavior? For example, if a class activity was switched from morning to afternoon could that help the child? Could the child eat at a different lunch table? Join a different group for recess?

d. Could transition times be handled differently (e.g., more or less structure depending on the needs of the child)? Instead of downtime, could the child be given an activity to complete? Asked to assist the teacher or another child? Allowed to do whatever he or she wanted to do for a few mintues?

e. Would changes in traffic patterns have a positive outcome on a child's behavior (e.g., reroute children through several doors to go to recess, dismiss children at staggered times to reduce the congestion and the possibility of unnecessary roughhousing)?

5. Additional (more traditional) questions that may also be explored related to the child's behavior:

a. Any other clues as to why the behavior might be occurring?

b. Has the behavior occurred before? When? Is the behavior likely to be temporary? Will the behavior go away if left unaddressed?

c. What is happening just prior to the onset of the behavior?

d. What happens after the behavior has occurred?

e. Does the child understand what the expected behavior is and when it should be performed? (If not, teach the behavior.)

f. Does the child have the desired behavior in their repertoire? (If not, teach the behavior.)

6. Could this behavior be better addressed by a collaborative team of people?

a. Have I discussed the situation with at least one other person who will provide me with honest feedback? What is their understanding of the situation?

(continued)

FIGURE 12.3 *(continued)*

b. Have I spoken with the child's family about the behavior? Do they see the behavior at home? Is it an issue for them?

c. Am I the best one to address this behavior?

d. Should I be talking about the behavior to anyone else? If so, to whom?

e. Do I have the knowledge, skills, attitudes, motivation, confidence, and experience to address the behavior? If not, what resources are available to me?

f. What support might the child need from others? What support might the other children in the class need from others? What support might the family need from others? What support might I need from others?

g. Do I have the collaborative problem skills I can share with others on a solution? If not, what training would be helpful? Where can I get it?

7. What are the ethical issues involved with changing this behavior?

a. Am I being sensitive to ethnic, religious, gender, or other issues that may be impacting the child's behavior (e.g., language, family values, parental and self-expectations, attitudes)?

b. Can I (or the team) find a solution that will maintain or promote the child's self esteem and dignity?

c. Have I involved the family?

d. Have I tried positive methods of intervention before trying any other method?

e. Are there legal procedural safeguards that need to be considered? Who would know what these are?

f. Are there other environments (e.g., home, other classrooms at school, the cafeteria) we should also consider? Who else needs to be involved?

should become familiar with any precautions and situations that signal that a child may be experiencing difficulty with the technology. The child's family and doctor will be valuable resources to the teacher and other school personnel. In addition, resources are available that outline guidelines to follow, precautions, and problems that may require immediate attention for some of the most common types of situations that teachers who are working with students who are medically dependent may face (Haynie et al., 1989).

In most situations, the classroom environment will not need to be altered a great deal to accommodate a student who is medically dependent on technology. However, some of the procedures that need to be performed will require privacy (for example, emptying colostomy and catheter bags, tube feeding, suctioning) and a clean environment. Often the nurse's office may be the most appropriate place for these procedures. If the school does not have a nurse's office, a suitable environment will have to be located.

Both teachers and students who are unfamiliar with medical technology may be hesitant or frightened at first with the situation. School nurses, public health nurses, the student's doctor, or the student's family can play an important role in helping others feel comfortable with the medical technology. Generally, elementary school children will adjust quickly to the situation, and we should allow children an opportunity to ask questions about the technology and why their peer requires the technology. At the same time, we should be sensitive to children using the technology. Depending on factors such as (a) how long the child has been using the technology, (b) the type of technology required, and (c) people's reactions to the technology, the child may or may not be comfortable with using the technology. If the child has adjusted well and has adequate communication skills, the child may be the best person to answer classmates' questions. For a child who is still struggling with acceptance of using the technology, we might answer questions without the child present. Yet for other students, being present when questions are being asked may facilitate acceptance by peers. In another strategy, one of the child's family members may provide information and answer questions either with or without the child present. These issues should be thoroughly discussed with the child (if appropriate) and the child's family prior to the child's attending school.

Teaching Children with Dual Sensory Impairments in the General Education Classroom

As previously mentioned, some students with severe disabilities may also have dual sensory impairments. Downing and Eichinger (1990) have outlined a variety of instructional strategies that can be used to integrate students with dual sensory impairments into the general education classroom. These strategies include enhancing visual and auditory stimuli, using tactile teaching techniques, determining whether activities require vision or hearing, targeting visual and auditory skills within meaningful contexts, teaching in small groups and cooperative learning strategies, and providing partial participation.

EVALUATION AND GRADING

Frequently, general education teachers and administrators, special education teachers, and the families of students with severe disabilities are concerned about how to evaluate progress being made by students with severe disabilities. In addition, they wonder how students with severe disabilities in the general education classroom will be graded if they are not working at grade level. Discussing these issues with the IEP/support/collaborative team prior to beginning instruction is critical. The issues of evaluation and grading are briefly discussed in the following sections.

Evaluating Academic, Behavioral, and Social Progress

Probably the most basic evaluation question is, Are IEP goals and objectives being met? If goals and objectives are being met, the team should determine if additional IEP goals and objectives need to be developed. If goals and objectives are not being met, the IEP team should determine the reason why. If this occurs, the team should explore the following questions:

1. Do the current IEP objectives accurately reflect the academic, behavioral, and social needs of the student? If not, either the current objectives should be modified or totally new objectives should be developed by the team.
2. Are the IEP objectives realistic as they are currently written? Sometimes initial IEP objectives are simply not appropriate for a student, a situation especially true at the elementary school level where educators may be working with the student for the first time. For example, predicting how a student will interact with other students in the general education classroom for the first time is difficult. Initial objectives may be (a) too difficult for the student, (b) too easy for the student, (c) unnecessary, or (d) simply off target. If this situation occurs, the team should revise the IEP immediately. Students with severe disabilities simply do not have educational time to waste. Consequently, the revised IEP should be carefully monitored to ensure it is on target and that progress is being made as quickly as possible.
3. Are there obvious noninstructional reasons that the objectives are not being met? For example, has the student missed an excessive amount of school due to an extended illness or tardiness? Has the student's medication changed, and is the student having difficulty staying awake or attending? Is there a new student in the class who triggers undesirable behaviors in the student with severe disabilities?
4. Are there instructional reasons the objectives are not being met? For example, has the instructional aide been absent for an extended period of time and no substitute provided? Has the class size been increased as the year has progressed and thus become unmanageable for the support assigned to the class? Have materials not been adapted to the extent they should be because of inadequate fiscal resources or broken equipment?

If social goals are not being met, the teacher may look at the social opportunities available in the general education classroom. Because of the very nature of social goals, teachers often rely on the willingness or ability of students without disabilities to interact with the students with severe disabilities. Consequently, sometimes the teacher may need to elicit assistance from students without disabilities in order for social goals to be met. A variety of strategies have been used to address this issue. These may include activities that (a) involve problem solving (Giangreco, 1993), (b) require adults to assist in facilitating friendship and social network building (Stainback & Stainback, 1985), or (c) address negative attitudes of peers through a variety of attitude change strategies (Salend, 1994).

Another means of evaluating whether social goals are being met involves asking, Is the quality of life improving for the student with severe disabilities? This could be measured by looking at the number of invitations to birthday parties and after-school and weekend activities with peers. Are these types of social opportunities increasing? If not, what could be done to expand these opportunities?

Students with severe disabilities, like all students, should be closely monitored to ensure that adequate progress is being made. The team that monitors student progress should be skilled in appropriate assessment techniques, making curriculum modifications, collaborative problem-solving strategies, and working effectively with others, particularly the families of the students.

Grading Students with Severe Disabilities in the General Education Classroom

Openly discussing this issue is critical for several reasons: (a) all those involved will have a clear understanding of what to expect prior to grading time, (b) there will be ample opportunity to gain administrative support if the proposed grading practices deviate from school or district grading policies, and (c) the differential grading practices can be discussed with the students without disabilities, if necessary, to ensure that the issue of fairness has been addressed.

Salend (1994) discusses a variety of possible alternative grading systems. These include (a) using the student's IEP to serve as the foundation for grading, (b) student self-comparison (student and teacher identify the goals that will be evaluated), (c) contract grading, (d) pass/fail systems, (e) mastery level/criterion systems, (f) checklists (mastery of delineated competencies), (g) multiple grading (grades are given for areas such as ability, effort, and achievement or are averaged into one grade), (h) level grading (can use a subscript grade to indicate the level of difficulty on which the student's grades are based), (i) shared grading (more than one teacher evaluates a student's progress and assigns a collaborative grade), and (j) descriptive grading (descriptive comments and examples are provided in lieu of grades). This list is by no means exhaustive. The important point to remember is that grading decisions should be determined as the child enters the general education classroom.

RESOURCES AVAILABLE

Numerous resources are available (see Vandercook et al., 1995) to assist teachers, administrators, and families as they begin transitioning to inclusive schooling practices. Consequently, there should be little need to "reinvent the wheel"; rather, materials may need to be tailored to meet the needs of the local school community that will be using the materials. The references cited at the end of this chapter contain a wealth of information about many aspects of inclusive schooling; therefore, the readers are strongly encouraged to review materials. A very brief listing of several resources is provided in Figure 12.4. Because most of these resources have been supported with federal dollars, many of the materials that have been developed often can be purchased for a reasonable cost (for example, the cost of duplication). In addition, Figure 12.5 provides a listing of written materials that also might be helpful, including professional journals that regularly publish articles regarding inclusive schooling. Because the knowledge base is

FIGURE 12.4 Resources to Help the Transition to Inclusive Models for Students with Severe Disabilities

Consortium on Inclusive Schooling Practices
Child and Family Studies Program
Allegheny-Singer Research Institute
320 E. North Ave.
Pittsburgh, PA 15212
(412) 359-1600

National Information Center for Children and Youth with Disabilities (NICHCY)
P.O. Box 1492
Washington, DC 20013
(800) 695-0285 (voice/TTY)
Outstanding resource for general educators who have limited knowledge about children with disabilities, including toll-free numbers of disability-related organizations, special education laws and regulations, family and sibling issues, "A Guide to Children's Literature and Disability," and numerous publications available in Spanish.

Teaching Research Assistance to Children Experiencing Sensory Impairments (TRACES)
Western Oregon State College
Teaching Research Division
345 N. Monmouth Ave.
Monmouth, OR 97361
(503) 838-8401 (voice)
(503) 838-8821 (TTY)

The National Information Clearinghouse on Children Who Are Deaf-Blind (DB-LINK)
Western Oregon State College
Teaching Research Division
345 N. Monmouth Ave.
Monmouth, OR 97361
(800) 438-9376 (voice)
(503) 854-7013 (TTY)

developing quickly, persons interested in inclusive schooling should seek information that will assist them in remaining professionally current.

IS INCLUSIVE SCHOOLING ACTUALLY WORTH THE WORK AND GOOD FOR CHILDREN AND OTHERS?

Without a doubt, transitioning to an inclusive schooling model of education is a tremendous amount of work. Although from a value perspective inclusive schooling appears to be the right thing to do, is it actually good for children and others? Numerous benefits to children with severe disabilities, typical children, teachers, families of children with severe disabilities, and the school community have been identified in the growing body of literature on inclusive schooling (McGregor, 1993).

FIGURE 12.5 Written Materials on Inclusive Schooling

A listing of all current U.S. Department of Education, Office of Special Education, projects (research, systems change, model development, outreach, in-service training) targeted to serve children with severe disabilities in inclusive schools can be obtained from:

U.S. Department of Education
Office of Special Education Programs
330 C Street S.W.
Washington, DC 20202

Inclusive Education for Learners with Disabilities: Print and Media Resource (6th ed.). (1995). Compiled by T. Vandercook, L. Walz, M. B. Doyle, J. York, and S. Wolff at the Institute on Community Integration. This publication provides the reader with resources about theory, research, and effective practices. Resources listed in the publication include journal articles, books and chapters, manuals, research papers, newsletters, journals, organizations, children's books, and videotapes addressing inclusive education. Copies may be ordered by contacting:

Publications Office
Institute on Community Integration
University of Minnesota
109 Pattee Hall, 150 Pillsbury Dr. SE
Minneapolis, MN 55455
(612) 624-4512

A Reader's Guide: For Parents of Children with Mental, Physical, or Emotional Disabilities (3rd ed.). (1990). This extensive annotated bibliography is authored by Cory Moore. Though the title indicates the book was designed for parents, the information contained in this guide is invaluable to teachers and administrators as well as to librarians and school counselors. The publication is available through Woodbine Press, Rockville, MD.

Journals that regularly publish articles related to special education include these:

American Psychologist
Education and Training in Mental Retardation
Educational Leadership
Exceptional Children
Exceptional Parent
Focus on Exceptional Children
Holistic Education Review
Intervention in School and Clinic
Journal of Learning Disabilities
Teaching Tolerance
The Journal of Special Education
The Journal of the Association for Persons with Severe Handicaps
Phi Delta Kappan
Preventing School Failure
Remedial and Special Education
School Psychology Review

The literature contains numerous examples of the benefits of students with severe disabilities being educated with their peers without disabilities. One of the first studies to document such advantages was conducted by Brinker and Thorpe (1984). They found the degree of integration, as measured by interaction with typical students, was a predictor of educational progress, as measured by the proportion of IEP objectives met. Similarly, general education teachers have reported that students with severe disabilities who were educated in the general education classroom were more aware and responsive to others in the environment and learned a variety of communication, social, motor, academic skills (Giangreco et al., 1993). In addition, parents of children with severe disabilities who have received their education in the general education classroom have reported they have seen (a) dramatic improvement and growth in speech, language and communication skills of their children, (b) more interactions with peers, (c) more friendship, (d) less inappropriate behaviors (self-stimulatory behaviors, self-injurious behaviors, attention-seeking behaviors), (e) increased self-confidence and greater independence, and (f) increased self-initiation by their children (Ryndak, Downing, Jacqueline, & Morrison, 1995). Interestingly, parents in this study also noticed a change in the demeanor of their children, who appeared happier and had more positive attitudes toward both school and learning.

Numerous benefits to children without disabilities have also been noted. Giangreco et al. (1993) found that general education teachers reported that students in the general education class became more aware of the needs of people with disabilities and demonstrated an increased level of social-emotional development, flexibility, and empathy. Similarly, Peck, Donaldson, and Pezzoli (1990) found that adolescents who had social experiences with peers with severe disabilities perceived that as a result of these interactions (a) their self-concept improved, (b) they grew in social cognition, (c) they were more tolerant of others, (d) fear of human differences was reduced, (e) they developed personal principles, and (f) they developed relaxed and accepting friendships.

General education teachers have also reported that they benefited both personally and professionally from having a student with a severe disability in their classroom. General education teachers have reported that (a) they experienced a sense of pride in their ability to remain open to change, (b) they had more confidence as a result of the experience, and (c) the experience impacted the way they taught all students (for example, better planning, incorporating new ideas into teaching) (Giangreco et al., 1993).

With benefits such as those identified earlier, despite the work inclusive schooling requires (especially as schools are transitioning to this type of service delivery model), the benefits to children and their families, teachers, and the larger school community are certainly worth the effort.

CONCLUSION: THE CHALLENGE BEFORE US

So, we ask, are we there yet? In some parts of the United States inclusive education for students with severe disabilities is a reality; however, in most places we are not there yet. To date, we have more inclusive schools at the elementary school level than we do at the secondary school level. However, as elementary school children grow older, we are now seeing a great deal of development at the secondary school level. Although we have many successful models of inclusive schooling, many challenges remain, including limited attitudes, personnel preparation programs that are not preparing teachers for inclusive schools, state licensing and credentialing issues, and assessment matters. Probably the greatest challenge is getting best practice into practice in all schools.

We have an opportunity before us. Let us share our knowledge and learn from each other. Let us channel our energies and solve the educational challenges that face us together. Together we can make a difference for all children. Together we can reach our ultimate goal—a world in which all children are included in their schools and communities as valued human beings.

REFERENCES

Beane, J. A., & Apple, M. W. (1995). The case for democratic schools. In M. W. Apple & J. A. Beane (Eds.), *Democratic schools*. Alexandria, VA: Association for Supervision and Curriculum Development.

Board of Education Sacramento City Unified School District v. Holland, 786 F. Supp. 874 (E.D. Cal. 1992).

Brinker, R. P., & Thorpe, M. E. (1984). Integration of severely handicapped students and the proportion of IEP objectives achieved. *Exceptional Children, 51,* 168–175.

Catlett, S., Hunter, D., & Brady, M. (1998). *Becoming an inclusive school: A predictable venture*. Manuscript in preparation, Florida International University, Miami.

Charney, R. S. (1994). *Teaching children to care: Management in the responsive classroom*. Greenfield, MA: Northeast Foundation for Children.

Daniel R.R. v. State Board of Education, 874 F. 2nd 1036 (5th Cir. 1989).

Downing, J., & Eichinger, J. (1990). Instructional strategies for learners with dual sensory impairments in integrated settings. *Journal of the Association for Persons with Severe Handicaps, 15,* 98–105.

Ebling, D., Deschenes, C., & Sprague, J. (1994). *Adapting curriculum and instruction in inclusive classrooms: A staff development kit*. Bloomington, IN: Institute for the Study of Developmental Disabilities, Center for School and Community Integration.

Epanchin, B., Townsend, B., & Stoddard, K. (1994). *Constructive classroom management: Strategies for creating positive learning environments*. Pacific Grove, CA: Brooks/Cole.

Evans, I., Salisbury, C., Palombaro, M., & Goldberg, J. (1994). Children's perception of fairness in classroom and interpersonal situations involving peers with severe disabilities. *Journal of the Association for Persons with Severe Handicaps, 19,* 326–332.

Ford, A., Davern, L., & Schnorr, R. (1992). Inclusive education: "Making sense" of the curriculum. In S. Stainback & W. Stainback (Eds.), *Curriculum considerations in inclusive classrooms: Facilitating learning for all students* (pp. 37–61). Baltimore: Brookes.

Fox, T., & Williams, W. (1991). *Best practice guidelines for meeting the needs of students in local schools*. Burlington: University of Vermont, Center for Developmental Disabilities.

Giangreco, M. F. (1993). Using creative problem solving methods to include students with severe disabilities in general education class activities. *Journal of Educational and Psychological Consultation, 4,* 113–135.

Giangreco, M. F., Cloninger, C. J., & Salce-Iverson, V. (1992). *Choosing options and accommodations for children (COACH): A guide to planning inclusive education*. Baltimore: Brookes.

Giangreco, M., Dennis, R. E., Cloninger, C., Edelman, S., & Schattman, R. (1993). "I've counted Jon": Transformational experiences of teachers educating students with disabilities. *Exceptional Children, 59,* 359–372.

Giangreco, M. F., Dennis, R. E., Edelman, S. W., & Cloninger, C. J. (1994). Dressing your IEPs for the general education climate: Analysis of IEP goals and objectives for students with multiple disabilities. *Remedial and Special Education, 15,* 288–296.

Graden, J. L., & Bauer, A. M. (1992). Using a collaborative approach to support students and teachers in inclusive classrooms. In S. Stainback & W. Stainback (Eds.), *Curriculum considerations in inclusive classrooms: Facilitating learning for all students* (pp. 85–100). Baltimore: Brookes.

Haynie, M., Porter, S. M., & Palfrey, J. (1989). *Children assisted by medical technology: Guidelines for care.* Boston: Children's Hospital, Project School Care.

Hunter, D. (1994, June). *The ultimate goal: Inclusive education for all.* Paper presented at the World Conference Special Needs Education: Access and Quality, Salamanca, Spain.

Institute on Disability at the University of New Hampshire. (1990). *Materials developed by the INSTEPP and Statewide Systems Change Projects.* Durham, NH: Author.

Johnson, L. J., Pugach, M. C., & Hammitte, D. (1988). Barriers to effective special education consultation. *Remedial and Special Education, 9*(6), 41–47.

Knight, D., & Wadsworth, D. (1993, Summer). Physically challenged students: Inclusive classrooms. *Childhood Education,* pp. 211–215.

Kronberg, R., & Filbin, J. (1993). *Ideas and suggestions for curricular adaptations at the elementary school level.* Denver: Colorado Department of Education.

Margolis, H., & McGettigan, J. (1988). Managing resistance to instructional modifications in mainstreamed environments. *Remedial and Special Education, 9,* 15–21.

McCoy, K. M. (1995). *Teaching special learners in the general education classroom: Methods and techniques.* Denver: Love.

McGregor, G. (1993). Inclusion: A powerful pedagogy. *Front Line, 2*(1), 8–10. Temple University: Philadelphia, PA.

Mead, M. (1935). *Sex and temperament in three primitive societies.* New York: Morrow.

Meyer, L. H., Eichinger, J., & Downing, J. (1994). *Program quality indicators (PQI): A checklist of most promising practices in educational programs for students with severe disabilities* (3rd ed.). Syracuse, NY: Syracuse University, Center on Human Policy.

Morsink, C., Thomas, C., & Correa, V. (1995). *Interactive teaming: Consultation and collaboration in special programs.* New York: Macmillan.

Neary, T. (1992). Curriculum adaptations: Student-specific strategies. In T. Neary, A. Halversen, R. Kronberg, & D. Kelly (Eds.), *Curriculum adaptation for inclusive classrooms.* San Francisco: California Research Institute, San Francisco State University.

Neary, T., Halversen, A., Kronberg, R., & Kelly, D. (Eds.). (1992). *Curriculum adaptation for inclusive classrooms.* San Francisco: California Research Institute, San Francisco State University.

Oberti v. Clementon Board of Education, 995 F. 2nd 1204 (3rd Cir. 1993).

Osborne, A. (1963). *Applied imagination.* New York: Scribner.

Parnes, S. (1981). *The magic of your mind.* Buffalo, NY: Creative Education Foundation, in association with Bearly Limited.

Parnes, S. (1985). *A facilitating style of leadership.* Buffalo, NY: Creative Education Foundation.

Parnes, S. (1988). *Visioning: State-of-the-art processes for encouraging innovative excellence.* East Aurora, NY: DOK.

Peck, C. A., Donaldson, J., & Pezzoli, M. (1990). Some benefits nonhandicapped adolescents perceive for themselves from their social relationships with peers who have severe handicaps. *Journal of Association for Persons with Severe Handicaps, 15,* 241–249.

Pugach, M. C., & Johnson, L. J. (1990). Meeting diverse needs through professional peer collaboration. In W. Stainback & S. Stainback (Eds.), *Support networks for inclusive schooling: Interdependent integrated education* (pp. 123–137). Baltimore: Brookes.

Pugach, M. C., & Johnson, L. J. (1995). *Collaborative practitioners, collaborative schools.* Denver: Love.

Ronker v. Walters, 700 F. 2nd 1058 (6th Cir. 1983), cert. den'd, 464 U.S. 864, 104 S.Ct. 196, 78 L.Ed. 2nd 171 (1983).

Ryndak, D. L., Downing, J. E., Jacqueline, L. R., & Morrison, A. P. (1995). Parents' perceptions after inclusion of their children with moderate or severe disabilities. *Journal of the Association for Persons with Severe Handicaps, 20,* 147–157.

Salend, S. J. (1994). *Effective mainstreaming: Creative inclusive classrooms.* Upper Saddle River, NJ: Prentice Hall.

Sontag, J. C., & Schacht, R. (1994). An ethnic comparison of parent participation and information needs in early intervention. *Exceptional Children, 60,* 422–433.

Stainback, S., & Stainback, W. (1992). *Curriculum considerations in inclusive classrooms: Facilitating learning for all students.* Baltimore: Brookes.

Sugai, G. M., & Tindal, G. A. (1993). *Effective school consultation: An interactive approach.* Pacific Grove, CA: Brooks/Cole.

Tashie, C., Shapiro-Barnard, S., Schuh, M., Jorgensen, C., Dillion, A. D., Dixon, J., & Nisbet, J. (1990). *From special to regular, from ordinary to extraordinary.* Durham: Institute on Disability/University Affiliated Program, University of New Hampshire.

Thousand, J., & Villa, R. (1992). Collaborative teams: A powerful tool in school restructuring. In R. Villa, J. Thousand, W. Stainback, & S. Stainback (Eds.), *Restructuring for caring and effective education: An administrative guide to creating heterogeneous schools.* Baltimore: Brookes.

Turnbull, A., P., Turnbull, H. R., Shank, M., & Leal, D. (1995). *Exceptional lives: Special education in today's schools.* Upper Saddle River, NJ: Prentice Hall.

Vandercook, T., Walz, L., Doyle, M. B., York, J., & Wolff, S. (1995). *Inclusive education for learners with disabilities: Print and media resource* (6th ed.). Minneapolis: Institute on Community Integration, University of Minnesota.

Wood, J. W. (1992). *Adapting instruction for mainstreamed and at-risk students.* New York: Macmillan.

York, J., Giangreco, M. F., Vandercook, T., & Macdonald, C. (1992). Integrating support personnel in the inclusive classroom. In S. Stainback & W. Stainback (Eds.), *Curriculum considerations in inclusive classrooms: Facilitating learning for all students* (pp. 101–116). Baltimore: Brookes.

Zins, J. E., Curtis, M. J., Graden, J. L., & Ponti, C. R. (1988). *Helping students succeed in the regular classroom.* San Francisco: Jossey-Bass.

13

Integration in the Secondary School of Students with Mild or Moderate Disabilities

ALISA C. YORK
H. ELIZABETH WYCOFF

Students with mild or moderate disabilities are being included in regular education classrooms in increasing numbers, and with varying degrees of success. Programs can and are being implemented that increase the chances that the experience will be a positive one for all concerned. This chapter presents a brief history of attempts to serve this population, describes data used to evaluate success from a number of viewpoints, and discusses some programs designed to promote the success of such efforts. Elements of a model for maximizing success and monitoring progress toward goals for all students are included. Data are presented comparing students' rates of progress in reading fluency related to placement conditions, identified disabilities, and program supports. Finally, future directions are discussed, including a recap of effective programming elements.

The Education of All Handicapped Children Act of 1975 (EHA) and its successor, the Individuals with Disabilities Education Act (IDEA), affirmed the right of all students, including those with severe disabilities, to a public education. The intent of the law was clearly that students with disabilities should be educated with their nondisabled peers whenever possible (Snell, 1991). Special education services within the schools have generally been divided into (a) regular education with resource assistance less than 50 percent of the day and (b) self-contained instructional programs, where assistance is provided for more than 50 percent of the day.

HOW WELL DOES SEPARATE SPECIAL EDUCATION WORK?

How well does special education under IDEA and the current system serve students? According to the National Longitudinal Transition Study of Special Education Students (Wagner, D'Amico, Marder, Newman, & Blackorby, 1992; Wagner et al., 1991), special education and related services programs are failing a significant percentage of youth with disabilities as measured by graduation rate, employment, and levels of independence. Some studies report unemployment rates as high as 69 percent, even though graduation rates are as high as 75 percent ("Louis Harris Poll," 1994). Even when eventually served, some children are forced to fail before they can qualify for special education and related services. For these and other reasons, many researchers have felt that there has been a lack of evidence available to support benefits of segregated programs (Gartner & Lipsky, 1989; Wang & Baker, 1986).

Such has been the prevailing opinion, until recently. Having looked closely at both the methodology of studies of special education effectiveness and at the details of the programs being studied, Fuchs and Fuchs (1994) conclude that the more carefully designed studies show some benefits of special education for some students. For example, students classified as behavior disordered (BD), including those designated as seriously emotionally disturbed (SED), tend to show more gains in self-contained classrooms (Carlberg & Kavale, 1980), while students with learning disabilities (LD) are more likely to benefit from inclusion in regular classrooms. In addition, effective teaching techniques, designed primarily for use in special education programs, have demonstrated improved gains for all students (Bear & Proctor, 1990; Jenkins, Jewell, Leicester, O'Connor, & Troutner, 1994; Wang & Birch, 1984). The question of whether special education, as a general concept, is effective cannot be answered with a simple yes or no. To evaluate an educational program, especially for students with special needs, we must look at individual student characteristics and learning styles and at the type and amount of service provided. Later in this chapter, we will describe the academic progress of ten students as they transitioned from self-contained classrooms to inclusion in regular classrooms. Results are linked to personal and programmatic variables.

INCLUSION/MAINSTREAMING

What options do we have in serving students with mild or moderate disabilities, in addition to self-contained and resource (or pull-out) special education services? Historically, programs under the names of Regular Education Initiative (REI), mainstreaming, and inclusion have been used to educate students with special needs in their Least Restrictive Environment. Hocutt, Martin, and McKinney (1991) cite research dating back to 1986, calling for increased mainstreaming in the public schools, with key concepts being integration of children with and without special needs, individualized services, and clear roles for school personnel. The term *mainstreaming,* however, has typically been used to mean placing students with special needs in regular classrooms, without aides or other special modifications, and expecting them to perform at least as well as the lowest-functioning student in that regular education class.

In contrast to this "sink or swim" approach, inclusion is often defined as "the education of students with disabilities in the classrooms and school they would attend if not identified as disabled, with the provision of the appropriate supports and services necessary for the students to derive educational benefit" (Illinois School Psychologists Association Task Force, 1994, p. 5).

We must emphasize that appropriate supports and services are essential; without them a program is not inclusion, no matter how many disabled students are placed in the classroom. We will discuss the effects of inclusion on different aspects of the school experience in this context.

How Well Has Inclusion/Supported Mainstreaming Been Implemented?

Major questions persist concerning whether these necessary supports are provided. For example, results of surveys and interviews with high school teachers in Texas concerning mainstreaming with accommodations (defined here as inclusion) indicated that, according to teacher perceptions:

- Mainstreaming is not working as it should.

- Teachers use few accommodative strategies for LD students.
- Schools provide little or no training of any sort for teaching students with disabilities.
- School districts impose constraints that keep teachers from using accommodative strategies; and
- Administrators, operating under constraints imposed by governmental agencies, are complying with the law, but not allocating necessary resources to provide the training, supervision, materials, and/or personnel that would help train teachers to use accommodative strategies. (Betancourt-Smith, 1992)

How Has Inclusion Been Working?

Given the caveat that accommodation strategies are often implemented ineffectively (or not at all), what do we know about how well programs are working? Because of our interest in constructing a model, we focus on variables related to the students we wish to serve. Three areas of student performance have been assessed to evaluate inclusion, or mainstreaming, programs (Lloyd, Singh, & Repp, 1991; Rogers, 1994): (a) academic performance—with achievement in content areas measured using norm-referenced, criterion-referenced, or curriculum-based instruments; (b) attitudes—of students, parents, teachers, administration, legislators, and the general public; and (c) process—the types of interactions among teachers, peers, and students with special needs.

The impact of inclusion on regular education peers has been an area of interest and concern, in terms of both social and academic outcomes. Inclusion has gained support based on the perceived benefits for regular education students as well as students with disabilities, although these benefits have been primarily felt to be a change in attitude of teachers and students toward their peers with disabilities, rather than in benefits of an academic nature. Some studies have reported social benefits of inclusion for all students (Staub & Peck, 1995) and lack of detrimental effect on academic progress of nondisabled students (Cooke, Ruskus, Apolloni, & Peck, 1981; Odom, Deklyen, & Jenkins, 1984; Sharpe, York, & Knight, 1994; Staub & Peck, 1995). These studies have primarily addressed the impact of inclusion on younger students and have based their support on the reaction to more severe populations.

In one study that addressed secondary populations, Peck, Donaldson, and Pezzoli (1990) conducted semistructured interviews with classmates of twenty-one high school students with moderate or severe disabilities included in regular classrooms. Characteristics of the students with disabilities included severe mental retardation (MR), multiple disabilities, autism, and moderate MR, with the preponderance being moderate MR. The nondisabled classmates had at least weekly contact with their included peers. Perceived benefits reported by classmates included the following:

- Self-concept—gaining a better understanding of their own personal characteristics (62 percent)

- Social cognition—better understanding of feelings and beliefs of others (66 percent)
- Reduced fear of differences between self and others who are different (38 percent)
- Increased tolerance of others and their differences (66 percent)
- Development of personal principles—for example, "This is my friend; I don't care what others say" (48 percent)
- Relaxed and accepting friendships with students with disabilities (48 percent)

Students with mild or moderate disabilities have not been systematically studied, perhaps because the perceived impact for most LD and educable mentally retarded (EMR) populations is negligible. These students have had many more mainstream experiences over time, with little question as to the academic or social impact of their placement on peers.

Alternately, BD populations have also had mainstream experiences that, in many cases, have resulted in their removal from the regular education classroom. The impact of their behavior on classrooms would appear to be a factor that has been addressed primarily through the case study process, not through other systematic research.

In terms of academic progress, little information exists on the outcomes for either students with mild disabilities or their classmates at the secondary level. What we do know is that individual student characteristics account for only one piece of the whole picture of whether inclusion can be successful at the secondary level. Assessment of individual student progress can, however, assist in determining what additional structures need to be considered.

Inclusion as an option in special education has dealt with a variety of disability types, across age groups from preschool through high school (Staub & Peck, 1995). The focus of the remainder of this chapter is on practices that affect secondary students with mild or moderate disabilities, including LD, BD, and EMR.

Demonstrated Effects on Students with Disabilities and on Their Nondisabled Classmates

Using programmatic structures that support inclusion, several examples have demonstrated positive effects, not only for students identified with special needs but also for their unidentified classmates. These structures include detracking, cooperative learning, and individualized programming. We will discuss some of these structures in greater detail later in this chapter.

Rewards for improved performance and high expectations for performance of all students were demonstrated in classrooms using an approach consistent with inclusion, one that concentrated on providing a unified educational approach for all students. Steinberg and Wheelock (1992/1994) report the results of "untracking" in several middle schools, located in different parts of the country. In one model, all students (not just the straight A students) were encouraged to work toward honors. Honors depended on a combination of work completion, consistent school attendance, and raising grades from one quarter to the next.

Steinberg and Wheelock (1992/1994) cite cooperation with and respect for others as benefits in several of the programs in which emphasis was placed more on developing projects and following themes through coursework than on simple recall of information. One student reported benefits that included (a) working more often in groups, as opposed to lecture; (b) developing responsibility toward both peers and the teacher; and (c) development of respect for others' interests and talents. For example, when a project required making a movie based on class assignments, the formerly "lower-track" students showed the most creativity.

Another example of a unified educational approach demonstrates alternative teaching strategies for all. The Williston Central School, near Burlington, Vermont, uses computers to help provide an individualized education for all students in a full-inclusion setting (Schultz, 1992). Software allows teachers to formulate individual plans, establish broad educational goals, and link these goals to requisite skills in spelling, math, and other areas. The school is open each day for four hours beyond the time students are required to be in attendance. A measure of student enthusiasm is that they regularly attend for extra time, before and after normal school hours.

Schultz (1992) reports that several schools in other parts of the country allow students to use the computer for such things as writing assignments and that both the special education students and their classmates have produced creative reports of excellent quality. Positive results are reported in terms of the quality of products produced, enthusiasm on the part of both teachers and students, and allowing students with special needs to concentrate on the subject matter itself, rather than the mechanics of writing. In addition, a more familiar use of the computer for math and spelling drills provides extended practice, immediate feedback for students, and nonjudgmental reporting of progress.

Benefits for Students with Special Needs: "Fitting In" to Regular Classes

A study of junior high students in New York City (Truesdell, 1990) found no significant differences between students with special needs and their classmates in a lower-track class, with respect to achievement scores in math and reading, report card grades, or teacher ratings of classroom behaviors. Observed behaviors, however, showed that the students with disabilities participated less in class discussion and were less attentive.

In two Midwestern high schools, SED students and their nondisabled peers (ND) did not differ significantly in any classroom or group behaviors observed in mainstream vocational education classes (Denny, Epstein, & Rose, 1992). Both groups showed high rates of on-task behavior, and little extraneous interaction was observed between students or between students and teachers. This "blending" of SED and ND students occurred in spite of the fact that the class format was not one recommended for students in special education; it was mostly lecture and demonstration rather than hands-on group or individual work. In this type of situation, one might expect either disruptive behavior or withdrawal and lower participation rates.

Newman and Cameto (1993) report that students who were mainstreamed in high school academic classes were more likely to go on to postsecondary education, in academic or vocational areas. This information comes from a six-year study based on data from the National Longitudinal Transition Study of Special Education Students (NLTS) for eight thousand students, ages thirteen through twenty-one, with disabilities.

WHAT IS NEEDED FOR SUCCESSFUL INCLUSION? RESTRUCTURING SECONDARY SCHOOLS

The outcome for students must be the acquisition of usable skills in society. To be successful, schools must graduate students who can meet the educational goals set forth in Goals 2000 (Council for Exceptional Children and the National Association of State Boards of Education, 1994). How can one then accommodate the diversity that is present at the secondary level in terms of skills that students bring to the tasks required of them? In the past, the practice has been to track, segregate, and separate students based on their skills and behaviors. Mildly disabled populations, as noted previously, have been placed in programs in which school personnel hoped they could be successful within the lower ranges of classroom performance.

Secondary classrooms, however, have been designed to impart great quantities of knowledge; the more knowledge imparted, the more successful the course. Advanced classes have been revered for the amount of information that could be presented and absorbed by students. Assessment of success in many cases has been based on the student's ability to recall large quantities of factual information. How then could students with mild/moderate disabilities be included when they could not hope to match the pace of any course but the remedial or basic level courses? Adaptations of curriculum and modification of requirements are a short-term solution for many students; but, in the long run, other avenues may be more beneficial.

Many authors have expressed concerns about the education that we currently provide for all students at the secondary level (for example, Brandt, 1993; Giangreco, 1992; Sizer, 1992; Steinberg & Wheelock, 1992/1994). What changes must be made to the system for inclusion to work? Giangreco (1992) states that the goal for inclusion-oriented personnel should be to improve the lives of students as a result of their being in school. The goals should go beyond academics to include social and vocational as well, as students need to develop social networks and life experiences to apply what they have learned.

Development of the Coalition of Essential Schools has been another outcome of these concerns. This group has supported a restructuring of education for all students at the secondary level (Sizer, 1992). At the base of this philosophy is the concept that students must be able to use the information they learn in meaningful ways that allow them to be thoughtful and responsible individuals. Only through using and integrating the information they receive can they truly become educated citizens. The concept of student as a worker—using and connecting information—is paramount, instead of perceiving a student as a vessel to be flooded with information. Some of the other core beliefs of the Coalition of Essential Schools are as follows (Sizer, 1992):

- Coverage of topics without mastery is not coverage at all.
- Development of a set of essential skills in which each student will demonstrate mastery should be based on the types of intellectual skills a student will need in the future. Means to that end will vary with each student.
- Teaching and learning should be personalized—teachers need to know students to be able to teach them.
- There should be no specific time line for students to demonstrate competency and mastery in order to earn a diploma—it will vary for each student.
- The school must stress high expectations, trust, and the values of fairness and tolerance.

Demonstration of outcomes is accomplished through exhibitions—a way for students to demonstrate their ability to understand and integrate their coursework. Unlike typical tests, these exhibitions are accomplished over longer periods of time. Schools expect that students will apply information to a variety of life experiences, thus demonstrating its utility.

When these concepts are applied to a school, the concept of inclusion within this restructuring becomes a viable one. Several schools have been able to build on this philosophy and have included all students (Jorgensen, 1995; Nisbet, Jorgensen, & Heron, 1994; P. Vedovatti, personal communication, March 7, 1995). In New Hampshire's Souhegan High School, the critical parts of this philosophy for inclusion have been that collaborative planning time is available, much like the middle school concept (Jorgensen, 1995). At the high school level, staff use the term "Houses" for groupings of students whose teachers interact and collaborate in lesson planning and implementation. This includes special and regular education students and teachers. The use of "Essential Questions" when planning instruction for any unit is critical to success (Jorgensen, 1995). These questions guide the format and suggested outcomes of any unit, and they are designed to build success for all students, from the outset. The questions are as follows:

- How accommodating will the program be for students with different learning styles, interests, and challenges?
- Will it challenge the most well-read student in the class?
- Will it motivate and engage students who are not terribly interested in school?

- Are there high-interest, low-level reading materials on the topic for students who do not read or who read with great difficulty?
- What accommodations will be made for students with extraordinary learning challenges who may not understand the topic regardless of how it is presented? How can they be fully included in every class period?
- What are the students expected to remember about this unit? What should they be able to do a year from now when they have forgotten all the details?
- Can all students achieve some of these outcomes? (Jorgenson, 1995, pp. 52–53)

This type of questioning and planning helps all students gain from instruction. Instruction in this scenario is not geared to the average or above-average student but to all students, based on knowledge about individual students and what they bring to the learning environment. Flexibility can be provided, based on the level of challenge they wish to pursue (Jorgensen, 1995).

What, then, of schools that are not in a position to complete the transition to restructuring such as that posited by the Coalition of Essential Schools? In terms of students with mild or moderate disabilities, a promising approach for instruction is that of the Center for Research in Learning (Deshler & Lenz, 1989). The goal of instruction here is to make learning meaningful to all students. Rather than focus on the individual student, this approach takes the position that restructuring must occur at two levels: one for the individual child (strategies for independent learning that the student brings to the classroom) and another for the classroom teacher (in terms of how content is identified and presented).

Schumaker and Deshler's (1995) model proposes that both students and teachers in a secondary setting be involved in strategic instruction. Students learn specific strategies for dealing with the demands of the regular classroom. For example, students use paraphrasing (Schumaker, Denton, Pegi, & Deshler, 1984) for learning a systematic approach to putting information into their own words and first letter mnemonics (Nagel, Schumaker, & Deshler, 1986) for learning not only how to make up mnemonics to aid in recall but also how to determine key words that signal that the information may be important. Many other strategies assist all students in learning information that is critical to success. Teachers, for their part, teach more strategically by providing "road maps" for students in the form of lesson organizers (Lenz, Marrs, Schumaker, & Deshler, 1993) and unit organizers (Lenz, Bulgren, Schumaker, Deshler, & Boudah, 1994). These procedures include a systematic way of presenting instruction as well as visual organizers to assist students in understanding critical relationships.

Another component of these road maps is the addition of structures or routines within the instruction that help students relate important concepts to known information and to broader categories of knowledge. These types of road signs allow students with a variety of skill levels to become successful in regular classrooms. For example, the Concept Mastery Routine (Bulgren, Deshler, & Schumaker, 1993) assists students in understanding a critical concept, seeing its relationship to broader concepts, and identifying the specific characteristics that define the concept. Another example is the Concept Anchoring Routine (Bulgren, Schumaker, & Deshler, 1994), in which a student builds on characteristics of a known concept to develop an understanding of new information.

The essential components for successful use of this model appear to be a shift for regular class teachers to accept the idea that strategy instruction must be a part of content instruction, and a shift for special educators to see their role as not only teaching strategies to students but also as assisting students in using these strategies in a variety of settings. Special educators can assist in making the routines presented in classrooms explicit for all students (Schumaker & Deshler, 1995; Schumaker, Deshler, & McKnight, 1991). In a scenario in which restructuring has not taken place, this model allows teachers to move toward the goals of making content more meaningful, using the knowledge base students have, and determining the most critical outcomes for each content area.

HOW DO WE DOCUMENT AND MONITOR ACADEMIC PROGRESS?

Some previous research on academic progress has used standardized norm-referenced achievement tests such as the Metropolitan Achievement Tests (MAT) or criterion-referenced tests directed at assessment of a particular skill (for example, assessment of progress in learning math concepts). Shinn (1989) has criticized the use of these tests for monitoring academic progress, for several reasons: (a) they do not consistently overlap with teaching material; (b) they are not suitable for monitoring progress using repeated measurement; (c) the information obtained is limited and does not allow an error analysis that may lead to intervention; (d) fluency is not taken into account, although it is a relevant factor in comprehension; and (e) these instruments are designed to measure differences between, not within, individuals and may not be valid for the latter.

A comprehensive discussion of the use of curriculum-based measurement (CBM) is beyond the scope of this chapter; for examples of use of these techniques, we refer the reader to Fuchs, Deno, and Mirkin (1984); Fuchs, Fuchs, and Fernstrom (1993); Shinn (1989); Shinn, Knutson, Good, Tilly, and Collins (1992); Shinn and McConnell (1994); and Stainback and Stainback (1992). Curriculum-based measurement has been used to track academic performance in reading, math, spelling, and other content areas. Reading fluency, in particular, correlates highly with standardized measures of academic achievement (Fuchs & Fuchs, 1992; Shinn et al., 1992). Fuchs et al. (1993) report successful integration of resource elementary students into regular math classes, including improved academic performance when preparation included CBA and transenvironmental programming.

Advantages of CBM are that (a) it is a direct measure of performance in the curriculum; (b) it is a production-type response where students are observed using a particular skill; (c) the person observing may assess the process, as well as the product, produced; (d) there is a high degree of technical adequacy; (e) it can be used as a repeated measure, over time, and provides an opportunity for monitoring individual progress; (f) in situations where interstudent comparisons are required, local norms may be developed for the classroom, school, or district, providing an indication of what may be expected in the regular education environment (Shinn, 1989).

An Example of Academic Progress Monitoring

We conducted a study during three school years, beginning in the fall of 1991. Our purpose was to document progress in math and reading fluency, as students identified with mild or moderate disabilities moved from self-contained educational placements to inclusion in regular education classrooms. Because some advantages for an inclusion model have been demonstrated elsewhere, we suggest that if academic progress for these students is comparable in both settings, they may benefit from other aspects of inclusion with their peers, without worsening their academic prognosis. As noted previously, social benefits for both students with disabilities and without have been demonstrated in some classrooms where students with disabilities were included. In addition, a greater percentage of students with disabilities who attended regular classes to go on to postsecondary education (Newman & Cameto, 1993). These data would support the argument for inclusion if academic progress were demonstrated.

Data were collected in three Midwestern suburban school districts over three years. Data here represent only one of the districts, because teachers in this district more consistently collected data. Inclusion was mandated for this district by the school board and scheduled for a phase-in beginning the second year of this project. All students were in self-contained classes for the first year, some moved to inclusion in the second year, and all moved to inclusion by the third year. Although we collected data on both elementary and junior high school students, we included only those students who were in junior high (grades 7–8) for at least one year of the project. Further, we will discuss data for only those students for whom data were available for all three years. Attrition was caused by students moving from or being placed outside the district and by inconsistent administration of scheduled probes.

Ten students meet the aforementioned criteria: one whose primary disability was behavior disorder (BD), two who were classified as LD but had significant behavioral/emotional concerns, one student who was originally classified as moderately mentally disabled but later as LD, and the remaining six who were classified as LD. The primary minority group in the district is Hispanic.

In self-contained classes, class size ranged from ten to fifteen, including students at several grade levels and, in some cases, students with different disability classifications (EMR, LD, BD). Instruction was typically a combination of large-group, small-group, and individual strategies. Material was presented at the students' instructional level. For inclusion, the schools provided different levels of support in different settings. Conditions are described more completely, with respect to individual students, later in this chapter.

Measurement We used CBM to track individual academic progress over a three-year period, including both reading fluency and math measures. Reading fluency is highlighted here, as it has more relevance to the broad spectrum of academic requirements and has been shown to correlate with a number of academic success predictors, as described earlier. The dependent variable for reading was words correct per minute. Omissions, substitutions, and incorrectly pronounced words were counted as errors, with the exception of pronunciation consistent with ethnic dialect and mispronunciation of proper nouns. This format allowed repeated measures over time and comparisons across placement for individual students. In addition, CBM allowed ongoing decision making about the level of support required to derive educational benefit.

To assess the effects of the program, we looked at slope of improvement, variability, and overlap, all important dimensions in evaluating data collected over time (Shinn, 1989). Slope indicates rate of change in one variable as a function of an increase in another variable (in this case, with reading fluency, the change in number of correct words per minute by months elapsed during the school year). Two acceptable methods for determining slope, the split middle technique and the ordinary least-squares (OLS) method, have been described in the literature (Parker, Tindall, & Stein, 1992). In a classroom situation, the split middle technique may be used by graphing the data, taking the average of the first two and last two data points, and drawing a line between these averages. In the current study, we determined slope using the OLS method because this measure is more precise than the split middle technique in estimating the slope of student progress using CBM (Good & Shinn, 1990; Shinn, Good, & Stein, 1989).

Overlap is the most comprehensive measure, because it is a function of both slope and variability. A range of scores, bounded by the highest and lowest scores during the baseline period (year 1 of this study), is projected into subsequent measurement periods. In this study, continued performance within the overlap band of the first phase suggests comparable progress, or at least lack of deterioration, as placement changes. Since lack of deterioration of academic skills is defined here as the minimal measure of success in inclusion, only data points below the overlap band are of concern. Data points above the overlap band represent higher levels of performance during the second or third years, compared with any recorded during the first year.

Administration and Scoring Procedures We based the selection of probes for monitoring progress on each student's instructional level in reading and math. Students completed reading and math probes approximately once per month during the school year, across the three-year period. We could not implement the schedule precisely because, as is often the case in natural environmental research, program changes, alternate schedule days, student illness, and so forth, interfered with the planned schedule.

We determined the appropriate level of reading probe by using the median score of three probes for each of the students. This procedure provided a more accurate base level and gave students an opportunity to feel comfortable with the procedure. A single math probe was completed (two minutes). Subsequent sessions consisted of a single one-minute reading probe and a two-minute math probe. We used multiple forms of the reading probes for each level (that is, students read a different passage each time).

Design The design of the study was a multiple baseline across subjects, with placement conditions as the independent variable. Some students had two years of baseline (self-contained), followed by one year of inclusion placement; some had one year of baseline and two of inclusion. The procedure allowed comparison of students with their own progress. Discussion here is concentrated on reading fluency measures, because standards for growth in reading are better documented in the literature and because reading continues to be an area of need through one's academic career, impacting virtually all subject areas. Further, as already discussed, reading fluency correlates highly with a variety of other academic outcome measures.

Results Table 13.1 provides the slopes for each of the three years of the project, along with grade, placement, and qualifying disability. Asterisks within the table indicate that for the year indicated the level of difficulty of the reading probe increased.

In a comparison of progress across conditions, only one student showed a steady rise in slope over three years. James was originally classified as EMR, but later as LD, and also had some issues related to his ability in English. His rate of improvement, indicated by the slope, rose slightly from the first year to the second. He made an even more impressive gain the third year, even though he was tested on a more advanced level probe.

A steady decline in slope was shown by three students: Matt, Carl, and Alex. Alex's primary qualification for special education was BD; Matt and Carl were classified as LD, but both had significant behavioral/emotional concerns. We maintained the same level of reading probe difficulty for all three students, across all three years.

Changes in slope, related to services provided, were shown by six students: Gene, Erin, Hillary, Mick, Ellie,and Amanda. For the first five of these students, the second year of the project showed a drop in slope, followed by an improvement in the third year. For all but Mick, the third year showed a positive slope; Mick's slope was less negative the third year than the second year (from -1.9 to -0.2). For the sixth student in this group, there was an increase from 1.4 to 5.8 from the first year to the second but a drop to 3.0 in the third year. We should note that the drop for all students was in the year they were first included in a regular classroom. For those having two years of experience in inclusion, improvement was noted in the second year of inclusion, related to programmatic supports discussed later.

Data for two students are presented here as examples of monitoring student progress. Figure 13.1 represents data collected over the three-year period for Ellie. In the 1992–1993 school year, she made a school change (elementary to junior high) and a placement change (self-contained to inclusion). By the end of

Table 13.1 Reading Fluency Slopes Representing Average Monthly Change in Words Correct per Minute

Grade	Name	Years in Self-Contained	1991–1992	1992–1993	1993–1994
6–8	Gene (LD)	1	3.9	−0.9	3.3*
	Erin (LD)	1	3.4	2.4	3.1*
	Matt (LD/BD)	1	5.0	2.3	−1.7
	Carl (LD/BD)	1	3.4	1.8	−0.4
	Hillary (LD)	1	1.1	−1.3	2.3
	Mick (LD)	1	1.0	−1.9	−0.2
5–7	Ellie (LD)	1	5.4	2.2	7.0
	Alex (BD)	1	1.9	−0.5	−1.4
	James (LD)	2	2.1	2.7	3.3*
	Amanda (LD)	2	1.4	5.8*	3.0*

NOTE: An asterisk indicates an increased level of reading probe difficulty as compared with the previous year.

the first month in this setting, Ellie's reading fluency, measured by the same level of probe difficulty as the previous year, had dropped dramatically. Although she did attain a positive slope, it was much "flatter" than in the previous year. Also, the number of data points below the overlap band increased. During her second year of inclusion (the third year of the project), Ellie showed the highest slope of any of the ten students reported here (slope = 7.0), had less variability among data points than in the first year, and had her final data point above the overlap band. Associated program variables are discussed later.

Alex (Figure 13.2) also changed schools each year. As for Ellie, the second year (first year of inclusion) showed a decline, not only in slope of improvement but also in levels of correct words per minute, even with probes of the same difficulty level. All but one of the data points for the second year are below the overlap band. For 1993–1994, although the slope of improvement continued to decline, the number of correct words per minute increased, and two of the five data points were above the overlap band established during the first year.

Discussion Students eligible for special education often display inconsistent performance of skills, verified again by visual inspection of this study's graphs. Therefore, in spite of fluctuations, the authors feel that a positive slope is evidence of skill development in reading and math, even though the "goodness of fit" of the slope line is less than optimal in most cases. Accuracy, and probably goodness of fit, may increase with a greater number of data points per year and per session.

For comparison purposes, students in regular education are expected to gain approximately 1.9 correct words per week in reading fluency. Data presented here are based on monthly recording; therefore, expectations for regular educa-

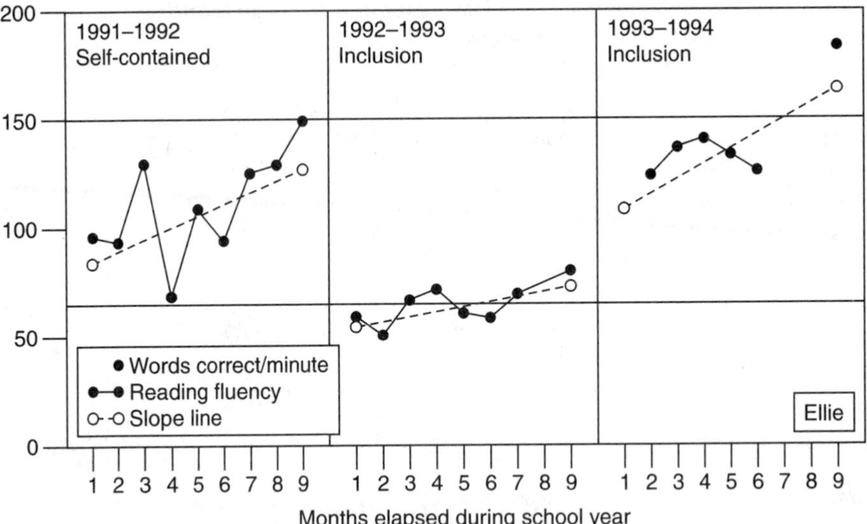

FIGURE 13.1 Reading Fluency Data for Ellie, with Superimposed Slope Lines Indicating Rate of Improvement

NOTE: The shaded area represents high and low scores for the first year, projected into subsequent years.

tion students would be a gain of approximately eight words per month during the instructional phase. None of the students in the current study reached that level of improvement, although Ellie's slope was 7.0 in the third year of the project, the second year of inclusion.

Some have suggested that students with behavioral/emotional disorders may do less well in inclusive settings than their special education counterparts with learning disabilities. All three of the students with consistently declining slopes in this study had emotional/behavioral concerns—one was qualified for services under the BD criteria; the others had LD as their primary qualification.

Ellie, who had already attained a high level of reading fluency, dropped to a level less than half of her former proficiency by the end of her first month in an inclusion setting. How could conditions associated with her change in setting be described? The team to which she was assigned during her first year in inclusion was not supportive; they were not willing to make modifications to the course requirements or to provide any more extra assistance than they would to any regular education student—the "sink or swim" approach. In addition, the special education teachers in the building had been assigned other duties that precluded them from giving a significant amount of assistance to inclusion students. In contrast, program changes had been made by the beginning of the 1993–1994 school year. Partly in response to documentation of students' difficulties using project probes, the school provided the inclusion students opportunities for additional assistance. Provisions included a study hall where individual help was available and an opportunity to take a study skills course. Whenever possible, administra-

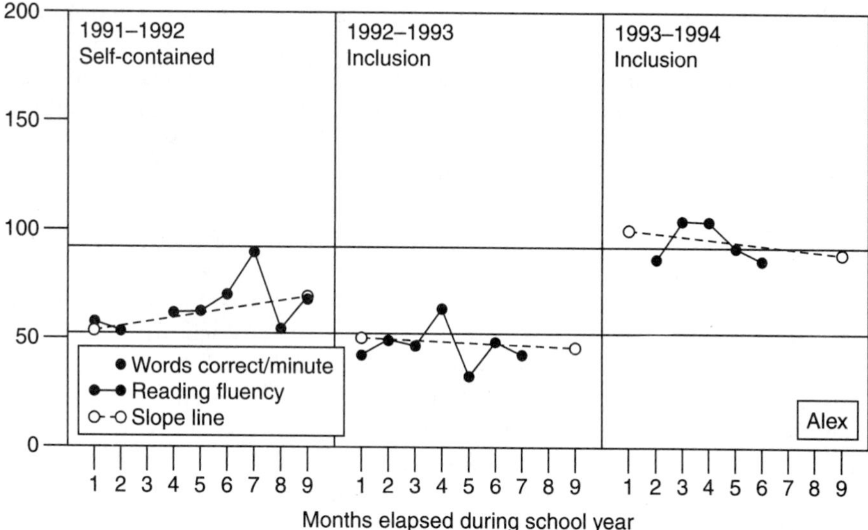

FIGURE 13.2 Reading Fluency Data for Alex, with Superimposed Slope Lines Indicating Rate of Improvement

NOTE: The shaded area represents high and low scores for the first year, projected into subsequent years.

tion assigned inclusion students to a team that was more supportive and gave the special education teachers time in their schedules to work with these students. Additional study sessions were available after school, and several of the students took part in these. The school encouraged team members to monitor progress using the probes, identify problems early, and intervene as quickly as possible. Ellie's results, although showing the most dramatic increase, are not an isolated positive incidence—others included in this study, and many others in the larger database, showed positive results with the increased support.

The results of this study suggest that inclusion may be successful academically for individual students if supports and adaptations are provided. In some cases, however, even with the supports in place, students did not make academic progress (as measured in reading fluency). Therefore, ongoing monitoring of progress is crucial, as is modifying the individual student's educational program on an as-needed basis.

WHERE DO WE GO FROM HERE? A RECAP

Successful inclusion of students with mild or moderate disabilities at the secondary level is interconnected with a process in which we consider the needs of all students. Structures such as "Essential Questions," strategy instruction, cooperative learning, and flexibility in scheduling and teaching routines help meet the needs of individuals. In these areas, secondary schools can learn much from implementation of successful elementary programs. Wang (1992) thoroughly describes these structures at the elementary level. In schools in which restructuring for all students has occurred, the inclusion of students with mild disabilities can be provided in the initial planning for any academic unit (Jorgensen, 1995). Options and choices within the curriculum allow teachers to address the needs of all students.

The learning strategies of Deshler and Schumaker (1988) present ways for students to learn to be successful in conjunction with teaching routines that support looking at the "critical content." Also critical is the need to assist students in integrating information into their own knowledge base. When these factors are present, inclusion can be very successful at the secondary level.

Another necessary component of a successful inclusion program—specifically, assessing progress—is using measures that are relevant to the curriculum. Without this type of information, decisions cannot be made reliably about the supports and adaptations necessary to include students with disabilities. The types of measures described in the study reported here (curriculum-based) as well as other authentic (classroom-based) assessments provide specific information that can lead to intervention and positive change for student programming. Repeated measures (such as curriculum-based measurement) provide a means of obtaining reliable information on student progress within the curriculum.

What should successful inclusion programs look like for mild or moderately disabled populations? Three key elements have been described here:

1. Restructuring of secondary schools to promote mastery of content over coverage. The goal of instruction must be to help students understand relationships between critical pieces of information and to apply these to real problems.
2. Teaching learning strategies. Students with disabilities are at a disadvantage in regular classrooms in many cases. Their skill in acquiring information is often much less developed than that of their regular peers. These students need the opportunity to learn strategies for information acquisition. In addition, teachers must assist by helping students identify important outcomes; one method is the use of teaching routines described by Deshler and Schumaker (1995).
3. Progress monitoring. Ongoing progress monitoring in course content and in skill and strategy acquisition must take place to determine whether the outcomes planned are being achieved.

Ideally, inclusion should be an individual decision based on evaluation of the progress of particular students and the instructional environments in which they learn. Under these conditions, the experience can be beneficial to all.

REFERENCES

Bear, G. G., & Proctor, W. (1990). Impact of a full-time integrated program on the achievement of non-handicapped and mildly handicapped children. *Exceptionality, 1,* 227–235.

Betancourt-Smith, M. (1992, January). *Accommodative strategies for mainstreamed LD students: High school teachers' perceptions of reasonableness and use.* Paper presented at the Annual Meeting of the Southwest Educational Research Association, Houston, TX.

Brandt, R. (1993, December–January). On outcome-based education: A conversation with Bill Spady. *Educational Leadership,* pp. 66–70.

Bulgren, J. A., Deshler, D. D., & Schumaker, J. B. (1993). *The Concept Mastery Routine.* Lawrence, KS: Edge Enterprises.

Bulgren, J. A., Schumaker, J. B., & Deshler, D. D. (1994). *The Concept Anchoring Routine.* Lawrence, KS: Edge Enterprises.

Carlberg, C., & Kavale, K. (1980). The efficacy of special versus regular class placement for exceptional children: A meta-analysis. *Journal of Special Education, 14,* 293–309.

Cooke, T. P., Ruskus, J. A., Apolloni, T., & Peck, C. A. (1981). Handicapped preschool children in the mainstream: Background, outcomes, and clinical suggestions. *Topics in Early Childhood Special Education, 1,* 73–83.

Council for Exceptional Children and the National Association of State Boards of Education. (1994). What is Goals 2000: The Educate America Act? GTE Educational Network Services, Inc. Newsgroups: cec.news; date: Fri, 7 Oct 1994 02:58:30 GMT.

Denny, R. K., Epstein, M. H., & Rose, E. (1992). Direct observation of adolescents with serious emotional disturbance and their nonhandicapped peers in mainstream vocational education classrooms. *Behavioral Disorders, 18,* 33–41.

Deshler, D. D., & Lenz, B. K. (1989). The Strategies Instructional Approach. *International Journal of Disability, Development and Education, 36,* 203–224.

Deshler, D. D., & Schumaker, J. B. (1988). An instructional model for teaching students how to learn. In J. L. Graden, J. E. Zins, & M. L. Curtis (Eds.), *Alternative educational delivery systems* (pp. 391–411). Washington, DC: National Association of School Psychologists.

Education of All Handicapped Children Act of 1975, 20 U.S.C. 1401 (1978).

Fuchs, D., & Fuchs, L. S. (1994). Counterpoint: Special education—Ineffective? Immoral? *Exceptional Children, 61,* 303–306.

Fuchs, D., Fuchs, L. S., & Fernstrom, P. (1993). A conservative approach to special education reform: Mainstreaming through transenvironmental programming and curriculum-based measurement. *American Educational Research Journal, 30,* 149–177.

Fuchs, L. S., Deno, S. N., & Mirkin, P. K. (1984). The effects of frequent curriculum-based measurement and evaluation on pedagogy, student achievement, and student awareness of learning. *American Educational Research Journal, 21,* 449–460.

Fuchs, L. S., & Fuchs, D. (1992). Identifying a measure for monitoring student reading progress. *School Psychology Review, 32,* 45–58.

Gartner, A., & Lipsky, D. K. (Eds.). (1989). *Beyond separate education: Quality education for all.* Baltimore: Brookes.

Giangreco, M. F. (1992). Curriculum in inclusion-oriented schools: Trends, issues, challenges and potential solutions. In *Curriculum considerations in inclusive classrooms: Facilitating learning for all students.* Baltimore: Brookes.

Good, R. H., & Shinn, M. R. (1990). Forecasting accuracy of slope estimates for reading curriculum-based measurement: Empirical evidence. *Behavioral Assessment, 12,* 179–193.

Hocutt, A. M., Martin, E. W., & McKinney, J. D. (1991). Historical and legal context of mainstreaming. In J. W. Lloyd, N. N. Singh, & A. C. Repp (Eds.), *The Regular Education Initiative: Alternative perspectives on concepts, issues, and models* (pp. 17–28). Sycamore, IL: Sycamore.

Individuals with Disabilities Education Act of 1990, PL 101-476 (1990).

Illinois School Psychologists Association Task Force. (1994). *Manual for best practices on inclusion.* Springfield: Author.

Jenkins, J. R., Jewell, M., Leicester, N., O'Connor, R. E., Jenkins, L. M., & Troutner, N. M. (1994). Accommodations for individual differences without classroom ability groups: An experiment in school restructuring. *Exceptional Children, 60,* 344–358.

Jorgensen, C. M. (1995). Essential questions–Inclusive answers. *Educational Leadership, 52,* 52–55.

Lenz, B. K., Bulgren, J., Schumaker, J., Deshler, D. D., & Boudah, D. (1994). *The Unit Organizer Routine.* Lawrence, KS: Edge Enterprises.

Lenz, B. K., Marrs, R. W., Schumaker, J. B., & Deshler, D. D. (1993). *The Lesson Organizer Routine.* Lawrence, KS: Edge Enterprises.

Lloyd, J. W., Singh, N. N., & Repp, A. C. (Eds.). (1991). *The Regular Education Initiative: Alternative perspectives on concepts, issues, and models.* Sycamore, IL: Sycamore.

Louis Harris poll conducted for the National Organization on Disability. (1994). GTE Educational Network Services, Inc. Newsgroups: school.psych; date: Thu, 15 Sep 1994 12:35:41 GMT.

Nagel, D. R., Schumaker, J. B., & Deshler, D. D. (1986). *The First-Letter Mnemonic Strategy.* Lawrence, KS: Excel Enterprises.

Newman, L., & Cameto, R. (1993, April). *What makes a difference? Factors related to postsecondary school attendance for young people with disabilities.* Paper presented at the Annual Meeting of the American Educational Research Association, Atlanta, GA.

Nisbet, J., Jorgensen, C. M., & Heron, L. (1994, Spring). *Equity and excellence.* Available from Restructuring and Inclusion Project, Institute on Disability, Heidelberg-Harris Building, University of New Hampshire, Durham, NH 03824.

Odom, S. L., Deklyen, M., & Jenkins, J. R. (1984). Integrating handicapped and nonhandicapped preschoolers: Developmental impact on nonhandicapped children. *Exceptional Children, 51,* 41–48.

Parker, R., Tindall, G., & Stein, S. (1992). Estimating trend in progress monitoring data: A comparison of simple line-fitting methods. *School Psychology Review, 21,* 300–312.

Peck, C. A., Donaldson, J., & Pezzoli, M. (1990). Some benefits nonhandicapped adolescents perceive for themselves from their social relationships with peers who have severe handicaps. *Journal of the Association for Persons with Severe Handicaps, 15,* 241–249.

Rogers, J. (Ed.). (1994). *Inclusion: Moving beyond our fears.* Bloomington, IN: Center for Evaluation, Development, and Research.

Schultz, S. (1992). High marks for multimedia: Use of computers in education. *Computer Graphics World.* (Reprinted in *Inclusion: Moving beyond our fears,* by J. Rogers, Ed., 1994, Bloomington, IN: Center for Evaluation, Development, and Research)

Schumaker, J. B., Denton, J., Pegi, H., & Deshler, D. D. (1984). *The Paraphrasing Strategy.* Lawrence: University of Kansas Press.

Schumaker, J. B., & Deshler, D. D. (1995). Secondary classes can be inclusive, too. *Educational Leadership, 52*(4), 50–51.

Schumaker, J. B., Deshler, D. D., & McKnight, P. C. (1991). Teaching routines for content areas at the secondary level. In G. Stover, M. R. Shinn, & H. M. Walker (Eds.), *Interventions for achievement and behavior problems* (pp. 473–494). Washington, DC: National Association of School Psychologists.

Sharpe, M. N., York, J. N., & Knight, J. (1994). Effects of inclusion on the academic performance of classmates without disabilities: A preliminary study. *Remedial and Special Education, 15,* 281–287.

Shinn, M. R. (Ed.). (1989). *Curriculum-based measurement: Assessing special children.* New York: Guilford.

Shinn, M. R., Good, R. H., & Stein, S. (1989). Summarizing trend in student achievement: A comparison of methods. *School Psychology Review, 18,* 356–370.

Shinn, M. R., Knutson, N., Good, R. H., Tilly, W. D., & Collins, V. L. (1992). Curriculum-based measurement of oral reading fluency: A confirmatory analysis of its relation to reading. *School Psychology Review, 21,* 459–479.

Shinn, M. R., & McConnell, S. (1994). Improving general education instruction: Relevance to school psychologists. *School Psychology Review, 23,* 351–371.

Sizer, T. R. (1992). *Horace's school: Redesigning the American high school.* Boston: Houghton Mifflin.

Snell, M. E. (1991). Schools are for all kids: The importance of integration for students with severe disabilities and their peers. In J. W. Lloyd, N. N. Singh, & A. C. Repp (Eds.), *The regular education initiative: Alternative perspectives on concepts, issues, and models* (pp. 133–148). Sycamore, IL: Sycamore.

Stainback, S., & Stainback, W. (1992). *Curriculum considerations in inclusive classrooms: Facilitating learning for all students.* Baltimore: Brookes.

Staub, D., & Peck, C. A. (1995). What are the outcomes for nondisabled students? *Educational Leadership, 52,* 36–40.

Steinberg, A., & Wheelock, A. (1992/1994). After tracking—What? Middle schools find new answers. *Harvard Education Letter, 8.* (Reprinted in *Inclusion: Moving beyond our fears,* by J. Rogers, Ed., 1994, Bloomington, IN: Center for Evaluation, Development, and Research)

Truesdell, L. A. (1990). Behavior and achievement of mainstreamed junior high special class students. *Journal of Special Education, 24,* 234–245.

Wagner, M., D'Amico, R., Marder, C., Newman, L., & Blackorby, J. (1992). *What happens next? Trends in postschool outcomes of youth with disabilities.* Washington, DC: U.S. Department of Education.

Wagner, M., Newman, L., D'Amico, R., Jay, E. D., Butler-Nalin, P., Marder, C., & Cox, R. (1991). *Youth with disabilities: How are they doing?* Washington, DC: U.S. Department of Education.

Wang, M. C. (1992). *Adaptive education strategies: Building on diversity.* Baltimore: Brookes.

Wang, M., C., & Baker, E. (1986). Mainstreaming programs: Design features and effect. *Journal of Special Education, 19,* 503–521.

Wang, M. C., & Birch, J. W. (1984). Comparison of a full-time mainstreaming program and a resource room approach. *Exceptional Children, 51,* 33–40.

14

Integration in the Secondary School for Students with Severe Disabilities

DANIEL E. STEERE
ERNEST ROSE
MARY SUSAN E. FISHBAUGH

Perhaps the most perceived challenge to the concept of inclusive education is that of adolescents with severe disabilities in secondary schools. That challenge would appear insurmountable if secondary schooling were looked upon as an exclusively academic curriculum contained within the walls of a school building. Fortunately, this is not the case. For adolescents with severe disabilities, the school, home, and community have become integral domains of the curriculum and productive environments for teaching and learning. A key part of this approach is the role of the teacher, not as the individual of sole responsibility for the education of the student but as a team coordinator who works with families, other teachers, and school administrators, related services specialists, adult service providers, community businesses, and employers.

A DEFINITION OF INCLUSIVE EDUCATION

For purposes of this chapter, inclusive education is defined as the education of all children and youth, regardless of the existence of a disability and the severity of that disability, in an educational setting with either same-age peers or mixed-age individuals some of whom are the same age. The majority of these peers and other individuals do not have a defined disability, and the ratio of those with and without disabilities should approximate that which is found in the general population.

This definition is supported by Hunt and Farron-Davis (1992), who suggest that the following characteristics are indicative of inclusive practice: (a) students with disabilities attend their neighborhood or home school like all other children within a common school boundary, (b) there is a natural proportion of students with severe disabilities attending the school and general education classes, (c) students with disabilities are members of a same-aged general education classroom, (d) special classrooms are places for integrated activities and available to a variety of educational support programs, (e) IEPs for students with severe disabilities are written and implemented by both general and special education teachers, and (f) students with disabilities receive support in general education classes from special education personnel. Sailor, Gee, and Karasoff (1992) have added individual, outcomes-based decision making and site team coordination of services as key elements in their definition of inclusion.

THE LOOK OF AN INCLUSIVE HIGH SCHOOL

Over the past ten years, a number of descriptions of the inclusive school have emerged (Gartner & Lipsky, 1987; Lipsky & Gartner, 1989, 1991; Snell, 1991; Stainback & Stainback, 1985, 1992). These descriptions have the following features in common: (a) the school is a regular neighborhood school; (b) children attending the school are not labeled as "special," "at risk," "disabled," "gifted," and so forth; (c) teachers are not designated as regular or special educators; (d) children who have been traditionally labeled are not pulled out of regular classrooms but are accommodated within those classrooms; and (e) social interaction among students with and without disabilities is as important, or perhaps more so, as academic learning (Fuchs & Fuchs, 1994). The look of our inclusive high school (IHS) is a character composite of current descriptions along with some features we and other educators would like to see in the near future (for example, Wang, Walberg, & Reynolds, 1992).

Collaborative Teaming

The inclusive high school has teams of teachers that work across content areas. For each subject there is a lead teacher, but the leader in one subject will play a supportive role in another subject. The teachers on each team have been prepared to handle students with diverse needs and paces of learning.

Effective Instruction

Unlike traditional high schools, the inclusive high school does not have standard times for all classes. Some classes in the IHS do not meet every day, but some meet on Saturdays. However, when they do meet a high percentage of instructional engagement occurs, there is parental involvement, and supports are provided for students who may find the pace of instruction too fast or too slow. Materials are individualized, but learning is a cooperative experience for all members of the class.

Evaluation

In the IHS, evaluation is for everyone. The focus of evaluation is not solely on students but on programs, teachers, administration, and supporting services. The emphasis is on what works well and why, not on deficits from the normative mean. Categorical labels such as mental retardation and severe disabilities are not used. Students work toward outcomes reflective of community, state, and national goals.

Serving Diversity

The inclusive high school uses available technology to educate students with diverse needs including severe disabilities. Hardware, software, and adaptive controls enable students with disabilities to communicate in the classroom and at home with the help of a telephone and modem. A teaching team member is available until 10:00 P.M. to take on-line questions and check assignments.

School-Linked Services

Special school district programs, community and county agency services, and state agency services are coordinated through the IHS. Children and their parents go through only one application process to qualify for specialized school support services and services provided by vocational rehabilitation, mental health, developmental disabilities, family services, Medicaid, and other programs. Agency representatives and providers are available at the school on a regular basis.

The inclusive high school provides educational opportunities and services to all students within the contexts of school, home, and community. The philosophy embraces the school's obligation to provide a foundation of literacy while offering ample opportunities for practical application (Dewey, 1944).

In this chapter we will discuss the topics of academic and social inclusion within the contexts of home, school, and community. We will do this, in part, through the lives of two individuals with severe disabilities who have real dreams and real fears like other adolescents in secondary schools.

We will also describe what we believe to be important factors for an inclusive education, including aspects that are not clearly known at this time but are critical to the development of inclusive education in secondary schools.

MEET NICK AND ROBIN

Nick

Nick is a sixteen-year-old with a label of autism and mental retardation. He is six feet tall and a bit overweight. He is often seen speaking or mumbling to himself, and he will engage in stereotypic behaviors such as waving his hands and humming in a falsetto voice. Nick prefers to be alone, avoiding people unless he wishes to interact with them. He loves to eat, and he particularly loves Diet Mountain Dew.

The profile of Nick that his parents have developed shows that he has many positive characteristics: he is gentle with his younger siblings; he is able to remember dates, significant people, and significant events long after most other people have forgotten them; he can take care of his dressing, grooming, and meal needs; he can use the bus system without assistance; and he reads most written material he encounters in his daily life. Nick also has an extremely supportive family who have taken an active role in his educational program. They want Nick to have the opportunity to live, work, and recreate in inclusive community environments. Mostly, they want him to develop fulfilling and meaningful relationships so that he will have a network of caring support at all times.

Recently, Nick has demonstrated an increasing oversensitivity to noises. Concurrently, he has developed extremely challenging behavior, including screaming, throwing furniture and other objects, and striking other people. These behaviors have created increasing difficulties, both at home and at school. His teachers continue to want to see Nick succeed, but they are frustrated and confused by his behavior. In addition, Nick's nondisabled school peers are concerned and at times frightened by his behavior. No one appears to understand fully the reason for these behaviors, and predicting when outbursts will occur is difficult. Nick's parents and his team are baffled by these outbursts, and they have not come to agreement about what causes these reactions and what to do about them. Despite these current problems, Nick's family and his educational team remain committed to affording him full options for life in an inclusive community.

Robin

Robin is sixteen years old and has mental retardation. She is rather overweight and has webbed fingers and a slight speech disorder. Robin is a pleasant, friendly person with a tendency to engage in stereotypical behavior. She can become quite upset, almost hysterical, if teased or taunted. Robin has long red hair that her mother fixes in a single braid in back. Her most common stereotypy is to pull her braid to the front, hold it in her right hand, and flick it back and forth while holding her left hand to her cheek and moving it in a waving motion. She is obsessed with canvas mail bags and frequently talks about how fearful she is of mail bags and anything of a like texture. There is speculation that some children put a mail bag over her head when she was younger, but there is no documentation, and Robin has never verified such a story.

Robin's academic skills are barely at a first-grade level, and she has problems participating in academic activities in high school courses. Robin does benefit from the social atmosphere, and she has begun to interact more appropriately with other students at the school. Robin's parents and teachers agree that she needs a program that will enable her to continue to make progress in appropriate social interactions, while preparing her for meaningful and gainful employment during her adult years. Robin's training as a hotel maid has gone slowly. Her performance in both quality and rate has been unacceptable for employment standards.

Robin also has problems in preparing for more independent living arrangements. She will not make her bed without prompting and rarely volunteers for tasks that need to be done. She can perform only the simplest meal preparation tasks (such as making cold cereal, toast, microwave popcorn). She can wash and dry her clothes with some modeling but cannot fold them without continued guidance. Robin is quite dependent on her parents, and they are beginning to question how well she will fare once they are too old to care for her. Nevertheless, they and Robin's teachers are committed to preparing her for life in an inclusive community.

FOUNDATIONS OF INCLUSIVE SECONDARY SCHOOLS

Policy and Law

Although inclusive practice is not a mandate of the Individuals with Disabilities Education Act (IDEA), it is in fact the spirit of IDEA's Least Restrictive Environment (LRE) clause, Section 504 of the Rehabilitation Act of 1973, and the Americans with Disabilities Act (ADA). IDEA requires that a team meet to determine the best program for a student with disabilities by developing educational goals and objectives, and then deciding on a placement that will support achievement of the proposed program. The assumption is that this placement will be the mainstream of regular education. A more restrictive setting is suggested only if the individual's education cannot be achieved in a normalized environment with supplementary aids and services.

Section 504 demands that regular educators make regular program adaptations and regular curricular modifications for students who have or are perceived to have a "disability" as defined by that law. All special education students are candidates for Section 504 services, but not all Section 504 students qualify under the thirteen disabling categories as defined by IDEA. Section 504 mandates that we not discriminate against students by denying them either the access or the opportunity to enjoy educational programs because they do not fit our preconceived curricular mold.

The Learning Disabilities Association of America (1994) cites a 1993 Senate Education Committee report that suggests the premise on which the Americans with Disabilities Act rests is that disabilities is a natural part of the human experience. Individuals with disabilities have the right to live independently, make choices, contribute to society, and enjoy full inclusion and integration in all aspects of American society. The ADA impacts all aspects of American life, including education.

Case law, resulting from court responses to both IDEA and Section 504, consistently reinforces inclusive practice (*Board of Education v. Rowley,* 1982; *Irving Independent School District v. Tatro,* 1984). Through the case *Daniel R.R. v. State Board of Education,* the court reinforced four principles for deciding on the appropriateness of inclusion: (a) educational benefit for the student with disabilities, (b) nonacademic benefit, (c) effect of the student's presence on the other students and, (d) cost of inclusion with supplementary aids and services (*Daniel R.R. v. State Board of Education,* 1989; *Roncker v. Walter,* 1983). Using this balancing test, the courts have found in favor of including both Rachel Holland, a child with moderate mental retardation (*Board of Education of Sacramento Unified School District v. Holland,* 1992), and a boy with Down's syndrome and significant behavioral disabilities in regular educational settings (*Oberti v. Clementon Board of Education,* 1993). Thus, the courts have determined that the burden of proof for restrictive educational programming, in settings removed from the educational mainstream, lies with the school and is increasingly difficult to support.

The most recent federal initiative in education is the Goals 2000: Educate America Act. According to the Senate Education Committee report (Learning Disabilities Association, 1994), the needs of students with disabilities have been considered throughout this legislation, so that America's educational goals are applicable to all students. The committee has addressed students with disabilities in each of the six national education goals: school readiness; school completion; student achievement and citizenship; mathematics and science; adult literacy and lifelong learning; and safe, disciplined, and drug-free schools. The intent of both Section 504 and the ADA has been applied to Goals 2000, so that rather than discriminating against persons with disabilities, the mandates of the Goals 2000 Act can be appropriately adapted and modified.

Policy statements from professional education organizations seem polarized, but on closer scrutiny they may be perceived as mere arguments in semantics. The American Federation of Teachers (AFT; Gorman & Rose, 1994) and the Learning Disabilities Association of America (LDA; 1994) have both made strong position statements against full inclusion. Their opposition, however, rests on implementation of inclusive practice without attention to class size, teacher education, and needed supports. Both groups state that expecting all students to achieve equally in the same manner is unrealistic and detrimental to all students' achievement. Groups such as the National Education Association (NEA; 1994) and the Council of Administrators of Special Education (CASE; 1993) strongly support inclusion and would not disagree with the specific objections voiced by the AFT and LDA. Clearly, inclusive practice is supported by federal legislation, by state and federal case law, and by professional organization policy statements.

Demonstrations

Initial demonstrations of the development of successful inclusion at the secondary level include those in Vermont (Cross & Villa, 1992; Schattman, 1992) and Wisconsin (Brown et al., 1989). Since the development of these initial demonstration projects, additional demonstrations of secondary-level inclusion have occurred in many other parts of the United States and Canada, including San Francisco, New Brunswick, and other cities.

Some of the most compelling pioneering work in demonstrating inclusion at all grade and age levels occurred in the Madison Metropolitan School District in Wisconsin (Brown et al., 1987). Since the 1970s, Brown and his colleagues at the University of Wisconsin–Madison have reported the abilities of students to succeed in integrated and inclusive schools. With Brown's leadership, Madison has become an example of a district that has made major strides toward inclusion.

Vermont's demonstrations have included those in the Winooski School System, a suburb of Burlington, and the Franklin Northwest Supervisory Union, a collection of five independent school districts in the northwest part of the state (Cross & Villa, 1992; Schattman, 1992). Like the demonstrations in Wisconsin and other parts of the country, those in Vermont are reported as being a longitudinal metamorphosis from a traditional approach to education to a restructured organization that supports inclusion (Schattman, 1992).

We should note that, at present, more demonstrations have been reported at the elementary level than at the secondary level. We believe that more secondary-level demonstrations will emerge as students who have been educated in inclusive settings at the elementary level enter high school and as more districts make a commitment to inclusion at all levels.

Research

The major research that has occurred in the area of inclusion has been in the form of case studies of school districts that have moved to total inclusion (Brown et al., 1987; Cross & Villa, 1992; Schattman, 1992). We should note that these case studies typically reflect districts that have made a major commitment to inclusion at the philosophical/mission and policy levels. Thus, these case studies do not focus on whether inclusion works but rather how it works, what challenges are encountered, and how they have been addressed.

The commitment to inclusion is based on earlier research in the development of integrated schools for students with severe disabilities. Much of this research highlighted the enhancement of positive attitudes by nondisabled learners when they spent time in close, personal interaction with peers with disabilities (Brinker & Thorpe, 1983; Schnorr, 1990; Voeltz, 1980, 1982). The inclusion movement is also fueled by criticisms of the continuum approach to services at both the educational level (Taylor, 1988) and the adult service level (Bellamy, Rhodes, Bourbeau, & Mank, 1986). These writings highlighted the failure of a continuum approach to facilitate movement of children, youth, or adults to inclusive environments. Taken together, the attitude change studies and those that document the failure of a continuum approach to education and adult services support the position that social inclusion is the desired outcome for all students and that other approaches to "getting ready for inclusion" have not demonstrated success.

Finally, emerging research is documenting additional outcomes of inclusive education. For example, Kennedy and Itkonen (1994) used single-subject research methodology to document increases in durable, frequent social contacts for three students with severe disabilities as a result of inclusion in regular classrooms. Continuing to extend this type of research will be extremely beneficial. It should refine our knowledge regarding the implementation of teaching practices within inclusive settings that enhance social interaction both within school and in other environments.

ORGANIZING THE SECONDARY-LEVEL CURRICULUM

Choosing Desirable Outcomes

One practical way to begin developing inclusive practice for secondary students with severe disabilities is using the McGill Action Planning System (MAPS) (Forest & Pearpoint, 1992). Through this process, optimal educational outcomes and the best settings in which to achieve them can be decided. Analogous to a map that provides direction for a road trip, this educational "MAP" provides a starting point, ending point, and direction from one to the other for an individual educational journey. This direction is acquired through answers to seven questions: (a) Who is the student? (b) What is his or her story? (c) What are his or her unique talents? (d) What are his or her unique needs? (e) What are his or her dreams? (f) What are his or her nightmares? (g) How do we avoid the nightmares and make the dreams come true? (Forest & Pearpoint, 1992). These questions are posed to anyone with an interest in normalizing and improving the quality of life for and with the student.

The sequence of events for developing a MAP might progress as follows. In the spring of Nick's eighth-grade year, an IEP annual review meeting was scheduled to determine progress on current goals and objectives and to discuss his future transition from high school to the world of work. But this meeting was different from any that Nick's parents had previously attended. Nick's teacher told Nick's mother that it was time for his annual review but that she wanted to try a novel process and asked when it would be convenient for both parents to meet for a couple of hours. She encouraged Nick's mother to invite any other friends or relatives who knew Nick well and might have insight into his future needs. Two weeks later on a warm spring evening, Nick, his parents, and a family friend who had known Nick since birth arrived at school and were ushered into the school's new "living room." Formerly an unused smokers' lounge, this living room had been transformed by community donations and volunteer labor into an attractive room complete with comfortable chairs, ceiling fans, and an espresso machine. There was ample room for Nick's special education teacher, classroom aide, the junior and senior high school principals, the high school guidance counselor, Nick, his parents, and their friend. For the first time in their experience, Nick's parents were given an unhurried opportunity to talk to the school personnel about their son, and Nick had a chance to express his own desires and fears. The educators asked the MAPS questions listed earlier, listened, and took notes on big sheets of chart paper that were then displayed around the room for everyone to read and reflect on. After the meeting, the special education teacher and counselor translated minutes of the meeting into formal IEP goals and objectives for Nick's freshman year in high school.

The process of developing a MAP promotes inclusive practice through its focus on the person. Traditional IEP meetings frequently occur in a sterile school environment that may be uncomfortable to the point of threatening for parents. The IEP goals and objectives are viewed from the perspective of available school programs and disability labels rather than from the personal perspective of the student. Educators talk, parents listen, and routine decisions result. The use of MAPS embodies the spirit of IDEA by directing everyone's attention to the student. Segregated settings become less defensible when we consider the gifts, needs, dreams, and nightmares of each unique student.

MAPS is only one of several possible ways currently being used to develop meaningful and truly individualized educational plans. The reader is referred to the positive futures planning approach described by Mount and Zwernik (1988) or to lifestyle planning described by O'Brien (1987) for alternative planning methods.

Functional Curriculum Domains

Early efforts in curriculum design for students with severe disabilities were based on the acquisition of skills. That is, isolated skill areas, such as self-care skills or language skills, were targeted for remediation. A more functional and community-referenced approach to curriculum development, the domain-based curriculum, was clarified by Brown and his colleagues from the University of

Wisconsin–Madison during the 1970s (Brown, Branston-McLean, Baumgart, Vincent, Falvey, & Schroeder, 1979; Brown, Nietupski, & Hamre-Nietupski, 1976). This curricular approach organized all educational activities into four domains of daily living: domestic, vocational, leisure, and community. The underlying rationale for a domain-based approach to curriculum development is that community life in general is not organized by skills but rather by broad areas of activity in which most members of local communities engage. Rather than addressing isolated remedial skill development, such as a specific self-care lesson conducted at a specific time within a classroom, teachers provide activities within a natural context and at appropriate times. For example, one learns to tie shoes and get dressed during the natural activity of gym class, not during an isolated and artificial dressing lesson.

Wilcox and Bellamy (1987) refined the domain-based curriculum approach to include three domains: employment, leisure, and personal management. Employment domain activities involve all of those related to working in general community environments. Leisure domain activities include all nonwork activities that are done for enjoyment. Personal management activities entail all activities intended to maintain one's health and appearance, one's home, and so forth.

A major facet of a domain-based curriculum is that specific activities to be taught under each domain are determined through a detailed analysis of current and likely future environments. This ecological inventory strategy (Brown et al., 1979) increases the likelihood that the curriculum reflects the demands of current and future local communities. In addition, activities are selected for instruction that reflect environments that are or will be frequented by specific students. Thus, individualization of curricular content is enhanced.

The major impact of the domain-based approach to curriculum development is that it avoids isolated skills development, conducting instead activities within a logical framework of community life. From this perspective, a domain-based curriculum is community referenced; that is, it reflects the true demands of living within a particular community.

Using Functional Activities Across Domains

Once teachers, service providers, and parents begin using a domain-based approach to educating students with severe disabilities, similar activities across domains are used to emphasize maintenance and generalization of acquired behaviors. For example, on most school days Nick eats in the high school cafeteria. Unlike the cafeterias of old, he can now order a hot lunch, sandwiches from the grill, or prepackaged sandwiches, salads, and other fare. When he is in the community, Nick is learning to order foods at fast-food restaurants. Several similarities exist:

- He must wait in line.
- He must read from overhead menus.
- He must make selections from different sections of the menu if he wants additional items with his meal.

- He must clearly communicate what foods he wants to the employee.
- He will either pay for his food or present a meal card.
- He will probably have to use a self-service station for a tray, utensils, and, perhaps, beverages.
- He must carry his food to a table.
- When he has finished eating, he must carry his tray to a cleanup area and will most likely have to separate dishware, utensils, and trash into separate receptacles.

Additionally, Nick will learn this routine from a number of different people, including his parents and siblings, teachers, and peer advocates from school. Consistency in their understanding of the routine and use of a prompting hierarchy is essential for Nick to acquire, maintain, and generalize the routine at school and in the community. Because Nick likes to eat, learning the routine has a built-in reward.

In Robin's case, her parents and teachers have identified increasing Robin's rate of dressing as an important objective under her personal management domain. There are three occasions per week when Robin must dress twice during the school day. Dressing for school is the first, and dressing after her aerobics class is the other. If she is too slow in the morning, she will miss her ride to school. If she is too slow after her aerobics class, she will miss the most direct route bus back to her neighborhood. The ultimate goal is to increase Robin's personal independence so that she will not have to rely on intensive prompting from individuals to make sure she meets time lines and transitions. She has made progress, but, predictably, it has been slow.

FACTORS FOR SUCCESS

We have endorsed the domain-based approach to curriculum as an effective framework for inclusive education. But for this approach to bring about a true integration, the participation of a variety of people is essential. Quite obviously, family and teachers will be involved, but the participation of peers with and without disabilities is also a key to success (Stainback, Stainback, East, & Sapon-Shevin, 1994).

Three factors create opportunities for interaction: the setting, the individual(s), and the situation. As professionals, we have written generally about settings for teaching and learning. We write about schools, and we believe we have an understanding of their promise and their shortcomings. We write about homes and communities, and we think we understand their uses as educational environments. However, as educators we rarely investigate the private worlds and social milieus of teenagers as do our colleagues in sociology, anthropology, and, occasionally, journalism (Ventura, 1993). We are concerned about the potential for isolation and depression of adolescents with disabilities, but our discussions are often fragmented and not considered within the holistic context of society. For example, we really do not know much about teenagers with disabilities who are homeless, who commit violent crimes, who are addicted to alcohol and other drugs.

As we consider the positive side of integration, we must also concede that we will have less control over situations that will affect the safety and well-being of adolescents with disabilities. They will have to consider and make decisions they may not have made before and begin to trust the advice of peers much more than ever. One of our greatest challenges will be to organize increasing opportunities for choices while teaching the responsibility that comes with making choices, for all adolescents, not just those with disabilities.

Meaningful Choices

Until recently, people with disabilities have been afforded few opportunities to learn how to make choices and then exercise their rights to do so (Guess, Benson, & Siegel-Causey, 1985). Both small issues (what one eats, how one dresses, and so forth) and larger choices (where one lives or spends each day) have been left to professionals who were presumed to have the knowledge and expertise to make such choices.

Increasingly, attention has turned toward active instruction in choice making from an early age. In addition, as highlighted earlier, planning processes such as positive futures planning (Mount & Zwernik, 1988) have reasserted the focus person's role in making their own decisions with support from caring others. Efforts to teach students with severe disabilities to make choices is an essential issue at the secondary level. All adolescents are faced with numerous decisions, including those regarding employment, housing, relationships, and many other aspects of community living. Students with severe disabilities will need both increased support to learn how to make choices and numerous opportunities to practice the exercise of choices.

A key consideration in enhancing students' abilities to make meaningful choices is the provision of a sufficient range of experiences to allow informed choices. This issue alone provides a strong rationale for a school curriculum rich with community-based and community-referenced activities. Syzmanski (1994) offers excellent recommendations for a longitudinal, "life span" approach to transition planning, with particular emphasis on career awareness, as a strategy for empowering adolescents to make more informed choices. For example, she highlights the importance of providing opportunities for career fantasizing so that, from a young age, students learn about different careers and their positive and negative aspects.

Systematic Instruction

Learners with severe disabilities require systematic instruction that is provided in a precise and persistent manner. Educators must begin with an assumption that students will need to be taught to participate in valued school and community activities and that without such instruction, students' abilities to participate will be severely limited.

Steere and Pancsofar (1995) define the instructional process to be one of assisting students with severe disabilities to (a) recognize and attend to salient environmental and social cues and then (b) respond appropriately to these cues. This definition focuses on the need for all members of complex community environments to be able not only to discriminate among the myriad sounds, sights, textures, odors, and so forth, but also then to act on those that are most relevant or important (Horner, Sprague, & Wilcox, 1984). These complex stimuli, which exist in abundance in all school and community environments, may be referred to as natural cues (Pancsofar, 1992). The purpose of systematic instruction, then, is to help draw attention to natural cues and the desired responses to them.

A key orientation to systematic instruction is that of Gold (1980), who asserts that when an individual with severe disabilities fails to learn a task, the instructor has not brought sufficient teaching power to the instructional situation. In essence, this orientation states that people can learn if instructors structure the learning situation carefully. Instructors must, therefore, develop strategies for teaching that use careful and systematic environmental analyses to organize the teaching situation so that salient natural cues are highlighted (Bellamy, Horner, & Inman, 1979).

Pancsofar and Blackwell (1986) recommend organizing strategies for systematic instruction into three categories: (a) those that are used before the learner responds to the natural cues (antecedent strategies), (b) those that follow a response (respondent strategies), and (c) those that modify the task in some manner (task modification strategies). Using an analogy that systematic instructional strategies are "tools of the trade," we can view these three categories as sections of the toolbox (Pancsofar, 1992).

One important antecedent strategy is the use of prompting sequences or hierarchies. A least prompting sequence is one in which assistance to draw attention to a salient natural cue is arranged in a sequence of providing the least amount of assistance that may elicit a correct response to a controlling prompt that is certain to elicit the response (Doyle, Wolery, Ault, & Gast, 1988). For example, a least prompting sequence to draw attention to the natural cue of the price label on a grocery item might be as follows:

1. Allow opportunity for the learner to respond to the cue.
2. If no response occurs, ask a nonspecific verbal prompt such as "Robin, where is the price tag?"
3. Allow response. If no response occurs, then add a more specific verbal prompt such as, "Robin, the price tag is on the bottom of the box."
4. Allow response. If no response occurs, then add a verbal and gestural prompt: "Look here on the bottom of the box."

This is only one example of a least prompting sequence. As with all instructional strategies, least prompting must be adapted to the needs of each learner.

Consequent strategies include the use of effective reinforcers, including those that naturally occur in community environments, such as compliments, paychecks, and so forth. Learners often need multiple, longitudinal experiences with such natural reinforcers before they become motivated by them. Educators must remember that students with severe disabilities can learn to respond to natural reinforcers over time if these reinforcers are systematically paired with current motivators. For example, a paycheck may have little meaning until it is associated with currency, which is in turn associated with a current reinforcer such as going out to lunch.

Task modification strategies include the use of more detailed or "branched" task analyses, as well as adaptations or modifications to an activity or the materials used to accomplish it. Changing the sequence of steps on a complex activity is an example.

These are only a few strategies for systematic instruction, and presenting a comprehensive overview of all well-documented strategies is beyond the scope of this chapter. Specific strategies for teaching are, as Pancsofar (1992) notes, merely tools of the trade and cannot replace the creativity and problem solving that is necessary to use them effectively. The most important ingredients for successful use of systematic instruction is a belief that all students can learn to respond to natural cues if instruction is structured and presented effectively.

Issues Related to Professional Development

Although the strategies of systematic instruction are well known to teachers prepared to educate students with severe disabilities, these are not strategies commonly taught in elementary and secondary teacher education programs; nor are they routinely offered at professional development workshops for veteran teachers. In fact, teachers receive their professional preparation in separate teacher education programs—one for general education and one for special education. Except for a few professional core courses, there is typically little contact between the two groups (Rose, 1994).

Changing this programmatic structure will be a critical element in the movement toward widespread inclusive education. We cannot expect teachers, with the many responsibilities they already have, to embrace the appearance of added work in a time of shrinking resources. Inclusion is a concept that must be considered in the broadest context of educational reform and restructuring (Skrtic, 1991). We must recognize children with disabilities within this context, which includes issues related to multicultural diversity, as well as gender and cultural access and equity.

The importance of consulting, collaborating, and teaming has been well documented as it regards benefiting both students and teachers (Friend, 1984; Morsink, Thomas, & Correa, 1991). If we accept these practices as positive, they must be embraced in teacher education programs. That is, professors should be demonstrating these practices as they teach curriculum theory and development and use instructional methods related to the variety of content taught at the elementary and secondary levels. Therefore, if we expect teachers in general and special education to consult, collaborate, and team in our high schools, professors who teach these subjects should do so in our teacher education programs in colleges and universities. Such a practice would thus mirror the reform and restructuring taking place in the K–12 school system.

Likewise, continued professional development for teachers from induction periods onward should emphasize methods for including students with all types of special needs, including severe disabilities. The point, of course, is not that the regular education teacher is the primary instructor for all students but that he or she has a repertoire of strategies to ensure inclusion through examples such as co-operative learning, peer coaching, and support from paraprofessionals or parents.

Functional Assessments

Functional assessment, as opposed to traditional norm-referenced, intelligence, and achievement measures, is a means of evaluating a student's competence in areas directly related to the student's life experience. Functional assessment is essential for successful inclusion. Inclusive practice demands that educational excellence as required by Goals 2000 be defined on a student-by-student basis. What constitutes a challenging education for one student will vary for other students. Ecologically referenced functional assessment is the means for defining educational outcomes to be expected of students with severe disabilities.

Wiggins (1993) has discussed the need for more authentic testing at length. He criticizes the decontextualization of most tests and the simplistic nature of individual test items. He calls for a new look at "face validity." Does a test appear to measure what it purports to measure? A good test will require application of principles to contextualized situations. Functional assessment is exactly that—evaluation of skill competence in the context where that skill is needed and used.

Pancsofar, Steere, and Wood (1993) have listed ten factors to be considered in assessment for supported employment. With minimal modification, these ten factors apply to functional assessment for school inclusion. First, the assessment should emphasize competence, rather than deficiency. Second, assessment should identify supports needed rather than serve as a means of screening students out of the mainstream. Third, in relationship to the planning process, assessment is the compass from which to chart an individual's educational course. Fourth, there should be some choice as to the means and formatting of assessment delivery. Fifth, results of assessments should be analyzed by the family, the student, if possible, and the assessor. Sixth, from an ecological perspective, assessment should emphasize understanding relationships in the individual's present and future life. Seventh, assessing the school environment is as important as assessing the individual. Eighth, standardized assessments have little predictive validity for the student's success in achieving individual educational goals and objectives. Ninth, assessment should measure outcomes from an educational program related to quality of life, which may be more important than academic skill for a student with severe disabilities. Finally, the primary purpose for educational assessment should be to help answer how to include an individual with severe disabilities in regular educational programs.

Increasingly, portfolios are being used for student evaluation (DeFina, 1992; Glazer & Brown, 1993; O'Neil, 1993), a practice that allows a teacher to see progress through a student's products. Portfolios are framed in many styles depending on the purpose. Likewise, items chosen as portfolio exhibits differ depending on the portfolio's purpose. Such a measure can provide a better, more thorough, more well-rounded perspective of student academic achievement and social growth than either norm-referenced or criterion-referenced tests.

Family Support and Involvement

Inclusion demands a collaborative community. Obviously, that collaboration involves educators, but it also involves parents and students. Inclusive educational practice means opening the high school doors for parents. It means respecting the student's family by making the following assumptions: (a) the best place to grow is in a family, (b) each family is a system, (c) parents know their child's needs, (d) the family is the child's best advocate, (e) families want to be involved, (f) educators should support families, (g) parents can question educators, (h) an individual's disability need not be negative and is not the only aspect of the person, and (i) everyone's concern should be the long term (Powell, Hecimovic, & Christensen, 1992).

Employing the MAPS process (Forest & Pearpoint, 1992) for educational planning (described earlier) is an excellent start for parental involvement. Listening to parents and the student in that process provides a form of moral support. Knowing what parents face during the student's out-of-school hours helps educators and parents plan in-school programs that become neither an additional burden to parents nor an additional source of frustration to teachers.

What might Robin's family support look like? Because Robin's parents both work, they cannot be as involved in her high school day as they might like. Although Robin's father is comanager of an office supply business and works during the day, her mother is a nurse and works at night in a hospital emergency room. For the teachers to ask for much weekday follow-up to Robin's daily school tasks is often unrealistic. But teachers and parents agreed that Robin might practice her maid's training by folding laundry, a help to her mother, and might improve her independent living skills by warming leftovers in the microwave for supper, a load off her dad's mind. In addition, Robin and her parents have been referred to the supported employment project at a local university so they can begin now, during her high school sophomore year, to plan for her involvement in this project after she graduates.

Supporting the student's family demonstrates respect for them by school personnel. As opposed to one more duty assigned to the teachers, involving families in planning and implementing a student's educational plan can itself be a source of support for both the family and the teachers. The teamwork that ensues from such a collaborative effort can actually lessen the burden of responsibility on any one of the team members and can allow each member time to enjoy the student's personal development and educational progress.

A Focus on Transition

Even with the best curriculum, the desired outcome of a smooth transition from educational services into employment and community living does not happen without proactive planning. Ongoing studies have confirmed that posteducational outcomes are generally poor for students with disabilities, and particularly those with severe disabilities such as Nick and Robin (DeStefano & Wagner, 1992; Peraino, 1992). In reauthorizing PL 94-142 (the Education of All Handicapped Children Act) as the Individuals with Disabilities Education Act (IDEA, PL 101-476), Congress added a mandate for transition planning for all students with disabilities no later than age sixteen and as early as age fourteen. With the passage of IDEA, a clear national agenda has been established to enhance the outcomes of transition so that students with disabilities leave school to begin productive lives of employment and community living in inclusive community environments.

Transition planning involves agreement by educational team members of desired posteducational outcomes for specific students (Wehman, 1992). This planning, however, requires the difficult work of clarifying a vision of postschool success on an individual basis. This is difficult for any young person, as issues of self-image, increasing independence, mobility, and sexuality emerge during adolescence (Wehman, 1992). For students with severe disabilities and their families, this task can become even more daunting.

Several elements contribute to more successful transition outcomes for students with severe disabilities. First, a commitment by educators to listening to the dreams and fears of students and their families for their futures is essential. This implies that students and families are able to plan and review information in environments that are comfortable for them and conducive to collaborative planning. Second, students and their families require accurate and complete information about funded services that are available upon graduation, as well as referral processes, waiting lists, and so forth. Third, they require assistance in organizing their own informal, nonpaid networks of family members and friends who can be counted on to assist with job searches, location of apartments, and other essential activities.

An additional element that clearly enhances transition outcomes is collaboration among service agencies and the schools (Wehman, 1992). Several authors have expanded this consideration to include collaboration among other community members who should have a vested interested in the success of transition efforts (Minnesota Department of Education Interagency Office on Transition Services, 1989). These community members include local business and political leaders, representatives from postsecondary educational agencies, and other educators. As Wehman (1992) asserts, "[T]ransition is predominantly a local challenge, and local forces within communities must pull together to make transition a reality" (p. 81).

Finally, as discussed earlier in relation to curriculum, students require a range of community experiences to make informed choices. Expecting young people, regardless of disability, to make informed decisions about their futures is unreasonable if they have not experienced and reflected on different work and general community activities. Although the number and type of community experiences that can be provided or arranged will clearly be limited to some degree by school staff and other resources, the impact of a curriculum rich in community experience on effective transition planning cannot be overemphasized.

Assistive Technology

Recent legislation, including IDEA and the 1988 Technology-Related Assistance for Individuals with Disabilities Act, or Tech Act (PL 100-407), have asserted the essential role of assistive technology as a potential support for individuals with severe disabilities. The potential benefits of assistive technology in the areas of vocational preparation for secondary-level students with severe disabilities have received increased attention (Sowers & Powers, 1991), as has the area of augmentative and alternative communication systems (Baumgart, Johnson, & Helmstetter, 1990). It is clear that the rapid development of assistive technology holds great promise for opening expanded opportunities in the areas of employment and community living for individuals with severe disabilities.

A persistent and serious challenge to the effective use of assistive technology is technology abandonment, or the cessation of use of technology by people with disabilities (Phillips & Zhao, 1993). Although users of technology apparently cease to use particular devices for a variety of reasons (for example, changes in lifestyle, advances in technology, and so forth), a major predictor of technology abandonment is the lack of consideration for the opinion of the user (Phillips & Zhao, 1993). That is, people with disabilities are apparently more likely to abandon assistive technology devices if they are not involved in the decision-making process for obtaining technology. This effect is not surprising as assistive technology is not simply a set of devices but part of a broader system of supports that must fit within the overall lifestyle of the individual.

In response to this issue, an alternative planning process called the Solution Circle was developed by the Alliance for Technology Access (Kelker, 1993). Based on other approaches to lifestyle planning, such as the MAPS process described earlier, the Solution Circle process relies on a team of individuals who know the target individual well and care about him or her. The process begins with a clarification of the individual's strengths, abilities, dreams, and aspirations as the context for the selection of technology. Technology is only discussed within the context of broader lifestyle issues as a potential "solution" to challenges that impede the attainment of dreams and aspirations. This approach is substantially different from a traditional approach to technology prescription based solely on evaluation by professionals with expertise in assistive technology.

Transdisciplinary Teaming

Morsink et al. (1991) suggest that there are three types of teaming: (a) multidisciplinary, in which all members report to the leader; (b) interdisciplinary, in which each member has their own say as participant of an assessment meeting; and (c) transdisciplinary, in which members hold and release roles depending on their individual interest and expertise for assessment, program, and placement decisions. The transdisciplinary team is a group of persons who interact with parity. Members of such a team have roles and responsibilities that change as the student's needs change. The transdisciplinary team is based on mutual respect and a sense of community among individual members. It is the transdisciplinary team that will be most effective for inclusion of students with severe disabilities in high school.

Meeting the educational needs of students with one or more intensive challenges involves many professionals and paraprofessionals from different areas of expertise. In addition to teachers and school administrators, counselors, school psychologists, occupational and physical therapists, speech and language pathologists, classroom aides, biological and/or foster parents, medical personnel, community agency representatives, and others will also engage in the process. All these people, together and individually, have an important role to play in providing a quality educational program for students. No one of these team members is always in a position to lead the team. The importance of their individual roles within the team structure should ebb and flow depending on the current needs of an individual student. At some times, a team member may serve as a consultant to the other members (Idol, Nevin, & Paolucci-Whitcomb, 1994). At other times, he or she may be a peer coach for a teammate. And at regular intervals, the team should meet as a whole to redefine goals, clarify direction, and interact as a transdisciplinary body. Such intensive collaboration, based on a common vision and mutual respect, should result in valid inclusive practice.

Teaching for Generalization

A significant challenge for many students with severe disabilities is the generalization or transfer of abilities from one set of conditions to another (Stokes & Baer, 1977; Brown et al., 1976). Brown et al. (1976) assert that educators should adopt a "zero degree inference" strategy; that is, they should assume that no generalization occurs unless active and systematic efforts to teach for generalization have occurred. They go on to indicate that educators should not be satisfied that generalization has occurred until the student can complete a targeted activity in three different environments, with three different people or instructors, and with three different sets of materials. The clear message from these recommendations is that educators must not assume that students with severe disabilities will generalize their skills to a new set of conditions. Instead, specific strategies must be employed during the instructional process to enhance the likelihood that generalization will indeed occur in a variety of novel situations.

One powerful strategy for enhancing generalization is referred to as general case programming. Adapting the work of Becker and Engelmann in the area of academic instruction to students with learning disabilities (Becker, Engelmann & Thomas, 1975; Engelmann & Carnine, 1982), Horner and his colleagues at the University of Oregon demonstrated the efficacy of general case programming with a range of functional activities required in most community environments (Horner, Sprague, & Wilcox, 1984). In general case programming, an instructor surveys community environments to determine the range of conditions under which a targeted community activity is completed. The full range of conditions that might be encountered is then documented and analyzed. From a detailed analysis of this information, a set of teaching examples is drawn that samples the range of possible variation in the targeted activity. Instruction is conducted across these teaching examples, while generalization is assessed on a parallel set of probe examples chosen from the same analysis. The general case strategy has been documented as effective in teaching a range of community activities, including crossing streets (Horner, Jones, & Williams, 1985), using soap dispensers (Pancsofar & Bates, 1985), opening containers in fast-food restaurants (Steere, Strauch, Powell, & Butterworth, 1990), operating coin-operated vending machines (Sprague & Horner, 1984), participating in vocational assembly activities (Horner & McDonald, 1982), busing cafeteria tables (Horner, Eberhard, & Sheehan, 1986), selecting items in a grocery store (Horner, Albin, & Ralph, 1986), and putting on pullover shirts (Day & Horner, 1986). The use of a general case programming strategy to teaching community activities increases the likelihood that students with severe disabilities will generalize their abilities to a range of situations in their local communities.

BEYOND EIGHTEEN: IS HIGH SCHOOL THE BEST PLACE?

For many years, special educators have discussed the importance of age-appropriate settings and curriculum for students with severe disabilities (Brown et al., 1979; McDonnell & Hardman, 1986; Wilcox & Bellamy, 1982, 1987). The same issues go beyond high school into extended education and preparation for employment. Earlier in this chapter we have discussed the need and provided some examples for developing social contacts and friendships among students with and without disabilities. The concept behind this work is violated if the advocates and friends of individuals without disabilities move on to other phases of their lives and their peers with disabilities do not.

The high school can be a convenience. In many ways it is a single-point service provider, and parents may prefer it over the variety of community and state agencies that provide services for adults. Nevertheless, in the seven years of service eligibility (ages fifteen to twenty-one), the entire student body of a high school will have turned over almost two times. Rightly, the attention and efforts of teachers and parents should be focused on the social integration of students with disabilities in the current four-year class groups, not those who have graduated.

Fortunately, now more and better options are available for individuals with disabilities outside high school as the primary setting (see Rusch, 1990; Rusch, DeStefano, Chadsey-Rusch, Phelps, & Syzmanski, 1992). Some of these options include adult education centers, community colleges, vocational-technical schools, and independent living centers. We will point out again the importance of using the community as an extended classroom and the need for thoughtful transition planning and implementation. These frameworks allow for the development of friends and advocates in the context of community as well as in school and continue educational experiences related to living and working in the community. As educators of students with severe disabilities, we must attempt to set our transition outcomes for age eighteen and then transfer service and training provisions to our adult service counterparts. As advocates for individuals with severe disabilities, we must work to see that adequate service and training funds are available from ages eighteen through twenty-one in organizations other than schools, when appropriate.

FOLLOW-UP OF GRADUATES

The true impact of an inclusive secondary educational program is best assessed through follow-up information gathered about students who have graduated or left the auspices of educational services. On a national level, follow-up studies of individuals with disabilities paint a dismal picture of students leaving school unprepared to live in inclusive communities (DeStefano & Wagner, 1992; Peraino, 1992). With transition planning now mandated through the IDEA, Congress has clarified the urgent need to improve the current situation and increase the number of students with severe disabilities who leave the auspices of educational services with a paid community job in hand, a place to live in their community, and the abilities and supports to succeed in complex community environments.

Follow-up of graduates is equally important on a local level. It is important to note that follow-up, like other aspects of a comprehensive transition program, is not the sole province of the schools. Instead, transition is viewed as a shared community responsibility in which multiple agencies and community members share a vested interest (Wehman, 1992). Many communities form local transition boards or committees to oversee and evaluate the success of transition efforts in their communities, and some states, such as Illinois and Minnesota, have state legislation that mandates such boards on a local (county) level. An essential function of these boards is to conduct ongoing assessment of the status of students leaving the educational program (Minnesota Department of Education Interagency Office on Transition Services, 1989).

Hess (1992) recommends that follow-up evaluation efforts go beyond simple analyses of wages, hours worked, and location of residence. Instead, she urges that follow-up efforts focus on broader issues of quality of life and degree of inclusion. In addition, because individuals with disabilities will require lifelong support in many areas, describing the nature of supports being used is more meaningful than describing whether independence has been achieved. Hess (1992) suggests that questions focus on the quality of choices and decisions that are made, the quality of relationships that are formed, and the richness of daily schedules of activity. Although such information is more difficult to obtain and analyze, it can provide schools and communities with a more complete picture about services that work well and those that must be enhanced or changed.

CHALLENGES TO AN INCLUSION EDUCATION

The Need for a Problem-Solving Approach

There is no formula for successful inclusion. There is no one model to follow. Just as there are many models of teaching and many styles of learning, there are many strategies for successfully implementing inclusion. What constitutes effective inclusive practice will vary over students, time, and setting. What is important are a school vision and faculty commitment.

Joyce and Weil (1992) have organized teaching into four families: Social, Information Processing, Personal, and Behavioral Systems. The model chosen by a teacher for a lesson depends on the lesson objective. Although any one model may achieve many objectives, each model has both direct and nurturant effects specific to that model. The best model to choose is that which will most directly affect the purpose of the lesson. Being aware of different ways to teach and having practice in different teaching models will allow teachers to have a variety of means for working with their students, whatever their abilities.

Strategies that have been successful include those that are discussed in several sections of this chapter. Collaboration among teachers in the form of peer coaching and among students in the form of cooperative learning groups or peer tutors should be used consistently. Proactive behavior plans and curricular modifications should be a given. More important than adaptations, however, is the concept of different expectations. As educators, we should not expect the same outcomes for all students; each student should be expected to achieve excellence, however that is defined for the individual. Team planning is essential on many levels—teacher to teacher, teacher with parents and students, and school with community agencies.

Inclusion may mean change at any level of education but probably entails major shifts in mind-set, course delivery, student grouping, and scheduling in secondary schools. As people adapt to change, they go through several phases, similar to the stages of grief. Villa and Thousand (1992) outline the following four steps in the progression toward change: (a) visioning; (b) introducing, which involves creating discomfort, chaos, and outrage; (c) expanding; and (d) maintaining change and change processes. Glickman (1990) discusses stages of concern about innovation. We progress from awareness of impending change to refocusing our own belief or practice through informational, personal, management, consequence, and collaboration stages. Assessing an individual school to determine at which stage it is before implementing inclusion can prevent unnecessary sabotage and so facilitate the change process.

Earlier we discussed professional development in the context of preparing regular educators in best practices for students with severe disabilities. In a problem-solving approach, this training should be viewed as a springboard for teacher implementation, modification, and continuing refinement rather than a means of providing the one right way to teach. Johnson, Pugach, and Cook (1993) have described a process of peer collaboration for prereferral. This same process can be used by teachers as they struggle to make secondary programs meaningful for students with severe disabilities. The process involves one teacher as initiator of a problem and the other as facilitator. The facilitating teacher guides the problem initiator through a series of steps for describing and clarifying the problem, summarizing, developing interventions and predicting outcomes, and developing an evaluation plan.

Inclusive practice means constant change and demands both individual and institutional flexibility. The natural correlate is an understanding of change with a commitment to continual problem solving. The components for successfully implementing inclusion are those for successful implementation of change: vision, common goals and objectives, administrative support, action strategies, evaluation techniques, and perception of obstacles to progress as problems to be solved.

Problem Behaviors

> Dear Teacher: A child with frequent temper tantrums is not ready for mainstreaming. Moreover, it is unfair to the other students as well as the teacher to subject them to such disruption. It should be up to the principal to call the shots.
>
> ANN LANDERS, AUGUST 2, 1994

This response by a national columnist highlights all too well the reactions that many citizens have to students with challenging behavior. This orientation may support inclusion, but only for those that are "ready." Within this framework, students with severe behavioral challenges are considered simply not ready and are therefore segregated.

We do not agree with this premise. Inclusion, as defined earlier in this chapter, is not an exclusionary approach that only applies to those with whom it can be easily accomplished. The question is not "Should students with severe challenging behavior be educated in inclusive schools?"; rather, it is "How should students be included?" Educators must continue to develop advanced skills in strategies of positive behavioral support—that is, approaches to instruction that are nonaversive and that allow individuals with disabilities to live in integrated community environments (Horner et al., 1990).

In this section we address some key current issues regarding positive behavioral support of students with severe disabilities. We must note that, like many of the topics discussed in this chapter, this is an emerging area of research and practice. In addition, we are only able to touch on broad themes in this section, and readers are urged to look to the works referenced here as well as other resources for more detailed descriptions of support strategies.

Horner and his colleagues at the Research and Training Center on Community-Referenced Positive Behavioral Support (Horner et al., 1990) describe several themes that are key in addressing positive support strategies. First, they assert that approaches should result not merely in behavior change but in lifestyle change. For example, a reduction in hitting may be a positive step, but a concomitant increase in participation in school and community activities is an equally important measure of change. A second and essential theme is on understanding the function or purpose of behavior (O'Neill, Horner, Albin, Storey, & Sprague, 1990). Detailed approaches to functional analysis allow teachers to predict when challenging behavior is most and least likely to occur and, in doing so, to develop working hypotheses for why students engage in specific behavior (LaVigna & Donnellan, 1986; Meyer & Evans, 1989; O'Neill et al., 1990). A third important theme views challenging behavior as a communication (Carr & Durand, 1985; Hitzing, 1992). This orientation leads to the fourth theme, viewing problem behavior as an instructional challenge. That is, the challenge is reframed as "How can we teach this individual an alternative way to communicate wishes and reactions to us?" This is a formidable challenge that requires a full understanding of the function of a behavior and creativity to teach an alternative that is equally efficient for the learner. A fifth theme focuses on environmental analysis and change as an approach to positive behavioral support. Horner et al. (1990) recommend an analysis of the instructional and social environments in addition to the physical environments. Often, changes in the physical setting (physical environment), schedule or content of instruction (instructional environment), or interactions (social environment) can produce positive behavior changes. Finally, Horner et al. (1990) describe the need for multicomponent behavior support plans that encompass environmental analysis and change, lifestyle planning, communication training, and so forth.

A final point in this section is that a team approach to positive behavioral support is essential and that no behavior expert is sufficient to "solve" a challenging behavior. Instead, all members of the educational team, working in a transdisciplinary fashion, come together to ask relevant questions about the function of behavior and then to make environmental changes and teach alternative communication strategies based on their functional analyses. Most important, a continued commitment to meaningful social inclusion as the most relevant measure of success in arranging positive behavioral support is essential.

Time Management

Time is an expensive commodity in our fast-paced society. Inclusion demands teaming and teaming demands time, yet teachers consistently complain about their lack of time. At the secondary school level, with five to six classes, one preparation period, and a twenty- to thirty-minute minute lunch "hour," finding the time for collaboration may be one of the greatest challenges to inclusion. Yet, with commitment to inclusive practice, teachers and school administrators have discovered the needed, yet elusive time.

Raywid (1993) cites the following examples of creative scheduling: (a) schedule lunch and preparation periods within the same time block;, (b) divide teachers and students into working teams so that while students are with one team, the other can meet; (c) divide teachers into common content areas and schedule meetings on a curricular basis; (d) increase class sizes so that the surplus teachers serve as substitutes; (e) adopt a year-round calendar with three-week intersessions when teachers can be compensated for concentrated planning; (f) divide periodic staff development days into more frequent two-hour sessions; (g) convert state-legislated instructional days into staff development time; (h) dismiss students early one or more days each week to allow for instructional planning; (i) lengthen the school day for students four days and dismiss them at noon on the fifth; (j) have supplemental staff plan a half-day program for subunits of the school so that every two weeks, each subunit of teachers has collaborative time; (k) plan student community service activities with community agencies and permit teachers to use this half day for planning; (l) meet state time requirements with early morning classes so that faculty can have a free half day for meeting; and (m) schedule the teacher day for one to two hours longer than the student day. One school even added meeting days to their school year and teachers to the staff. By assigning six teachers to four classes, teachers were freed on a rotating basis for collaboration (Raywid, 1993).

Once collaboration time has been created in the school schedule, it can easily be dissipated unless collaborative teams concentrate on using it efficiently and effectively. Villa and Thousand (1992) suggest that teams meet frequently enough to respond to a limited number of issues at any one time. Infrequent meetings can result in an overwhelming and unmanageable agenda. Meeting time is maximized by prioritizing tasks, recording and sharing minutes, designating responsibilities for both during and after the meeting, and beginning and ending the collaborative time promptly (York, Giangreco, Vandercook, & Macdonald, 1992). Although a seeming impossibility, collaborative time can be achieved through imagination, creativity, and flexibility on the part of each team member.

Resource Management

The implementation of a quality inclusive educational program requires both sufficient staffing and other resources. Inclusion within the school in regular classes and school events relies on the effective use of instructional assistants, teachers, and related services personnel who are willing and able to serve as facilitators of inclusion. This implies that these professionals are not only strongly committed to inclusion for students but also able to work effectively with other educators and with nondisabled students to facilitate meaningful participation in school activities.

Because a substantial portion of instruction for secondary-level students with severe disabilities occurs in community environments, personnel must be made available to support students during these activities. Teachers must become skilled at deploying support staff to allow the maximum community-based instruction for all students. In addition to personnel, resources to support community-based instruction, such as transportation, are necessary. Transportation is clearly easier in urban areas in which public transportation is available, but the time for transportation to and from community job sites and other community locations is a challenge for all programs.

Finally, obtaining needed educational materials can be a challenge for teachers. An effective community-referenced and community-based curriculum rarely uses commercially available curricula, so teachers are forced to become creative in obtaining materials that reflect the true demands of local communities. Teachers who have positive, ongoing relationships with area employers and other community members are most often successful in this regard.

A DAY IN HIGH SCHOOL

Nick

Nick arrives at school at 8:00 and immediately catches the local bus to a community-based work site where he is learning to perform clerical tasks. This is the second such job Nick has had, and his team is planning to have him experience at least four paid jobs prior to graduation. Nick works with support from a job coach who is an employee of the school. His job coach uses individualized systematic instructional strategies to help Nick learn essential job functions. In addition, he helps "broker" interactions between Nick and nondisabled coworkers by facilitating joint breaks and shared work tasks.

Nick works for two hours and then again uses public transportation to return to school. Nick has progressed to the point where he no longer needs assistance to use public transportation, so he is able to use the public bus without support. This ability is the result of years of systematic instruction within community environments.

Back at school, Nick eats lunch in the school cafeteria. This is a challenging time for him, as the noise of the cafeteria bothers him. However, this is also a time during which he can interact with his nondisabled school peers on a regular basis. He typically sits at a table near the far corner of the cafeteria, and one or two students who know him join him. Occasionally he sits alone.

Following lunch, Nick attends a work study class within the high school. The curriculum for this class, which focuses on developing resumes, interviewing strategies, and various career paths, has been adapted so that Nick can participate. An instructional assistant provides additional support for Nick during the class. On this particular day, students are using role-playing to learn strategies for successful interviews. Although the questions are adapted and modified for Nick, he participates as an equal member of the class.

During the latter part of the day, Nick receives community-based instruction in the use of community resources. In particular, he is learning to use ATM banking machines and public telephones. A general case strategy is used so that he will be more likely to be successful with new examples of these activities that he may encounter. His instruction on these activities is followed by a snack at a local restaurant, where he is learning to order from a menu.

Robin

Robin arrives at school around 8:15 each day. She is part of a car pool of four students who live on her street. Sometimes a parent drives; sometimes one of the two students who are seventeen and participate as peer advocates for Robin at the high school drives. Classes begin at 8:30, and Robin's peer advocates remind her to head directly to her locker to get materials for a first period art class. The students in this class are working on compositions in watercolor. Robin's work does not have nearly the technical quality of other students, but she is learning that painting is a relaxing recreational activity for many people and something she can continue as a hobby throughout her adult life. The art teacher and other students encourage Robin to talk about her painting and why she has chosen to use certain colors in her composition.

Robin's next class is academically challenging. She participates in an American history course for high school freshmen, and she has not been able to discuss or write about the political, social, and economic factors that precipitated important events in our history. However, she has been able to talk about some of the groups important to American history such as American Indians, the pilgrims, and African Americans. She is particularly interested in the clothes people wore and the foods they ate. She has been included in role-playing scenes from early American history put on by her cooperative learning group and in contributing magazine pictures to help illustrate group reports. The history teacher and Robin's special education teacher meet twice a week to plan and discuss activities related to the class that will be academically and socially meaningful for Robin and the other students. During the first semester, an instructional assistant attended the class with Robin, but this semester, the history teacher wanted to see whether other students could take over the support Robin needs to be an active participant. So far, everyone is satisfied with the results.

At 10:15, Robin takes the local bus to a downtown hotel where she is a trainee in the maid service program. Robin's job coach greets her at the employee entrance and waits to see whether she will self-initiate the first steps in preparing for work. Today, Robin has brought a picture from her art class that she wants to share with her job coach. Her coach says she would like to talk about the picture when it is time for a break or at lunch but prompts Robin that she needs to move toward the time clock. After Robin has punched in and changed into her hotel uniform, her job coach tells her she will be vacuuming hallways on the tenth, eleventh, and twelfth floors. As Robin works, hotel employees come by and say hello and compliment her on her work. Robin does the vacuuming thoroughly and methodically, but slower than typically acceptable for this task.

When it is time for lunch, Robin joins others in the employee lounge and asks her job coach to assist her in buying a sandwich and a soft drink from the vending machines. She talks about her watercolor with her job coach, and two regular employees join in the conversation.

At 2:00, Robin leaves work and catches the bus to a community recreation center. Her parents and teachers believe she will benefit more from an aerobics course than a traditional physical education class at the school. A teacher aid meets Robin and another female student with a disability in the lobby, and they head for the locker room to change. After a vigorous workout and a shower, Robin takes the bus home. She cannot wait to tell her parents about the day she has had!

SUMMARY

We have discussed a considerable amount of content as it relates to the inclusive education of students with severe disabilities in high school. However, some key factors and challenges bear repeating to emphasize their importance.

Factors for Success

Meaningful Choices A major step in the implementation of inclusive education is the opportunity for students with severe disabilities and their families to work as equals with educators in selecting meaningful programs with authentic activities in real-life settings. This creates a different level of risk and a higher level of reward.

Systematic Instruction Although inclusive educational settings are less controllable than traditional special education classrooms, teachers must use the systematic instructional methods that have proven successful for many years with many different learners. In fact, systematic instruction should become part of the preservice and continuing professional development of all teachers and support personnel, not just those in special education.

Functional Assessments For assessment to be functional, it must be meaningful and, thus, usable. This statement means that assessment is a much broader activity than evaluating the performance of individuals, although that is part of the function. However, it is broader in the sense that programs, support features, environments, and other people are included in the assessment endeavor. A functional assessment creates an overall picture of the quality of one's life.

Family Support and Involvement Developing and nurturing partnerships with parents is an important element in inclusive education. This is particularly true when we deliver education in the contexts of home and community as well as in school buildings. The successful acquisition, maintenance, and generalization of adaptive behaviors in these settings is unlikely to occur without strong family support and involvement.

A Focus on Transition Special educators agree nearly unanimously about the importance of transition planning and preparation for youth with severe disabilities. Numerous studies have demonstrated the need for and success of transition. The many benefits of an inclusive education could be lost if transition from school to adult life is not part of the curricular effort.

Assistive Technology The proliferation of assistive technology in its many forms enables individuals with severe disabilities to access environments and activities that seemed impossible just a few years ago. As with other aspects of the educational experience, participation in the choices of technology is an important issue to both the individual and family.

Transdisciplinary Approach This teaming model stresses equity and responsibility in the decision-making process. It is an approach that uses the strengths of family support and involvement with the knowledge and experience of professionals.

Teaching for Generalization Educating individuals in inclusive settings makes attention to generalization an imperative. Natural environments have few controls beyond their original designs. Thus, finding and teaching "likeness" within and across curriculum domains is critical for individuals with severe disabilities to behave in successful and satisfying ways whether they are in their schools, homes, or communities.

Challenges to an Inclusive Education

A Need for Problem-Solving Approaches Among the things we do know about inclusion is that there are no pat answers. New ground is being broken, which is at once exciting and frustrating. Rule 1 is that school personnel and families must be committed to inclusion. Rule 2 is that we must be willing to take risks. Rule 3 is to remember rules 1 and 2 when difficulties arise.

Problem Behaviors Not surprisingly, a high percentage of regular education teachers are most worried about highly disruptive behaviors in their classrooms. They worry that these behaviors will interfere with the learning opportunities of students without disabilities. This concern is legitimate. The approach to this concern is to provide adequate support for students with behavior problems in the learning environment, not to make them wait for inclusion until the problem has gone away.

Time Management Time today seems to be more foe than friend. Creating new environments, materials, and activities for learning means that we will also need to be creative in our scheduling and use of time so that all people can participate in employment, family, and community activities. This includes teachers as well as students.

Resource Management The most expensive resource is people, and inclusion is a people-intensive enterprise. Federal, state, and local governments must look at inclusive education as a long-term investment in people. We cannot at present say whether there will be a cost savings because of inclusion. What is fair to say, however, is that inclusion is unlikely to add to the cost we currently spend on individuals with severe disabilities if we factor in the costs of ongoing support services and entitlements when these individuals become adults. That is, inclusion may cost more than we currently spend on special education, but it may create a savings if individuals with disabilities become more independent and employable as adults. What our federal and state governments must be willing to do is reallocate their current resources in ways that support school and community inclusion.

We have attempted to describe the best practices available for the inclusive education of individuals with severe disabilities in high schools. Though we have learned enough to be fully committed to this endeavor, much more remains to be to learned. That in itself is the joy of education, the continuous journey of discovery.

REFERENCES

Americans with Disabilities Act of 1990, PL 101-336, 2, 104 Stat. 328 (1991).

Baumgart, D., Johnson, J., & Helmstetter, E. (1990). *Augmentative and alternative communication systems for persons with moderate and severe disabilities.* Baltimore: Brookes.

Becker, W., Engelmann, S., & Thomas, D. (1975). *Teaching 2: Cognitive learning and instruction.* Chicago: Science Research Associates.

Bellamy, G. T., Horner, R. H., & Inman, D. (1979). *Vocational habilitation of severely retarded adults: A direct service technology.* Baltimore: University Park Press.

Bellamy, G. T., Rhodes, L., Bourbeau, P., & Mank, D. (1986). Mental retardation services in sheltered workshops and day activity programs: Consumer benefits and policy alternatives. In F. R. Rusch (Ed.), *Competitive employment issues and strategies* (pp. 257–271). Baltimore: Brookes.

Board of Education v. Rowley, 458 U.S. 176, 102 S.Ct. 3034, 73 L.Ed., 2d 690 (1982).

Board of Education of Sacramento Unified School District v. Holland, 786 F. Supp. 847 (E.D. Cal., 1992).

Brinker, R., & Thorpe, M. (1983). *Evaluation of integration of severely handicapped students in regular classrooms and community settings.* Princeton, NJ: Educational Testing Service.

Brown, L., Branston-McLean, M., Baumgart, D., Vincent, L., Falvey, M., & Schroeder, J. (1979). Using the characteristics of current and subsequent least restrictive environments in the development of curricular content for severely handicapped students. *AAESPH Review, 4,* 407–424.

Brown, L., Long, E., Udvari-Solner, A., Davis, L., VanDeventer, P., Ahlgren, C., Johnson, F. Gruenewald. L., & Jorgenson, J. (1989). The home school: Why students with severe intellectual disabilities must attend the schools of their brothers, sisters, friends, and neighbors. *Journal of the Association for Persons with Severe Handicaps, 14,* 1–7.

Brown, L., Nietupski, J., & Hamre-Nietupski, S. (1976). The criterion of ultimate functioning and public school services for the severely handicapped student. In M. A. Thomas (Ed.), *Hey! Don't forget about me! Education's investment in the severely, profoundly, and multiply handicapped.* Reston, VA: Council for Exceptional Children.

Brown, L., Rogan, P., Shiraga, B., Zanella-Albright, K., Kessler, K., Bryson, F., VanDeventer, P., & Loomis, R. (1987). A vocational follow-up evaluation of the 1984–1986 Madison Metropolitan School District graduates with severe intellectual disabilities (Research Monograph). *Association for Persons with Severe Handicaps, 2.*

Carr, E., & Durand, M. (1985). Reducing behavior problems through functional communication training. *Journal of Applied Behavior Analysis, 18,* 111–126.

Council of Administrators of Special Education. (1993). *CASE future agenda for special education: Creating a unified education system.* Reston, VA: Council for Exceptional Children.

Cross, G., & Villa, R. (1992). The Winooski School System: An evolutionary perspective of a school restructuring for diversity. In R. Villa, J., Thousand, W. Stainback, & S. Stainback (Eds.), *Restructuring for caring and effective education: An administrative guide to creating heterogeneous schools* (pp. 219–237). Baltimore: Brookes.

Daniel R.R. v. State Board of Education, 874 F. 2d 1036 (5th Cir. 1989).

Day, M., & Horner, R. H. (1986). Response variation and the generalization of a dressing skill: Comparison of single instance and general case instruction. *Applied Research in Mental Retardation, 7,* 189–202.

DeFina, S. S. (1992). *Portfolio assessment: Getting started.* New York: Scholastic.

DeStefano, L., & Wagner, M. (1992). Outcome assessment in special education: What lessons have we learned? In F. R. Rusch, L. DeStefano, J. Chadsey-Rusch, L. Phelps, & E. Syzmanski (Eds.), *Transition from school to adult life: Models, linkages and policies* (pp. 173–207). Sycamore, IL: Sycamore.

Dewey, J. (1944). *Democracy and education.* New York: Free Press.

Doyle, P., Wolery, M., Ault, M., & Gast, D. (1988). System of least prompts: A literature review of procedural parameters. *Journal of the Association for Persons with Severe Handicaps, 13,* 28–40.

Education of All Handicapped Children Act, PL 94-142, U.S.C. 1401 (1975).

Engelmann, S., & Carnine, D. (1982). *Theory of instruction: Principles and applications.* New York: Irvington.

Forest, M., & Pearpoint, J. C. (1992). Putting all kids on the MAP. *Educational Leadership, 50,* 26–31.

Friend, M. (1984). Consultation skills for resource teachers. *Learning Disability Quarterly, 7,* 246–250.

Fuchs, D., & Fuchs, L. S. (1994). Inclusive schools movement and the radicalization of special education reform. *Exceptional Children, 60,* 294–309.

Gartner, A., & Lipsky, D. K. (1987). Beyond special education: Toward a quality system for all students. *Harvard Educational Review, 57,* 367–395.

Glazer, S. M., & Brown, C. S. (1993). *Portfolios and beyond: Collaborative assessment in reading and writing.* Norwood, MA: Gordon.

Glickman, C. D. (1990). *Supervision of instruction.* Needham Heights, MA: Allyn & Bacon.

Gold, M. (1980). *Marc Gold: "Did I say that?": Articles and commentary on the Try Another Way System.* Champaign, IL: Research Press.

Gorman, T., & Rose, M. (1994). Inclusion: Taking a stand. *American Teacher, 78,* 9–12.

Guess, D., Benson, H., & Siegel-Causey, E. (1985). Concepts and issues related to choice-making and autonomy among persons with severe disabilities. *Journal of the Association for Persons with Severe Disabilities, 10,* 79–86.

Hess, C. (1992). Applications with youth with severe disabilities. In P. Wehman (Ed.), *Beyond the classroom: Transition strategies for young people with disabilities* (pp. 261–276). Baltimore: Brookes.

Hitzing, W. (1992). Support and positive teaching strategies. In S. Stainback & W. Stainback (Eds.), *Curriculum considerations in inclusive classrooms: Facilitating learning for all students* (pp. 143–158). Baltimore: Brookes.

Horner, R. H., Albin, R., & Ralph, G. (1986). Generalization with precision: The role of negative teaching examples in the instruction of generalized grocery item selection. *Journal of the Association for Persons with Severe Handicaps, 11,* 100–108.

Horner, R. H., Dunlap, G., Koegel, R., Carr, E., Sailor, W., Anderson, J., Albin, R., & O'Neill, R. (1990). Toward a technology of "nonaversive" positive behavioral support. *Journal of the Association for Persons with Severe Handicaps, 15,* 125–132.

Horner, R. H., Eberhard, J., & Sheehan, M. (1986). Teaching generalized table bussing: The importance of negative teaching examples. *Behavior Modification, 10,* 457–471.

Horner, R. H., Jones, D., & Williams, J. (1985). A functional approach to teaching generalized street crossing. *Journal of the Association for Persons with Severe Handicaps, 10,* 71–78.

Horner, R. H., & McDonald, R. (1982). Comparison of single instance and general case instruction in teaching a generalized vocational skill. *Journal of the Association for Persons with Severe Handicaps, 7,* 7–21.

Horner, R. H., Sprague, J., & Wilcox, B. (1984). General case programming for community activities. In B. Wilcox & G. T. Bellamy (Eds.), *Design of high school programs for severely handicapped students* (pp. 61–98). Baltimore: Brookes.

Hunt, P., & Ferron-Davis, F. (1992). A preliminary investigation of IEP quality and content associated with placement in general education versus special education classes. *JASH, 17,* 247–253.

Idol, L., Nevin, A., & Paolucci-Whitcomb, P. (1994). *Collaborative consultation* (2nd ed.). Austin, TX: PRO-ED.

Individuals with Disabilities Education Act, PL 101-336. U.S.C. 1401–1468 (1990).

Irving Independent School District v. Tatro, 468 U.S. 883, 104 S.Ct. 3371, 82 L.Ed. 2d. 664 (1984).

Johnson, L. J., Pugach, M. C., & Cook, R. (1993). Peer collaboration as a means to facilitate collegial support to reduce teacher isolation and facilitate classroom problem solving in rural areas. *Rural Special Education Quarterly, 12,* 21–26.

Joyce, B., & Weil, M. (1992). *Models of teaching* (4th ed.). Needham Heights, MA: Allyn & Bacon.

Kelker, K. (1993). *Solution Circle.* Billings: Parents, Let's Unite for Kids (PLUK), Eastern Montana College.

Kennedy, C., & Itkonen, T. (1994). Some effects of regular class placement on the social contacts and social networks of high school students with severe disabilities. *Journal of the Association for Persons with Severe Handicaps, 19,* 1–10.

LaVigna, G., & Donnellan, A. (1986). *Alternatives to punishment: Solving behavior problems with non-aversive strategies.* New York: Irvington.

Learning Disabilities Association of America. (1994, May/June). Inclusion. *LDA/Newsbriefs.*

Lipsky, D. K., & Gartner, A. (1989). *Beyond separate education: Quality education for all.* Baltimore: Brookes.

Lipsky, D. K., & Gartner A. (1991). Restructuring for quality. In J. W. Lloyd, A. C. Repp, & N. N. Singh (Eds.), *The regular education initiative: Alternative perspectives on concepts, issues, and models* (pp. 45–56). Sycamore, IL: Sycamore.

McDonnell, J., & Hardman, M. L. (1986). Planning transition of severely handicapped youth from school to adult services: A framework for high school programs. *Education and Training of the Mentally Retarded, 20,* 275–286.

Meyer, L., & Evans, I. (1989). *Nonaversive intervention for behavior problems: A manual for home and community.* Baltimore: Brookes.

Minnesota Department of Education Interagency Office on Transition Services. (1989). *Community transition interagency committees: Yearly summary.* Minneapolis: Minneapolis Institute on Community Integration, University of Minnesota.

Morsink, C. V., Thomas, C. C., Correa, V. I. (1991). *Interactive teaming: Consultation and collaboration in special programs.* Upper Saddle River, NJ: Merrill/Prentice Hall.

Mount, B., & Zwernik, K. (1988). *It's never too early, it's never too late: A booklet about personal futures planning.* Mears Park Center, MN: Metropolitan Council.

National Education Association. (1994). *NEA Today, 13,* 16–17.

Oberti v. Clementon Board of Education, 995 F. 2nd 1204 (3rd Cir. 1993).

O'Brien, J. (1987). A guide to lifestyle planning: Using the Activities Catalog to integrate services and natural support systems. In B. Wilcox & G. T. Bellamy (Eds.), *The Activities Catalog: An alternative curriculum design for youth and adults with severe disabilities* (pp. 175–189). Baltimore: Brookes.

O'Neil, J. (1993). The promise of portfolios. *ASCD Update, 35,* 1–5.

O'Neill, R., Horner, R., Albin, R., Storey, K., & Sprague, J. (1990). *Functional analysis of problem behavior: A practical assessment guide.* Sycamore, IL: Sycamore.

Pancsofar, E. (Ed.). (1992). *Community connections.* Manchester, CT: Communitas.

Pancsofar, E., & Bates, P. (1985). The impact of acquisition of successive training exemplars on generalization. *Journal of the Association for Persons with Severe Handicaps, 10,* 95–104

Pancsofar, E., & Blackwell, R. (1986). *A user's guide to community entry for the severely handicapped.* Albany: State University of New York Press.

Pancsofar, E., Steere, D., & Wood, R. (1993). Consumer assessment: Ten important considerations. *The Advance, 4,* 1–3.

Peraino, J. (1992). Post-21 follow-up studies: How do special education graduates fare? In P. Wehman (Ed.), *Beyond the classroom: Transition strategies for young people with disabilities* (pp. 21–70). Baltimore: Brookes.

Phillips, B., & Zhao, H. (1993). Predictors of assistive technology abandonment. *Assistive Technology, 5,* 36–45.

Powell, T. H., Hecimovic, A., & Christensen, L. (1992). Meeting the unique needs of families. In D. Berkell (Ed.), *Autism: Identification, education, and treatment* (pp. 187–224). Hillsdale, NJ: Erlbaum.

Raywid, M. A. (1993). Finding time for collaboration. *Educational Leadership, 51,* 30–35.

Rehabilitation Act of 1973, Section 504. 29 U.S.C. 794 (1978).

Roncker v. Walters, 700 F. 2nd 1058 (6th Cir 1983), cert. den'd, 464 U.S. 864, 104 S.Ct. 196, 78 L.Ed. 2d 171 (1983).

Rose, E. (1994, February). *Developing models for inclusive teacher education programs.* Paper presented at the annual meeting of the American Association of Colleges for Teacher Education, Chicago.

Rusch, F. R. (1990). *Supported employment: Models, methods, and issues.* Sycamore, IL: Sycamore.

Rusch, F. R., DeStefano, L., Chadsey-Rusch, J., Phelps, L. A., & Szymanski, E. (1992). *Transition from school to adult life: Models, linkages, and policy.* Sycamore, IL: Sycamore.

Sailor, W., Gee, K., & Karasoff, P. (1993). Full inclusion and school restructuring. In M. E. Snell (Ed.), *Systematic instruction of persons with severe handicaps* (4th ed.). Upper Saddle River, NJ: Merrill/Prentice Hall.

Schattman, R. (1992). The Franklin Northwest Supervisory Union: A case study of an inclusive school system. In R. Villa, J. Thousand, W. Stainback, & S. Stainback (Eds.), *Restructuring for caring and effective education: An administrative guide to creating heterogeneous schools* (pp. 143–159). Baltimore: Brookes.

Schnorr, R. (1990). "Peter? He comes and goes...": First graders' perspectives on a part-time mainstream student. *Journal of the Association for Persons with Severe Disabilities, 15,* 231–240.

Skrtic, T. M. (1991). *Behind special education: A critical analysis of professional culture and school organization.* Denver: Love.

Snell, M. E. (1991). Schools are for all kids: The importance of integration for students with severe disabilities and their peers. In J. W. Lloyd, A. C. Repp, & N. N. Singh (Eds.), *The regular education initiative: Alternative perspectives on concepts, issues, and models* (pp. 133–148). Sycamore, IL: Sycamore.

Sowers, J., & Powers, L. (1991). *Vocational preparation of students with physical and multiple disabilities.* Baltimore: Brookes.

Sprague, J., & Horner, R. H. (1984). The effects of single instance, multiple instance, and general case instruction on teaching generalized vending machine use by moderately and severely handicapped students. *Journal of Applied Behavior Analysis, 17,* 273–278.

Stainback, S., & Stainback, W. (1985). *Integration of students with severe handicaps into regular schools.* Reston, VA: Council for Exceptional Children. (ERIC Document Reproduction Service No. ED 255009)

Stainback, S., & Stainback, W. (1992). *Curriculum considerations in inclusive classrooms: Facilitating learning for all students.* Baltimore: Brookes.

Stainback, S., Stainback, W., East, K., & Sapon-Shevin, M. (1994). A commentary on inclusion and the development of a positive self-identity by people with disabilities. *Exceptional Children, 60,* 486–490.

Steere, D., & Pancsofar, E. (1995). Cues, prompts, and correction procedures. In W. Woolcock & J. Domaracki (Eds.), *Instructional strategies in the community: A resource guide for community instruction for persons with disabilities* (pp. 35–54). Austin, TX: PRO-ED.

Steere, D., Strauch, J., Powell, T., & Butterworth, J. (1990). Promoting generalization from a teaching setting to a community-based setting among persons with severe disabilities: A general case programming approach. *Education and Treatment of Children, 13,* 5–20.

Stokes, T., & Baer, D. (1977). An implicit technology of generalization. *Journal of Applied Behavior Analysis, 10,* 349–367.

Syzmanski, E. M. (1994). Transition: Life-span and life-space considerations for empowerment. *Exceptional children, 60,* 402–410.

Taylor, S. (1988). Caught in the continuum: A critical analysis of the principle of the least restrictive environment. *Journal of the Association for Persons with Severe Handicaps, 13,* 41–53.

Technology-Related Assistance for Individuals with Disabilities Act, PL 100-407 (1988).

Ventura, M. (1993). *Letters at 3 AM: Reports on endarkenment.* New York: Spring.

Villa, R. A., & Thousand, J. S. (1992). Restructuring public school systems. In R. A. Villa, J. S. Thousand, W. Stainback, & S. Stainback (Eds.), *Restructuring for caring and effective education* (pp. 109–137). Baltimore: Brookes.

Voeltz, L. (1980). Children's attitudes toward handicapped peers. *American Journal of Mental Deficiency, 84,* 455–464.

Voeltz, L. (1982). Effects of structured interactions with severely handicapped peers on children's attitudes. *American Journal of Mental Deficiency, 86,* 380–390.

Wang, M. C., Walberg, H., & Reynolds, M. C. (1992). A scenario for better-not separate-special education. *Educational Leadership, 50,* 35–38.

Wehman, P. (1992). *Life beyond the classroom: Transition strategies for young people with disabilities.* Baltimore: Brookes.

Wiggins, G. (1993). Assessment: Authenticity, content, and validity. *Phi Delta Kappan, 756,* 200–215.

Wilcox, B., & Bellamy, G. T. (1982). *Design of high school programs for severely handicapped students.* Baltimore: Brookes.

Wilcox, B., & Bellamy, G. T. (Eds.). (1987). *A comprehensive guide to the Activities Catalog: An alternative curriculum for youth and adults with severe disabilities.* Baltimore: Brookes.

York, J., Giangreco, M. F., Vandercook, T., & Macdonald, C. (1992). Integrating support personnel in the inclusive classroom. In S. Stainback & W. Stainback (Eds.), *Curriculum considerations in inclusive classrooms.* Baltimore: Brookes.

15

Transition from School to Adult Life

Issues of Inclusion

BARBARA GUY
SUSAN BRODY HASAZI
DAVID R. JOHNSON

Societal changes in the 1980s such as decreased demands for products, increased imports, and workforce reductions influenced the nation's economy and increased the number of people who were unemployed and without housing or health care. A multitude of disciplines were moved by these and other factors to examine approaches to education and the types of preparation that all workers received. Reports such as those prepared by the William T. Grant Foundation Commission on Work, Family and Citizenship (1988a, 1988b) revealed that a great portion of American youth do not go to college. To succeed, these youth must often work more than one job, live longer with family, delay marriage, and take whatever training they can to further their careers. In an attempt to provide *all* youth increased opportunities to achieve successful outcomes after leaving school, federal legislation has established a national reform agenda for education that is tied to results (Goals 2000: Educate America Act), stresses the importance of preparing students for future concerns (School-to-Work Opportunity Act of 1994), and increases postsecondary education opportunities (Higher Education Amendments of 1992).

Numerous follow-up studies conducted during the past decade reveal that large numbers of youth with disabilities who exit special education programs experience substantial difficulties in achieving the desired goals of employment, independent living, and access to postsecondary education programs (Hasazi, Gordon, & Roe, 1985a; Mithaug, Horiuchi, & Fanning, 1985; Wagner, 1989; Wehman, Kregel, & Seyforth, 1985). These studies report the following findings:

1. More than 30 percent of students who received special education services at the secondary level dropped out of school before graduating.
2. Fewer than 15 percent of former special education students who were out of school longer than one year participated in postsecondary education and training.
3. Thirty to 40 percent of students were unemployed following exit from school; of those who were employed, only about half were working full-time.
4. Many students with disabilities were not linked up with adult community services and educational agencies before graduation.
5. Young women with disabilities were unemployed at rates significantly higher than young men with disabilities or young women without disabilities.
6. Of the small percentage of people with moderate/severe disabilities who are working, very few work in community jobs (0–20 percent).
7. Many young people with disabilities are placed on long waiting lists for community services following school completion.

These findings have led to an increased emphasis on issues related to the transition of students with disabilities from school to adult life. In its narrowest sense, transition is defined as the process for ensuring that students successfully move from school to the world of work (Clark & Kolstoe, 1990). A broader interpretation views transition as a comprehensive process that focuses on improving the quality of a student's employment outcomes, residential options, and interpersonal networks following exit from school (Halpern, 1985). In yet other applications, transition refers simply to the delivery of services to youth with disabilities.

In this chapter, the term *transition* is used to encompass the series of purposeful activities designed to ensure that students have the skills, opportunities, and supports needed to locate and maintain employment, pursue postsecondary education and training, live and participate in the social fabric of the community, and make decisions about their lives. An overview of the legislative definitions and requirements regarding transition will be presented in this chapter, as well as a summary of the assessment, planning, implementation, and programmatic activities that are necessary for youth with disabilities to successfully obtain beneficial outcomes in inclusive settings.

FEDERAL LEGISLATION RELATING TO THE TRANSITION OF YOUTH WITH DISABILITIES

Individuals with Disabilities Education Act

The Individuals with Disabilities Education Act (IDEA, PL 101-476) was signed into law in October 1990. This act, which served to amend the Education of the Handicapped Act Amendments, introduced new requirements concerning the transition of youth with disabilities from school to adult life. IDEA mandates that for students, beginning no later than sixteen years of age (and at a younger age, if determined appropriate), one of the purposes of the annual meeting will be the planning of transition services. Transition services are defined in Section 300.18 of IDEA as

> (a) a coordinated set of activities for a student, designed within an outcome oriented process that promotes movement from school to postschool activities, including post-secondary education, vocational training, integrated employment (including supported employment), continuing and adult education, adult services, independent living, or community participation.

In addition to requiring the planning of transition, IDEA establishes important criteria concerning the conduct of the planning meeting: (a) notification, (b) participation in meetings, (c) content of the IEP, and (d) agency responsibility.

Notification Section 300.345 requires that if the purpose of a meeting is to plan transition services, the notice to parents must indicate this purpose, indicate that the student will be invited, and identify any other agency that will be invited. It is likely that this change was intended to ensure that parents are informed in advance that transition issues will be discussed at the IEP meeting, thus providing them with the opportunity to prepare for the discussion. An understanding of the agencies to be invited also allows parents to request additional or alternate agencies be included.

Participation in Meetings In IEP meetings in which transition will be discussed, IDEA expands participation to include the student and a representative of any other agency that is likely to be responsible for providing or paying for transition services. The mandate to involve students in the discussion of their future goals and plans reflects the concepts and values of self-determination, personal empowerment, and shared responsibility. For many students, this will mean that well before the IEP meeting, both in and out of school, they must participate in activities designed to enhance their knowledge base and decision-making and communication skills. If the student chooses not to attend, IDEA mandates that IEP teams must ensure that the student's preferences and interests are considered prior to determining transition services.

The requirement to involve agencies responsible for providing or paying for services reflects the values of long-term, child-centered planning; coordination; and shared responsibility. It places responsibility on school personnel to become knowledgeable about the services and policies of community agencies. The agencies, in turn, should expand their role to include interaction with students who are still in school. These agencies might include vocational rehabilitation, recreation, employment and training, mental health, mental retardation/developmental disabilities, social security, housing, and others relevant to the individual needs and preferences of the student. These agencies are not required to attend the IEP meeting. If they do not attend, the education agency is required to "take other steps to obtain their participation" in the planning of transition services. Although not specified in the law, these steps might include forwarding a copy of the IEP to the agency (with student and parent approval), arranging for a subsequent IEP meeting to discuss transition specific issues, involving advocacy groups, maintaining contact with the agency to promote involvement, and encouraging parents and students to initiate contact and request involvement.

Content of the IEP The term *coordinated set of activities* used in the definition of transition services is further defined in Section 300.18 as (b) The coordinated set of activities described in paragraph (a) of this section must:

> (1) Be based on the individual student's needs, taking into account the student's preferences and interests; and (2) Include (i) instruction, (ii) community experiences, (iii) the development of employment and other post-school adult living objectives, and (iv) if appropriate, acquisition of daily living skills and functional vocational evaluation.

At a minimum, the IEP team must now address each of the areas including instruction, community experiences, and the development of employment and other postschool adult living objectives. In most cases, each of the four areas, and possibly some others, will be included in students' IEPs. However, if the IEP team determines that no services are needed within any one of the four designated areas, a statement to that effect and the basis on which that decision was made must be included in the IEP. This requirement is designed to ensure that the IEP team and the resulting IEP addresses all areas that are critical to successful postschool outcomes for an individual student.

Transition services may be special education, if they are provided as specially designed instruction, or related services, if they are required to assist a student to benefit from special education. They may be provided by the education agency or, as we will see in the next section, by agencies outside the school. In either case, they should be written into the IEP and the responsible party noted.

Agency Responsibilities In addition to inviting representatives of outside agencies to the IEP meeting when transition is being discussed, IDEA states that IEP should also include statements of each public and participating agency's responsibilities or linkage (or both) before the student leaves the school setting. This section should also include a commitment by the participating agency to meet the financial responsibility associated with provision of services. This is most important if a state or local agency other than the school is responsible for providing or paying for needed services

If an agency, other than the school responsible for the student's education, fails to provide an agreed-on transition service, the school needs to convene a meeting to identify alternative strategies to meet the transition objectives and, if necessary, revise the student's IEP. These provisions, as stated in Section 300.347, clearly do not imply that the burden for services, programs, or financial responsibility falls solely on the educational agency when things do not turn out as planned. By giving parents and students a means to reengage with the planning team when things go wrong, the provision seeks to prevent students "falling through the cracks" with no place to go for assistance and advocacy. The strength of this provision relies on the existence of local or state interagency agreements that clearly delineate the financial and legal responsibilities of agencies involved in transition services. Without such agreements, the reconvention process may be ineffectual.

Representation of Youth with Disabilities in Other Federal Legislation

A second important piece of legislation passed by Congress in 1990 was the Americans with Disabilities Act (ADA). Although not specifically targeted at the transition from school to adult life, this legislation has important implications for students with disabilities. The ADA provides "civil rights protection to individuals with disabilities in private sector employment, all public services, public accommodations, transportation, and telecommunications." It includes a variety of provisions related to ensuring accommodations for, and accessibility to, services and employment opportunities for individuals with disabilities.

The Carl Perkins Vocational and Applied Technology and Education Act of 1990 includes a number of provisions designed to improve the access to vocational education programs for students with disabilities. For example, the act specifies that prior to the beginning of the ninth grade, all students with disabilities and their parents must be informed of the vocational programs and accompanying entry requirements offered by vocational education. In addition, the act provides for counseling services designed to facilitate the transition from school to postschool employment and career opportunities, as well as adaptation of curricula, instructional equipment, and facilities. Finally, the act requires that local vocational education programs assure equal access to the full range of vocational program options and involve special education personnel in the planning of program modifications for students with disabilities.

One of the most promising opportunities for the inclusion of youth with disabilities in the transition activities for all youth is within the School-to-Work Opportunities Act of 1994. This act is part of a broader national initiative for comprehensive education reform, which also includes Goals 2000: Educate America Act and the National Skill Standards Act of 1994. The act provides states and localities with federal funds that are to be used as venture capital to underwrite the initial costs of planning and establishing statewide School-to-Work Opportunities systems. It seeks to improve the knowledge and skills of *all* American youth by integrating academic and occupational learning, integrating school-based and work-based learning, and building effective linkages between secondary and postsecondary education. In addition to a set of general program requirements, the act calls for the planning, development, and integration of a school-based learning component, a work-based learning component, and a connecting activities component. Although it has yet to be implemented in a majority of states, the activities specified in the act provide opportunities for youth with disabilities to learn the skills they need alongside youth without disabilities.

DETERMINING NECESSARY AND APPROPRIATE TRANSITION SERVICES

Unemployment, underemployment, social isolation, and dependency are too frequently the plight of adults with disabilities. To ensure that youth with disabilities leave school to achieve success in employment, living, social, and postsecondary options in the community, transition planning and instruction must be thorough and begin as early as possible. Parents and educators make formal instructional decisions for students with disabilities from the moment they enter the special education system. In theory, the Individualized Education Plan (IEP) builds upon itself, leading toward a culmination of skills that will benefit the student after graduation. In practice, however, the IEP may focus on remediation skills or graduation requirements that have little or no relationship to the skills the youth will need to live independently in their communities as adults. Students must begin to learn self-advocacy and self-determination skills, as well as specific academic skills and tasks at a very young age. If elementary and middle school programs fail to address these skills, the task of preparing secondary-aged students for transition is next to impossible. The development of transition skills is a continuing and never-ending process of extension and refinement. The techniques and strategies necessary for this process are further described here in terms of preference and skill identification, individualized transition planning, and the selection and follow-up of transition strategies and activities.

Preference and Skill Identification

Although parent input to the identification of IEP goals is sought throughout students' educational careers, the determination of specific goals are most often based on the students' skills (or strengths and weaknesses). The transition process requires greater student and family input and a balance between the use of preferences and skills to determine not only IEP goals but long-term outcomes.

Preferences, in this sense, are the involvements, experiences, and opportunities that an individual likes or desires. In some cases, they may not be compatible. For example, Matt, age sixteen, likes the out-of-doors, animals, and solitude but hopes to live downtown in a large, urban city and work as a parking valet. He has expressed a preference for living and working in areas that are completely different from the things he currently likes to do. Until Matt was asked his long-term dreams, however, these differences were not identified. The long-term outcomes set by his parents and other members of the IEP team were for Matt to live in a rural town as a veterinary assistant. Matt's plan now includes a variety of experiences to help him determine which situation he would like best and will result in outcomes that are meaningful to him.

Students, parents, and professionals may all have different preferences for the outcomes of one individual. Identifying the similarities and differences in these preferences prior to the IEP meeting will help ensure that the meeting itself is focused on the specifics of what will be done and how it will be done. The process of identification may be done shortly before the IEP meeting using an informal interview or over a period of time using a combination of techniques including interviews, surveys, and planning games. Individuals with short attention spans, as well as individuals who have difficulty answering abstract questions, may require multiple opportunities to discuss a minimum number of preferences.

Skill assessment is a critical component of transition planning. Formal and/or informal assessments should be made of the student's current skills, needs, and opportunities in the areas of employment, residential placement, postsecondary education, recreation and leisure, transportation, medical needs, income and insurance needs, and interpersonal relationships. Together, the results of the assessment and the student's vision of the future should guide the development of transition services within the IEP.

Individualized Transition Planning

The transition planning process provides the framework for identifying, planning, and carrying out activities that will help a student make a successful transition to adult life. It identifies the specifics of the type of skills to be learned, which transition services will be provided, when they will be provided, and the party responsible for providing the services. The planning process is individualized in the sense that it focuses on the unique needs of the student, and collaborative in that it involves a team of people drawn from different parts of the student's school and community life.

Given the individualized nature of this process, no two transition plans will look alike. A generic set of factors, however, can guide the transition planning steps—for example, assembling a team, inviting student participation, implementing the planning process, selecting strategies and activities, and following up on identified activities.

Assembling a Transition Team Transition planning for high school students with disabilities should be accomplished through the IEP process as specified in Part B of IDEA. Because the entitlement to educational services ends in most states at age twenty-one, and because adult services are not mandatory for all individuals who need services, it is essential that the IEP include components that focus on vocational, postsecondary education, and community participation concerns. To facilitate this, transition planning teams need to include representatives from a variety of disciplines, each of whom may offer different perspectives on objectives, strategies, and resource availability. The composition of a transition team should reflect individual student needs. For example, a team for a student interested in attending a postsecondary technical school might be composed of the student, one or more family members, a special education teacher, a vocational education teacher, a representative from the technical school, a representative from a local community agency connected with residential options, and a community member. Other transition planning teams might include representatives from Rehabilitation Services. *Only invite representatives whose agencies represent the needs of the student.* Their attendance at meetings will be higher if they have a defined role and relevant input.

Student Participation at IEP Meetings Concern has been growing among individuals connected with transition planning that educators and adult services professionals have assumed too much responsibility for decisions that govern the lives of their students and clients. The empowerment movement is dedicated to the belief that individuals with disabilities have the right to direct their own lives through making choices, speaking for themselves, and resisting dependence on specialized services.

The issue is critical for any student about to transition from high school to adult life, but it appears especially difficult for students with disabilities. On the one hand, students must make a host of choices about where and how to live, work, and become an active member of a complex, adult world. On the other hand, they may have a few real choices in the community and little experience in making decisions that concern where and how to live, work, and become involved in their community.

Family members, friends, and professionals may be well meaning, but they may also be prone to making decisions for, rather than with, students (Gould & McTaggart, 1988–1989). This pattern may be detrimental for a number of reasons. First, students who are not involved in making choices and planning their educational programs in high school may not be personally invested in the choices made for them. As a result, otherwise well-designed strategies may fail. Second, students who are not encouraged to make their own decisions may not develop a sense of responsibility for their own actions. Finally, students who are not encouraged to speak for themselves in school will be less likely and perhaps less able to make choices in the adult world.

Empowerment of students represents a variety of skills including independence, self-expression, choice making, and self-representation (Lakin, 1992). Students who are empowered have the skills of self-determination that help them identify what they want and the self-advocacy skills to obtain their goals and needs. For young people to focus on personal goals and needs, they need an opportunity to sample a variety of jobs and acquire an understanding of the kinds of living situations, activities, and resources that will be available to them in their communities. A high school curriculum that provides a variety of options and experiences (for example, paid work and community experiences, vocational classes, traditional academic classes, extracurricular activities) and ensures that students are actively involved in developing their own programs will promote empowerment. Instructional strategies such as peer partnerships and cooperative learning indirectly promote empowerment by encouraging students to speak for themselves in the context of a group.

IDEA recognizes the need for student participation by requiring that students must be invited to their IEP meetings when transition will be discussed. Actual participation at meetings, however, may be quite different than mere attendance. Most students will need to be given opportunity, encouragement, support, and training to participate fully. With preparation and training some students can lead their own IEP meetings. Others who may not yet feel comfortable leading the meeting can participate in a variety of ways, such as collecting assessment information from their teachers, asking friends to come to the meetings, listing their strengths and needs, learning about resources, or preparing questions to ask at the meeting.

The focus on self-determination and choice means little if educators and other professionals do not provide students with opportunities and skills to plan their lives. For some, this will mean changing interaction styles. Not only do students need to be given the opportunity to provide input, their answers need to be respected (instead of dismissed as too idealistic or unrealistic), and action needs to be based on their input. When questions are posed to students, they should be open ended and not directed to obtaining a specific answer.

Peters (1990) provides these hints for including students in the IEP meeting: (a) inform parents, administrators, and other team members that the student will be attending the conference; (b) provide students with preconference preparation such as viewing videotaped IEP meetings or practicing a meeting; (c) address the student directly and maintain eye contact; (d) use nontechnical language; (e) highlight student's strengths, keep remarks positive, and make specific suggestions regarding needs; (f) provide the student opportunities to ask questions and request clarity; and (g) provide opportunities for student contributions and reactions.

Implementing the Transition Planning Process Transition planning processes need to ensure that students' needs are recognized and pursued. Planning strategies such as Personal Futures Planning (O'Brien, 1987) and the McGill Action Planning System (Forest & Lusthaus, 1990; O'Brien, Forest, Snow, & Hasbury, 1989) make conscious attempts to personalize the planning process and address the issues of empowerment. They also focus on creative approaches to meeting students' needs and support students and their families to finding solutions in informal community networks instead of adult human service agencies (Perske & Perske, 1988). Rather than describing the process of conducting a planning meeting, the information presented here will focus on the slight differences in determining transition goals.

Long-term outcomes based on preferences and skills are first determined for each transition area. A long-term outcome states a concrete activity that will be achieved after exit from high school. It does not refer to the process the student will complete. For example, "Matt will graduate from postsecondary training as a veterinarian's assistant" is a long-term outcome. "Matt will apply to postsecondary institutions in the major of his choice" is a process statement that does not describe the outcome (that is, we do not know whether he wants to get accepted or finish or what his desired area of study is). Long-term outcomes can, and should, change as a student gains more experience and refines his or her choices. Table 15.1 provides further examples of Matt's long-term outcomes. The annual goals presented in the table demonstrate how goals should build toward the achievement of the long-term outcome.

Although IDEA uses the terms *instruction, community experiences, employment, postschool adult living objectives, daily living skills,* and *functional vocational evaluation,* each state, and sometimes school district, may have other terms to identify areas of transition. Regardless of the semantics, a long-term outcome statement should be written for each content area. Although not required by federal law, it is helpful to write the long-term outcome statement on the IEP. This will help each future IEP team to review progress and reevaluate the meaningfulness of the long-term outcome.

Selecting Transition Strategies and Activities The selection of transition strategies and activities must consider both opportunities to be with peers without disabilities and the best place to learn a given skill. These two factors are most compatible when inclusion is defined as including *all* youth into the wider community.

Youth with and without disabilities often have difficulty establishing a good career, suitable living arrangements, and a wide social network after high school (Kazis, 1993). Over one-third of high school graduates without disabilities have not found stable employment by the time they are 30 (Osterman, 1992). The statistic is even higher for those who did not complete high school. For those men who are entering their thirties, over 51 percent of them have worked one year or less in their jobs (Osterman, 1992). Unemployment periods of four weeks or more have been reported for over one-third of the people entering their thirties who do not have college degrees (Osterman, 1992). The outcomes for youth with disabilities are even bleaker (see Edgar, 1987; Hasazi et al., 1985a; Hasazi, Gordon, Roe, Hull, Finck, & Salembier, 1985b; Johnson, Bruininks, & Thurlow, 1987; Mithaug et al., 1985; Sitlington, Frank, & Carson, 1991; Wagner, 1989; Wehman et al., 1985). It is apparent, therefore, that both youth with and without disabilities need more assistance in learning skills that will help them as adults.

The issue, then, is to develop both school- and community-based educational opportunities for all youth that are related to their individual long-term

Table 15.1 Sample Transition Goals and Long-Term Outcomes for Matt

Transition Area	Long-Term Outcome	Annual Goal
Postsecondary education	Matt will graduate from postsecondary training as a veterinarian's assistant.	**10th Grade** Matt will identify and demonstrate organizational study skills that he needs. **11th Grade** Matt will identify and demonstrate study skills and content knowledge necessary for successful completion of the SAT. **12th Grade** Matt will graduate from high school with a GPA sufficient for admission to a postsecondary institution.
Integrated employment	Matt will work part-time as a parking valet, while attending school to become a veterinarian's assistant.	**10th Grade** Matt will get his driver's license. Matt will have work experience within an animal hospital or similar setting. **11th Grade** Matt will be able to drive a manual and automatic transmission **12th Grade** Matt will work part-time as a parking valet.
Independent living	Matt will live independently in an apartment downtown.	**10th Grade** Matt will demonstrate ability to plan, purchase, and prepare balanced meals. **11th Grade** Matt will demonstrate the ability to establish a budget and manage his finances. **12th Grade** Matt will select an apartment of his choice and successfully complete the application process.
Community participation	Matt will be able to move independently within the . state using multiple modes of transportation, including his personal car.	**10th Grade** Matt will be able to maintain his car. **11th Grade** Matt will be able to use a map to get to any destination in the city or suburbs. **12th Grade** Matt will be able to use a map to get to any destination within 100 miles of his home.

outcomes. School-based programs should expose students to a broad array of career opportunities and facilitate the selection of a course of study that will lead to a first job. Student knowledge and skills should be enhanced in school-based programs through the integration of academic and occupational learning and strong linkages with postsecondary programs. Community-based programs are most often considered work-based and stress the importance of workplaces as active learning environments. They should build on and advance activities such as tech-prep education, career academics, school-to-apprenticeship programs, youth apprenticeships, school-sponsored enterprises, business-education compacts, and promising strategies that assist school dropouts. Work-based activities may include work experience, job training, job shadowing, and workplace mentoring.

Career awareness, exploration, and counseling are essential for all students. Students with disabilities, however, may require special assistance in making informed decisions regarding future careers. In this regard, it is important that families, counselors, and other school staff assisting students be familiar with the full range of assistive technology devices, environmental accommodations, and other types of supports needed by individuals to participate fully in school- and community-based learning.

Youth with disabilities who participate in some type of work-based learning are more likely to stay in school. Students with disabilities, for example, who took a concentration of vocational courses, as well as those who enrolled in survey courses in a variety of occupational areas, were significantly less likely than nonvocational or prevocational students to drop out of school (Wagner, 1991). Participating in a work experience program as a part of their vocational program further enhanced the probability that students would stay in school. Postschool employment outcomes were greatly enhanced for those who participated in vocational education and work experience programs.

The development of programs that are both school- and community-based and include all youth preempts the discussion of inclusion versus community-based placement. Youth with disabilities will be educated with their peers, regardless of the setting, because their peers without disabilities also will be receiving both school and community experiences. The challenge simply becomes the determination of the best setting for the student and the skill to be learned. There are three general considerations for determining the settings where instruction should occur: (a) the anticipated work, living, and social communities of individual students; (b) the degree to which students wish to be included in those communities, and; (c) the relationship of their long-term outcomes to their learning characteristics, age, motivation, and ability to generalize. Students with significant disabilities, or whose learning characteristics indicate a slow learning curve, will typically require additional time to learn the skills necessary to achieve their long-term outcomes. Transition planning for these students should begin as early as possible, at least by age fourteen, but preferably sooner.

Following Up on Identified Activities The IEP meeting should also be a time to identify the specific responsibilities of the planning team members for completion of the goals and objectives and to establish patterns of communication regarding the effects of the plan. Formal communication on a regularly scheduled basis will help assure the continued participation of team members throughout the postschool implementation of the plan. As students come closer to their year of exit from school, emphasis should be placed on the shift of students from schools to receiving agencies (Maddox & Edgar, 1985). Students in high school typically have had little contact with adult service agencies, and neither they nor their families are prepared for the myriad of complex steps involved in obtaining services from these agencies. Steps for obtaining additional training and services (for example, filling out applications and eligibility paperwork), doing final student assessment, identifying transition resources and supports, and assigning responsibilities for implementing the postschool transition services should all be part of planning in students' last few years in school.

Schools can assist in this process by providing parents and students with structured training programs that teach the process of adult agency referral, effective approaches for supporting the efforts of a working student, strategies for accessing adult community services, and other information specific to their community. Parental participation in such training is increased if there is a parent facilitator specialist on the transition team who can visit the family to explain the transition program and the parent involvement opportunities. Additional incentives include transportation assistance, child care relief, stipends, and scheduling convenience.

COMPONENTS AND STRATEGIES OF INCLUSIVE TRANSITION IN SCHOOLS AND COMMUNITY SETTINGS

An important step in the transition planning process is to provide experiences that meet individual student needs and ensure that transition goals will be met. These strategies and experiences are the "how-to's" of transition planning, in that they provide the vehicle for accomplishing transition goals specified by students and their families. It is unlikely that a single transition plan would contain all of these strategies, but planning teams and students need to be aware of these "promising practices" that have been shown to be effective in increasing students' opportunities and abilities to live, work, and participate in the community.

Experiences and approaches specifically associated with transition include academic experience within regular education classes, participation in paid work experiences, vocational training at community sites, and vocational education and job seeking skills. Other promising practices—such as learning strategies, cooperative group learning, peer tutoring, and peer partnerships—are more typically associated with strategies to improve overall classroom instruction. They may be equally important to transition planning, however, because they increase students' opportunities to acquire academic skills and widen their social networks.

In general, the more opportunities students have in high school to make decisions about the future, engage in paid work experience, and interact with peers and adults in regular classroom environments, at work, and in the community, the more likely it seems that they will have positive experiences in the transition from school to adult life. A brief description of promising practices in student-centered strategies and their importance to transition planning follows.

Academic Participation in Regular Education

In an effort to obtain a better understanding of the types of programs that students with disabilities experience in secondary schools, and their impact on postschool outcomes, the National Longitudinal Transition Study (NLTS) was initiated. *The Sixteenth Annual Report to Congress on the Implementation of the Individuals with Disabilities Education Act* (U.S. Department of Education, 1994) presents highlights from the NLTS regarding selected aspects of the performance of the 92 percent of students with disabilities within their sample who attended regular secondary schools. These data suggest that regular education academic classes of the 1980s were difficult environments for students with disabilities. Students who spent more of their class time in regular academic classes were significantly more likely to fail courses than other students. Course failure, with its accompanying loss of credit toward graduation, was among the most accurate predicators of students dropping out of school. In another study, it was found that students who spent more than half of their high school careers in academic courses indicated that they would rather be involved in vocational training or employment programs (Newman & Camento, 1993). Interviews with students who had dropped out of school showed that many were frustrated with academic classes and wanted to learn vocational skills that would help prepare them for future jobs (DeStefano, Hasazi, McGinty, & Topper, 1993). It is apparent from these findings that students who are enrolled in regular education classes need to be highly motivated and feel engaged in their coursework. Educators can help the success of students in regular academic classes by providing accommodations in instructional delivery, curriculum options, and standards.

Participation in Vocational Education Programs

Vocational education at the secondary level is generally provided for half the school day during the junior and senior years. The goals of vocational education include assisting students to acquire (a) personal skills and attitudes, (b) communication and computational skills and technological literacy, (c) employability skills, (d) broad and specific skills and knowledge, and (e) foundations for career planning and lifelong learning.

Various social skills have proven to be critical for maintaining employment. Karge, Patton, and de la Garza (1992) note that students with mild disabilities are "jeopardized by the 'hidden' disability which manifests in the work place as inappropriate socialization, lack of initiative, poor attitude, defiance, and other behaviors which cause loss of jobs early on" (p. 61). They recommend that every student participate in a one-semester course that covers such job-keeping behaviors as dressing appropriately on the job, filling out time cards, getting along with supervisor and coworkers, asking for assistance, giving and accepting praise, and interacting with the public. In addition, on-the-job teaching of skills, job coaching, crisis intervention, and close employer communication are effective strategies for promoting job maintenance skills.

Vocational education is organized around three major components: in-school vocational skill instruction, out-of-school work experience, and vocational student organizations. Historically, students with disabilities have had difficulty gaining access to regular vocational education, particularly to the work experience and student organization components (Birchneall & Wanat, 1981). Research has indicated, however, that students with mild disabilities who did gain access to regular in-school vocational instruction were later employed in the jobs that paid higher wages than those students who did not participate in regular vocational education (Hasazi et al., 1985a, 1985b).

In recent years, vocational educators and special educators have placed greater emphasis on collaborating to provide the supports necessary for students with disabilities to succeed in vocational classes (Hasazi & Clark, 1988). Vocational classes provide a practical hands-on education for these students, but as society has become more technical, the vocational courses that are in place to train students have also become more technical, requiring more in the way of reading, math, and problem-solving skills (Touzel, 1989). Most vocational centers employ a full- or part-time vocational resource teacher who works with vocational educators to plan, monitor and/or implement, and evaluate strategies to meet the needs of individual students.

The level of support provided to teachers and students varies according to individual needs and classroom demands. For example, in-service training could be provided to vocational instructors to help make them aware of whole-class, effective teaching strategies such as modeling and questioning for understanding (Brookover et al., 1982; Christenson, Ysseldyke, & Thurlow, 1989). An auto mechanics teacher might find that one student in his class understands the concepts of auto mechanics but has difficulty memorizing vocabulary words for written tests. This student's needs could be met through a peer partnership program developed jointly by the vocational class teacher and vocational resources teacher, in which a peer who typically finishes class assignments early is trained to work with the student on vocabulary comprehension. A second student in the class may have trouble expressing herself in writing; she could be allowed to take tests orally with the vocational resource teacher. A student experiencing greater difficulties learning the auto mechanics curriculum might require more significant curriculum modifications. In this case, the vocational instructor and vocational resource teacher would consider the student's strengths and learning style in light of curriculum demands, determining which curriculum competencies could be met as written and which would need to be adapted so that the student could realistically attain them (Eddy, Mack, & Ringe, 1989).

Paid Work Experience

Students with disabilities who hold paying jobs while in high school are more likely to be employed following graduation than those who do not (Edgar, 1987; Hasazi et al., 1985a). They also are more apt to remain in school, seek postsecondary education opportunities, and become self-supporting adults (Edgar,

1987). However, only about 6 percent of students with mild disabilities receive community-based instruction (Halpern & Benz, 1987).

Paid work experiences may help students acquire an understanding of the contingencies associated with earning wages and learn to observe and collaborate with coworkers. The manner in which these experiences might occur include supervised part-time work after school or on weekends, part-time or full-time summer work, or a combination of these options. Only through actual paid employment experiences will students acquire appreciation for the social ecology of the workplace and the natural consequences inherent in real work. For example, it is essential to learn that break time in a work environment has a beginning and an end, and it usually involves some form of social interaction between coworkers. It is also critical to experience the relationship between work accomplishments and tangible rewards such as money and increased participation in leisure activities that require financial resources.

Vocational Training at Employment Sites

Research has demonstrated that instruction provided in community work settings is an essential component of a vocational program to prepare students for employment (Cobb, Hasazi, Collins, & Salembier, 1988). The range of potential difficulties that may occur at a work site cannot be anticipated and accommodated in a classroom-based vocational education environment and, for many students, can best be addressed at the actual workplace. Specific vocational skills are more effectively taught in the environments in which skills are naturally utilized and rewarded. Vocational training at employment sites can include a variety of support services. An individual might require short-term, intensive training provided by a job trainer, which would include a planned process for fading the training support. Another individual might require only that the trainer provide intermittent follow-up support to monitor changes in the work routine by the employer and provide retraining if necessary. Yet another individual might not require direct training or monitoring but might need support in relationships with coworkers or supervisors.

COMMUNITY AND AGENCY COLLABORATION

Strong parent-professional partnerships, a team approach to the delivery of special education at the secondary level, interagency collaboration, and use of community resources are all programmatic and organizational issues related to the overall delivery of successful transition services. Schools and communities with these strategies in place tend to foster communication and collaboration, making them conducive to transition planning efforts and welcoming to young people with disabilities. Promising practices relative to these issues are discussed in the following sections.

Parent and Professional Partnerships

Strong partnerships between parents of students with disabilities and professionals are critical to the success of transition planning efforts. Successful working relationships between parents and professionals are characterized by openness, honesty, and acceptance. Strong parent-professional partnerships are important to the success of program-centered strategies in the same way that empowerment among students is important to the successful achievement of student outcomes. Schools and transition teams may initiate well-meaning programs and plans, but if these lack parent support, they are not likely to succeed. Parents who feel they have a true voice in determining their child's future are more likely to feel connected to their schools and communities and empowered to influence high school and adult programs to be more responsive to the needs of students in transition to adult life (Ferguson et al., 1988; Hanley-Maxwell, Whitney-Thomas, & Pogoloff, 1995; Wilcox, 1987).

Transition teams that value and encourage parent participation are likely to conduct more in-depth and accurate assessments of students, set clearer and more meaningful goals, have a greater likelihood of follow-through, and have a reduced dependency on external resources than are teams that ignore or devalue the contributions of family members. The value of parent participation on individual planning teams seems quite apparent. These same contributions, however, have been made to those systems that encourage parent participation in activities such as policy review and development, or the design, development, and implementation of training materials.

Interagency Collaboration

A secondary level program with employment or further education and training as one of its primary goals requires the use of resources from both generic and specialized service agencies. An excellent mechanism for identifying human and financial resources is through the development of local interagency agreements between vocational education, special education, vocational rehabilitation, and employment and training agencies (Stodden & Boone, 1987). The purpose of these agreements is to minimize service duplication while maximizing the availability and quality of services provided by different agencies. Increased interagency collaboration has been a federal-level priority, resulting in written joint policy statements between the office of Special Education Programs and the offices of Community Health Services, Vocational Education, Vocational Rehabilitation, and Social Security Administration (Johnson et al., 1987). Federal mandates have encouraged many states to establish local interagency agreements. Interagency agreements should specify the underlying values and beliefs of service agencies and policies; the services provided by each agency; procedures for identifying the extent and range of need at the local level; provisions for developing a local plan to meet those needs procedures for identifying and informing potential consumers of the services available; procedures for monitoring consumer services and programs; provisions for development and delivery of jointly sponsored in-service training for professionals from the various agencies; and procedures for monitoring, evaluating, and revising the local agreement. These procedures need to be clearly articulated in language that avoids agency jargon and demonstrates consensus as to the purpose and type of service provided by each agency. In formulating the local agreement, particular attention should be directed toward including generic agencies or programs such as community colleges, area vocational-technical schools, adult education programs, and state employment and training services.

Interagency agreements improve the transition planning process by overcoming expressed barriers to service provision. Barriers identified by parents and service providers include a lack of coordination among services, a lack of information about available services, difficulties interpreting varying bureaucratic procedures (for example, application procedures, fiscal cycles), and problems assessing available services. Interagency agreements provide transition planning teams with accurate, up-to-date information that has been gathered from a variety of sources and coordinated in an understandable way. In the act of producing interagency agreements, local agencies tend to improve their efforts to streamline and coordinate services, thus creating a service system that is easier to access and more capable of meeting the needs of young adults in transition. When one or more transition planning teams identify needed improvements in service provision or coordination, the agreement can be used as a mechanism for systems change. Finally, monitoring and evaluation procedures developed through interagency agreements may be used by transition planning teams who wish to analyze the outcomes and costs and benefits of a particular service (Johnson et al., 1987). Although many states and regions need to further develop the kinds of agreements specified here, it seems clear that interagency agreements are important to the success of transition planning efforts.

Team Approach

Earlier descriptions of the transition planning process discussed the importance of a collaborative, team approach to planning and delivering services. A successful transition planning effort requires parents and professionals to be flexible in their roles and responsibilities in planning and delivering services. At one time, the responsibilities of special educators, vocational educators, and vocational rehabilitation counselors were quite separate from one another. Special educators tended to focus on direct instruction in the context of the high school, vocational educators were primarily concerned with providing instruction in vocational classes, and rehabilitation counselors dealt with employment issues. Today, educators and adult service providers are faced with the reality and challenge of meeting students' needs in a variety of school, vocational, and community-based settings. Students making the transition from school to adult life are especially likely to participate in activities and programs that cross disciplines and involve adults with a variety of "professional hats." For these reasons, it is important to conceptualize transition services in a holistic way that acknowledges classroom educators, special educators, vocational educators, rehabilitation counselors, postsecondary educators, employers, parents, and community members as equal partners in the education of students with disabilities. These partnerships must be formed on the basis of collaboration and teamwork, and the educators and other professionals involved in them must be trained in the skills and knowledge to work collaboratively with one another.

Use of Community Resources

Given the broad range of skills and opportunities that students will need to make a successful transition from school to adult life, the entire community needs to be viewed as a learning environment in which students may apply the strategies outlined earlier. Resources such as institutions of higher education (including community colleges, vocational technical schools, and universities) may provide invaluable exploration experiences for students considering postsecondary schooling and may assist in identifying and developing the supports that students will need to be successful in these environments. Community organizations and clubs may provide both work experiences and opportunities for socialization that lead to the development of long-term social networks. For example, most communities have recreational clubs that encourage noncompetitive leisure activities. Participation in one of these could lead to the development of a lifelong interest in a given sport and encourage stable and valued friendships based on mutual interest. It is essential that students acquire an understanding of the resources available to them in the community that are compatible with their long-term outcomes, for it is only through connections with community members that students with disabilities can gain access to the full range of opportunities available to all citizens.

Organization Strategies

Schools wishing to foster the transition planning process can create environments that are conducive to collaborative teamwork. To begin with, teachers and administrators must believe in the value of helping students plan for the transition from school to adult life. This ideal is most likely to be realized if it is included in a written school philosophy or statement of purpose that views the transition to a meaningful life in the community as an important educational goal for all students.

Use of the teaming approach also requires schools to be organized to allow teachers and administrators sufficient planning time and flexibility in their schedules. Master schedules need to be designed so that team members have overlapping planning time, preferably at least two periods per week. Transition specialists responsible for establishing job sites and training students may need to work afternoons and early evenings, or early mornings and afternoons, in cases where students' work experiences or jobs do not correspond with traditional school hours. Similarly, many of the social and recreational events offered in the community occur in the evening. If teachers are needed to attend meetings, provide transportation, or consult with sponsoring agencies, they must be allowed some flexible scheduling.

If effective transition services are not already in place, teachers and administrators must be prepared to advocate for changes in the system that will lead to their establishment and implementation. Systems change efforts require planners to identify potential barriers to the delivery of services, set goals for improving service delivery, brainstorm and carry out activities designed to accomplish these goals, and evaluate activities and strategies. Examples of systems change strategies that might be used to implement effective transition planning include development of a school philosophy that includes transition planning and delivery as a goal, in-service training in peer power strategies, establishment of a work experience program, or a restructuring of special education service delivery.

Obtaining and Using Outcome Measures

To determine whether transition efforts have been successful at the program level, schools need to establish evaluation procedures that will yield data on students' success in achieving independence, employment, and community participation. One effective means of doing this is to establish outcome measures in each of these areas and develop an accompanying questionnaire that can be used to conduct interviews with former students. Interviews should be conducted either on the telephone or in person, eight to twelve months following graduation, and reviewed from an individual and programmatic perspective. For example, information regarding a particular youth may indicate that a referral to an appropriate adult service agency is required. In addition, responses across all of the interviews need to be analyzed to determine whether there are trends that point to effective and less effective programs and services. Although the information acquired through the questionnaires may not be conclusive, it will provide a framework for continuing to examine programs and services as they relate to postschool outcomes.

SUMMARY

The period of transition from school to adult life is a challenging one for students with disabilities and their families. The current statistics regarding the postschool employment, living arrangements, and social outcomes of youth with disabilities are discouraging. It is imperative, therefore, that youth exit school with skills that will generalize to the maximum number of environments as possible. To do this, we need to move beyond a discussion of inclusion versus community-based placement, academic versus functional curriculums to the educational aspirations and needs of individual youth. Transition planning needs to be based on student preferences and skills and ease students' movement from school to adult living. Experiences in paid work and vocational education, as well as curricula for student empowerment, are designed to increase students' academic, vocational, and life skills along with opportunities for meaningful social interactions with peers and adults in a variety of school and community settings.

Finally, successful delivery of transition services includes program-centered strategies that promote a philosophy of community integration for students with disabilities and create opportunities for collaboration among students, families, school personnel, adult human service providers, and community members. These strategies include efforts to create strong parent-professional partnerships, interagency collaboration, a team approach to the delivery of special education, utilization of community resources, and organizational patterns that promote teamwork in schools.

Successful transition to adulthood is built on the academic, personal-social, community living, and vocational skills that all students develop throughout their school careers. Use of school- and community-based educational programs will ensure that not only are youth with disabilities learning with their peers without disabilities, but both groups of students will receive the educational experiences they need. The instructional approaches described throughout this book lay the foundation for planning and implementing programs that facilitate the lifelong success of all students.

REFERENCES

Birchneall, J., & Wanat, J. (1981). Serving the handicapped in vocational student organizations. *Vocational Education, 56,* 51–54.

Brookover, W., Beamer, L., Eftheim, H., Hathaway, D., Lezotte, L., Miller, S., Passalacqua, J., & Tornatzky, L. (1982). *Creating effective schools.* Holmes Beach, FL: Learning Publications.

Christenson, S., Ysseldyke, J., & Thurlow, M. (1989). Critical instruction factors for students with mild handicaps: An integrative review. *Remedial and Special Education, 10*(5), 21–31.

Clark, G. M., & Kolstoe, O. P. (1990). *Career development and transition education for adolescents with disabilities.* Needham Heights, MA: Allyn & Bacon.

Cobb, R. B., Hasazi, S. B., Collins, C. M., & Salembier, G. (1988). Preparing school-based employment specialists. *Teacher Education and Special Education, 11*(2), 64–71.

DeStefano, L. S., Hasazi, S. B., McGinty, S. T., & Topper, U. V. (1993, April). *Special education is too slow, regular education is too fast: A qualitative study of youth with disabilities.* Paper presented at the annual meeting of the American Educational Research Association, Atlanta, GA.

Eddy, J., Mack, K., & Ringe, J. (1989). Vocational outreach services: A joint vocational education/special education program. In G. F. Elrod (Ed.), *Career education for special needs individuals: Learning, earning and contributing.* Columbia, SC: Dance Graphics.

Edgar, E. (1987). Secondary programs in special education: Are many of them justifiable? *Exceptional Children, 53*(7), 555–561.

Ferguson, M. P., Ferguson, D. L., & Jones, D. (1988). Generations of hope: Parental perspectives on the transitions of their children with severe mental retardation from school to adult life. *Journal of the Association for Persons with Severe Handicaps, 13*(3), 177–187.

Forest, M., & Lusthaus, E. (1990). Promoting educational equality for all students: Circles and maps. In S. Stainback, W. Stainback, & M. Forest (Eds.), *Educating all students in the mainstream of regular education.* Baltimore: Brookes.

Gould, M., & McTaggart, N. (1988–1989, Winter). Self-advocacy for transition: Indications of student leadership potential today. *American Rehabilitation,* pp. 6–28.

Halpern, A. (1985). Transition: A look at the foundations. *Exceptional Children, 51,* 479–486.

Halpern, A. S., & Benz, M. R. (1987). A statewide examination of secondary special education for students with mild disabilities: Implications for the high school curriculum. *Exceptional Children, 54,* 122–129.

Hanley-Maxwell, C., Whitney-Thomas, J & Pogoloff, S. M. (1995). The second shock: A qualitative study of parents' perspectives and needs during their child's transition from school to adult life. *Journal of the Association for Persons with Severe Handicaps, 20,* 3–15.

Hasazi, S. B., & Clark, G. M. (1988). Vocational preparation for high school students labeled mentally retarded: Employment as a graduation goal. *Mental Retardation, 26*(6), 323–349.

Hasazi, S. B., Gordon, L. R., & Roe, C. A. (1985a). Factors associated with the employment status of handicapped youth exiting high school from 1979 to 1983. *Exceptional Children, 51*(6), 455–496.

Hasazi, S. B., Gordon, L. R., Roe, C. A., Hull, M., Finck, K., & Salembier, G. (1985b). A statewide follow-up on post high school employment and residential status of students labeled "mentally retarded." *Education and Training of the Mentally Retarded, 20*(6) 222–234.

Johnson, D. R., Bruininks, R. H. & Thurlow, M. L. (1987). Meeting the challenge of transition service planning through improved interagency cooperation. *Exceptional Children, 2*(1), 40–47.

Karge, B. D., Patton, P. L., & de la Garza. (1991). Transition services for youth with mild disabilities: Do they exist, are they needed? *Career Development for Exceptional Individuals.*

Kazis, R. (1993). *Improving the Transition from School-to-Work in the United States.* Washington, DC: American Youth Policy Forum, Competitiveness Policy Council and Jobs for the Future.

Lakin, C. (1992). Improving the quality of community living to empower people with mental retardation. *Office of Special Education and Rehabilitative Services, 5*(2), 30–35.

Maddox, M., & Edgar, E. (1985). Maneuvering through the maze: Transition planning for human service agency clients. In J. Chadsey-Rusch (Eds.), *Enhancing transition from school to the workplace for handicapped youth* (pp. 58–69). Urbana: National Network for Professional Development in Vocational Special Education, University of Illinois.

Mithaug, D. E., Horiuchi, C. N. & Fanning, P. N. (1985). A report on the Colorado statewide follow-up survey of special education students. *Exceptional Children, 51,* 397–404.

Newman, L., & Camento, R. (1993, April). *What makes a difference? Factors related to postsecondary school attendance for young people with disabilities.* Unpublished manuscript.

O'Brien, J. (1987). A guide to personal futures planning. In G. T. Bellamy & B. Wilcox (Eds.), *The Activities Catalog: A community programming guide for youth and adults with severe disabilities.* Baltimore: Brookes.

O'Brien, J., Forest, M., Snow, J., & Hasbury, D. (1989). *Action for inclusion.* Toronto: Frontier College Press.

Osterman, P. (1992, February). *Is there a problem with the youth labor market and if so how should we fix it? Lessons for the United States from American and European experience.* Unpublished manuscript, Sloan School, Massachusetts Institute of Technology, Cambridge.

Perske, R., & Perske, M. (1988). *Circles of friends: People with disabilities and their friends enrich the lives of one another.* Nashville, TN: Parthenon.

Peters, M. T. (1990, Summer). Someone's missing: The student as an overlooked participant in the IEP process. *Preventing School Failure,* pp. 32–36.

Sitlington, P. L., Frank, A. R., & Carson, R. (1991). *Iowa's statewide follow-up study: Adult adjustment of individuals with severe/profound mental disabilities one and three years after leaving high school.* Des Moines: Iowa Department of Education.

Stodden, R., & Boone, R. (1987). Assessing transition services for handicapped youth: A cooperative interagency approach. *Exceptional Children, 53*(6), 537–545.

Touzel, S. (1989). Motivating vocational educators to work with special needs students. In G. F. Elrod (Ed.), *Career education for special needs individuals: Learning, earning, and contributing.* Columbia, SC: Dance Graphics.

U.S. Department of Education. (1994). *The sixteenth annual report to Congress on the implementation of the Individuals with Disabilities Education Act.* Washington, DC: Government Printing Office.

Wagner, M. (1989). *The transition experience of youths with disabilities: A report from the National Longitudinal Transition Study.* Menlo Park, CA: SRI International.

Wagner, M. (1991). *Dropouts with disabilities: What do we know? What can we do?* Menlo Park, CA: SRI International.

Wehman, P., Kregel, & Seyforth, J. (1985). Transition from school to work for individuals with severe handicaps: A follow-up study. *Journal of the Association for Persons with Severe Disabilities, 10*(3), 132–139.

Wilcox, B. (1987, September). High school programs for students with disabilities. *The Exceptional Parent,* pp. 31–41.

William T. Grant Foundation Commission on Work, Family and Citizenship. (1988a). *The forgotten half: Non-college-bound youth in America.* Washington, DC: Author.

William T. Grant Foundation Commission on Work, Family and Citizenship (1988b). *The forgotten half: Pathways to success for America's youth and young families.* Washington, DC

Index